Praise for *Burt Lancaster: An American Life*

"[Lancaster] had a fierce soul locked up in that buff body, and Buford has done full justice to it with her intelligent, discerning biography; better still, she has done justice to Lancaster's career, which becomes more intriguing the more one considers it."

—LOUIS BAYARD, *WASHINGTON POST BOOK WORLD*

"An extraordinary story of a kid from East Harlem who became a movie star in his first minutes onscreen. . . . Lancaster is captured in all his complexity."

—*SAN FRANCISCO CHRONICLE*

"Outstanding. Sets a standard against which other Hollywood biographies can be measured."

—NEAL GABLER

"Probing. . . . Buford teases out the contrasts in Lancaster, and shows how the actor used them to create a composite portrait of how a man comes to terms with his masculinity."

—*PHILADELPHIA INQUIRER*

"A straightforward account, avoiding the perils of psychobiography and placing Lancaster in the context of his times."

—*PITTSBURGH POST-GAZETTE*

"An excellent book."

—NEAL TRAVIS, *NEW YORK POST*

"An admiring portrait of a man who treated his movie career with the same daring he once applied to a flying trapeze."

—*ATLANTA JOURNAL-CONSTITUTION*

"Splendid."

—*ST. LOUIS POST-DISPATCH*

"By carefully contextualizing Lancaster's more than 50-year career within the tumultuous political and economic changes of the postwar years, Buford's finely detailed, sensitive biography ranks among the best of its genre."

—*PUBLISHERS WEEKLY* (STARRED)

"An authoritative and unflinching biography."

—*BALTIMORE SUN*

"Absorbing. An admirable chronicle."

—SALON.COM

"Well-researched, well-written."

—*BOSTON PHOENIX*

"A fascinating, honest, terrific read. A must for all Burt fans!"

—JOHN TURTURRO

"A wonderful look into the complicated life and influences that made this extraordinary man. . . . It reminded me that politics and art have always been intertwined and that celebrities who think independently can make a difference."

—SUSAN SARANDON

"Precisely observed and shrewdly insightful . . . Burt Lancaster was never more fascinating than he is in these pages. Buford's portrait is witty, compassionate, a helluva read, and—I suspect—definitive."

—STEVEN BACH, AUTHOR OF *FINAL CUT*

"Kate Buford has done something remarkable with Burt Lancaster. . . . The book is as good as it is because she never denies the abiding mystery of the man."

—DAVID THOMSON

"A serious biography of the Adonis who wanted to be considered a thinker."

—*KIRKUS REVIEWS*

BURT LANCASTER

BURT
LANCASTER

AN AMERICAN LIFE

KATE BUFORD

DA CAPO PRESS

Cataloging-in-Publication data for this book
is available from the Library of Congress.

ISBN 0-306-81019-0
First Da Capo Press edition 2001
Reprinted by arrangement with Alfred A. Knopf,
a division of Random House, Inc.

Published by Da Capo Press
A Member of the Perseus Books Group
http://www.dacapopress.com

Da Capo Press books are available at special discounts for bulk purchases
in the U.S. by corporations, institutions, and other organizations.
For more information, please contact the Special Markets Department
at the Perseus Books Group, 11 Cambridge Center,
Cambridge, MA 02142, or call (617) 252-5298.

1 2 3 4 5 6 7 8 9—04 03 02 01

To the people sitting in the dark, watching

. . . Mr. Lancaster's remarkable—
though not often remarked about—career.

—Vincent Canby

Contents

Illustrations follow pages 86, 182, and 278

BURT LANCASTER

Prologue

British director Alexander "Sandy" Mackendrick, nerves raw from trying to shriek sense into a movie shoot that was out of control, threw up his hands and cried, "Cut!" Bing Crosby had stumbled out the front door of Manhattan's "21" Club on Fifty-second Street into the middle of a scene from *Sweet Smell of Success.* In the back of a nearby prop truck screenwriter Clifford Odets, typewriter on his lap and a blanket thrown over his shoulders against the icy wind, glanced up at the commotion and continued punching out dialogue for the next scene. It was January 1957, deep in the night.

Waiting for the next set-up, Tony Curtis paced nervously, pitching moves to Burt Lancaster, the star of the movie. "You stand still," he suggested, "and I'll circle around you." Mackendrick had told them to model this key scene on the predatory dance in Ben Jonson's *Volpone:* the slimy press agent Sidney Falco orbits around Lancaster's J.J. Hunsecker, the megalomaniacal, all-powerful newspaper columnist who uses Falco to do his dirty work in exchange for printing the agent's gossip "items." But Curtis preferred the good old Laurel and Hardy routine: "You take the shovel, I'll take the bucket. No, *you* take the shovel. . . ." Lancaster, silent, older, stared down at him through his thick prop spectacles and said, "Do whatever you want, kid."

The camera rolled for their first take. Hunsecker walked to the edge of the sidewalk and sucked in the night air. "I love this dirty town," he barked, Lancaster's famous voice, teeth, chopping up the words into bloody bits of raw meat. The dialogue fit his Big Apple diction, so tight and sharp. And he did love this dirty town, his hometown, the Manhattan bedrock that would not yield. One of the most powerful stars in 1957 Hollywood, Lancaster sunk his big white capped teeth into the part of Hunsecker like a mastiff loose in the city, his prey dead but still twitching. "The cat's in the bag and the bag's in the river," says Falco, dancing around him, reassuring him that the plot to destroy his sister's boyfriend is in play, that she will be saved for Hunsecker's own incestuous self.

Lancaster's independent production company made this acid movie about American celebrity, ambition, greed, and lust, and then it drowned in a river of red ink and popular repugnance. "*Sweet Smell of Success* destroyed us all," said its director just before he died. The movie certainly killed the indie, then hung on for decades as a cult favorite and is now a Library of Congress–registered American classic.

But success isn't everything, as the movie so effectively demonstrated. "The moments of your greatest fear," concluded Mackendrick, unwittingly voicing Lancaster's credo, "are also the moments you look back on as your greatest thrill. The danger is an aphrodisiac. It *must* be."

Burt Lancaster is so much a part of the fabric of American popular culture that he blends into our collective memory like a famous uncle who was once a great athlete. Gestures and intonations remain in the mind, perhaps a bit hazy. In the final episode of *Seinfeld* in 1998, Kramer looks up at the sky and says, with carny zest, that there's something in the air, he can feel it. Jerry replies, "You know you're turning into Burt Lancaster?"

Lancaster's achievement was uneven and he did not court acclaim— hence the uncertain memories. *From Here to Eternity* or *Elmer Gantry* is matched by a quirky *Come Back, Little Sheba* or a banal *Airport*. But there are not many of the last. More representative of his ambition is *The Swimmer*. What seemed a disjointed failure in 1968 now plays like a long-repressed American nightmare. Lancaster's more flamboyant failures were often deliberate attempts to stretch his range, to take the untutored talent he had and make it do more. "Bear with me," he once said to his audience in an interview, wryly pleading for patience while he got better at his craft.

His restlessness often gave his performances a brittle, mannered flatness. But when the work is accumulated he streaks across the screen like a quixotic American meteor aimed only at its destination. Lancaster did not make films, he made *movies*. The best of the work—*The Killers, All My Sons, From Here to Eternity, Sweet Smell of Success, Elmer Gantry, Birdman of Alcatraz, Seven Days in May, The Swimmer, Ulzana's Raid, Go Tell the Spartans, Atlantic City*—charts the arc of postwar mainstream American life, a coherent story with chapters and themes. He lived a self-inventing life, trying on different identities like an artist shifting into different periods, assuming new personae on- and off-screen. He died in 1994 without funeral or epitaph. By then he had lost the mainstream audience even though the story he was telling was their own. They got confused along the way by the conflicting signals beaming out from his deepening persona and lumped him together with Kirk Douglas, Robert Mitchum, and Charlton Heston.

From 1946 to 1990, he alternated the artsy with the commercial movie, financing one with the profits of the other to keep himself in play. At the same time, he manipulated his star image back on itself, sabotaging, refining, and ultimately discarding it altogether to arrive at something more than stardom. Part of the "sandwich" generation of male stars that slipped in between World War II and Marlon Brando's arrival in Hollywood in 1950, he had to shape his career in opposition to the one sure audience sector that had emerged by the mid-fifties: fifteen-to-twenty-year-olds. What Robert Brustein has called the "Zola realism" of such films as *East of Eden* featured a young, doomed protagonist as a victim of forces beyond his control—the perspective of youth or of adults so overwhelmed by postwar fear that they regress. Over another decade this attitude would evolve into the retributive nihilism of Clint Eastwood and, in another turn of time, into the apocalyptic fantasies of Arnold Schwarzenegger. As sustained myth or antimyth, it can be the stance of despair, a retreat from the complexity and change that marked life in the latter half of the twentieth century.

Lancaster resisted this tide. Too earnest to be chic, he hungered to make what he considered grown-up movies that engaged, productively, with the circumstances of his era. As time went on, he equally resisted relaxing into a comfortable heroic cliché. "I hate looking backward," he said in 1986, "but every once in a while it sneaks up on you. You have to fight against being an antique—an artifact of a culture's past and not a part of its future." As the country reinvented itself, his hero reinvented his own myth.

The dimensions of his stardom—what Roddy McDowall called his "outlandishly popular and potent *mega*stardom"—were unique. Known around the world as "Mr. Muscles and Teeth" after his overnight leap into the Hollywood frenzy in 1946, he quickly learned to treat his hypermasculine American good looks—electric blue eyes, blond hair, tall, god-like body, panther grace, clipped, clear voice, disciplined energy, and those teeth—as one big commodity. He understood early that movie fame gave him an even better weapon in the brave new world of postwar Hollywood: power. The 1950s troika of Lancaster, agent Lew Wasserman, and United Artists led the way to one of the biggest shifts in the industry since the talkies: from studio domination to widespread independent production. Lancaster's company, Hecht-Lancaster, later Hecht-Hill-Lancaster, became the biggest actor-managed indie of the decade, virtually a ministudio.

Making his own synthesis of fame and big bucks, he started adding, slowly, a bit of art to it. There were no rules in that post–Golden Age, so he made them up as he went along. Starting from a core belief in personal freedom, an insistence that he define himself as he wished, he created the *ur*-model of the unfettered star in charge of his own destiny.

Sweet Smell of Success was pivotal for his career, the failure that pointed the way to the real success, and it is not coincidental that it is set on the streets of New York. That is where his performing life began, in the politically progressive, immigrant slum of East Harlem where he was born and raised. He would remain a New Yorker, proud to consider himself, in that city's street phrase, the best of the best and worst of the worst. "That is who I *am*," he said, proudly.

He became a creature of the grubby Depression-era circus where he toiled as an acrobat. His discipline, physical courage, and glow-in-the-dark glamor are pure big top. When he arrived in Hollywood after World War II and immediately summed it up as "nothing more than a big circus," he had already found his key to Tinseltown: make the act fresh and sharp, wow the audience, do your own stunts, keep the show on the road. To his fingertips, he was a product of the raucous popular culture that bred him—and which he refused to regard as cheap or secondary.

His ambition took its toll. His is not a straightforward story like those of James Stewart, Gregory Peck, or John Wayne. He was a highly intelligent, demanding, six-foot-one-inch bundle of contradictory impulses. Cruel (he reduced Kirk Douglas to tears by teasing him about elevator shoes), selfless (he kept old friends on his payroll for decades), and deadpan funny (when Ernest Lehman told him he was at work writing *The Sound of Music,* Lancaster replied, incredulously, "Jesus, you must need the money")—Luchino Visconti, no open book himself, called him "the most *perfectly* mysterious man I ever met." Lancaster, ever the artful dodger, countered that he was only mimicking Visconti. If Lancaster's humanness is difficult to see at certain periods of his life, it is because he disappeared from himself.

He tried to balance it all by fanatically keeping his personal life private. It was a cagey way to elude cheap definition, to maintain the real star's mystery. He had his secrets to hide. Lancaster was a serious, compulsive womanizer, and the father of five children by his second wife. That moral juxtaposition was perhaps one source of the melancholy that lurked behind the ice-blue eyes. There is compelling evidence that he was bisexual, but one suspects that in his own mind at least he moved beyond such categories—he was sexual, period, the puzzle of his sexuality only another prism through which to watch the multifaceted body of work refract even more. The core of his character was an intense, obsessive, physical energy. He did not just move across the screen, he dominated it. Off-screen, he let his physicality, an expression of his curiosity, take him wherever it would.

The biographer is left with a certain respect for a complicated personal life adroitly lived.

Like fellow New Yorkers Cagney and Bogart, he remained the wary city kid who took nothing for granted, and this gave him his fundamental integrity. It also kept him aloof and suspicious of the very success he so craved—and, for a long time, of the love and affection he claimed not to need. He relished the role of protector of friends, family, new talent, and the generally disenfranchised. Like so many men of his generation, he saw himself as a warrior, fighting the good fight, alone. Yet the biggest battle he fought was with himself. Slowly, he had to loosen up to life, to put down the sword. His intelligence demanded, ultimately, that he turn his commitment to change back on himself—with problematic results. As he mellowed, he remained a frightening contradiction, even to himself. "Burt was a gentle person," Ernest Lehman said, "maybe because he knew he could kill someone."

His beautiful body was his fortune and its disciplined strength the proof of the one quality on which almost everyone, friend or enemy, agrees: his professionalism. He could be as skeptical as the most jaded movie veteran but he stopped short of cynicism. To the end, he retained what Amanda Plummer called a "sense of wonder" at the process of making movies and his own great luck at being able to be a part of it. He respected the work.

In the passion of his striving is the poignant, brassy heart of his story. The American movie was dignified by his ambition and he always gave the movies credit for being able to change hearts and minds. Entertainer that he was, he never forgot the people out there watching him in the dark, the polyglot mass of Americans he had grown up with. "Burt dared us to do more, be better, push harder," said Bruce Dern. "We were all his sons."

While his sense of purpose prompted him to make remarkable choices, he was only generally aware that they created a pattern. "We don't know these things," said Robert Altman, his director in *Buffalo Bill and the Indians*, "until someone taps us on the shoulder and says, 'Excuse me . . . ?' Then we see that all our work has just been chapters of the same book."

PART ONE

THE SET-UP

1913 – 1945

I walked out of class one day
and I never went back.

—Burt Lancaster

CHAPTER ONE

New York City Boy

There was a child went forth every day,
And the first object he look'd upon, that object he became,
And that object became part of him for the day
or a certain part of the day,
Or for many years or stretching cycles of years.

—Walt Whitman, "There Was a Child Went Forth," *Leaves of Grass*

The story of Burt Lancaster begins with the idea of America, with the belief that you can journey to another place and become another person. His ancestors crossed to England from France in the Norman invasion of 1066 and took the name de Lancastre. Most likely concocted from the Roman word *castra* (legionary camp) and the river Lune whose name may come from the Gaelic *slan* (healthy, salubrious), Lancaster came to mean simply one who comes from Lancaster, the county town of Lancashire. Blond hair and blue eyes would persist over a millennium as a characteristic of Norman or Teutonic origin, showing up in odd places like Sicily. The coats of arms of several Lancaster families feature golden lions but at least one has a leopard, rampant.

His immediate ancestors left England for Ireland, easily accessible across the Irish Sea. Later, eager publicists would claim that he was a descendant of John of Gaunt and his father would tell a tale of lost House of Lancaster fortunes confiscated by Oliver Cromwell, but Lancaster dismissed such stories. Not much would survive of his Irishness except two instinctive responses: a reverence for the single human singing voice and a belief that the declamatory persuasion of live drama, theater, could change the world.

By the second half of the nineteenth century, the Lancasters and the Roberts family, his mother's Belfast people—working-class Northern Irish Protestants—were poor and trapped by the island's limitations. His paternal grandfather James emigrated to New York in the mid-1860s, more than a decade after the Great Famine, part of the human migration to America that provided labor for the vast technological changes that swept the country after the Civil War. James had two key advantages as an Irish Protestant: he was educated enough to read and he was a skilled worker, a cooper, having served a five-to-six-year apprenticeship before landing in America. He settled on the Lower East Side of Manhattan, at 40 Essex Street. In the twisting streets and dark brick buildings lived harness makers, peddlers, grocers, bakers, carpenters, and barbers, Germans from Hesse-Darmstadt and Bavaria, Russians, Austrians, and thousands of Irish—one of the most horrific concentrations of tenement-jammed humanity in the world.

By 1880 the next great wave of immigration filled New York's Tenth Ward around Essex Street with Eastern European Jews fleeing pogroms and starvation. James married Susannah Murray, another Irish immigrant five years his senior, and they had five children, including James Henry (Jim), Burt's father, born December 6, 1876. James Sr. moved the family uptown to 619 First Avenue between East Thirty-fifth and Thirty-sixth Streets. Perched on the edge of the island next to the East River, just south of today's Queens-Midtown Tunnel, the Lancasters settled amid a new mix of midtown working-class neighbors—butchers, machinists, florists, and varnishers.

Up the East Coast in the busy seaport town of Norwalk, Connecticut, in 1880, four-year-old Elizabeth "Lizzie" Roberts, Lancaster's mother, was living at 194 Main Street and developing the dominating traits of the first-born. In addition to her father, James, 35, and her mother, Jennie Smith Roberts, 28, plus baby brother, George, the house was filled with members of the extended Roberts family. Her parents had emigrated from Belfast around 1875; Lizzie was born in Norwalk on May 13, 1876. James was a shoemaker and the family lived surrounded by neighbors—carriage makers and hat trimmers—whose skills catered to a refined clientele.

The family proudly claimed to be related to Frederick Sleigh Roberts, the British field marshal who was later named the 1st Earl Roberts of Kandahar, Pretoria, and Waterford. The last person to hold the title of commander in chief of the British Army, Earl Roberts was from 1857 until his death in 1914 an outstanding combat leader in famous imperial battles from India to Afghanistan and, at the end of the century, South Africa. The elderly mustachioed man staring out of the John Singer Sargent portrait in the National Portrait Gallery in London has the look of Burt Lancaster: the strong, well-shaped head, the straight chiseled nose, and what Laurence Olivier would describe as Lancaster's "steely-steady" eyes.

The Roberts family left Norwalk for Manhattan shortly after 1880, probably sailing the usual route down through the notorious whirlpools of

Hell Gate on the East River. They were part of a land rush to the southeast section of the neighborhood of Harlem, an area that would become one of the most densely populated and volatile in New York City. For the first half of the nineteenth century, the flat plain, later to be called East Harlem, was a bucolic area of farms sloping down to the Harlem River on its northeastern border and loosely bounded by Ninety-sixth and 125th Streets, with the mansions and museums facing Central Park on the west. By the 1860s, the "Harlem Flats" was the site of breweries spewing malt and brew odors into the air, slaughter houses, coal yards, junkyards, and saw mills clustered along the river frontage. Isolated clusters of small four-story brownstones, built to house the workers, popped up like mushrooms in the middle of the fields that filled in the empty grid of future cross-streets. Irish shanty towns lined the water.

The rapacious northward growth of the city that followed the construction of the Second and Third Avenue elevated railway lines in 1878 and 1880 further engulfed the area with Irish and German immigrants. Speculators threw up row upon row of unregulated tenements with as many as four hundred people crammed into structures designed to house fifty. The New York Central railroad track ran aboveground up Park Avenue from Ninety-seventh Street, the dark stone viaduct further slicing up the neighborhood.

By the turn of the century four out of five New Yorkers were immigrants or the children of immigrants, with East Harlem absorbing each wave of newcomers. Rag peddlers trolled through the neighborhood's trash-filled yards and dead animals floated in flooded cellars. By 1904 there were over one hundred saloons in a forty-block area. From this rattling rhythm of immigrant change, poverty, and backbreaking labor was bred Lancaster's energy and taste for work. The tone of the slum was set: working-class immigrant, the lowest rentals. Years later he would remember crossing the de facto border of Ninety-sixth Street, sauntering down Fifth and Park Avenues to look at the rich people.

In 1900 James Roberts—a widower now, with two more children, Minnie and Stephen—rented an apartment at 2068 Second Avenue, near the corner of 106th Street in the shadow of the El. Lizzie, twenty-four, took on the responsibilities of mother of the family. Four years later, James bought what his grandson would call a "very poor little house," a narrow four-story brownstone down the street at 209 East 106th Street between Second and Third Avenues, built around 1880 on the north side of the street. The house had been divided into three rental floors, with a moving business on the ground floor. As one of the periodic broad streets that broke up the narrow Manhattan grid, 106th, even with the superstructures of the two Els marking both ends of the block, was less confined and claustrophobic than other nearby streets. The light was stronger and brighter all day long. A very young Walter Winchell and his parents briefly lived up the street between Fifth and Madison Avenues.

The Roberts family took over the second-floor apartment, a classic coldwater railroad flat with windows only in the front and back. Lancaster would describe it as "long, dreary, one room after the other" with a toilet out in the hall and a coal stove in the kitchen providing the only heat in winter. The big bay window protruding from the front façade was a perfect vantage point from which to view the busy street. The family derived additional income from the tenants, $16 a month per family by the 1920s. A landowner in the slums, no matter how shabby the house, was somebody.

Shortly after settling into the new house, Lizzie met a handsome, talented young man who looks in photographs like the lean and cunning James Joyce. Jim Lancaster had moved uptown and become fairly well known in the area for using his Irish tenor voice to win prizes on amateur nights at the local theaters with a song-and-dance routine called "The Broadway Swell and the Bowery Bum." According to various accounts, he played an old guitar, the ukelele, the accordion, and the harmonica. To Lizzie's take-charge assumption of authority, he was gentle. Both were remembered by their children as being in their youthful primes two of the best-looking people on the East Side, Lizzie attracting wolf whistles well into middle-age. Neither would ever have much inclination for daydreaming about life's impractical possibilities. They were married on August 8, 1908, and Jim moved in with his new wife's family. Over thirty at the time of her marriage, Lizzie lost no time in having three children over the next four years: Jennie Dorothea (Jane), James Robert (Jim) Jr., and William Henry (Willie).

In 1913—a year that would be remembered for several firsts, including the founding by Jesse Lasky of a motion picture company later called Paramount Pictures, and the opening of the tallest "skyscraper" of the new Manhattan skyline, the sixty-story Woolworth Building—Jim took a job as a postal clerk at the brand-new McKim, Mead and White–designed General Post Office. Not only was he working in a salaried white-collar position in an edifice which took up two full blocks between West Thirty-first and Thirty-third Streets, he got to wear a uniform. He may as well have been working on Wall Street.

On November 2, Lizzie, age thirty-seven, gave birth at home to her third son, Burton Stephen. A crowd of friends and neighbors gathered outside in the street cheered at the news shouted down from the bay window. The baby was named for Lizzie's brother, Stephen, and the attending physician, Burton Thom. Though Thom was a well-loved doctor in the neighborhood, known for his generosity and stiff white collars, mothers did not usually name a child for the doctor unless he had done something extraordinary, such as save the life of the baby—or the mother.

The young Burton became acquainted with death early. On April 28, 1918, Florence, Lizzie's last child, barely a year old, died at Willow Park Hospital of diphtheria, a victim of one of the epidemics that frequently ravaged the slums. Four-year-old Burton was back to being the baby of the family. Four months later, Dr. Thom was called to the house on the night of August 12 to confirm James Roberts's sudden death of apoplexy at the age of seventy-two. Lizzie buried her father, the last direct link with Ireland, next to her daughter at Cypress Hills Cemetery in Brooklyn.

Roberts's will divided an estate of about $1,800 into four equal parts among George, Stephen, Minnie, and Lizzie's four children, each of whom were to receive their share of the estate upon turning twenty-one. (The house was legally the property of the two sons; each would sell his share to Lizzie, who would own the house outright by 1927.) That $112 plus interest was waiting for him was another indication to Burton—like his blond hair, blue eyes, Anglo name, property-owning parents, and Protestant faith— that he was different from the poorer, foreign people he lived among. But to his uncles George, now a stockbroker living in upper Manhattan, and Stephen, a manager of Gents Furnishing living north of Yankee Stadium in the Bronx, East Harlem was a place you left. This consciousness of being a holdover in the old neighborhood produced in the boy a jumpy belligerence. He was never sure just where he fit in.

As he approached the age of seven, the raggedy, dissonant city that defined him was growing up too. The U.S. census of 1920 confirmed that for the first time America was an urban nation, with New York elevated to a new status as capital not only of the postwar country but of the world. When mass immigration was stopped in 1924, only one million of New York's six million residents were white, native-born Protestants, and only a handful of these lived in East Harlem.

Arbiter of all that was new and fresh and dangerous, the city was the nexus of popular entertainment during the 1920s. Led by the vaudeville revue, a slick mannered pose was elevated to iconic status. The city sort of ran itself; Prohibition was a joke. The "City on a Still" sobriquet mocked not only the civic ideals of the previous generation but the decade's compulsion, as Frederick Lewis Allen would write, to use the Bible to "point the lessons of business and of business to point the lessons of the Bible." Sinclair Lewis's hustling evangelist Elmer Gantry personified the overlap in his 1927 novel of the same name, which earned Lewis in 1930 the first Nobel

Prize for literature awarded to an American. By the end of the decade, Walter Winchell and Mark Hellinger were creating in their enormously popular newspaper columns the idea of the urban wiseguy on whom nothing—scandal, pathos, politicians, showgirls, cops, criminals—was lost.

Growing up in this Manhattan was like growing up in imperial Rome. You were marked for life as someone unique, elite, ready for anything the planet might dish out. East Harlem, however, existed on the fringe of the whirl and light. When Washington politicians went on about America's universal postwar prosperity, Fiorello La Guardia, the neighborhood's contrary Twentieth District congressman from 1923 to 1933, leapt to his feet and yelled, "Not in East Harlem!"

Though Eastern European Jews remained a significant presence in the neighborhood east of Third Avenue—Burton's first childhood pals were Jewish—immigrant Italians from Naples, Calabria, Sicily, and Salerno now dominated the quarter. Burton, who would play the Sicilian Prince of Salina in *The Leopard* and would truly regret that he did not get the part of Don Corleone in *The Godfather*, may as well have, he often recalled, grown up Italian. East Harlem's Little Italy was not only three times more populous than the downtown section, it was the largest concentration of Italians in the country. More than three-quarters of them unskilled, almost half illiterate, these Italians were refugees of *la miseria*, the perpetual poverty and disease that centuries of *mezzogiorno* peasants in the south of Italy had accepted as their destiny. Entire Italian villages occupied a given block making the East Harlem street grid a patchwork of the southern Italian boot. Slowly making his way along 106th Street, the 1920 U.S. census taker got so tired of writing "Italy" as the place of birth after each name, that the word became an illegible scrawl. The Sicilian Black Hand, a precursor to the Mafia, thrived just south of the Lancasters on Second Avenue between 104th and 105th Streets; the greatest concentration of the city's Neapolitan organ grinders lived on 106th and 108th Streets. From 107th to 116th Streets the pushcart vendors and hawkers at the First Avenue market offered oils, cheese, sea urchins, olives, bread, garlic, macaroni hung on racks to dry—the smell of minestrone, espresso, cigar smoke like a rich ether come all the way from Palermo.

The house on 106th Street had been further subdivided during the wartime housing shortage with the result that five families, thirty-seven people, now lived in the building. All, except for the seven Lancasters, were Italians. On the top floor, the Marsalise family with eight children and a grandfather squeezed into little more than two rooms. Outside was the clatter of the Els, all night long, sirens shrieking, trucks roaring down Third Avenue, the clop of horses' hooves on cobblestones, the reek of the toilets out in the hall, the stench of the East River at low tide. No secrets, no phony attitudes, no pretensions. The density enveloped Burton with the raw sustenance of a womb.

Burton's father was what the family called a "fun father," with a family trip to the great amusement parks of Steeplechase and Luna Park at Coney Island a rare treat. The usual routine was for Jim to arrive home after a day's work at the post office, change into overalls, and patch plaster, paint, fix the plumbing, or repair the roof of the house. He was a fine mason with fingers so calloused he could pick a piece of coal from the fire with his bare hands. Burton's job was to bring tea and sandwiches to a busy father who seemed to work all the time.

Like thousands of other hardworking East Harlem dwellers, Jim's favorite relaxation was to sit on the front stoop on a summer's night and sing. The Victorola was new, most music was still self-made, and the poignant sound of the human voice, needing no money or position or influence to be beautiful, was revered by both Italians and Irish as a divine gift. Jim sang tunes like "Kathleen Mavourneen," popularized by the ardent tenor John McCormack, and sometimes little Burton, with his wavy pompadour hair and boy soprano voice, would join in with his party piece, "My Wild Irish Rose." One evening Jim stopped singing and let his son continue solo for the gathered crowd. The applause was a revelation. Later, his famous speaking voice would always have an Irish, cocky, romantic lilt— with an Ulster edge.

Once a five-foot-nine-inch beauty, Lizzie after five children weighed 250 pounds, and she had a terrifying temper. Her bulk loomed large in the dark, narrow rooms of the flat and her extremism, like a genetic wild card, was inherited by her youngest son. "Mother beat the hell out of us," he would recall, once specifying that he "got the strap." "She'd have wild outbursts, then cuddle us and overcompensate for the lickings." He admitted that if he was a "terror," she was "more of a terror. I was always in mortal fear of her." Under threat of punishment, he developed a tactic of beaming his blue eyes up at her, throwing his arms around her neck, and saying, "Mother, dear, you don't love me anymore!" Lizzie would relent to the "utter disgust," as father Jim later described it, of his two other sons, "no charm boys" they. When she came at him with a switch, Burton broke into "When Irish Eyes Are Smiling."

The exchange of music for mercy created a profound emotional response in the little boy. All his life music had the power to take him back to that primary connection with his mother, back to the inchoate center where the rages began, and bring calm, even when he, who would have an exceptional memory, could no longer recall any clear image of her.

Together they listened to Lily Pons and Guisseppe de Luca on the radio and to her collection of McCormack records. She took him to the Metropolitan Opera house on Broadway and Thirty-ninth Street to sing in the children's chorus or stand in the family circle for $1.10. The old building overflowed with props and costumes, with extra sets placed out on the sidewalk. The backstage bustle and onstage drama were an exaggerated version of the peaks and valleys of life he saw every day on the streets of East Harlem, an art form he would love with a religious intensity. "Burt always lived his life as if it were an opera," recalled a friend, one of many who made the same analogy. Jim, home from the post office, would often trip over Burton, sprawled out on the sitting room floor, his head stuck all the way under the Victrola, his legs twitching to the music.

With the fanatic self-consciousness of the displaced ethnic, Lizzie insisted that her children distinguish themselves from the hoi polloi by scrupulous honesty. Coming out of the local Corn Exchange Bank one day, Burton saw a twenty-dollar bill lying on the sidewalk. Instead of grabbing it and taking off, he decided to cover the bill with his foot and wait twenty minutes to see if anyone came. When an elderly Jewish neighbor appeared, obviously distressed, and asked if he had seen a twenty-dollar bill, Burton reluctantly handed it over and cursed himself all the way home. More than sixty years after the fact he would recall in detail on the *Donahue* television show, hosted by Phil Donahue, when his mother, furious, made him return five cents in incorrect change to the local grocery store. An old man by then, as he acted out the story he stood poised, ready to dodge a blow.

With a strong dose of noblesse oblige, Lizzie showed by example that the Lancasters had an obligation to give to those less fortunate, which covered just about everyone in the neighborhood. The word on the street was that Mrs. Lancaster, after chewing you out for being a bum, would feed you and send you on your way. Burton watched these transactions, listened as his mother purposely simplified her speech to "Second Avenue English," had black neighbors in to tea, and shared what little they had. The actions became what he would call his "Bible." "You are your own slum area," she admonished him. "You can make it as mean or as meaningful as you wish."

Burton looked up to his older brother Jim, a natural leader and athlete who was nicknamed "Dutch" in the neighborhood for his bright blond hair. But Burton did not hesitate to hit his brother over the head with a baseball bat when Jim said the ball was out of bounds and Burton, "Little Dutch," said it wasn't. The bulwark of older siblings produced in him an obliviousness to the more boring demands of family life such as coming home on time. He was always getting lost, especially at the annual Coney Island clambake for the city's postal workers. When Willie finally found him among the packed bodies on the beach at the end of the day, he complained to his father, "Aw, Dad, all I ever do around here is retrieve Burt!"

Neighborhood fights were like a huge game with the playing board marked off by the corners, alleys, and doorways of New York City. "If you want to know about love," said Lizzie, "stay in the house. If you want to know about life, go out in the streets." Groups of boys banded together by block, which usually meant by ethnic group. Every day of his life, Burton would recall, he had a fight. His short height made him an unseen target for the automobile that was taking over the city streets, chugging through swarms of game-playing children. He was hit eight times, once by a taxicab that knocked him thirty feet in the air. His five lower teeth were bashed in when he went through a windshield. He broke his nose after falling two stories from a fire escape. With his pal Tony "Moby Dick" Iovieno, he swam off an old gravel barge at the end of 104th Street, dodging floating chunks of human excrement and water rats to cross the East River a quarter mile to Wards Island. The boys tested their balance teetering along the tops of the fences that divided buildings like the Lancasters' that had backyards, leaping off to raid the candy store or snatch apples from a pushcart. Burton developed a total lack of—or willed command over—physical fear.

On Saturday mornings the next-door cleaners would let him deliver clothes for tips, which provided enough money for the movies. He had a paper route and set up a shoeshine business one summer in front of Macy's department store on Broadway and Thirty-fourth Street. In an unguarded moment, he summed up his youth as "the cold"—there were never quite enough clothes to keep warm in the winter—"and the scrounging for jobs." He remembered his childhood as running, running to stay warm, always in trouble for something, singing at the top of his lungs to get out of trouble, always a little hungry, and his mother—"half her life," he remembered—hanging out the bay window calling for him: "Burton!"

If his life lessons had been learned solely on the streets, his future might have been limited to what was waiting for many of his slum pals—the boxing ring, the rackets, or the slammer. Luckily, a remarkable group of New York City institutions was ready to offer him an alternative.

Lancaster would credit Union Settlement House on East 104th Street as the single most important influence, after his mother, on his childhood and youth. An experiment in making the Christian Kingdom of God—the "City of the Light"—manifest in the slums, Union was founded in 1895 by a group of alumni from the Protestant Union Theological Seminary in Manhattan. Underwritten by contributors like Mrs. J.D. Rockefeller Jr. and

Mrs. Andrew Carnegie, it was created to serve the as yet unnamed area devoid of civil services north of East Ninety-sixth Street. One of at least fifty settlement houses set up around the country by 1895, Union was based on the activist charity work of Jane Addams's Hull House in Chicago. *"Hail the glorious Golden City,/Pictured by the seers of old!"* went one settlement house hymn of the time. *"Only righteous men and women/Dwell within its gleaming walls/Wrong is banished from its border/Justice reigns supreme o'er all/We are the builders of that city . . . All our lives are building stones. . . ."*

At their best such experiments in the "social gospel" tapped into the ardent hope that America might be the fulfillment of Old Testament prophecies of a heavenly kingdom for all people, a place where racism and class conflict wither in the glorious light of justice. Union's "special gift," as Janet Murray, widow of former Settlement House director Clyde Murray, described it, was to have settlement workers "literally go down, 'settle,' and live in crowded immigrant communities as neighbors," and then help the residents put pressure on the city and federal governments to make changes. The movement was a training ground for the progressive era of the first two decades of the twentieth century, often described as a golden age of American politics. While Union quickly shed any religious affiliation as inappropriate for its mission in a Jewish/Catholic neighborhood, its ethos remained religious in its insistence that the American experiment have an applied meaning.

Happily unaware of all this idealistic freight, Burton trooped down a couple of blocks to the settlement house almost every day to have fun. It was his home away from home, buzzing with boxing matches and other sporting events, and classes in painting, drama, English, hygiene, sewing, and dancing. Countless clubs taught the rules of parliamentary procedure: changing the world began with meetings. A large gym with an indoor track around the perimeter took up the entire top floor. "All this belonged to us," Lancaster would recall, "the local kids."

On Sundays the Lancaster family attended the Union-affiliated Church of the Son of Man, a Protestant island at 227 East 104th Street. Called "the church in a house" because it was indistinguishable from any other building in the neighborhood, the small, plain church was deliberately austere, stripped down to the essentials of the Christian mission. "Isn't it more satisfying to touch a few lives deep down at their roots," asked the pastor, Harris Ely Adriance, in one of his sermons, "than a larger number who 'hit the trail' and then forget what it's all about?"

Burton was one of those so touched. The names of Adriance and his assistant, David Morrison, turn up, again and again, in interviews throughout the actor's life. The two men were like emissaries from another planet, pointing the way to a different kind of life. Though Adriance, a skilled preacher, was constantly wooed by "[t]he rich Fifth Avenue churches," Burton would remember he turned down all offers in order to stay with them. A literate, intent man, slim with a small face, big eyes, receding hair, and a large forehead, his central message was St. Paul's plea for a noble life. "Lives that tell," he exhorted from the pulpit in the tiny wainscotted church room, "are those that are thus spread out to the full octave" of justice and fairness. One Sunday, Burton watched the pastor stop his sermon to welcome and seat a black woman who stepped into his church for the first time. "Not to be blinded, not to be controlled by prejudice, not to be warped, not to be unreasonable, these are the things," the preacher insisted, "for the spiritual man to battle for." Planted like a seed in the head of young Burton, these ideas would grow.

David Morrison was an exotic character born in Punjab to English missionary parents. He was also an artist who taught drawing classes at the settlement house and at the private Allen-Stephenson School on East Seventy-eighth Street. Using his drawings to illustrate Bible lessons, he gave children's sermons which in fact taught the children about art, how to *see* what they saw. Burton watched and listened, taking in Morrison's lesson that art, supposedly an elitist preserve, was a natural expression of life.

Most of the time, however, Burton was what his Sunday-school teacher, Carrie Nester—like Lizzie, a stalwart of the church—remembered as just another "snuffle-nosed little boy." He was the star of the children's choir until he was fifteen, his pure soprano voice revered even more than a tenor's. He had his first acting role as a shepherd (some accounts say angel) at the age of three in the church's annual Christmas pageant. Bundled into a burlap sack, he had no words to speak, but halfway through the production, when the angels, sheep, and shepherds usually get restless, Burton, center stage in front of the altar, discovered a wad of chewing gum on the bottom of his shoe. He sat down and started to work at pulling it off. "After much exasperated pulling," his father would remember, "he snarled at the top of his little voice, 'How'd this damn gum get on my shoe?'" A roar of laughter burst from the audience, who had been watching this bit of distracting business intently. "Mrs. Lancaster," her husband recalled, "was not amused" and whisked Burton off the stage.

Adriance got the eleven-year-old Burton to try out for his first proper acting role in 1924, the lead in a settlement-house production of *Three Pills in a Bottle*. Participation in the one-act play by Rachel Field earned him credits toward two weeks at Union's Nathan Hale summer camp across the Hudson River on the shores of Lake Stahahe in the Palisades Interstate Park. A popular sentimental work performed all over the country by amateur theatrical groups of the time, the play featured a poor crippled boy in a wheelchair—Burton's part—who gives away three magic pills to the imagined disembodied souls of three people more needy than himself. He sees a reality no one else sees and shows the other characters the better way—motifs that would mark many of Lancaster's film roles all the way to his last, *Field of Dreams*. If Adriance saw the experience as a vehicle to give the child a different idea of himself, Burton mainly remembered his hair. The director told him it stood straight up as if he had been "suddenly frightened." His tousled mop was already a signature.

When, on the strength of his performance, scouts from a brand-new theater company offered him a scholarship, he was brought into contact with the New York avant-garde theatrical ferment of the early 1920s, what Ann Douglas has called "the peak of American theatrical production . . . the decade's and city's most striking and deepest-rooted characteristic." Evolving away from the fin-de-siècle tradition of stylized gestures and histrionic emotings codified by François Delsarte into a method of matching voice with gesture to indicate emotion, a new American style of acting developed in the workshop ambience of the settlement house—the natural environment for what Harold Clurman would call "a sense of the theater in relation to society." These amateur productions showcased some of the more innovative theater work in New York. Jimmy Cagney gave credit to the Lenox East settlement house for his first acting part and a young Lee Strasberg performed and directed at the Chrystie Street settlement house.

This local experimentation was given a quantum shove forward by the 1923 visit to New York of Konstantin Stanislavsky and his Moscow Art Theater, hailed as "the most celebrated theater in Europe." The Soviet ensemble demonstrated not only the organic integrity of a repertory troupe in which no one was a star, but also presented what one reviewer called "the fresh vision of the Russian soul." The fact that no one attending the performances in Al Jolson's big "music hall" at the corner of Fifty-ninth Street and Seventh Avenue understood a word, except the ecstatic Russian immigrants from the Lower East Side who mobbed the director during the intermissions, only added to the mystique. Audiences embraced an acting Alexander Woolcott called "true and vivid and telling" in which the actor found an emotion within himself and then gave expression to it onstage. So soon after the Russian Revolution of 1917, a communal humanity seemed to surge across the footlights bringing Americans a blast of the faraway economic and spiritual devastation of postwar Europe. It was an early, potent exposure to the allure of the Soviet experiment.

Immediately after the tour, Stanislavsky's former Moscow stage manager Richard Boleslavsky and Maria Ouspenskaya, also from the Moscow theater, formed the American Laboratory ("Lab") Theater on East Fifty-eighth Street as both a repertory troupe and a training school for actors in the Russian method. One of their first pupils was Lee Strasberg; Stella

Adler also joined the company and Harold Clurman met her when he took courses in directing from Boleslavsky. These three, with Cheryl Crawford, would found the Group Theater, "America's first true theatrical collective," in 1931. The Lab immediately offered a few tuition-free scholarships for its three-year program to "promising students," the requirements being a strong coordinated body that Boleslavsky likened to the actor's "violin," a voice as free as possible from diction handicaps, and an ability to do hard, concentrated work. When Lab representatives climbed the stairs of the Lancaster apartment to offer the young star of *Three Pills in a Bottle* the company's first scholarship, Burton bolted out onto the fire escape. He persuaded his mother to say he was not interested. He got bored playing the same role night after night and was only doing it to earn camp credits. And it was too "sissy."

Lancaster, the star who was supposed never to have had an acting lesson, was in fact involved in play after play at Union and other settlement houses directed by new disciples of Boleslavsky. ("Hey, you heard?" Basil Natoli, a childhood pal, remembered asking the local gang on the street corner. "Burt's in a play tonight. Wanna go?") He would express contempt for the famously exclusive Actors Studio "Method" style that Strasberg evolved from Stanislavsky, the Lab, and the Group Theater. Later reaction against the Method would claim that it ignored movement, one of Lancaster's most distinctive characteristics, and that it detached itself from Stanislavsky's original insistence that drama connect to the outer world, to its time: "Above all," wrote Boleslavsky, "do not forget your fellow men. Be sensitive to every change in the manifestation of their existence. Answer that change always with a new and higher level of your own Rhythm. This is the secret of existence, perseverance and activity. This is what the world really is." It was no wonder that Lancaster later claimed that when he hid on the fire escape he was running away from his destiny: Boleslavsky's rhythm was a secular expression of the social gospel.

The Lab's theater opened for its first season in 1925 without him, presenting *The Sea Woman's Cloak* by Princess Troubetzkoy. Playing the part of a fisherman in the play was Harold Adolph Hecht, an ambitious, idealistic Jewish actor, born in 1907 in Yorkville, a product of a Bronx settlement house who remained a regular member of the Lab for the rest of the decade. A quarter century later he would watch Lancaster, a complete unknown, on the stage in New York and realize he was seeing his future.

Burton had no intention of playing dour Russian peasants when he could dream of emulating Douglas Fairbanks. In 1920 he saw *The Mark of Zorro* at the local Atlas Theater and became hooked on the brave, insouciant loveliness of the man often considered the first great male movie star. He kept going back to the theater, entering when it opened at 11 a.m. and staying through every show, skipping lunch and dinner until Willie was sent to drag him home. Sitting in the dark movie house filled with raucous kids, the little boy watched the glorious man on the screen and memorized his every move. From the title frame announcing the theme of "oppression" from which "a champion arises," the boy absorbed the image of a graceful hero doing battle against the bad guys, armed with little besides a big toothy grin and an agile body. "Are your pulses *dead*?" demands Fairbanks, exhorting the reluctant *caballeros* to action. Burton was already primed to thrill to the hero's exclamation in the last title shot: "Justice for All!" This was the star in charge.

The most seductive element was what the Russian filmmaker Lev Kuleshov most admired in Fairbanks: a physical expressiveness that emphasized the rhetoric of movement over feeling, a kind of updated Delsarte. The watching eye in the audience followed the body on the screen because the way it moved told a story. When the short, pudgy Burton got home and began imitating his new idol, jumping off, on, and over every piece of furniture in the apartment, he was only practicing to be a movie star, to tell stories with his body.

There were even more brave tales behind the fanciful Herts & Tallant–designed façade of the Aguilar Free Library a few blocks away on 110th Street. One of the earliest Manhattan circulating libraries, it became Burton's other home-away-from-home by the time he was twelve, a safe place because the gangs never went there, a perfect incubator for romantic dreams. By fourteen he claimed to have read the whole library: Lang's *Fairy Tales*, Shakespeare, Schopenhauer, Kant, Bertrand Russell, Spinoza, the brothers Grimm. He liked their words even if he did not understand them and imagined himself a character in every book he read. At home, when Lizzie came in to say goodnight after the gas was turned off, Burton would "give her a big loving kiss," recalled his father, and pretend to snuggle down just long enough to be sure the door was shut. Then he would take the flashlight from under the pillow where he hid it and read a Frank Merriwell adventure under the covers. Jefferey Farnol's 1910 "long novel of the open road," *The Broad Highway*, was a particular favorite and provided yet another potent archetype: the scholarly aristocrat, adept with his fists, who takes to the road to find adventure with highwaymen, gypsies, and beautiful ladies in distress.

A more current hero/model was his supposed relative. Burton often read "Lord Roberts," the poem Rudyard Kipling wrote in honor of the commander when he died in 1914 while visiting British troops in France: "Clean, simple, valiant, well-beloved/Flawless in faith and fame/Whom neither ease nor honors moved/An hair's-breadth from his aim." Part of the man Burton grew up to be would want to be like Roberts, especially the flawless part, especially the aim.

The discovery of movies, books, and poems was fortuitous. He had started to have run-ins with the local police that could have taken a dangerous turn. Lizzie knew when to distrust cops, however. One night at 2 a.m., when her son ran home from a movie theater followed by a policeman, she threw the cop down the stairs. His mother stuck up for Burton, even against the law—another chapter and verse of his "Bible."

His hungry mind loved the idea of school, if not its onerous reality. He entered P.S. 21 on 102nd Street in February 1920, and graduated from P.S. 83 on 110th Street on June 30, 1926—at age twelve, the smallest boy in the class. He raced through his homework at the last minute, cramming for tests the night before. His omnivorous reading and the fact that, unlike most of the neighborhood boys, he was continuing on to high school, left him open to taunts of being a sissy—a *short* sissy.

Then, just after he turned thirteen, he began to shoot up in height, continuing to grow over the next several years until he reached his adult height of six feet one inch, taller than either of his brothers. He also discovered he was an athlete. His body was coordinated and muscular; it moved well, responded to training. Like his star athlete brother, he excelled in basketball. No one had ever expected Burton, the bookish little scrapper, to be tall. Now he could hold his own, not have to battle his way through life as a short guy. The change was also frightening. People looked at his size and his emerging beauty with a different set of expectations. For the rest of his life, the body armor nature gave him like a surprise bonus would encase the wary child within.

In September 1926 he branched out from the self-contained world of the slum to the diverse, challenging universe of one of the great public schools of the era. Lizzie not only insisted he follow his brothers on to high school, but she chose the most academically demanding of the three best schools open to a New York City eighth grader of the time. Unlike Jim, who was attending Stuyvesant High School or Willie at Commerce High School and Jane at Hunter High, Burton went to De Witt Clinton High School for boys on Tenth Avenue between Fifty-eighth and Fifty-ninth Streets. In the midst of the railroads, rumbling trucks, market wagons, and penny-pretzel men of Hell's Kitchen, Clinton's motto was—and is—*nihil sine labore:* nothing without work.

The massive Dutch Colonial–style structure built just up from the eastern bank of the Hudson River was a response to the huge growth in public school enrollment since the Civil War and an expression of the same burst of national and civic pride and social activism that had inspired the creation of Union Settlement. Reportedly the largest high school in the country at the time of its opening in 1906, by 1926 Clinton had six thousand students, all boys. Hollywood press reports later claimed that Lancaster had little education, but in fact a Clinton diploma was an achievement to be proud of. James Baldwin, Richard Avedon, George Cukor, Richard Rodgers, Daniel Schorr, Thomas "Fats" Waller, Lionel Trilling, Countee Cullen, and Paddy Chayefsky are among its distinguished alumni. A laboratory for the progressive educational philosophy of John Dewey, the school prepared young men to be fully engaged in the world, skeptical of the status quo, ready for change through social interdependence. "We [are] young iconoclasts," bragged a yearbook commentary, "with blood and gall and salt burning within our spindly frames."

His course schedule was demanding. Four years each of English, French, physical training, and elocution—plus several terms of history, chemistry, hygiene, Spanish, biology, algebra, geometry, economics, and, perhaps at the suggestion of David Morrison from Union, two years of drawing—refined the self-taught jumble of romance, history, and philosophy in his head. His grades bounced around, ranging from 65 to 90; the more studious or active classmates' memories of him are vague. His instinctive defensiveness may have made him feel second-best in the midst of so many brainy adolescents and he never liked being second-best anywhere. During his free periods he built up his spindly frame in the gym on the parallel bars. Morris Meislik, Class of '29, remembers practicing gymnastic moves with him: "He was a strong kid . . . already pretty good at it."

In the spring of 1929 the school moved to a brand-new, collegiate-looking edifice in the middle of a green field just south of Van Cortlandt Park in the Bronx. Burton rode the El for a nickel, passing Yankee Stadium twice each day, and finally made his appearance in the yearbook in his senior year of 1929–30. At a scrawny 140 pounds (his voice had changed only a year before) and "so damn weak I couldn't even chin myself," he had come into his own as a fast-running ballplayer. He was a forward on the "brilliant" varsity basketball team of that season, and in their first game he scored twelve points—"like fifty points nowadays," he recalled in 1978, claiming he had earned a mention in the *New York Times*.

Graduating from Clinton in June 1930 at the age of sixteen, he faced his future without the person who had been his driving force. On November 29, 1929—one month to the day after "Black Tuesday" saw the inflated stock wealth of millions drown in a sea of ticker tape—Lizzie Lancaster died. Ill with what the death certificate recorded as "chronic intestinal nephritis," the immediate cause of death was a cerebral hemorrhage. Her body was laid out on a table in the apartment for the wake, a sight Lancaster never forgot and spoke of rarely and then only to family. She was buried at Cypress Hills on December 2, the third person Burton had seen die in his home. Jane took on the duties of the mother of the family, as Lizzie had done more than thirty years before.

His mother was the wall against which Burton had flung himself, secure in the knowledge that it would not give way. There had not been time for him to come to terms with where her overwhelming personality stopped and his as yet unformed character began. She had defined love for him as something absolute, violent, passionate, and loyal, and now she was gone. The hole she left behind in his mind and heart would never be filled.

One of the first things Burton—now called Burt—did after his mother's death, his father remembered, was throw away his comb. From now on he just ran his fingers through his unruly hair and let it go at that.

CHAPTER TWO

The Daring Young Man

*A circus is like a mother in whom one can confide
and who rewards and punishes.*

—Burt Lancaster

In June 1930, Burt was selected for a Union scholarship to enter New York University in the fall. He was obligated to put in time at the settlement to earn the $300 they would pay toward books and tuition. Basketball coach to the nine- and ten-year-old boys two nights and three afternoons a week, he also worked one evening as locker-room boy in the gym. For two weeks he was a junior counselor at the summer camp, as he had been the previous summer. Union noted for its records that while his father, who was now working intermittently at the post office in the neighborhood, would be able to contribute to his son's education, "Burton is anxious to be as nearly independent as possible." He took his responsibilities seriously, maybe a little arrogantly.

One night that month he climbed the stairs to the empty gym on the fourth floor checking that no one had snuck in unauthorized. Suddenly JoJo Tomasetti and a pal, Charlie, burst in with a message for Burt from a worker downstairs. He didn't recognize them and yelled, "Get outta here!" When he tried to hustle them out, Charlie pulled a knife and stabbed him in the thigh, close to the groin. Horrified, JoJo and Charlie ran down the stairs to find Helen Harris, Union's director. Burt followed, staggering and bleeding. When he collapsed, a staff member, later claiming to have "saved Burt Lancaster for future generations," stanched the blood until an ambulance arrived to take him to Mt. Sinai Hospital, a few blocks away on Fifth Avenue. When a streptococcus infection developed, he was moved to Lenox Hill Hospital, where he stayed, according to an account written later by Harris, for several months. "That little incident almost did Burt in," she remembered. "The Depression was in full swing and a major revolt was going on inside every boy, including Burt." His scholarship money was shifted, for a while, to his brother Willie.

Burt now had a year to kill, time to rethink his future. Most of East Harlem's wage-earning residents, who worked in manufacturing and construction, had abruptly lost their jobs with the onset of the Depression. More than a thousand men lined up on 104th Street one day in 1931 to register at Union Settlement under the Emergency Work Act. Local boys hung out on street corners, in candy stores or cigar shops under the El, shooting craps. Youthful ambition vanished and in its place came a sickening fear that was reinforced by the sight of families sitting on sidewalks surrounded by their possessions, evicted for nonpayment of rent. Groucho Marx cracked that things must be bad because the pigeons in Central Park were feeding the people.

The last days of Prohibition played out, spectacularly, on the impoverished streets of East Harlem during Burt's recovery year. With Mussolini's assumption of power in Italy in 1922 and his subsequent crackdown on the Sicilian Mafia, many of the *mafiosi* had moved to New York, fought the Black Hand, and taken over East Harlem. "Big Tee," a big-time bookmaker on 106th Street, "Dogs" Gazzola on 105th, and the infamous "Lucky" Luciano on 107th, were the crime bosses of the "East Side underworld" that fanned out around the Lancaster house. In 1930 and 1931, cutting in on the "big money" from the wine, beer, and hard liquor rackets centered in Harlem and the Bronx, an ambitious group of young gangsters led by Vincent "Mad Dog" Coll, age twenty-two and dubbed by Winchell as "The Town's Capone," were picking off the older gang leaders in a series of brazen murders that shocked the city.

One block north of the Lancaster brownstone just after six o'clock on the hot, humid evening of July 28, 1931, a large touring car carrying Coll and several of his men came up 107th Street through a swarm of children skipping rope and playing hopscotch. As the car slowed in front of the local Italian club located on the ground floor of a brownstone which abutted the back of the Lancaster property, a burst of gunfire from tommy guns shot up the walls of the clubhouse and the adjacent tenements. The bullets, aimed at a man lounging in front of the club, hit five children instead, killing a five-year-old boy. When the police tried to question the Sicilian neighbors, hardly anyone could be found who would admit even to having seen the car. Governor Franklin Roosevelt condemned the killing as "a damnable outrage," the tabloids headlined "the baby massacre," and a major manhunt began for Coll with police ordered to shoot to kill.

The sounds of the shots and screams drifted in through the open windows of the neighborhood apartments like the soundtrack of the newest

Warner Bros. movie. In 1929 the gangster flick surpassed the cowboy saga as the subject of choice for Hollywood filmmakers and, with Darryl Zanuck as head of production, Warner's skimmed the headlines for plot ideas, mythologizing the urban milieu. On April 24, 1931, *The Public Enemy* had opened at the Strand, the studio's flagship theater on Times Square. Fresh as a bomb in the minds of millions of adolescent boys would be the image of its star, Jimmy Cagney. His manic energy, slangy talk, defensiveness, grace, and electric speed had an added shock of recognition for Lancaster: he was looking at himself. Not only was Cagney the city boy incarnate, a totally new movie type inspired by real-life characters utterly familiar to the Strand audience, he was also an Upper East Side Irish boy, a product of the same ethnic soup.

The parallels in the lives of the two men are striking. Born in 1899, Cagney moved with his family to East Ninety-sixth Street, ten blocks south of the Roberts/Lancaster house, a few years before Lancaster was born. Surrounded by immigrants, both men learned early that with the hands and the body stories could be told without words. Cagney's mother was another pugnacious Irishwoman whom Cagney credited with keeping him on the straight and narrow by belting him into shape—"we loved the great staunchness of her," he would say. His father, like Jim Lancaster, was gentle and graceful, no match for his wife.

Both actors would insist that they had never been "poor," but for Cagney this was a distinction more of pride than accuracy. Like Burt, he got his first exposure to acting on a settlement house stage and went to settlement summer camp. He had an older brother who was a "flawless athlete," a younger sister who died in infancy, and a father who died the same year as James Roberts, a victim of the influenza epidemic. Cagney's "break-in" to vaudeville as part of an act (he lasted one performance) was at Fox's Star Theater at 107th Street and Lexington Avenue around 1921, when Burt was eight. Both men would credit vaudeville with giving them the live performer's desire to please the audience who, after all, bought the tickets and so had the right to decide what was good or bad. At the end of his life Cagney recognized the "unmistakable touch of the gutter" in him, which he made no attempt to hide, and the "wonderful, remarkable" people of his neighborhood. He remained tenaciously loyal, as Burt would, to the slum code of never forgetting a favor.

When Warner Bros. production head Hal Wallis saw early screenings of the studio's 1934 release, *St. Louis Kid,* and asked director Ray Enright if Cagney was in fact directing the picture, Lancaster's future boss at Paramount was posing what would be a key question for fifties Hollywood and for Lancaster's career. With his financial support that same year of strikes by the Mexican farmworkers of the Cannery and Agricultural Workers Industrial Union in California, Cagney made headlines as the first major movie industry figure reportedly involved with an activity whose leadership identified with the Communist Party. His loyalty to where he came from was expressed, at this stage of his life, politically. Not just tough on-screen, Cagney was city-smart through and through, as fearless and fast on his feet as the New York light fantastic, the very model of the movie star engagé.

Suggestible, antsy from his year-long recovery, Burt entered NYU's School of Education as a physical education major in the fall of 1931. What a settlement house report described as Burt's "existing condition" (probably the knife wound) kept him from joining the freshman basketball team. The lecture classes were huge in this commuter institution of thirty thousand students, with the School of Education alone enrolling about seven thousand. In college because his mother had expected it of him, he found that the work load was nothing compared to what Clinton had demanded. Sitting around in classrooms made him feel trapped. Nothing was active enough, tough enough.

He escaped to the roofs to fly birds with friends and watch the trained pigeons and tipplets swoop through the air, away and free. "Burt knew his birds," recalled Jim Zanghi, a neighborhood friend, "he knew how to handle them." Settlement house plays continued to absorb him and he mugged in the mirror at the Muschio Brothers barber shop on Third Avenue, telling everybody he was going to be an actor someday. Girls made him nervous. When he was sixteen he had his first romance with a Jewish girlfriend, Esther (some accounts say Hester), who became "the only girl" in his life for two years. When he had money he would go to a dime-a-dance hall on Broadway with one of his more experienced pals and hope for introductions. "He wasn't much with the girls," remembered Natoli. "It's not that he wasn't interested. He didn't have a way with them."

A couple of times he walked Emily Hernandez, one of the prettiest girls at the settlement house and a May Festival queen, to her home on Ninety-sixth Street. "I found him to be a little conceited," she recalled. "He was very ambitious even then. He would put down people and ask me things like, 'Why don't you raise yourself above this?' I didn't like him for that, for putting down the fellows he hung out with—when he hung out, which was very, very rare. He was a good basketball player so the fellows looked up to him, but I don't think too many of them were very fond of him. He was not a dead-end kid like he wanted everyone to think he was. Burt was above all that, in a little class by himself."

Honoring his now-reactivated Union scholarship, he arrived one afternoon at the settlement house gym, a little early for his 3 p.m. basketball class. He wanted to take advantage of the quiet to study. Over in the corner he noticed a man working out on a single horizontal bar. He watched the man's body swing through space—precise, controlled, intense, pushing the air away. Burt was tall and skinny and beautifully coordinated, but this was something different. He was mesmerized by the movement.

"I wish I could do that," Burt said to the man.

"I could teach you," the man replied.

That deal was, he would say later, like discovering his calling. The man was a former circus acrobat named "Curly" Brent who had a history right out of a Tarzan movie—or a vivid imagination. He said he was born into a wealthy English family on an estate in the interior of New Zealand, stolen by Maoris, and found by a missionary when he was fourteen, only to run away to join a traveling circus where he learned to perform on the trapeze and bars. By the time Burt met him, he was installing window awnings on skyscrapers and living in a boardinghouse on 105th Street. Hokum or truth, his story was right out of any one of Burt's favorite books, a confirmation that real life could be high romance.

The bar act is an ancient skill, dating back to Greek and Roman gymnastics. Revived in nineteenth-century European and American gymnasiums, the classic single-bar routine developed into a two- and three-bar sequence of grace and beauty that was claimed by circus pros to be the purest form of human physical display. By the turn of the century, thousands of young boys were signing up for tumbling classes and setting up bars in their backyards, as Burt eventually did. "Can you do bars?" asked small-time circus employers in the 1920s and 1930s, referring to the skill which could be added to clowning and tumbling by a versatile performer.

Supplanted over the decade by the movies, the glittering circus spectacle of exotic wild animals and amazing physical feats by international stars reached its peak as Burt grew up in the 1920s. "Great circus immortals" such as Ringling aerialist Lillian Leitzel, had a true and unique stardom according to circus historian Robert Lewis Taylor: "In their time of crisis, the split-second of something-gone-wrong, they showed courage worthy of their station." Not just glamorous, the feats were dangerous, a fact easy to forget because the art was in making it look easy—an equipoise irresistible to the young Lancaster. There was also something boldly sexual about the circus, the preening display of the scantily-clad human body, the heart-stopping risks, the ecstatic rhythm of the *saut perilieux*—the perilous leap into the dark, the unknown, the series of highs from which it is impossible, once addicted, to come down. "To grow up in America without dreaming about the circus," he once wrote, "is not to have lived."

THE SET-UP

After some sessions with Brent, Burt decided to bring along a short, tough Italian pal, Nick Cuccia (the family pronounced the name "Coochee"), to work out with him. It was the beginning of a relationship mythic in its mutual devotion and classic dissimilarities. "They were like Damon and Pythias," said Tina Cuccia-Cravat, Nick's daughter. "Burt couldn't be without Nick and Nick couldn't be without Burt," recalled Nick's sister, Frances Cuccia Rossi. "Any look at Burt begins and ends with Nick," screenwriter J.P. Miller insisted. Though they had known each other since summer camp, the friendship was sparked a few months after Burt entered NYU by the opening of the movie version of Mary Shelley's novel *Frankenstein*. Rounding the corner of 104th Street one night after coaching basketball, Burt ran into Nick, who was insisting to his gang of pals that there was something more than just a horror flick in this odd tale of the creator and his monster. "Let's ask Burt what he thinks," he said. "He's educated." When Burt agreed with him, there was a moment of mutual recognition— "It was like, 'friends!' " said Cuccia-Cravat—and Nick invited his new best friend to his mother's apartment on 104th Street for dinner the next Sunday. After lasagna and stuffed artichokes, the three of them listened to Mrs. Cuccia's Enrico Caruso records and talked and talked. Burt nicknamed his new friend Nicodemus, the name of the New Testament Pharisee to whom Jesus talks, in cryptic analogies, about the Son of Man and his promise of eternal life.

Nick was the Frankenstein terror of the neighborhood. "Animal" and "Little Dempsey" were his nicknames, the latter given in recognition of his Golden Glove career as an amateur bantamweight and lightweight boxer who was fast with his hands. Helen White, the settlement house drama teacher of the time, said with gentle understatement, "Nick had a few odd moments." The brutish frustration of Boris Karloff's monster who knows not what he does must have touched something in the Italian who had an almost pathological temper and would always be considered the real tough to Burt's softie. His mother, a Sicilian immigrant widowed with five young children, had put him in a New Jersey Catholic children's home for several years while she learned the seamstress trade. When the nuns beat him and confiscated his mother's gifts, he became alternately hostile or an aggressive clown and, by the time he returned home at around age eight, something had been destroyed. It did not help that he never grew beyond five feet two inches tall and left school after the eighth grade.

Burt felt an instinctive protectiveness toward this underdog, thanks to his mother's conditioning. It was the first of many such relationships. He claimed he could see the sensitive soul in the tight, powerful little body, and he liked being the educated one. Each knew the other would sense the slightest pretension. "I think my father never felt very important so he overcompensated by these overstrong opinions on things he didn't know any-thing about," Marcy Overway-Cravat, Nick's older daughter, suggested. "Burt knew more but he, too, would get a little cocky about his opinions and wasn't always right."

Remembered by his friend Zanghi as rarely smiling on the street, Burt had found not only a soulmate in Nick, but in his white-haired, kindly mother, a substitute for his own dead parent. "How he would laugh!" recalled Rossi of the many times Burt came to the Cuccia apartment for coffee and stories. "He'd crack a joke and we'd laugh like hell." Mrs. Cuccia could translate the Italian arias, heightening the exaltation of the music that produced a shiver in him, like the blood running under his skin: "You had to go out of the room because they listened so *intense,*" said Rossi. When Jim Lancaster kicked him out of the apartment for too seriously wooing a girl with the gift of a wristwatch and talk of marriage, Burt stayed with the Cuccias until his father calmed down. Years later, whenever he spoke of Mrs. Cuccia, he cried.

Curly Brent taught the two boys to make their own wooden bars on the set-tlement house lathe which they then set up in the backyard of the Lancaster brownstone. Burt thought he was doing Nick a favor by introducing him to gymnastics; Nick saw his future not only in gymnastics, but in Burt, the educated, good-looking "American," and refused to get a regular job, spending all his time practicing. Brent regaled them with tantalizing tales of the sawdust trail and the boys began to flirt with the idea that they might be circus performers themselves.

In November 1932, the worst year of the Depression, Roosevelt was elected President in an atmosphere of national crisis. The prospect of a cir-cus life now dangled in front of the boys like a glittering dream. From the movie *Cimarron,* starring Richard Dix, which had opened in 1931, they appropriated for Nick the surname of Dix's character, Yancy Cravat, as a stage name: Nick Cravat. Burt shortened the bulky "Lancaster" to the snappy "Lang," and "Lang & Cravat" instantly transformed them into something more than the sum of their wannabe parts. Burt quit NYU after the 1932 fall term and began to practice on the bars all day, every day. In early spring 1933, the boys snuck into the Ringling Bros. and Barnum & Bailey Circus at Madison Square Garden. With the confidence of specta-tors, they thought they could do some of the horizontal bar act moves just as well or better. Alfredo Codona, one of the aerialist stars of the Greatest Show on Earth, performed his famous triple somersault—the *salto mortale,* somersault of death—in the center ring, combining skill and energy with what Lancaster would recall more than fifty years later as a "beautiful style and grace." When the Kay Bros. Circus, a truck show formed in 1932, advertised in *Billboard* for new acts to fill the coming spring/summer season, Burt sent a letter to their winter headquarters in Petersburg, Virginia, explaining that he and his partner didn't really have an act, just a bunch of routines, but they were willing to work and learn. There was no reply.

Impatient to step into their new life, the boys decided to intercept the circus en route and take their chances. For forty dollars they bought the body of a Ford Model T into which was put a brand-new motor by a mechanic cousin of Nick's. Anxious to hold the family together so soon after their mother's death, Burt's brother Jim and his sister Jane were upset; Willie, who was closer to Burt, felt his brother should just go and get it over with. Later, Burt would think the phrase "run off to join the circus" described exactly his flight from responsibility, respectability, the ghost of his mother, East Harlem, the Depression.

Shortly after newly inaugurated FDR closed the country's banks for four days, Burt and Nick took off from East Harlem one morning, their rigging and second-hand tights stashed in the backseat of the car. Burt insisted, often, that they headed for Petersburg, arriving around April 15. But Bob and Mary Ellen Peters, the children of the circus owner Bill "Ketrow" Peters, remember a dumpy Model T showing up in Plainfield, New Jersey with two very green kids inside who had a lot to learn.

"They were very polite and mannerly and very quiet," recalled Mary Ellen. "Burt was very well-spoken," she added, in what was important code at the time for well brought up, educated. Their audition—a cutaway, or forward somersault between bars—was a disaster of falls, ripped tights, and bloody knees, a classic circus burlesque of anticipated success and actual failure he would never forget. "I was so excited," Burt recalled, "I fell right off. I got up from the ground, surprised and woozy, and tried it again. It was a trick I *knew* I could do, but after the sixth plunge of eight feet, as I lay on my back, my tights ripped and each vertebra separated from its brothers . . . I knew it was no use. If I could have accomplished the darn thing, the old-timers were too weak from laughing to appreciate it." It was unusual for a circus to hire anyone with no experience, especially in the worst period of the Depression. But Ketrow had only one excellent but aging bar performer, Paul LeRoy, and recognized the visual appeal of two incongruous figures working off each other as a team. The boys, said Mary Ellen, "sort of fit in."

The Kay Bros. one-ring show consisted of twenty-five people, a dog-and-pony-show format, and one elephant. It was "motorized," as opposed to the old horse-drawn "mud shows," which were too small and modest to travel by rail. Tootling along in fancifully painted trucks, the little circus made daily "jumps" of about fifty miles along country back roads. Up through New England to the tip of Maine and back on down the coast, through towns such as Hancock and Vestal, New York, across Pennsylvania, it ended up about nine thousand circuitous miles and seven months later in the tobacco and cotton country of Georgia. Lancaster, who had never been outside of New York City except for summer camp, found the New England countryside "beautiful beyond description." The troupe did two shows a day with Sundays off, for which Burt and Nick were initially paid three dollars a week each, plus board. After the first month, they were raised to five dollars a week. They loved telling the story of peeking into their first pay envelopes and realizing there was no way they could quit now: How could they admit to anybody in East Harlem that they were making only three bucks a week?

The boys were seeing the world—and from a vantage point that made them feel important. Circus people, Lancaster would recall, were "the only ones who had traveled everywhere and had seen everything." The fuzzy toot-toot of the calliope could be heard for two miles as the cumbersome, colorful troupe came from far away bringing wonders. Forming patterns of exhausting, nonstop labor that became addictive, Burt adapted to a life with the repetitive rigor of a military campaign. He and Nick slept on army cots in a tent, getting up each morning at five for a breakfast of sausages, eggs, bacon, ham, and bottles of milk. On the road by six, the circus would arrive in the next town about two hours later. If the trucks bogged down on an unpaved back road in a summer rain, the elephant pushed them out of the muddy ruts, literally keeping the show on the road. Pitching the big tent was the first priority at each destination, with everyone helping. Then Burt and Nick put up their own rigging, driving in eight stakes to hold down three parallel hickory "sticks" or bars, about seven feet high, six feet long, and seven feet apart. From ten to eleven in the morning they practiced and warmed up for the first show at 2:30, which would last about two hours, then more practice, supper, and the second show at 8:30. Sometime after 11 p.m., the circus gear would be loaded on the trucks and they slept until the next morning at five. Then they rolled up their tent and cots, threw them on a truck, and faced another seventeen-hour day. "When you're nineteen years old," Burt would recall, "you thrive on it."

On the road, LeRoy taught the neophytes. Because of the bar performers' momentum off the stationary bars, the act was considered one of the most dangerous in the circus. There were no nets, as with high-wire and trapeze artists; one missed cue and the "bar boy" went flying off, unprotected, in any direction—sometimes to his death. Cuccia-Cravat remembered her father saying, often, that he and Burt had "no padding." Burt admitted he had to swallow a lump in his throat and wipe his sweaty palms every time he looked up at "those bars." Because of the years of hard training and practice required to perfect it, the act was highly respected. Foreigners usually dominated because it was a "dumb" act, that is, requiring no speech.

Burt's solo routine began by his jumping up to catch the first bar with his hands and then building up a rhythm by swinging back and forth until he soared into a series of giant swings—a full circle in the air around the bar. He then launched himself into somersaults, flying from one bar to the next. Eventually he developed his star trick: letting go of one bar at the height of a giant swing, arching up through the air to land on his feet on the next bar, six feet away, poised and stationary like a big bird. Performing a variation called a "swing around" several times each day, he got an essential life lesson in showmanship when several layers of skin blistered off the back of his knees. "Lay off that trick for a while," Ketrow suggested, "and fill in with something else" while the legs healed. Burt stood there, "sort of paralyzed. It just hadn't occurred to me that although 'the show must go on,' there might be a less harrowing way of continuing it." Always being in motion, perfecting something, alternating back and forth to find a rhythm of sustained effort—the dance of the circus.

By the end of the season Burt and Nick were no longer, in the taunting lingo of the circus, "First of May guys." They were seasoned "Johnny Come Latelys" with a "fair, not top notch by any means" act, according to Bob Peters. "We were a family group just as real as any I have ever known," Burt later said. "When the box office was low, salaries had to be skipped but we always knew that no one else was doing much better. . . . We learned everything there is to know about trouping. And we learned about 'heart.' " The little troupe was indeed the first of many surrogate, self-assembled "families" in his life. He was hooked on what Taylor called "the fugitive bustle" of the circus, the life of "detachment and anonymity" in which it was bad form to ask where you were from.

Heading north in November to "winter" at home like an old circus hand, Burt returned to a jubilant East Harlem. La Guardia, "America's most liberal congressman," the half-Italian, half-Jewish gadfly who had argued against nativist hysteria for a larger, broader vision of immigrant America, had just been elected mayor of New York City. He stubbornly continued to live in a tenement apartment on 109th Street and Fifth Avenue, three blocks north of the Lancasters. When he championed Roosevelt's New

Deal, East Harlem residents gained in "solidarity and empathy," recalled neighbor Jim Giorgi. What would later seem in Hollywood like extreme behavior from Lancaster was very like La Guardia's. "The Little Flower," about five feet, four inches tall, freely admitted he was "inconsiderate, arbitrary, authoritarian, difficult, complicated, intolerant—a somewhat theatrical person." He also liked humiliating people and would routinely test a new victim to see if he would fight back. "Arguments based on precedent," according to biographer Thomas Kessner, "made him seethe," and Helen Harris described his "electrifying" speeches at the settlement house, where he denounced "tin-horn gamblers and sin generally." The only thing that could stop and quiet him was music.

As Burt refined his routines at the settlement house and plotted his next circus season, La Guardia took office on January 1, 1934, in one of the worst winters in New York history, during which the temperature dropped to a record minus 14F. More than eighty percent of East Harlem housing, including the Lancaster building, lacked central heating and fuel chits were distributed, redeemable at an East River pier for hundred-pound bags of coal, which people hauled home through the snow-blocked streets in baby carriages, wagons, or on their backs. Eighteen million Americans were out of work and East Harlem claimed the largest number of unemployed of any neighborhood in a city that itself had the greatest number of people on some form of relief (one estimate was 23 percent). La Guardia insisted that it was the duty not of charitable "hell-fearing millionaires" but of government—of society—to give direct relief. Lancaster would vividly remember the soul-destroying side of chits and queues: "The Depression brought change," he said later. "Despair. Hating the dole."

Not only the Depression, but talking movies, radio, and paved roads were squeezing the diversity and spontaneity out of the old forms of popular fun into which Burt's skills now took him. Smaller circus shows sprang up to take advantage of abandoned routes when Ringling was forced to end its Depression-scorched 1931 season on September 14, the earliest closing date in its long history. Many performers turned to aerial routines—the flying trapeze—which were more spectacular than a little bar act down on the ground. Or they switched to comedy, discovering that one clown/bar performer catching his coat on the corner of a bar and flopping to the ground got more immediate audience reaction than the studied beauty of the gymnastic routine.

Burt and Nick doggedly worked against these trends. They perfected a kind of syncopated routine in which each would work from the opposite end of the bars, executing full twisters and the giant swing finish with in-air somersaults back to the ground. Eventually their act expanded to include a comedy/bar routine with Burt playing the straight man to Nick's clown.

Burt's tall, gangling body did not really suit what he was making it do; he had to bend his knees as he swung to avoid hitting the next bar. But the oddity of his size worked in a business where anything that set you off from everybody else was an asset. The incongruity suited his nature. He made his own music of motion, an opera of the air, learning to use his body as an instrument of style.

The May 19, 1934, issue of *Billboard* listed only "B. Lancaster boss props" for the Russell Bros. Circus. Nick may have been recovering from a fall at the end of the Kay Bros.'s season, or the two may have had one of their periodic fights. The 120-foot big-top Russell Bros. Circus was another small to mid-sized troupe featuring trapeze acts, Central American sloths, trained elephants, a sideshow with a double-faced pygmy, and the "added attraction" of a four-legged girl. Starting off in Harrisburg, Illinois, the troupe progressed by quick jumps to Dunkirk, New York, and trekked up through New England playing a town a day (Burlington, Laconia, Holyoke), and back down through Pennsylvania, Maryland, Virginia, Alabama, and further south. With more New Deal cash jingling in people's pockets (circus receipts rose 33 percent from 1933 to 1934), there were so many motorized shows on the road that season that they ended up racing each other to be first to a given locality. On November 10 the season ended in Tunica, a northwest Mississippi town south of Memphis in a county that Jesse Jackson, in 1985, would call "America's Ethiopia." Somewhere in Alabama, intersecting with another circus, Burt met the woman who would be his first wife.

A short, chunky, pretty performer with fluffy hair, June Ernst was, Burt proudly claimed, "the only woman in America who could do horizontal bar tricks." Initially he may have had his eye on the skill and circus connections of her mother, a bar performer and aerialist named Ora Blush Ernst. She and her twin sister Pauline were the Loretta Twins, famous during the teens and twenties for an aerial bar and trampoline act and as the "World's Greatest Lady Performers on the Horizontal Bar." An ad in the June 30, 1917, issue of *Billboard* claimed the "Ernstonian" aerial troupe—the twins and their husbands—featured "Ladies doing Double and Triple Somersaults"; if true, they are forgotten in the male-dominated history of the once-elusive "triple." Burt—the future producer and star of *Trapeze,* the 1956 movie about mastering the triple—would have heard the circus talk about Ora and her heyday circus tours to Australia and Cuba and her stints with Barnum and Bailey. When he met her, she was performing a high single bar act with no net.

Lancaster claimed he fell in love with June in one February 1935 moment when the Ernsts, Nick, and Burt were all piled into one of the string of Chevrolets that Lang & Cravat bought on time throughout the decade. They were heading south to a quick gig at the Orange Festival in Winter Haven, Florida. June looked out at the cold New Jersey landscape and said, "Look at the trees in their brown little dresses!" Everybody laughed. Burt and June were married within a month. The entrée by marriage into this tight little world of circus greats was a perfect move for an ambitious young performer. All the more so because, according to Gracie Hanneford, daughter of circus equestrian clown legend "Poodles" Hanneford, who met Burt the following spring, it was "sort of looked down on to marry an outsider."

The unexpected marriage caused Burt immediate problems with his old partner. They were contracted to start the coming season in York, South Carolina, with the bigger, three-ring Barnett Bros. Circus at $35 a week. But the Ernsts were going with the Gorman Bros. Circus and expected Burt to join them for the opening in Hackensack, New Jersey, in April. Though Nick insisted Burt go with his bride, and found someone to replace him in the act, he was not happy. "My dad liked having Burt to himself," said Overway-Cravat. "He took the place of a girlfriend or a wife."

Two of America's greatest circus families were Gorman Bros. headliners with Ora that 1935 season: the Hannefords and the Clarkes. Poodles Hanneford, "the funniest man on horseback"—his 1915 record for twenty-six running leaps on and off horseback while running behind and holding onto the back of a galloping horse still stands—shared the bill with his famous daredevil flyer brother-in-law, Ernest Clarke, the first male flier to do the back triple aerial somersault. Hanneford had the extra Hollywood aura of having been tapped by Fatty Arbuckle to appear in films under Arbuckle's pseudonymous direction after a 1921 manslaughter case ruined the actor's on-screen career. (Though Arbuckle died in 1933, Poodles could be seen that season doing a version of his act in the Shirley Temple movie *Our Little Girl*.)

Under the critical eyes of such pros, Burt's performing skills improved. While June swung alone on a single trapeze, he performed a triple horizontal bar act—"The Lancasters"—with June's siblings, Mary and J.G. "For a big guy, Burt had a very good style—and the smile," said Tommy Hanneford, Poodles's nephew. "The bar act used to be called a 'stick act' and is considered the hardest act to perform, hard on your body and all muscle. That's why you don't see it anymore." Tommy and Gracie remember the newlyweds sleeping in the back of a station wagon. "June was very nice, sweet, arty," recalled Gracie, "a quiet person, small with dark hair. Pretty but plain. Burt was different. He was personable, a nice fellow."

There were now four railroad shows on the road in addition to about a dozen motorized shows. Towns were plastered with circus posters, often for three troupes simultaneously. The newly formed Interstate Commerce Commission enacted trucking regulations that added costs and red tape to what had been a happily unregulated business. When Gorman Bros. kept getting bogged down in rainy, windy weather, Burt and June decided to leave in July, mid-season, something circus performers rarely did (Gorman Bros. later closed, early, on August 10). After eleven weeks with the "Honest Bill" Newton circus, for which he was never paid, Burt finished off the season back home working for four weeks at Coney Island's Luna Park, the "Electric Eden" of thousands of brilliant lights bedecking exotic minaret towers and a neck-snapping Shoot the Chutes ride. Burt fit right in hawking the show to the eager crowds, a carny veteran now. Over the entrance to his favorite attraction, Steeplechase Park, a famous sign hung for nearly seventy years. The Steeplechase Man, it was a strange, leering Cheshire cat face, which some people thought obscene, with two even rows of grinning, super-white teeth. Its rictus grin is spookily like the Chiclets grimace of "Mr. Muscles and Teeth" of postwar Hollywood, Burt Lancaster.

By the fall of 1935 Burt was back in New York City in time to be a part of an explosive chapter in American entertainment, one that would be for him, as for so many others, a kind of conversion experience. In the New York theater of the mid-1930s, play and playwright seemed to have the power to dissolve the barrier between performer and audience, to make them into one charged entity ready to exit the theater and change the world. "Everybody was on WPA," Burt recalled, referring to the Works Progress Administration, the New Deal federal relief program, "nobody had a dime—but the vitality, the hope, the imagination! The theater was alive—*Dead End*, Lillian Hellman's *The Children's Hour*, the Group Theater, Clifford Odets, *Julius Caesar* in modern dress—it was a thrilling time." All his life he would recall "the entire audience standing up to hiss that little girl at the end of the second act of *The Children's Hour* . . . that was the place and that was the time."

Because he was on relief, he qualified to work for the WPA circus, one of the many arms of the Federal Theater Project (FTP), a WPA initiative designed to put unemployed entertainment professionals to work. Across the country more than forty-two thousand performances—dramas, puppet and marionette shows, children's plays, and dramatizations of current events called *The Living Newspaper*—brought live performances, often free of charge, to twenty million Americans. Many of them had never seen any kind of play before. The result was what *Fortune* called, in 1937, "an astonishment needled with excitement such as neither the American artist nor the American audience had ever felt before." The sheer size of the effort was, wrote Brooks Atkinson in the *New York Times* the same year, "beyond the scale of anything that had ever been done in the theater before." Of the more than twelve thousand FTP workers, almost half were employed in New York City, and army engineer officer Brehon B. Somervell was called in to administer the behemoth. The circus alone was a three-ring extravaganza employing 375 people, including the "world's largest circus band" of fifty-five musicians and a whopping sixty clowns. It was all expressly created to make Depression children laugh.

Burt cabled Nick in Chicago and told him to get on relief quick so he could qualify for the WPA salary of $23.86 a week and then he bided his time before the opening of the 1935–36 winter season. He and June were living in an apartment on Forty-seventh Street where June, entranced with the style of German expressionist dancer Mary Wigman, spun out dreams of the two of them becoming a dance team. For three weeks he took ballet lessons then quit out of embarrassment.

The winter WPA season started off at Ridgewood Grove, a boxing arena in Brooklyn, and circulated around the five boroughs of the city, continuing into the new year. Starting up again for the 1936 summer tenting season of twenty-one weeks from May to October, the circus performed during one of the hottest summers on record. Children from city settlement houses, orphanages, and detention houses, few of whom had ever seen a circus, were herded into packed performances, with one matinee playing to an audience of fourteen thousand, the largest audience for any WPA show. Eventually the circus's slogan would be "Two and a half million children can't be wrong." The hyperbole of the 1937–38 winter season program touted Lang & Cravat in Ring Two in a comedy/triple-bar routine of "daring conjunctive giant swings and far and fearless fly-overs." At the Harlem River Speedway in August 1937, as Hollywood star Estelle Taylor—known in the popular press as "the former wife of Jack Dempsey"—watched with a group of children, Nick attempted a back somersault between the second and third bars, missed, and crashed twenty feet to the ground, smashing his face. In late September he was injured again and remained out of the show for several weeks.

By the next spring opening in 1938, after more than two years with the FTP, Burt and Nick had each made other plans. They may have sensed which way the political wind was blowing and decided to get out before the big top blew in on them. When the FTP was created in 1935, what had started with the American Lab Theater as admiration for Russian repertory theater and its collective emphasis on the performing whole had been transformed by real economic hardship into what theater artists like Adler and Strasberg saw as a chance to test their mettle, to be, as Clurman would write, "devoted, courageous and boldly creative," like the Russians. Clifford Odets was "the King of Broadway" in 1935, his *Waiting for Lefty*, with its electrifying curtain call to "Strike!," playing simultaneously in about sixty American cities. By 1938, a midterm election year, conservative politicians were more than alarmed by a sequence of events including Roosevelt's attempt to "pack" the Supreme Court with liberal justices, the 1937 Memorial Day Massacre by Chicago police of striking steelworkers, and Odets's appearing on the cover of *Time*. The safe, careful country they thought they knew was threatened from all sides, but especially from within by communist radicals. The FTP was assumed to be riddled with Communists—at best a New Deal propaganda machine, at worst a patronage boondoggle for fellow travelers.

In July 1938, J. Parnell Thomas, a pudgy Republican congressman from New Jersey and a junior member of the newly formed House Special Committee on Un-American Activities (HUAC), released an unfavorable opinion of the FTP, calling it a "hotbed for Communists." Chaired by Rep. Martin Dies of Mississippi, the HUAC was charged with the mandate to find and expose "politically subversive activity" in not only the FTP but also the Federal Writers' Project and the American Civil Liberties Union. Roosevelt blasted the effort as "flagrantly unfair and un-American." By August, Dies was holding hearings and calling witnesses, including the FTP's head, Hallie Flanagan. Representative Everett Dirksen called the project's productions "salacious tripe" and one congressman asked Flanagan if Christopher Marlowe, the Elizabethan dramatist, was a Communist.

Hollywood tried to defend against what was seen, after Republicans won control of Congress in November, as the "quickest game" to start deconstruction of the New Deal. Tallulah Bankhead made a well-publicized trip to Washington to plead the FTP's case before the Senate. Lillian Hellman, Bette Davis, Katharine Hepburn, Clifford Odets, Jimmy Cagney, and others twisted the arms of congressmen and sent telegrams. A precedent for coast-to-coast radio appeals was set as major figures from the actor, director, and screenwriter guilds united into one committee to produce two radio broadcasts from Hollywood on June 25 and June 26. On June 30, 1939, the Federal Theater Project was killed.

The celebrity effort to save the FTP and the principles at stake left a mark on Lancaster. Freedom of individual expression, especially when different from majority opinion, and the mildly collective vision of America that inspired the FTP, were all in line with what he had been brought up to believe. The HUAC would resurface less than ten years later, with many of the same pieces and players in place but with the stakes much higher. He would be right in the middle of the game.

The swan song of the New York City FTP was *Sing for Your Supper,* a musical revue that opened in April 1939 with a cast of more than one hundred. One defiant quartet song, "Leaning on a Shovel," rebutted the common taunt directed against relief workers—that they did nothing but lean against their government-issue shovels—by explaining that only by leaning on them could they have built so many roads, parks, dams, bridges, and public schools. The director of this emblematic flop, years in the making as Congress kept cutting the funding, was Harold Hecht. After dancing with Mikhail Mordkin, the Metropolitan Opera ballet corps in Stravinsky's *Les Noces,* the Martha Graham dance company, and a song and dance act in the Grand Street Follies, Hecht followed Boleslavsky out to Hollywood in 1930 to choreograph dance numbers in Paramount and Fox talkies. When the production of musicals was cut back, he returned to New York in 1935 to join the FTP and the Communist Party. After the FTP folded, he went to work for the Nat Goldstone Agency in Hollywood as a literary agent specializing in theatrical properties—and formulated a plan. All he needed to succeed in this crazy business was a star. Then he could cluster the scripts and the directors around him and become a David O. Selznick.

Together with Ora, J.G., and Mary, Burt joined the Newton Bros. Circus in the spring of 1938, opening on March 30 in Greenville, Alabama. With twenty trucks, three elephants, eight clowns, nine high-diving dogs, a ten-piece band, and a drunk horse, Ora and Mary were the "ace number" of the program, according to *Billboard.* Burt and J.G. were the comedy/bar act. June was not listed on the line-up because the marriage was over. Burt would always speak well of his first wife, claiming that the two of them just drifted apart, too young to be married. She had bigger dreams than the circus, but he had married her *because* of her connection to the sawdust trail. But one close circus friend recalls that the relationship abruptly ended when Burt discovered June with another man. Personal loyalty, which was considered the paramount "male" virtue at the time, at least between men, was becoming what Pete Martin of the *Saturday Evening Post* would later call his "religion." He stood by people; they should stand by him. If they didn't, then what, under this big blue American heaven, could he count on?

An unexpected and severe economic slump made the summer of 1938 in the circus business the worst ever. Too many truck-and-wagon circuses had been created in response to the economic upturn of 1937 and they found themselves overlapping in towns too small to support more than one troupe at the best of times. Then the rains started. The smaller outfits bogged down in seas of mud that slowed the jumps between towns and cut back the already diminished audiences. By July 1, two of the five railroad circuses had folded. When Ringling-Barnum closed suddenly due to a strike, there was a mad scramble by the motorized troupes to claim their New England dates. In one of the heaviest rains of the season, the Newton Bros. outfit ground to a halt in Corry, Pennsylvania, and closed early in Willoughby, Ohio, on August 10. In early September the largest truck show, the Tom Mix Circus, closed forever. Showmen everywhere, said one account, were left "beaten and bewildered."

For Burt, it was 1935 all over again. Even Ora could not get him bookings now. Of his five years in the circus, he would only regret that he had not been good enough or lucky enough to have made it his real life. Like anybody so smitten, he was not in it for the security. He fed off the *insecu*-rity. "[N]o responsibilities, no bills to pay, no household to keep up. . . . A nice life," a wistful Lancaster told a *New York Times* reporter in 1953, summing up one of the most rigorous, dangerous performance arts as "comfortable, easy."

He was now forced into the lowest bookings—fairs, carnivals, the dying vaudeville circuits, and burlesque houses. After 1938 he and Nick operated out of Chicago, the hub of the booking agencies listing the acts used in the less sophisticated circuits of the South, Midwest, and West. In a kind of performer/agent cockfight, each season's dates were lined up at the Barnes-Carruthers Fair Booking Association, located on Chicago's Clark Street in what one of Burt's later press releases would call "a particularly realistic section" of the city. More than one hundred agents representing everything from amusement parks to road houses held court while Burt and Nick raced the other acts up and down the staircase from floor to floor. They stepped over drunken has-beens, going from agent to agent, datebooks in hand.

Acrobatic acts like theirs were a dime a dozen, not quite good or exciting or funny enough. Hurtling through the dark in their Chevys to one gig after another, Nick, always the driver, claimed to have racked up a million miles by the early 1940s. He would remember closing one gig in Kansas City and driving over icy roads to Milwaukee to report for a dress rehearsal the next morning. Exhausted, he and Burt had slept in their dressing room on the canvas equipment covers. At least one night a cop took pity on them and let them bunk in the local jail.

Every penny was saved, squirrel-like, for the New York winter when one weekend of work in five weeks was doing well. When that wasn't enough, a restaurant on Forty-sixth Street gave them open credit. Come the spring, the two men borrowed enough to pay for the gas to their first fair date, then they mailed off money orders to pay back their debts and the cycle began again. Bedouins of the heartland, they pitched tents near sum-mer fairgrounds and were fed by the local women's clubs all the homemade pies and roast meat they could eat for thirty-five cents. Feral, brown from the sun and the outdoors life, with a mop of tousled blond hair, bad teeth, and preternaturally bright blue eyes that already had seen a lot. In 1939 Burt turned twenty-six.

In 1940 they teamed up with a WPA circus headliner, Jack McCarthy, to form a new act called The Three Toppers. To the triple-bar routine, a perch pole stunt was added in which Nick balanced a wooden pole verti-cally in the air on his head while Burt shimmied to the top and, by the strength of his upper arms, swung his body out at a right angle to the pole and kept it there, like a flag. It was a light, fast, flexible act that could be set up virtually anywhere. They found themselves riding the jitterbug craze that pulled in huge audiences for the joyful rhythm-blast of swing. Lesser acts like theirs were clustered around the "bandshows" now performing in movie theaters between screenings of the opening run of a Hollywood fea-ture. The biggest names—Harry James, either Dorsey brother, Benny Goodman—were able to specify the "A" pictures they would agree to appear with. Weak "B" movies, of which there were many at the end of the 1930s, now needed the enhancement of some kind of stage show to ensure a decent-sized audience. All over the country, small-town theaters had to come up with weekly revues to "draw [the audience] away from Mickey Rooney–Clark Gable flickers," complained one harried manager to *Bill-board* in 1939.

Burt and Nick got brief bookings, typically lasting about a week, with top acts such as Ozzie Nelson's band, and at the Drake and Blackstone Hotels in Chicago. On New Year's Eve 1939, they appeared in a stage show with the Harry James orchestra at Shea's Theater in Albany, New York, opening *Balalaika*, an MGM musical. The headliner was radio comedian and former circus clown Red Skelton, at his peak as one of the highest-paid entertainers in show business, and the band singer was Frank Sinatra (who joined Tommy Dorsey's band immediately after this booking). Both Skelton and Sinatra would remember Burt on that show ("swinging on those crazy bars," said the singer), but neither of two reviews in *Billboard* lists any such act or person. He was merely an acrobat filling in before the name star.

Toward the end of the 1940 season, The Three Toppers arrived in Los Angeles on tour with the West Coast Burt Levey vaudeville circuit. Burt noted the "lazy tang" of the orange-scented air, the big "sprawling country town" with silver-haired ladies playing bridge in hotel lobbies and orange-juice stands on each corner. In an era when men still wore hats and jackets everywhere but to the beach, Los Angeles men walked around in shirtsleeves. A telegram arrived from Burt's New York agent, Eddy

Smith, informing him that an appointment had been set up with Steve Trilling, head of casting at Warner Bros. Smith thought his client might be Fairbanks-like movie material—or at least another Richard Talmadge, the star's stuntman (and reportedly the first "kid," at age 14, to do the triple for Barnum and Bailey). Burt was driven out to the new, modern studio in Burbank and, after meeting Solly Biano, Trilling's genial assistant, he sat around for about half an hour, feeling nervous. Inside Trilling's office he had to wait another ten minutes while he was pointedly ignored. Suddenly Trilling looked up, as if seeing him for the first time, and snapped, "What did you do, bribe your agent?" Burt claimed he went up to Trilling and said, "You're a rude, stupid little man," and left the room. He probably said worse. What did he care? It was only another humiliating indicator that he did not have much of a future in any kind of performing career.

The periods of no work were increasingly frequent and he went back to East Harlem to stay with his father and sister and hang around Town Hall in hopes of being able to sneak in to the opera. During a matinee appearance with the Nelson band, Burt's beat-up equipment broke and Ozzie and Harriet Nelson lent him the enormous sum of $1,000 to fix it. Over the next few years they received envelopes containing money until, one night when they were all in the same town, Burt came up to their dinner table, plunked down $25, and said, "This pays me off." Then he brought out a notebook in which all the payments were listed and asked Ozzie, "Will you mark it *paid* please?"

Like a big, brutal incarnation of the Keatsian boy with his nose pressed to the sweet shop window, he knew what success looked like, but he could not claim it as his own. He was smaller than small-time, the cruel vaudeville term for performers either on their way up or on their way out. At some point he was reportedly reduced to posing for what were called "meat magazines" for men, not quite nude, his body arranged in quaintly Greco-Roman stances. (Almost thirty years later a candid frontal nude shot of a young man carefully identified as "could be Burt Lancaster," smiling with taunting affection at the camera, would turn up in *Blueboy* and in a special retro Hollywood spread in *Playgirl* and even later on the Internet.) It was back to Lang & Cravat in 1941 and to playing the raunchy burlesque houses of Cincinnati, St. Louis, and Kansas City. "There's never a payoff," he told Nick. "We go without food, and without even subway fare just like when we started. I'm fed up." Nick was convinced they could still make it, but Burt insisted, "I'm not a kid anymore. . . . It's time I tried something else." In November he cut a finger on his right hand. When it became badly infected he decided to call it quits. After training a replacement for the act, Burt left for Chicago.

Thinking he would take advantage of the Christmas 1941 holiday rush to get a job as a delivery truck driver for the Marshall Field department store, he instead found himself hired, just after the Japanese bombing of Pearl Harbor on December 7, as a floorwalker in women's lingerie at $25 a week. The personnel director thought the handsome, college-educated circus performer was ideal to handle the women customers returning brassieres, nightgowns, and girdles. "I . . . learned," he recalled, "how to con those dames along" and he was kept on into the new year when he decided his path to success was as a 5 percent commission salesman in men's furnishings. He had always had an eye for good clothes and a hole in his pocket. If he had $100 with him and needed a suit, he would buy a $100 suit.

But selling was not as easy as it looked. "I was starving," he recalled— and so grew, as he put it, a notion. "My lack of success . . . was related to my slow starting sales pitch, which in turn was related to an inability to attract attention." He started doing handstands on the counters and then did a few cartwheels in the aisle, "distinguishing myself," as he described it, "from the wallpaper." He became the third-best salesman in the department, earning about $80 a week—good money in 1942. "Sell yourself first," he would say later, "if you want to sell anything." Through a local music critic he found a new circle of music-loving friends and was able to move into a North Side boardinghouse. A fellow salesman who occasionally worked at WGN radio in Chicago suggested he try for a job with the New York–based Community Concerts Bureau, Inc., a Columbia Broadcasting System (CBS) subsidiary. It would involve, as Burt later described it, "selling culture in lieu of shirts," traveling across America persuading communities to book top orchestras, opera companies, and ballets on tour.

Waiting for a response after an interview with a CBS rep, he took a summer job with the Fulton Market Refrigeration Company in the heart of the Chicago meat-packing district. With the same carny passion he had used to sell underwear, he took on the bloody butchers of Chicago. Seventy meat coolers had to be adjusted twice a day but Burt decided to make three rounds, "disciplin[ing] the butchers," as he described it. "I became," he said, "their pal." At the end of the summer the butchers signed a petition asking the company to hire Burt permanently. They had never had a cooler inspector who cared so much.

Just as he got a call to come back to New York for an interview with the head of Community Concerts in July 1942, his draft papers arrived. He moved in with his father and took a temporary weekend job as a singing waiter across the Hudson River in a Jersey City "night box," doing the odd after-midnight rendition of "Paper Doll." In the dockyard setting of gamblers and bookies, his quaintly formal way of asking the roughest customer for his order, please, instead of growling the usual, "Waddya want?" stood out. Some trace of Sunday school propriety had survived the years on the road.

"I never let it get up to my conscious mind," he recalled of the long string of grubby jobs now coming to an end, ". . . that all the time I was trying to be an actor. There was the pattern for me to read, spread out before me. But I wouldn't. Nobody—but nobody—can make a good life for himself if he keeps on denying his own pattern, his own drive, his real self. That was what I was doing."

On the night of January 11, 1943, along with the 101 other enlisted soldiers assigned to the Twenty-first Special Service Division of the U.S. Army, Burt arrived at Fort Riley, Kansas. Inducted into the armed forces in New York on January 2, he was now put through what his field artillery captain would later describe as "a thorough and gruelling basic training." By March, Private Lancaster had a forty-one-inch chest and looked the part of an all-American fighting soldier.

His basketball, circus, and vaudeville skills made him a perfect candidate for the Army Service Forces (ASF), a brand-new experiment in U.S. military organization. The functions of induction, deployment, demobilization, procurement, and delivery of matériel, as well as anything else that might need doing—especially the morale-building entertainment of soldiers—were assumed by the ASF, thereby, in theory, freeing Chief of Staff George C. Marshall and the field generals to focus on strategy and winning the war. The man chosen to run "the biggest headache in the War Department" was General Somervell, the same man who had administered the New York WPA. Out of the long and demoralizing trench warfare of World War I, General Pershing had emerged with an insight that became the motto of the new division: "Give me a thousand men who are entertained over 10,000 men who have had no entertainment." Not only was this to be a different kind of war, it would be fought by a different kind of army, a "smart" army manned by the first generation of Americans to have benefited from free general public education.

Before being shipped out for duty to a destination as yet unknown, the Twenty-first moved on to Camp Sibert in Attalla, Alabama, where they were taught a new curriculum designed to enable mobile units behind the front lines anywhere in the world to offer sports, a library, games, and soldier shows. For the musicians, all of whom were big-band professionals, the unit's commanding officer wrangled the equipment for a fourteen-piece orchestra, including a Steinway "Victory piano" that weighed five hundred pounds and was painted olive drab. While awaiting orders, the Twenty-first developed its first revue appropriately called "Let's Go!" Lancaster's duties expanded to include routines in the show and he was upgraded to an "entertainment specialist." When the division sailed from Norfolk, Virginia, in July, he was part of a group of seasoned performers who made up another of his self-created "families," friends he would keep for the rest of his life.

Well out to sea and safe from the loose lips that sank ships, the men were told their destination: Casablanca. The Allied forces, after landing in Casablanca in November 1942 and running the Axis troops out of North Africa, had just landed in Sicily. The invasion was facilitated, it was rumored, by the Mafia connections of old East Harlem neighbor Lucky Luciano; during an April preinvasion bombing of Palermo, the *palazzo* of Giuseppe de Lampedusa, the future author of *The Leopard*, was destroyed. The goal was the swift capture of Rome, after which, it was assumed, the rest of the campaign would be a straightforward march up what Churchill described as Italy's "soft underbelly," with a last-ditch stand by the German army at the northern border of the Alps. While due note was taken of the dangers—five hundred miles of rough mountainous terrain on which tanks would be useless—nothing could be allowed to slow down the advance. The fate of Europe in the summer of 1943 was thought to hang on the Italian campaign.

Burt became inseparable during basic training from violinist Arnold Belnick and pianist Boris Barere, two classically trained musicians assigned to the Twenty-first. Belnick was a culturally savvy New Yorker, while Barere had recently emigrated from Russia and barely spoke English (his father was Simon Barere, the "heartstopping piano virtuoso" who dropped dead of a cerebral hemorrhage at Carnegie Hall on April 2, 1951, while playing Grieg's piano concerto). They began giving concerts—Burt was Barere's page-turner—for the local radio station in Casablanca and were detached from the Twenty-first to play for the troops in hospitals and camps in Bizerte, Tunis, and Rabat. The trio floated free across the North African coast for the last months of 1943, "bad-mouthed as troublemakers," according to Belnick, by mistrustful, envious officers, and finally court-martialed in December for refusing to carry out what they considered an unfair task assigned by a sergeant. As punishment they were demoted back to privates.

They rejoined the Twenty-first at Caserta, just north of Naples, at the beginning of 1944. The division was assigned to follow the U.S. Fifth Army in its brutal fight for what would seem like every river, mountain, and hill town up the Italian boot. After the Italian government had surrendered on September 8, and Naples, wrecked and booby-trapped by the retreating

Germans, was liberated on October 1, Salerno, Anzio, and Monte Cassino became horrific highlights in the history of modern warfare. Bogged down in one hard-won Apennines ridge after another, the Allied effort was plagued by freezing rain, snow, mud, hypothermia, mines, dysentery, hepatitis, foot infections, and syphilis. When Somervell's global trouble-shooter, Major General Leroy Lutes, was later asked which theater of World War II had the worst conditions of all, he answered the mountains of Italy in winter. It took the Fifth Army and the Twenty-first Special Service Division nine months after the liberation of Naples, during what Lancaster would call a "starving, stinking winter," to reach Rome on June 5, 1944.

From then on, the Italian campaign was of dubious strategic value and the character of the top leaders who had staked so much to beat the Normandy invasion by one day became the subject of bitter sarcasm among the troops. Fifth Army General Mark Clark in particular was derided for his love of publicity and his inability, unlike General Douglas MacArthur in the Pacific, to plan and execute strategy that would both outwit the enemy and save lives. Ten, fifteen, twenty, even forty years later—especially when he began to subvert his heroic persona in the service of what a veteran could recognize as something like the truth—Lancaster brought to his military roles the wary stance of someone who had been there. No phony heroics, no vainglory.

He fell in love with the country that had colored so much of his childhood: the teeming streets of Naples; the Italian women "sensational," he said, "in their will to live"; Mt. Vesuvius erupting as if in sympathy with the devastation below. Wartime Italy was a landscape all the more surreal for the complaisant beauty of a vanquished people eager for Hershey bars and packs of cigarettes, awed by tall soldiers with straight teeth who seemed as beautiful as gods.

The Twenty-first performed the first live show to play on the Anzio beachfront—"G.I. Joe from Anzio"—after the Allied breakthrough in spring 1944. "Stars & Gripes," a minstrel show revue developed somewhere between Casablanca and Tunis in fall 1943, became the signature of the division and was the first American show to be staged in newly liberated Rome. Goofy and irreverent, it was a typical "soldier show" combining music, vocal solos, a quiz, a "stirring patriotic number" or a popular tune for sing-alongs, and funny skits about the daily gripes of war and old favorites like "Who's on First?" Anything lying around was salvaged for props and costumes—mop heads for wigs, coffee cans for floodlights. Burt ransacked bombed-out Italian opera houses for props and scenery. In the absence of women, the drag "chorus line" was a constant feature as were jitterbug jam sessions held in boxing rings with men dressed in skirts made from G.I. tents. In a 1946 *Screenland* interview, Burt recalled that "Stars & Gripes" received "commendations from Generals Clark and [Lucien] Truscott as the finest morale-builder in any theater of the ETO [European Theater of Operations]."

He would dismiss any kind of danger in his wartime career. But in fact, the Twenty-first often performed a mile or so from the enemy in the midst of what the official history of the division described as "severe" bombings and nightly shelling that made it impossible for anyone to bivouac. The Italian winter snow, rain, and frigid cold "forced the bandsmen to play while wearing overcoats and woolen gloves," noted the history, "and caus[ed] the 'girls' in the can-can chorus to come out with knees blue with cold."

Thanks to the Twenty-first's theatrical director, a New York actor and director named Thom Conroy, the shows provided Burt with a chance to speak onstage—a key link between his circus and movie careers. Two years older than Burt, Conroy had appeared on stage with Ruth Chatterton, Jean Muir, Spencer Tracy, and Tyrone Power, and was director for several seasons of Connecticut's Hartford Civic Theater. Burt loved this gay man's humor, loyalty, skill at bridge, and ability to play any of a huge repertoire of show tunes on the piano as he lit one cigarette from the last, sipping endless martinis. Writing sketches and helping work out production numbers for the constantly changing revue, Burt often acted as MC. For one act, he sat on the knee of another New York actor who was half his size, vaudeville comic Irving Burns (né Bernstein), for a take-off on one of the best-loved songs of the time, an Al Jolson hit, "Sonny Boy." When he found an Italian mechanic in Caserta to turn out bars on a lathe, he added a version of his old circus act to the revue mix.

He was learning to create spectacle out of nothing, to engage a shell-shocked audience in an elemental kind of theater poised between life and death. Fully aware that the average soldier from the front despised the entertainers behind the lines and often vented that anger by picking fights with them, he and Conroy incorporated the belligerence into their skits. The soldiers laughed at themselves, many of them for the last time. Casualties would reach 70 percent in some Allied units before the final breakthrough over the Apennines into the Lombardy plain in a rush toward the Po River in April 1945.

Belnick recalled that Private Lancaster was a quiet soldier revealing "tremendous enthusiasm and vitality" only to those he trusted. Barere claimed Burt "never gambled or drank," although there was evidence—knife wounds, a hair-trigger aggressiveness when challenged—that suggested his rough past. Ted Post, who would direct him in one of his finest movies, *Go Tell the Spartans*, was also assigned to a Special Service Division in

Italy and remembered the handsome acrobat as always reading and asking permission to go to the opera. "Burt had a very private life," he said. "He hugged it to himself." At thirty, he was older than most of his fellow soldiers and, Barere recalled, somewhat "depressed" about his future. But he had begun to formulate what Post described as a kind of "vision." In the midst of a world war being fought on the rubble of old cultures, "he was very aware of the difficulties of our civilization—he had lots of ideas." When his two musician pals—short, Jewish, and subject, as Belnick recalled, to constant "incidents of anti-Semitism"—were taunted once too often one afternoon at an outdoor restaurant, Burt leaped up on a table and "threatened anyone" to take him on instead. "I was always sticking up for the little fellows," he later said, "and fighting their battles for them."

The Twenty-first moved north from Rome to Cecina, Certaldo, and Florence in fall 1944, setting up another rest center, including six theaters, for the frontline troops at the ancient thermal spa of Montecatini-Terme in the Arno River valley of Tuscany between Lucca and Pistoia. Toward the end of the year a USO unit, including six actresses from New York, arrived to perform for the troops. Captain Phillip Leslie Tomalin, a singer with big bands in the 1930s, Susan Sarandon's father, and the officer who had escorted Danny Thomas and Marlene Dietrich into Anzio for their brave performance under fire, had just been named head of Entertainment Special Services for the Mediterranean Theater of Operations. With five days to write a musical comedy for the USO group, he created a take-off on Dumas's *The Three Musketeers*, written in jive lingo. For the part of the innkeeper's daughter he cast a petite, vivacious, twenty-seven-year-old, blond stenographer named Norma Anderson, substituted at the last minute in New York for an ill USO girl. Anderson was a girl who had what Tomalin recalled as a "wonderful sense of humor." On seeing Burt in the crowd that thronged the jeep on the way into town from the airport, she turned to the officer next to her and said something like, "Who is that good-looking soldier and is he married?" The officer set up a blind date for that evening.

The future star's second wife and the mother of his five children, Norma was born in 1917 in the far northwest corner of Wisconsin in the farm hamlet of Webster from immigrant stock with a set of political values very like those of East Harlem's residents. The Scandinavian farmers of Wisconsin, having fled the rigid inheritance laws of their homelands, were ripe for Robert La Follette's campaign to break the power of the lumber barons, rail bosses, and utilities companies; by the turn of the century, the city of Milwaukee had a socialist government. Norma's father, Charles Anderson, was a Swedish Lutheran farmer who settled in the area in 1896 and believed that every American should have an equal opportunity to make of his life what he could. Her mother, Mary Elizabeth "Mae" Carroll

Anderson, was a Roman Catholic of Irish descent who was working as a schoolteacher in the local one-room schoolhouse when she met and married Anderson. After the family moved to Opa-locka, Florida (Charles worked as the town's first gardener), in the 1920s in hopes that the climate would ameliorate Mae's asthma, Norma graduated from Miami Edison High School in 1933—her yearbook nickname was "Hot-Cha"—and arrived in New York just before the war ready for the high life of the big city. Pretty enough to work as a hatcheck girl at the Russian Tea Room, Norma was also smart enough to study at Columbia University's Teachers' College.

The story of the wartime romance as precursor to one of Hollywood's longer-lasting marriages would get spun many ways. Lancaster himself would remember observing that Norma made a point of dancing with the enlisted men at a USO dance, letting them cut in every couple of minutes. Later, he said of their first encounter, "love hit me again—and again in an offbeat, theatrical kind of way," implying a comparison with his sudden falling for June ten years earlier. He had a lifelong weakness for the bolt-of-lightning love that zaps but is maybe not so smart. It was often claimed in studio press releases that he and Norma were so in love they went temporarily AWOL that winter of 1944 and got married two days later in a civil ceremony in Pisa after Lancaster proposed inside the Leaning Tower. On Louella Parsons's radio show in 1948, Lancaster said that Norma was "locked up for three weeks" on her return to base and that he had to propose "through the bars."

Not only did the different versions of the same story conflict, they were all made up. Millions of postwar GIs could identify with such romances, so Lancaster's story was inflated to serve the expectations of the audience— and with even more contradiction and confusion, to cover for the out-of-wedlock birth of the couple's first child. What did happen in Montecatini, according to Tomalin, was that when Burt and Norma stayed out past the 10 p.m. curfew one night, Tomalin gave orders to the MPs that they be returned to their respective quarters and that was that. Burt told the pretty, sympathetic woman that he wanted four children, and she said she wanted a big family, too. She dubbed him "H.B.L." for Handsome Burt Lancaster, a nickname that would last between them for years.

Nine days after the Fifth Army reached the Po River, General von Vietinghoff conceded unconditional surrender of all German forces in Italy and on May 8 the end of the war in Europe was officially celebrated as V-E Day. The Twenty-first, which was in Ferrara on the Adriatic to put on "Stars & Gripes" for the British Eighth Army, followed the troops' pell-mell rush north into lower Austria, stopping at the town of Klagenfurt, which bristled with Yugoslav partisans eager to claim Trieste. Ordered back to Montecatini, the men dawdled along the way in Venice. One day Burt went alone to Padua, maybe acting on an old injunction of David Morrison, to see the Giotto frescoes already under postwar repair.

In mid-June, the Twenty-first received orders for shipment to the Pacific Theater via the United States and in August boarded the SS *Cody Victory* bound for Hampton Roads, Virginia. Five days out at sea the announcement came over the ship's loudspeakers: Japan had surrendered, the war was over. Lancaster and his band of entertainers arrived home just in time for V-J Day, September 2, 1945.

PART TWO

THE PLAY

1945 — 1960

*They were fun days and we set the town on fire
with every movie we did.*

—Burt Lancaster

CHAPTER THREE

Discovery

New York, September 1945, was an exciting place to be.
Fresh currents, people back from the war, a new order was beginning;
there was a certain ferment in the air.

—Irene Mayer Selznick

When Lancaster arrived home, 106th Street was a little quieter. The Second Avenue El had been torn down. Only the Third Avenue El clattered along on its dark metal girders now. The sudden end of the war surprised everyone and he was one of thousands of uniformed soldiers thronging the city, choking the armed services bureaucracy, which was unable to demobilize them fast enough. Manhattan was once again what it had been in the 1920s: the unbombed, intact center of the free world that had won the war. Nobody knew what was coming next. Whatever it was, it would surface in New York any minute now.

Burt's sister Jane, with a master's degree from Columbia Teachers' College, was teaching locally at P.S. 113 and living at home, unmarried, with her father in the dingy old apartment. Willie, with a law degree from St. John's University in Brooklyn, was now a lawyer and married to Ruth Thorkalson, a pretty Swedish girl from the neighborhood who had often played the Virgin Mary at the settlement house Christmas pageant. Older brother Jim was a cop. Only Burt, on a forty-five-day terminal leave, was unsettled, as ever. Nick, who had spent most of the war doing USO shows in the Pacific and married a fellow performer, Arlene, got him to re-sign with a Barnes & Carruthers route to do their horizontal bar act for the coming winter.

Toward the end of September Burt made a lunch date with Norma Anderson. She had returned to New York to work as secretary to Raymond Knight, the radio producer who had sent her off in the USO show to Italy and a media pioneer who had originated one of the earliest comedy variety shows, *The Cuckoo Hour,* in 1930 for NBC. Norma—now twenty-eight years old, unmarried, anxious to secure a happy ending to her wartime love story—suggested that Lancaster come see her boss, a very useful contact in the postwar job scramble, in his three-room suite on the fourth floor of the Royalton Hotel on Forty-fourth Street.

From this lunch date began one of Hollywood's most famous star-discovery stories. It was retold and punched up so many times it became another Horatio Alger of the movies tale, as arbitrary as myth. In fact, Lancaster's overnight ascent was a series of convergences, each building on the next, of circumstance, timing, personality, street smarts, popular yearning, and sheer dumb luck. Lancaster would say over and over again in counterpoint to the deus ex machina spin Hollywood gave the story that when luck finally walked into his thirty-two-year-old life, he knew exactly what to do with it.

Riding up in the Royalton elevator—still in uniform, "one hell of a good-looking soldier," one observer recalled—he noticed a man standing next to him putting "the mince pies on me," street lingo for point-blank staring. When the doors opened at the fourth floor, Lancaster walked down to Knight's office, the other man following behind and disappearing around the corner as soon as Lancaster opened the door.

He had barely been introduced to Knight when the phone on Norma's desk rang. Knight took the call and, according to one of Lancaster's many recollections, said dryly, "He's right here now. Sure he's a great actor, another Barrymore." The caller, the man who had seen Lancaster on the elevator, was Jack Mahor, a scout for Broadway producer Irving Jacobs. As the pool of likely looking actors was still at its wartime low, Jacobs wanted to know if the soldier would be interested in reading for the part of a sergeant in *A Sound of Hunting*, a fall season war drama by new playwright Harry Brown. Lancaster said sure, and Mahor rushed down the hall, handed him a script, and told him to be at the Green Room of the Warwick Hotel on Sixth Avenue at Fifty-fourth Street at six o'clock that evening for a reading. When he showed up, Thom Conroy was there as a friend of the director Anthony Brown (no relation to Harry) and later claimed to have done, on the spot, "a good advance job of selling" his army buddy to Brown. For his efforts he was on Lancaster's payroll as dialogue coach for the rest of his life.

There were high hopes that *A Sound of Hunting* would be the first postvictory dugout drama hit, another *What Price Glory?* The plot involved a group of GIs modeled on the infantrymen of the Thirty-fourth Division of General Clark's Fifth Army who are squeezed into one room of a bombed-out house on the outskirts of Monte Cassino and must decide whether to save one of the group who is stranded, perhaps dead, out in the no-man's-land under the German guns. Lancaster's Sergeant Mooney, the senior officer on the stage, is the "mother" of his squad, propelling the action. The theme of the play is the responsibility of each for all, all for each—cornerstone of the career to come.

The group assembled to put on the play were Broadway pros. Anthony Brown had directed both *Tobacco Road*, which had a record-breaking Broadway run from 1933 to 1941, and *Marching Song*, John Howard Lawson's 1930s "militant workers' drama." Playing Private Colucci, the wise-ass New Yorker–type who emerges as the unlikely hero of the play when he retrieves the missing, dead squad member, was Sam Levene. Patient, humorous, he was a natural teacher who helped found the Actors Lab school in Hollywood and in the 1950 smash stage hit, *Guys and Dolls*, would create what his *Variety* obituary termed "among the classic comedy portrayals in U.S. musical legit theater," Nathan Detroit.

At 11 a.m. on October 14, the day before rehearsals started, Lancaster, a little bleary from hunting down a sympathetic army chaplain to spring him out of the army early, showed up straight off the train from Fort Dix, New Jersey, for first run-throughs at the Hotel des Artistes on West Sixty-seventh Street. After a couple of weeks of what he would recall as twenty-four-hour-a-day rehearsals during which he had to learn not only lines but basic pacing and movement, *A Sound of Hunting* opened at the Locust Street Theater in Philadelphia for tryouts at the end of the month.

Hollywood studio scouts flocked to check out the new play only to discover a new star. When it officially opened in New York on November 21 at the Lyceum Theater on West Forty-fifth Street, representatives from all the major movie studios were in the audience. An intimate theatrical space with elaborate carved wood decoration built by the same architects—Herts and Tallant—who designed Lancaster's childhood public library, the Lyceum was ideal for an intense drama with a cast of twelve. The bombed-out stage set banked in mud looked like a piece of the wartime battlefield shipped home, especially when Lancaster barked out timely lines like, "Jesus Christ, what I'd give to do what I want to do for once in my life!" Max Youngstein, scouting talent for 20th Century-Fox, watched him "bounce off that stage with a vitality to him like a mountain cat." George Tyne, another cast member, would recall to John Guare that in the middle of an important line of what Tyne hoped would be his breakthrough role, he looked out at the audience expecting a sea of rapt faces. Instead, all eyes were focused on the tall, blond, iconic newcomer, silent in the corner.

Irene Leigh (later Diamond), scouting for Hal Wallis, suggested that the producer, who had recently left Warner Bros. to set up his own independent production unit at Paramount, check out this new talent. As contract offers flooded in from, reportedly, seven studios, with the best offers from Selznick International Pictures and Paramount, Levene began gently taunting his protégé. When Sergeant Mooney had to say the line, "Calling CP!" (Command Post), Levene, his back to the audience, whispered, "Calling Paramount!" Initially Lancaster decided to go with the man who made *Gone With the Wind*, but Selznick decided he looked too much like Guy Madison, the new star of his 1944 film *Since You Went Away*. Levene then informed the new discovery that what he needed was a "pirate" to steer him through the free lunch circuit of agents, producers, and scouts—and Levene knew just the one.

Enter Harold Hecht, in his element at last. After serving in the war as a staff sergeant in the air force movie division, he had returned to Hollywood and formed his own agency in 1945 with fellow agent Louis Rantz. Five-feet three-inches tall and thirty-eight years old, *Photoplay*'s Ruth Waterbury called him "a small-time agent," adding that there was nothing "much smaller in Hollywood" than that. Acting on a suggestion of Lillian Schary, Dore Schary's sister, Hecht came to see the play once and then came again, convinced he had found his star ticket to Selznickdom. Lancaster, meanwhile, "didn't try to sell myself to anyone," as he recalled later. "Instead I listened to what was being offered. And there was a lot to listen to for a guy who previously had had many jobs but no profession. . . . Then before the last performance of the play a small, intense man with a big smile came to my dressing room and offered me something the others hadn't even mentioned. 'Come with me,' he said, 'and we'll be producing our own pictures in five years.' " The postwar times demanded, the pair agreed, different, more realistic movies and they would be the ones to make them.

When not much remained of their original rapport, a respect for this first common purpose would bind them, as well as common backgrounds: Upper East Side of New York, settlement houses, Boleslavsky and his disciples, the Federal Theater Project. In Hecht he got not just an agent, but a former actor, dancer, and choreographer. "Burt had a natural survivor's instinct," recalled Post. "But he was also very touchy and needed to stay objective. He needed somebody to front for him." Wallis, alone among the majors, offered, in addition to a seven-year contract, the option of one outside, independent, picture a year, above and beyond any "loanouts" of Lancaster to other studios, and Hecht grabbed it. After meeting with the producer at the Waldorf-Astoria Hotel on Park Avenue, Lancaster signed with the studio famous for Gloria Swanson, Rudolph Valentino, and Gary Cooper.

As if in collusion with his destiny, *A Sound of Hunting* quickly closed. Despite some good reviews—*Cue*: ". . . a brilliant cast. . . . It looks, sounds, almost smells real"—the play lasted a bare two weeks, a victim of a war-jaded backlash to the victory jolt that had launched it three months before.

But for that brief period of postwar fervor, the handsome GI who had never fought in any battle was the personification of the victorious but haunted American soldier back from the war, what one critic would later call his "wounded colossus."

Wallis sent Lancaster a round-trip, first-class Pullman train ticket to Los Angeles plus a hundred dollars a week for his one-month option. If the producer did not like the screen test, the acrobat was "back in New York," he recalled. "Nowhere." He hopped the train leaving behind one problem that would continue along like a backbeat to all that was to happen in the next six months. Norma was pregnant and he had never gotten around to divorcing June.

Hollywood in January 1946 was a Sleeping Beauty–like kingdom waking up after a long sleep of depression and war. Uppermost in the minds of studio producers were the end of the busy, profitable manufacture of upbeat wartime pictures and the reality that many of the prewar stars were five years older and, well, prewar. Nineteen forty-six would be a banner year, with box office grosses reaching a record of $1.69 billion from an audience of close to ninety million who still showed up in droves just to watch a movie. The castle denizens stretched and yawned, largely unaware they had slept above an underground fault line that now began to shift, signaling the coming of a cataclysmic explosion.

Some tremors: in 1944 Olivia de Havilland won a suit against Warner Bros., establishing the principle that a studio could not, without violating a law against involuntary servitude, hold an employee under contract for more than seven years and the U.S. Justice Department reopened a 1938 antitrust suit against the majors, charging that their vertical integration of production, distribution, and exhibition of motion picture product was monopolistic. As people looked again at the craft of making movies for a brave new age, the huge studio structure looked suspiciously like the kind of dictatorship the nation had gone to war to defeat.

Hal Brent Wallis at Paramount was what *Life* would describe a decade later as "a pioneer among independents and prototype of them." He began as head of studio publicity at Warner Bros. in the silent era, in 1927 promoting Al Jolson's *The Jazz Singer*, the first talkie, which changed the industry. After Darryl Zanuck left Warner Bros. in 1933 to form 20th Century-Fox, Wallis took his place as executive producer in charge of production at the fast-paced, frugal Burbank studio nicknamed San Quentin. He blanketed offices and stage sets with studio pink slips printed with the motto "Verbal Messages Cause Misunderstandings and Delays (Please Put

Them in Writing)," forming a paper trail attesting to the producer's immersion in every phase and detail of moviemaking, from script to casting to lighting to editing.

The hot, up-to-the-minute Warner style that showcased talents like Cagney, Bogart, Edward G. Robinson, John Garfield, and Bette Davis had been as much the result of Wallis's obsessive cost and quality control as any artistic principle. Working with equally tough administrators like Trilling, he found a lucrative balance between the melodrama of *Little Caesar,* biopics, and Errol Flynn costume adventure hits and then set up his own independent unit within the studio producing pictures like *Yankee Doodle Dandy.* But when Jack Warner beat Wallis to the dais on Academy Award night in 1943 to accept the Best Picture Oscar for Wallis's own *Casablanca,* the furious producer quit for greater independence at Paramount. A well-dressed, solid-looking man, Wallis was also, remembered Max Youngstein, "one of the most obnoxious men you could ever meet."

On January 27, 1946, Sheilah Graham marked in her syndicated gossip column that Wallis's independent unit was exactly one year old. She noted that Wallis had recently signed newcomers Lizabeth Scott, Kirk Douglas ("a young Spencer Tracy"), and Wendell Corey ("a Bogart type"), as well as veteran Barbara Stanwyck. It is an indication of both the frantic race for new talent and Lancaster's unique presence that Wallis offered the acrobat, who had yet to appear in one *un*independent picture, the kind of flexibility given to bankable stars like Bogart or Cagney.

Burt arrived in Hollywood with borrowed clothes, a cherry red tie, and hair that "jutted like the tailfeathers of a disturbed cockatoo." "Who is this bum?" asked a casting assistant when Lancaster walked through the imposing Paramount studio gate on Melrose Avenue for the screen test dressed in corduroy pants and a sweatshirt. Byron Haskin, in Hollywood since 1918 and a director of photography at the time, was assigned to oversee the new boy's test and found himself first having to listen to an earful about what was wrong with the movies. Nevertheless he was immediately struck by what he would describe with professional precision as Lancaster's "complete naturalness . . . the rugged frame, the well-formed head and the regular features make him a cameraman's delight. All the angles are good . . . a voice which is low and well-modulated . . . a swell sense of humor which is reflected in his ease of performance . . . his memory for lines is almost photographic. . . ."

The test consisted of a couple of scenes from a film to be called *Desert Fury,* one with the impassively blond Lizabeth Scott—who told Youngstein that Lancaster was "one of the best-looking boys I've ever seen in my life"—and the other with Corey. When Haskin ran the rushes it was obvious the quirky guy had what director Robert Wise would call "a gene for the screen." No one bothered to tell Lancaster, however, and he dragged through the rest of the thirty days, staying in a San Fernando Valley garage.

At the end of the month, Wallis picked up Burt's option: for the first of a series of films he would be paid $1,250 per week; his salary would climb to $1,500 a week for the next series, and then by $500 increments up to $5,000. He would be paid $200 a week for now and, pending a better idea, his screen name would be Stuart Chase. Until filming on *Desert Fury* began in August, he was free to return to New York. Hecht bought him a car to drive home and Lancaster packed his bags, such as they were. By the end of the week, he was to be on his way.

If he had gone home to Manhattan for those six months his career would have been very different. *Desert Fury* would not have launched anybody, he later said, dismissing it as having "starred a station wagon." Instead, Wallis's assistant Martin Jurow, another New Yorker who had been at Warner Bros. during the Wallis era as an office boy for former newspaperman-turned-producer Mark Hellinger, saw the screen test and had an idea. Like everybody else in Hollywood, he knew that Hellinger, after burning through Wallis and then Zanuck at Fox and now in business for himself as an independent producer with Universal-International, was desperately searching for the right face to play the lead in his first film, *The Killers*. It was based on Ernest Hemingway's famously minimal short story which had burst onto the American literary scene in 1927 and out of which, it would be said more than seventy years later, "whole libraries of American fiction descend." Jurow wanted to return a favor to Hellinger, the man who never, ever let anybody pick up a check. Who better, he suggested, to play the lumpen fall guy in Hellinger's picture than the tall blond newcomer with an outside option?

Hellinger was another Upper East Side native, born in Yorkville in 1903. Winchell's old sidekick, the best pal of Bogart and mobsters, a prodigious drinker and tipper, a spinner for a reported twenty-two million readers in his famous *New York Mirror* column of "short, swift, sobby little tales" of Broadway so sentimental they could only have been written by a cynic, he was also a story writer for the 1930s hit movies *Broadway Bill* and *The Roaring Twenties*. He had a newspaperman's instinct for the story behind what were called, then, "the little people," with what Youngstein recalled as "the sharpness of Winchell, but none of the viciousness." His wife was former Ziegfeld Follies showgirl Gladys Glad and he speeded around Hollywood in a huge black Cadillac town car, a death-bed gift from a Manhattan mobster. Out of the car, he moved with what journalist Pete Martin called "the cocky strut of George M. Cohan," his behavior informed, said director Jules Dassin, by "that gangster honor."

The burning question for Tinseltown was, Could Hellinger craft a hit now? Hemingway's story involved two hit men in search of their victim, described as "a big Swede." Because the killing and the motive were not described or explained, Hellinger sketched out a backstory based on a Brooklyn heist that had always intrigued him, a robbery so well planned that everyone initially escaped but later "fully half the gang," he recalled, "had been kicked off and the money had slipped away from the rest of 'em." For the death-bed revelations of one character, Hellinger would claim inspiration from the dying ravings of Mad Dog Coll's nemesis, gangster Dutch Schultz.

He wanted the instant audience draw of Hemingway, but first he had to buy the rights from the author who had refused all previous requests. After Hemingway haggled with his "old friend" Hellinger, a price of $36,700 was agreed upon. Hemingway was not told quite yet the full extent of the liberties that would be taken with his story, title, and name. ("[I]t might be a very good idea," read one nervous prerelease internal memo at Universal, "to have Mr. Hemingway bumped off before releasing the picture.") The producer's story ideas were passed on to Richard Brooks and then to John Huston in late 1945 to draft into a script. The screenwriter of *High Sierra* and an exuberant adventurer in the Hellinger mold, Huston was moonlighting from both the army and his Warner's contract—he received no screen credit for *The Killers*. By Valentine's Day the storyline had been straightened out and polished by Anthony Veiller and was sent with Hellinger's detailed suggestions to Broadway producer and director Jed Harris to read. Nothing was being left to chance.

Except the lead. Rejecting the use of stars such as Bogart for fear they would swamp what was supposed to be a *story*-driven movie, not to mention his budget, Hellinger initially wanted to use Warner's big, blond Wayne Morris. The studio took its time giving him an answer and in the end he had to scramble to find an actor. "I was going slightly smorgasbord," he wrote later. "If somebody had suggested Garbo, I would have tested her too." Lancaster cut through the hype: "I was the cheapest thing in town, so he signed me."

This second discovery that launched Lancaster's screen career was, of course, more nuanced than that. Hecht managed to get a copy of the script and prepped his client thoroughly. He later claimed to have borrowed a suede jacket from Robert Preston so Lancaster would have something to put over his sweatshirt. When the producer came back from lunch the day after talking with Jurow, sitting on the porch of producer Walter Wanger's bungalow at Universal was what he described as a "character," absorbed in reading a letter.

"This guy was big," wrote Hellinger. "Really big. His hair was tousled. He needed a shave. No tie. And his suit looked as though it hadn't been pressed since C. Aubrey Smith [a British character actor] wore short pants. But there was something about him—

" 'You Lancaster?' I asked.

" 'Yeah,' he replied slowly. 'You Hellinger?'

"Fine way for an actor to talk to a producer! For a second, I thought I was back at Warner's."

One of the most graceful and voluble of men when he wanted to be, Lancaster moved and spoke slowly, fumbled with his coffee. If Hellinger wanted a stupid, schmuck Swede, he would give him one. But the ain't-seen-nothin'-yet worldview of 1920s Manhattan instantly joined the two men. This "big, brawny bird," as Hellinger affectionately dubbed Lancaster, was just a beautiful city boy from one block south of the Coll baby massacre who said funny, Runyonesque things like, "The *soyvice* was impeccable." And Lancaster knew as well as any American at the time that if Hellinger could use him, that was a good thing.

When asked if he liked the script, Lancaster replied that it was fair or maybe worse. It was the first one he'd ever seen. When Hellinger told him that although he looked the part, there would have to be another screen test for Universal's use, Lancaster said, No, he was going to New York on Saturday; the Paramount test would have to be sufficient. Then he left for the garage in the Valley. Nonplussed, Hellinger called him and pleaded that if he just did the test, he'd be a star, guaranteed. Lancaster finally said OK as long as he was out of town by Saturday. Thursday evening Hellinger took him to director Billy Wilder's house to rehearse with starlet Constance Dowling and the test was done the next day. Thrilled with the rushes, Hellinger called his discovery early Saturday morning to tell him he was on for *The Killers*, starting in late April. After the first film, for which he would be paid $20,000, he would make two more at $45,000 and $65,000 respectively. Burt headed east knowing he was now secure with two contracts.

As soon as he returned to Hollywood, Hellinger took him under his wing, guiding and shaping him for press conferences and appearances. Lancaster "handles himself well, is free and relaxed and 'gives,' " reported one Hellinger interoffice memo. "We should have no trouble with him. He sells himself without being a goddamn bore about it." The two men clicked, going to boxing matches, Ciro's nightclub, the usual round of Hollywood nightlife. With shooting scheduled to begin on April 30 and to end on June 28, a good part of this preproduction time was spent getting the script past the objections of the Production Code Office of film censors to the "overemphasis on violence and murder"—especially a three-minute crane shot of the payroll robbery which showed in too much detail how to pull off a successful heist.

Lancaster was not the only actor whose fate Hellinger had riding on the picture. After he saw MGM starlet Ava Gardner as a gun moll in *Whistle Stop*, he knew he had found his Kitty Collins, the slippery female who almost outwits everybody in *The Killers* script. Robert Siodmak, the movie's director, insisted she wash off the regulation MGM makeup, revealing what some consider the most beautiful face on the Hollywood screen. When Lancaster first kissed her, age twenty-three, in front of the camera, he was so "deeply stirred," as he slyly recalled years later on the *Donahue* television show, Siodmak closed down the set except for the two stars, himself, and the cameraman. Playing the dogged insurance investigator who unravels the *Citizen Kane*–like mystery of who killed the Swede and why was another New Yorker, Edmond O'Brien. Sam Levene, perhaps due to Lancaster, was cast as the detective who sends his old pal, the Swede, up the river, and Albert Dekker played the big-shot heist leader, Colefax.

In his balding, beady-eyed director, Hellinger found the person perhaps most responsible for showcasing Lancaster as a star. Siodmak was born in Tennessee but brought up in Germany and codirected with E. G. Ulmer the 1929 classic *Menschen am Sonntag*. After his 1945 hit, *The Spiral Staircase*, he was, as *Time* reported when Hellinger announced his casting of the Swede, "now regarded with considerable awe as 'the new master of suspense.' " For *The Killers* he would be called a *vater* of film *noir*. Lancaster, much later, appreciated what he called Siodmak's "UFA style," referring to the German pre–World War II studio known for dark expressionist shadows and angled shots that told the story as much as any hard-boiled dialogue.

Working with director of photography Elwood Bredell, Siodmak found the planes of Lancaster's face and body and shot the light and dark off them like a piece of kinetic composition. When the Swede, just out of prison where he's taken the rap for Kitty, arrives at the heist's planning meeting and turns and sees her on the bed, the camera stops just close enough to mark his face turning inside out like an adolescent's. The director also gave Lancaster's tall body room to move for the camera, which it did, like a cat. "So help me," shouted Hellinger when he saw the first rushes, "may all my actors be acrobats!" Lancaster shook so badly with fear during the filming that when he later saw himself on the screen in those same rushes, he was amazed there were not two or three of him up there at once.

When somebody pointed out that Stuart Chase was also the name of the prominent living economist who had come up with the phrase "New Deal," appropriated by FDR for his 1932 presidential campaign, Hellinger's secretary Myrtle looked up from her typewriter and said what about "Burt Lancaster"? Another core authenticity remained all his screen life: because Hellinger wanted the pivotal boxing scene in *The Killers* to look real—the Swede, a boxer, loses the match and his career because of a broken hand, thereby setting himself up for a switch into the criminal world of Colefax and Kitty—no doubles were used. Lancaster learned about moving fast and fluidly for the screen and very rarely if ever used a double for the next forty-five years.

There remained the last prerelease hurdle. Hellinger dispatched a publicity man with a cut of the film up to Sun Valley, Idaho, where Hemingway was working during the off-season. The author gave his blessing and Hellinger relaxed, a little. When the movie previewed for the press in Los Angeles in the first days of July, the reporters hoped it wouldn't be *too* bad, thereby putting them in an awkward position with their pal. Instead they saw a terrific example of what was called not highfalutin *noir* but a "crime thriller." Lancaster showed up for an initial screening but took off for the East Coast immediately afterward. On July 19 Hellinger fired off a telegram to his discovery: "PICTURE MET WITH REALLY GREAT RECEPTION AND SEEMS PRETTY MUCH WHAT WE DREAMED ABOUT. I AM AFRAID YOU'RE DESTINED TO BE A BIG STAR, YOU POOR GUY. CALL ME ON MONDAY. KINDEST REGARDS. MARK HELLINGER."

The wire was sent to 135 North Newport Avenue in Ventnor, New Jersey, where Lancaster was vacationing just off the boardwalk in Atlantic City. When the Swede makes off with the cash and Kitty, he goes to a cheap hotel room in Atlantic City. When Kitty in turn ditches the Swede, returning herself and the cash to Colefax, the ringleader sets up a contracting business in Atlantic City. More than thirty years later, the tawdry seaside town and Lancaster would make a comeback together, the old star looking oddly at home there for reasons long forgotten.

Hellinger mapped out a special publicity campaign to hand-carry his Swede around the country and introduce him to his old friends in the press. No one, not even Winchell, had more such friends and it resulted, as one in-house publicity memo happily observed, "in considerable space." Before *The Killers* opened in September, and before Lancaster had to report back to Paramount for *Desert Fury* in mid-August, Hellinger and his wife, Lancaster, and O'Brien went out on a prerelease warmup tour to twenty cities including Chicago, Detroit, Boston, Pittsburgh, Cleveland, and Los Angeles. In New York, everybody's hometown, the legendary Toots Shor hosted a party upstairs in his restaurant on Fifty-second Street. Eddie Duchin played piano, O'Brien did his party piece—a Shakespeare soliloquy—Toots cried, and everybody went home at 4 a.m.

When the movie opened, the reviews were all Hellinger could have wished for. His star was called "the brawny Apollo," "the brute with the eyes of an angel." From his first scene, speaking his first line, "There's nothing I can do about it," he was presented as a star. The long, single shot begins on Nick Adams, the friend running to warn him, and then moves up to the rooming house bedroom, across to the door, and back over to the figure of Lancaster lying passive on the bed, his face obscured in the shadows. Closing in, the camera stays on his face for more than twenty seconds as he rises up into the light and hears the sound of his killers on the stairs. "He came out of that screen and he was a knockout," recalled director and friend John Berry. "It's a goddamned cliché, but he was a hell of a good-looking man, an absolutely marvelous portrait of a virile, straightforward male."

It was an extraordinary debut for a complete unknown. Overnight he was a star with a meteoric rise "faster than Gable's, Garbo's or Lana Turner," as *Cosmopolitan* said years later. The movie played twenty-four hours a day at the Winter Garden theater in New York, where over 120,000 picture-goers filled the 1,300-seat theater in the first two weeks, figures *Variety* called "unbelievably sensational." Among the congratulatory notes flooding into Hellinger's office was one with "high praise" from Fritz Lang. Critic Bosley Crowther in the *New York Times* mused on Lancaster's "lanky, wistful" presence, a "nice guy who's wooed to his ruin"; Manny Farber in *The New Republic* described him as "a fascinating, unstereotyped movie tough" with "a dreamy, peaceful, introspective air that dissociates him from everything earthly." Looking back over the movies of 1946, *Life* rated *The Killers* the "best gangster film since the days of *Little Caesar* . . . a minor masterpiece." Siodmak, Veiller, and Miklos Rozsa, whose dum-ta-dum-dum music theme was later used in the *Dragnet* television series, all got Academy Award nominations. Hellinger bought his director a Cadillac.

And the people sitting in the dark, watching? A queasy, shell-shocked feeling had set in with the ticket-buyers Hellinger's scouts now identified as "a normal man and woman crowd," men wary of the women they didn't know anymore, and women frightened of the changed boys who had seen too much too soon. The immediate postwar years had a black undercurrent, *noir*. If Lancaster was so frightened of the camera he shook, the fear in the beauty of his young face wrenched something in the hearts of the viewers Gore Vidal would describe as "that passionate, hungry postwar audience that no longer exists." The Swede is killed because he thinks he should be. The stoic Hemingway stance that had produced so many imitations mutated in Lancaster's Swede into an almost voluptuous embrace of death. "The story was about coming back from the war," said Hemingway, "but there was no mention of the war in it."

The new star did not recognize his voice up there on the screen, and thought his hair "looked like a bird's nest, going all over the place." Part of him was indeed the tough city boy/warrior Hemingway so admired as a type. Another, much deeper core trapped in the big, god-like body was the soft Swede, the sucker, Hellinger's little man of the streets. It would be Lancaster's peculiar destiny to look like the American hero but to grow into the American man he really was. And he would do it on-screen, telling his story back to his audience, who in turn saw its own story.

The rewards of instant discovery came fast. He moved into a house rented from actor Conrad Nagel that hung over the ocean at 24142 Roosevelt Highway, Pacific Palisades, today's Pacific Coast Road in Malibu. And, according to Mickey Knox, another Wallis actor signed on shortly after Lancaster and a very close friend of Burt's at the time, he took up with Marlene Dietrich.

Back in town from Europe for the first time since the end of the war to shoot Paramount's *Golden Earrings*, Dietrich was forty-five and had just ended her wartime love affair with French actor Jean Gabin. She and Lancaster were photographed out on the town at clubs and restaurants and when he was asked by Louella Parsons which star he would most like to appear in a picture with, he answered, "Dietrich"—otherwise not the most obvious choice. "She wouldn't have looked at him if he hadn't been a star," says Knox. "Marlene was like that." In Malibu she got up at six in the morning to cook breakfast, also packing bagels, lox, cheese, and fresh doughnuts for him to take to the studio for lunch. The high priestess of the silver screen who had followed the Fifth Army into Rome initiated the new boy into the mysteries of Lotusland. The liaison was brief. At the end of the year, Dietrich sailed back to Europe.

Wallis, meanwhile, had hustled to catch up with Hellinger. Lancaster's role as a stolid deputy sheriff in *Desert Fury* was enlarged and the movie filmed in 110-degree heat from mid-August into October in and around Sedona, Arizona. A sunny *noir* oxymoron of surreal color and huge lumbering cars, the script had gangsters, gambling queens, cops, and the blond Lizabeth Scott all snarling at each other while squinting into the sun. "To the good old days," says one character. "What was good about 'em?" snaps back another. *Time* called the movie "impossible to take with a straight face" when it was released a year later.

Lancaster brought his brother Willie and his wife, Ruth, plus his father out to live with him in Malibu in early November. But on the twenty-third, the favorite brother who was going to protect Burt from the Hollywood sharks as he had always managed to find him in the crowds at Coney Island, dropped dead at the age of thirty-four of a heart attack at the seaside house. He was the fourth close family member to die in Burt's lifetime so far. Years later, Lancaster was still saying, "My brother lost to me."

Because of this recent death, it was announced in the *Los Angeles Examiner* of December 28, 1946, that there would be no reception or party after the marriage in Yuma, Arizona, that day of film star Burt Lancaster and Norma Anderson. Yuma called itself "The Wedding Capital" because couples could get married just over the California-Arizona border without the California waiting period. The bride was officially described as a former USO entertainer, a widow, and the mother of a six-month-old son by her first marriage to an army flyer who had died in the war. Irving Burns was Lancaster's best man. Parsons announced that the quickie marriage would "still the rumors that [Lancaster] was romancing with this and that Hollywood girl."

Only the parts about Willie, the USO, and Burns in the wedding announcement were fact. There was no previous marriage to an army flyer. The son was Lancaster's. During the first summer press preview of *The Killers,* which Lancaster had abruptly left to head home, Norma had given birth back East on June 30 to a baby boy, his son. Conception had taken place sometime during rehearsals for *The Sound of Hunting* and turned a postwar fling into something a lot more complicated. Though Lancaster tried "frantically," recalls another friend, to raise money for an abortion, that solution for Norma, raised a Catholic, was out of the question. The baby was named James Stephen and called Jimmy. Burt's divorce from June was not finalized until the end of December.

A cable in early July from Hellinger's Universal office to a New York rep specified that Lancaster was arriving in New York July 7; by the fourteenth he was in Atlantic City, not the logical place for a new mother and baby, but ideal for a bachelor whose life had been a whirl for ten months. Another Hellinger memo insisted the new star was to "lay low until Mark [Hellinger] comes east"; ". . . offer any courtesies," ordered the studio, "but don't use him for publicity or reveal his presence in New York." Walter Seltzer, publicity director for Wallis at the time, says that Paramount was also aware of the threat of scandal. Knox recalls that Wallis put "a lot of pressure" on Lancaster to marry Norma.

To be at last on the brink of major fame and faced with fatherhood and another marriage was like the self-set trap his *noir* suckers would keep walking into. Worse, Norma was a serious alcoholic who had kept a bottle of whiskey in her desk drawer at Knight's office and the baby was born with a foot deformation. Each week for the first eight months of his life, fresh casts were applied to the leg, Jimmy screaming in pain and shock each time; Norma later claimed the process had a permanent effect on the child. Lancaster called Nick Cravat in Michigan City, Indiana, where he had settled after the war and asked, agonized, what he should do. "Give the child a name," said his friend. "The rest can take care of itself." In the end his personal code demanded he help anyone who had ever helped him, and without Norma he would not have gotten the part in *A Sound of Hunting.* He made the best of it and willed himself to make it work. Hellinger's warnings that Lancaster would be in debt in no time with such a string of obligations were ignored. He would now be Big Daddy, needed but needing no one.

The family ménage moved into the rented Malibu house, a raffish place with dusty ship models on the mantels. In a matter of weeks Conroy, Burns, and what Hellinger called "grubby old acrobats" moved in too. The Wisconsin farm girl in Norma was happy cooking for whomever showed up although one acquaintance remembers her as being drunk most evenings. Clyde Murray, the director of Union Settlement, in Los Angeles once for a conference during these early years of Lancaster's marriage, was struck by the simplicity of their non-Hollywood lifestyle, seemingly modeled on the values Union had worked to instill into its now most famous protégé. While Lancaster made aggressive public comments like, "I've made up my mind that Hollywood isn't going to get me. I'm going to be one guy who won't let it rot his soul," to Murray he confided a fear that his sudden success would turn out to be a fluke. "Well, I was lucky," he said, "but this may be the only one."

The circumstances of his marriage required him to take a defensive attitude to the press, a stance he was only too ready to assume. "Burt was not impressed with Hopper, Parsons, and Graham," said Walter Seltzer, referring to the three most influential Hollywood gossip columnists of the time. "He didn't give a damn. Obviously it didn't inhibit his success." He was one of the last great stars to get the elaborately artificial campaign of personal appearances and fan magazine coverage that carefully built up an acceptable image to the ticket-buying public. With obvious athletic gifts but little experience with organized sports other than basketball and gymnastics, he was taken by Seltzer one day to sports locales around town for a magazine photo shoot. "We took him to a baseball batting cage," Seltzer recounts, "and Burt took off as though he'd been doing it all his life. We took him to a golf driving range—he'd never played golf in his life—and he was swatting with the best of them."

The physical control of a natural athlete centered him. "Burt was a tough guy to deal with," recalls Seltzer of these early days, "yet very engaging, very pleasant and independent right from the beginning. He was very, very self-contained, very matter-of-fact, not starstruck. He knew he had a large career ahead of him and was not full of himself, but full of confidence."

By the end of 1946, Lancaster was in the middle of shooting his next Wallis film, *I Walk Alone*, from which he took a midproduction break to get married. Martin Scorsese later called this "underrated" nightclub thriller "one of the first pictures to show the underworld, prewar to postwar, which became high profile respectable like big business." Lancaster plays one-time bootlegger Frankie Madison, a Prohibition Rip Van Winkle out of stir in 1947 for the first time since 1933. He is hoping to pick up again with his old partner, now a successful legit nightclub owner, played by Kirk Douglas. When the club's sommelier offers him a 1933 bottle of wine, "a very good year," Lancaster rages back, "For *you*, maybe!" and proceeds to get his dignity and Lizabeth Scott back from two-timing Douglas through the use of good old street smarts and guns. When the movie came out in early 1948, Crowther sniped that "the sympathy was for the mug who did the 'stretch' as though he were some kind of martyr." The audience, feeling not unlike Rip Van Winkles themselves, got the point. *I Walk Alone* was a box office success.

With three pictures to his credit, Lancaster began to realize what had happened to him. "This isn't fun," he complained to a reporter for *PM*, sitting like a big spoiled baby in an expensive suite at New York's Sherry-Netherlands Hotel, forty-seven blocks south of the old family apartment. "It's like—like losing your identity to gain an identity. The identity I'm gaining is that of a movie star. The identity I'm losing is *me*." Wherever he went, "There's *Burt Lancaster*!" buzzed in the air. He said he felt like Grant's Tomb. No longer could he roam around Manhattan at four in the morning, soaking in the dawn air. The "cartwheel of dough" was terrific, but with so many instant dependents it was as much burden as boon. When his brother Jim insisted he come to dinner, Lancaster mused, "What the hell, my brother never had me to dinner in his life."

That the publicity and hype accrued around the person and personality of the performer and not the work, angered and baffled him—as it would all his life. "It's the old formula," he said, "the parade with the mayor and the brass band and the soldier hero passing by. People's lives are dull, they stop to watch the parade. I never had that feeling for anyone."

There was one good thing about instant fame: he had a lot of power. All by himself he could make things happen. Deciding Hollywood was just one big circus, he began to push the perimeter of the ring Wallis had put him in, options or no options. "Lancaster will do a tour for *Desert Fury* 'if he's not too tired,' " Paul Nathan, Paramount's savvy, wry publicity head resignedly memoed Wallis. In March 1947, Nathan wrote that he had met the head of a Universal fan magazine who grilled him about "our Mr. Lancaster": "Said he was impossible . . . that he was constantly quarrelling with his director . . . that he tried to write, direct and produce every scene . . . that they were all trembling for the day he gets two or three more good pictures under his belt. No, there is absolutely nothing you or any of us can do," concluded Nathan, ". . . it just will happen."

A few weeks later, it did. On April 9, 1947, Lancaster tried to break his seven-year Paramount contract claiming it violated his freelance deal and that he did not want to work with Lizabeth Scott anyway. Kirk Douglas had recently broken his contract with Wallis, but that arrangement was not, according to Nathan, the same long-term, multipicture deal as Lancaster's. Wallis, mid-Atlantic on the *Queen Elizabeth,* wired Nathan back: "[E]xercise second option immediately." Hecht proposed that Lancaster's two studio pictures a year be reduced to one and that his outside pictures be increased to two per year; Lancaster turned down all Wallis's counterproposals. On April 23 Nathan wrote the producer that "Harold has assured me that Burt wants his freedom. . . . I wonder how strong a hold Hellinger has been playing, and how soon we will be reading of Hellinger, Bogart, Lancaster Productions. . . . I can't even sign this 'best regards' since I am too depressed. I remember at one time in my life I thought all people were nice; and if you did something good for them they were grateful."

Lancaster stayed at Paramount with a sweeter deal, including the second outside option; he and Hecht now had time to regroup and think ahead. Meanwhile, Lancaster, the man Seltzer called "an intellectual from the streets," embarked on a stormy relationship with Wallis. "I'm going to pick you up, you son of a bitch, and throw you out the window of this office!" he raged at the producer in one early discussion about money whereupon Wallis backed down. Much later up the ladder of success, James Hill, a future partner of Lancaster, would recall agent Lew Wasserman telling him that Wallis was terrified of the star. And no wonder: Lancaster was picking up where the old Warner's gang had left off, pushing further against the restraints of the studio contract as the very idea of a classic contract died—as, indeed, Lancaster, by his contrary, aggressive example, drove the stake further through its heart.

While battling Wallis that spring, Lancaster shot *Brute Force,* his second Hellinger/Universal picture. Several of *The Killers* cast were reunited (Sam Levene, Charles McGraw) and Hellinger persuaded William Daniels, the great MGM cinematographer of Greta Garbo, to come back to active work. Richard Brooks wrote the grim script of repression, sadism, and thwarted revenge based, according to its director Jules Dassin, on a story idea of Hellinger's taken from an article written by a former convict. For Dassin, recently escaped from a "slave contract" at MGM, *Brute Force* was also a welcome exercise in "making a film about people locked in at a time when I had achieved liberation."

Crafted to showcase Lancaster, his lead role of Joe Collins, the prisoner who leads his fellow inmates in a doomed escape attempt, was a corollary for the star's own growing dreams of independence. Digging through the "drainpipe," where Hume Cronyn's Wagner-loving, truncheon-wielding Captain Munsey sends prisoners as punishment, Collins and crew plan to take the observation tower, open the prison gates, and escape. Munsey is tipped off by a character considered in the movies to be the lowest creature on the face of the earth—the stool pigeon, the canary, the rat—and installs a machine gun at the top of the tower, gleefully ready to mow down the prisoners as they emerge on the tracks leading out of the drainpipe. The prisoners strap the screaming stoolie onto the front of the handcar so he will get killed first, after which Collins, shot in the back and dying, struggles up the tower stairs to get Munsey and silence the gun. Hoisting the puny villain up over his head like a doll, he hurls him down to the prison yard below. "Nobody escapes," is the movie's last line. "Nobody really escapes."

As much as any scene in *The Killers,* this one made Lancaster's reputation. "If you saw *Brute Force,*" said Berry, "Burt was nuts. I'm not talking about whether he was a great actor. I'm talking about that ability to commit, to try and make it." Collins is the prototype of all his tough guy roles to come: strong, utterly focused, body bent, yearning, pushing through space toward the goal. The big, powerful man fighting to break free is an image beyond words, and Daniels lit his face to beam out of the darkness around it, the bars of Cell R-17 striking down his cheeks like brand marks. Unlike the doomed Swede, Collins at least tries to free himself. "He wasn't stupid," Lancaster said of Collins. "No prison should hold anybody—that's the way he felt." Yet as a postwar parable, the movie is deeply sad. The Nazi-type Munsey is vanquished only to have the heroes who killed him either dead or still in prison.

The shoot also marked what may have been the first of Lancaster's long string of off-screen liaisons with costars. One of the women waiting for the men on "the outside" in *Brute Force* was played by Yvonne De Carlo, a Universal starlet. In her autobiography she described Lancaster off-screen as knowing "exactly what he wanted, and at the moment it was me." Underneath an oleander bush, on top of her mink coat, they "went down together," she recalled in silver screen prose, "in an embrace that . . . was so spontaneous and explosive. . . . Talk about being swept away!"

Dassin found Lancaster "a great amount of fun," a "gay, marvelous boy," and the two men made a daily entrance onto the set, the diminutive director perched on the star's shoulders. "There was a scene," he recalled, "when Burt was going to be betrayed and realized who the betrayer was and I got into this whole Stanislavskian monologue about what he should feel. At the end of my discourse he said, 'You mean I give 'em the old snake eye?' " Dassin laughed, "That taught me much."

After several drastic cuts because of the Production Code Office's objections to "excessive" brutality, *Brute Force* opened in summer, 1947, and set first-week records at movie houses across the country. It was considered

Hollywood's most violent prison film to date. Coming after the war years, when critical examinations of problems on the home front were considered unpatriotic, the movie was one of a brief group of hard-hitting "problem pictures" that harked back to the prewar, even pre–Production Code censor, era. By siding with the convicts against venal and/or incompetent authorities, *Brute Force* redrew the old battle lines of the 1930s when sympathy for the underdog, the "underprivileged," was seen as implicitly leftist. Hostile critics made much of how *Brute Force*, even with cuts, violated just about every tenet of the Code. "If Daumier knocks off a sketch of a rat, eating out a woman's eye," said Lancaster, "by God, you say it's art, but if Joe Blow writes it for Hellinger, you say it's obscene. I don't get it." *Variety* raved that the producer's "gamble with Lancaster as a potential star in *The Killers* is paying off in spades with *Brute Force*" and noted that the box-office hit showed that "Hollywood can still turn out top grossers without breaking the bankers." Hellinger filed the reviews in his *Brute Force* folder. His independence was paying off, for everybody. Hecht and Lancaster also took note. If Hellinger could do this, why not them?

Lancaster was now Hollywood's newest tough guy, the fantasy figure who takes nothing from nobody. That same summer, in a new play she was producing, Irene Mayer Selznick was considering casting him as Stanley Kowalski, a tough guy who needs his Stella and is not afraid to say so. It was the plum male lead in Tennessee Williams's *A Streetcar Named Desire*, to be directed by Elia Kazan. John Garfield had been cast, but withdrew; Marlon Brando, a member of the Stanislavsky-inspired Actors Workshop founded by American Lab veteran Lee Strasberg, was, according to Brando biographer Peter Manso, initially rejected as too young at age twenty-three and "too pretty." The "only other prospect," recalled Selznick, was Lancaster. She arranged a meeting in New York when he and Hecht were on tour with Hellinger for *Brute Force*. Lancaster "yearned to do the part," she would recall, but his partner nixed the idea, taking the time to explain the movie business to the daughter of MGM mogul Louis B. Mayer and estranged wife of David O. Selznick. Lancaster let himself be persuaded to turn down perhaps the greatest male role of the American postwar theater. On December 3, Brando stepped onto the stage of the Ethel Barrymore Theater and what William Goldman described as a "sound, . . . some kind of visceral recognition of greatness" rumbled out of the audience.

Lancaster would not have been the great Kowalski of Brando and he knew it. "Genius is a pretty dangerous thing to have," he admitted later. "Genius is too erratic. It's better just to be talented." But when the other actor scooped up four Oscar nominations in a row after arriving in Hollywood in 1950, winning the Academy Award in 1954 for *On the Waterfront*,

Lancaster responded by pushing for the kind of roles he—not Hecht—thought he should play. Quixotic, sometimes bizarre, his choices make sense when seen, partially, as attempts to make up for missing Kowalski. He came to acting with the Irish city boy's instinctive aversion to the Method's open, emotional display based on affective memory. He mistrusted any director who would probe and pry too much behind the hard-earned façade, instinctively more comfortable with Kuleshov's dictum that "people performing organized, efficient work appear best on the screen." The role of Hecht, who would have been in on long discussions of acting theory at Boleslavsky's Lab, is an intriguing factor: Did he reinforce Lancaster's version of the "supple, demonstrative, highly codified style" of Delsarte, as Naremore described it, so useful for the new art of cinema created out of sequence, assembled by montage? At his best, Lancaster would *move* with the movies. A joy in the discipline of performing would stay with him and in the end distinguish him from Brando.

In May 1947 J. Parnell Thomas, elevated to new chairman of HUAC, announced to the press that "hundreds of very prominent film capital people have been named as Communists to us." The FBI had been gathering data on "Communist activity" in Hollywood since 1942 and there was now enough data from "friendly witnesses," Thomas claimed, to launch a formal, public "trial" in Washington that fall. With the GOP the majority party in both the House and Senate and the Soviet Union again the evil enemy, conditions were ripe to pick up where the battle against the performing arts had left off with the cancellation of the Federal Theater Project in 1939.

The committee had had one brief star turn in 1940 when Chairman Dies absolved Bogart and Cagney of charges that they were at least sympathizers and perhaps members of the Communist Party. Though the *New York Times* ran a front-page headline, "Hollywood Stars Accused as Reds," the incident was a dubious precedent. HUAC had better have its facts straight when it targeted popular, lucrative movie stars. On August 7, 1947, as *Brute Force* was playing in theaters around the country, a report was filed with the FBI on the movie's "Communist Connections." The picture was an example, claimed the report, of the effort to corrupt by "introducing small casual bits of propaganda into innocent stories." Dassin was identified as having been a Communist from 1944 to 1945 (in fact, he joined the party after opening night of *Waiting for Lefty* in 1935).

Lancaster's name again came before the FBI with the announcement of his next project, a movie version for Universal of *All My Sons*. In the disintegrating political climate, the new play by dramatist Arthur Miller, which had won the New York Critics Circle award for best drama of the 1946–47 season, now seemed a last, suspect hurrah for social community. Joe Keller, a scrappy, self-made industrialist, played by Edward G. Robinson in the movie, knowingly ships out defective airplane parts during World War II so as not to lose a lucrative contract. Twenty-one airmen die as a result and Keller's son, also a pilot, deliberately flies to his death to atone for his father's act. At a time when *Variety* was reporting that "the mistakes, chicanery and treachery on the home front" during the war had become the stuff of daily postwar headlines, the play insisted that a social structure that could tolerate such private greed at the expense of others was flawed. "You can be better," was one line from the play. "Once and for all you can know that the whole earth comes in through those fences. That there's a universe outside and you're responsible for it."

By the time the movie script was finished the producer/screenwriter Chester Erskine—"no doubt on higher instructions," the *New York Times* would suggest—had carefully deleted from the original play anything that might explicitly suggest that there are "faults in the capitalist system" and had "confined the drama to the greed . . . of one man." But the play's shocking climax was not easily changed. Prompted by his other son Chris, played by Lancaster, Keller realizes that the airmen were "all his sons," his responsibility no less for their not being his own children, and he kills himself.

Ignoring Wallis's doubts and Erskine's protests that signing him was "like casting Boris Karloff as a babysitter," Lancaster pushed hard for the untough guy loanout part of Chris, which he had seen performed in New York by Arthur Kennedy. "I wanted to play Chris Keller," he told one reporter, "because he had the courage to make his father realize that he was just as responsible for the deaths of many servicemen as if he had murdered them." Happy for the chance to portray "an average guy—a solid character with high standards," his own best dream of himself, he insisted his choice was a step forward in the direction he, not any studio, had chosen. The overnight star that Universal called "the hottest thing in pictures" was not acting like one.

From September 22 to December 5, shooting on *All My Sons* proceeded through two weeks of exteriors shot in Santa Rosa, then back to Universal and the Western Stove Factory, serving as Keller's plant, in Culver City. In October, an informant supplied the FBI with the movie's script. Aware that *Newsweek* had reported on August 31 that Robinson was "persistently found in Communist fronts," the Bureau found *All My Sons*'s "open attack" on the family "sickening" (a favorite FBI word) and blatantly collectivist. When filming started, pink subpoenas had been sent out from HUAC to over forty Hollywood professionals, termed "friendly" or "unfriendly," requesting that they appear at hearings in Washington, which would open October 20. At 4:30 on the afternoon of October 2, FBI special agents conducted a surveillance of Robinson's home where Hollywood citizens had convened to organize opposition to the HUAC hearings and to support those of the subpoenaed witnesses HUAC deemed unfriendly, now known as the Hollywood Nineteen.

To oppose HUAC, William Wyler, John Huston, actor Alexander Knox, and screenwriter Philip Dunne had called the first meeting of the Committee for the First Amendment and proceeded to gather over three hundred petition signatures. Reprinted in the Hollywood *Reporter* on October 21, the text read: "We hold that these hearings are morally wrong because: Any investigation into the political beliefs of the individual is contrary to the basic principles of our democracy; Any attempt to curb freedom of expression and to set arbitrary standards of Americanism is in itself disloyal to both the spirit and the letter of our Constitution. . . ." The FBI labeled the committee a communist front.

Lancaster signed, as did many of the principals involved in *All My Sons,* including Henry Morgan, Howard Duff, Edward G. Robinson, Arlene Francis, and director Irving Reis. During the first week of hearings, "friendly" witness Jack Warner testified that he had seen Miller's play and that he thought the author was a Communist. When the "unfriendlies" pleaded with the Committee for the First Amendment to do more than just send a petition, another meeting was called on October 25 at Ira Gershwin's home at 1021 Roxbury Drive. Outside the enthusiastic, packed gathering, an informant took down license plate numbers of the cars parked in front of the house and fed them to the FBI. Lancaster was noted as present, as were *le tout* of liberal Hollywood including Humphrey Bogart, Lauren Bacall, Rita Hayworth, Groucho Marx, Frank Sinatra, Gene Kelly, and Frederic March. Lancaster was new to Hollywood compared to others in this group and he was vulnerable at the first surge of his new stardom. But the principles set out in the petition were a credo right out of his East Harlem childhood.

Because of his obligation to *All My Sons,* he was unable to join Bogart, Bacall, Wyler, Dunne, Huston, and the rest of the fourteen committee members on what became a well-publicized plane trip to Washington on October 26 to support the unfriendlies. As the group was in the air, the first of two Committee for the First Amendment–sponsored nationwide radio broadcasts, "Hollywood Fights Back," was beamed out to the nation by ABC. The comments of those on the plane had been prerecorded and, it was announced, "except for studio commitments" all the broadcast participants would have been on their way to Washington too. The voices of Judy Garland, Gene Kelly, Danny Kaye, and others—a total of forty-three top stage and screen stars—came on the air speaking brief messages. Lancaster was sandwiched between Evelyn Keyes and Paul Henreid. "This is Burt Lancaster. Gerald L.K. Smith says, and I quote, 'You have seen the newspaper accounts of the plan to investigate the traitors of Hollywood who are attempting to use the great film industry to undermine our American government. Be sure to write a letter to Congressman John Rankin congratulating him and his committee.' Who is Gerald L.K. Smith? He is a rabble-rouser, a professional anti-Semite and one-time speaker for the German-American Bund!" Lancaster spat out the last word with characteristic diction and vigor. The Reverend Smith was indeed the anti-Semitic extreme of the far right and had done much to inspire and inflame HUAC through his bully pulpit, a periodical called—with Elmer Gantry flair—*The Cross and the Flag.*

The headline-grabbing use of star power for political purposes was ill-fated and brief. As Thomas banged his brand-new gavel so hard it broke, a straightforward defense based on the First Amendment was rejected in favor of what were called "uncooperative" challenges to the committee's authority to question the witnesses at all and refusals to answer the query: "Are you now or have you ever been a member of the Communist Party?" The Hollywood group sitting at the back of the chamber was deeply shaken by the truculence of the unfriendlies and returned to Hollywood thoroughly discouraged. Chairman Thomas, fairly shaken himself, cut the hearings short. On November 24, the House of Representatives overwhelmingly voted to cite the unruly witnesses, now abbreviated to the Hollywood Ten, in contempt of Congress.

The same day, at a meeting of the Motion Picture Association of America at the Waldorf-Astoria Hotel in New York, a group of top executives and financial backers from the major studios met to confront this new challenge to their economic security. Independent organizations such as United Artists, still privately held by Mary Pickford and Charlie Chaplin, were absent—a fact that would be very important to Lancaster and the industry a few years later. The Waldorf Statement was issued in which the majors basically caved in to HUAC, agreeing to fire those five of the Hollywood Ten still under contract and not to hire, knowingly, a Communist or anyone else who advocated the overthrow of the U.S. government unless he or she had been "purged"—an as yet undefined process. Movie box-office receipts were just starting their long postwar decline and studio corporate executives realized they needed, more than previously, to placate banks for production loans. "Wall Street," quipped columnist Ed Sullivan, "jiggled the strings." Suddenly it was dangerous, Lauren Bacall later wrote, even to be a Democrat.

After a brief attempt to carry on the anti-HUAC fight with something called the Committee of One Thousand, the Committee for the First Amendment dwindled to a smaller group dedicated mainly to the defense of the Hollywood Ten. The FBI kept track of all the meetings, rallies, and fund-raisers called to support the Ten, accumulating them as proofs of guilt. Subpoenaed to testify before state Senator Jack Tenney's Un-American Activities Committee in Los Angeles in February 1948, Ira Gershwin denied he had ever been a Communist and then identified "a number of people from a prepared committee list as having been in attendance at the meeting" held at his home the previous October. Lancaster was one of them. He was also listed in the committee's 1948 annual report as one of the signers of a full-page ad protesting the Washington hearings in the October 24, 1947, *Hollywood Reporter* and, erroneously, as a sponsor of a dinner the following March at the Beverly Wilshire Hotel given by what the report cited as another front, the Freedom From Fear Committee.

When *All My Sons* was released in March 1948, *The New Republic*, then a liberal periodical, reported that "in the present state of political weather a citation for unusual heroism under fire" was due both the director and the studio for producing and distributing the picture. That same month Bogart publicly purged himself in the pages of *Modern Screen* in an article entitled "I'm No Communist." John Howard Lawson and Dalton Trumbo, standing as representatives of the Ten, were convicted for contempt of Congress. When the decision was upheld on appeal, and the case, in turn, submitted for possible review to the U.S. Supreme Court, an uneasy waiting period began, what Ronald Brownstein has called a "false spring."

Lancaster had never been a Communist. His peripatetic pre-Hollywood life had not even let him be especially political. But that Hecht had once been a Red now hung over both of them like the shoe that must drop.

Taking Charge of the Asylum

This kid has made one picture out here,
and already he knows more than anyone on the lot.
Two more pictures and he'll land flat on his can.
He's a frustrated Freudian, a body in search of a brain,
Mr. Know-It-All for the Big Town.

—Mark Hellinger

Hungry for action, life going his way, Lancaster began to come out of his shell. "Cinderella," he joked, thumbing his chest, "me." Norma gave birth to a second son at St. John's Hospital in Santa Monica in early November 1947. William—Billy—was named for Lancaster's dead brother, and to the parents' relief was without disability. The father dubbed the two blond sons his "little Vikings" and the publicity machines at Paramount and Universal started thinking of ways to spin the softer family man angle. It was time to find a bigger house, away from the beach and thus less appealing to the circus veterans who kept showing up. The family moved to a house on Conway Avenue in Westwood with the handsome, big, park-like campus of UCLA only a few blocks west. The beach house was kept for weekends, an arrangement, with different houses, that would be kept up for years.

In Lancaster's early months in Hollywood, stories had circulated about his abrupt behavior at parties where he would sit, silent, and then burst out with angry criticisms about the phoniness of it all or just move to another room and open a book. Of one such party Lucy Kibbee, wife of screenwriter Roland Kibbee, recalled: "I didn't know who he was. There were a lot of people and he was sitting in another room. I grabbed Kibbee and said, 'My God, there's a Greek god sitting over there!' He was so gorgeous and tall and beautiful and had this great body, physically above everyone in the room, and he never opened his mouth. Then [*The Killers*] came out and suddenly he became the most verbal of verbal men that ever lived. 'Jesus,'

I'd say, 'now you never shut up.' He was very insecure with all these Hollywood people, but, boy did he get secure in a hurry." By 1947, columnist Sidney Skolsky reported that Lancaster's favorite indoor and outdoor sport was talking.

With a disarming eagerness, he sought out people who knew more than he did about books, plays, movies, philosophy, and politics and pumped them for guidance. "I was amazed at this enormous desire to know," recalled friend Mickey Knox. "Burt was not intimidated by people who knew more than he did. He was no dummy, but he wanted to consider himself an intellectual. He read voraciously—we would be up until four in the morning talking about books." One day while thumbing through Kant, he came across the phrase "categorical imperative." "Mickey," he asked, "what is it?" The phrase obsessed him and he cornered anybody he thought might enlighten him, a gambit he kept up all his life. When he had mastered the new fact he owned it and made sure everyone around him knew he knew it. Then he moved on. "He was more interested in the history of philosophy," said Knox, "than in what the philosophy was really about."

He brought the same autodidactic obsession to the myriad details of making movies, moving beyond the basics into more esoteric levels of craft. As a practical matter, he simply decided to treat the new job as if he were any professional, in any trade: he had to think, learn, and practice. Paramount veterans remembered that "he went to work like a man resolved to one day own the company," shadowing the director and the cameraman, studying the daily rushes "while re-mouthing his lines," and hanging around the front office to see what producers did. Grace Houston Case, a Universal costume designer assigned to *All My Sons,* remembered a day when he came into her office to grill her on designs, "fitting actors, working toward shooting deadlines, etc." A former dancer with the Rockettes who had appeared in such 1930s films as *Ziegfeld Follies,* she recognized that a desire for self-improvement after years of vaudeville and circus work took "much ambition and courage."

In September, newspapers reported that Hellinger was starting his own independent company, Mark Hellinger Productions, at the end of the year. With the Selznick Releasing Organization he would produce six films in the next two years; his partner, Humphrey Bogart, would star in three of them. With Lancaster and Daniels already allied to him, Hellinger was set. The producer had realized what his biographer Jim Bishop would call "the dream—the long, long dream of no bosses."

But he was now competing with the very monster he had created. On August 1, Louella Parsons had led off her column with a real scoop: "Talk about zooming to the top—Burt Lancaster, an unknown two movies back, has been given his own independent production company at U-I [Universal-International] at least for one fling. Not since Clark Gable has any actor hit as hard as this Lancaster who is hotter than the so-called breeze trying to sneak through my window. Most actors wait years to get important enough to put their feet on a desk and boss the works. But not this baby."

His new production company was called Norma Productions, after his wife, who suggested the career balance he kept up for the rest of his life: "Make one movie for the bank, one for your art." He announced that acting was only a temporary gig. Producing was what he really wanted to do. Hellinger teased him, saying that when he took a call from Lancaster he never knew which incarnation he was speaking to. The star began to spout off what would be a lifetime of earnest, revealing babble: "I believe," he said, "that if I tell you I'm a bad fellow—and glory in the fact—I *am* a bad fellow. But, maybe, I'm a fellow who does something you consider 'bad' but do it with good in my heart. When the deed is not evil, I'd like to prove that the popularly drawn lines of good and evil are not ones which necessarily will stand up." With a whiff of settlement house pedagogy, he explained that he and Hecht wanted to make movies that prepared people in the audience to "make the decisions as to how they want their own societies to move." He courted risk, he told the *New York Times*, because, "Take the feeling of hunger out of your gut and you're no longer a champion." The rest of Hollywood indulged the cocky know-it-all. Talk was cheap. Everybody wanted to be a producer.

The postwar surge to independent production was the newest twist on a conflict almost as old as movies themselves: How could the stars, without whom the industry would not exist, tip the business, the profits, the residuals, the control, in their favor? Established actors such as John Garfield, Joan Fontaine, Errol Flynn, and Cary Grant went independent after the war for a mixture of motives—tax advantages, desire for control of the product that showcased their image, dreams of a direct tap into the money flow: a cut of the gross. The few precedents for the successful actor-producer came largely from the pretalkie era, before the industry hardened into studio monoliths. United Artists (UA), the distribution company formed in 1919 by Charlie Chaplin, Mary Pickford, director D.W. Griffith, and Douglas Fairbanks, was an early attempt to control both the product and, in the case of the actors, the exploitation of their unprecedented star appeal.

In that primeval time when everybody was creating the medium as they went along, Richard Rowland, head of what was then Metro Pictures, famously quipped that with the formation of UA, "the lunatics have taken charge of the asylum." Arthur Mayer later rebutted that the founders of United Artists displayed the same brand of lunacy as Rockefeller, Morgan, and du Pont. Directors like Cecil B. DeMille or Frank Capra later became producers as more natural extensions of their organizational skills behind the camera, and mavericks like David O. Selznick and Sam Goldwyn functioned not only independently but almost as ministudios. Most actors, experience would show, did not really want to be producers. They just wanted to think they were.

That was not true of Cagney, perhaps the most instructive model for Lancaster. Cagney did not try on independent production once for size and then discard it, as so many actors had and would. He kept trying to find the way to make the kind of movies he wanted to act in or to back. He did not want to make solely personal star vehicles, but rather to gather contract players, writers, and directors to function as a kind of studio of his own that would turn out several pictures a year. Like fellow New Yorkers Bogart and Garfield, he rebelled long and hard against Warner Bros. with the issue not so much money as the freedom to shape his career the way he wanted.

When he signed a distribution deal with UA in 1942 for Cagney Productions, the industry noted that no successful independent production unit had been set up by a performer since the studio system consolidated in the 1920s (Chaplin continued into the early 1950s to make independent movies with his own UA primarily to showcase himself). Periodically Cagney would return to the studio fold or strike a deal after the war to let him make independent pictures under Warner Bros.'s aegis, but the time was not yet right for what he wanted to do, nor was his partner-brother William suited for the role of producer/buffer/shark. When conditions became more favorable, Cagney was past his electric prime. A younger star in a different era with a savvy partner fronting for him would make good the promise Cagney tried to realize. Not the first actor to set up an independent production unit after the war, Lancaster risked independence sooner than any other *new* star. Much more important, he stuck with it.

In the middle of this indie ferment, Hellinger suddenly died of a heart attack on December 21, 1947, at the age of forty-four. Lancaster, who had watched him almost pass out ringside at a Tony Zale–Rocky Graziano fight in Chicago, joined Selznick, Mayer, Bogart, and others at the Hollywood memorial service. Hellinger's death was a major loss to his protégé.

Norma Productions's first project—*Kiss the Blood Off My Hands*—was indeed a Hellinger-like clone and the title gave headaches to everyone from radio announcers to newspaper editors to the censors who enforced the Production Code, the Motion Picture Association of America (MPAA),

Burton Stephen Lancaster, circa 1918

Jim Lancaster, Burton's father, in a rare moment of relaxation

Union Settlement, on East 104th Street in New York City's East Harlem, around the turn of the century

Burton (second row, second from left) graduating from P.S. 83, in June 1926

Burt and Nick Cravat (center), "First of May Guys," with the Kay Bros. Circus clowns, spring 1933. Their bar teacher, Paul LeRoy, is second from the right.

The daring young man of the
Depression-era circus

On the road with the Ernst circus family. From left: Mary Ernst, J.G. Ernst, Ora Ernst,
and Burt. Smiling in the background is June, Burt's first wife and "the only woman in
America," Burt boasted, "who could do horizontal bar tricks."

The "starving, stinking" Italian campaign, World War II, autumn 1944: Burt is on the right, taking a break from entertaining the U.S. Fifth Army troops.

The "dugout drama" performance that launched a megastar career: Lancaster (right) with costar Sam Levene in *A Sound of Hunting*, the Lyceum Theater, New York, November 1945

"I did something wrong, once." Lancaster's first, electrifying screen appearance, as the "wounded colossus" back from the war, in *The Killers* (1946)

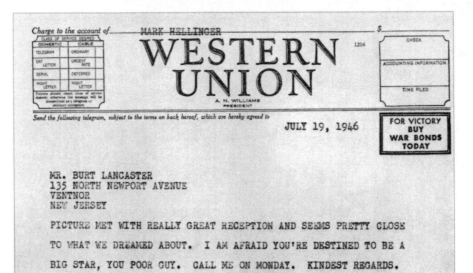

Charge to the account of...... MARK HELLINGER ...... $ ......

WESTERN UNION

1206

A. N. WILLIAMS
PRESIDENT

Send the following telegram, subject to the terms on back hereof, which are hereby agreed to

JULY 19, 1946

FOR VICTORY
BUY
WAR BONDS
TODAY

    MR. BURT LANCASTER
    135 NORTH NEWPORT AVENUE
    VENTNOR
    NEW JERSEY

    PICTURE MET WITH REALLY GREAT RECEPTION AND SEEMS PRETTY CLOSE

    TO WHAT WE DREAMED ABOUT. I AM AFRAID YOU'RE DESTINED TO BE A

    BIG STAR, YOU POOR GUY. CALL ME ON MONDAY. KINDEST REGARDS.

                                        MARK HELLINGER

The telegram Mark Hellinger, the Universal producer of *The Killers*, sent to Lancaster after the first showing of the movie to the press. At the time, Lancaster was staying near Atlantic City, just off the boardwalk.

The early days of Norma Productions, Lancaster's independent production company, founded in 1947, which would chart the course of seismic change in the industry. Burt discusses a script—probably *The First Time* (1952)—with Hugo Butler. His partner, Harold Hecht, is sitting at the desk.

Lancaster arriving at a Hollywood screening in the late 1940s with Norma Anderson, his second wife and the mother of his five children

Paramount producer Hal Wallis—"a pioneer among independents and prototype of them"—and Lancaster in an amicable moment

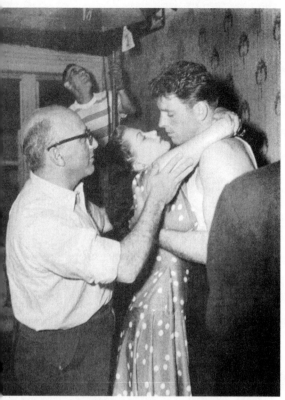

Director Robert Siodmak adjusts the embrace of doomed couple Steve and Anna (Yvonne De Carlo and Lancaster) in his *noir* masterpiece, *Criss Cross* (1949).

"Nobody," said director John Frankenheimer, "has ever looked like Burt Lancaster in *The Crimson Pirate* [1952]."

ncaster kept Nick Cravat, his treasured friend, on his payroll for as his trainer and sometime costar.

"I get a funny feeling," said the real Jim Thorpe, who was named, in 1950, the greatest football player and athlete of the first half of the century, "sitting there watching Burt doing the things I did. . . . I don't think I was ever that handsome." *Jim Thorpe—All American* (1951)

Star, producer, *bête du cinéma:* Lancaster on the back lot of Columbia studios while filming Norma Productions's legionnaire spoof, *Ten Tall Men*, March 1951

who called it "obscene." It was part of a double Universal deal cut on *All My Sons* with Joan Fontaine's new Universal-based indie, Rampart Productions. Fontaine got top billing as a lonely nurse, Jane Wharton, and Lancaster costarred as Bill Saunders, a traumatized former POW with a hair-trigger temper whose inadvertent murder of a fellow London pub crawler kicks off the film. Hecht hired Walter Bernstein, one of his clients, along with the more experienced Ben Maddow to adapt the best-selling British novel of the same title into a grim thriller, what Bernstein calls in "the good tradition of tired vet" postwar films.

Cameras started rolling at the studio on March 15, 1948, as publicists worked hard to spin the dubious angle that the movie was "undoubtedly the first film costarring two producers." Critics pounced, pointing out that it was the sort of movie one would expect from two stars without a studio. But Hecht and Lancaster were thrilled with the solid group of talent they had assembled: Robert Newton of *Odd Man Out* fame as Harry Carter, the blackmailing Cockney whom Fontaine stabs with a pair of scissors; after a brief try for Gregg Toland, Russell Metty, who had just done *The Stranger* for Orson Welles, as cinematographer; as director, Norman Foster, the credited director of *Journey Into Fear*, originally another Welles project. Siodmak was pulled in to do a few last-minute "exterior" tag shots of dock streets on Stage 21 and the script was "improved" by Leonardo Bercovici. The Hellinger-like touch was assured with music by Miklos Rosza, now a two-time Oscar winner.

Lancaster's newness was given quick depth playing against an actress who came trailing clouds of glory from great movies like Hitchcock's *Rebecca* (1940) and *Suspicion* (1941). The end effect, as Fontaine staggered in and out of dark, foggy, "London" alleys in her cable-stitch twinset, was of a cartoon-like expressionism with moments of sudden beauty when the camera fixed on the faces of the two stars. Lancaster later told Hedda Hopper that the project was his "bloodbath in production." Fontaine was in the early stages of pregnancy and threw up every morning at the top of the Sepulveda Pass on the way to work. The fog machine was unreliable. Lancaster was often late to the set as he ran around wearing the two hats of actor and producer. Rain held up many of the outdoor sequences, including one in Griffith Park Zoo where Saunders has a dissociative fit seeing all the caged animals: "Never been in a zoo?" Fontaine's nurse asks. "Been in one all my life," replied the recent star of *Brute Force*. Though not a rave success when it opened at New York's Criterion Theater in November, the thing was done, their first production, what *Variety* called "an intensely moody melodrama." "Hey!" crowed Lancaster. "Producers!" He and Hecht even ended up with a $50,000 nut for the next project.

By the end of 1948, *New York Times* film editor Thomas Pryor was assessing Lancaster in Hollywood as "a refreshing, puzzling type for the tight little town to contemplate." The paper of record noted that "even in a business where spectacular ascents are now more or less commonplace, the rise of Burt Lancaster is regarded as something extraordinary." His name on a theater marquee was now said to be good for at least $1 million in ticket sales. When he was blocked at the door of Manhattan's Stork Club and only let in when the bartender whispered "That's Burt Lancaster!" in the bouncer's ear, or when he walked out on a woman writer at the Colony Club, claiming that the "fancy-pants dame was tolerating us," the stories quickly became part of the Lancaster antilegend. Of himself he said, truthfully, "Most people . . . seem to think I'm the kind of guy who shaves with a blowtorch. Actually I'm inclined to be bookish and worrisome."

When *The Saturday Evening Post* told star reporter Pete Martin to catch a 1948 "movie comet by the tail," he chose Lancaster. Loping around the writer's hotel room with his "springy pantherlike stride," griping about how too much courting of publicity would turn him into "nothing but a high-class Hollywood male prostitute," Lancaster accused Martin of missing the mark in a previous piece on another star. When Martin replied that Lancaster was demanding perfection, the star retorted, "Why not? . . . I try for perfection." Well, said Martin, he wasn't so perfect in *Desert Fury.* "You're right," Lancaster admitted, kneading his hands. "But in *I Walk Alone,* I think I was about eighty percent perfect. In *The Killers,* though, I came close to hitting one hundred. . . ." As Martin listened to the musical, persuasive clarity of Lancaster's voice he thought, "what a sawdust trail evangelist" he would have made.

The tight little town waited for the comet to crash land on its face. Not factored in was the circus acrobat's expectation that he would fall, often, and break each fall by using the downward momentum to bounce back up. Lancaster liked the uncertainty and risk of something completely different *because* it was just beyond his reach at the time. A Universal press release zinged him as behaving with his stardom like "a crap shooter with hot dice."

There was also something monstrous. Bernstein saw the unformed Lancaster of this period as the golem, the mythic Adam-like creature created out of base clay to serve his creator but who then evolves into a destructive monster. To the industry that is exactly what he was: the star-being waking up. In the big body Knox called that "perfect masculine figure, not overly-muscular, long legs, long muscles," there was the look of a creature crafted for a purpose not quite human. His form in repose, John Le Carré would later tell Sydney Pollack, was "sculptural." In an industry that dealt in making small people look big on-screen, Lancaster was not only actually big (press releases claimed six feet two inches), he was actually powerful. In his disciplined command of that strength, he was also extraordinarily graceful—"a thing of beauty," as future partner James Hill described his early presence.

To take charge of the asylum, it wasn't enough to be a lunatic. The leader of the crazies had to be the strongest, prettiest, biggest, most indefatigable of them all.

Hecht hustled, buying indie properties for Lancaster. He told Parsons six months after the opening of *Streetcar* that he was flying to New York to offer Brando a contract to costar with Lancaster in a movie of John Galsworthy's novel *The First and the Last;* the project never got past the idea stage. When *Kiss the Blood Off My Hands* wrapped, Hecht distributed gift baskets to the crew and associates. "[A] lavish and gracious gesture for such a brand-new company," gushed a press release no doubt written by Hecht. Unproduced-but-paid-for product and lavish gestures were not good patterns to establish so early in the game.

Other patterns were also forming. The dark, diminutive Hecht and the blond, tall Lancaster had developed what several people describe as a symbiotic relationship. Lancaster's real and imagined exploits with women fascinated his partner. Hecht, who had been in and around Hollywood for years, would ask Bernstein, who had just arrived, if he "knew any nice girls." To Jack Berry, there was "something not quite right" in "fast buck man" Hecht's use of Lancaster. "I always felt," he said, "that he was in some way using the relationship."

The symbiosis affected their attitudes toward story material, the bedrock of their new enterprise. Hecht's eagerness made his analyses often "shallow" at this stage, according to Bernstein and others. Lancaster, on the other hand, was trying to think through thoughts and feelings that were still unformed. Hecht loved publicity not only for the company and the films but, according to Seltzer, for "himself personally." Lancaster could not have cared less and began zapping his voyeuristic partner with razor-sharp, humiliating put-downs. Hecht reportedly hired a gag writer for a while to give him comeback lines against "the tall, blond gentile" in his life.

It was a classic Hollywood trade-off. The agent turns producer for his star and they both go independent. The star, secure in his bankable persona, sees success as the freedom to make meaningful movies that make a difference. His producer partner has visions of money, women, art, cars, yachts, and respect. Both Hecht and Lancaster wanted to make the good commercial movie with a little social heft that was a common model immediately after the war, and to make a lot of money. But the star never sought what he described as the "big outfit with a lot of fancy names under contract." The producer wanted it so badly he could taste it. It was the partnership's weak core, a vulnerable bit of rot ripe for exploitation by a third party.

Kiss the Blood Off My Hands was released in October 1948 just as the big change Hollywood had been dreading came to pass. In May, a month before the commencement of the Berlin airlift, the U.S. Supreme Court had decided that the movie studio system was an exclusionary conspiracy. The Justice Department now reaffirmed that the practical application of the court's decision would be the divestiture by the studios of the approximately fourteen hundred theaters they owned around the country. When RKO capitulated at the end of October, the rest of the studios followed, and a consent decree ended the so-called Golden Age of Hollywood.

The fad for independent production took a nose dive as one new company after another—including Fontaine's—folded. Studio contracts were canceled and the workforce cut by half. Net profits plummeted by $40 million in 1948; the halcyon peak of $121 million in 1946 seemed as far away as the white cliffs of Dover. Television, the little box now cursed as "The Monster," was no longer the butt of jokes as one million sets were sold in 1948. By the turn of the decade there would be more than eleven million screens beaming into the living rooms of America.

Norma Productions should have been one more victim of the biggest series of challenges to the industry since sound. But what looked like bad news was, if you had the stomach for it, one big opportunity. Lancaster stayed afloat in part because he balanced his independent experiments with studio pictures that guaranteed money. It was a sequence he would repeat all his working life, forming in the very momentum a new standard of successful, productive stardom. The making of *Kiss the Blood Off My Hands* was sandwiched between *Sorry, Wrong Number,* a quick Paramount project shot in the early months of 1948, and *Criss Cross,* Lancaster's last commitment to the Hellinger contract. As he shuttled between Paramount and Universal during the first seven months of 1948, news reports followed the moves like a tennis match: Lancaster the producer; Lancaster the star. He turned down a chance to work with Bette Davis on *Winter Meeting* for Warner Bros. When Steve Trilling, now head of production, asked why, Lancaster told him scene-by-scene what was wrong with the script. Now that he was a producer, he knew from scripts. *Then* he reminded the executive of their first meeting, in 1940. Hecht collapsed in laughter at the dumbfounded expression on Trilling's face.

When Wallis described *Sorry, Wrong Number*—Henry Stevenson, a boy-toy weakling, tries to get out from under the control of his rich invalid wife,

Barbara Stanwyck's queen bitch, Leona, by having her murdered—Lancaster said, "Why not me?" Wallis objected that he was too strong for the part of Stevenson, but Lancaster insisted that the audience would be more interested in watching a strong man become weak. In the first of what would be a series of roles in which the star was cast against type, Wallis gave in. It was also the beginning of another career motif for Lancaster: getting himself cast opposite strong, experienced, intimidating women.

His part was expanded from the original, hugely popular radio play by Lucille Fletcher, and a sequence of flashbacks was added to alternate with the footage of an increasingly terrified Stanwyck, bedridden and helplessly privy to the plot against her. Though Lancaster was six years her junior in her biggest role since *Double Indemnity*, they were well matched. When Leona tries to lure Stevenson away from his frumpy girlfriend on the dance floor with an offer to sit out the next number in her brand-new Lagonda, parked outside, Stanwyck purrs, "Come on, for once, I'm not kidding." Lancaster, with a cool, assessing, sexual look that would rarely show up again on-screen, answers, "Neither am I, Miss Cotterell," and walks away. The next sequence opens with a close-up of the Lagonda hood ornament and then moves up to the two of them inside the car, Leona smugly poised for the kill.

Critics were not impressed when the movie opened in the early fall of 1948, weeks before *Kiss the Blood Off My Hands*. Stanwyck received an Oscar nomination—the first of several female costars to get the Academy nod playing opposite Lancaster, what he would describe as his "good luck charm" function—but *Life* called the movie "the most extended emotional jag in recent movie history." Lancaster's hysteria-tinged performance was judged "adequate but not remarkably successful" by *Cue*. But he was pleased, claiming that for the first time he did not recognize his more assured self up on the screen. The confidence had indeed informed the performance. When conflicts arose between the movie's worldly-wise Paramount director, Anatole Litvak, and Lancaster, the uppity star said, "OK, let's leave it up to the studio: Either you leave or I leave and who the fuck do you think is gonna be out?"

He was forced to honor the last commitment to Hellinger when Gladys Glad exerted her fiduciary right and insisted he make *Criss Cross* in June, six months after the producer's death. When he tried to get 20th Century-Fox to buy out the Hellinger obligation so he could make *To the Sea in Ships* for them instead as a loanout, the studio balked at paying the $237,000 Universal had offered Glad for the property. The star pleaded that his career was at stake. Toots Shor flew out from New York and persuaded him to do right by Glad, and so he—plus Siodmak, Rozsa, De Carlo, cinematographer Franz Planer, and the rest of the troupe—was stuck making this piece of "celluloid trash." But without Hellinger, who had intended that *Criss Cross* do for Los Angeles what *The Naked City* had done for New York, what was the point?

With no one to care, Siodmak made a little masterpiece. Roaming around a late 1940s landscape of Union Station, Bunker Hill, a factory on Terminal Island, with references to Bakersfield and Monrovia, Lancaster and De Carlo helplessly, stupidly spin through a series of doublecrosses from which there is no escape. All the interior sets were constructed on the single Stage 21 at Universal. The nightclub/bar where De Carlo's Anna rhumbas across the screen with the unknown Tony Curtis to the beat of "Brazilian Rhapsody" is the tight trap in which the doomed plans fester. As in *The Killers*, there is a long robbery sequence, but one more complex, brilliant in its unraveling chaos.

"Tell the truth, Steve," the detective asks Lancaster's feckless Steve Thompson. "Didn't they work you for the prize sucker of all time?" The big, sad star lights up cigarette after cigarette, his actions no less beautiful for being incidental, unthinking. He is at home in this movie. His Swede isn't any smarter this time, but he is less passive, with a slick instinct for the wrong girl, the wrong choice, all the while blaming it on fate. The cluster of the three *noir* movies formed a de facto trilogy, each of his characters a study of male desperation and despair. After *Criss Cross* his screen personality hardens. No more soft *noir* chumps who embrace easeful death. He—and the audience—had changed.

Between June 3 and July 29, 1948, while *Criss Cross* was being shot, the Lancaster brood moved again, this time into a Dutch Colonial house at 830 Linda Flora Drive, in the middle of a two-acre piece of land high in the hills over the Sepulveda Pass. A spectacular view of the city spread out far away below to the south. They would live at that address for the next twenty years—telephone exchange Granite 2—the area then a relatively undeveloped part of west Los Angeles that Lancaster called "poor man's Bel Air." The family was now about as removed from the taint of Hollywood as you could get and still live and work in the place. The isolation fed the fantasy that he could keep one part of his life as it should be, a good island of the soul into which he could go at will and pretend that he was normal and that he had a normal life.

He and Norma put more than $100,000 into extensive renovations, adding a big kitchen—the hub of the house—that circled around what they called "a real family table" designed to withstand bangs, scrapes, and spills. A playroom off the kitchen filled with blocks, blackboards, radio, and TV, plus a huge living room with a projection booth to allow movie screenings and a formal dining room were included in the upgrade. Unlike many other star families, only one servant was hired and then only on a daily basis, and there was no cook. Lancaster and Norma insisted they would bring up the children themselves, making dinner the special family time with big meals of steaks, spaghetti Milanese (Lancaster's own specialty), Caesar salad, lots of vegetables, and what Pete Martin described as "heaping plates of hot bread."

The couple stood out in social Hollywood by avoiding the party circuit to stay home and play bridge with couples such as the Knoxes, Berrys, and, later, the Norman Mailers. In a heavy-drinking town, Norma's alcoholism was noted as bad, but it was tolerated. Entertaining at home was the safer option. To listen to his now huge record collection, Lancaster stretched out on the floor, as he always had. His father continued to live with the family, an affable man who whipped out *Variety* to brag about his son and talk the latest hix pix grosses to anybody who would listen.

As the babies kept coming—by 1954 there were five children—Lancaster had the typical dilemma of the Hollywood star: how to be a meaningful parent in a business that provides every excuse to flee the task. His tenacious attempts to maintain a connection during his childrens' formative years were atypical. "Burt was lovely with the boys," recalled Knox of these years. "Very affectionate." The two sons and their acrobat father played a game each night on top of their beds called "handsies," during which Lancaster would hold their feet up, teaching them to walk on their hands. When one child sprained his thumb and the other his wrist during one of these sessions, Lancaster insisted they come right back after a fall, as he had been taught. "They wouldn't sleep until they figured out their mistakes," he said. "Teach them early to have fun instead of fear and they have an easier outlook on taking chances in life." He did not consider the more insidious fear of not being able to live up to the expectations of a dad who could seemingly do anything.

Friends were struck with the beauty of Jimmy. "I was sitting in the living room and Burt was sitting across from me in a chair," said Lucy Kibbee. "This little boy was crying upstairs and Norma went up and got him and put him in Burt's lap. He was absolutely the most beautiful child I have ever seen. It was like a Bernini sculpture: this exquisite child and this exquisite man." The child Lancaster described as a "dreamer"—shy, sensitive, intensely musical, highly intelligent with an IQ of 140—was also emotionally disturbed. The early experience with foot casts had left a legacy of nighttime screaming as he dreamed people were reaching under the covers for his feet. He largely withdrew from children his own age into a world of his own, drawing witty cartoons and playing the piano by ear. The more sensitive among the Lancasters' friends had a special affection for Jimmy;

others thought him very odd. When he was six years old, he was enrolled in a special school for children with similar disabilities. His father drove him there the first day and told a friend he could hardly bear to watch the little boy vanish through the big front doors of the building.

Billy was also handsome, but more energetic and husky. Lancaster proudly called him an "out-and-out athlete—strong as any child of his age I've ever seen." Like most athletic fathers, he looked forward to a future of sharing his love and knowledge of physical activity with his son. When the girls came along, they would be expected to learn to walk on their hands too. When *Photoplay* ran a piece on the family in 1954 with photographs, it was the first formal coverage of Norma and the children and done only because a fan letter had accused him of fabricating a phantom wife and children.

After a series of long-distance phone calls during which Nick Cravat would hang up because they were costing his friend too much money, Lancaster persuaded his old partner to come out to Hollywood from Indiana in 1947. "Dad didn't want to come," his daughter Tina said. "Burt wanted him out here, to have him close by. It was a natural impulse—like Elvis buying everybody Cadillacs." Hollywood was baffled by the relationship. With huge powerful shoulders that formed a big V down to hips that looked barely bigger around than twelve inches, Nick was a rough remnant of a past the star had been able to transcend. Some assumed there had to be something sexual in the friendship. How else, in an industry filled with new best friends, to account for such loyalty? "It was incredible," said Berry of the friendship. "Nick was a tough little bastard who only wanted his own goddamned way. They were so close—I remember the two of them being together all the time. They worked out, they ran. In some ways it was Lenny and George in *Of Mice and Men*." Lancaster told Nick that he would pay him as his trainer, to help keep him in shape. The hook worked and the arrangement lasted for decades.

Nick quickly came up with the idea of reviving their old vaudeville act and taking it on the road. This time they were paid $10,000 a week for a seven-week tour starting at the Oriental Theater in Chicago, followed by one week in Milwaukee, and then the big time—three weeks from Christmas 1948 into the New Year at the Capitol Theater in New York. Lancaster took a suite at the Sherry-Netherlands Hotel and brought Norma, the children, and his father to stay with him. Appearing with Julie Wilson—a singer later well-known in the 1950s Manhattan nightclub scene—and Skitch Henderson and his orchestra, he did a little bit of Shakespeare, sang with Wilson, did a comedy routine, and for the finale, got back on the parallel bars with Nick. Thousands of fans came for the show, headlined with the RKO comedy *Every Girl Should Be Married,* starring Cary Grant and Betsy

Blair. Earl Wilson in the *New York Daily News* reported that "little girls are squealing for Burt at the Capitol Theater like they swooned for Frank Sinatra . . . and as they shrieked for Rudy Vallee a generation ago."

One afternoon he returned to the Union Settlement House at the invitation of Clyde Murray. Hecht tried to talk him out of it but Lancaster insisted: "I was nurtured by them and I owe it to them." The visit was a disaster. Teenage girls packed the stairwells and screamed so loudly at the sight of him he could not be heard. Murray told his wife, Janet, to wait out back on 105th Street in the car with the motor running, then he and Lancaster fled through the mob out the back door to the car. With them were Charlie, the kid who had knifed Lancaster years before and since been forgiven, and a fourth young man who turned out to be a hitchhiker so determined to see the star he had snuck into the car.

"He started to talk to Burt," Janet recalled of the stranger, "and talked with him all the way downtown. It was one of the most fascinating conversations I've ever heard. *Brute Force* had just come out and had made a big impression. 'I've been in stir, Burt,' the boy said. 'That's nothing to be ashamed of if you're determined to keep straight now,' said Burt. 'It's up to you as to what you do after that.' 'You were lucky,' said the boy. 'You got into the movies.' 'It was luck I got noticed,' said Burt. 'But I had the experience and discipline that when I had the opportunity, I was able to take advantage of it.' The conversation went on like that all the way downtown and then the young man disappeared."

When they arrived at the Capitol Theater, Janet recalled that "for the first time in my life I had a sense of a particular kind of animal magnetism coming out of Burt. He had some sort of aura, a strong sexual component." Indeed, like an animal, Lancaster was watching the crowds around him carefully. "Burt had done something to someone in the past," said Janet, "and the relatives were out to get him." On Christmas Eve, Nick, fronting for Burt, was arrested for beating up William Miller, an eighteen-year-old delivery boy at the theater's stage door. Miller, according to the *New York Herald Tribune*, had come to try to discuss the death of his father, an acrobat who had appeared with Lancaster in a stage show. Lancaster testified in Nick's defense and the following May Nick was acquitted of simple assault by a three-judge panel of the special sessions court of New York City. "It had nothing to do with Nicky at all," remembered his sister. "Burt had a fresh mouth at times." The incident may have been an attempt to capitalize on Lancaster's new fame. Or maybe not. If audiences and critics saw in his eyes the memory of things he would rather forget, perhaps Miller's father was one of them.

Sitting in the stage show audience was a scout for the Cole Bros. Circus, a railroad show second in size only to Ringling Bros. and Barnum & Bailey.

He noticed how loudly the "saddle-shoe set" screamed each time Lancaster whirled through the air and offered him and his partner a spot with the troupe for one month the next April. They accepted. Just before leaving for the Louisville opening, Lancaster squeezed in his last picture of the decade and the one he would remember as the worst movie in which he ever appeared, *Rope of Sand*. A weak *Casablanca* variation, the picture was quickly shot in Arizona near Yuma and had the sole benefit in his mind of fulfilling his Wallis/Paramount obligation for the year.

At $11,000 a week for four weeks, Lancaster's Cole Bros. salary was the highest paid to any circus performer, breaking Tom Mix's $10,000 record. He was given a private railroad car, painted white with his name and a strong-man pose splashed across the side, and a private chef. But three days out of Louisville, Lancaster reverted to type: "I couldn't stand the comfort and the food was too rich for my blood." He appropriated the manager's Cadillac and drove himself from town to town. "Some difference, huh, Nick?" he kept saying, handing out money to anyone who asked. In fact, the circus comeback, like the Manhattan homecoming, was bittersweet. Tommy Hanneford, also in the show with a comedy riding act, recalls that there were problems with Nick. "He really wasn't a nice guy," says Hanneford. "He thought he was the star and it really was Burt." By the time the troupe had done the sawdust-and-peanut circuit in Toledo, Ohio, and Gary, Indiana, and into Pennsylvania, Lancaster had decided that it wasn't so much fun going back.

But his return only reinforced the alert performance style. "There was one thing about Burt that I loved," said Berry, "which was that circus background. It gave him something very, very unusual. You see circus performers, when the act is over, the way in which they take a bow, the way in which they relate to an audience, which is with great dignity and a certain way of sharing their whole set-up. Burt could be a pain in the ass, but he was *generous*."

Outside the studio walls, the "brave days of 1948" turned into the more dangerous political year of 1949. There was increasingly less middle ground as people waited to see what would happen to the Hollywood Ten and what HUAC had up its sleeve for the industry. Since Alger Hiss, a former New Deal state department official, had been identified as a communist spy by former *Time* editor Whittaker Chambers in August 1948, the fear that subversives might be working from within Washington was now plausible.

Lancaster's name appeared in various pamphlets that sprouted up around the country like mushrooms, listing names of suspected celebrities.

"Red Stars in Hollywood: Their Helpers . . . Fellow Travelers . . . and Co-Conspirators" was a slim tract ("100 copies for $1") that showed up in La Crosse, Wisconsin, in early 1949 and claimed that the names listed were those that newspapers were "afraid to publish." Citizens were encouraged to refuse to see any movie those mentioned had anything to do with. Charlie Chaplin, Douglas Fairbanks Jr., Henry Fonda, John Garfield, Gene Kelly, Myrna Loy, Frederic March, Robert Siodmak, Frank Sinatra, Orson Welles—these and others were said to be friends of Russia and enemies of America.

His new role as producer made Lancaster suddenly aware of the restrictions blacklisting posed to his growing professional power and freedom. In January 1949 he was the key speaker at a rally in New York at the Commodore Hotel calling for the abolition of HUAC and its "scare tactics." The event was sponsored by what the anticommunist newsletter *Counterattack* termed "the CP's [Communist Party's] top cultural front"—the National Council of Arts, Sciences and Professions (NCASP), whose members included W.E.B. Du Bois, Walter Gropius, Lillian Hellman, Garson Kanin, Norman Mailer, Arthur Miller, and Mark Van Doren. Described as "the new cave man star" by the right-wing Hearst newspapers, Lancaster joined Hollywood Ten defendant Lester Cole, Rep. Adam Clayton Powell, and a "weird array of toe dancers, movie stars, Broadway producers and astronomers [including Harvard professor Harlow Shapley, chairman of NCASP]" up on the dais. The other congressman in attendance was one of the most unapologetic leftists in public life, La Guardia's protégé and successor in his East Harlem seat, Vito Marcantonio. To stand up with this group in 1949 was not a frivolous step.

"Can anything be more un-American than the Un-American Committee?" Lancaster asked in the first political speech of his life. He had recently read a book by one of the Hollywood Ten that he thought had movie possibilities and observed, "If I buy this writer's book, the technique of the Un-American Committee would be to attack the purchase, the picture, the exhibitors, and everybody who has anything to do with it. The banks, of course, would be reluctant to put up money for the production. I recognize no limits to my right of free speech and it remains to be shown that being a member of the film industry alters that condition." By January 21, *Counterattack* was urging its readers to tell movie and radio stations and networks "AT ONCE" of their objections to the appearance of Burt Lancaster at communist-front meetings. The FBI noted in its files not only Lancaster's speech but that the NCASP event was well covered in the communist newspaper, the *Daily Worker.*

The California State Senate Committee on Un-American Activities published its fifth biennial report in June, which included a list of several hundred Hollywood figures suspected of having "followed or appeased some of the Communist party line." The Hollywood Ten was now, potentially, the Hollywood Hundreds. For the October term of the U.S. Supreme Court, Lancaster signed the *amici curiae* brief filed in support of the Hollywood Ten's request that the court review the conviction of Trumbo and Lawson for contempt of Congress. Over two hundred Hollywood professionals and almost as many luminaries from what *Variety* called "other arts and sciences" also signed including Berry, Bercovici, Howard Duff, Hecht, Kibbee, Mickey Knox, Maddow, Arthur Miller, Reis, Waldo Salt, and George Tyne. No more Bogart, Bacall, or Gershwin.

Meanwhile, the Soviet Union, gobbling up one Eastern European country after another, exploded its own atomic bomb in September. By January 1, 1950, Chinese Communists had taken over mainland China and Hiss had been convicted of perjury.

On July 5, 1949, Norma gave birth to the couple's third child in four years and the first girl. Susan Elizabeth was partly named for Lizzie and quickly nicknamed Susabet. Behind the delight in having the children and the shared focus on the needs of so many offspring so quickly, it was evident to many that the Lancasters had little in common. Norma was a "functioning" alcoholic—up at seven every morning, drinking only after five and never while pregnant. A fairly accomplished person, she nevertheless did not follow her husband in his new intellectual pursuits. She was, said one sympathetic friend, "not strong enough" to weather being married to a Hollywood star, much less to Lancaster. A family member would later say she was "destroyed" by the marriage.

There evolved a tacit agreement that her husband could do what he wanted as long as she remained Mrs. Burt Lancaster for the community. "Burt came and went as he pleased," said Knox, "as a lot of guys did in those days." Yet if she thought her husband was having an affair, Norma "fell apart," setting off another cycle of drinking. "I said to her," said Lucy Kibbee, " 'Jesus Christ, Norma, you shouldn't be so unhappy. He loves you as much as he is capable of loving a woman. He loves himself.' " She added, "I know friends of hers that betrayed her and of course I never told her. They went after him, he didn't go after them. It fed his ego, for God's sake. Burt didn't seek out women. They came to him with mattresses on their backs."

His immersion in the art, business, and politics of anti-HUAC Hollywood threw him together with a fellow enthusiast, Shelley Winters. She was cast opposite Garfield in *He Ran All the Way* and thus placed smack in the middle of the blacklisted world of the movie's director, Berry, and coscreenwriter, Hugo Butler, both Communists. She signed the *amici curiae* brief, she was at all the meetings, she attended the Gene Kelly/Betsy Blair liberal parties made up of like-minded liberals such as Hecht, Mailer, Lancaster, and Garfield. A blond actress with a brassy, New York edge, Winters hooked Lancaster with a sudden, overwhelming, emotional force. For the man who had women falling at his feet, this was an affair of love, sex, *and* politics. "Politically Shelley was very progressive," said Lucy Kibbee, "and I know she introduced Burt to a lot of music and art and stuff he really loved. He was hungry for it." He also gave her books to read like *The Naked and the Dead:* "[Burt] was always," Winters recalled, "trying to educate me." In her autobiography, she described Lancaster as "charming and funny and, oh, God, so handsome! And he was, I think one of the most gracefully athletic men I've ever seen. Just watching him walk was almost a physical pleasure."

Winters was an uninhibited city girl who had, Berry recalled, no qualms about affairs with married men—indeed she would describe Lancaster as being unfaithful to her when he made love to his wife. "Shelley had a kind of moxie about her," said Knox, "a kind of Jewishness that Jewish girls have, that he fell for, that was so different from Norma who was a WASP." When their liaison did not move quickly and definitively enough, she confided in Berry and others during the fall 1950 filming of *He Ran All the Way,* asking advice on how to "nail the guy" or at least get him to spend the night. She stubbornly refused to reveal his name. Her confidantes suggested a sexual technique—versions differ—that she initially rejected, laughing, as unthinkable. A week or two passed. One night Berry and his friends were standing out on the sidewalk in front of Schwab's drugstore on Sunset Boulevard when they heard a woman yell out, "Hey, Jack!" An open convertible passed by with Winters standing up in the car waving like a prom queen. "It worked!" she cried. Lancaster was driving the car.

He came very close to leaving Norma for Winters, the only time he would be so seriously tempted for more than twenty years. By 1951, what Winters called their "lovely and sad backstreet romance" was over. Lancaster reportedly continued to be obsessed with her, sitting in his car outside her apartment for three to four hours a night, watching for who came to see her. Brando was his successor, a further chagrin. Like the *noir* chumps he played with such aching stolidity, like a character in the operas he loved, he yearned for the grand passion. That was not his to have.

Their romance had taken place at the end of Hollywood's adolescence as a movie "colony" insulated from real life, a time Norman Mailer remembers as "a sweet time, quiet, peaceful, kind of middle-class where family and friends got together and played bridge or charades." The lionized young writer of *The Naked and the Dead,* the sensational 1948 combat novel, Mailer was newly arrived in the movie capital to campaign for Henry Wallace, the Progressive Party's 1948 presidential candidate, and to try his hand at the business. He observed that Lancaster was much more handsome off-screen than on, always "the biggest man in the room," with the most chilling blue eyes he had ever seen. What Lancaster really wanted at this time, Mailer observed, like Knox, was "to become a brain." One day he bought about ten books, including Proust's *Remembrance of Things Past,* and told Mailer how he was going to read all of them, so many pages a day. "I literally began to feel faint after a while," the writer recalled, "because he overawed me. He had so much energy and the whole feeling was, Jesus, I don't even belong in the same ballpark with this guy."

Mailer experienced some of Lancaster's most characteristic behaviors across the bridge table. "Burt was a very good player," he said. "That answers the question about his intelligence. You can't be a good bridge player without some intelligence. But he was a pain in the ass to play with because he was as condemnatory as hell if you fucked up. He hated to lose. You could feel the athlete in him. God, he hated to lose!"

CHAPTER FIVE

The Hero Business

... THE TROUBLE WITH BUSINESS IS
EVERYBODY STILL THINKS THIS IS 1945, 1946, AND 1947
AND ALL VALUES ARE BUILT AROUND THAT
WHICH I BLAME MUCH NOT ONLY ON THE
MO PIC COMPANIES BUT ON AGENTS
ARTISTS AND EVERYONE WHO IS GREEDY
FOR A BUCK INCLUDING MYSELF ESPECIALLY. ...

—Cable from Jack Warner to agent Charles Feldman, June 15, 1950

As fledgling independents folded left and right, Lancaster and Hecht had to find a replacement for the Hellinger alliance. They needed a studio that would distribute Lancaster's two annual options from outside Paramount and, as news reports emphasized, also let the indie make pictures *without* the star, like real producers.

It was essential to keep the momentum going, to keep nourishing Lancaster's white-hot stardom. The options, the choices, the rejections he and Hecht went through in their quest for the right deal were not just on the front edge of Hollywood pushing into the new decade—they were the edge itself. Lancaster used the chaos to his advantage. Divesture of theaters from production opened up the market, as it was intended to do, for independent companies like Norma to provide more varied, better product, the supposed answer to the great split of the postwar American audience between studio movies and television. As Lancaster would say a decade later, "It was the best thing that ever happened to the movies."

But there were other developments that would make the 1950s one of the most baffling, challenging decades of American movie history. In 1950, box-office receipts continued their decline, shrinking by a quarter of a billion dollars. The studios stripped down their cozy overhead apparatus and fired long-time contract players they could no longer afford to keep like thoroughbreds twitching their tails in the stable. Remembering the last time the industry had sustained such a shock to the system with the introduction of sound in 1927, Hollywood began to spin out one technological gimmick and cartoon-like star after another, hoping to lure the audience back: Vista-Vision, 3-D, Marilyn Monroe, Martin and Lewis, Elvis Presley. Wider screens and more vivid color technology would demand bigger if not better movies like *The Robe, The Ten Commandments, The King and I, War and Peace*—all the way to the end of the decade with *Ben-Hur* and *Spartacus.* The fickle audience, however, stayed home to make babies, mow the lawn, and watch TV. The fabulous movie palaces built on America's Main Streets in the flush heyday of the twenties were stranded: between 1954 and 1958, more than two thousand of them across the country shut their doors forever. From 1946 to 1962, the number of Americans going to the movies declined by 73.4 percent, the vacuum partially created and then filled by the phenomenal market for television.

The wild card nobody counted on was politics. Without it, independent production might have been a normal all-American foray, with the usual risks, into a new way to express yourself and make money at the same time. Instead, fear choked the energy at its source. When *All My Sons* opened, one critic predicted the industry would react as it always had to political unrest, "by an all-consuming pre-occupation with the affairs of Blondie, Dracula and Lassie." When HUAC's J. Parnell Thomas went to prison for fraud in 1949, the movie colony waited uneasily, hoping the invaders would just go away. Banks, studios, would-be indies, old stars, and new stars were living in a world turned upside down. Freedom to compete was fine but how, exactly, did you do it safely?

Lancaster's first preference as an independent studio partner was the producer he most admired, Darryl Zanuck at Fox. He agreed to star in *Twelve O'Clock High* if Zanuck would make a three-picture deal with Norma Productions. But the producer of *The Grapes of Wrath* and *Gentleman's Agreement* did not think he could convince the New York money men in the unsettled economic climate to give Lancaster and Hecht such independent authority. (Gregory Peck got the part and an Oscar nomination.)

The next best choice was Columbia. By now the partners had a new story idea to peddle. "Harold and I were wracking our brains what to do next," Lancaster recalled, when Nick came up with a bright idea: Fairbanks. Fresh from the enthusiastic circus and stage show crowds and noting the highly successful reissue of two Errol Flynn hits—*The Sea Hawk* (1940) in 1947 and *The Adventures of Robin Hood* (1938) in 1948—they asked themselves who else could do on-screen what Burt's hero used to do? It would be a complete departure for Lancaster, a calculated risk with the audience's insistence that stars stay true to type. But what was the point of being independent if you didn't try something different? Hollywood Nineteen screenwriter Waldo Salt wrote an original story, later titled *The Flame and the Arrow*, based on William Tell, the heroic resister of Switzerland and transposed to Lombardy. Hecht took it to Columbia as the hook to bait them into a multi-picture deal but the studio turned them down for a classic studio reason: they wanted Lancaster to make another gangster flick, not some oddball costume period romp.

The only likely major left was Warner Bros. On March 18, 1949, Louella Parsons reported that Jack Warner, "out to corner all the lads who play he-man roles," had signed Lancaster. The tough guy star was still, she reassured her readers, under contract to Wallis. The tyrannical Warner was now running the Burbank studio through what he called "turbulent times" by trying both to give established stars like Bogart more money and leeway with options, scripts, and directors, and to restock the studio with new talent. With UA teetering so unsteadily that banks had cut production funds, Cagney returned to Warner Bros. in May with an agreement that allowed him to make three outside pictures with his own company, to be distributed by Warner Bros., in exchange for three pictures for the studio in which he starred. On July 8, Norma Productions and Warner Bros. signed a six-picture deal, which the *Times* reported as "almost exactly duplicat[ing] the deal made recently by Warner's with the Cagney brothers." The parallels between the two stars were now exact.

There were actually two Lancaster/Warner agreements, one with Norma Productions for the independent productions and the other with Lancaster for his services in the studio's upcoming *Jim Thorpe—All American*, *South Sea Woman*, and a third as yet unspecified film. Norma Productions was to receive ten percent of the gross up to $75,000 "and no more" after the deduction of a 27.5 percent North American distribution allowance; the same percentage would apply to the Warner pictures starring Lancaster. The studio would completely finance each of the three Norma pictures, the casting, director, final editing, and scoring of which would be subjected to the written approval of Jack Warner. Important for future, better deals was Warner's insistence that the Norma "photoplays shall not be grouped or considered as a single unit for the purpose of accounting," meaning that the indie could not offset any losses with a heavy-grossing hit, a potential budget morass. Hecht and Lancaster took new office space at 8747 Sunset Boulevard in West Hollywood. Warner approved the Salt story as long as, to keep total costs down to $1.6 million, costumes and sets were used from *The Adventures of Robin Hood* and another Flynn swashbuckler, *The Adventures of Don Juan*, just completed.

Shooting began at the end of the year on the seemingly innocuous yarn full of sword fights, horses charging in and out of the forest, bull's-eye arrow marksmanship, pretty ladies with long hair, sinister Hessian overlords with

British accents, brave Lombardy outlaws—all in glorious non-*noir* Technicolor. With Warner Bros. busy switching to Doris Day musicals, the movie fell right in with the spirit of the new decade. Max Steiner's gay, rompy music kept up with each beat of the plot in which feisty princess Virginia Mayo falls in love with Lancaster's outlaw hero, Dardo (the name means "arrow"). The twist was Salt's campy humor, which Jacques Tourneur, who had directed *The Cat People* in 1942, happily blended with his own visual grace and energy. "The roof leaks!" exclaims one of Lancaster's band as they arrive at their forest hideout, an artfully classic ruin of no known period constructed on Warner's huge Stage 21 with no roof at all.

Nick was cast as the mute sidekick Piccolo because his East Harlem accent was too strong, even for this broad farcical picture. Lancaster had to taunt him before he would agree to perform at all. He stormed off the set several times and hit his friend on the head so hard with a horseshoe during one take that Lancaster protested, "That's the way they kill cattle, Nick. . . . The camera will never know if you hit me easy or hard."

The two men trained for weeks with Shotsy O'Brien, one of the great acrobats of the old Palace Theater in New York, and so named because he had been shot out of a cannon since the age of nine. He brushed up their perch pole routine (with a 225-foot climb at the top of which Lancaster could still hold himself out like a flag), parallel bar flips, hand-over-hand rope climbs up a thirty-foot rope done with no camera cuts, somersaults and pirouettes from horizontal bars twenty feet above the ground, and so on. Up at 5 a.m., they ran three miles, did tumbling workouts, archery, sword and dagger practice, memorized lines, and—significant for the star's future work—took lots of horseback riding lessons. Lancaster's hands got so greasy eating trencher food à la Errol Flynn in *Robin Hood,* he had trouble shooting arrows in the following scenes. "What these babies wouldn't have given for a bowl of Wheaties," he grumbled, loving every minute of it. In the middle of a pell-mell acrobat scene, Warner walked onto the set and bumped into Lancaster dressed in striped leggings, a big red clown nose stuck in the middle of his face. Behind him, Nick scurried up a rope. "What the fuck is this?" the mogul roared. *"Midsummer Night's Dream?"* In the grand finale, Lancaster flung himself into the air off a castle roof grabbing the first of a row of flaming horizontal flag poles, soaring into his old routine of giant swings from one to the next, alighting on his feet on top of one bar only to fall back into the air as if into open arms.

When *The Flame and the Arrow* opened July 15, 1950, reviewers seized on the formerly "large and laconic" Lancaster as now "the liveliest swashbuckler of them all" because, unlike his predecessors, he did all his own stunts. "[T]he producers," wrote the *New York Times,* "are not trying to kid anybody that their film is meant to be viewed in rapt amazement such as greeted old Fairbanks films. They have let it be such obvious hokum—such broad, carefree, candid, circus stuff—that you can laugh at it more than you can gasp." Warner Bros. stuntmen signed an affidavit claiming that no star in any one picture had ever performed such ambitious, often dangerous stunts. To back up its offer of a $1 million reward to anybody who could prove otherwise, the studio sent Lancaster and Nick on a grand publicity tour in July 1950. They whirled through thirteen cities in as many days, performing practice sessions on the platforms alongside the Union Pacific Streamliner as it chugged across the country to Chicago. Legs wrapped around the top of the perch pole, Lancaster was interviewed face-to-face by a critic hanging out a window of the *Cleveland Press* building. In a Cincinnati street crowd was his first circus boss, Bill Ketrow, then eighty-two. "Burt was on top of the pole," his son Bob Peters said, "and he spied my father down in the audience. He came down off the perch, leaped over a convertible, grabbed my father in his arms and hugged him and my dad started crying."

Rare in the history of movie stardom—but essential to circus celebrity—a particular kind of trust and admiration of the risk taken was established between performer and viewer in *The Flame and the Arrow*. So instinctive that nobody thought much about it, in the truthful grace of Lancaster's movements there was something god-like, an ancient presumption of the good. If he was authentic on-screen, perhaps he was the same off-screen. If he could move through space with joy and beauty, he was what the earthbound people sitting in the dark watching him wished they could be. Underlying so many of the roles that were to come would be this first memory of him flying free in the air, no net. "This," he said, delighted at the change of pace, "is the hero business."

Hidden within the movie's Forest of Arden frivolity was a clever, subversive edge. Salt had been scheduled to testify in 1947 at the HUAC Washington hearings after Bertolt Brecht but was never called. Fired from RKO, at the turn of the decade he was working for independents such as Hecht and Lancaster in a political climate in which "[n]othing was above suspicion." Salt's tale of little guys rising up against oppressive overlords was seen by some as clearly leftist. Dardo, facing the gallows, tells his son the value of friends in language that indeed sounds like code: "A man can't live by himself alone. . . . But a man who has friends . . . who are willing to risk their lives for someone else, a man who has friends like that will never really die." True to the genre, *The Flame and the Arrow* is a story of the hero's moral awakening to his role in the fate of his fellow men and women, the most dangerous message of all.

While Lancaster was chasing Hessians in January 1950, the Los Angeles outpost of the FBI advised the home office in Washington that he and

Hecht had established a new, additional production company, Halburt Productions with Columbia, and they were hiring suspicious people. The studio's head, Harry Cohn, had taken another look at the indie and decided to contract with them after all to make two independent pictures. Among the suspect Halburt employees were Salt, and left-wing screenwriter Hugo Butler and his wife, writer Jean Rouveral. Norma Productions over at Warner Bros., the informant also reported, were known to be hiring "a number of individuals . . . who are suspected of being CP members or Communist sympathizers." The following month, Republican Senator Joseph R. McCarthy stood up in Wheeling, West Virginia, with what he claimed was a list of 205 Communists working in the state department. In March, New York FBI agents sent out an "internal security" report on current Hollywood activities reporting that the closely watched José Ferrer was scheduled to work for Lancaster and Hecht as the star of *Catbird Seat*, based on a James Thurber story, one of a trilogy of shorts to be called *Spice of Life*.

The two producers had just cut a subsidiary Paramount agreement with *Spice of Life* as the first picture. Wallis retained "complete final authority" plus the right to terminate if the movie's budget exceeded $700,000. The *New York Daily News* called the comedy/tragedy/drama trilogy "something of an experiment in the motion picture industry." Already at work adapting *Catbird Seat* into a script that he was also slated to direct was Frank Tashlin, a future Jerry Lewis writer. A Ring Lardner story, *Love Nest*, was being scripted by Salt.

As Lancaster began work on a Wallis loanout in April, the case of Trumbo, Lawson, and the rest of the Hollywood Ten was denied review by the Supreme Court and the men went off to prison. Having signed the *amici curiae* brief on their behalf was suddenly a dangerous thing to have done. In a period of crisis John Cogley called "a kind of anti-communists' *Ten Days That Shook the World*," *Red Channels* was published on June 22. The booklet listed radio and television professionals with suspect activities itemized after each name, and was created by the same three ex-FBI agents who put out *Counterattack*. It soon was dubbed with a mixture of fear and contempt as the "Bible of Madison Avenue." On June 24, North Korean troops crossed the 38th parallel and invaded South Korea.

Five years after World War II, the country was at war again and with a communist adversary. The reactionary wing of the Republican Party, HUAC, and the FBI now settled in for the fight to the finish. Rumors flew of a forthcoming Hollywood version of *Red Channels*. *Counterattack* reported on August 4 that Lancaster, as well as Marlon Brando and Elia Kazan, had a "Communist front record." On September 27, *Daily Variety* headlined news of a probe, aided by the men at *Counterattack*, of Hollywood professionals who "may be members or associated with organizations branded 'subversive' by the Department of Justice." In October the American Legion, a major force in the anticommunist campaign, published the entire list of those who had signed the Supreme Court brief. By the end of this first year of the decade, Hecht announced he would not hire any more Communists. It was clear conditions were perfect for reopening the hearings into communist infiltration of the motion picture business. The only question was when.

Lancaster responded to what was for many a paralyzing situation by finding even more movie opportunities. "Burt is sliced more ways than a watermelon contractually," claimed one press release: two studio star contracts; three indie contracts; offices at Warner Bros., Columbia Studios, and Norma's home office in West Hollywood. The *New York Herald-Tribune* chided that "if anything, [Lancaster's] Norma company has too many choices to pick from." There were no real studio affiliations for many of the story acquisitions dangled in the press, yet Hecht made a point of saying he was "pursuing a fairly unique course" in acquiring so many properties and in giving writers greater control in the development and directing of many of them. Salt had already informally apprenticed on the set of *Flame* with the idea that he would direct the Theodore Dreiser story *St. Columba and the River*. Dreiser, who had died in 1945, was a provocative choice. The author of controversial, naturalistic novels like *Sister Carrie*, he had been a very public member of the U.S. Communist Party.

The indie's biggest coup was getting the rights to *The Naked and the Dead*. Hecht and Lancaster saw the project more as a chance to make their "big movie" than as a vehicle for Lancaster, who would play Red Valsen, the coal miner's son described in the novel as having blue eyes, a "boiled and angry face," and "a rough voice braying out with a contemptuous inviolate mirth." The partners readily gave Mailer script approval and assigned the project to writers Philip Stevenson and Joseph Mischel (both of whom were later blacklisted). Admitting he never really thought Hollywood would make a movie of his graphic novel of GI despair and apathy, the author, recalling himself as a "prodigious innocent," figured that it may as well be attempted by friends no matter how thin their experience. He was always skeptical of Hecht. Though he recalled the producer as "a man of the left" clearly sympathetic to the intent of the book, he also felt that "you really couldn't trust [Hecht] to get things done, you couldn't quite trust his word."

The author's instincts about the project were correct. In October 1950, Parsons announced that Lancaster had decided this was not the time to make an antiwar film. In any case, it had proved impossible, said Mailer, to come up with an acceptable script. Paramount, meanwhile, may have found the clever idea of the *Spice of Life* trilogy too risky and fey and, Oscar aside, the leftist politics of Ferrer, not to mention Salt, were liabilities to a careful career man like Wallis. In any case, Lancaster and Hecht could not stomach the idea of the Paramount mogul having final control. The aborted projects taught the partners much about what to look for next—and what to avoid.

Spice of Life was initially postponed so Lancaster could do two loanouts for Wallis: Fox's *Mister 880*, a winsome drama based on a true-life counterfeiting case; and MGM's *Vengeance Valley*, a soap-opera Western based on the relationship dramas of unwed pregnancy and sibling rivalry. Lancaster complained that as soon as he set up a date for a Norma picture, Wallis intervened with his own project. "I want to clean up those contracts as fast as possible," he said of the Paramount obligations, "so I can get busy on some of my own productions—and also so I can pick and choose what outside pictures I do." When Wallis scheduled him to star in Paramount's thriller *Dark City* with Lizabeth Scott, Lancaster insisted that he did not want to do another melodrama and certainly not one with Scott. Wallis, who rarely met a loanout he didn't like, instead signed his hot star, without consulting him about the production timing, at Fox and MGM, each for $150,000. Lancaster's original role in *Dark City* went to Charlton Heston as his Hollywood debut.

On April 5, 1950, Lancaster reported for work on *Mister 880* at Fox studios and barely ten days after it wrapped, started shooting *Vengeance Valley* in July outside Canyon City, Colorado. "A typical John Wayne part," reported Nathan to Wallis of Lancaster's good-guy rancher, the solid foster brother foil to Robert Walker Jr.'s no-count. "Slow-thinking, slow-moving, and very heroic." About a quarter of Lancaster's career would be devoted to Westerns and in this, his first (not counting *Desert Fury*), he indeed moves slowly like Wayne, and sits well on a horse. His jeans did not yet look natural on him but the industry saw he could also do Westerns.

The immediate effect on Lancaster of two loanouts in a row was rage against Wallis. The producer was in the equivocal position of being the one fixed piece in the career puzzle, the Big Bad Daddy from whom one could borrow money for personal and professional needs and resent the necessity to do so at the same time. Though Lancaster was now theoretically a full-fledged production partner, Wallis continued to act as if the star owed him everything and to pester him with written reminders about irritating details like his discolored and damaged teeth. ("Burt didn't care," recalled Knox, "but Hal Wallis was the old school—everybody had to be a movie star with beautiful white teeth.") On October 2, 1950, he wrote a letter to his boss, itemizing "a number of grievances." It is a key document of this transitional time in Hollywood history, a movie star *j'accuse*. He began by assuring Wallis that he would never "refuse to be in any picture" he was assigned to, but that he felt it was his "right" to voice his honest opinion and to be consulted about future projects. Promised there would not be many loanouts, he was then lent out twice; when he tried to discuss his career with Wallis, he found it "impossible" to reach him by phone and was forced to deliver messages through a third party. He reminded Wallis that he had made a great deal of money for Paramount of which he felt he should have "some share." Wallis not only "refused" to give him any part of the loanout profits, a "really inexcusable" move because loanouts do "not even require the producer's risk in his work," he also insisted on appropriating most of the money Lancaster received from the two outside studios. "There are other things," concluded the star. "I am interested in being in pictures that I would like to see, with parts I would like to play—human, believable people."

There is no record of Wallis's formal reply among his papers. But a copy of a "letter, not sent" of October 12 reads as the response of the old guard to the upstarts who are—in Lancaster's case, anyway—maybe not so lunatic after all. "Many things have transpired since the time of our original discussions with you and Harold at the Waldorf-Astoria in New York," wrote Wallis, "which have been as unpleasant and disappointing to me as have the grievances which you have enumerated in your letter. . . . We are gaining nothing by this except a spreading out of the remaining pictures while you are being given the privilege of improving your position handsomely."

As if to flaunt his rebellion, Lancaster's next project was not only *not* for Paramount, but a biopic of the man a 1950 Associated Press poll had chosen as the greatest football player and athlete of the first half of the twentieth century, Jim Thorpe. With Lancaster under contract, Warner Bros. decided the time was finally right to make the story that had kicked around Hollywood for years. A Native American from Oklahoma of the Sauk and Fox tribes, Thorpe was a superb track athlete and football star under coach Glenn S. "Pop" Warner at the Carlisle Indian School in Pennsylvania, winner of the pentathlon and decathlon events at the 1912 Olympic Games, a great professional football player at the dawn of the pro league, and a fallen hero stripped of his medals when it was revealed that he had played professional minor league baseball in the East Carolina league in the summer of 1909 for $2 a day.

Making the movie was fraught with the sad realities of the aged athlete's real life, which Lancaster described as "gone to pot." That Thorpe had been reduced to playing, as James Robert Parish described it, "stereotyped Indians in ever cheaper and more stupid productions" was left out of the movie as Warner Bros. received preproduction letters from all over the country pleading with the studio to do right by their hero. The story had the unbeatable combination of athletic prowess and racial prejudice and

Americans knew it by heart: "No peeps from fans," warned the *New York Morning Telegraph,* "about bloopers." Released after *Broken Arrow,* the story of the Apache chief Cochise, in 1950, and with dialogue like "White man lick Indian: he win great battle. Indian lick white man: massacre," *Jim Thorpe— All American* was part of the beginning of a big change in perception. In real life, Thorpe died in 1953 and his medals were not restored to him, posthumously, until 1982.

The movie was directed on location for four weeks from late August into September 1950 at Bacone College outside Muskogee, Oklahoma, and at the Los Angeles Coliseum, the site of the 1932 Olympics. The part of Thorpe was an awesome challenge: how to portray convincingly to the camera the grace, strength, and skill of the athlete who could run the one-hundred-yard dash in ten seconds flat, as well as kick, block, pole-vault, sprint, throw the javelin, and high jump. Jess Hill, the University of Southern California's track coach, and the University of California at Los Angeles football coach Bill Spaulding, plus "Mushy" Callahan, former junior welterweight champion and Kirk Douglas's trainer on *Champion,* were all hired to coach the star. Thorpe was hired as a consultant. Every morning at 6:30 Callahan had Lancaster running around Bacone's baseball field, getting him down to 175 pounds and into what Lancaster recalled as "really wonderful condition."

He had to learn how to play football. Roughly the same height and weight as Thorpe at his collegiate prime, Lancaster insisted he could hold his own against the bigger, brawnier collegiate players drafted from the UCLA and USC teams. For the other athletic feats, with the exception of a couple of pole-vault and long-jump shots, the star did his own jock work. All he had to do, he said, was "look pretty good doing it"—the distances could be manipulated—as if that were simple. He turned his knee twice, tore a thigh muscle, burned a foot when his spike shoes penetrated an electric cable, and put the shot forty-eight feet on his first try. His hair was dyed black and makeup darkened his skin, shading in the appearance of high cheekbones. "I get a funny feeling," said the real Thorpe, "sitting there watching Burt doing the things I did. . . . I don't think I was ever that handsome." Phyllis Thaxter, cast as Thorpe's first wife, made a claim that was perhaps the secret to what a fellow professional later called Lancaster's "impeccable blocking": because he did not like doing love scenes and "wished to hide his feelings from the camera," she said, he carefully rehearsed every move with her in front of a mirror.

Director Michael Curtiz, the Hungarian-born workhorse who had shaped Errol Flynn in swashbucklers and Cagney in *Yankee Doodle Dandy,* was largely past his peak in this, his seventy-fifth Warner picture. He and Lancaster clashed often. But with the intensity of the immigrant, Curtiz was sentimentally captivated by the story of a man, as the *New York Times* said in praise of Lancaster's portrayal, "who found joy and sadness in competition," the all-American boy. In a key scene, Thorpe smashes up a room after being stripped of his medals—the athlete in anguish at the effort annulled. Time's toll on the superior body and the role of self-discipline in staving off the worst a little longer was implicit in the casting of Lancaster. The star was almost thirty-seven years old when playing the collegiate Thorpe.

The athlete in Lancaster and the audience watching him saw the story as their own, the metaphor of striving to the perfect action that hooks fans to sports and movies alike. *Jim Thorpe—All American* ends with Thorpe, old and battered, driving a truck for a living, stopping in a rundown railroad yard in the middle of a group of kids. They hand him a football and there is a quick cut to a crane shot from high above looking down on him as he steps back to drop-kick the ball. As his leg springs up, the camera moves in to meet him and follows the ball up into the air until it leaves the screen. Holding for a split-second midsky, the lens then turns with a beautiful carefulness and plunges back down and in to the lone figure of Lancaster. Ball, athlete, and space—the coordinates of sport.

A month after sending off his angry letter to Wallis, he finished up studio work on *Jim Thorpe* while Norma took Jimmy, Billy, and fifteen-month-old Susan to the Apple Valley Inn outside of Los Angeles to give them a chance to splash around in a pool before winter. Back home, a few days before his third birthday, Billy developed a spasm in his left leg and a high fever that would not come down. With Norma at his side, he was rushed to Los Angeles General Hospital in an ambulance, his fever still raging. The major fear of parents in the early 1950s had been realized by the Lancasters: Billy had contracted polio.

For the next several days, Lancaster continued work on *Jim Thorpe*, staying in constant touch with the hospital; at night, he and Norma sat vigil by the boy, isolated in the polio ward. The fever, a symptom of the dreaded virus for which Jonas Salk would not develop the vaccine until 1953, did not go down fast enough and the muscles in the child's left leg were permanently affected. Billy would need therapy and braces, and although his parents would hope for several years that he would eventually recover the full use of his leg, the sturdy little boy who had showed such early athletic promise would limp for the rest of his life. "When I heard Billy got polio," remembered Knox, "I cried."

A key element in *Jim Thorpe* are the sequences in which the athlete is shown doting on his son, training him to carry on in the great Thorpe tradition. When the child dies suddenly of influenza, the tragedy is a further trigger for Thorpe's downfall. For Lancaster, the experience of watching the hospital's reaction to his son's emergency was what he described as "a revelation." He realized he needed to pay back, to get involved on a more positive level, instead of just mouthing off. Despite a dread of the water left over from an accident at Lake Stahahe when he had got trapped under a pier, Burt built a pool and began to swim with Billy, almost on a daily basis, to work out the leg. And he started to show up at event after event in support of worthy causes.

He became even more protective of his children. At one of what were regular Sunday afternoon pool parties at Walter Seltzer's home in Woodland Hills, the publicist was watching over the guests' children after their parents had gone into the house. He was "horrified" to see the two Lancaster boys standing on the edge, peeing into the pool. "I grabbed each one by the shoulder," he recalled, "and shook them and yelled at them. Burt saw me and, furious, said, 'No one, *no one* treats my kids that way.' " When Seltzer protested that urinating in the pool was a destructive thing to do, Lancaster shot back, "I don't care what they did. No one treats them like that." The boys overheard the entire exchange. The two men did not talk to each other for a year.

His "revelations" were dismissed by many who saw no visible improvement in his one-on-one attitude to his fellow man—indeed, he would get a lot worse before he got better. Composed of what Seltzer calls "warring elements, very complex, respectful, without sham, with a great sense of moral rectitude even with all the peccadillos," his character was marked by a dissonance the publicist chalked up to simple rebellion mixed with "Burt's never losing sight of the original training." But an evolution had begun. Max Youngstein, soon to be the United Artists executive vice-president with whom Lancaster would work for years, called the star's slow process of personal change over the next two decades "the coming out of a cocoon."

The career now had a momentum beyond the early fits and starts. Valiant Swashbuckler followed by the Greatest Athlete of the Century—good guys both, but with a particular Lancaster twist. The star looked heroic, certainly, but there was something else lurking behind the eyes. A remnant of *noir* desperation? A gleeful wit that detached him—saved him, maybe—from the whole business? He was fully in his own skin now, in charge. Even the forgettable *Mister 880* provided grist for his ravenous mill: Zanuck and his meticulous daily production memos gave Lancaster a producer-model he could admire and use.

At the end of March 1951, the star began work on his other Columbia project, *Ten Tall Men*, a Foreign Legion spoof shot at Palm Canyon outside of Palm Springs. When the movie opened in October, one month after *Jim*

Thorpe, its inconsistencies were seen as part of the indie's new style. "These Norma people," wrote Crowther, "are the ones who played hob with the Robin Hood tradition in last year's *Flame*—to the utter delight and entertainment of millions . . . and now the same sort of gay abandon is being shown in their tossing around of a yarn of the Foreign Legion. Let's settle: they don't give a damn." *Ten Tall Men* marked the rapid inflation of Lancaster's star presence on the screen. A ferocity lashes from his legionnaire as he endures bare-chested torture, barks out commands, shoots bullets not arrows, and kills Riff natives dead. Also emerging was the style split of Lancaster's early 1950s career: serious effort followed by zany parody, each persona played off against the other with a circus performer's instinct for the next, quick surprise.

Ten Tall Men also snuck in front of the industry, Cohn, and the audience an image of Lancaster as in-charge military man that would pay off two years later. As the star played war games in the desert, *From Here to Eternity*, James Jones's sensational novel about the peacetime U.S. Army in Hawaii on the eve of Pearl Harbor, was published in February. Cohn bought the movie rights in March and by April the novel was the number-one best-seller in the country—an extraordinary feat for a first book by an unknown author. The search for the right script and cast was launched for the project the industry mocked as "Cohn's Folly." How could anybody in such dangerous times make a movie out of a big, fat, antiarmy book full of four-letter words and sex?

One of Lancaster's most enduring friendships and professional collaborations began on *Ten Tall Men*. Robert Schiffer, the makeup expert Columbia usually assigned to Rita Hayworth and later the director of makeup and hairdressing for the Walt Disney Company, had led a rambunctious life equal to Lancaster's, starting out as a sailor before the war, jumping ship in Shanghai where he peddled colored lard as "Robert Schiffer's Night Cream" until he realized the tin containers were giving his clients lead poisoning. Returning to Los Angeles, he worked on several MGM musicals including *The Great Ziegfeld* and *The Wizard of Oz,* and got a reputation for working well with Dietrich and Rosalind Russell, the "glamor girls" of the industry. Funny and always game for life's unexpected amusements, Schiffer relished Lancaster's obliviousness to the details of his appearance. "Most stars," he said, "are up in front of the mirror moving their head all over the place trying to get a look at themselves. Burt would sit in the chair and anything I put on him was fine." Years later, when he had become the star's regular makeup man, Schiffer painted a Groucho Marx moustache on him one morning; only when the crew started laughing and Lancaster knew he was not being particularly funny did he think to check a mirror.

The two men started a lifetime of what Schiffer, unmarried during *Ten*

Tall Men, calls "rousing good times." With a droll sense of the incongruous, he recalled that "Burt could never understand between the two of us why the women would end up with me. I would use him at a bar as bait and what happens psychologically is the women say, 'Who does this big star think he is, that he can take me and do what he likes with me? I'll go with this other guy.' . . ." The next morning Lancaster would come in, baffled, and Schiffer would say, "Burt, you just don't have it."

"What, *again?*" whined *Boxoffice* on March 3, 1951. HUAC had reopened its hearings on communist infiltration of the American movie business, marking a tacit deal with the studio hierarchies. The committee would leave movies and their possible subversive content alone and instead go after individuals who were, depending on money-making ability, expendable. In order to clear their own names of any red taint and go back to work, former Communists had to finger their comrades, or indeed anybody they might have seen at a party cell meeting.

The hearings were largely a publicity exercise. Through a network of informants, the FBI, and the American Legion, HUAC already knew all it needed to know. To a generation brought up on the movie stereotype of the rat who sells his soul to save his skin, this turn of events was a sickening kind of reverse wish fulfillment. Many of the people Lancaster had worked with during his brief Hollywood career were sent subpoenas to appear before the committee that spring: Salt, Robinson, Butler, Maddow, Dassin, and Berry. Walter Bernstein, like other former Communists, was not called to testify; blacklisted since 1950, he was effectively out of the film industry, working quietly in television. Knox was blacklisted and ended up in Italy. Berry, Butler, and Bercovici also left the country to avoid testifying. When *He Ran All the Way* was released in June, the names of its director and screenwriter were deleted from the promotional material. Dassin moved overseas. Salt and Dekker refused to cooperate with HUAC and were blacklisted. Maddow was also blacklisted but, much later, named names.

On April 4, Hecht's name showed up on one of the many lists flowing through the FBI but, according to the informant's report, he had not been seen at "any Party function." Though Norma Productions was only about three months old when the Waldorf Statement was signed in 1947 and was theoretically "independent," it was now allied with three studios, including Warner Bros., the studio Youngstein called "the worst" because, at the slightest suspicion, "they wouldn't let you work." If the persistent little indie wanted to make pictures, it had to conform like everybody else. With rumors of imminent Soviet production of the A-bomb, plus almost a year's worth of press barrage—"Commies' propaganda" are making a "horrible shroud for our GI dead in Korea" claimed the *Los Angeles Daily News*—the atmosphere surrounding the next set of hearings was toxic.

Norma's response was to wave a literal red flag—*The Crimson Pirate*—in front of the charging HUAC bull that was too thick-witted to quite get it. The original script of this second swashbuckler was written by Salt but, according to director Siodmak, if Hecht did not want to be "embarrassed . . . a great deal" by having to give a screen credit to the unemployable writer, the story had to be changed. The last-minute job of revising went to Kibbee, not exactly un-Red himself in the eyes of the committee. But Salt's spirit infused what critic Pauline Kael later called a "wonderful travesty of the buccaneer film," a fond homage to Fairbanks's 1926 hit *The Black Pirate*. In between the fun were slipped subversive messages: "All my life I've watched injustice and dishonesty fly the flag of decency," snarls a pirate. "I don't trust it."

The suspect theme of liberating the oppressed masses from their conquerors was camouflaged by costumes closely modeled on Howard Pyle's book illustrations of pirates and a plot so busy nobody has time to think. Lancaster's pirate hero, Vallo, cooks up a plan to sell his latest loot of guns from the king's navy to a rebel leader, El Libre, and then sell El Libre back to the king. When he falls in love with the rebel's daughter and agrees to let her father escape, a whirlwind of plot twists follows with balloons, disgruntled pirates, nitroglycerine explosions, cross-dressing, and lots of gymnastics by Lancaster and his sidekick, Ojo, played by Nick and based on the Black Pirate's mute accomplice, Bernardo. Vallo eludes his own pirate crew's revenge for his apostasy and saves the day. In 1992, Richard Koszarski, curator of the American Museum of the Moving Image, looked back at these early Lancaster action works and assessed that in their championing of "underclass characters" they were "very much from the Left," the beginning of what would be a career different from that of Charles Bronson, Clint Eastwood, or Wayne.

The Crimson Pirate was not only one of the most globally popular movies Lancaster ever made, it was also his arrival at a certain level of the Hollywood stratosphere where stars generate so much heat they glow in the dark. Utterly confident before the camera, he had a knife-edge of aggression that dared the audience to watch him and only him. The relaxed, joyous Dardo of *Flame* had inflated into a hypercreature with the streaked blond locks, huge shoulders, big teeth, tight hips, and tall grace of what the *New York Post* called "the young Sun god, gorgeously coiffed and windblown by nothing less than the ionosphere." "Nobody," said director John Frankenheimer, "has ever looked like Burt Lancaster in *The Crimson Pirate*."

The making of the movie also marked the arrival of the partners at the rung of power where producer and star felt they could throw their weight around, control the product, and make life miserable for director and studio. In 1951 such upstart antics were rare. Because so many independent star ventures had been either short-lived and/or failures, there were few precedents for something like Norma Productions, now on its fourth picture, including one big hit. With Hollywood in uncharted territory, Lancaster was the star swelling out to fill the power vacuum.

At the end of May 1951, while sailing on the *Queen Mary* for England en route to location in Italy and enjoying a romantic reprise with Dietrich onboard, he prepared his own version of sequences that would allow him to fulfill the old dream of wrapping storybook romance in progressive principle. The Technicolor "Caribbean" *Pirate* exteriors were to be shot on and off the island of Ischia in the Bay of Naples near Capri from June through September, with interiors completed over the following two months at the Warner Bros. base at Teddington Studios and at the Associated British Elstree Studios. Location shooting away from Hollywood had been done before, but not to the extent it would be in the coming decade. Costs and labor were cheaper abroad and the war had left "frozen" money reserves that could only be spent outside the U.S. (countries like Britain had quotas on the number of "American" films allowed to be shown in their country each year, increasing the pressure for films like *Pirate* to be technically British). Not least, authentic locations were a terrific marketing hook to lure in the dwindling audience.

Flamboyant production stories, a staple of mainstream news twenty-five years later for movies like *Apocalypse Now* and *Heaven's Gate*, were as exotic as the new locales. There would be those who thought *Pirate* turned out as well as it did *because* it was made far from the studio—a perfect test case for the new potential of independent production. Ischia was primitive, with no water, no airport, one good road, and only twenty-five telephones that shut down after 8 p.m. Most of the extras were Italians who spoke no English; the journalist assigned by the *New York Times* to the production reported back that director Siodmak was reduced to calling Silence, *Silenzio, Silence!* [in French] "virtually simultaneously." He was washed overboard at least once from his camera platform on deck. The big Technicolor machine had to be hoisted, precariously, up to a crow's-nest platform fifty feet in the air to shoot the scene of the pirate band boarding the frigate. Lancaster once disappeared underwater, hanging onto the rope he was crossing that had sagged as the ships suddenly surged toward each other; when a swell of water pulled the ships apart again, yanking the rope taut, he was snapped thirty feet in the air and back into the water. Luminaries such as Somerset Maugham and Arturo Toscanini came to visit Siodmak in his rented villa. Everybody was seasick most of the time.

All that was the easy part. Siodmak and the studio versus Lancaster and Hecht became locked in a bitter struggle for dominance utterly at variance with the light-hearted tone of the movie. The Salt script that Siodmak had agreed to direct had largely vanished, replaced by an unfinished story line that changed daily. On August 2, Hecht sent a cable to Trilling, production executive at Warner Bros. since Wallis's departure: "BURT VERY DISCOURAGED." By August 28, twenty-four pages and ninety-four scenes had been added to the script, increasing the budget from $1.25 million to $1.75 million and threatening both the quota requirement (80 percent of the labor cost paid to British subjects in order to qualify for the "blocked sterling") and the profitability of the entire picture. Hecht claimed Siodmak was doing two takes for every set-up. And there were surreal star stories, such as the one about Lancaster taking out his penis to urinate in full view of everybody, while barking orders to the crew. Trilling fired off a cable to Ischia demanding Hecht restore the script and insisting Siodmak be allowed to function properly. He signed off with the plea: "FOR PETE'S SAKE BOYS PIRATE IS EVERYBODY'S PROBLEM/MEET HEAD ON." When Hecht threatened a diversionary lawsuit over claims of studio accounting errors on *Flame* and began sending long cables in September justifying all extra expenses as part and parcel of a superior production, Trilling knew he was dealing with a new kind of problem that he started to call "Hechtomania."

At the end of September, Siodmak threatened to quit unless Hecht's "amateurish exuberance" was curbed. Lancaster he could handle, he thought. Four days later, Lancaster threatened to quit unless he were allowed, when the others moved on to England, to stay on Ischia and do some pick-up scenes and direct them himself. The studio smelled a rat, correctly guessing that the star, already claiming he had planned all the action sequences of the film, was planning to shoot the last eighteen-minute sea battle scene himself. Hecht claimed his star was tired and needed a couple of weeks' rest. Warner's started talking "major financial losses" and said Lancaster could rest in England. The star, pleading fear of flying and fatigue, stayed on Ischia and shot the end of the film. This was rebellion of a new sort.

Hecht was now at the happy place where he could claim that if the picture had come in at $1 million, he would have made all the requested cuts, but since the cost was going to be so much more, he wanted to "be assured that [the picture] was not jeopardized by any curtailment" on the part of Warner Bros. Siodmak would later voice the suspicions of many that if Norma Productions had not known the picture would go way over schedule in time and money they were "stupid," and if they knew, "dishonest."

Gerry Blattner, the director of British Warner Bros., suggested to Trilling that the studio start taking precautions now to avoid ever getting into another such set-up with Hecht and Lancaster. Siodmak told Lancaster that "even for a million dollars," he would never direct him again.

Siodmak then wrote a letter to Trilling which was not only a farewell to the new Hollywood—the director moved to Germany shortly thereafter—but an assessment of the new independent star, the ambitious, tyrannical, gorgeous golem, in all his monstrous power. After describing what he saw as Hecht's complete domination by Lancaster, he comes to "the most unpleasant and saddest point of this letter": "Burt Lancaster has gone through such a change [since *The Killers*]," he wrote, "that I cannot consider him normal any more. His complete inconsideration of others, his tantrums, his language—so filthy that the English crew wrote him an open letter one day . . . I think he suffers from megalomania and must be mentally sick—otherwise you couldn't explain his behavior. He . . . declared himself the final and undisputed judge in script, wardrobe, make-up and acting matters and asked me to explain every camera set-up, because if he didn't approve of it he wouldn't do it and would fire me on the spot. . . . Many times when I considered a sequence finished he insisted on close-up after close-up, which demanded practically reshooting the scene. I do not deny him a certain intelligence and showmanship, but he will never be able to overlook [*sic*] the *whole* of a picture. He is a very hard worker, but all his hard work is based on a terrific selfish and egocentric personality. And because he owns a large part of the profits, he is inconsiderate for costs. . . . He is absolute master of the whole situation and nobody could, or can, handle him."

The director ended with an eternal conundrum of Hollywood: "But we finished the job, and much as I wish he would make an unsuccessful film once, this time we certainly have an important and a good picture." By August 1952, when the *New York Times* raved that "any viewer with a drop of red blood in his veins and with fond memories of the Douglas Fairbanks Sr. school of derring-do should be happy to go on this last cruise of the crimson pirate," Siodmak's plaint had been filed away by Warner Bros. and forgotten.

Lancaster's abusive behavior may have been in part a displaced expression of his increasingly complicated personal life. In the middle of his battles with Siodmak and Trilling, Norma gave birth in Los Angeles in early July to the couple's fourth child, Joanna Mari. The baby was reportedly born with a foot deviation similar to Jimmy's, but this time it was decided to leave the problem alone to see if the child outgrew it. When Norma had recovered enough to travel, she left the newborn with her sister-in-law, Ruth, Willie's widow, and took the other children with her to join Lancaster in Italy; the father would not see his new daughter until she was almost six months old. Billy arrived in leg braces and crutches. His parents had been instructed by the doctor not to rush to him when he fell, but to let him pick himself up so that he could strengthen the leg muscles. The three-year-old fell often, struggling to pull himself back up and then awkwardly hobbling forward to rejoin the rest of the family. Burt and Norma were often in tears as they watched.

The Shelley Winters affair had recently ended. Friends, usually men, were baffled that Lancaster stayed married at all. "Norma kept having kids," said Cuccia-Cravat, recalling her father's version of events, "probably in order to save the marriage." For the next ten years, production correspondence and studio contracts detail his desire to include the children on his location shoots, to provide for Norma to join him, to get back home in time for Christmas. He did not want to be the kind of person who left an alcoholic wife and needy children in the lurch, so he messed around on the side and stayed married, a time-honored tradition in the town where, as the saying went, except for your mother and sister everybody was fair game. "Boris," Lancaster confided on the phone to his army buddy, Barere, calling him on impulse from Boston one night, "anything goes in this gig. Anything."

Stories about the star now whizzed around Tinseltown, some of them expressions of the spiteful envy that insists nobody that successful so fast got there on a straight and narrow path. Rumors surfaced from Ischia that he and the pudgy, mild, and droll Roland Kibbee were having a homosexual affair. The two men had become close friends and, according to Lucy Kibbee, the "bullshit" rumors began because Lancaster, rather than trek out between set-ups to the villa he had rented for himself and his family, came over to the hotel where Kibbee was staying and took quick naps. When Lucy arrived to join her husband, she had just had a baby and took frequent naps herself. One day she woke up and found Lancaster asleep next to her on the bed. "For Christ's sake!" she said, waking him up. "You didn't even make a pass! I would have turned you down, but. . . . Am I such a piece of nothing that you don't even think I'm female?" "I was screaming at him and he was dying laughing." Back in Hollywood the Kibbees went to a party and were talking to a *Life* reporter when, according to Lucy, he said to Roland, " 'Oh, I hear Burt and his head writer were having an affair down in Italy.' And Kibbee says, 'Who was that?' And the guy says, 'Some guy named Kibbee.' It was so funny because then Kibbee said, 'I am Roland Kibbee and this is my wife. . . .' If you could have seen that man's face."

The face to watch was Hecht's in Italy as he read a telegram from HUAC in September informing him he had just been named as a member of the Communist Party in a closed session of the committee. The informant was Martin Berkeley, a screenwriter and former Communist whom

Hollywood Ten writer Ring Lardner Jr. dismissed as a writer of animal movies such as *The Lone Wolf* because "[h]e couldn't write human dialogue." Berkeley set a kind of record, naming around 155 people at one go, among them Dorothy Parker, Dashiell Hammett, Lillian Hellman—and Kibbee, who had become a member of the party back in 1937, according to Victor Navasky, "by way of the Hollywood Anti-Nazi League and out three years later by way of the Nazi-Soviet Pact." His wife claimed he never knew Berkeley. Kibbee and Hecht persuaded HUAC that, as Berkeley's testimony had been private, they should be allowed also to respond privately before their names were made public. Both men thus bought more than a year of time, enough to consider their options: take the Fifth and avoid jail but, like Salt, be blacklisted; refuse to answer and either go to jail like the Ten or flee the country; or cooperate, name names, and stay in the business.

In December, Lancaster's name was prominent in an article—"Did the Movies Really Clean House?"—published in the *American Legion Magazine*. Though HUAC had dug up two hundred of the three hundred or so Hollywood Communists, the article claimed there still remained some unexposed big-name sympathizers. John Garfield, Judy Holliday, José Ferrer, Shelley Winters, Arthur Miller, and Clifford Odets were listed as was Lancaster, whose swashbucklers were cited as examples of productions harboring "recently exposed communists and collaborators with communist fronts." Legionnaires threatened to march and wave placards in front of theaters showing movies starring Reds who had been named in the magazine. Hollywood, as Cogley wrote in his 1956 history of the blacklist, *Report on Blacklisting*, was thrown "into a near panic."

In January, *Counterattack* again blasted Lancaster's leftist leanings. Via Norma Productions, he was accused of hiring Norman Corwin, a top writer/producer at CBS who had "over 50 instances . . . [of] support of CP fronts and causes." The star had "a record of his own," claimed *Counterattack*, from the Committee for the First Amendment to the *amici curiae* Supreme Court brief, any one of which had rated a listing in the *American Legion Magazine* article. In February, an informant wrote a personal letter from Beverly Hills to "Dear Edgar" Hoover at the FBI, reporting from the Hollywood front that "The Reds are just as active as ever." Norma Productions, "whose star is Burt Lancaster," was cited as an example of "the way the Reds help each other."

There were now so many names floating around, the pernicious idea of a clearance process emerged, ostensibly to "absolve" movie professionals like Lancaster who were not now nor ever had been Communists but were suspect all the same. After meetings that spring between studio executives and Legion representatives, a quasi-system was devised. If a person's name was on the Legion's new list that went out to the eight major studios, he or she would be asked by the studio to write a letter to the Legion in which past activities listed against them would be explained, put into context, and their repentance, or at least patriotism, avowed.

To facilitate this process, certain lawyers emerged who would guide the appeal along the right path. Chief among them was Martin Gang of the Los Angeles law firm of Gang, Kopp and Tyre. Famous as a tough negotiator, he had been Lancaster's attorney since the star's arrival in Hollywood and was the man who came up with the idea in 1944 that the standard seven-year Warner Bros. contract of his client Olivia de Havilland constituted involuntary servitude. Opinions differ about his methods and sincerity during the blacklist period. At one extreme were those like Charles Katz, attorney for the Hollywood Ten, who said years later that being asked to share a public dais with Gang was like asking him to appear with Torquemada's adjutant (Friar Tomás de Torquemada was the first Inquisitor General of the Spanish Inquisition, responsible for the burning at the stake of as many as two thousand Jewish converts to Christianity). Then there are those like Seltzer who remember Gang in that "trying and terrible time" as "very respectable and helpful."

Gang was an integral part of Lancaster's professional life at the beginning of the decade, the legal partner of the various subcorporations such as Halburt, which composed the star's increasingly complex executive profile. Although Gang insisted he made a minimal amount of money off his beleaguered clients, other people must have made plenty. "It took cash and it took a letter of repentance," recalled Seltzer, who had left Wallis to work as publicity director for Norma Productions. "We bought our way out of it. The 'process' was very expensive. Where the money went, into whose pocket, I don't know."

In Cogley's history of the blacklist there is a copy of one such "typical" clearance letter. Sent to James F. O'Neill, the Legion's man in Washington, it was written by a person Cogley described as "Z.Z., a top-flight Hollywood star." When the alleged subversive activities of Z.Z. are cross-checked, the only star, top flight or otherwise, whose name appears in connection with all of them is Lancaster.

The letter begins with the requisite affirmation that the "star" is not nor ever has been a Communist or "knowingly" a member of a communist front. He does not claim to have been a dupe. Each allegation is then answered in turn. Membership in the Committee for the First Amendment is acknowledged but defended as having come from "only the most patriotic of motives." "Even with the benefit of hindsight," reads the letter, "I cannot believe any fair-minded person would consider the use of my name in connection with that committee as the use of my name for a Communist front." Having signed the Supreme Court brief is also defended because the writer "felt that the Constitutional issues presented were of such importance that a decision by the Supreme Court would be helpful." A careful distinction is made between the desire for a hearing and sympathy or support for the actions of Trumbo or Lawson: "To my knowledge no signer of that petition in any way condoned the actions . . . or indicated any sympathy with the political beliefs of the men." The third allegation, sponsorship of the October 28, 1947, anti-HUAC ad in the Hollywood *Reporter*, is similarly justified as an expression of "honest beliefs." Another distinction is drawn between the "properly conducted" HUAC hearings since January 1951 and those of 1947, implying that the present ones are better. Referenced from the 1948 annual report of the California Un-American Activities Committee, the fourth and last allegation—sponsorship of the dinner benefit rally in Beverly Hills on March 5, 1948, for the Hollywood Ten—is denied, as was the giving of "any money to the Hollywood Ten."

Cogley recorded that "the actor's 'explanation' " went "to all the studios distributing either his own pictures or those made by the company he owns" and "was acceptable." Only about thirty of the names on the 1952 American Legion list refused to write a clearance letter and for the rest of his life Lancaster would imply he was one of them. For him, it was a rare reconstruction of the past, meant to camouflage the fact that once he had walked the walk.

While there were multiple references to Lancaster's activities in the bureau's files, in the pages of *Counterattack*, and elsewhere—a "file" that is more than an inch thick—there was, unbelievably, no single FBI "Lancaster" file. "There was always an implicit anti-Semitism that ran through the whole thing," says Bernstein. "They would go after a Garfield much more than they would go after a Burt. I don't think it was so much a fear of backlash, as feeling an affinity with this nice Aryan fellow." Knox was more trenchant: "They never got a star. The only one was Garfield and he was Jewish and was destroyed."

On May 21, having moved into the Warwick Hotel, where Lancaster's career had begun, a distraught, exhausted Garfield collapsed in the apartment of a friend and died of a heart attack at the age of thirty-nine. In September, as Lancaster's Vallo was swinging across screens around the country, Walter S. Clugson of Cambridge City, Indiana, wrote a letter to J. Edgar Hoover to which he got an immediate reply. "It might be a good idea to check the moving picture *Crimson Pirate*. In it Burt Lancaster makes a speech in which 'workers' is brought in. It sounds like a commie plug."

Lancaster confounded everyone's expectations by next agreeing to portray a defeated middle-aged loser in a claustrophobic story of broken dreams, small redemptions, and yearning for a lost little dog named Sheba. Cast as Doc Delaney in the Paramount screen version of William Inge's Broadway hit, *Come Back, Little Sheba,* he was shifting into a character actor part long before that would be all that was left.

Wallis, true to habit, had seen the play and bought it cheap when nobody else had touched it for six months. The studio was not enthusiastic: Who wanted to see a movie about what Lancaster described as a "disillusioned ex-alcoholic married to a pitiful frump"? But the star of the play was Shirley Booth, whose brilliant performance as Doc's wife, Lola, had won her both a Tony Award and a New York Drama Critics award. The cachet of having Booth in her first film performance being directed by her stage director, Daniel Mann, appealed to the producer's instinct for blue-chip product. If the movies were to outdraw TV, so one school of current Hollywood wisdom went, they should do better what they had always done—piggyback on the prestige and audience recognition of the New York theater. The black-and-white, small-scale artiness of the movie *Sheba* and the casting of the unglamorous, unyoung Booth was deliberate. This was Hollywood's new, serious, realistic filmmaking.

Though Lancaster later claimed that he asked Wallis to let him play Doc, the *New York Times* reported that not only did Lancaster initially find it difficult to imagine himself as the gloomy chiropractor, but it was Curtiz who suggested to both Wallis and Lancaster that the actor who had convincingly portrayed Thorpe's disintegration could also play Doc. Lancaster told Wallis that though the film was Booth's, he would be good box-office balance to her untried screen presence. He also tested for the part at his own request, wearing no make-up, a Brooks Brothers suit, and plastering down his hair to look old and tired. When shooting began in mid-February on Stage 17 at Paramount and on location in Los Angeles at Thirty-seventh Place and Vermont Avenue near USC, he had become immersed in the unlikely role. "I guess I wanted to play [Doc] more than any other part I ever got close to," he recalled. "[He] is the most human, if imperfect kind of guy. . . ."

And for the man who had lost out on *Streetcar, Sheba* was another chance. Doc Delaney was an alternate template for some of the most memorable roles of his career, the squishy *noir* core that kept seeping out. Though Norma and not he was the alcoholic and they were hardly childless like the Delaneys, the central regret of a shotgun marriage is common to both the movie and the life. "We all make mistakes," Doc pleads with Lola in one of the more convincing scenes. "So what? We've got to keep going, don't we?" When Lancaster is given more reactive things to do as Doc—attack Booth with a kitchen knife, collapse in a screaming, drunken fit—he forgets the circumscribed movements of an older man, the strange eyebrows slashed over half his forehead, and just emotes. Booth, working hard, as Lancaster would remember, to *un*learn her stage movements for the movie camera, cautioned him: "Burt, once in a while you hit a note of truth and you can hear a bell ring. But most of the time, I can see the wheels turning and your brain working." Yet, when she overheard someone deride the choice of "gymnast" Lancaster at a Chateau Marmont party during production, she countered, "Don't sell him short. He's called me at three in the morning, not even realizing what time it is, to ask me to explain a scene. One day he'll be a great actor."

The reviews were largely respectful when the picture was released at the end of the year, with raves for the performance that won the forty-five-year-old Booth an Oscar. Lancaster's new effort set him up for some ridicule, as he knew it would. "Burt Lancaster," reported the *The New Leader,* "far outside his normal range of habits, manages to give off an air of infinite repose, like a statue of Lincoln in a public park." But *The New Yorker*'s John McCarten marked the particular accomplishment: "To my astonishment and delight . . . a man I've always associated with the acrobats who used to perform while people were being seated in the old Keith [vaudeville] houses, is highly effective. . . ." Lancaster's own dry assessment was, "Alas, for the first time since I can remember, I was called on to really act. Bear with me." He delighted in what he rosily recalled as "extraordinarily interesting reviews for the first time," concluding, "that was a progression in my career."

The audience absorbed another twist in the Lancaster star zigzag. At the end of *Sheba,* Lola recounts a dream in which she and Doc are at the Olympics and suddenly her transformed husband picks up the javelin and throws it into the sky where it never comes down again. There is an eerie movie moment when Booth is looking at Lancaster and the audience is looking at the guy who just played Jim Thorpe.

He fed the ridicule by immediately switching back in summer 1952 to the flamboyant, crowd-pleasing mode to make *His Majesty O'Keefe,* a "spectacle picture" based, said one optimistic claim, on *Mutiny on the Bounty,* made in 1935. Lancaster was cast as O'Keefe, a true-life adventurer shipwrecked on the South Pacific island of Yap in the 1870s who is eventually crowned "His Majesty" by the natives. *Pirate* headaches in mind, Warner Bros. negotiated a slightly different deal: *O'Keefe,* another joint venture with British Warner Bros. for tax purposes, would be made in the village of Goloa on the primitive island of Viti Levu in the Fiji Islands with studio reps on the site.

Budgeted at $1 million, *O'Keefe,* before anything had been shot, had already cost $1.5 million in an industry climate of falling studio stock dividends. In June, Trilling complained to Hecht that rather than receiving the usual "fixed overhead" payments from the indie, the studio itself was bearing the costs, which could only be recouped out of "possible" future profits after everyone else had already recouped themselves. "I am sure," he concluded, "it is obvious to you that this is unfair."

Hecht was too busy to worry about issues of fairness. The new production circumstances were indeed like those of *The Crimson Pirate*, possibly worse: the location was six thousand miles from Hollywood. There was a "script" in name only by Borden Chase, the screenwriter of *Red River* who took his name from a dairy company and a bank. A ministudio had been created for the duration with a sound stage, production and accounting office blocks, and a Technicolor lab (press reports claimed it was the first time such elaborate movie facilities had been built so far from the center of the industry). Raindrops "the size of teacups" fell several times a day, producing "enervating" delays. "There were times," said Lancaster, "when the only thing idyllic about it was the Nadi airport where fast and comfortable planes took off constantly in a northeasterly direction for Hollywood."

The star had again taken charge. "The m.o.," recalled Byron Haskin, the movie's director, "was that when the slightest little bit of action was suggested, Burt would jump up and act it all over the room, breaking chairs and jumping over things, explaining as he went." Chase would try to come up with a few lines of script, which the producers would promptly kill. At three o'clock in the afternoon, everybody quit, exhausted, and started drinking Scotch at fourteen cents a glass (it was an era where remembered incidents are usually prefaced with: "Well, everybody had had a few drinks. . . ."). For the final coronation scene, with a throne designed by the islanders, Chase scribbled, "Burt is crowned." A new writer, James Hill, a friend of Chase, was added and fell right in with this company whose freewheeling ways didn't bother him a bit. The ad campaign was originally titled "The White Man is Chief" before somebody thought twice. *O'Keefe*, Haskin recalled, was "just a narrative featuring Burt's new caps on his teeth."

The teeth were not a trivial detail. He had them capped by the favored Dr. William Goodley to the tune of $5,000 and Schiffer always thought they were too big. They inflated his chin just enough to harden the profile. The Chiclets teeth, the sneer, the grin, and the laugh would now become as much a part of his style as his hair, eyes, voice, and body. He was Mr. Muscles *and* Teeth. Hecht, too, had his teeth fixed. Zipping his finger over his bright, new, clenched choppers, Lancaster would jibe, "Harold has my old teeth."

The press made much of the fact that Lancaster transplanted the family (except Joanna, who stayed home with a nurse) to Fiji. The children ran naked up and down the beach and learned to count to five in Fijian. Norma abandoned nude sunbathing when she discovered islanders hanging out of the palm trees watching her, and filled her time organizing a campaign to care for the more than forty thousand wild dogs on the island. It was all a refreshing example to the public of the star's devotion to his family, and Burt delighted in having them waiting in his rented thatched hut at the end of every crazy day. It was easier being a family away from home. All this world traveling reminded his father, back in Bel Air, of "that little towhead" whose curiosity had propelled him out into the masses on Coney Island beach, happily unaware that he was lost.

Burt's original Paramount deal was now whittled down to about four more pictures, the Columbia arrangement would dissolve by the end of the year, and the separate Wallis deal had been abandoned. Norma Productions tossed another of its juggling balls in the air with the 1952 Columbia release of *The First Time*, a "weak farce" written by Butler and Rouveral that spun off the gimmick of the infant who tells his own story of living with his parents. The film died a quick death, but the indie had made its first movie not starring Lancaster—and one without a trace of politics—and survived.

Lancaster moved quickly to wrap up the Warner Bros. contract with two quickies—another Pacific island fantasy, *South Sea Woman*, plus a cameo slot on a different Warner Bros. sound stage with Sam Levene in *Three Sailors and a Girl*. Both were shot concurrently in early 1953, no doubt to Trilling's relief. *South Sea Woman* was a forgettable World War II buddy tale with the loose integrity of a veteran's reverie (girls, guns, jokes, and heroics) and produced in exact counterpoint to *His Majesty O'Keefe*. An entire South Sea island was created on a single sound stage with mountains, jungles, and sea vista backdrops painted on a 360-degree canvas cyclorama; for the exterior sea sequences, the cast, including Virginia Mayo, and crew chugged out to Catalina Island. Lancaster's marine pal in the movie, Chuck Connors, was a tall, lanky, first baseman for the minor-league Los Angeles Angels and would later say he owed his career to Lancaster, who pushed him for the part and coached him for his screen test. The two men ribbed each other—"I'm on my honeymoon," says Connors to a snoopy island Factotum in one scene; "I'm on his honeymoon, too," says his best pal— with a naturalness that both reinforced a new set of underground rumors that they were romantically involved and might have prompted goofy buddy sequels if the star were anybody but no-sequel Lancaster.

On a sweltering night in August 1953, Dietrich called Fred Zinnemann in Los Angeles at midnight Eastern Standard Time from New York to tell him there was a line around the block at the Capitol Theater for a 1 a.m. extra showing of *From Here to Eternity*. Incredulous, the movie's director protested that there had been no publicity. Dietrich replied, "They smell it."

World War II was eight years over and the Korean armistice had been signed a month before, on July 27. With Dwight Eisenhower the new Republican president, McCarthy's Senate subcommittee and HUAC had unleashed an unprecedented "epidemic of investigations" into communist subversion. But behind the raging hysteria perceptions were beginning to change. Ex-President Truman, a Democrat, would be harassed by a flimsy charge from HUAC in November, three months after *From Here to Eternity* opened, and Eisenhower would oppose it. There were limits to this witch hunt.

The crowds packing movie houses across the country knew the movie was a summing-up of the national character, a reminder that "American-ism" was not a single, simple thing. Daniel Taradash's script toned down the book's sex, language, sadism, and bitter view of the army, but the characters burst frank and fresh on the American screen thwarting themselves in their various quests for love and integrity on the eve of war as much as they are thwarted by circumstance. Ernest Borgnine's cruelty as Fatso and the dumb, stubborn endurance of Montgomery Clift's Private Robert E. Lee Prewitt entwine with Frank Sinatra's guileless Maggio and the sanity of Lancaster's Sergeant Warden. There is no happy ending: Deborah Kerr and Donna Reed sail off to a certain future as women who will drink and smoke too much.

The audience watching saw the personification of whatever mixture of qualities it was that had won the war—themselves. Often overlooked later in favor of the bravura performances of Clift and Sinatra, Lancaster reached the 1953 audience on a completely different level. *From Here to Eternity* ends on the morning of December 7, 1941; the one character still alive and able to lead the defense against the surprise Japanese attack on Pearl Harbor is Sergeant Warden. As Lancaster galvanized to the task on-screen, a generation of moviegoers around the world took that image into its psyche as surely as any of the other, more fashionable antiheroes of the postwar decade. The wounded colossus was whole again. Tough, gentle, fair, virile, brave, and focused, Warden was an apotheosis of postwar American manhood.

In an era of extravagant wide-screen gimmicks, this tight, spare, black-and-white movie was made at the normal screen ratio. The careers of the principal players jumped to another level and the stories that swirled around its making became movie legend: Sinatra's big comeback as the scrappy Maggio who gets beaten to death in the stockade by Fatso; Clift's obsession with his "fuck-up," doomed, bugle-playing Prewitt and his monu-mental, destructive, mostly off-screen drinking; the surprise casting of Kerr as the promiscuous officer's wife who falls in love with Warden and of Reed as a prostitute; Zinnemann's scrupulous oversight; the scandal of the famous beach scene, where Lancaster and Kerr not only embrace, prone, on the sand as the surging waves wash over them, but Kerr is on top. The movie was nominated for thirteen Academy Awards, won the most—eight—since *Gone With the Wind*, and, by the end of 1954, grossed over $12 million to a cost of just under $2.4 million. Clift and Lancaster were both nominated for Academy Awards as Best Actor (William Holden won for his role in Billy Wilder's *Stalag 17*), and Oscars went to the picture, Zinnemann, Taradash, cameraman Burnett Guffey, Sinatra, and Reed.

The movie's spit-and-polish style was also an example, in the midst of independent turmoil, of what the great studios could still produce if the tyrannical vision of the one person at the top was brought to bear. Cohn was involved in every detail, pushing Zinnemann to wrap in forty-one days and at absolutely no longer than two hours, always pushing Guffey for the tighter cut. "One shot of the waves is sufficient," he insisted in a typical midproduction note. "Having three shots is ridiculous."

That Lancaster's sergeant flourishes amid such talent has often been taken for granted. Lancaster was only acting himself, it has been said, playing to type. In fact, he had never portrayed a character of such breadth and centrality in the midst of such a troupe. Zinnemann brought with him the prestige and clout of his first hit, *High Noon;* the star could not crush him as he had Siodmak. For the first time, too, he was matched with real male competition. Clift was at the peak of his stardom, the brilliant performer of *Red River* and *A Place in the Sun* as yet unmarred by the car accident that wrecked his face. Clift resented Lancaster's top billing and complained to friends that he was no actor and the "most unctuous man" he had ever met. Prewitt was the more complex role, but Warden, as Zinnemann later said, was "the catalyst, the commentator on the whole situation." Clift could not get around the fact that while Prewitt is getting himself killed, as he must, Warden is on-screen for the start of America's entrance into World War II.

Lancaster respected Clift's professionalism—"He approached the script like a scientist," he observed, "I've never seen anyone so meticulous"—and he hid his admiration behind a wary, defensive pose, knowing he was looking at the kind of emotionally fearless acting he was incapable of. "The only time I was ever really afraid as an actor was that first scene with Clift," he recalled. "It was *my* scene, understand: I was the sergeant, I gave the orders, he was just a private under me. Well, when we started, I couldn't stop my knees from shaking. I thought they might have to stop because my trembling would show. . . . I was afraid he was going to blow me right off the screen." When he tried his own version of meticulous, repeatedly arguing with Zinnemann for changes in his lines, the director, according to Clift biographer Robert LaGuardia, told Lancaster to go screw himself.

During the shoot—two weeks at the studio, three weeks at Schofield Barracks in Honolulu during March and April 1953—Clift, Sinatra, and author Jones formed a tight little group with epic drinking bouts. Lancaster got so used to carrying Sinatra and Clift, dead drunk, to their rooms each night, undressing them, and putting them to bed, that on his birthday for years afterward he would get a telegram from Sinatra with the message "Happy Birthday, Mom." He practiced his own form of stress control by learning everybody else's lines, jogging, working out, and having an affair, so he later confided to a few close friends, with Kerr. Together the unlikely pair practiced lines and perfected the beach scene. And the woman previously known for her British lady-like roles developed an aptitude for on-screen passion that astonished everybody.

Zinnemann's detailed analysis of each beat of loyalty, conformity, individuality, and love shaped Lancaster's performance. Again and again the director scribbled the word "tempo" in the margins of his leather-bound copy of the script. For the scene where Lancaster and Kerr first embrace, he penciled, "How much nerve does this guy have?" The pacing of the man *un*nerving the woman, moving in on her, the camera alternating between medium and close-up shots, was plotted like a tight little piece of music. "That scene," said Taradash, "the intonations, the insinuations— Burt got everything out of it."

The beach scene—Scene #106—was shot with a crew of one hundred in three days on Holcona Cove, left of the Halona Blowhole at the eastern end of Oahu, and set a record in time, manpower, and equipment for a single movie love scene. "MEDIUM CLOSE SHOT KAREN AND WARDEN," read the script, "at edge of beach, side by side, as if they have just surfed in. They are still in a few inches of water and it runs over their faces as they kiss." After first suggesting that "either Karen or Warden put on a beach robe or some other type of clothing before they go into the embrace," the Production Code Office insisted that four seconds be cut. The objectionable element was the water. Certain publicity shots taken on the beach could not be used at all.

Often running shorter than it should—projectionists have snipped out frames as souvenirs—the open, confident lovemaking of the beach scene remains a literal high-water mark of screen eroticism. Warden looks beyond Karen's promiscuous past and makes love to her as ardently as the surf pulses onto the beach. Never again would Lancaster approach such adult, reciprocal sexuality on-screen. Neither, it was argued, would anybody else: "The passion of Lancaster for Kerr in *From Here to Eternity*," wrote Joan Mellen more than twenty years later of a performance she extolls as that of "a fully realized man" who leaves "no doubt" that he prefers making love to a woman rather than a man, "never quite reappears in the American film." The director would muse of Scene #106, "It is a curious contribution we have made to popular culture."

The movie was full of 1953 masculine exemplars, but *Time* set Lancaster apart: "As Sergeant Warden [he] is the model of a man among men, absolutely convincing in an instinctive awareness of the subtle, elaborate structure of force and honor on which a male society is based." The role was also for Lancaster what *Yankee Doodle Dandy*'s George M. Cohan had been for Cagney in 1942: irrefutable proof of all-American patriotism. The New York Film Critics Circle awarded him their Best Actor prize for the first time.

One family was lastingly affected by the movie. Growing up in Queens and Brooklyn in the late 1950s, John Turturro, as well as his parents, brothers, aunts, uncles, and cousins, regarded Lancaster as a member of their Italian-American family, the main man. His walk, talk, and hand movements were analyzed and copied. "Doing a Burt" was to betray by a shift of the shoulders, a fluid grace in the walk, the desire to *be* Lancaster. In an immigrant culture in which each person developed a nonverbal signature flourish, they shared an Italian delight in the male *bella figura*, the beauty of great style. The finesse of power held in reserve.

When Turturro wrote, directed, and starred in *Mac*, a movie loosely based on his own father and the winner of the 1993 *Camera d'Or* at Cannes for a first-time director, he inserted an homage to his childhood hero. The irascible, work-obsessed Italian-American contractor, Mac, played by Turturro, is sleepily watching *From Here to Eternity* one night. The barracks barroom fight scene comes on and he suddenly wakes up. Lancaster, with a smooth spin into the center of the floor, smashes off the top of a beer bottle and brandishes it in the air, coldly, calmly inviting Fatso to "Come on" and fight him instead of picking on Maggio. Mac sits up and shouts at the TV screen: "Get him, Burt! Get him! Get that Fatso! That's Burt, man, Burt Lancaster! You don't fuck with him, man!" Then he slumps back to sleep, exhausted from a long day's manual labor.

In the middle of the *Eternity* shoot, Shirley Booth won her Oscar for *Come Back, Little Sheba*, boosting by association her costar's attempt to broaden his range. But if Lancaster was riding high, his partner was not. On March 23, Hecht, obeying a summons mailed to him care of Martin Gang, sat down in front of HUAC chairman Harold H. Velde in the Los Angeles Federal Building and proceeded to name names. His attorney was Edward Bennett Williams, trial lawyer extraordinaire who had also represented Berkeley. He turned down, to his later regret, a ten percent interest in Hecht and Lancaster's company as payment.

Of particular interest to the committee was Hecht's revelation that, as head of the Federal Theater Project's *Sing for Your Supper* revue from 1937 to 1939 and as a Communist, he had been instructed by the party to fire "the outspoken anti-Communist" when he had the chance and retain the party members as the number of jobs dwindled under increasing federal cutbacks. To his credit, Hecht insisted the FTP had not been run by Communists and was "a hallmark in the history of the American Theater." But then he reeled off several names including John Howard Lawson, Albert Maltz, Budd Schulberg, Frank Tuttle—and Roland Kibbee (a wry blacklist story that circulated around Hollywood for years claimed that when Kibbee turned to Hecht for advice on how to handle his HUAC summons, Hecht graciously obliged, and then turned around and named him). During a midday recess, agent George Willner—a one-time editor of the Communist Party's magazine *New Masses* who had refused to testify—confronted Hecht, his former partner at the Goldstone agency, in a hallway and accused him of being a "stool pigeon." The epithet stuck. Hecht remains one of the most reviled namer of names. Perhaps because his career had tracked the development of American drama and politics from early New York Russian–inspired drama to FTP to Hollywood producer, his capitulation seemed worse. "That son of a bitch," said blacklisted director Abe Polonsky more than forty years later.

Lancaster's name never came up during Hecht's testimony, leading some to wonder if a deal had been struck to sacrifice Hecht and protect Lancaster. Knox and others scoffed at the idea: Hecht had too much to lose not to name names. Kibbee, who was in line for a partnership with Hecht and Lancaster, testified later that spring and mostly named those who had named him. He persuaded himself that he had not really cooperated with the committee and broke with Hecht.

Lancaster had been warned early by Kibbee to distance himself from HUAC. But Hecht's naming of a member of their inner circle only increased his contempt for his partner. And Kibbee's exit (he continued to work for the company on a freelance basis) left the producers in need of a story man. The person who worked his way into that slot claimed that HUAC testimony posed no difficulties: "All you had to do," recalled James Hill, "was rat." The cynicism of the comment marks the distance traveled from the first exuberant hopes and ambitions of Lancaster and Hecht in

1945. While Lancaster was able to protect himself from the worst compromises, he and his company had nonetheless been infected with the contagion. The new gig that had seemed to him at first just a bigger version of his beloved circus had turned into something much more problematic and soul-destroying.

CHAPTER SIX

Zenith

Hecht-Lancaster at its zenith? It was like Disney is now.

—Robert Schiffer, director of publicity, Hecht-Lancaster,
later Hecht-Hill-Lancaster

From the end of the Korean War to the first confidence-shattering A-flat *beep-beep* from the Soviet Sputnik satellite in the fall of 1957, the mid-decade years seemed a mythic interregnum of sunny skies, pretty women, happy children, and strong men—a global heyday of the white American male and all he stood for. Stalin was dead. Eisenhower was president. Burt Lancaster, larger than life, was the archetypal American movie star, absorbed into the bloodstream like red meat and Coca-Cola.

His every quirk was now a news item. He slept nude in the biggest bed in Hollywood. He almost never shaved. One day he showed up in an outfit of which everything was a different shade of brown. The industry was split between those who felt he would have won at least one Oscar had he been more diplomatic and those who envied the success achieved without "bowing to bigwigs." He let it wash off him, claiming to relish, instead, the chance to risk all and avoid "the easy, sure thing, like the circus or the Army." He freely talked of sessions with Jimmy's psychoanalyst that had uncovered problems in his own ability to value human relationships. There were reports that he was making greater efforts to be nice but *Look* magazine, in a 1953 profile, still labeled him "one of the rudest individuals in Hollywood."

Friends insisted there was a gentle side that negated the dictator. At the end of her life, Albert Dekker's widow, Esther Dekker, remembered his generosity during the blacklist, one of many examples of time taken and attention paid. After telling reporters that he abhorred talking about himself, he would run on for twenty unbroken minutes about very personal matters. To the *New York Times* he revealed that when Jimmy had shrunk from him in terror one day he realized, horrified, that he had been "doing what Mother used to do" and vowed never to spank his children again. Hedda Hopper got an earful about how he hated gyms and training, how he loved to "waste life," and decided that the star's most characteristic trait was "tenseness." He claimed to find neuroses in his emotional inability to accept himself as a movie star. "I keep worrying," he said, "and wondering why the hell they give me all that dough." But not for long. When asked if anybody had ever tried to take a swing at him, he replied, with refreshing self-mockery, "No. . . . So far they have been deterred by my size, my apparent strength, and my untested virility."

Such comments tantalized the people around him. The loneliness at the center of such constant activity and crushing responsibility was kept at bay with more work, more exercise, more acting challenges, more grueling stuntwork, more children. More everything. The *noir* transparency was gone. His eyes were guarded, sunken, glinting in the handsome head. He had become a force moving through space, parting the waves of sycophants, creating an electric charge just by walking down the street. Sitting in Yankee Stadium surrounded by awed fans one sunny day in the mid-1950s, he looked, remembered John J. O'Connor, future television critic for the *New York Times*, "supercool in sports jacket and sunglasses . . . quite simply bigger than life . . . the very essence of what is supposed to be a movie star." After proudly driving an old jalopy for years, he suddenly bought a brand-new Thunderbird.

Less than three months after Hecht's testimony, Norma Productions and Warner Bros. formally parted ways in a release agreement dated June 11, 1953. *O'Keefe* had been the last straw. In any case, the two producers were not optimistic about their future at the troubled studio. Lancaster was down to just the one Paramount contract.

But there were all these unmade properties, scripts in progress, and the star was poised for another breakthrough with the yet-to-be-released *Eternity*. It was time to put the indie pieces together in a completely different way, to use his stardom as no star had used his or hers before. The core issue, as always, was control: Who was calling the shots? How—and who—to marry the talent to the product?

Out of the crumbling woodwork of the old studio system emerged the agent to broker the new industry. Lew Wasserman was named president of the Music Corporation of America (MCA) talent agency the same year that Lancaster arrived in Hollywood and at the same age, thirty-three. The two men came from opposite ends of the prewar vaudeville twilight: the powerful agent at MCA's Hollywood office booking the likes of Harry James and the nobody acrobat opening the act. Intelligent, intensely private, with a notorious temper that could reportedly make strong men faint, Wasserman watched and perfected his new movie strategies as the industry lurched from change to change. When the studios, seeking ways to keep top talent, started giving profit shares of up to 33 percent in 1949, the agent dreamed up a fifty-percent-of-profits deal for client James Stewart to star in *Winchester '73*. When the actor—*actor*—made over half a million dollars, the industry blinked. Talent, as managed by the agent, had become, in Neal Gabler's phrase, "the new coin of the realm."

Wasserman drew the industry's unfocused power to himself like a human magnet and then doled it back out to his star clients: "He did it the same way that [Michael] Ovitz did it at CAA [Creative Artists Agency]," said Leon Kaplan, founding partner of Kaplan Livingston Goodwin Berkowitz & Selvin, a leading Hollywood law firm of the time, and Lancaster's attorney after Gang. "Lew represented so many important clients that they had to deal with him." By 1953 the agent was ready to step up to the next level—the production package itself. For that he would need a particular kind of star allied to a proven independent company.

In 1951, Arthur Krim and Robert Benjamin, aided by the movie business expertise of a cadre of professionals like Youngstein, began their revival of the almost-bankrupt United Artists. Turning a profit within twelve months and acquiring 50 percent of the company's stock, the two New York lawyers quietly launched a revolution in the industry. With no encumbering studio real estate or seven-year star contracts, they came up with a deceptively simple approach: attract talent not only by sharing the profits and ownership of the movies, but by financing production. They also had an ingenious notion perfectly suited to a creative business facing the open future of deregulation: once the basic movie package was approved—director, script, star—UA would for the most part leave the producers alone. There were to be no Wallis-style pink slips, no 30 to 50 percent studio overhead (reportedly 65 percent at MGM) added on to the cost of the picture; stage space, equipment, costumes, and lighting machines could be rented, allowing the independent to make the movie for hundreds of thousands of dollars less and thereby realize profits sooner. It was such a funky idea, nobody paid much attention at first. A few decades later, *Fortune* would call Krim and Benjamin "the Medicis of the movie business."

Thanks in part to the successes of UA-distributed hits *High Noon* and *The African Queen*, and the new willingness of banks to back the company, UA in 1953 was also ready for its next big step, a multipicture contract with a major star who could deliver the goods and carry the company into successful, on-going independent production—and lure other stars to UA by his example. The company wanted to be a model not just of lucrative entertainment but, as Sidney Lumet summed up Krim's goals years later, "entertainment *about* something."

On June 12, Lancaster informed Wallis that all future correspondence regarding any contractual agreements should now be directed to MCA. Wasserman had become his agent and would be, for the next several years, what Tony Curtis called "Burt's silent partner." Four days later, *Variety* confirmed the end of the Warner contract, revealing that the studio had insisted that the budget of future productions be trimmed to $900,000 and that the movies be made in Hollywood. In the midst of preproduction for *Apache,* their next production scheduled to start shooting in Sonora, Mexico, in October, the indie needed a new backer, fast, somebody with the flexibility to ride the crazy times with them.

Youngstein flew out to Los Angeles to meet with Wasserman and, by his account, refused to call it quits until the right deal had been struck. Ownership share in the picture was one persuasive lure, adding a tax advantage to profit participation. "At first Lew said, 'You're nuts,'" recalled Youngstein. "It was like owning a piece of the land, giving a piece of the land away." By the end of the month, UA had signed Norma Productions to a two-picture contract. *Apache* and their next feature, *Vera Cruz,* would be fully financed. Norma would get 75 percent of the profits plus an overhead allowance to keep developing new properties, and offices with UA at its lot, informally known as the Samuel Goldwyn Studios.

But, as Tino Balio wrote in *United Artists: The Company That Changed the Film Industry,* to get its first big star UA "nearly had to give away the store." Closely guarded as "the Lancaster terms," UA agreed to do what it had done only for Chaplin previously. It gave Lancaster special domestic distribution terms (the cut taken by the distributor, usually off the top, for the middleman costs of brokering the movie from the producer to the exhibitors) of 25 percent rather than the industry standard of 30 or even the 27.5 percent of the Warner contract; foreign distribution remained at 40 percent. Eight months later, on February 7, 1954, UA ripped up the old contract and signed an even bigger deal with what was now renamed Hecht-Lancaster (HL), giving the independent $12 million to produce seven pictures, five of which would star Lancaster. *From Here to Eternity* had opened the previous August and the rushes of *Apache* were so strong that UA—and Wasserman—realized that they had in Lancaster an even bigger winner. In the week of negotiations that preceded the signing of the new contract, Lancaster stopped the projector midscreening and acted out for the "suits" from Bankers Trust the rest of the *Apache* script himself.

The first two HL/UA movies were a bundle of thematic contradictions. Idealism was laced with despair in the tale of Massai, the last Apache still on the warpath after the surrender of Geronimo. In the odd-couple buddy Western of *Vera Cruz*, an exuberant cynicism was only slightly tempered by any so-called higher feelings. Both were directed by maverick Robert Aldrich, once assistant director to Polonsky on *Force of Evil* and to Chaplin on *Limelight*, production manager on *Ten Tall Men*, respected by Hecht as a superb technician able to make pictures look bigger than they cost. The films were Lancaster's first real Westerns, quantum leaps from *Vengeance Valley*. He deepened into yet another dimension of star repertoire, what he would affectionately call "the grubby old Westerner."

The Anglo star playing an Apache in a wig made an easy target for critics despite claims that Massai's eyes really were blue. The action, when not focused on Lancaster's usual feats, was slow. Particularly shocking was one scene in which Massai, thinking his squaw (Jean Peters) has betrayed him, slugs her. But the audience, watching the movie a month after the U.S. Supreme Court desegregation ruling in May 1954, responded to the deliberate spirit in which *Apache* was produced—"meant by all involved," recalled Lancaster, "to make a broader statement on the injustice of racism." It functioned as a prequel to *Jim Thorpe*, boosting Lancaster to a different level of myth and meaning. The warrior's bewilderment at the loss of his nation and his yearning for the freedom and wildness of the faraway mountains, stars, and rivers were emotions Lancaster would return to again and again in incarnations as seemingly unrelated as *The Leopard* and *The Swimmer*.

UA became nervous that Aldrich and HL were getting so carried away with Massai's tragedy they were putting the movie's profitability at risk. The overhead charged against *Apache* was less than 4 percent but transportation costs as well as an item vaguely termed "Studio General" were grossly over budget; a lavish $155,771 had been spent on HL "future product"—story purchases and writers' salaries. Not only had the original budget of $742,000 ballooned to nearly a million, but the ending eliminated Massai with a shot in the back, "*killing* the *hero*," as a later account in *Fortune* described it with mock horror. Krim figured that Lancaster's on-screen death would take $1 million off the gross.

Independent production was sometimes not so free after all. UA insisted, according to Lancaster, on the happier ending in which Massai survives to live a farmer's productive, emasculated existence; Krim claimed he, Krim, said nothing. The star and director forever regretted the change. *Apache* finished as the top-grossing Western of 1954, its success a mark not only of Lancaster's continuing box-office draw, but also of the heady power of the right star in the right vehicle to alter the audience's prejudices.

The game had changed again when cameras rolled near Cuernavaca for *Vera Cruz* in March 1954. UA watched as their new producers got bogged down in what were now typical snafus. Cortez-era bridges barely held the heavy trucks full of equipment, the entire 150-person cast and crew came down with insomnia or *touristos* or both, and the script was never finished. Aldrich had to work, like Siodmak, in a chaos antipathetic to his rigorous style. A greedy tale of gold and treachery in the 1866 Mexico of Emperor Maximilian, *Vera Cruz* was wrapped with all the gloss Techni-color/Superscope-enhanced location scenery could give it and saved from total cynicism by a subplot, à la *Flame* and *Pirate,* of downtrodden *juaristas* who end up with all the gold anyway. The violence is raw, especially toward women. For one shot in the movie that Andrew Sarris has called a piece of "elegant escapism," cinematographer Ernest Laszlo put a camera on a platform four feet above what Hecht proudly described as "the very top of the highest pyramid at Teotiaucan" to capture a spectacular fifty-mile vista. "Get a shot like that on a process stage?" asked the producer. "Never."

HL, with the help of UA, successfully wooed *High Noon* icon Gary Cooper to costar with Lancaster as the other cowboy lusting after the gold. He was an audacious choice to play what passes for a good guy in this story of shifting loyalties, and Lancaster gave the fifty-two-year-old star first billing plus a hefty percentage of the gross, the latter a first for UA and soon to be the industry norm. Cooper would make $1 million from *Vera Cruz* while boosting the profits, Lancaster bragged, by $2 million.

Scheduled to direct his own movie, *The Kentuckian,* in August, Lancaster ignored Aldrich and dominated the movie, stealing scene after scene of the script by James R. Webb and Roland Kibbee. His disarmingly degenerate character Joe Erin, dressed in dusty black, is tense, sharp, slightly stupid, and constantly flashing a big, white, taunting grin at his costar. "No such thing," he says to the Coop, "as an innocent man." When the MPAA cautioned that he could not mouth "You son of a bitch" and get away with it, he did. Yet Cooper's Ben Trane, a Southern, post–Civil War gentleman— "our Cause expert," says Erin—proved an artful match. The pair is symbolic of many things, not least the old and new Hollywood. "Next time you draw near me," says Lancaster, jumpy, pistol in hand in the first scene, "better say what you're aiming to shoot at." To which Cooper drawls, in passing, "If I have time, I will." The relationship builds to the inevitable shoot-out. Trane outdraws Erin, who remains standing and grinning for several tantalizing seconds before dropping to the ground, dead. In *MAD* Magazine's parody of the movie, published in July 1955, "Burt Lambaster," convinced he's won, shaves, dresses, and *then* drops dead while "Gary Chickencooper" hangs on long enough to get the girl and, hours later, crashes down dead himself.

As a piece of full-blown Lancasteriana, the movie has moments that remained for millions defining images of the star. "If I know anything about movie acting," actor/playwright Sam Shepard later claimed, "it's from practicing my Burt Lancaster sneer—from *Vera Cruz*—at sixteen in front of a bedroom mirror." Ostentatiously galloping with only one hand holding the reins, he rides as well as Cooper. Spinning his pistol backwards and forwards with a flamboyance that came from hours of practice, in one cocky sequence he shoots two men with a quick move of the gun from behind his back. Here was a bad guy who relished being bad because bad was fun and funny and much more interesting. Nobody seemed to notice that the star who was not allowed to die in *Apache* not only bites the dust in *Vera Cruz* but does so at the hands of Gary Cooper.

Most critics dismissed it as a violent, sordid mess, unseemly for such heroic stars, when it opened Christmas Day 1954. But the audience loved the anti-Western with *two* stars where the villain falls in love with the quasi-hero as the only friend he's ever had and the hero lets him. Louis Malle, among fans that included director Sergio Leone, considered *Vera Cruz* the best example of the American Western buddy movie and used it as a model for *Viva Maria!* in 1965, costarring female adventurers Brigitte Bardot and Jeanne Moreau.

In the emerging body of HL work up through *Vera Cruz*, there was a distinction, wrote James Morgan in *Sight and Sound* in the summer of 1955, that had "received somewhat cursory notice from most critics." Lancaster was incomplete and uncertain in these early movies, the critic observed, but with promise of better to come. "[T]his odd mixture of violence and decency," he quoted director and critic Lindsay Anderson on Lancaster, "this goodwill that has not quite found a satisfactory channel of expression," described the man with startling accuracy. The "shrug of irony" the two Britons saw as common to all Lancaster's independent efforts was indeed the expression of his own jagged personality.

When *Vera Cruz* wrapped in May, costs had escalated from the budgeted $850,000 to $1,250,000. Krim, a self-effacing, thorough man who gave his creative partners a very long rope, wrote Benjamin barely three months after signing the revised HL contract: "I have the completely helpless feeling of not knowing enough about the internal operations of Hecht-Lancaster." How much money was being spent on what was a disturbing puzzle. "[P]urchase and development of other properties . . . personal withdrawals for themselves . . . money [spent] unnecessarily on overhead or in any other direction"—all the weak points of the new alliance were even more evident when, a week later, "the boys" asked UA for $100,000 for "living expenses" in Mexico. Hecht was using the most fluid source of money, UA, for everything from legitimate movie expenses to hiring a bunch of "Indians," as an *Apache* publicity stunt, to bang war drums in Union Station as Lancaster, back from filming *Vera Cruz,* came up the tunnel from the train tracks. ("Get the Indians the hell out of here," Lancaster snapped at Seltzer, "or I'll tear the place down.") Twenty-five hundred dollars was needed to pay for the approximately twelve thousand studio photographs of the star requested each month. The company's financial officers were "continually aghast," Seltzer said, at the fiscal brinksmanship.

UA sent out accountants from New York to tighten up procedures and came up with some "cross-collateral" adjustments. The first profits of *Apache* would be held back to cover the overrun penalty on *Vera Cruz;* those monies, in turn, would be used as a promissory note for *The Kentuckian,* budgeted at $1.2 million. In the end, none of it mattered. *Apache,* which cost just under $1 million, grossed $3 million its first year and $6 million overall. *Vera Cruz,* which had gone over budget to a total cost of about $1.5 million, took in more than $9 million early on. As long as the star pulled in the audience, all was forgiven. HL's reputation was solidified as a star-driven independent production company with a cumulating body of work that actually made money. The new UA was officially launched, "the decisive factor" in its "rise to affluence," as David Shipman later judged, being "Burt Lancaster."

Lancaster declared he was leaving acting behind at age forty to become a director with *The Kentuckian*—a job, he said, Hollywood had accused him of doing for years anyway. "Where do I get off calling myself a director?" he asked in *The Hollywood Reporter.* "Well, they say I have a sense of planning, and a sense of story and dramatic values. And, of course, enthusiasm, and a will. In fact, I think you could describe it as a 'want.' I *want* to direct." His hunger to participate was the good actor's prerogative. "They're the ones who have to *do* it," he said, "so they have to have some concept as to what they want to do." In 1954, this was not the received wisdom of Tinseltown. The Directors Guild refused to admit him because of his "contempt" for the directing profession expressed in such jibes as "incompetent, high-minded, self-styled supermen"—exactly what many in the industry thought of him. He was finally granted a waiver to direct *The Kentuckian* without membership, but by then he was already filming near Owensboro, Kentucky.

Looking back to the 1930 movie that had inspired Nick's stage name, he called *The Kentuckian* a "*Cimarron*-type" story, and indeed, it moved with an operatic fulsomeness that tried to balance the disparate dreams that had swirled in his head since childhood. En route to the wilds of 1820s Texas with his young son, Lancaster's Kentuckian Eli Wakefield allows himself to be temporarily seduced by the lure of homecooking, song-singing civilization only to light out for the territories at the movie's end with woman and child in tow. In the script adapted from a Felix Holt novel by A.B. Guthrie

Jr., the Pulitzer Prize–winning novelist and screenwriter of *Shane*, Burt is meant to be the natural Davy Crockett democrat, slow to anger or even react, Cooper-like. Moments of finely evocative Americana, particularly the arrival of a riverboat, expand off the screen with a gentle simplicity.

The new director, remembering his battles with directors, wanted to institute on the set the free, open play of ideas with himself as the benevolent artiste. The reality was a revelation: it was much harder than it looked to be on the other side of the camera. He had put himself in a situation he detested but constantly sought—the know-nothing neophyte—to learn something new. It was lonely work. "I had no one to help me," he recalled, though Hill was supposedly his production ally, "just struggled through on my own." Walter Matthau, appearing in his screen debut as a whip-wielding villain, told him, "You don't know what the hell you're talking about, Burt." Finally, he ate crow and admitted that nobody worked harder than a director. Lancaster "did not," Schiffer recalled, "enjoy directing that thing."

At the end of filming, he went to Kansas City to have his portrait completed as "The Kentuckian" by Thomas Hart Benton. If Norman Rockwell could do a painting of Gary Cooper for use in advertising for *Along Came Jones* in 1945, why not Benton, painter of powerfully rhythmic paintings of a muscular, pulsing America, to idealize Lancaster as a New World pioneer striding out of the frame into the West? "You old reprobate," Lancaster growled while the painter, who hated modernist art, homosexuals, and New York, snapped back at his subject to sit still during the preliminary sittings he snatched between takes in Owensboro. The almost life-size oil painting became the motif of the movie's marketing campaign and now hangs at the end of a hall on the first floor of the Los Angeles County Art Museum, a gift from Lancaster.

The Kentuckian opened in July 1955 in the wake of *Vera Cruz* to grudging praise. Tweaking the movie as "Hollywood pastoral," *Time* recognized its "touches of poetry" and praised the directing: "the credit goes to Actor Lancaster . . . he demonstrates a refreshing preference for natural settings . . . and a remarkably pretty wit. Furthermore, [he] directs himself with more sense for his own limits than most other directors have shown." Though the movie was invited to be shown at the Venice Film Festival, Lancaster would not, with one minor exception, direct again. Perhaps he judged himself too harshly or he may have indeed recognized his limits. The "want" to direct remained a hunger that was never satisfied.

He asked for a month's postponement on his next Paramount commitment, claiming exhaustion when *The Kentuckian* went two weeks over schedule.

Wallis blew up, again. His star was scheduled to start work in Key West, Florida, on another of the producer's class-act properties in November, the film of Tennessee Williams's play *The Rose Tattoo*. Lancaster had insisted that Wallis cast him in the picture to be directed by *Sheba*'s Daniel Mann; Williams stipulated that the movie must star what *Time* described as "the most explosive emotional actress of her generation," Anna Magnani. Her arrival in America on the SS *Andrea Doria* from her native Italy—a publicity coup in itself—had already been delayed by a month to accommodate Lancaster's indie fling. "Jesus Christ Almighty," fumed Wallis, "we've knocked ourselves out for this man." Just before he got on the train in Kansas City to head south—his fear of flying had intensified—Schiffer told him he could not do Tennessee Williams with flowing *Kentuckian* hair. After a couple of drinks, the makeup man snipped the curls off with a pair of nail scissors borrowed from a hotel maid. The result was a cropped, haphazard mess that then had to be exactly maintained for the whole film.

The dawdling may have been an avoidance tactic. Magnani—forty-six in 1954—had given even Brando pause ("she would wipe me off the stage," he would say of the woman with whom, in 1960, when she was rather older, he eventually costarred in Williams's *The Fugitive Kind*) and he had been considered for the part of Alvaro Mangiacavallo, the buffoonish truck driver who woos Magnani's Serafina back to real life and love. Still chasing Kowalski, Lancaster welcomed—at least publicly—the challenge of facing off against the passionate, dark-haired *realismo* star of Roberto Rossellini's *Open City* and Jean Renoir's *The Golden Coach*. Given the limits of his talent, it was a courageous decision. At the same time, in this comedic drama of Sicilian immigrants transplanted to the Gulf Coast written especially for Magnani, Williams's friend, Lancaster was at home: East Harlem had been full of Serafinas. The essential part of him that responded to opera and *commedia dell'arte* glowed in his best moments with a surreal life force suited to what Williams hoped would be an opened-up version of his play, a "riotous and radiant thing . . . fully exploited to enormous advantage on the screen."

The two stars clashed often, both in the neighborhood of Williams's real-life house in Key West and back in Hollywood on the interior sets at Paramount. The playwright, acting as peacemaker, recalled that Lancaster once refused to return to the set until his costar stopped trying to direct him. Before leaving for New York to join Elia Kazan who was casting *Cat on a Hot Tin Roof*, Williams told Mann he hoped peace could be kept between the two leads "long enough to finish the picture." In fact, Magnani was "crazy about Burt before she ever met him," said Knox, who had just worked with her on *The Golden Coach* and was assigned from Italy as dia-

logue coach on *The Rose Tattoo*. In the last scene of Luchino Visconti's 1951
Bellissima, made in the grim period of Italian postwar recovery and about a
movie-obsessed mother who dreams that her plain daughter will be a star,
Magnani, weeping, hears an American voice through the bedroom window; coming from the soundtrack of an open-air movie playing on a
draped sheet in the next yard, it is the voice of Lancaster. *"Lo senti, ni?"* she
cries. *"Coso Burt Lancaster. Quant'e simpatico, quant'e simpatico!"* ("Do you hear
that? It's Burt Lancaster. How nice he is, how nice!")

In Magnani Lancaster recognized a chancer like himself who admitted
that if she had not found acting as an outlet for her enormous vitality, she
would have become "a great criminal." Knox recalled a champagne party
in Lancaster's Paramount bungalow one night after viewing rushes when a
jubilant Magnani jumped on her costar's back and rode around piggyback, clinging to his neck. When Lancaster pointedly offered to drive her
back to the Beverly Hills Hotel, she accepted with delight: *"Magnifique!"*
The next morning, when asked how things had gone, she made an Italian
gesture to indicate that Lancaster had been a disappointment. Knox
shrugged, "Anna could be pretty imposing."

Critics divided between contempt and varying degrees of admiration
for an impossible task creditably done when the movie came out at the end
of 1955. As with the stage version, some saw it as a stew of tragedy, farce,
and sexuality. Lancaster was satisfied to have done such a project at all, a
no-regrets philosophy that made him impervious to critical disdain.
"[D]on't come in til the 'third act,' " he breezily told one reporter, "but
when I do, it's like a gang buster."

Hecht, meanwhile, was deeply immersed in the making of the movie
that would remain the most famous feather in the Hecht-Lancaster cap:
Marty. More than forty years later, U.S. Representative Barney Frank of
Massachusetts would describe the general idleness of his colleagues in well-
loved lines from the movie: "We are less busy than the guys in *Marty,* standing around on the corner: 'Whadda you wanna do tonight?' 'I don't know.
Whadda *you* wanna do tonight?' "

Industry watchers assumed that if the indie was making a movie as
unlikely to succeed as this little black-and-white cheapie, it must be taking a
deliberate loss to offset all the cash that kept pouring in from *Apache* and later,
Vera Cruz. The jeers had an element of truth, but the real reasons the movie
version of a teleplay that had already been enormously successful ever got
off the ground reveal another important turn in the history of Hecht-
Lancaster: *Marty* became the poster child for independent production.

When East and West Coast television networks were linked in 1951,
creating a nationwide system, and when government restrictions limiting

the number of transmitting television stations were eased in 1952, "the tube" came into its own as the new American communications phenomenon. What had been a funny box owned by one family on the block was now a necessity bought by everybody, the new mass audience.

An enormous demand sprang up for new programming. Along with so-called low-to-middle-brow shows such as *I Love Lucy* and *The Honeymooners*, there was an explosion of top-quality weekly "anthology dramas" originating live from New York. Among the most distinguished were NBC's *Philco Television Playhouse* and *Goodyear Television Playhouse*. Under producer Fred Coe, young writers such as Horton Foote, David Shaw, Sumner Locke Elliot, and *Marty*'s writer, Paddy Chayefsky, were given the freedom and control usually granted to Broadway playwrights. Since Hollywood initially maintained a defensive disdain, refusing to sell screenplays to television, there was little flow of ideas and properties between the two camps. The result was a flowering of the emerging medium made all the more exciting by its simultaneous live transmission across the country. For a brief Golden Age, television seemed the magic ether that would bind the country together, reflect the nation's best hopes back to itself.

On Sunday night, May 24, 1953, as Lancaster was getting ready to leave Warner Bros. and sign the first two-picture contract with UA, a winsome little drama directed by Delbert Mann about the love life of a pudgy Bronx butcher named Marty was broadcast on the *Goodyear Television Playhouse* and became the around-the-water-cooler, over-the-back-fence TV show of the decade. Calls and letters poured into NBC's New York headquarters expressing amazement that Chayefsky could have known their life stories so exactly. Mailer—"What have the 1950s brought us but *Marty*?"— and others would deride the sentimentality of the story of ordinary people and their search for love, but the audience embraced it as their truth. Rod Steiger, the original Marty, recalled, "All the souls were singing at the same time."

Hecht had been introduced to Chayefsky by Knox in the late 1940s. The unknown playwright, testing the Hollywood waters, found a sympathetic ear for his hopes and ideas in the aspiring producer. Both men grew up in the same section of the Bronx, both were Jewish. "I'm sure," said Mann, "the pain and the loneliness and the sort of desire to find a life, to find a girl—Hecht saw himself in that. He was the one emotionally behind *Marty*." Eager to make his mark in a partnership dominated by his star, whatever remained in him of the years with Boleslavsky and the FTP also yearned to make a real art movie. Hecht wanted respect.

Chayefsky agreed to go to Hollywood as long as he could have a dream deal, including full control over the script and the original television director, Mann (who had never directed a movie). The producers would have no legal right to change any of the dialogue, "the first time," reported the *New York Herald-Tribune*, "that's happened in Hollywood." *Marty* was also the first major property to cross over from TV to the movies. Hecht and Lancaster agreed to everything. With the budget targeted at barely over $100,000, why not cede some control? This was art, not commerce.

Ernest Borgnine and Betsy Blair were cast instead of the original leads, Steiger and Nancy Marchand, because Hecht felt the audience would only pay to see a significantly different version. Lancaster's work with Borgnine on *From Here to Eternity* and *Vera Cruz,* plus the actor's portrayal of sympathetic characters in several TV dramas, made him seem a good, fresh choice to the star-producer, who actively promoted him for the part. Blair was more problematic. She had been graylisted for about four years because of her public support of suspect groups such as veterans of the Spanish Civil War. At Chayefsky's insistence, she read for the part of Marty's delicately plain girlfriend and as she left the HL/UA offices after the third reading, a secretary whispered to her, "I think you got the part. The great stone face"—Lancaster—"had a tear in his eye." To spring her off the graylist, Gene Kelly, her husband at the time, confronted Dore Schary, the head of Kelly's home studio, MGM, and a personal friend. " 'You play Charades with Betsy every Saturday,' " he told Schary, according to Blair. " 'She's not going to overthrow the country. She says it's a great part and if you don't do something, I'm going to start shooting.' So Dore called the American Legion in Washington in front of Gene and vouched for me."

HL's insistence on Blair was doubly risky because Lancaster was again under scrutiny. When he tried to renew his passport in December 1953, the State Department asked him for an affidavit "setting forth whether you are now or ever have been a Communist." In January he fired back a letter with a one-paragraph, notarized disclaimer—what Seltzer called "a kiss-off in a page"—stating: "I am not now a Communist. I have never been a Communist and I am not in sympathy with the Communist movement." It was not enough for the director of the passport office, R.B. Shipley, busy restricting the passports of other Hollywood suspects Salka Viertel and Edward G. Robinson (scrawled across the top of the file copy of Lancaster's letter was, cryptically, the word "Fraud"). He was issued a limited one-year passport, good for travel to Mexico only for *Vera Cruz.*

When he then requested a general passport with no limits, the star was told, via Edward Bennett Williams, that he must provide another more detailed affidavit. On December 16, 1954, with *Marty* in the can, a lengthy affidavit was sent from the Washington, D.C., law offices of Williams to the state department. Though McCarthy had been censured by the Senate two weeks earlier, signaling the beginning of the end of the right-wing tide, the almost defiant language of Lancaster's first clearance letter was selectively replaced by a fulsome, less edgy capitulation: he claims to believe that HUAC has "completely comported" with fair procedure and is "militantly opposed" to the Communist Party. Parts of both letters are identical, suggesting Williams used the earlier text as a template.

Trapeze was scheduled to start shooting in Paris in August 1955, and Lancaster was finally issued a new, unrestricted passport in April. Two years later, on a publicity tour for *Sweet Smell of Success* in Washington with Norma, Billy, Jimmy, his sister Jane, and her daughter Barbara, his request for a meeting with Hoover during a "very special tour" of the FBI was denied. "I will not [greet Lancaster]," the bureau director scribbled across the background check memorandum, "in view of his subversive associations."

Politics aside, UA carefully assessed the risk-quotient of the *Marty* package before any camera rolled. Just how much money got allocated to what became an exquisite exercise in the evolving dynamic of the new Hollywood. After praising *Marty*'s "tremendous opportunity for audience identification" in a preproduction letter to Krim in May 1954, Robert Blumofe, UA's West Coast production representative, drew a careful line between a too-expensive picture with no names and a $550,000 to $600,000 hit with "the strongest possible name"—like Brando, whom he strongly pushed for the lead. What Hecht saw as part and parcel of the UA/HL multipicture deal—his frosting-on-the-cake reward for jump-starting UA, like Lancaster's self-directed *The Kentuckian*—the distribution company saw as a chance to change the terms of their deal, at least for this one non-Lancaster picture. "UA would be in an extremely disadvantageous, embarrassing and indefensible position with other producers," as HL lawyer Kaplan restated UA's position in a letter to Krim, "if it were forced to admit that it gave the Lancaster terms to *Marty*."

Then Kaplan coolly countered. "So far as the precedent argument is concerned," he argued, "the feeling is that that should present no real problem to United Artists. If a producer comes to UA with a modest cost package without a star and demands the *Marty* terms, all United Artists would have to tell him is that he would get them if he would deliver several million dollar plus pictures starring Burt Lancaster. . . ."

Lancaster could have killed *Marty* without a second thought. "Who wants to see a picture about two ugly people?" is a statement often attributed to him, though he claimed the source was Youngstein. "[E]ven though the guys at UA were nice enough to admit we just about made them," he said in 1972, "they were dead set against *Marty*. . . . Why shouldn't they be willing to lose a little, if at the same time they would be encouraging new writers, new faces? . . . They did it because I told them that if they didn't, I wanted out of my contract." When more money was needed for retakes toward the end of filming, "Burt really went to the mat with UA," recalled Kaplan. "But he couldn't move them and he and Harold finally put up the end money, $75,000, on that deal." *Marty* eventually cost a reported $360,000, the usual cost of a second feature. The teleplay became a relatively expensive art film with more scenes, more extras, and no stars to offset the difference. A big floating overhead continued to accumulate for which no separate accounts were maintained.

The *Marty* shoot took a bare, if not consecutive, twenty days starting with location shooting in the east Bronx in September and ending in Hollywood in December 1954. The playwright and Mann were enrapt in what the director recalled as "a constant shot-by-shot preoccupation to move away from what we arrogantly felt was the non-realism of Hollywood to the essential realism of live television." A cut was ready to be shown to Lancaster and UA executives by the end of the year. First reactions were cautiously optimistic: *Marty* might make a good art house movie with limited distribution and very limited profits. When Hecht protested to his partner that Mann and Chayefsky would not "let" him shoot more footage, Lancaster reportedly grabbed Hecht by his jacket lapels and, lifting him up against the screening room wall, said, "What do you mean they wouldn't let you?" Just where had that end money gone, if not into more shots?

How to show and promote *Marty* became a model of modern movie marketing. As a regular theater circuit was out of the question, Youngstein, Seltzer, Hecht, and HL's New York publicist, Bernie Kamber, decided to focus on just one venue, the Sutton Theater on Manhattan's East Side. *Marty* would be built, as Seltzer recalled, "slowly and carefully." At the same time, Kamber—a Runyonesque New Yorker who knew everyone, including columnists Ed Sullivan and Earl Wilson—started having private screenings. "It was like a one-man religious campaign for Bernie with *Marty*," said Joe Hyams, who would soon work for HL himself as a publicist and, eventually, for Clint Eastwood as the star's Warner Bros. executive overseeing promotion. "All the guys at Lindy's liked *Marty*—it was their life story!" But not until Kamber ran into Winchell at a barber shop one night did the famous *Marty* groundswell begin. When the columnist predicted in his column the following week that HL's *Marty* would be one of the great sleepers of all time, Kamber's phone finally started to ring.

The movie opened at the Sutton in April 1955 to rave reviews— Chayefsky's "sentences . . . are so accurate that hearing them is like listening to your own heartbeat," reported *Cue*—and people started to fill the theater and kept filling it for an unprecedented thirty-nine weeks, coming in from the boroughs to stand in line around the block. However, when the local phenomenon was released west of the Hudson with virtually no publicity to create a national stir, it bombed. Meanwhile, UA had submitted the movie to the eighth annual Cannes Film Festival in France, a deliberate effort, as an in-house UA memo put it, to win the cheap publicity of "international acclaim" for the ugly duckling movie. Over heavy competition such as *Mister Roberts, Marty* was accepted as a U.S. entry for the May event. Gene Kelly was going to the festival anyway on an MGM junket, so Blair went along to moonlight as the one representative of *Marty.* A UA exec, Arnold Picker, would be there to help publicize a Stanley Kramer film, but otherwise not even Hecht, busy packaging *Trapeze,* bothered to go. In an era of plentiful, esteemed foreign films, no American entry had ever won Best Picture at Cannes.

When *Marty* won the *Palme d'Or* on May 11, Krim, Hecht, and others arrived, fast, for the awards ceremony. The international group sitting in the Palais du Festival embraced the movie with the happy *folie* of the prince who has found his unassuming little Cinderella: America had joined the *realismo* company of real people, real "art" movies. Blair, not Brigitte Bardot, was now the toast of the Riviera town for her award as Best Actress, and Borgnine split Best Actor with Spencer Tracy for Tracy's performance in *Bad Day at Black Rock.* A jubilant cablegram was fired off to UA's home office in New York: "FIRST TIME ANY AMERICAN FILM HAS WON CANNES GRAND PRIX . . . MARKS ANOTHER MILESTONE IN UA HISTORY. . . ."

The ad budget was tripled to $150,000 and *Marty* won the New York Film Critics Circle Award for Best Picture and for Best Actor, British Film Academy honors for Borgnine and Blair, the Writers' Guild award to Chayefsky, a Golden Globe for Borgnine, and the Directors Guild of America award for Mann. *Marty* was now Oscar material. Hecht, with the approval of Lancaster, poured money into publicity prior to the 1956 awards ceremony, less than a year away. "Harold couldn't spend enough," said Hyams. Seltzer crafted an Oscar promotion that would set another standard in the industry. "We put on a very expensive, intensive campaign that possibly cost more than the film," he recalled. "It was among the first asking for academy members to vote for your movie. We arranged to have a movie screening party in their [members'] home with food, a print, and a projectionist. Then there was a very intensive advertising campaign in the trades. This was not the normal way to do things at that time."

The new aggressiveness paid off. When Oscar nominations were announced on February 13, 1956, *Marty* had gathered seven: Best Picture, Director, Actor, Supporting Actress (Blair), Supporting Actor (Joseph Mantell), Cinematography (Joseph LaShelle), and Screenplay (Chayefsky). To celebrate at least their nominations, HL had Seltzer and his copublicist

George Glass (who testified before HUAC in 1952 and named names) prepare a big, expensive post-Oscar party at the Beverly Hills Hotel for the night of the ceremony on March 21. At the last minute, Hecht panicked. "What if we don't win?" Seltzer recalled him saying, to which Glass replied, "Don't worry, Harold. You'll have enough roast beef to feed your family for years to come." When Hecht, Lancaster, Borgnine, Blair, Seltzer, and the rest arrived at the RKO Pantages Theater in Hollywood that evening—Mann and Chayefsky were at the Century Theater in New York for a dual telecast—Hecht was drunk and getting drunker.

Marty won several awards on the countdown to Best Picture. First Chayefsky, then Mann, then Borgnine. Magnani won Best Actress for *The Rose Tattoo.* As Hecht gulped down cups of black coffee, Lancaster, on a break from filming Paramount's *Gunfight at the O.K. Corral,* agreed to be at the ready to accept the award if necessary. But when Audrey Hepburn read out *Marty* as the Best Picture for 1955, beating out *Picnic, The Rose Tattoo, Mister Roberts,* and *Love Is a Many Splendored Thing,* Hecht got to the stage and calmly, soberly accepted the award of his lifetime.

He then proceeded to get seriously drunk while Seltzer ran downtown to the newspaper offices and got the *Marty* ad reset to read "Four Academy Awards." When Seltzer got back to the party, hours later, with a copy of the newspaper with the new ad, no one was there but Hecht, "very drunk," and a few stragglers. "The paper was one of the first off the press and it was smudged," Seltzer said. "Hecht looked at it and said, 'Goddamn ad looks awful!' Well, I was so distraught that I remember rolling up the newspaper and beginning to beat Harold about the head and shoulders with this rolled-up newspaper. George said, 'Come on Walter, this is ridiculous.' And we left and never came back." Seltzer went to work for Brando and his independent company, Pennebaker Productions.

The industry went into another tailspin. What did *Marty*'s success *mean?* Even before the Oscars, *Variety* had noted: "Rarely has a single picture so influenced the film industry as has *Marty.* . . . The popular notion in the picture trade was that only major-scale product could make a meaningful profit." *Newsweek* reported that the movie marked the second time, following *On the Waterfront* in 1954, that a black-and-white movie shown on the "antiquated square screen" was voted best picture. Actually, it was the third time in a row, counting *From Here to Eternity* in 1953, but the magazine's theory as to why such non-blockbuster, non-Technicolor, non-wide-screen movies cleaned up at the Oscars was accurate. "[M]ajor studios no longer keep sixty to seventy stars under contract and thus do not hold the tremendous voting power they once did."

All the more indicative of some kind of sea change was the fact that the previous films had names to offset their spare style. "At last Hollywood,"

Parsons pronounced, "—with the small independent productions setting the pace—is keying itself into the experimental work TV can literally afford to do. . . . No major studio, with its vast overhead, could have produced *Marty* for a low figure like this. Hecht and Lancaster . . . have no miles of studio space, no swank offices." (HL were in fact busy pouring money into very swank offices.) Such kudos boosted the indie, Mann recalled, "to another level." If the pattern sounds familiar, it is. *Marty* is the model for the shoestring-budget indie with fresh faces that comes out of nowhere and runs away with all the prizes.

Building on that dream, Chayefsky wrote *The Bachelor Party,* another low-key, acutely observed drama about four men on an all-night bachelor bender in Greenwich Village directed by Mann for HL and released in 1957. It did not do well, despite hopes that it would surpass *Marty* in artistry and theme (which many, in the end, felt it did). After the Oscar hoopla died away, UA "brought out the ledgers. 'Burt,' " Lancaster recalled being told, " 'we're glad we did the picture, because we've won every award there is and people are coming to UA with exciting ideas . . . but. . . .' *Marty* grossed only half [Hecht claimed $6 million] of what *Vera Cruz* brought in." The movie's cost-profit ratio would be claimed as an industry record for years but there were not *enough* profits. Hecht told the Oscar audience he felt lucky "to be part of an industry where any picture, no matter how low its budget, can win an Oscar." Lancaster, the practical prime mover, assessed the story of the Bronx butcher as "a fluke."

As early as 1948, *Photoplay* had remarked on Lancaster's "ambition to write, produce or just act in a real circus story." What Michael Powell's *The Red Shoes* had done for ballet, he wanted to do for the greatest show of them all. He would show Tinseltown what real effort was, the discipline and heartache in bending the body to its own art form. Make the artist a trapeze performer who spins triple somersaults high in the air with "one split-second" to connect with his catcher and avoid breaking his neck, and the symbolic parallels with real life are obvious.

Lancaster had finessed his own Hollywood Triple: star, producer, director. In casting himself as Mike Ribble, the crippled master of the aerial feat, he threw his screen image into its own elegant spin. Ribble is not the star, he is the *ex*-star. The once-graceful body walks with a cane, its tensile frustration bristling off the screen. Bitter, isolated, reduced to tinkering with riggings, catching not flying, Ribble is contemptuous of the soft glitz of the new acts. The triple demands extreme physical rigor and mental clarity, qualities Lancaster saw himself as bringing to his profession.

Trapeze would be HL's biggest hit around the world, earning back its cost in Japan alone. The movie most critics patted on the head and relegated to the status of a spangled melodrama stuck in the minds of audiences like a fairy tale. This was a movie that *moved,* its vertiginous camera swings and angles drawing viewers into a tight little universe of its own making. *Trapeze* is as good an example as any of the movie memory, all the more powerful for being officially forgotten. The audience owned this movie as it owned the circus, as it had and would own many of Lancaster's movies. That was fine with him. He was speaking to them.

The hot indie now had the clout to make a movie that started out budgeted at $2.5 million and ended up costing close to what the *Los Angeles Times* called an "astronomical" $4 million. A reported $100,000 alone was spent on the script. The Paris-based movie was also a perfect example of what Hecht now called "The Global Look: An international array of world-renowned artists in a production of surpassing size and concept." The concept was partially a ploy to get at frozen foreign funds. Entire European circus acts from fifteen countries were hired to guarantee *Trapeze's* authenticity—and to fill the foreign quota. With almost 50 percent of Hollywood's movie revenue now coming from foreign markets, local talent was also an important audience draw abroad.

To insulate foreign distribution profits from U.S. taxation, *Trapeze* was built on a corporate structure of U.S. and foreign companies named for Lancaster's daughters: Susan Productions, Inc., was a California corporation contributing the "American ingredients" and controlling the distribution territories of the U.S. and Canada; Joanna Productions, A.G., was a Liechtenstein-based coproducer that had complete ownership of *Trapeze* for "all foreign territories." UA's European rep, Charles Smadja, cautioned Kaplan in a preproduction letter "not to inform me who is producing *in fact* the picture. For our French company, it is an American picture produced in France by HL."

The movie's glamorous scope made the distributor nervous. Early in 1955, before *Marty* had opened and with the profits of *Vera Cruz* only starting to come in, UA pushed Wasserman to "establish some brake" on HL's movie budgets. The indie, meanwhile, was trying to free *Trapeze,* in advance, from any penalties or cross-collateralizations, while preventing the ever-growing overhead disbursements from being adjusted retroactively onto the profits of *Apache* and *Vera Cruz.*

UA was left with the sinking feeling that it would end up paying through the nose for the privilege of working with HL. In February 1955, Krim wrote a confidential memo to himself for his files after two meetings with Wasserman. The agent agreed, he noted, that the problem was that HL "is unrealistic in spending as much money as they are without realizing it is their own money which they are spending." Krim noted that Lancaster wished more pressure on this score be exerted on Hecht. Wasserman "seemed impatient," Krim wrote, "with this kind of in-fighting on their part." He then recorded his deepest concerns about working with HL. "I was greatly troubled by our meeting on Saturday," he wrote. "I felt that we will be put to an unusual test in respect to *Trapeze*. I told Lew that if anybody else were to make *Trapeze*, it would cost $1,000,000 less, but he said, and I had to agree, that we had to take this operation as it was and either go ahead or drop the picture but not expect to change them." With Wasserman as the "statesman" of the situation, Krim was anxious to disprove the industry model of "great success breed[ing] divorce." Addressing a complaint from HL regarding the "millions of dollars that [UA] were going to make in distribution fees," Krim reminded Wasserman of the distributor's annual "load" of $13 million which it was a "fallacy" to consider as profit. "By clipping us," he added, "they would be reducing the very strength which has given them this kind of a home and now has given them competitors who can snipe at us and offer them seductive inducements for change." Here were the fresh parameters of the movie business a decade after the war—each side arguing from strength as equals.

Virtually all of *Trapeze* was shot in the fall of 1955 on location at the 103-year-old, five-thousand-seat Cirque d'Hiver (Winter Circus) in Paris. Carol Reed, Oscar nominee for *The Third Man*, was brought from England to direct. Tight with budgets, utterly focused, taller than Lancaster, he not only wanted to work with the star, he brought to the project the cameraman who had won an Oscar for *The Third Man*, Robert Krasker. Together they broke down the problem of shooting the high, wide, and fast (seventy-five miles per hour) swings of the trapeze in widescreen Cinemascope within the domed confines of the Cirque. There is a fond wit in Reed's use of big wild animals, their sudden noises, and a sly symbolism in the motifs of little gray rats and slimy snakes. The result is a vibrantly layered visual rhythm that caught the mania of the real thing. There is even, when Ribble gazes longingly at just about anything that swings in the air, a *Third Man*-ish echo of a Viennese zither.

Lancaster and Wasserman had to use considerable force to convince Universal to loan out Tony Curtis, one of their most lucrative stars at the height of his duck-tail-hairdo, teeny-bopper popularity, to play the eager student of the triple, Tino Orsini. "Burt"—whom Tony Curtis described as "the major force of the major players of that time"—" was the main reason I got that part," insisted Curtis. "He refused to relent." Lancaster liked Curtis—the two men worked out at the same gym—and enjoyed ribbing him to see how much he could take. The older star in turn inspired in Curtis, a fellow native of the Second Avenue El, something of his own attitude to the craft: "When they say 'it's only a movie,'" said Curtis, "—bullshit. It's not only a movie. You're eating up time, you're eating up your own sense of who you are and what you are." From the pattern of their teasing would come the deep, knowing rapport of *Sweet Smell of Success*.

Playing into another major trend of the mid-fifties, HL was delighted to announce that the foreign female bombshell Gina Lollobrigida, "La Lollo," would perform in her first American film as Lola, the woman who comes between Ribble and Orsini. She was persuaded, reported the *Los Angeles Times*, by "$160,000 . . . the largest film salary ever drawn by a European star." Katy Jurado, the Mexican-born actress who had just lost out as Best Supporting Actress for her performance in *Broken Lance* to Eva Marie Saint in *On the Waterfront*, was reportedly in the film not only for her almost-Oscar aura but also because of a romantic liaison with Lancaster.

And there were to be no peeps from circus fans either. In an early scene, Orsini rattles off the lineage of the famous triple masters: "Clarke, Concello, Codona. . . ." Lancaster was paying homage. Ernest Clarke, the first male triple star, had been with Lancaster on the Gorman Bros. Circus in 1935; when Lancaster saw triple master Alfredo Codona at Madison Square Garden in the early 1930s, Codona was appearing with the Flying Concellos, Art Concello and his wife, Antoinette. Catching for the Concellos was Eddie Ward Jr., who had been with Lancaster on the Cole Bros. Circus in 1948 and was now hired as the star's double; Ward's parents were the first famous American circus aerial trapeze artists, the Flying Wards. Fay Alexander, who had done the triple in practice at winter quarters, doubled for Curtis. Alexander had been crashed into so often by the Concellos he had, Lancaster recalled, "all false teeth and a terror of being hit in the mouth again." As a result, the central trick of the movie had to be faked.

The on-screen bickering and teasing between competitive performers carried over off the screen, sometimes turning ugly. Fed up with what he and Curtis saw as Lollobrigida's self-absorbed preening, Lancaster sat down at a table one day between takes with Lollobrigida, Curtis, and the movie's publicist, Michael Mindlin, and suddenly asked the Italian, whose English was shaky, how a particular part of her anatomy was doing. There was a shocked silence from the other two men during which Lollobrigida, confused by another English word she didn't know, said, "What does he mean? What does he mean?" Finally Curtis, whom Mindlin described as being "the least sophisticated by far" of the group, interjected, "Um, um . . . he means, ah . . . 'How's your *country*!' " which set Lollobrigida off on a riff about *la bella Italia*.

Lancaster's behavior was in keeping with the misogynist tale of *Trapeze* in which the scheming femme fatale intrudes on the male friendship of Ribble and Orsini and their quest for the triple. The original novel, *The Killing Frost*, on which James Webb's script for *Trapeze* was loosely based, had a homosexual twist: Orsini is executed for the murder of the woman who left him for Ribble, but the real killer was Ribble, who really wanted Orsini. The gay theme would not play in 1955, but the submerged intensity of feeling, the erotic imperative of art as in *The Red Shoes,* is there. "Right from the start," says Lola to Orsini, "[Mike] saw he might lose the only life he has, the life you give him." Ribble pleads with his acolyte, "Ribble and Orsini . . . or Orsini and Ribble. Doesn't matter which way you put it: It's the same person." With the male-dominated triple a metaphor for all kinds of bonding, it is a credit to Lollobrigida that the woman, however camped up, more than holds her own in this mid-1950s universe.

Conflicts never got a chance to fester, according to Curtis, because of Reed. Dressed in a quiet gray suit, he beamed calm and strength like "a lighthouse." When Lancaster insisted on retakes for scenes Reed privately felt had gone well on the first take, the director quietly gave in and then used the first take anyway. "I need him, so it's better I'm kind with him," he told Lollobrigida, knowing he had to get the star/producer's OK for any scene alteration.

Outside the Cirque, another real-life circus swirled around the production. At the Hotel George V, just off the Avenue des Champs-Elysées, the top echelon of the production staff of HL took over an entire, beautifully furnished floor and proceeded to trash it, getting drunk, breaking vases, staining rugs. Lancaster had a separate top-floor suite with a terrace and arranged for Curtis, free from the mothering of Universal and "really homesick, just like I was when I went away to camp or the navy," to have his room one floor below. Curtis took to climbing up the trestle, as if he were Orsini, and in through the window to Lancaster's suite. When he was invited up for an evening with three women and burst in through the window, one of them, he claimed, almost fainted.

The two men commiserated with each other about the burdens of blending work and family. "All Burt's kids showed up," Curtis recalled, "and then my brother came and all of a sudden we're worried where they're staying in the hotel, will they be cheated, where are they going to eat? The picture business, making movies, is a lot more complicated than that. You have to drive every other thought out of your brain." When Norma and the children, for whom he rented a fifteenth-century chateau on five hundred acres of French countryside near Versailles, returned to Beverly Hills, Lancaster went back to womanizing. Hill began to emerge as Lancaster's buddy and protector, adding a new strain to many of his key relationships. "I always felt," said Curtis, "that Burt hired Jim Hill just to piss off Harold Hecht." Norma assessed the situation as accurately as anyone: "You get off my husband's back," she said one night to Hill at dinner in a Paris restaurant, "and I mean that literally." Then she threw a glass of beer in his face. There was a new "remoteness" Curtis and others observed between the couple. Even though Waterbury did another *Photoplay* piece about the happy Lancaster family shuttling back and forth between the Cirque and Versailles, the image was beginning to be too much of a fiction to maintain.

Amid the critical groans that greeted the opening of *Trapeze*, there was one commentary, in *Saturday Review*, which saw the work as the audience saw it. "*Trapeze* is one of those rare pictures," wrote Stanley Kauffman, "that is inconceivable in any other medium. . . . [It] may lack the stature of a 'great' movie, but it's a perfect example of great movie-making." The picture was also a vindication of Hecht's Global Look, grossing close to $20 million worldwide, five times its cost. In Tehran, military police were called out to control the crowds "obsessed" with seeing the international hit. *Variety* raved in May 1957 that *Trapeze* "is now UA's biggest grosser in history . . . also UA's foreign record holder." HL, in spite of, or maybe because of its chaotic style, could seemingly do no wrong.

At four o'clock one morning in 1962, in a dumpy all-night theater on Forty-second Street in New York, a Mexican trampoline artist named Tito Gaona sat with his family watching a rerun of *Trapeze*. By the time the movie was finished, the fourteen-year-old so identified with Ribble and Orsini that he knew he had found his mission in life. Four years later, with Ringling Bros. and Barnum & Bailey Circus, Gaona became the first trapeze artist to consistently throw a triple since Codona. By 1974, *Sports Illustrated* reported that—shades of Jim Thorpe—Gaona "may be the finest athlete in the world." The logical next challenge was the one that had never been done: the quadruple. When asked his secret in trying to master the most dangerous, improbable feat of the human body, the flyer quoted his mantra, memorized verbatim from Lancaster's instructions to Curtis/ Orsini: "Remember, there's a little clock inside of you and a little clock inside of me—and we've got to keep those clocks ticking alongside of each other. . . ."

Life isn't a movie and Gaona never succeeded in doing the quad in public. But for millions around the world with less dramatic risks to take, what counted in *Trapeze* was the yearning to master the difficult task made vivid in a movie that needed no words. "[T]he higher the act," Lancaster would say decades later, finding the parallel with his own life, "the easier the act. . . . The higher you get, the tighter the wire can be stretched; it gets so tight that it's solid." Success was not the point. Aiming for it was.

Word of Lancaster's activities at the Hotel George V seeped back to *Confidential,* the infamous Hollywood scandal magazine with a circulation of five million. In May 1955, it reported what it claimed was one of several such incidents: Lancaster took Mrs. Bruce Cabot, once Francesca de Scaffa, "formerly the mistress of the Shah of Persia," into his office for a casting interview and promptly asked her to take off her clothes ("a $400 Jacques Fath dress"). When "international playgirl" Zina Rachevsky was invited into the star's bungalow one night in Palm Springs, the magazine claimed, and refused to "peel," Lancaster reportedly tore her clothes "to shreds" after which she bit him, putting him in the hospital. Of his antics in Paris, *Confidential* reported: "He's a star on the flying trapeze, but. . . . One night BURT LANCASTER was an acrobat in the *boudoir*" after which followed a tale of a French "dark-haired mannequin" with the star at the "George Cinque Hotel" at an 11 a.m. tryst, complete with chicken sandwiches and lemon tea. Afterwards, not only did the star not send flowers, he called the mannequin's friend to get the names of more "hot numbers." How dare he? vamped the magazine hardly anyone sued because the stories, while pumped up, were largely based on truth gathered from witnesses, private investigators, and what Ezra Goodman called "that great army of disgruntled movie people."

There were stories *Confidential* did not report. Ernest Lehman recalled that, as he sat in the offices at Canon Drive waiting for his first interview with Lancaster, the star walked in, late, smiling, and announced to the assembled group, "She swallowed it." While Lancaster was, said J.P. Miller, the HL writer who was also a drinking and womanizing buddy of Lancaster's, "a clear-headed, hard-working guy, not a drunk," on "extraordinary occasions, like everybody that's anybody," he could drink "quite a lot" and at those times, recalls another friend, "be quite cruel to women." Youngstein recalls a party one night in the early 1950s at the Norma Productions offices at Columbia studios during which Lancaster lifted a woman high up above his head as in *Brute Force* and flung her to the ground. "She was a gal about town," he says, "ready to flop into the sack if you had a big enough executive position. People were having a rousing good time about some successful picture and then some big quarrel started. It was terrible. Publicity people hushed it up. We got her into the hospital and the insurance covered it. It was pretty vicious." Referring to Lancaster, Youngstein added, "It was the whiskey."

It wasn't just women. Men recall being near him during this period, in an otherwise amicable context, and feeling, as Mindlin described it, "He's gonna hit me." Miller told of being with the star when he was "smashed," often after an argument with Norma: "The closest thing to it would be to say 'Would you walk up to a thousand-pound bomb and put your hand on it and realize that within that bomb was a thousand pounds of nitroglycerine and if it exploded you would be blown to bits?' "

With his father and the six-foot, one-hundred-ninety-pound stolid bulk of his brother Dutch, who came to work for him after retiring from the New York Police Department in 1955, he still had "that old sense of values," said one friend, and felt "guilty and ashamed even though he never flaunted himself, never made advances." Allowing for the fact that people put up with such behavior during this zenith period because he was a lucrative star, there were those who, knowing the worst, loved the best. Or rather they caught enough glimpses of the good to wait for the better in what seemed a daunting struggle composed of so many disparate elements. He inspired a tenacious loyalty among those like Knox who remain resolutely mum on the murkier aspects of the life. "Burt's life was his," he said, "and only his." A kind of Everyman writ large and extreme, Lancaster's best qualities—passion, discipline, loyalty, and courage—had within them the seeds of his worst.

There was no evidence or recollection of any physically abusive behavior with Norma; indeed the couple enjoyed, according to Lucy Kibbee, "a great physical relationship." Another friend saw them both as "embryos," people suspended in arrested modes of conduct—Lancaster the delayed adolescent, giving himself a feeling of importance by constantly having to make the decisions required by nonstop movies; Norma playing the dependent role of the movie star's wife, endlessly shopping and then giving half the purchases away, a sadly typical 1950s matron unable to capitalize on the wit and intelligence Tomalin had noted in 1944. The press detailed her growing collection of fur coats, useless in the Southern California warmth: "the full-length [mink] job so expensively brown it was practically black" and, for Christmas 1954, a Somali leopard sports coat to match her blond hair and brown eyes. Yet until well into the 1950s, Norma drove a 1948 station wagon and Lancaster the jalopy, confirming the general opinion that they were the least pretentious of the great movie star families.

After the birth in 1954 of Sighle, their fifth and last child, the couple began another remodeling of their home. Grandfather Lancaster, for a while, moved out to his own house in the San Fernando Valley for some peace and quiet. Part of the Bel Air property was converted into a baseball field for Jimmy and Billy. An entire room was devoted to Norma's major interest, the League of Women Voters, and crammed with printing presses and all the necessary supplies for mass mailings ("like putting out the *New York Times*," recalled Joel Douglas, Kirk's son). For contract bridge parties, a mix of studio people, actors, and writers was invited for big pots of baked beans, meat and cold cuts, and a bar where Norma mixed the drinks. As the evening progressed, one friend recalls, the hostess often got louder and louder. Lancaster was the king around whom the festivities circulated and the evening was considered a success if it ended without him loudly banning a guest from ever coming to his house again. When he'd had enough, he retreated into the den or his bedroom and listened to opera records.

As if to create some echo of East Harlem heat, there was a whirlwind of family activities—five sets of bedtime stories ("because my offspring resist the idea of forming an audience," he claimed), morning sessions for listening to all their dreams from the night before ("and I tell you, some are pretty weird"), fixing "whopping" breakfasts, and packing them all off to school—this after the two-and-a-half-mile daily run around the UCLA track. He trained all five to walk on their hands and the sight of them chatting away with their feet waving in the air, was, as one reporter described it, "quite a sight."

The two boys banded together with Billy the protector of his brother. The three girls formed a second subgroup and, as they matured, could in their solidarity seem cliquish and cold to outsiders such as the Cravat daughters. Joel Douglas recalled a family life that was "comfortable with the coming and going of kids." There was now an even bigger collection of games, toys, and sports equipment plus the fenced-off pool, a playroom that opened directly out onto the lawn where their athletic equipment was set up, and "recurrent batches" of kittens and dogs chosen at the pound for a dollar each.

Waterbury, a regular player at the Saturday night bridge parties and a seasoned Hollywood observer who had known Burt since *The Killers,* provided glimpses in her *Photoplay* articles of the family during this period. The marriage would continue for another decade, but this was the end of what Lancaster and Norma would insist were the first, best, ten years. Allowing for fan magazine gloss, Waterbury's sympathetic detail suggests the family life Burt wished to remember as "very, very happy." Her credibility is reinforced by negative tidbits such as the fact that work-obsessed Lancaster was capable of "forgetting" to come home to dinner nights in a row. "You stop that!" four-year-old Joanna, short and chunky, told her father, a compulsive nicknamer, when he once dubbed her "Stubby." "That's not my name!" When Lancaster asked her what her name was, she replied, "I'm Mrs. Mary Angry . . . and don't you ever forget it!" Susan's favorite activity for a while was counting her father's big white teeth while the two of them sat in the antique rocking chair that anchored the kitchen. When Jimmy drew a fanciful mural around all four wallpapered walls of his room one bridge party night, Lancaster made the whole group come upstairs to see the artwork—another masterpiece to add to the star's growing collection, downstairs, of Chagalls, Renoirs, Utrillos, and Vlamincks.

After a long period of consulting psychiatrists for the various "maladjustments" of their children, Lancaster finally said, "Norma, they are *our* kids. Let's bring them up in our own way." But their laissez-faire childrearing techniques were often perceived by outsiders as rationalized neglect, a state of liberated but unsettling chaos. Norma would ask what each child would like to eat for dinner and then honor the preference; dessert was a free-for-all with each child whipping up Jello, pudding, cakes. One friend recalled a dinner-table conversation when bodily organs and functions were thoroughly discussed by all ages with no limits imposed on the subject. There were no proscribed bedtimes, even on school nights. According to many family friends, Alberta and Adele, two maids with the family since the late 1940s, really brought up the children. When Bernie Kamber had to squeeze into a stateroom booked at the last minute on the SS *United States* bound for England in June 1958 with Lancaster, Billy, Susan, and Joanna, he was nonplussed by the childrens' lack of the most basic privacy inhibitions.

Younger observers like Joel Douglas did not see much "one-on-one" between Norma and the children, although she wrote plays for them to perform and carefully corrected their grammar as her schoolmarm mother had done. As an adult, Joel admitted that he had "loved the unstructured-ness" of the Lancaster house but "it's also a curse—you're floatin'." Joel and Billy met in the third grade when Joel's mother, Diana Dill, divorced from Kirk, married to producer and actor Bill Darrid, and living in West-port, Connecticut, agreed to let Joel and his brother Michael live with their father for a year in California. There was an immediate connection: both were the sons of major "tough guy" stars, one had a limp, and the other was overweight. Both were loners. "We were exactly the same ball of wax," said Joel, "and there was nothing materially that we wanted from each other."

The boys were shipped back and forth across the country for visits and, over the years, compared notes on everything from "The Business" to trust funds. "The house revolved around the dad," said Joel, "his schedule, his thing. Both of us being the second kid, the younger boy, there was always that confusion in trying to understand who your dad is and, as a result, Who am I?" The boys watched the electric and instantaneous reactions that people had to their fathers. "It'd be a very strange feeling," Joel recalled. "You'd wonder: What has he got? What are they seeing in him? Sometimes we felt like we were in competition with the human race for our fathers." When Joel told his father once about a particularly "nice man," he was told, "Do you know how much I pay that man to be nice?" Worst of all was the question: "Are you really Burt Lancaster's/Kirk Douglas's son? You don't look anything like him."

With Burt Lancaster a more physically adept man than Kirk Douglas, Billy's limp was all the more poignant. "It's one thing to be overweight," said Joel. "There's always that chance. But with the polio, you know you'll only be able to go so far and never any further." Billy created a sports link with his athlete father by playing in the baseball Pony League, which met on Saturday mornings on a field off Sepulveda Boulevard between Wilshire and Santa Monica Boulevards. His father was the coach and he was catcher, the one position that did not require much running. Billy was allowed to get to first, after which another teammate would take his place for the rest of the run around the bases. If he fell down, he had to get himself back up. "Billy could hit," said Joel, "and I think because baseball seemed contradictory to everyone because of his physical problems, that was the reason he chose it." A very Lancaster solution—and no one forgot the sight of Burt Lancaster's son dragging his foot behind him on the way to first base.

The key issue was time, "the gold," said Joel. "The biggest thing that Billy and I used to talk about is to have your father strictly doing something with you for you. We wanted that really special thing where you are prioritized, that wasn't connected to any other aspect of work." Especially with sons, these particular fathers "were not geared" to show vulnerability, to let the children in. And when they did turn the longed-for focus on the child, the intensity was often "overwhelming"—what one of Lancaster's children called "pretty scary"—and came out as anger and ferocity, the very attributes that made them stars. It became easy for the children to think everyone understood the star/father but them. As an adult, Joel came to understand that the lives of both men were organized around controlling and hiding their fear and surviving.

"It's not the easiest way to grow up," he said. Today he is the partner with his brother Michael in the Douglas family movie enterprises, proud and fond of his father, grateful for the concern he always felt from Lancaster. "Burt was a good man, a strong man, not a killer. It's a very big distinction: Most killers are weak, they're manipulative, figure out the situation and go for the throat. The strong guy takes what's dished and keeps pushing his principles and ideas forward. Bill and I used to fantasize that our dads were carpenters or plumbers where they knew we loved them for them and not because they were superstars and they came home every night at five and the only problem was getting food on the table and it seemed so clear."

But they weren't plumbers and *Cosmopolitan*'s Cameron Shipp, assigned to follow Lancaster on his daily Hollywood rounds mid-decade, reported that he resembled "an intense young college instructor who lettered in gym" when he was not otherwise "leaping, falling, stunting, fighting or dismembering executives." One typical morning began with telephone calls to the writers on his current movie project, progressed through chats with the film's editors, then broke for lunch with Wasserman. At 2 p.m. he hopped a train for San Diego for an afternoon meeting with distribution executives; after a quick dinner, he screened another movie, dictating comments to his secretary, and then met with production staff at the U.S. Grant Hotel until 2:30 a.m. Before bed, he took a quick break for a hamburger and a trip to an all-night drugstore to buy a toothbrush and razor—he still rarely traveled with any luggage.

The next morning there were breakfast meetings with his staff, followed by the 9 a.m. train ride back to Los Angeles, with the star playing gin rummy in the club car to pass the two-and-a-half-hour trip. Back at the office, he put in a call to Hecht at the Georges V in Paris and talked for an hour and a half. When Norma arrived, late, he lectured her for fifteen minutes on how to negotiate Los Angeles traffic. "The gist of it," wrote Shipp, "was that Mr. Lancaster drives defensively, as if all other motorists were retarded baboons with murder in their hearts. This reminded him of directing pictures. 'Why shouldn't anybody, including me, have an opinion about how a movie should be directed,' he inquired. 'Anybody who sees movies, if he has an adult mind, knows when a movie is badly directed, just as he knows bad automobile driving when he sees it.' "

If movies were the great popular art of the century, anybody could tell a good one from a bad one. If the elitist critics and guardians of high art derided such claims as, indeed, they still disparaged the movies, well, "tough titty," as Lancaster would tell critic Judith Crist twenty years later. It was a presumption that, coming from him, few took seriously. He had been so earnest for so long that he was getting boring. He still combed his hair with his fingers, admired the style of Stanwyck's "slim, taut figure," skipped lunch, smoked Camels, and in general did everything "hard." Here and there he would let slip that he wanted to stop "being the caricature of a he-man . . . [and] simply to be a man and enjoy life as others do." Lehman remembered him as "not stressful, rational, quiet, powerful" in private. When asked if he was happy, he replied, carefully, "I am reasonably happy, providing I keep busy." "That's the m.o.," said Joel of his father and Lancaster during this period. "Step up the pace so you don't have to face it."

With his contract star at the top of his form after the completion of *Trapeze* in December 1955, Wallis pounced. Lancaster would make two last big movies for Paramount, giving his first producer his money's worth before he finally let go. *Gunfight at the O.K. Corral* was filmed before *The Rainmaker* in 1956 but the Paramount releases were seen by audiences in the opposite order in 1957, splashing Lancaster's name on theater marquees across the country for months. Top hits at the peak of his 1950s stardom, both movies were powerfully mythic, celluloid light years away from the Swede of *The Killers*.

The Rainmaker was originally a play by N. Richard Nash, a regular contributor to Coe's *Philco Television Playhouse.* It aired on the *Goodyear Television Playhouse* in 1953 and went on to a Broadway run in 1954 and eventually ended up, in 1964, as a musical, *110 in the Shade.* When Lancaster read in Hopper's column that William Holden had bowed out of the role of Starbuck in the upcoming movie version, he asked to see the script. Burt had in fact been briefly considered for Starbuck before Holden and, when Nash had sent the first half of his screenplay to Wallis in March 1954, he wrote that he was "thrilled" with the idea of the Oscar nominee. "Aside possibly from Brando," Nash wrote, "there is no actor who combines more fully the attributes of romance, agility of mind and body and pungent sexuality. Matter of fact," he added, "I like him even better than Brando for this part. For Lancaster is more open, healthier, less turned inward upon himself." If Wallis would let him play Starbuck, Lancaster now offered, he would please the fans by doing a money-making Western and be out of his Paramount contract at last.

The timing of the role appealed to Lancaster. After playing the stunted, cynical Ribble, he could flip and soar into the exuberant role of the spellbinding charlatan who promises rain to drought-stricken 1913 Kansas and love to dried-up spinster Lizzie Curry—and then, to his own delighted surprise, delivers. Though Katharine Hepburn was easily twenty years older than the ideal Lizzie and six years older than Lancaster, the star of *The African Queen* and *Summertime* had been pursued by Wallis for the part of Lizzie since 1954 when she saw the play in New York and loved it. She signed with Wallis and in March 1956, three months before production, went to see *The Rose Tattoo* to research a model of the woman brought back to life by Lancaster. "He has a lovely face and a wonderful figure," she wrote the next day to the producer, "and looks healthy and gay and desperate—and he moved me so. . . . I think I'll get a Rose Tattoo on me—can't get over it."

On Paramount's Stage 16 from mid-June to mid-August 1956, reunited with old Paramount players like Wendell Corey, he faced the actress he described as "a hell-for-leather challenger if ever there was one." Unlike Booth and Magnani, Hepburn was a formidable legend, had been in the movies since 1932, and had a competitive presence to match—and exceed—his own. With a lot to gain by having her name up on a 1957 marquee with Lancaster's (he got first billing, on the left), she knew all her lines on the first day and berated her costar for showing up twenty-five minutes late.

He needed such correctives. He had decided he did not want to do what he he now called an unreal "bunch of crap" with a woman he privately saw as a cold fish. According to the director, Joseph Anthony, in Charles

Higham's biography of Hepburn, Lancaster was rude and aggressively impatient. Nervous that a rookie director—the director of the Broadway version of *The Rainmaker* and in the middle of a distinguished stage directing career, Anthony had never tackled a movie before—would compromise his performance on-screen, he pumped himself to cover up his own deficiencies and fussed about anything that struck him as inadequate. Finally, he got into the part, and he and Hepburn worked meticulously to revise, over Nash's objections, the tack room scene during which Starbuck kisses Lizzie—her first kiss ever—and gets her literally to let her hair down. Wallis enthused about the "overall cooperative spirit and enthusiasm" the two developed for the project: "I never dreamed," he memoed an associate after viewing the rushes, "that Lancaster could be this great an actor."

When the MPAA objected to the scene—reported Nathan to Wallis: "Half say it was a lay . . . half insist it wasn't"—and said the story amounted to "a glorification of illicit sex," Wallis exploded. "I am not going to tear my guts out," he wrote to Paramount associate producer Hazan, "to talk to a lot of bigoted people. . . . I would like to discuss with Paramount the matter of making this picture without a seal." With the political climate just beginning to calm after so much turmoil, and the Supreme Court having extended First Amendment protection to the movies in 1952, there was now room to challenge the arbiter of Hollywood's on-screen morals. *The Rainmaker* got its seal of approval and remains one of the movies for which Lancaster is most vividly remembered. "[T]he grace he has given is the grace he has received," wrote *Time* of Starbuck when the movie premiered on New Year's Eve 1956. "For the first time in his life, somebody believes he can really make rain; and for the first time in his life, he really can."

Though Hepburn gained an Oscar nomination for Lizzie, the Hollywood take on *The Rainmaker* was that without sexy Starbuck, the movie would have "died in the can": only in the mid-1950s would a woman pass up Starbuck for a slow but steady Corey—and stick to her decision even when it starts raining. Hepburn presented her costar with a tiny portrait she had painted of him as the rainmaker, a gesture he would recall with pride and gratitude decades later. Her work and example certainly contributed to his creating, three years later, a much more developed version of the same wily, smooth-talking creature of the heartland in *Elmer Gantry*.

Opening six months after *The Rainmaker*, in May 1957, *Gunfight at the O.K. Corral* had Lancaster striding across the screen as Western hero Wyatt Earp, the famous frontier lawman of Dodge City and Tombstone, Arizona. The title alone was instantly definitive, a shorthand phrase for the ultimate confrontation where everybody might be dead when the smoke clears. Wallis knew he was making a movie of a major American Western myth, the odd friendship of Earp with the consumptive, straight-shooting dentist, Doc Holliday, and how together, in thirty seconds, they wiped out most of the Clanton gang at about 2:47 on the afternoon of October 26, 1881, at the O.K. Corral (actually *behind* it) in the silver boomtown of Tombstone. The only person not dead or wounded when the real dust cleared was Wyatt Earp. When Wallis first sent Nathan a 1954 *Holiday* magazine article titled "The Killer," which focused on the relationship between Earp and Holliday as a possible story idea, his associate cabled back: "Doc Holliday a ruthless beast killing while dying of consumption. Is this good movie?"

There were other complicating factors. In 1946 director John Ford had made his nostalgic version of the famous gunfight in *My Darling Clementine*, reinforcing the popular, heroic version of the story by casting Henry Fonda as Earp. The ABC television network was planning a major series, *The Life and Legend of Wyatt Earp*, starring Hugh O'Brien, which would premiere in September 1955, six months before *O.K. Corral* was scheduled to start shooting in March 1956. A March 1955 article in the *Los Angeles Times* claimed that not only had the Earp clan hid their "dealings with shady characters" behind their official badges as officers of the law, but that they had "opened fire on a group of unarmed cowboys in the O.K. Corral and killed three of them," after which the local judge "whitewashed the incident" and set them free. Singled out for blame was the "tinsel glory" woven around the unheroic Earp by the dime-novel historians of the old West—principally Ned Buntline. There were still people alive who remembered the Earp brothers as "desperadoes" who had been hand-in-glove with the Clantons in a corrupt trade-off in which Earp would "arrest" the Clantons for the murder of a stage driver, thereby winning votes in his quest for the office of country sheriff, and then give the reward money to the Clantons. Then there were the legions of true believers who resented any suggestion that Wyatt had been anything less than all Buntline had claimed he was. For many of these supporters the gunslinger was the Cold War personification of the all-American hard line drawn in the Free World sand. The real Earp was astonished that the gunfight at the O.K. Corral, his one and only shootout, became a legend.

Wallis proceeded with a somewhat revisionist story line. Earp would drink and smoke, love a woman, have a mildly dubious past, and not look too gleeful—indeed glum—about what he has to do at the O.K. Corral. As late as January and February 1956, Wallis and Nathan were still scrambling to find a cast and a director. Leon Uris had been working on the screenplay since July after Stuart Lake, Earp's biographer and the former press secretary to Theodore Roosevelt, had been dismissed by Nathan from the project as a "sick, tired old man—and a big phoney to boot." Though Lancaster had been the choice for Earp almost from the beginning, as late as December 12, 1955, the star was saying he did not like the script and "would rather not do it," Paramount contract deal notwithstanding. After considerable shuffling of names and offers—Van Heflin, Jack Palance, Humphrey Bogart, Richard Widmark—Wallis settled on Lancaster, and Douglas as Holliday, with John Sturges as director.

Douglas had turned down the part of Holliday early on. He had not wanted to do another Western so soon after *The Indian Fighter,* made in 1955 by his own independent production company, Bryna Productions, which was formed under UA's wing in 1955 and would produce *The Vikings, Spartacus,* and *Paths of Glory,* among others. But after Lancaster committed, Douglas became interested again. He had solidified his reputation as an intense actor with a third Oscar nomination for his 1956 performance as Van Gogh in *Lust for Life.* His edge of wide-awake cynicism drew the eye on-screen and held it—his Holliday cough was masterful—and, off-screen, he had a reputation for bristling pugnacity: "On the floor, in the work," Tony Curtis recalled, "Kirk was a killer, much more than Burt. He would take no prisoners. If it [the camera shot] was over Kirk's shoulder on me, by the time the shot was over, it was over my shoulder on Kirk." Youngstein observed that Douglas, "always with a chip on his shoulder," did not have Lancaster's "ease with people." He was shorter than Lancaster by several inches and without the physical mass or grace of the athletic, slightly older star (Douglas was born in 1916). The fact that he was Jewish to Lancaster's WASP in the white-bread 1950s added, in Douglas's mind, according to his son Joel, to the rivalry. Not only did Lancaster have what Douglas later described as "certain qualities . . . I wish I had"—principally, "loyalty"—his fellow star had cleared the path for Bryna. He understood as well as anyone what such an achievement signified in the industry both men had sunk their teeth into: Douglas the feisty terrier, Lancaster the great big lion.

The older star's attitude to Douglas was harder to read. He admired the professionalism, what Joel described of both "temperamental" stars as "anger at other people who weren't prepared and who weren't doing their homework." He was tolerant of Douglas's quirks—after all, he put up with Nick Cravat—and fond, in a wry way, of his Sidney Falco–esque eagerness. During the filming of *O.K. Corral,* Lancaster reportedly told a group of autograph-seekers to go ask his costar for an autograph—that is, if they could find him without his elevator shoes on; Douglas was weeping by the time the ribbing was over. When their children were young the two families got together quite often socially, but the myth of a great personal affinity maintained over decades was largely a creation of Douglas and the Hollywood publicity machine. Lancaster sometimes obligingly corroborated the story and sometimes shot it down, as when he once abruptly said that he and Douglas had different ideas of friendship. The rapport began on location in Tucson, the two stars talking into the night, sharing for that one brief period the temporary bonding of a movie shoot.

In February Lancaster was calling Nathan two to three times a day (between more Wallis-mandated trips to the dentist), complaining there was "too much information and unnecessary dialogue" in the script. Though he had top billing, he wanted more about Earp's background inserted here and there. He suggested a scene in which Doc would say to Earp just before the gunfight, "Wyatt, you can't go in. You're a lawman and you're becoming me. What will happen to law and order here if the Earps lose . . . ?" Uris thought it was "phoney, contrived" and started privately calling Lancaster and Douglas the Bobsey Twins.

With the package barely complete, shooting began on location in Tucson on March 12, 1956. A week later, the company traveled back to Los Angeles and started shooting again the next day at Paramount. There were few clashes between Lancaster and Douglas because they were too busy harassing the director. DeForest Kelley, cast as Morgan Earp, Wyatt's brother and the Tombstone marshal, had a concept in his head of how to play his character but quickly discarded it when he saw how Lancaster dominated Sturges. "Lancaster and I were one of a group standing around on a porch in the first scene where Ike Clanton came riding into town," Kelley recalled. "Ike whips off his horse and walks up to Lancaster and begins to tell him off. I saw Lancaster walk over to the director and give him some sort of instructions that Lyle [Bettger, cast as Clanton] was coming on too strong to suit Burt. I saw this happen and I saw it happen another time and I thought, well, hell, I wouldn't be able to do what I wanted to do." The star duo reminded Kelley of Dean Martin and Jerry Lewis: Who's going to get the close-up? "They were both intelligent, bright guys who knew what they wanted," he said. "It was humorous at times because Douglas was just as obstinate as Burt was."

Lancaster took a liking to Dennis Hopper, whom Kelley recalled as "the wild young thing" who turned twenty on May 17, the day *Gunfight* wrapped. He had just come off *Giant* to play Billy Clanton, the confused kid whose death at the hands of Holliday ends the gunfight and the movie. One night over dinner at the Prairie Oyster Bar, a Tucson restaurant, after he had chewed and swallowed a few of what looked like breaded shrimp and scallops, he was told they were "bull's balls," prairie oysters. "I love 'em!" he cried, passing another one of Lancaster's tests. "Burt was wonderful to work with, very generous, very involved," Hopper said of a man he felt "protected" him. "A consummate professional. He always wanted to *rehearse*." Hopper observed what he calls a "clash of method acting versus classic film acting" on the set. Jo Van Fleet, the Broadway actress who won an Oscar for her movie debut performance in *East of Eden*, had been cast as Kate, Holliday's abused but loyal woman. She insisted that Douglas slap her, hard, before each of their scenes and Douglas, incredulous, asked Lancaster to come watch. When it came time for Lancaster and Hopper to work out the scene in which Earp grabs and slaps Billy in the alley the night before the shootout, Lancaster had a different approach. "Burt made it really easy," Hopper explained. "It was a very emotional scene, so many elements, with very complicated blocking. Burt was very good at it. He had a sense of that." Sometimes he was so good at it, he blocked the emotion right out.

Ignoring complaints from folks in the real Tombstone, the final gunfight scene was shot last in Old Tucson in May where the natural mountain backdrop and recreated Western town could be used to best advantage. During four grueling days, cast and crew began each morning at 7 a.m., working through thirteen to twenty-seven set-ups before calling it quits twelve hours later. For the death scene of Billy Clanton, the group returned to Hollywood the night of the fourteenth, to resume shooting the next morning at the studio. Uris wrote Nathan from Israel that he had his "toes crossed in deadly fear that the Bobsey Twins . . . didn't fart up the end of the picture."

As Lancaster had made such a point of fixing the script and fighting with Sturges, one has to assume that his hair-slicked-down, dour, rather boring Earp was his deliberate choice. That Douglas does not steal the show as the much more interesting Holliday may have been the result of an implicit bargain: the two men would create an almost exactly even star weight by being completely different. When the movie opened at the end of May 1957, it was seen as a return to what the *New York Times* called "the old gambling, boozing, boasting shooting type of Western . . . not *High Noon*." There had not been such a dual star casting since Lancaster was teamed with Cooper three years earlier—and, indeed, *Gunfight at the O.K. Corral* featured a variation on the buddy love of *Vera Cruz*. Describing the thick relationship between the two main characters, *Time* claimed Lancaster "looks like a man who is heading for nothing better than the electric chair" when he has to leave Holliday and ride off to join the heroine.

Audiences flocked to see it, spending $5 million on the first release through the summer of 1957, and eventually shelling out $11 million. Some would later claim *Gunfight at the O.K. Corral* was the last truly popular Western: with the exception of *Airport*, it was Lancaster's last truly popular movie, his farewell to the glory days. Easy to overlook now is the fact that Earp goes after the Clantons as a strictly personal fight. Lancaster knew the significance of the shift in hero ethics when he suggested Earp wanted to *be* the amoral killer Holliday. He throws his badge on the ground at the end of the movie, marking another step across the all-American line between law and lawlessness, good guys and bad guys, myth and reality that he first danced across in *Vera Cruz*.

CHAPTER SEVEN

A Cookie Full of Arsenic

This is life. Get used to it.

—*Sweet Smell of Success*

In the wake of the *Marty* Oscars, HL set another lavish indie precedent by moving out of grubby quarters in the Key West studios on Santa Monica Boulevard and into new offices in the "Golden Triangle" of Beverly Hills at 202 Canon Drive, one block north of Wilshire Boulevard at the northeast intersection of Clifton Way. The two-story, stucco building was originally the office of the William Morris Agency and on either side of the front entrance door remained two bas-relief medallions, the classic masks of the theater: laughing comedy on the right and weeping tragedy on the left. "Hecht-Lancaster Productions is the largest and most important independent production organization in Hollywood," bragged its star/producer in 1956. "We're worth $25 million and have made five pictures including *Marty,* have ten pictures in work, employ thirty-five people and own our own building. In the ten pictures coming up I'll appear in only two."

The white wall-to-wall carpeting was so thick that Kamber claims Hecht lost several inches off his already short self when he stood on it. There was a barber on the premises for Lancaster to have a shave every morning; a manicurist was on call. An atrium full of hundreds of twittering canaries and finches in the double-story entrance foyer gave something for all the aspiring actors to look at while waiting to see casting director Max Arnow, whom Trilling had replaced at Warner Bros. in 1937. The $15,000 executive washroom had a purple velvet sofa, onyx fixtures, gold plumbing, and "HL" embroidered in real gold thread on special hand towels. Art work—Utrillo, Corot, El Greco—owned or rented, plastered the walls. Hecht bought a ninety-foot company yacht, the *Pursuit,* hung a Renoir in it, and hired Schiffer, an accomplished yachtsman, as West Coast director of publicity in charge of the yacht. He also ordered a black custom Cadillac station wagon, one of two in Hollywood, and took a pied-à-terre on Wilshire Boulevard for general corporate use. Publicist Joe Hyams briefly stayed there when he first came out from New York to work for the company and each day he was asked by the butler which outfit among his one blazer and two pair of pants he should "put out" for Mr. Hyams to wear. One employee thought the whole set-up "looked like a scene out of *Citizen Kane.*"

Lancaster, the raison d'être of all this mogul glamor, breezed down the office halls singing show tunes in his would-be opera voice, taking breaks to "go play" with Curtis. He took golf lessons from Hyams and got hooked, for life, on the game. A series of Rouault studies of circus acrobats hung on the walls of his office and an adjustable indoor waterfall gurgled in the background. If he got bored or did not want to listen to someone, he just turned the cascade's volume up to a roar. "It doesn't matter if we have $250,000 or $2,500,000," he told *Time* in September 1956. "The thing from now on is the fun of moviemaking."

On December 30, 1956, the day before *The Rainmaker* was to premiere, he called Hyams into his office. "Joesy," the publicist remembered him saying, "could you get the press over here?" Hyams asked what it was about so he could write something up in advance to hand out. "No," said Lancaster. "You don't have to write anything. I'll announce it when they get here." A few minutes later Hecht walked into Hyams's office. "You having a press conference?" he asked. "What's it about?" When Hyams said he didn't know, Hecht started in: "Don't lie to me!" Hyams replied, "I'm not lying to you. Go to your partner and ask him."

Several witnesses recall that Hecht's face turned white when Lancaster stood up to announce that, as of January 1, the name of the firm would be Hecht-Hill-Lancaster (HHL) with partner Jim Hill in charge of stories, writers, and scripts. Hecht did not blanch because he was surprised. *Time* had announced the previous September that Hill was slated to become partner in the top indie where everybody worked seven days a week, ten hours a day. The shock was rather a combination of Hecht's hope against hope that Lancaster would not insist upon elevating Hill and the knowledge that Lancaster had deliberately chosen to piggyback his announcement onto just the moment that meant the most to Hecht. Recalled Seltzer, "It was the cruelest thing Burt could have done."

The press was in fact already headed to Canon Drive to hear the news that what the *New York Times* called the "extraordinarily successful" independent production company of Hecht-Lancaster, after the "unusual good fortune of making a profit on each of the eleven movies they had produced" would now be making no less than nine pictures in the coming year at a projected cost of $25 million. This upgraded what *Variety* announced the previous April, midway through production on *Gunfight at the O.K. Corral* and just after the *Marty* Oscars, as the "largest independent motion picture deal in Hollywood history" between HL and UA: $40 million dollars over three years. The distribution percentage problem was solved by a special bonus provision, which Lancaster suggested. If the indie grossed a minimum of $45 million over the next three years and each picture broke even, UA would pay them $50,000 per each additional $1 million the pictures generated.

The niggling about overhead was scrapped. In exchange for covering HL's $5,000 weekly operating cost, UA expected the company to exercise more discipline over their productions, to plan better; if they did not, the cost came out of their own profits. If the indie went over budget on a given movie, as it did all the time, it would be liable for that amount.

A roster of projects was announced that was as ambitious as any in the industry: George Bernard Shaw's *The Devil's Disciple* with Laurence Olivier, to be directed by Alexander Mackendrick; *Separate Tables,* from a stage play by Terrence Rattigan, the British playwright who "ruled the West End" of London theater; *The Rabbit Trap* with a script by J.P. Miller from his own hit teleplay about a Long Island City construction worker's conflicts between his ethics and work; *Take a Giant Step,* a Broadway racial drama with an all-black cast. Other properties yet to be scripted and produced included Peter Viertel's *White Hunter, Black Heart,* to be made on location in Burma; *The Catbird Seat,* on the shelf since 1948, to be scripted by George Axelrod this time around; *The Ballad of Cat Ballou* from the novel by Roy Chandler; *The Hitchhiker* by George Simenon with Peter Brook as director; and Turgenev's *First Love* possibly starring Audrey Hepburn. Five million dollars alone was budgeted for *The Way West,* to star Lancaster, James Stewart, and "possibly" Gary Cooper; Odets would write the script from the Pulitzer Prize–winning novel by A.B. Guthrie Jr. For Irwin Shaw's novel *Lucy Crown,* the *New York Times* reported that HL had paid a "record price for pre-publication screen rights" of $400,000.

The company's overhead supported a number of innovations that sprouted up like vigorous signs of fresh, new growth. Sherlee Weingarten Lantz was hired in 1955 as the company's New York story editor to match former Alfred A. Knopf editor Bernard Smith, her West Coast counterpart. A former casting director for the Theater Guild who had worked closely with Eugene O'Neill, Lantz was installed in the UA headquarters at 729 Seventh Avenue with the job of persuading publishers who were, she recalls, "not very interested in movie deals" in the first place, to consider working with the maverick independent. In a neighboring office was Bernie Kamber, now elevated to head of publicity for HHL. Foreign publicity offices—some of them more hype than reality—were set up in London,

Paris, and the Far East, another indie first. UA, worried about yet another expensive new precedent, grumbled quietly.

As the profits from *Trapeze* poured in, actors were put under contract—Ernest Borgnine, Marty Milner, Sophia Loren, and others. After Borgnine sued for monies owed for loanouts plus his cut of *Marty*'s profits (he claimed the producers had skimmed off more than they should have before computing his share), and Loren backed out of her two-picture deal, Lancaster and Hecht restructured their boilerplate contract to include one outside option for every two HHL movies plus full payment to the actor for any loanout deals. Writers were similarly hired as in-house talent and along with two secretaries were given offices in another building behind the Canon Drive headquarters. At one time or another the script staff included Paddy Chayefsky, Clifford Odets, J.P. Miller, Ernest Lehman, John Gay, Phil Leacock, Julius Epstein, Roger MacDougal, and Ray Bradbury.

If the new modus operandi of the independents was what Arthur Mayer called "packaging"—star-driven alliances between actors, directors, producers, and writers—HHL, constantly guided by Wasserman, was showing the industry how. Behind the hoopla was a mission, the mature moviemaking that would now follow the firm's action-picture adolescence. It may well have been their ultimate downfall, but the fact that Lancaster and Hecht articulated a particular vision of what the movies needed in this transitional time reinforced their image—and bankability—as seeming prophets of a new celluloid age. "[S]omewhere in between Hollywood's so-called 'blockbuster' entertainment and the quickie-type melodramas and westerns," wrote Hecht in the *Hollywood Reporter* in 1955, "there lies what should be a fertile field." The great middle area was thought to be where "the classes and the masses are in step," where intelligent movies with an emotional heat cross over into art. These movies, he thought, should cost no more than $300,000, ensuring that they have a shot at earning back twice the movie's cost, at which point the picture's revenues move into profits (today, the multiple is over three times the production cost). It was a tantalizing concept that shimmers no less seductively almost half a century later. "Hecht-Lancaster never gave us crap," said Youngstein.

HHL came into being in a year that would be one of the worst ever in the movie business. After lurching from one technological innovation to another, clutching at blockbusters like *The Robe* or slice-of-life sleepers like *Marty*, the industry was stumped. More film was now being turned out for television than for theaters, with Lucille Ball and Desi Arnaz's Desilu Productions enjoying the stature of a major studio. The old cinemas continued to close, declining from 14,700 to 12,300 between 1954 and 1958. Drive-ins now accounted for about twenty-five percent of the studios' annual income.

Actors, studio personnel, secondary features, cartoons—all continued to be stripped back. Arthur Mayer, writing in *The Saturday Review* in April 1956, the same month UA and HL signed the $40 million contract renewal, declared that movie attendance had fallen from the immediate postwar peak of ninety million to a "probably still overestimated" sixty million.

Ezra Goodman, in his 1961 book, *The Fifty-Year Decline and Fall of Hollywood*, would blame the stars—"[t]he overpaid profiles"—and "their grasping agents," principally MCA, for having put a "stranglehold" on the industry. Though the public still hungered for new personalities and fan magazines had bigger circulations than ever, Hollywood was driven by a handful of megastars. "You either pay Cary Grant ten percent from the first dollar or you go without," lamented Mayer. One star was no longer enough to carry a film. Inspired by *Vera Cruz*, a blockbuster was now, by definition, a very expensive multistar package. Without foreign markets accounting for 50 percent of Hollywood's revenues, the movie business would have been a total disaster.

The national crisis of confidence produced by the Soviet launching of Sputnik only accelerated the tailspin. Beginning to emerge from the worst of the blacklist, the industry, Paul Jacobs claimed in May 1958, was in such tough shape that "if they thought they could turn a buck doing it, they might even hire Paul Robeson to sing in a musical written by Dalton Trumbo and produced by Adrian Scott," all "notorious" left-wing figures. "Majors Worth More Dead Than Alive," headlined *Daily Variety*.

Hecht and Lancaster's ability to buck the statistics, doom, and gloom seemed uncanny. In 1921 Hollywood had turned out 854 features; in 1955 the output was 324, of which one-third were produced by independents. During 1957, of 291 productions, 58 percent would be made by independents and half of those distributed by UA, whose cornerstone was Lancaster and his company. HL had set the standard of the new Hollywood, the dream of lucrative freedom. Its last five pictures had cost $7,343,000, marveled *Time*, and grossed $42 million.

So why Hill? asked a mystified Tinseltown. With a partner obsessed with being another Selznick, the forty-four-year-old Lancaster was in fact ripe for relief, escape. He now taunted his original partner as "the Mole" and Hecht's head sunk into his shoulders as if weathering a blast. Hecht even played into it, answering the phone, "Mole speaking." Lancaster's practical nature found the rented El Grecos, the Cadillac, and the yacht beside the point—or worse. "You dirty little Jew bastard," Miller recalled Lancaster yelling at Hecht at Canon Drive. "I ought to step on you and squash you like a fucking bug!" Half an hour later, they were both back at work, together: "[I]f you want to keep on working," Hecht told Chayefsky, "both of you need a short memory." As a peace offering, Lancaster once walked into his partner's art-filled office and presented him with a painting by Utrillo, carried under his arm like a newspaper.

Into this mix slipped the man Hyams described as "a guy who used to give you goosebumps without opening his mouth." Born in Indiana in 1916, the tall, good-looking, athletic Hill graduated from the University of Washington on scholarship, came to New York to work for NBC as a page boy, then shifted to MGM in Hollywood as a junior contract writer thanks to a connection with actor and screenwriter Frank Butler. He returned to the studio after World War II and managed to leverage relationships with people like writers Vincent Lawrence and Borden Chase into entrées to the next job. After being introduced to Roland Kibbee by mutual friend and screenwriter Guy Trosper, he was brought into Norma/HL. He and Lancaster barely overlapped during the crazy Fiji script drama of *His Majesty O'Keefe* and by his own account began to connect on *Apache,* then on *Vera Cruz,* and finally with his accompanying Lancaster to *The Kentuckian.* Actual script credits are tough to pin down. Hill insisted he disliked taking credit for his work and preferred ceding it to the other guy, thus artfully implying that he was essential to many productions. With Lancaster he recalled no particular effort: "He heard me talking story and it impressed him and he gradually came into my orbit. It was really my world he came into."

It was a strange world. In addition to heavy drinking—Hill was reportedly an alcoholic, as was Hecht—playing around with the truth was one of his favorite games. "Burt called me one of the great liars of all time," he said. "I said, 'That's true, Burt. I don't believe in telling the truth because the lie I'm about to tell is gonna create a little excitement and the truth won't create any.' " Hill was also a great charmer when he wanted to be— "He was so darling," said Lucy Kibbee. "You just wanted to kiss him"— and the charm was finely calculated. J.P. Miller recalled being challenged by Hill one day in his office to answer the question, "What's the biggest star you ever fucked?" Behind the carefully studied appearance of unconcern was an ace manipulator, what Youngstein called an Iago. "That was what he was all about," said Miller, who went on to write *Days of Wine and Roses.* "Anybody who was nobody he didn't want to shake hands with. Of all the people I've ever known in Hollywood, he was the champion starfucker."

A certain portion of Hollywood that was eager, always, to find Lancaster's Achilles' heel *and* figure out how a nonentity like Hill got elevated to partner in the top independent, assumed that the two men, already renowned as womanizers, had a bisexual relationship. Hill, with his fondness for the wild, unsettling lie that also pumped up his own power, may well have been a source of the speculation. Other titillating behavior reinforced the rumor mill. When Schiffer asked Lancaster why he always hired "homosexual personal secretaries," providing fodder for the gossip mongers, the star said, "They're the best. They protect you. I know they're out there telling their homosexual friends that we're having a big affair or something." Camping it up in front of the camera was another favorite tease Schiffer warned him against: "Jesus Christ," he would say, "don't do that. You're a big star. This is going to be misinterpreted." Lancaster ignored him.

While insiders like Seltzer, Schiffer, and Kamber didn't "put much stock" in the stories about Hill and Lancaster, and Curtis insisted "there's no way Burt would be homosexual—he only liked girls with big knockers and I learned that from him," there was a fascination of each for the other. "Whether active or not," said Miller, "Burt and Jim had a very strange physical relationship. I don't say they were homosexually involved or anything like that. . . . Burt lifted weights every morning and I would see Jim admiring him. If I came in, Jim would say to me, 'I bet you can't put that weight above your head.' It was like a hero-worship thing in the physical sense." Curtis chalked the bond up to a shared worldview: "They were both athletic Irishmen—they had the same soul, so to speak. They saw life, if not aggressively, a little more adventurously." To Kamber, Lancaster's adoption of a man "nobody really liked" was "the old underdog thing"—the same impulse that drove him to protect and remain loyal to Nick. But back in 1954, Waterbury had observed that Lancaster had a "perfectly open admiration" for phonys—if they were getting away with it.

The two men partied, drank, shared women in the swaggering Rat Pack mode of the time, and set each other off in childish escapades. On a seventeen-hour plane trip back to New York from the *Trapeze* shoot, Hill and Lancaster started roughhousing while passengers looked on, uncertain whether they were watching a real fight. When Lancaster slammed Hill against a seat, the backrest crashed down within inches of concert pianist Arthur Rubinstein (some accounts name Artur Schnabel) who cried out, "My hands!" as he snatched them free just in time.

Forty years later, people are still careful to distance themselves from what Miller called "those parties." "Hecht tried to get me to come," he said. "I was told in roundabout ways that all kinds of interesting things were going on—interesting if you liked that sort of thing." Miller made it clear he was not interested in what were portrayed as "extremely complicated bisexual relationships" and was left alone. Curtis recalled that he "appreciated" the fact that he was not approached to participate in the antics of Hecht and Hill in Paris. One HHL employee, while vacationing with his wife in Palm Springs, was approached by Hecht and Hill, who had come to entice him with "some scheme" involving a quick trip to Mexico with them and two women. He never found out exactly what they had in mind or why he seemed a likely player.

The homophobic FBI kept track of Lancaster's supposed sexual history. An informant in the bureau's New York office reported in November 1955 that he had seen Lancaster at "parties at the home of a wealthy homosexual." In April 1956, the Office of Naval Intelligence received a "signed statement from a sailor who had deserted" who claimed he had attended several "homosexual parties" in Beverly Hills and that he had seen Lancaster at one of them. At the end of the decade, under the heading "Hollywood Vice," a report was filed detailing a raid conducted in January 1960 by the "combined forces" of LAPD vice officers and the Office of Naval Intelligence on the home of a "millionaire dillitante [*sic*] who frequents the Hollywood night spots and is a notorious homosexual." Behind his mansion "surrounded by a high wire fence and guarded with a $10,000 electric alarm and shocking system," were organized, claimed the report, "large-scale homosexual orgies . . . at which guests were required to register their names and at which many of them were surreptitiously photographed." Files of guests' names were confiscated with the result that "many prominent individuals" were revealed "as apparently participants in these orgies," including Rock Hudson and Lancaster. The military was called in because, in addition to an unnamed fleet admiral, there were reportedly about fifty marines involved from the Twenty-nine Palms Marine base east of Los Angeles, all from the First 75th AAA Battalion, and "some 200" marines from Camp Pendleton. The report suggested that many of these soldiers might be "opportunists" rather than "actual homosexuals."

Norma "hated" Hill, assuming he was the person who got her husband women and maybe more. But, as Kamber and many others have affirmed, "Burt didn't need anybody to get him anybody." Like Schiffer on *Ten Tall Men*, Hill found that although women naturally gravitated to the star, they often ended up with him instead. When asked how he could trust "his women" when he was with the much more handsome Lancaster, Hill said he always replied that his friend's taste in women was so bad, there was nothing to worry about. "When I think of the dames he sorta liked—that terrible broad that wrote a book about him, Winters, and that Mexican, Katy Jurado . . . ," he said, "Burt certainly wasn't a ladies' man. Unless they wanted to do what he said to do, whatever it might be. I don't think women just meant very much to him, that's all. Occasionally he'd run into somebody like Anita Ekberg who thought he was God Almighty, but they never lasted. That's why I didn't mind using him because I knew it didn't make that much difference to him."

That he played such destructive games with the enterprise he had worked so hard to create is indicative of the corrosive effect that ten years of Hollywood had had on Lancaster. If Hill was a spoiler, ready to plant artful seeds of doubt that grew to choke the zest and energy of the indie, Lancaster was ready to be spoiled. "Burt was still going through a transitional phase at that time," said Youngstein, aware, as the UA executive in closest rapport with HHL, that he was watching a serious threat to his company's crown jewel. "He could be influenced if you vaselined him—that's a gutter way of explaining it—with enough compliments. Hill did that."

Lancaster's rages, promiscuity, and mood swings suggest some kind of conflict or confusion about sexual identity, at least. Odets eventually decided there was not one Lancaster but at least seven: Inscrutable Burt who, even when he was there seemed not to be; Cocky Burt, utterly confident and maybe contemptuous; Wild Man Burt, with an overpowering voltage of energy and enthusiasm; Big Daddy Burt, the paternal caregiver who took over when weaker persons needed him; Monster Golem Burt who could instantly transform into a cruelty machine; "Marquis de Lancaster" Burt, the grand old courtier of precious gestures and mincing words, a caricature of nobility; and, juggling life with grace and mischief and laughter, Hustler Burt, the con man who revealed nothing to no one. "Burt," said Hill, "was like a clam."

In July 1957, barely a month after his Wyatt Earp received "socko" and "whopping" raves, UA went public. Buying out first Chaplin then Pickford, it was the last so-called major to step up to Wall Street, the corporate offering a signal of the company's remarkable success in a foundering industry. At the peak of his own remarkable success, hoping his bait-and-switch career rhythm would allow the mythic power of Earp to carry his fans over to try a very different movie, Lancaster opened during the July 4 holiday in *Sweet Smell of Success.*

Half a century later, it is for many *the* hip American movie. A swan song to *noir,* the gleefully cynical exposé of the sleazy link between celebrity and the press, between naked ambition and corrupting success, stands in stark contrast to the musicals and biblicals of 1950s Hollywood. Martin Scorsese's *Mean Streets* and *Taxi Driver* are said to have been inspired by the movie's vicious urban rhythms and hyperkinetic camera moves. In Barry Levinson's *Diner,* a character obsessively spouts chunks of its acid dialogue ("I'd like to take a bite out of you. You're a cookie full of arsenic."); Dustin Hoffman wanders in on his brother's lovemaking in Levinson's *Rain Man,* to stare, transfixed, at a scene from *Sweet Smell* playing on TV. "This is a feel-

bad movie," exulted Curtis. When it flopped, the unique apparatus clustered around Lancaster took its first big fall. A signal went out to the industry: independent production, no matter how big the star, has its limits.

As for the movie itself, the story behind the story begins at the end of the 1930s, when Ernest Lehman, a slight, witty man with a sudden smile, found himself working for the celebrity press agent Irving Hoffman in Manhattan and playing into a nocturnal Broadway underworld of nightclubs, cigarette girls, brutal cops, and the treacherous innuendo of celebrity gossip. Repelled and fascinated, Lehman serviced powerful columnists of the time like Winchell with gossip "items"—real or fabricated—in exchange for "mentions" of his clients in the columns.

His original story, published as a novelette in *Cosmopolitan* in 1950, posited the ultimate trade-off. Press agent Sidney Falco is asked to do a dirty deed for the Winchell-type columnist J.J. Hunsecker that will be both his ticket to success and his sentence to moral perdition. He must wreck a romance between J.J.'s kid sister, Susie, and a young jazz musician by framing him on a drugs charge, thereby setting him up for a brutal beating by a corrupt cop beholden to J.J. If Sidney can pull it off, he gets to write Hunsecker's nationally syndicated column. There is a total disregard for useless guilt. With a string of sexually loaded plot twists and the real-life Winchell an enthusiastic Red-baiter still too influential to cross, no producer—let alone the censors—would touch it, except for Hecht, who immediately saw the lurid potential. But Lehman did not want "the risk of having my story done by these people who did pirate pictures."

Time passed and HL, big UA contract in hand, *Marty* and *Trapeze* two huge hits, was on the verge of becoming HHL. Lehman, coming off *Sabrina* and heading into *The King and I*, one of the hottest screenwriters in Hollywood, decided to take a chance. He began work on *Sweet Smell of Success* in the early months of 1956 with himself as writer and director, only to be told by HL that UA was too nervous with a first-time director. "But you never knew with these guys," he said. The indie was known for hiring top talent, then mistrusting its own good judgment and backing off.

He was renamed writer-producer and one morning, sitting at the typewriter, was approached by Hill who told him to put a fresh sheet of paper in the machine and write a fulsome note to go with the three dozen roses he had just ordered for Barbara Nichols, the actress who was being considered to play Rita, Falco's cigarette girl and sometime lover. Why? asked Lehman, only to be told a long tale, the gist of which was that after interviewing, wining, dining, and sleeping with Nichols and telling her he loved her, Hill had left her apartment at 2 a.m., met another woman from the same building walking her dog outside on the sidewalk, come back with her into her apartment and into her bed. Suddenly Nichols, a friend of the woman, showed up ready to have a girl-talk visit in the middle of the night, saw Hill, and got "hysterical." " 'If you want her in this picture,' " Lehman recalled Hill telling him, " 'you'd better write this note.' " The screenwriter, feeling like he was trapped in his own screenplay, crafted what he calls a "terrific" billet-doux.

Alexander Mackendrick took over as director. A tall Briton with a bemused look of irony playing over his face, he had been brought over by HL in 1956 from the newly defunct Ealing Studios in England. But the director of the brilliant Alec Guinness comedies *The Man in the White Suit* and *The Ladykillers* discovered that the "extraordinarily ruthless producers" of Hollywood were not his Anglo cup of tea. Advised by Elizabeth Taylor and Montgomery Clift to avoid working with the boys—"monsters," the two actors called them—and warned by Lehman that "Lancaster chews directors alive," Mackendrick wanted to go home. The indie reminded him that he was under contract and assigned him to *Sweet Smell.*

UA immediately upped the ante after Lancaster, lying on a Canon Drive sofa listening to a discussion about casting Hunsecker—Orson Welles was one possibility—said, "How about me?" He started weighing in with his interpretation of the script and one day, looking across the table at Lehman, who had taken to clutching his stomach during the endless story conferences so maddeningly typical of HL, mused, "Someday we'll all be standing around Ernie's grave and there'll be a stomach tree growing out of it." When the screenwriter was ordered by his doctor to get on a slow boat to Tahiti to unkink a tension-induced spastic colon the size of a fist, Lancaster said, "Gee, Ernie, I hope we're not the cause of this," his big arm around the much smaller Lehman's shoulder as he left. A uniquely observant and articulate fly on the HHL wall, the writer left loathing Hecht and Hill, but liking the "kindliness" and "warmth" of Lancaster.

The usual production chaos was in full play—no script, no schedule, no budget to speak of—as Hill replaced Lehman as producer. Odets stepped in as screenwriter, an aging, elfin, somewhat pathetic has-been reduced, Curtis recalled, to selling paintings from his collection to make ends meet. He had not had a full screen credit in ten years, "a symbol," said Lehman, "of Hollywood corrupting artists, of the man who had sold out." He was also revered by virtually everyone involved with *Sweet Smell* as a once-great writer who was now their very own under-contract genius.

Believing success to be the "peritonitis of the soul," Odets took to this Manhattan melodrama with the bittersweet passion of a once-great New Yorker and proceeded to deconstruct the language. "Odets came in to clarify scenes," said Curtis, "so the dialogue fit them, like a custom-made suit.

He wasn't allowed to touch Ernie's structure." (Many of Lehman's lines survived, however: "Suppose I give you a *lovely* reason. . . ."; "I was too busy laughing, no, make that *screaming*. . . .") The result was dialectic interactions and sexually charged dialogue made up of some of the most crackerjack language in American movies.

With temperatures averaging well below freezing, the exteriors were shot on location in New York from late December 1956 into January 1957 with James "Jimmy" Wong Howe as cinematographer. Lancaster brought the great artist of black-and-white film to the production because he liked his work on *Come Back, Little Sheba* and *The Rose Tattoo*. Back on his old glory ground, Odets went into an emotional tailspin (John Turturro would act out a version of Odetsian angst in *Barton Fink*). Staying in the Essex House on Central Park South with the rest of the principals, he insisted that Mackendrick, who had been given a better room at the front of the hotel, switch with him. Then he began to obsess about the light coming in through the window and blotted it out with curtains so he could sleep all day, work all night, and slip the pages under his door to Mackendrick at dawn. Mackendrick slept from dawn to midday after which, he said, "we cut the pages by half—Clifford never noticed—right on the floor, with the actors, for shooting at seven, eight o'clock that night."

Because no one could yet agree on an ending, the script-in-flux had to be, within the limitations of each location, shot in continuity. In December the Motion Picture Production Code, originally drafted by a group of Catholic clergy and laymen in 1930, was liberalized for the first time. Pages of the *Sweet Smell* script flew back and forth between the coasts, the provocative plot and raw language pushing just about every button of the new Code. "Sidney's use of the word 'spic' is a specific violation," advised the censors; Rita was to be played as a "crushed" woman; Kello, the sadistic cop played by Emile Meyer, must be portrayed, somehow, as a "disgrace to the force." All of this was ignored.

The New York shoot was done at night, all night. Using real-life locations such as the Palace Theater, the Brill Building, Tin Pan Alley, and Duffy Square, the filming frequently collided with the nighttime Manhattan swirling around it. Mackendrick insisted that every scene begin and end out on the sidewalk so that the audience would never forget that this movie was about a city. Much of the fluidity and speed comes from his labyrinthine, claustrophobic use—often in dizzying multiples—of doorways and entrances. For certain scenes, Howe used the fifteen minutes of dawn and dusk to get a very particular light-in-the-dark. "A twelve-to-fourteen-hour day," said Curtis, "and you got two scenes. You can see the pressure that was put on that movie." Standing over Lancaster with a spotlight aimed to create the malevolent skull shadows over his face, Howe rubbed Hunsecker's black-framed prop spectacles with a dab of Vaseline to distort the star's eyes and disorient him, producing a more baleful stare.

Marty Milner, the fresh-faced Midwesterner cast in his breakout role as the young jazz guitarist in love with Susie, "never quite connected," he said, with Mackendrick and took direction from Lancaster, who had brought him to the production from *Gunfight at the O.K. Corral.* Slipping happily through the shoals, Curtis thrived on the tension, getting so smooth on the first take Mackendrick had to suggest obstacles, unexpected moves, to slow him down. Feeding lines to Odets, Curtis became Falco. "Look at the way Sidney looked," he said. "So . . . *perfect.* Good-looking, lean, silk shirts, tapered trousers. Couldn't get out of that environment. He's there forever."

Used to careful rehearsal and elaborate, even elegant, storyboards, Mackendrick found himself caught in the mid-Manhattan rush hour "at the mercy of the material." Lancaster stepped into the gap as the rival director, challenging Mackendrick's interpretation of how the movie should look and feel. Manhattan was his town. The script came out of his mouth like his own words punched black and blue. If *Trapeze* was his ode to the circus, *Sweet Smell of Success* was his loving screed to the city that had made him, and was no less passionate for being utterly cynical. He would out-Hellinger Hellinger.

"[Sandy] was like a mad professor who worked in a world of his own," Lancaster later said. "No matter what you did, no matter how good it really was, it wasn't good enough. He was always reaching for that extra dimension that was beyond anyone's grasp." The star's own madness grew as the shoot progressed. Like an evil mutant of his Crimson Pirate, J.J. is the movie *monstre sacré* made flesh, the star in control not only of the work but pushing the whole industry. "Look at the way J.J. operates in that movie," said Curtis. "He has to manipulate and control everybody. Don't you think that was a little reflection of the making of the film? Burt was a guy trying to hold on to all his own faculties and slowly he's losing it. And that's what happens when someone has an important fix on a movie and it ends up in the hands of someone else. I know Burt felt that way. He wanted to direct that movie. And he was an important producer, he didn't lay back. More than anyone else, he had an idea of this picture. He could have taken it in any direction."

The interiors of the script with no ending were shot, with a couple of exceptions, from February through March on Stage 8 of the Goldwyn Studios. Howe and long-time HHL art director Edward Carrere, who later won an Oscar for his work on *Camelot,* re-created the "21" Club and Toots Shor's nightclub on sets built two feet off the floor to accommodate the spewing smoke pots and with walls washed with oil to give them a slimy sheen. With such meticulous attention to detail for the look, sound, and feel of the movie, no one seemed to be tending to the big picture. UA began to watch the project more closely.

In late February, the production ground to a halt. Three times Odets was ordered to rewrite the climax scene in Hunsecker's apartment at the top of the Brill Building in which Susie Hunsecker, played by eighteen-year-old unknown Susan Harrison, wise at last to what J.J. and Sidney have been doing to her, manipulates Sidney into a violent confrontation with her brother. This was the big, obligatory star finale between Lancaster and Curtis, but without giving some power to the woman there was no scene. If she left before the men fought, what were they fighting about? If she left afterward, she stole their scene. "Nobody then in America," said Mackendrick, "could see strength coming from the woman." The constant tension erupted one night in Hill's office at Canon Drive. "It was a late-night session," said Mackendrick. "We'd been drinking a little. Burt started shouting at me—and he's scary. Then he came at me across the room with that coiled-spring animal energy, like a panther, and vaulted over a sofa in one of the most graceful movements I've ever seen, [as if] to attack me. I stood up and said, 'No, Burt,' and he stopped. That took every atom of performance possible. The reason I had that strength was that just as he came across the sofa I thought, 'He's *beautiful!*' "

Mackendrick was tipped off by the movie's editor, Alan Crosland, that HHL was going to wait until the end of shooting, dismiss Mackendrick, and cut the picture themselves with the big star scene coming after the girl leaves. "I became devious, as a director has to be," said Mackendrick, "and decided to shoot it so it could be cut in two versions; Tony's departure could be spliced in either before or after the girl leaves Hunsecker. And I shot the whole thing with a moving camera, which makes it much harder to cut. I wanted to be sure they couldn't massacre the scene."

Because Lancaster was, Mackendrick recognized, "very good on staging," he kept making changes in moves midscene that messed up the director's secret plan. "What the fuck are you doing?" said Lancaster one day, sneaking up behind the director who was hidden behind a flat, frantically reworking the intricate pattern of tape marks. "So I confessed," said Mackendrick. "Burt laughed and said, 'You're out of your mind. You don't know how the movie business works. The last shoot-out has to be between the two stars and that's it!'" Mackendrick asked Hecht if he could stay on at his own expense and sit in on the cutting. Hecht agreed but said, "We'll do what we want with it." When the rough cut was run, it was clear that the producers' version did not work. "Then they ran it my way," said Mackendrick, "and there was a *delicious* silence. It worked. The girl delivered the

"Bear with me," Lancaster asked his audience as he began to break out of his star mold, taking "stretch parts" like the alcoholic Doc Delaney in *Come Back, Little Sheba* (1952).

The real *From Here to Eternity* scene #106—"the beach scene"—as cut by the censors: Deborah Kerr and Lancaster, just left of the Halona Blowhole at the eastern end of Oahu, 1953

Sergeant Warden—*Time*'s "man among men"—rallies the troops on December 7, 1941, in *From Here to Eternity* (1953).

Norma, daughter Susan, and Burt in the village of Goloa on the island of Viti Levu in the Fiji Islands, during the filming of Norma Productions's escapist yarn *His Majesty O'Keefe*, in 1953. Lancaster remembered the first ten years of his marriage to Norma as "very, very happy."

Blue-eyed Massai, the last Apache still on the warpath after the surrender of Geronimo. *Apache* (1954) was the first project of the newly named Hecht-Lancaster with United Artists—the union marked a major creative regrouping amid the deconstructing chaos of postwar Hollywood.

Lancaster and the Coop—Gary Cooper—as odd-couple buddies in quest of gold in Hecht-Lancaster's *Vera Cruz* (1954)

Goes upstairs to wash up . . . shaves . . . dresses . . . and as . . . you're convinced he won . . . he falls on his face dead

A 1955 *MAD* Magazine spoof of the final shootout scene in *Vera Cruz* (1954), with Lancaster as "Burt Lambaster"

Lancaster directed himself in *The Kentuckian* in 1954. While he was on location, Thomas Hart Benton painted him in his role as the New World New Man.

A gala circus parade down the Champs-Elysées in Paris, 1955, before the start of the *Trapeze* (1956) shoot at the Cirque d'Hiver. From left: Tony Curtis, Katy Jurado, Gina Lollobrigida, Lancaster

For *Life* magazine in 1955, cartoonist Al Hirschfeld contrasted the old Hollywood (studio mogul surrounded by sycophants) with this, the new "talent take-over" industry. Lancaster is now waited on by the once-powerful studio boss.

Gunfight at the O.K. Corral (1957). From left: Kirk Douglas, Lancaster, John Hudson, DeForest Kelley

It took four days in 1956 to film the movie version of a shootout that lasted barely thirty seconds in 1881. This layout is attributed to the director, John Sturges.

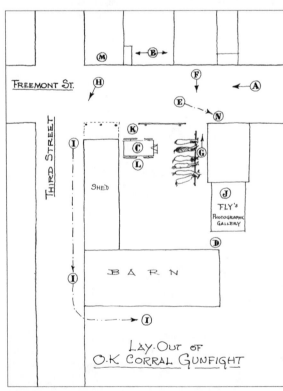

FREEMONT ST.

THIRD STREET

SHED

BARN

FLY'S PHOTOGRAPHIC GALLERY

LAY·OUT OF O·K CORRAL GUNFIGHT

"Match me, Sidney,"
Lancaster's command to
Tony Curtis in *Sweet Smell
of Success* (1957), became
a catchphrase.

James Hill, Lancaster, and
Harold Hecht—Hecht-
Hill-Lancaster—in New
York at their peak, 1957.
HHL brought Terence
Rattigan's *Separate Tables*
from London to New York
and then made the Oscar-
winning movie version
in 1958.

"Burt's Bouncing Brood" on the deck
of the SS *United States* ocean liner at
Southhampton, England, July 2, 1958:
Lancaster; Jimmy, 12; Billy, 10; Susan, 9;
Joanna, 7; and Sighle, 4

Newlyweds James Hill and Rita
Hayworth in England for the filming
of *The Devil's Disciple* (1959). The
bandage over Hill's eye was blamed
on a "fall," but later accounts told of
a fight during which Hayworth hit
him with a telephone.

final coup de grace." The director who later called the auteur theory "rot" had saved the film.

After the first preview at the United Artists theater in San Francisco in June, Lancaster scooped Odets into a delighted bear hug and waltzed him around the lobby floor. Hecht, certain he had a financial disaster on his hands, stood in a corner whispering, "I hate, hate, hate this picture!" The director, confident going into the screening that he had played the salacious script "fast and high" enough for the audience, observed something quite different from what he expected. "The effect of *Sweet Smell* on the people sitting in front of me was like dripping lemon on an oyster," he said. "They cringed with the body language of folding arms, crossing legs, shrinking from the screen."

The sordid slice of life alienated just about everyone and was savaged as a "lip-smacking peep show" by the heartland press. Lehman remembers one preview card which read: "Don't touch a foot of this film. Burn the whole thing." Opening in a problematic market and competing with fluff movies like *Tammy and the Bachelor, Sweet Smell of Success,* despite being named one of the best movies of 1957 by *Time,* was a box-office failure. To the *Marty*-obsessed industry the movie represented a lot of things, principally what happens when a $600,000 labor of love balloons into a $2.6 (maybe $3.4) million disaster, of which $300,000 alone went to Odets for the script.

Recriminations flew like shrapnel. "You didn't have to go to Tahiti," Lancaster said to Lehman at a postpremiere party at the HHL Wilshire Boulevard apartment. ". . . I oughta punch you in the jaw." "Go ahead," replied Lehman, "I need the money." Hecht blamed Hill, telling him he had destroyed the company with its first big expensive flop. Youngstein noticed a distinct falling off of energy at HHL after *Sweet Smell* and he concurred with Hecht on who was responsible for what one player called "the most outrageously incompetent of any production I have been involved in." Hill was pleasantly cavalier: "You make the movie you have to make. Whether the audience likes it or not is another story."

Of course, if *Sweet Smell* had been a success, Hill would have been a genius producer. The real reason the movie failed was what one reviewer called the "shock casting." The audience could not stomach two major stars playing such venal characters. If Curtis's brilliant performance set his career in the direction of Billy Wilder's *Some Like It Hot,* Lancaster took the bigger risk: if his star persona could not die in *Apache,* it certainly could not be Hunsecker and hope to survive in the same league as Stewart, Peck, and Cooper. "Stars have a persona that stays the same, therefore they must be uninteresting monoliths that never change," said Mackendrick. "Burt was better than a star. He had a moral courage at playing roles that are quite against any star image."

But for Lancaster, who persisted in the populist belief, throughout a career of risky experiments, that a movie's financial success was a proof that it had "communicated," the box-office failure of *Sweet Smell of Success* was a huge disappointment. The black hole of antistardom was dark indeed.

The movie as good as finished Odets. Two years before his death in 1961, at the age of fifty-seven, he recorded in his diary a dream he had been having all week. He is playing a game with Hill, Lancaster, and Hecht of dice and dominoes, three to a hand. When he finds he can't throw or grasp all three, he switches to two dice but still keeps losing. "Then I go over to a baby pig," he wrote, "and cut strips of fat off its face and eat them. The pig is waiting till the layers get lower to eat some of its own fat off its own face!"

CHAPTER EIGHT

The Fall

I bought a boat for the company—eighty-five feet—for $39,000.
I put $120,000 into it and sold it for $35,000.
That's Hecht-Hill-Lancaster!

—Robert Schiffer, director of publicity, Hecht-Hill-Lancaster

While financial and administrative problems would destroy HHL, its choice of material only hastened the demise. Seeking a surefire commercial hit, the company took on *Run Silent, Run Deep,* a World War II submarine tale set in the Pacific one year after Pearl Harbor, directed by Robert Wise. The momentum is highly abstract, strategic, its real tension seeping in, like the vast ocean around the sub, from the Cold War anxiety pervading the planet. Clark Gable's aging Commander Richardson is on a mission to sink a Japanese destroyer with an audacious torpedo technique involving a thirty-two-second bow shot followed by a quick *Dive! Dive!* maneuver executed by a crew that included a young Don Rickles. Lancaster plays the lieutenant, Jim Bledsoe, and his *From Here to Eternity* Warden-like form fills the claustrophobically accurate sub dimensions mandated by Wise, slipping through the corridors and hatch doors as if in an underwater ballet. After constant script battles, the decision by Lancaster and Hill to cut the picture themselves prompted Wise to quit; when it was released, the movie Crowther called "all-male and all-submarine" made only a ripple at the box office. The indie that could do no wrong was continuing to sink.

One of the males patrolling the movie's Bungo Straits was Nick Cravat. He had branched off on his own for a while, appearing in movies like *Veils of Bagdad* and *King Richard and the Crusaders;* marrying Ceil Brink, the mother of his daughters in 1959, after the death of his wife, Adele; and nursing grudges that he should have made more money from his swashbuckler costar roles and gotten the Curtis part in *Trapeze.* The rift was finally healed, but one of the pair had ended up a star and the other never would be. Lancaster told J.P. Miller that Nick had a job "forever" and the screenwriter thought, "Whatever this guy's other dimensions may be, he's a solid human being, he's a real man." All the more when Lancaster, laughing, said, "I just got a call from Nick. He really laid me out: 'Where the hell is my check?' "

While Hollywood retrenched, HHL announced it would be producing twelve movies in 1958 at a total cost of $25 million. Two of the most ambitious were *The Unforgiven*, from a Western novel by Alan LeMay, and *The Summer of the Seventeenth Doll*, an Australian play currently the Laurence Olivier–directed hit of the London season. At least three of the twelve, reported *Variety*, would be holdovers from the earlier $25-million UA deal of the year before, with "no mention" of all the other previously announced projects.

Falling in step with the cost-conscious antiblockbuster mood, HHL also announced a new program of four "modest budget" $500,000 features to be produced by Harry Kleiner, who would write the 1968 Steve McQueen cop thriller, *Bullitt*. In February 1958, *Variety* reported that "the leading indie theatrical film outfit" was now branching into television with four series planned, each based on one of the company's features—*Vera Cruz, Apache, His Majesty O'Keefe*, and *Bachelor Party*. "This TV is big," enthused Lancaster. "We want to get our feet wet." Nat Perrin, who had a long Hollywood history as a writer for the Marx Brothers and other comedians, was hired to head the TV division (he would produce "The Addams Family" in the 1960s for ABC-TV). And, if "the boys" could sign French bombshell Brigitte Bardot—"exceedingly interested," wrote HHL's Paris publicity rep, Marc Spiegel, to Hecht, "in a film co-starring Burt"—who was also coveted by Selznick, MGM, and Fox after her role in . . . *And God Created Woman*, that would prove HHL was right up there with the majors. The company's plans, said the *Los Angeles Times*, "are enormous."

The one project the company was actually shooting, under the direction of Delbert Mann on Goldwyn Studios' Stage 5, was *Separate Tables*. The black-and-white, highly artificial British drama reeked with the repressed desires of fake majors, spinster daughters, drunk Americans, and aging beauties cooped up in a Bournemouth hotel and gave Lancaster the opportunity to debut his new, dour, "mature" screen image. He and Hecht had brought to Broadway the Terence Rattigan stage play from London starring Margaret Leighton and Eric Portman, which featured the theatrical trick of two actors playing four roles. When UA and HHL decided that a movie version would be more marketable with *four* stars, including Lancaster and Rita Hayworth, Laurence Olivier, who was both to direct and costar with his wife Vivien Leigh, quit. Rattigan floundered, making the necessary adjustments to the script, and then turned down, *Variety* reported, a $600,000 HHL contract for four screenplays over seven years with the right to choose his own stories. The playwright had had enough of Hollywood parties, "interminable [HHL] story conferences," and the industry's use of tranquillizers—"little pills that keep you working by keeping your temper."

The decision to create two more roles was, in part, a result of Hill's ambition to showcase in a breakthrough "serious" role—and thereby woo—his newest love interest, Hayworth. Schiffer had befriended the star while doing her makeup for *The Loves of Carmen* and *The Lady from Shanghai* and introduced her to Hill at a New Year's party just after Hill was made partner (Hill claimed he "used" Lancaster to set them up earlier). Hill was on his way up, Hayworth well on her way down, and they intersected in what would be a sad, exploitative relationship. She was still, barely, Gilda, the beautiful, auburn-haired dancing star of the 1946 movie of the same name, the famous pin-up girl poised on the bed. Now, the ex-wife of four husbands, including Orson Welles, she was facing her fortieth birthday a sad, confused woman, easily crushed, drinking too much. Hill believed she had a performance potential that had never been explored. He would be her Svengali.

Replacing Olivier, Mann was initially apprehensive about directing such an English effort packed with what Sheridan Morley has called "the last great stand of the Hollywood English"—Gladys Cooper, Cathleen Nesbit, Wendy Hiller, and Felix Aylmer, with Deborah Kerr and David Niven as the other star pair. He was allowed by Hecht to rehearse for three weeks with the entire cast, all on salary, with a catered lunch served each day by the Brown Derby restaurant.

When shooting began, egged on by Hill's "sniggering on the sidelines," said Mann, Lancaster began to taunt Hiller with crude jokes. The cool, passionate British stage actress and screen star of the 1937 movie version of Shaw's *Pygmalion* "just withdrew," recalled the director, "pulled herself within and didn't respond to them like a true lady." Hayworth was intimidated not only by her costars (Cooper reportedly fell asleep and snored during the Hayworth/Lancaster scenes), but also by her part as Lancaster's aging ex-wife. "Rita was scared of it," Mann recalled. "I know that the role spoke to some of her own fears of growing old and lonely and alone." When Lancaster wrenches her head up to the light so as to see the wrinkles better in their big scene together, it is a cruel movie moment.

As the production moved closer to the climactic scene of the movie, the mood grew tense. Niven's Major Pollack, now exposed as a creepy fondler of women at the "local cinema," must enter the hotel dining room full of separate tables at which sit his fellow residents, his countrymen, his jury.

Normally so funny—Mann still remembers how his stomach ached with laughter listening to his stories—Niven was facing the role of his career, a brave portrayal of the underside of his own culture's jaunty cheerio! mask.

At the same time, Lancaster and Hill began to use their power—"[Burt's] authority was one of the devastating things about that picture," said the movie's editor, Marjorie Fowler—to ensure that there was more and more footage of the parallel plot involving the two American stars. Lancaster and Hill took over the editing from Mann, Hecht, and Fowler, snipping out more of Kerr's early scenes. When a cheesy theme song, "Separate Tables," was added to what Mann called the "astringent score" of David Raskin without the director's knowledge, Mann told his agent, "Get me out of my Hecht-Hill-Lancaster contract. I will never work for them again."

Separate Tables won Oscars for Niven and Hiller and five other nominations—for Kerr, for cinematographer Charles Lang, for Raskin, for Rattigan's and John Gay's screenplay, and for best picture. Of Lancaster's earnest performance, what remains in the mind are the *un*conscious bits of business: a couple of quick studies in how to light, inhale, and settle into smoking a cigarette; his fluid grace as he pulls on a raincoat while walking across the hotel lobby.

The movie's critical success seemed to give HHL a brief, bright reprieve from its doldrums but was in fact the indie's blue-chip farewell. A short while later, Mann heard Hill boasting at a big party at Hecht's Beverly Hills home with "everyone reasonably drunk" that he was going to replace Hecht. The firm would become Hill-Lancaster. J.P. Miller heard the same claim. When Mann got home he telephoned Hecht to warn him. "Oh, Del," said Hecht, "don't say things like that." While *Separate Tables* was shooting in Hollywood, Hecht took Sherlee Lantz out to lunch at the St. Regis Hotel in New York and told her HHL was shutting down her story office because of "financial difficulties." When she inquired further, he said "I can't!," burst into tears and left, leaving her at the table with "a very big check."

What Siodmak had called Hecht's "amateur exuberance" was now hysterical frenzy with too many projects, the brunt borne by HHL employees who swapped "how to kill Harold" stories. Lehman recalled that the producer was "inebriated" most of the time. He had also been stuck since 1948 in a miserable marriage to Gloria Buzzell, twenty years his junior and niece of director Eddie Buzzell. Three children later, the couple provided observers with lots of Hollywood stories. One HHL employee, ordered to tail Mrs. Hecht in her husband's Cadillac station wagon for a day to see if she was up to anything suspicious, reminded Hecht that the car was one of only two such cars in Los Angeles, which might make *her* suspicious. The producer insisted anyway. Odets noted in his diary in early 1958 that Gloria Hecht, "tight [tipsy]," confided to him one night at 3 a.m. as he escorted her home that her husband locked his door against her.

On February 2, 1958, Hill and Hayworth were married, adding a third improbable ménage to the partnership. Hecht threw a big party for the couple at Romanoff's that Lancaster did not attend because he was playing golf with Norma in Palm Springs. By the time the Lancasters returned the week after the wedding, Hill had already temporarily moved out of the newlywed house at 914 Hartford Drive, behind the Beverly Hills Hotel, and into the company apartment.

HHL's true situation was known only to close insiders in its tenth anniversary year of 1958. But its unprecedented success caught the attention of a foundering studio, once the biggest, richest, most fabulous home of "more stars than there are in the heavens," MGM. In 1957 the major showed a loss for the first time, going almost half a million dollars into the red. After Joseph Vogel, the president of the parent company, Loew's, Inc., ousted studio head Dore Schary in 1956, the studio operated without a leader while Vogel battled both the board of Loew's and the studio's founding mogul, Louis B. Mayer, now angling to reassume control.

MGM's problems were seen as epitomizing Hollywood's "economic revolution" and it was a measure of how far HHL had come that Vogel turned to the independent as the solution. The courtship began in June 1957 when the *New York Times* reported both a "possible production-distribution alignment" of MGM and HHL and the fact that Wasserman was in New York for talks with Vogel to clarify the numbers of pictures to be involved. Another point of discussion, according to the *Times*, was MGM's desire to cast Lancaster, as part of the deal, in what Gore Vidal called "the biggest role there is in town"—Ben-Hur. On July 10, *Variety* reported that MGM would release *The Devil's Disciple*, star Lancaster in *Ben-Hur*, and back an as yet undefined number of the "heavy backlog" of HHL properties; UA, "which reportedly does not feel miffed," would "of course" recoup its investment in all those scripts and stories.

The Loew's board, half of them fiercely anti-Vogel anyway, passed on the idea of letting this trio who made movies like *Sweet Smell of Success* and *Marty* take over the studio. HHL had insisted on retaining its autonomy and its deal with UA. Hill, who said that it was Wasserman who wanted them to take over MGM, remembered the three partners being shown through the Culver City headquarters. "None of us wanted to do it," he said. "What am I going to do, be Thalberg?" In any case, Lancaster refused to play Ben-Hur. Though ostensibly an atheist since circus days, he found the movie "a belittling picture of Christianity as I understand it," and probably felt an instinctive aversion to the huge epic in which even he might get lost. "Why," he asked the movie's director, William Wyler, "do you want to do this piece of crap?"

He continued to refuse even though the *Los Angeles Times* reported a year and a half later, in January 1959, that "1958 will go down in twentieth-century annals as a record maker: Jet transport set a new record for transcontinental and transoceanic flights and an actor named Burt Lancaster toppled previous salary records [$750,000, for Holden, Wayne, Brando, Taylor, and Audrey Hepburn] by asking $1 million for the privilege of adding his name to the cast of a motion picture." In fact, it was MGM that had offered the star the million dollars if he would play Ben-Hur, sweetening the deal by offering to take over the $2.5 million worth of unproduced scripts and put the trio in charge of "all MGM feature production." Lancaster's unprecedented million, the *Los Angeles Times* concluded, represented the final, complete "realignment of the relations between . . . stars and the studios." With the postwar liquidation of the majors' star rosters, the "single picture deal," built around the star and negotiated by his or her agent, had now become "the basis of bargaining." Who better than Lancaster to be the first one offered that magic million?

When he and Norma decided, with the design advice of California modernist architect Harold Levitt, to add on, again, to their house and grounds, Tinseltown buzzed. The man who had turned down $1 million for *Ben-Hur* out of principle (the movie won eleven Oscars and grossed more than $35 million over the years) had paid $300,000 to upgrade his house.

The tragedy, if that is the right concept, of HHL is that it was unable to build on such recognition. The scaling-down was apparent in Lancaster's next movie, *The Devil's Disciple*. A would-be Shavian in his own mind, Lancaster had been talking about making a movie of Shaw's satire of the American Revolution ever since seeing a Maurice Evans revival earlier in the decade. Originally a $3 million color extravaganza, worthy of the $600,000 paid to the playwright's estate for the property, the movie was now budgeted as a mere black-and-white, eighty-two-minute, $1.5 million project. UA agreed to Kirk Douglas's suggestion that his Bryna Productions and HHL jointly produce the movie with Mackendrick to direct. As the price of his involvement, Douglas got the prime part of Dick Dudgeon, the black sheep "devil's disciple" out to avenge the hanging death of his father by the forces of Olivier's British General Burgoyne. Lancaster settled for the thankless role of Anthony Anderson, the reluctant patriot who only puts on his buckskins to fight the redcoats in the last act.

After *The Indian Fighter*, Douglas had spent two years putting together Bryna's *The Vikings*, a huge hit in 1958. Following the Lancaster pattern, Bryna also put out a batch of UA-financed, low-budget movies in 1957 that did not star Douglas and did not make money. Douglas could now identify himself with his friend and rival's much bigger, older, more successful company, and HHL, wavering, could bolster itself by alliance with Douglas, whose *Vikings* had come in almost a million dollars *under* budget.

During preproduction, the two stars cleverly spun their buddy image in a skit performed at the 1958 Academy Awards ceremony. Reading through the list of Best Actor nominees—at the mention of Brando, nominated for *Sayonara*, Lancaster interjected, "Him and that corny southern drawl!" and the camera cut to Brando in the audience, laughing—the two stars realize that neither of their names is on it. Disgusted, they break into a song, "It's Great Not to Be Nominated," written especially for the occasion by Sammy Cahn and Jimmy Van Heusen: *"Since we can't be bested,/We're not interested./But who stuck those knives in our backs?"* The two men shuffled a little soft shoe, bowed, and left the stage to huge applause and laughter. Congratulatory telegrams flooded in and Douglas wrote to Dick Powell, "Burt and I almost feel like we won some kind of award. It's getting so it doesn't pay to win anymore—you do better if you lose."

Neither star believed that, of course. But the skit was smart publicity— and a broad Oscar hint—for their mutual project, which started shooting July 15 on location at a Rothschild estate, Tring Park, in Hertfordshire, and at Elstree Studios. All the Lancaster children and Norma came along and the family took to riding bicycles everywhere, a line of blond heads speeding across the green countryside. One week into the tight, forty-eight-day schedule, the too-meticulous Mackendrick was fired and Guy Hamilton, future director of several James Bond hits, took over. Olivier was in the middle of a personal and professional crisis. An extramarital love affair with actress Joan Plowright had evolved to a point of no return (they would marry in 1961) and Vivien Leigh was behaving, according to Douglas, "like Blanche Du Bois in *Streetcar*," her role in the 1951 movie. Olivier later wrote in his autobiography, "I just couldn't seem to handle the normal problems of acting any more," and he repeatedly confused Burt—"the boss"—with Kirk. Lancaster, aloof, would look at him "straight and steely-steady" and quietly repeat, "Burt," while Douglas, Kamber recalled, followed the great British actor around "like a puppy dog." In the end, Olivier's Burgoyne had his delicious, throwaway moments of fine British impatience as he strode about in a ridiculous hat. And, as Lancaster would remember, he was the only one who got any money out of the deal, "somewhere between $150,000 and $200,000."

The film, which could have been a sophisticated progression for HHL, was instead a tepid failure when it opened in August 1959. A movie he had wanted to make for so long, an intriguing match to *The Kentuckian*, the failure was a sad disappointment for Lancaster. If this was all he was getting out of his own company, it was time for something different.

Back at Canon Drive, Hyams began to get nervous. "Burt," he asked, "tell me what's happening because Harold doesn't tell me anything." Lancaster replied, "You're not going to be let go, I promise you. But, meanwhile, look for something." When Hyams repeated, "What's happening?" Lancaster said, "I'm closing down this company."

When UA absorbed the expense—"a fortune," said Youngstein—of renovating the entire floor of the Hotel George V post-*Trapeze*, it did so because the end product had been their biggest hit. When *Sweet Smell of Success* went over budget and then failed, spectacularly, and Hecht kept announcing in the pages of *Variety* ever more projects, Krim, Benjamin, and Youngstein had to admit the fair-haired child of their postwar renaissance had not matured well.

The distributor decided to set some limits and by March 1959 UA had made an accounting: five profit pictures for which HL/HHL had received compensation of approximately $550,000 and a profit share to date of a little over $5 million, with a share of about $1 million "still to come"; an estimated loss of $2,600,000 on *Bachelor Party, Sweet Smell of Success,* and *Run Silent, Run Deep;* two completed features, *Separate Tables* and *The Devil's Disciple*, with profits, if any, yet to come; plus the four low-budget pictures which had all gone over budget without script consultation or approval by UA. Dragging down the whole cross-collateralized apparatus were commitments to unfinished or abandoned projects. Five hundred thousand dollars was owed to various screenwriters. Eight pictures were in stages of incompletion which added another $700,000 of damages.

By April, in "heavy negotiations with Lew Wasserman," UA determined that it had already shelled out $300,000 for three more unmade "little pictures" and did not see the point, now, of "throwing good money after bad." The three remaining scheduled projects were: *Kimberly*, a South African diamond mine robbery blockbuster set in 1883 to be directed by Carol Reed; *The Way West*, with $545,000 charged against it, mostly to Odets; and *The Unforgiven*, already underway in Durango, Mexico, with John Huston having replaced Delbert Mann as director and starring Lancaster and Audrey Hepburn. All three were big-budget movies that would, it was hoped, recoup some of these losses and debits.

Hecht continued to deny anything was the matter as the press scrupulously marked each decline in the company's fortunes as spring turned into summer: the HHL Paris office had closed in June 1958, only four months after opening; if there ever had been other foreign offices or even reps, they disappeared, too; and Kamber, Smith, Hyams, and production manager Gil Kurland—the man Hill said really produced his pictures—were all let go. From June 15 to September 15, the HHL weekly overhead was reduced from $5,000 to $1,500. The Canon Drive offices were leased to a firm of advisers to the government on missile development and vacated in mid-July. The big, complex corporate structure of some twenty HHL subsidiary companies was dismantled, leaving the two original principals with about $2 million in "obligations" to work off. UA would still be open to separate production deals on any of the undone properties but was no longer holding the bag if they never got done.

The Unforgiven now had the added freight of having to be a success. The story, whose original script was by J.P. Miller from the Alan LeMay novel, reversed the situation of The Searchers, the 1956 film written by LeMay and directed by John Ford: the Indians, Kiowas, demand the return of the girl, one of their own, from the Anglo settler family headed by Lancaster who has taken over their land. After Miller and then Mann quit the project, the story was redone, to no one's satisfaction, by Ben Maddow. At the last minute Huston, who had cowritten his 1950 film Asphalt Jungle with Maddow, agreed to direct, as much to pursue some of his other enthusiasms in the blisteringly hot, bleak, cobalt blue–skied Durango as to craft what the producers still liked to call a serious story of frontier intolerance.

For making a movie he did not believe in, Huston later said that some "celestial vengeance" was loosed on him. Sun, fleas, flies, bad water, local banditos, and terrible food had most of the cast and crew cooking on hot plates in their motel rooms along the highway. Audrey Hepburn, improbably cast as the Indian girl, fell off a stallion, forcing an expensive three-week break. Audie Murphy, the most decorated American soldier of World War II, compulsively shot rabbits as they scampered across the desert and he almost drowned. Lillian Gish, cast as Lancaster's mother, pestered everyone with constant comparisons to her mentor and director, D.W. Griffith: "Well, D.W. never did that!" In one of the movie's more improbable scenes, the great silent film star plays Mozart's C Minor "Fantasia" on a grand piano set up in front of the family's sod hut because it's too big to fit inside.

Lancaster liked and respected Huston's Hellinger-Hemingway crackle, if not his taste for destructive practical jokes. The director actually listened to him, took in his ideas even if he did not use them. Huston decided he did not particularly like Lancaster and the two men wrangled for days over one scene before Huston finally gave up. By the end, The Unforgiven had become a Burt With His Back to the Wall exercise, an apt correlative to the past ten years of independent production. He melts down tin soldiers for bullets, teaches the women to shoot, sets fire to the roof of the hut to drive off the cattle, then hunkers down in the root cellar as the Kiowas close in. When cast and crew returned to Hollywood, HHL was history. *Kimberly* and *The Way West* were shelved as, over the next year, the intake from *Separate Tables, The Devil's Disciple,* and *The Unforgiven* did little to offset the previous losses.

Hill and Hayworth formed their own production company, Hillworth, made one disastrous movie with UA, *The Happy Thieves,* and divorced in 1961. Hill would write a book about their relationship which the *New York Daily News* called "reprehensible" because Hayworth, by then ill with Alzheimer's disease, was unable to respond. When the money ran out, Lancaster, without hesitation, wrote his friend a check for $75,000. Twenty or so years later, Seltzer ran into Hill late one night at a liquor store. "I said, 'What a pity that those days are gone,'" recalled Seltzer. "And Jim said, 'Not at all. That company should have been broken up and I'm proud of my part in breaking it up.'"

Gloria Hecht swallowed enough sleeping pills "to kill a horse" in the summer of 1959 and survived. By 1961 the couple who argued about everything from "chicken cutlets to the TV antenna" was also divorced and the *Los Angeles Examiner* itemized an estate worth $2–$4 million, including the yacht and Van Gogh's *L'Arléssienne.* It was always understood that Hecht could use Lancaster's name if it helped jump-start a project, the star remaining loyal to the man who had first offered him the better deal. Hecht would rehabilitate himself from alcoholism and tenaciously hang on in the industry for another ten years. After making a few more projects with Lancaster, he would produce one hit (*Cat Ballou*), followed by *The Way West* ("a jerk's idea of an epic," Pauline Kael wrote), and the flops *Taras Bulba* and *Flight from Ashiya.*

Lancaster was, as Seltzer said, "distracted, disillusioned." The juggernaut was over. UA remained ready, anytime, to sign a deal with him. "When you make ten pictures with anybody, that is a minor miracle," said Youngstein. By the middle of the next decade, UA would have contracts with over sixty independent producers and, in the 1970s, pull off the still-unmatched triple of winning three Best Picture Oscars in a row. As a star, Lancaster had almost pulled off a lucrative balance between a big popular Technicolor hit like *Trapeze,* and a gamble like *Sweet Smell of Success,* brokering with his persona what Steven Bach has called "the dominating central issue of American motion pictures"—art versus business. As Hollywood would water down "independent production" to mean restrictive studio-financed deals without seasoned in-house executive producers, Lancaster, claimed Kaplan, had "very good instincts, better than other stars" and he gave them, undivided, to the work at hand. "A very secure man, he called the shots," said Hyams. "I don't even know what he was doing with such a big company." The transition from studios to stars, as Alexander Walker noted, had so many unexpected problems that it came to seem "less like emancipation than slavery by other means."

What Kaplan called the "crucial error" of HHL's spending as much as a major on the development and acquisition of scripts that never got made, without more huge hits to absorb the difference, eventually swamped them. "Had they acted sensibly," reflected the attorney, "they probably would have had several million more dollars in the bank and that would have enabled them to continue instead of breaking up. It would have given Burt even more control when he had reached the peak of his power at the beginning of the sixties." The game was always about control.

The *New York World-Telegram* in September 1959 pronounced a postmortem of the company as "the biggest of the independents . . . [that] triggered the new era of film making, with stars heading companies that rivaled the major studios." One camp of former employees claimed that working for the indie had driven them "to the psychoanalyst's couch." But a secretary insisted "all the gals in town were dying to work there. They paid the highest salaries; they were the first to give writers and directors a share of the profits. They were innovators in this town, and they were *alive*."

Lancaster was philosophical. "But what the hell, Kirk," he wrote Douglas from Durango, consoling him for what they both considered a botched reprise of their Oscar routine at the 1959 ceremonies. "Let's face it, life is sad—a girl told me today that I looked twenty years older than my picture, so there you are! Just when I was thinking that I never looked better in my life."

PART THREE

THE PAYOFF

1960 – 1990

*I always try to improve, to find new ways of expressing myself,
to keep looking for truth and originality. And sometimes . . .
I only succeed in beating myself to death.*

—Burt Lancaster, 1961

He was locked right inside his own time.

—Roddy McDowall, 1998

CHAPTER NINE

Embracing the Zeitgeist

The period of good looks and sex is disappearing.
I think the industry is growing up.

—Burt Lancaster, *Los Angeles Times*, April 10, 1960

The nation plunged into a fresh, new presidential campaign at the start of a new decade. Politics were not only safe but chic once again. Lancaster now spoke as the "Golden Boy" of the New Frontier industry. "[T]he original model of Hollywood's present elite," said *Life*, "—the actor-producer who for the past dozen years has controlled the industry," he was also "the showiest specimen of this exotic breed that Hollywood has ever seen." Spray-painted gold, he reportedly showed up at a Hollywood costume party wearing only a G-string, looking exactly like the Oscar, animate.

What to make of this hybrid who did not see any distinction between serious art (the theater) and popular art (the movies)? "We in Hollywood have a sacred position," he told one reporter. "I believe we should appeal to people at the higher levels." Movies shouldn't just entertain, they should be "the voice of society." He really meant it, continuing to inspire resentment for his ability to break whatever rules there were left and not to show up at any important parties. And he still looked very good—tall, strong, lithe, and graceful, a full head of hair, the same bright blue eyes.

Now he dared to think that his talent, stretched beyond its natural limits only because he had forced it, might mutate into art. Auteur of his own career, truly independent at last, he would reap the benefit of all that 1950s megastar strategy.

When Richard Brooks failed to clear his war novel, *The Brick Foxhole*, through marine corps censors before publication in 1944 and was threatened with a court martial, Sinclair Lewis was among the group of distinguished authors rounded up by the publisher to intercede, successfully, on his behalf. Soon afterward, Lewis cautioned the budding screenwriter entranced with *Elmer Gantry*, Lewis's muckraking tale of an errant Protestant evangelist, not to be afraid of turning the book into a better movie. While filming *Brute Force*, Brooks told Lancaster, the star who could not yet act, to read Lewis's novel because someday they were going to make a movie out of it.

As Brooks kept renewing the option over the next decade, he had trouble finding a studio willing to touch the story of the smoking, drinking charlatan who seduces, loves, and uses the charismatic woman preacher, Sister Sharon Falconer, only to be brought down by a prostitute he had launched on her own road to ruin. But by 1959 Brooks had made *The Blackboard Jungle* and Lancaster, supremely bankable, wanted to play the role to which he could bring all he was: Irish shaman, Church of the Son of Man choirboy, settlement house do-gooder who opposed evangelism as a sapping of the will to work for change, backroads circus hustler, and progeny of the 1920s Manhattan which had embraced the novels of Lewis. Above all, *Elmer Gantry* played into his enduring fascination with the duality of good and evil within one person, within himself. Lancaster *was* the venal preacherman.

Beholden, with Hecht, to UA, during this first half of the 1960s he had to compensate, personally, for the 1950s excesses of HHL by making four movies—*The Young Savages, Birdman of Alcatraz, The Train,* and *The Hallelujah Trail*—at a salary of $150,000 each rather than his usual fee of $750,000. Though *Elmer Gantry* was made just before he "went into slavery," as he put it, his new UA contract made the distributor eager both to get more money's worth out of him and to make what Youngstein described to Krim as "one of the most explosive pieces of picture material" he had ever read. After Lancaster rejected one of the early drafts as too long and cumbersome, Brooks told him he could forget golf or anything else because they would rewrite it together. Holed up in a $45-a-month rented office on the Columbia lot on Gower Street, the two fractious men fought it out for seven months. They built the script, as Brooks later said, "brick by brick, like a wall."

The director had amassed a collection of articles on the two key figures, Billy Sunday and Aimee Semple McPherson, of the great revivalist wave that swept across America in the teens and 1920s. An ex–baseball player who used his superbly proportioned and coordinated body to sensational effect during his world-famous revival meetings, Sunday vaulted onto the platform "as beautiful," wrote journalist John Reed, "as a Greek runner," crying, "O-o-o-o-oh, come to Jesus!" More controversial because of her gender (only "fringe sects" had women preachers), McPherson roared down the aisle of her Anglus Temple in Los Angeles on a motorcycle, shouting, "Stop! You're speeding to Hell!" and was the most photographed woman in America by the late 1920s.

Billy Graham was the other model for Gantry, a fact carefully denied by the director and star. Several months after Lancaster's anti-HUAC speech at the Commodore Hotel in January 1949, thirty-year-old William Franklin Graham converted six thousand Californians under a huge canvas tent, exhorting them with fiery rhetoric to find the answers to their postwar fears in Jesus (a *Gantry* press release claimed the movie was shot in Los Angeles because the area had "spawned so many religious cults and sects that it seemed only fair"). In what became his great evangelist "crusade" of the 1950s, during which sales of bibles reached an all-time high, Graham had a style markedly similar to Sunday and McPherson, only more mainstream and global. Brooks kept a file labeled "Billy Graham" stuffed with newspaper and magazine articles on which he pencil-marked the salient characteristics. Graham's delivery was at "machine-gun speed" with "restless pacing on the platform" often covering a mile and a half in one session, leaving him soaking with sweat. His original style of dress was gaudy—he wore a pistachio-green gabardine suit to his first visit with President Truman. In 1958 the *Los Angeles Times* reported that his crusade had swelled to "staggering dimensions" for a revival at Madison Square Garden. The preacher who reminded the faithful that the word evangelist came from the Greek word *euvangélion*, meaning "good news," admitted he got his start selling Fuller brushes door-to-door.

To play Sister Sharon, Brooks chose Jean Simmons, the beautiful Sister Sarah of the 1955 movie version of *Guys and Dolls*. Arthur Kennedy was cast as Jim Lefferts, the cynical reporter who watches, laughs, reports, and understands everyone, especially Gantry. A fine back-up cast included Edward Andrews as an appropriately fatuous George Babbitt, the title character from Lewis's other notorious novel of the 1920s, *Babbitt*. To fill the movie's revival tents with true believers, nonprofessional revival-goers who knew the hymns by heart were bused in from Long Beach.

When Lancaster saw Shirley Jones play an alcoholic who commits suicide in a *Playhouse 90* television drama with Red Skelton called *The Big Slide*, he suggested her to Brooks for the part of Lulu Baines, the prostitute who brings him down. Her Emmy nomination notwithstanding, the director dismissed the idea of casting the blond, wholesome star of *Oklahoma!* and *Carousel* but Lancaster insisted and Jones came to the Gower Street production offices to read for the part. "She arrived with the old Maidenform pushed up as high as it would go," recalled Hoagy Carmichael Jr., the songwriter's nineteen-year-old son and a golfing partner of Lancaster's, who had been hired as a production gofer, "and with her hair down, high heels, she looked like she didn't know how to spell *Oklahoma*." Brooks was still unconvinced, but Lancaster assured him he would help her in their difficult scenes together and invited her to come down to the set weeks before she was due to perform. "I wanted his advice desperately," Jones recalled. "What Burt did for me was allow me to get to know him."

He was also ensuring, as filming progressed during summer 1959, that she got used to Brooks. Tom Shaw, *Gantry*'s assistant director who went on to work twenty-five years with the director and loved and admired him, insisted that Brooks's intimidating behavior was a calculated pose: "He was a faker. His whole goal in life was to reach that pedestal where everybody would say, 'Don't work with that son of a bitch.' " His phobia about revealing an entire script to anyone was, according to Jones, a mixture of paranoid fear that people would steal his work plus a desire to play Svengali with his actors. "Brooks was hard on actors, hard on the crew," recalled Jones. "I saw him slap this extra and make her cry. He was a screamer. Poor Jean Simmons was in tears most of the time because of him." Simmons began an affair with the director during *Gantry* and later married him.

The one person the director would not cross was Lancaster, a standoff which gave the impression, according to Jones, of "two elephant bulls on the stage." In the unusual position of conciliator, Lancaster set about explaining the director's impossible outbursts so the show could go on. "Guys respect that toughness," said Carmichael of the two men. "The difference was that Burt could walk in and say, 'Look, this is what we're going to do. I would like for us all to pull together for the next twenty minutes and do this task.' Brooks would come in and go, 'You! You get over here!' "

Not that the star was all sweetness and light. Shaw isolated a characteristic behavior pattern on *Gantry* that endured all Lancaster's acting life. If he was invested in a particular project, his engagement was total; if someone tried to penetrate the force field with what he saw as an irrelevant distraction, the result was explosive. "I think truly," said Shaw, "that nothing meant more to Burt—women, whatever you want to say—than the piece. Whatever we were doing at that time, that was *it*. Burt took it to a degree that I'd never seen before. He went down underneath, it was his function." Jones, too, recalled Lancaster as "the hardest-working human being I ever saw," always dealing with the most minute details. "Another actor would say, 'Oh, well, it's only a movie. We can cross that off and go on to something else.' Burt would never do that," she said. "There was no crossing anything off." After blasting someone away, Lancaster invariably came back later and he or she, nonplussed, was treated to the solicitous, gentlemanly Lancaster.

Six days were budgeted for shooting the spectacular fire climax scene in which Sister Sharon's brand-new Tabernacle—and Sister Sharon—go up in smoke. The exteriors were shot at the back of a skating rink at the end of an old Santa Monica pier, but six days were not nearly enough for what Brooks claimed was Hollywood's first "mass interior fire scene." Lancaster got UA to allow him and Brooks to take the extra $200,000 needed from their fees and the scene was then shot in about five weeks using highly flammable old nitrate films from the Columbia vault to speed the conflagration.

To avoid unnecessary prerelease controversies, the sets at Columbia and on the backlots of other studios with "1920s streets" were closed to everyone but carefully screened visitors. In fact, *Gantry* was calibrated to offend only so much and only those least likely to pose any real threat to the movie. While Lulu Baines's recounting of her early seduction by Gantry— "He got to howlin' 'Repent! Repent!' and I got to moanin' 'Save me! Save me!' and the first thing I knew he rammed the fear of God into me"—got the movie banned in Boston, the Protestant mainstream was not, by nature, easily galvanized into group action nor did it feel comfortable defending fundamentalist evangelism. The only group happy with the idea of the movie was the Catholic Legion of Decency, which comprised the Production Code censors. Catholics were not allowed to attend Graham's revivals, listen to his radio program, read his speeches, nor were they allowed to join Masonic orders (Babbitt is referred to as a Mason in the movie). As a portrait of Protestant vice and venality, *Elmer Gantry* seemed a justification of the Catholic Church's vigilance, through the Code, as guardians of American morality. Worldly, carnal, passionate, and dangerous, Gantry personified the American religious alter ego. There, but for the Catholic Church, went the nation.

Angry letters came in to Lancaster and Brooks during production asking why nobody in Hollywood had the guts to take on the "evils and shortcomings" of the Catholic Church. It seemed unfair that the denomination that had been so integral a part of the political, ideological, and social conformity of the postwar era should benefit from *Elmer Gantry.* "Make a sequel about a Roman Catholic priest who is a louse," wrote someone from New Jersey. "I'll even write it from my own experience—a story of a . . . priest who is a fornicator, an adulterer, a drunk, a gambler, and a general no-good bum. We'll call it *Father O'Reilly*, or *Father Mozzarelli*, or *Father Foulzanski.* We'll get Bing Crosby for the role of the priest and we can even let him sing a song or two—140 million non-Catholics will see it." A "businessman" from Indianapolis suggested that Brooks make a movie that mentioned the "connection between the Roman Catholic Church and Senator McCarthy."

The movie got a "B" rating from the Legion of Decency ("Objectionable in part for all"). No one under sixteen was allowed to see it without a parent and an explanatory prologue was thrown in as an added warning. *Variety* recorded that the restriction was "the first time that such an adults-only classification has been brought into play." Now the picture was officially notorious with whatever boost that might bring to the box-office take, and the Code administration, having passed it, was in the odd position of having to defend not only its decision, but the movie.

The cracks in the Production Code were now all too obvious. Sex, violence, and religion were passed without question in a "biblical" like *The Ten Commandments*. A single word in a contemporary movie came under scrutiny regardless of context or intent. The last line of *Gantry* was a case in point. The original script called for Lefferts to say to Gantry as he heads out of town, "See you around, brother," to which Gantry replies, "See you in hell, brother." The Legion objected and either Brooks or Lancaster—each claimed the solo experience—had to sit for the better part of three days discussing with three Jesuits in New York their intent with Gantry's parting shot. Did he *know* he was damned? The title character could not willingly, knowingly send himself to hell. The line was cut, Lancaster keeping it in reserve to use at a later, different time.

Nonetheless, *Elmer Gantry* symbolized a "new boldness," *Variety* reported at the time of its release in July 1960. The postwar emergence of the independents, unhampered by the "timidity of the top brass" in the old studios, had led, claimed the trade paper, to a "general revolution in Hollywood picture-making." And who better than Lancaster to personify these changes? His performance was hailed as the role of his career. "For once," raved the *Hollywood Reporter*, "Burt Lancaster has a role into which his full-blown talents can flow and fill." He did not have to act in *Elmer Gantry*, he bragged, he was just himself. His model, the star later claimed, was the "mannerisms, the charming demeanor" of Huston. Said Brooks, "Burt just . . . blossomed." In his graceful, lithe Gantry who runs, jumps, slides, and shouts to heaven "Can you hear me, Jesus?" older reviewers indeed saw Billy Sunday. Cameraman John Alton, Oscar winner for *An American in Paris*, shot the film in the classic screen ratio of 1:1.33, recognizing the original intent of the medium to eliminate space. Lancaster's gritty, grifting two-cent tabloid preacher burst through the screen, commanding his captive audience out there in the dark to listen and believe.

Criticizing the movie for not coming clear on the value of religion or the authenticity of evangelism, some reviews missed the intent of the filmmakers. For Brooks and Lancaster *Elmer Gantry* was a portrait of the vulgar, slickly charming, huckster soul of America in love with success because it is the mark of the elect. Flaunt yourself, your body, sell your God-fearing soul. Lure attention to yourself because that is all you have in this big lonely land with no past. In that transaction is the glamorous, corrupt heart of the circus, vaudeville, the movies, Babbitt's commerce, the politics of democracy, religion. Only in the new nation filled with restless people looking for roots, certainty, a leader, home does it matter so much to find the answers, to make it all add up.

Gantry is *the* seducer in a movie that reviewers remarked as being about the many kinds of seduction. He even seduces himself. The act of engaging attention, keeping it, and exploiting it is the seducer's—and the evangelist's—first sally. Cutting through the holy hype, the actual seduction scene in *Gantry* is a meeting of two consenting adults, two erotic equals. "I want you so bad, I'm in pain half the time," says Gantry to Sister Sharon. "I'd like to tear those holy wings off you and make a real woman out of you. I'd show you what heaven's like: no golden stairways, or harp music, or silvery clouds. Just ecstasy comin' and goin'. . . . When are you going to make up your mind to take it?"

Behind the bombast was an alert, nuanced portrayal of the man Brooks described as wanting "what everyone is supposed to want—money, sex, religion. He's the All-American boy." In the end, Gantry—as Lancaster felt he had done when he left religion behind in East Harlem—no longer looks through a glass darkly or speaks as a child. He has grown up but at a price. He will remain enough of a believer to know his eternal destination is hell, the apostate fleeing the hound of heaven. Lancaster's personal heroes were Lincoln, Jefferson, Galileo—and Jesus Christ. Shaw, watching him on the set, felt he "really believed in the bullshit he was preaching." The audience could decide for itself whether to believe Gantry or not. This was a movie for grown-ups.

In the midst of prerelease flurry for *Gantry*, and already obsessing on his next big passionate project, *Birdman of Alcatraz*, Lancaster was obligated to squeeze in thirty-five days to make *The Young Savages*. He left it to Hecht to sign television wunderkind director John Frankenheimer for his first significant Hollywood picture. His edgy, experimental work had appeared on CBS's *Climax!* and *Danger*, NBC's *Ford Startime*, and many productions for *Playhouse 90*, including J.P. Miller's *Days of Wine and Roses*. After the intimate, thrilling collaboration with the seasoned Brooks, Lancaster, forty-seven, was impatient with the abrupt adjustment to working with a less experienced thirty-year-old. And perhaps old anxieties and guilt for having left it were set off by being back on the streets, on location in his old neighborhood, now often called Spanish Harlem.

The script by Edward Anhalt and J.P. Miller was based on an Evan Hunter novel, *A Matter of Conviction*, which had in turn been inspired by newspaper accounts of gang feuds in East Harlem between entrenched Italians and Puerto Rican newcomers. Lancaster's character, assistant district attorney Hank Bell, originally from the neighborhood but now up, out, and married to a WASP socialite with a social conscience played by Dina Merrill, is assigned by an ambitious D.A. to prosecute to an advantageous conviction the murder of a Puerto Rican boy by an Italian gang. In the end, he chooses integrity over political ambition.

Lancaster showed up cold for the shoot, never having taken the trouble to meet with Frankenheimer. He later described the director as "tough and arrogant and terribly demanding on the set, sometimes to his own detriment." Blond, cool, typecast Merrill, a New Yorker who had done volunteer work in East Harlem, found her costar "very supportive and very easy to work with" while Frankenheimer "nearly drove me," she recalled, "out of the business"; Lancaster became an ally. "Well, you must be feeling pretty good today, John," she heard Lancaster say one morning. "Yeah, why?" replied Frankenheimer. "It's almost noon," said Lancaster, "and you haven't picked on Dina yet."

The working atmosphere was not improved by the sudden replacement of Lee Grant, cast as Bell's old girlfriend from the neighborhood and the mother of one of the Italian boys, by Shelley Winters. One of the best scenes in the uneven movie, shot in a cramped slum room, was a confrontation between Lancaster and Winters. She accuses Bell of deserting his people and he responds by accusing her of not being a good mother and leaving her child prey to the lure of gangs and crime. As cameras rolled, "Shelley was complaining about something," Frankenheimer recalled, "and Burt started screaming at her and she started screaming at Burt." The language was "appalling," recalled Winters, and a security guard from a block away came running, gun in hand. Later she wondered if they were confronting each other for the personal disappointments—for her, two failed marriages—each had dealt with in the decade since their love affair. The anger went much further back than that for Lancaster. Grant had quit or been fired by Frankenheimer after the same scene had produced the same explosive response from Lancaster, the man adandoned by his mother when he needed her most.

Frankenheimer admitted that even with the problems he learned a lot from his first experience directing Lancaster. "Burt knew how to make movies. He was the one that I learned from to rehearse the scene, thoroughly. He was extremely professional," he insisted. "Extremely." Frankenheimer claimed not to remember the notorious story, told by Ed Asner among others as Tinseltown folklore, of the day Lancaster bodily lifted the tall director, acknowledged to be a master of the camera, and plonked him where he, the star, thought the camera should go. At the end of the shoot he told Hecht he would love to direct *Birdman of Alcatraz* and Hecht said that would never happen because the star had decided he would never work with him again.

Lancaster's post-HHL career was marked by sustained relationships with certain directors—including, eventually, Frankenheimer—and another such rapport began on *The Young Savages*. As acting coach to the three young nonprofessionals playing the accused gang members, Frankenheimer hired twenty-six-year-old Sydney Pollack, a young Sanford Meissner–trained actor and teacher at the Neighborhood Playhouse who had worked with him in television. Lancaster was both curious and suspicious: "Hey, kid," he asked. "What are you saying to those young men?" Gradually, said Pollack, "I saw that he honestly wanted to know and I said, 'I'm just talking about the scene.' 'What kind of things are you saying about the scene?' he would ask. And then he said to me once, 'What do you think about *my* scene? What do you think I'm doing in this scene?' And I started to talk to him about it."

The day he was due to fly back to his family in New York after the movie wrapped, Pollack got a call from Ted DeBuys, Lancaster's big, gentle secretary: "Mr. Lancaster wants to see you." He suggested Pollack cancel his flight and come over to Gower Street. Lancaster was waiting for him. "I think you should be a director," he said. With no such plans, Pollack was taken aback. Lancaster then picked up the phone and called Wasserman, a name that meant nothing, yet, to the actor. "I'm sitting here with a young man named Sydney Pollack," said the star to his now former agent, who as head of the newly formed MCA Productions was looking for new TV directors. "I'm gonna send him over to see you. I'll be honest with you, Lew—I haven't seen anything he's directed, but I've got a strong hunch about him and, in any case, he can't be any worse than those bums you've got working with you now." Pollack signed an option contract with Universal, found an apartment over a garage, and did not see Lancaster again for about three years.

The movie version of *West Side Story* opened in 1961, the same year as *The Young Savages*. It swamped the well-intentioned, black-and-white picture which seemed weak and contrived, not as glamorous as the musical, nor as powerful as the litter-strewn streets and raw language of the real East Harlem. Lancaster's tense, scowling performance went largely unnoticed. He had only been passing time until *Birdman of Alcatraz* could absorb his every waking moment.

Thomas E. Gaddis's biography of Robert Stroud, the "Birdman of Alcatraz," was published in 1955 and immediately gripped Lancaster. In 1958 20th Century-Fox toyed with the idea of making a movie of the story of the convicted murderer who had served the longest term in solitary confinement of any U.S. prisoner—forty years by 1960 of what would be a fifty-four-year incarceration—and dropped it, reportedly due to pressure from the Federal Bureau of Prisons. In 1960, when Hecht and Lancaster revived the old Norma company title for this one movie to be distributed by Columbia, the bureau was no more ready to cooperate with a production that ostensibly glorified a murderer. Except for exterior scenes filmed carefully just outside the watery perimeter in the San Francisco Bay of the real Alcatraz, still in use, the entire movie—including a re-creation of an Alcatraz cell block—would be made on Columbia's backlot.

Lancaster immersed himself in a study of Stroud's strange life. After nursing a sick sparrow back to health in 1920, the prisoner with only a third-grade education became an amateur ornithologist, an expert on caged birds, and the author of *Stroud's Digest of the Diseases of Birds*, the standard sourcebook on the subject before the advent of sulpha drugs. At his bird-keeping peak Stroud had more than three hundred canaries in his cell in cotes made from old cigar boxes. Lancaster studied penal law and tried, with no immediate success, to meet the prisoner or any member of his family, pressuring Edward Bennett Williams, Stroud's attorney, for access. He read volumes on the case and all of Stroud's letters. Never before and never again would he, obsessive by nature, be obsessed to this level with a movie. If Elmer Gantry was who Lancaster really was, Stroud was who he wanted to be. "Stroud will not kowtow," Lancaster said in 1963. "He will not make polite amends for what he has done. He will not say 'Daddy.' "

Lancaster came to believe the movie would be the vehicle to free the prisoner, so persuasive that the implacable Feds would relent and grant him a pardon. The fact that Stroud was what *Time* described as "a homicidal threat to society" who, after being convicted for shooting a bartender in Juneau, Alaska, in 1909 in a fight over a prostitute, had then knifed to death a prison guard in Leavenworth Prison in 1916, did not matter. It was what he had done *since* the murders that sucked Lancaster in. A keeper of birds, confined, like himself, in cages, Stroud "took a miserable, unnatural existence," Lancaster said, "and yet made it a meaningful thing." Such persistence appealed deeply to his autodidactic soul and the simple visual symbolism took him back to the pigeons and tipplets he used to handle on the roofs of East Harlem. He put everything on hold, turned down other, more lucrative movies to, as Hecht later described it, "tinker" and groom this very uncommercial project. It was his masterwork, a creation out of the prison of his own self.

A team of familiar faces from the best of the good old days was gathered in: Edmond O'Brien; Whit Bissell (*Brute Force, Gunfight at the O.K. Corral*); *From Here to Eternity* cameraman Burnett Guffey; Gilbert Kurland, the long-suffering HHL production manager; and Schiffer, Shaw, and Carrere.

Old over-budget guarantees from *Sweet Smell of Success* and *The Bachelor Party* were added by UA to the negative cost to make a final budget of $2,650,000. Though UA had initially wanted Jules Dassin to direct, a suggestion that "delighted" Lancaster, shooting began at the end of 1960 with Briton Charles Crichton, of *The Lavender Hill Mob* renown.

In the middle of a divorce, Frankenheimer was avoiding California for various settlement reasons as *Birdman* commenced. When Hecht called to say he had to come out from New York to fix "cutting problems" on *Savages,* he retorted, "There are no problems on *Young Savages,*" but reluctantly flew out to Los Angeles. Lancaster was at the airport to meet him. "If I'd asked you to come out here," he explained, "you wouldn't have come. I saw *The Young Savages* last week. I think you did a brilliant job on it. I want you to take over *Birdman*." Crichton had lasted less than a month, a casualty of the actor's impatience and the director's own unsuitability for the subject; Frankenheimer recognized "the chance of a lifetime" and accepted. Actor and director joined forces on the massive script by Guy Trosper. Recalling how excited the actor was at the change, Carmichael said, "Frankenheimer meant a new voice at just the time Burt needed it."

Each day, in what the director called "a very collaborative effort," the two men hammered out the movie. "We blocked scenes. We decided to do the whole business of building the birdcage, of finding the first bird, of working with the birds—everything. Once Burt respected somebody," he said, "it was a whole other ballgame." To make the process of Stroud's on-screen aging over more than half a century smoother—and to intensify his equally cumulative triumph in confinement—the movie was made in sequence. After deciding that spending half an hour every day putting on a bald cap on which to build the thinning, graying hair was "baloney," Schiffer shaved Lancaster's head halfway back and every day applied each white and gray hair individually, eventually winning an Oscar for his effort. Off the set, the actor went around with half his hair missing.

Two thousand canaries were flown in from Japan. Lancaster spent two weeks working with them as well as with sparrows, taping birdseed to his finger and patiently waiting for the creatures to hop onto his hand. A trainer clipped the birds' feathers to prevent them from flying and eventually some of them ended up on Lancaster's finger while the camera was running. Most of the time the birds, according to Frankenheimer, would do just what was wanted "while we were loading film." When what Schiffer called "a crazy birdman" in charge of caring for the birds went around twisting their necks one day, Lancaster shouted, "What the hell are you doing, for Christ's sake?" "Well," said the real birdman, "they're no good anymore." Years later, at a Frankenheimer retrospective, Lancaster drew gasps from the audience when he revealed that the same bird handler had prepped the birds for the scenes in which they get sick and fall from their perches by pouring lighter fluid down their throats.

The feeling grew that they were making what the *New York Herald-Tribune* called "an important film." At one point tears rolled down Lancaster's cheeks as his immersion in the character of Stroud became complete. Delighted, Frankenheimer wanted to continue filming but the actor, in a defensiveness that went back beyond vaudeville, the circus, and Boleslavsky said: "Oh, no, John, let the audience cry—not me."

One week after John Kennedy was inaugurated in January 1961, Lancaster's brother Jim, age fifty, dropped dead of a heart attack while standing next to a telephone at Columbia studios before the filming of the 1946 Alcatraz riot scene. Big, genial, tough, he was the sixth close family member lost to Lancaster. After first calling his sister in New York, he decided to go right back to work after the body was taken away. "A lot of people thought that was not the right thing to do," said Schiffer. "But I think it was a tremendous blow to him. He loved his brother. He didn't want to sit up there and brood in that office and let it build up in him." Back home in Bel Air, Lucy Kibbee was keeping Lancaster's dying father company when his last son arrived home to tell him the news. "I'll never forget," she recalled, "Burt carried him into the bathroom and he had to tell him about the death of his brother. And the manner in which he did it was so exquisite. His gentleness, his kindness in telling his father was so beautiful and so sincere. I just remember thinking, My God, he does have a soul."

When Frankenheimer sat Hecht and Lancaster down some weeks later for a preliminary screening of *Birdman*, it ran four and a half hours. After a week of trying to cut it, it was agreed that while Lancaster left to fulfill a six-week commitment to Stanley Kramer's *Judgment at Nuremberg* in February and March, the first half of the story would be rewritten. Filming was suspended with a core group kept on payroll and UA ponied up the extra money needed to remake almost half of an already uncommercial movie. Lancaster, just nominated for an Oscar for *Gantry*, would be humored. And after the scary slump of 1957 and 1958, industry box-office receipts were headed toward the third annual rise in a row, hitting $1.5 billion in 1961, the highest total since 1948. UA could afford Lancaster.

As filming of *Judgment at Nuremberg* began at the Revue Studios on the old Universal-International lot at the end of February 1961, director Luchino Visconti, in Italy, was trying to interest Olivier in playing his elegiac Sicilian Prince Salina in a movie version of Giuseppi di Lampedusa's *The Leopard*.

Lancaster could not have been further from the mind of the aristocratic Italian postwar director in search of not only the perfect prince, but of the tons of money required to transform the best-selling chronicle of time, change, and democracy in nineteenth-century Italy into a sumptuous epic as operatic as any of his famed productions at La Scala. Eventually he would screen a print of *Judgment at Nuremberg* and see in Lancaster's Ernst Janning, the Nazi jurist who sees the errors of his civilization, a hint, a *possibility*, of his prince.

Kramer's production was an expansion of a 1959 *Playhouse 90* television drama written by Abby Mann as a re-creation of an actual 1947 Nuremberg trial of ninety-nine German judges and prosecutors held after the more famous prosecution of Hermann Goering, Rudolph Hess, and Albert Speer. As there had been no precedent for the horrors of Nazi Germany, there had never been such a series of trials for crimes against humanity and the impetus for the teleplay came from Mann's startling discovery ten years after the trials that not one of the jurists—all had been found guilty—was still serving any kind of sentence. The motives that led to their release were, he came to suspect, "the very philosophy that enabled the Nazis to come to power" in the first place. And with Germany now America's staunch ally against the Soviet Union, it was considered "a breach of good manners in polite society," he recalled, "to bring up the subject of German guilt or the victims of the Third Reich." The television drama had a tremendous impact, reinforced by the publication of Günter Grass's *The Tin Drum* in 1959 and, in 1960, of CBS war correspondent William L. Shirer's best-seller *The Rise and Fall of the Third Reich*.

During the preceding decade Kramer had accumulated a reputation for producing and/or directing controversial, self-consciously "important" pictures such as *Champion, High Noon, The Defiant Ones,* and *The Caine Mutiny.* His was a highly symbolic, classically heart-on-sleeve movie style that has remained in the public's consciousness in spite of the fact that much of his work was not commercially successful. For this difficult project, UA insisted that he gather a star-studded cast to provide some kind of insurance: Spencer Tracy, who had just starred in Kramer's 1960 dramatization of the Scopes trial, *Inherit the Wind,* was the American judge; Judy Garland in her first major screen performance since *A Star Is Born;* a shattered Montgomery Clift performing for free; Maximilian Schell as the German prosecutor; and Richard Widmark playing his American counterpart, a role Lancaster had turned down. Dietrich, the original *Blaue Engel,* was cast as the "good German" Mme. Bertholt who befriends Tracy.

Lancaster was also a last-minute replacement for Olivier, who was obligated to an extended run of *Becket* and whose flitting in and out of Lancaster's story in these years highlights how the former acrobat's reputation had transformed. Kramer sought Lancaster to play Janning because, he recalled, "it was not the obvious choice. His character was guilty and he was aware of it—that gave him a hook and I think he grabbed it. Also, Burt had a general background knowledge beyond the ordinary actor, in terms of the times in which he lived. He was interested, always, in going beyond the pale to achieve an honesty and I respected that."

Whatever risk Lancaster took, it was highly calculated. With the Academy Awards coming up in April, this prestige effort could only reinforce his new, heavyweight direction. Once he had secured Kramer's guarantee that he would not have to shoot on location in Berlin and Nuremberg—"It is important to Lancaster," wrote his attorney Kaplan to Kramer prior to shooting, "not to be separated from his family while his children are at school"—*Judgment* was an ideal miniproject.

And there was the money. Lancaster, the biggest star of the movie, was paid $750,000, his full going salary, for one scene plus many shots of him sitting in the courtroom, waiting his turn to testify; the size and position of his name above the title plus any picture or "likeness" was contractually to be exactly the same as Tracy's. When a journalist told Tracy, who had made a career out of being crusty and honest, that Lancaster said he would be paid very little money but would "do it for nothing because I think it should be done," Tracy, who was paid "something in excess of $400,000" to carry the movie, enlightened him that his costar was getting half a million dollars (perhaps the true figure was kept secret) for seven pages of dialogue. "Now why don't you go back," he suggested, "and ask Mr. Lancaster about the billing he's going to get for his small, underpaid part?"

Midway through the making of *Judgment*, on the night of April 17, 1961, the money seemed justified when Greer Garson opened the envelope for Best Actor in the Santa Monica Civic Auditorium and read Lancaster's name as the winner for Best Actor in *Elmer Gantry*. "This," she added, "is really rightly deserved." Later he told a friend that because Shirley Jones had just won as Best Supporting Actress for her performance as Lulu Baines, he was sure he would be the one who lost, that his performance would, as usual, be only a catalyst for other winners even though he had also won the esteemed New York Film Critics Circle Award for Best Actor for the second time. When he heard his name he thought Garson was still reading the list of nominees and would claim he had no memory of kissing Norma and running up to the stage with, it was noted, the bounding grace of Gantry himself. He thanked "all" who voted for him. "I'd even like to thank," he added, with exact Lancaster humor, "those who voted against me." Exultant, he brought the Oscar statue in to work to show Tracy. A few months later, Lancaster was named the number-one box-office star in the country for the first time by the Motion Picture Exhibitors of America. "Hollywood no longer snickers," marked the *New York Morning Telegraph,* "when Lancaster sets out to do something."

On the *Judgment* set, Kramer and Lancaster clashed over certain elements of the Prussian's characterization but both professionals, said Kramer, "were driving toward the same thing." Janning's dramatic about-face acceptance of the collective guilt of his nation is the climax of *Judgment.* He is a good German who should have known better. Guardian of one of the richest cultures of Europe who nonetheless colluded, as a *Junker,* a member of the Prussian military aristocratic class who unified the German nation under Bismarck, he loathes both the bourgeoisie and the Nazi party hacks. In this privileged detachment from most of his countrymen he is indeed cousin to Visconti's Leopard. He hoped, as did the prince, that by giving in a little to the forces of change, he would ensure that nothing fundamental changed. "Where were we?" he asks the courtroom and his people. "Where were we when Hitler began shrieking his hate in the Reichstag. . . . Were we deaf, dumb and blind?" His previously silent presence in the courtroom, the references by other witnesses to his actions in the past, his cumulating reactions are the connecting web of the drama. He gives flesh to the words very much in the minds of the movie's makers from the finale of Thomas Mann's *Dr. Faustus:* "God be merciful to thy poor soul, my friend, my Fatherland." Unlike the Prince, the consequences of Janning's bargain with the devil were catastrophic.

As the actor showed his character accepting his guilt and saying so to the world, the big swing of *Kentuckian* cinematographer Ernest Laszlo's camera eye completely circling Janning in the dock had, said Kramer, "to trace that development." In the coordinated rhythm, the director and the actor were in sync. Although both Kramer and Mann said privately at the time that Lancaster was miscast, the director later came to think that the actor did "one hell of a job making a Nazi into a universal character." With time, his portrayal plays more convincingly than the histrionic work of Schell, with whom he had well-publicized clashes during filming. The actor was so bound up with *Birdman* that the stolid, repressed, haunted quality of one bled into the other and he came onto the set of *Judgment* in a Stroud daze. His hair was growing back, and it took Schiffer, also assigned to *Judgment,* an hour and a half each day to apply the makeup for this other older character. Janning is last seen in his prison cell where he receives Tracy and argues, like Stroud, that he is exempt from the rigor of judgment, that his intent counted more than his actions.

There were some three hundred reporters on hand from more than twenty countries when the movie had its gala premiere at the end of 1961 at the Kongress Halle in Berlin seven hundred yards from the newly armed

Berlin border. Lancaster and Dietrich were absent due to prior commitments, a conspicuous lack that only added to the disastrous reaction of the German audience. "[T]he locals were stunned into silence," reported *Variety*, while others were stunned by the three-hour length. Reviews ranged from the respectful to the derisive. "Kramer," pronounced *Film* magazine in London, "is a sucker for ideas." The premiere was "shrewdly timed," noted *Time*, to coincide with the reading of the judgment at the trial of Nazi war criminal Adolf Eichmann, which had taken place in Israel at the same time as the movie's filming and postproduction. Eichmann was hanged the following May.

The ambitious movie cost $3 million, lost $1.5 million, and grossed only $6 million. With numbers like that, Lancaster's salary was even more impressive. Nominated for eight Oscars, at the ceremonies in 1962 it ended up with two: Mann for Best Screenplay and Schell beating out Tracy for Best Actor. Pointedly *not* nominated was Lancaster. He was too big a star to be put up for Supporting Actor and his limited, if crucial, speaking part did not equate—in another finely parsed Hollywood computation—with those of Tracy and Schell.

Back reshooting *Birdman* in May, he began a long process that would include, by his reckoning, three months alone of editing the picture with Trosper after Frankenheimer left to start work on *The Manchurian Candidate*. Looking ahead to the film's opening in summer 1962, he began his campaign to get Stroud pardoned. Even after U.S. Attorney General Robert F. Kennedy turned down Lancaster's personal plea, the star kept up the pressure, appearing before press and club groups across the country. In April 1962, when television newsman Mike Wallace, hosting *PM*, a late-night interview show on New York's Channel 5, tried to question Lancaster about his altercation with Schell and his "murderous temper" rather than *Birdman*, the star stood up and left the taping. "My temper," he insisted, "belongs to me." As a parting shot, he called the newsman, already famous for his own kind of confrontations, a name Wallace would not repeat to the next-day's audience. It was the first time in seventeen years of interviewing, said Wallace, that a guest had walked out on him in the middle of a show. Commentators agreed that both the movie and the campaign for Stroud got a lot of publicity out of it.

Lancaster's campaign died a quick death, however, when it was revealed that one of the reasons prison officials had been reluctant through twenty-four pardon requests to free the convict who insisted on total unsupervised freedom was that he was what the FBI called a "violent homosexual." Years later Lancaster would claim that the real fear was that, as a senile old man, the Birdman "might get involved in some sexual perversion

THE PAYOFF

with little children." After a screening for a group of media writers and federal officials at the Georgetown Theater in Washington in early May, Senator Edward V. Long, Chairman of a Senate subcommittee on federal prisons, asked Lancaster point-blank about the rumors. The star deferred to one of Stroud's lawyers. "Stroud has insisted," said Stanley A. Furman, "he never forced his attention on anyone" and that "any homosexual arrangements he indulges in are mutual. . . . The man is seventy-two," he concluded, "the juices have simmered." That last comment, reported *Variety,* "got a laugh."

Birdman did earn Lancaster his third Oscar nomination in 1963, the Best Actor award at the 1962 Venice Film Festival, and the Best Foreign Actor award from the British Film Academy. Restraining Frankenheimer's jumpy camera lens to stay within the walls of a prison cell and fixed on the imploding energy of Lancaster produced an inverse power ideal for a story that moved in incremental shutter clicks. And it was a remarkable performance. Lancaster handled the tiny birds with an exquisite gentleness. Where Gantry's voice and flow of words define him, the Birdman is silent: turn off the soundtrack and you miss little.

As several critics pointed out, *Birdman of Alcatraz* was not really a prison flick. Stroud, clomping around the prison yard, watching the years go by, frees himself with his mind and his will without ever getting out of stir. The movie is Lancaster's secular bow to the Christian ideal of redemption he had been brought up with. He hoped *Birdman* would galvanize the audience to free the real-life prisoner. Instead, the people sitting in the dark around the world didn't give a damn about Stroud, prisons, or penal theory: in Lancaster's Birdman, they saw themselves. For fifteen years Burt had been at the mercy of his moods, of an unpredictable rage that left him racked with guilt. "Why did I do that?" he would ask a friend, a costar, sometimes anybody who would listen, after recounting an incident of swearing at Norma or verbally lacerating a coworker. At the same time, there was the gentleness Lehman had noted that came from knowing he, like Stroud, could kill. Ida Turner, the widow of the guard Stroud killed in 1916, could be counted on to protest to any Hollywood studio even thinking of making a movie glorifying her husband's killer. In 1956 she wrote the *Des Moines Tribune* with a chilling insight: "His only reason for having birds was [to] destroy them and thereby in a small way satisfy his desire to kill."

Toward the end of the 1960s Kenneth Branagh, about eight or nine years old, was sitting in front of the television set in his family's Belfast, Northern Ireland, home watching a matinee rerun of *Birdman of Alcatraz.* Aware he was watching the star of *The Crimson Pirate* and *Trapeze,* "in those whompy singlets and that unruly hair of his, very romantic unruly hair . . . a rough diamond powerhouse of energy which felt very American and exotic to me," Branagh was struck then and still "by what an amazing medium it was that could provide a performance like that, that haunted you and made you think and moved you. And which seemed so clearly bound up, in this case, with the actor himself."

An actor, director, and producer himself now, Branagh was born in the dour, prisonlike city of Lancaster's mother's family and his Irish face looks like Cagney's. All three actors have a wariness that could be Irish, a protective sense of reserve, mystery. "You always felt that Lancaster was withholding something very intriguing," Branagh said. "He had a sense that certainly Cagney had of danger. A sort of bravura, élan—a great flourish. Like Cagney, for all his—for want of a better phrase—'working-class origins,' there was always something very stylish and aristocratic about Lancaster. Spiritually, you felt that he was a gent."

On an early November morning in 1961, Carmichael walked up to the twelfth hole of the Bel Air Country Club golf course and noticed what looked like a "little bit of smoke" up in the hills near Lancaster's home. The *New York Post* reported that, by late afternoon, a "mammoth fire" was raging across the Santa Monica hills, engulfing the neighborhoods of Brentwood and Bel Air. Residents fled to the Beverly Hills Hotel and by November 8 Los Angeles officials were calling the disaster the worst fire in Southern California history with estimated damage of more than $15 million.

Three hundred houses were destroyed, including the Lancaster's on Linda Flora, of which there was nothing left but a lone chimney sticking up out of the rubble. The *Los Angeles Times* ran a large photograph of Lancaster and ten-year-old Joanna walking through the smoking ruins. The star, on first seeing what was left of his house, turned to the mailbox, still standing, and made a crack to reporters that *Variety* claimed went around the world on the AP and other news wires: "I just came," he said, ". . . to pick up my *Variety*." In a town that lives almost totally in the present, reactions to the fire were not always the usual ones of shock and regret. "The fire?" says Schiffer, whose family silver service was melted down to a little ball of metal. "It was like cleaning out your closet."

The Lancasters were lucky. While Zsa Zsa Gabor lost a reported forty-five paintings, the Lancaster collection of gouaches by Leger, Chagall, and Roualt, an etching by Chagall, oils by Renoir, Vlaminck, Rousseau, Dufy, and Utrillo, plus eleven small Henry Moore *maquettes* happened to be on display at the time at the Los Angeles County Art Museum. The only real loss, said Lancaster, were all the photos of the children. Also up in flames were paintings by the five young Lancasters which had hung, framed and lighted, alongside the more famous works. The family moved into a rented home at 711 North Beverly Drive in Beverly Hills and started planning, like everybody else, to rebuild.

The fire ended a year of milestone events in Lancaster's life that had begun with winning the Oscar in April. In September, his father, age eighty-five, had died of a heart attack in the Linda Flora house where he had been living for the last four years, surviving Jim by only eight months. All that was left of his original family was his sister Jane living in Port Washington, Long Island. The cluster of wrenching events marked the kind of shift one searches to find later, when all has disappeared. A "helpless feeling" grew within the family as Norma's alcoholism dragged on, observed Joel Douglas and others, "a lot of sadness, a disintegration of a family structure."

In reaction, Lancaster tried to return to some of the simplicities of the early days in Malibu. The time not devoted to making or planning or finishing a movie was filled with adversarial bridge with Thom Conroy and his companion, or watching the Gillette Friday night fights on television with Callaghan, Carmichael, and others: he loved "the ambiance of the thing," recalled one friend, "the seamy underbelly" and the lightning timing. He coached Billy's baseball team in the West Los Angeles Pony League ("I need this like a hole in the head," he joked, missing only one event in the summer 1961 season of forty-five games and twelve practice sessions) and bragged of his catcher son, "He hits like a mule." His golf game progressed slowly. As with bridge, the fascination with the sport that can never be fully mastered totally absorbed him. "I never saw a guy work harder on a golf game," said Carmichael. "Burt was very stiff, not a natural golfer. He couldn't relax. I don't think Burt would ever tell you he was comfortable with his game."

Nick continued to come at least three times a week to work out with him. On the set when everybody broke for lunch, he and Lancaster skipped the meal and flipped through the old routines on the bars. A common observation at the time was that the forty-eight-year-old Lancaster looked a decade younger with the same "monkey butt" and a belly as flat and muscle-ridged as ever; free weights, he told Carmichael, only made the muscles tight, while acrobatics lengthened them. In an era redolent of cigarette smoke and three-martini lunches, reporters continued to record, incredulously, that the star, after running his usual early morning miles around the UCLA track, had skim milk, orange juice, coffee, and a couple of soft-boiled eggs for breakfast, and one big meal at the end of the day. He smoked unfiltered Camels, one after another. Off-camera he wore heavy-rimmed glasses that looked odd, like spectacles on an eagle. His sudden roars of laughter—usually a delight in the incongruous—were disarming and infectious and made the floor vibrate underfoot.

Now that he was relentlessly making "important" intellectual movies, the old question cropped up again: Was Lancaster really *intelligent*? Like art, it depended on how you defined it. "Burt was smart," said Carmichael. "You know what I mean by 'smart': He was always an East Coast guy. He knew how he got up there. I consider it intelligence when you are just as happy sitting on the back of one of the sound trucks with Mushy [Callagan] sharing a sandwich. People who are smart about themselves don't dispose of people."

Pete Martin, the *Saturday Evening Post* writer who had interviewed the star as a rising comet in 1948, broke his perfect record of never repeating a profile, and returned to examine Lancaster around the time of his Oscar award in 1961. Lancaster frankly admitted to him that he had had "periods of depression" and setbacks, but that he had lost his "fear of Hollywood," the terror that had fueled his famous temper. "Everybody changes," he said. "I hope I have. I hope I have more understanding of what I'm doing. I hope I'm better at my work. . . . I feel," he suggested in a simple sentence that, however, had been hard-earned, "that I am a good actor." When Martin asked Brooks if Lancaster had changed since *Brute Force*, the director replied, "Of course, he's changed. . . . He's tougher than he used to be, but at the same time, he's more elastic."

While an irony of Lancaster's career is that some of his best later work would be a mystery to any mass audience at the time of its release and only make sense later, with the perspective of time, he claimed to Martin, in typical Lancasterese, that he did not believe in art for art's sake: "If what [an actor] has to say remains a mystery to people who see it, I don't think he's done a job. All worthwhile creative work has a kind of universality. . . . If it doesn't measure up to that, then it's not art, it's bad." When someone asked him at a UCLA lecture that same year why better pictures were not being made, Lancaster snapped, "Better pictures *are* being made."

His next project was one of the most personally heartfelt films he would ever make—and one of his most ambitious failures. Kramer knew Lancaster had "a troubled child" and would be susceptible to a story inspired by a 1957 nine-minute TV short written by Abby Mann on the subject of "mentally disturbed" children—*A Child Is Waiting*. Starting the month after the Berlin premiere of *Judgment at Nuremberg*, Lancaster became deeply engaged, again, in a message-laden Kramer project at Revue Studios for UA. Playing the director of a state mental institution for children, he is a strict, disciplined professional who insists to the more protective, emotional music teacher, played by Judy Garland, that the impaired children be taught the dignity of independence and accomplishment—his own approach with Jimmy. Though the movie would seem like an aberration in the flow of his work, its theme of respecting the individual's right to be himself, no matter how bizarre he may seem to others, is in keeping with his work dating back to *Kiss the Blood Off My Hands*. When it was released in 1963, Brendan Gill wrote in *The New Yorker*, "It is almost unbearable to be made to observe and admire the delicacy of the acting skill of Mr. Lancaster and Miss Garland as they move—the charming, the successful, the famously gifted ones—among that host of pitiful children." (Handicapped children were cast in the movie as themselves.) But for Lancaster that was the point. "Suppose," he asked a reporter, "you or I were born into a race of Einsteins?'"

The movie was made on the cheap and directed by newcomer John Cassavetes, whose underground hit *Shadows*, released in 1960, was the first of a string of films that would make him what David Thomson has called "the first modern American independent" director. Shooting began in January at Pomona State Hospital in Pomona, California, with the handicapped children and "normals," including, among the latter, seven-year-old Sighle Lancaster as "Jennie." Most of the impaired children could only concentrate on any given instruction for about fifteen seconds, with the result that Cassavetes had to shoot what editor Gene Fowler called "an inordinate amount of film." The director's newness to the craft also guaranteed problems with Lancaster. Worse, his improv style matched with this particular subject matter and cast—Garland, already drinking, was rendered even more fragile and unpredictable by working with the children—was anathema to the actor's linear mind.

Lancaster, having spent two months at the hospital, observing, started coaching Garland on the side. Kramer, reviewing the rushes, joined with Lancaster in opposing Cassavetes, often scene by scene. When the director insisted Lancaster erupt furiously at Garland in one take, "tear her to pieces, tell her she's a fucking idiot," the star objected, claiming that, as a doctor, he would never overreact in such an unprofessional manner. When Kramer saw the scene, he thought, according to Lancaster's retelling, that the star indeed looked "ridiculous" and it was reshot. During the editing process, Kramer yanked the movie away from Cassavetes and finished it himself, with Fowler. Cassavetes disowned it and, according to his biographer, Raymond Carney, it is a "stretching point to consider it a Cassavetes film at all."

By the time Kramer had cut the movie in October, Lancaster was in Rome filming the last interior scenes for *The Leopard*. The producer declined to send a print of the film to the Grand Hotel, writing to the actor that the movie had already cost a half million too much, which was, coincidentally, the amount of Lancaster's salary. While Lancaster was "heartsick" at what had been left out, his sense of humor remained intact. Writing Kramer from Sicily, he sympathized that the director had had to make both *Judgment at Nuremberg* and *A Child Is Waiting* surrounded by "atomic egos," with the former salvaged by "someone as solid as old Spence." He asked Kramer to give Tracy his love and to "tell him they hate Mr. Schell in Europe too. Which reminds me," he added, "I have heard some brilliant things about a young director called John Cassavetes and if you like I will try to sign him for about seventeen years for your exclusive use. . . ." Ten years later—*Faces* just behind him, *Woman Under the Influence* just ahead—Cassavetes would breeze into Lancaster's office on the Universal lot. "You ought to do another [picture] with me," he told Lancaster. "I know a lot more, now."

Lancaster was getting older, forty-eight years old in 1962. The flesh was starting, barely, to shift. Never, in his almost half-century on the planet, had he looked back, but now he would portray a character whose entire existence was predicated on the past. *Il Gattopardo* was written by Giussepe di Lampedusa partially as a response to the Allied bombing of Palermo in April 1943 which virtually destroyed the palazzo of his aristocratic family. The wave of change and development that swept postwar Italy further accelerated the end of everything his class knew and valued. The author looked back to the previous big change of his culture and history— Garibaldi's fight against feudalism and privilege and the triumph of the bourgeoisie in the new, nonfeudal, unified nation-state of modern Italy in the 1860s—to bury his people with full literary honors. Di Lampedusa's only book, *Il Gattopardo,* was published in 1958 shortly after his death and became a surprise best-seller, even in America.

His *gattopardo,* the Sicilian Leopard Prince of Salina was, Lancaster said, "inimical to me." At first glance, he was right: Don Fabrizio of Salina is an aristocrat with an exquisite fatalism about life, death, history, his own class, his own person. Missing nothing, he is yet so detached from the immediate life around him that a measure of his distance is his absorption in the study of the stars. He is not defined by what he has made of himself; he is who he always has been. The idea of change and progress has no meaning for him except, as the novel famously said, to ensure that nothing changes. He bestirs himself to act strategically, like a retreating commandant, only in response to the *Risorgimento,* Garibaldi's revolt.

Lancaster lived for change, for the act of transforming himself in response to the changing world around him. He knew from years of observation the East Harlem legacy of Italian feudalism: torpor, despair, brutal manual labor, fear of education, squalor. Nick was one of the dark, small, faceless minions Don Fabrizio would have been aware of only as a paternalistic obligation lurking at the back of the stable. As Salina, he had to play the kind of man whose inability to change had caused one of the greatest human migrations of modern times. As Burt Lancaster, he was for millions of non-Americans *the* American, whose presence and avid energy and natural grace seemed emblematic of a new nation.

Yet there were in the American elements of the Italian Leopard, the big cat whose paws bent silver teaspoons during fits of rage. Salina was graceful, strong, magnificently, drolly oblivious, and so was Lancaster. In the multilayered personality Odets had found so contradictory, there was a strong streak of noblesse oblige. The prince is, supremely, a patriarch and so was Lancaster, the male who will take care of everyone whether they wish to be cared for or not. To be depended upon is a kind of power that Lancaster relished, and the ultimate anguish of the Prince of Salina comes when he knows that he and his class are now useless, needed by no one.

When Visconti viewed *Birdman of Alcatraz* before agreeing to cast Lancaster as the Leopard, he would have seen the actor's hands rolling cigarettes and gently building the cages, coaxing and stroking the birds— nature's gentleman with the long, slim, knowing, uncalloused fingers of an aristocrat, that manipulate with incredible finesse. Visconti later described the prince as "a very complex character—at times autocratic, rude, strong; at times romantic, understanding, sometimes even stupid and above all, mysterious," and then admitted that Lancaster was all these things too. The Lampedusa coat of arms, like that of the de Lancastres, is a leopard, rampant.

The Duke of Modrone of Milan; the director of *Senso, Bellissima,* and opera productions at La Scala; the reputed lover of Maria Callas; sexual connoisseur of blond young men and boys, Visconti was attracted by this tale that hit an aristocratic tone between passion and irony. He was regarded in 1962 as one of the great directors of Europe, a master of postwar neorealist cinema. His *Rocco and His Brothers* had come out in 1960, the same year as Federico Fellini's *La Dolce Vita* and Michaelangelo Antonioni's *L'Avventura,* and the trio were central to the renaissance of Italian film. Though a public and enthusiastic Marxist, Visconti's luxurious lifestyle conformed to his class and background. He revered the form and grace of a beautiful body, especially the supposedly "higher" form of the masculine physique, and his various homes were filled with precious *objets,* attractive people, and servants. By showing the end of a class whose dignity and distinction had come at such a human cost, he could yet pay homage with the passion of an insider to a style and beauty the world would never see again.

Goffredo Lombardo, the Neopolitan producer of *Rocco and His Brothers* and head of Titanus Films, bought the rights to the novel and entered into a production agreement with 20th Century-Fox in order to secure the lavish budget. When Visconti's first three choices for his Leopard—Nikolai Cherkasov, the lead in Sergei Eisenstein's 1938 *Alexander Nevsky,* Brando, and Olivier—were, for one reason or another, not available, Fox stipulated that the lead must be one of four American box-office stars: Gregory Peck, Anthony Quinn, Spencer Tracy, or Lancaster. The director countered with his own demand that he at least be allowed to interview any candidate first, but Lombardo offered the part to Lancaster who accepted before Visconti had a chance to meet him. The director had to settle for the screenings of *Judgment* and *Birdman* after which he said, in effect, according to Lancaster, "Well, *maybe.*" Alain Delon, Claudia Cardinale, and several of Italy's finest actors, including Romolo Valli and Lucilla Morlacchi, were also cast. Lancaster, who had read and admired the book, accepted only after Lombardo screened *Rocco and His Brothers* for *him. The Leopard* was not only a chance to become a so-called international star in the movie already being touted as the European *Gone With the Wind,* but also an exposure to a director working at an entirely different level of craft. The industry consensus was that it was "the most blatant piece of miscasting of the year."

The result of the casting mix-up was that, even before the star arrived in Sicily on May 14, 1962, to begin work on the five-month project, his director bore a big grudge. Visconti's attitude to his *gattopardo* was bound to be complex: Lancaster was playing an idealized version of Visconti. Having prepared with his customary exactitude for months before the shoot the Sicilian locations, sets, and props—using the expert services of di Lampedusa's adopted son Gioacchino Lanza Tomasi, Duke of Palma, to scout out locations and to advise on the multitude of historical details—Visconti now turned the full force of his demanding nature on the work of transforming his American movie star, his barbarian, to meet his exacting vision.

It was an excruciating experience for Lancaster. He had immersed himself in Italian history and arrived eager to learn from a new director who could teach him much. "I didn't for one moment," he later said, "pretend that I could do what he was doing better than Visconti could do it himself." But he was treated like the cowboy, the gangster Visconti assumed he was. The director already had a reputation for setting up cruel challenges to those around him and then, according to biographer Gaia Serviado, idolizing those who "resisted." If Lancaster was going to play his *gattopardo,* it was necessary for Visconti to test him, to find his breaking point. Initially, the director did not speak to his star or consult with him about the script or the role other than giving vague instructions about letting the Leopard come to him, as if through the air. As an extra snub, Lancaster was excluded from the dinners Visconti gave for the other actors in the lavishly decorated house in Palermo that he rented for the shoot.

"Lancaster had the wisdom," recalled Suso Cecchi D'Amico, the director's esteemed and trusted screenwriter, "to pretend that he hadn't noticed the coldness aimed at him." Instead, he built up the trust of the rest of the cast and crew who dubbed him "the anti-star" for his quiet, studious demeanor. "As further proof of his intelligence," added D'Amico, "Lancaster took advantage of the interest his presence aroused in Palermo's high society. He ably chose which surroundings to frequent in order to observe the behavior and movements of real Italian aristocrats, such as Prince Scalea, whose villa on the coast he rented. He learned, on his own initiative, how to move with ease around the antique furniture and an infinity of paintings and objects crowding those surroundings so different from the elegant but aseptic dwellings he knew in Los Angeles." When he realized the other, non–English-speaking actors were not only struggling with the stipulation in his contract that his scenes be shot in English, but that their performances were much better in their native tongues, he asked Visconti to disregard his contract and let each actor speak as he or she wished. The director accepted the offer, but "did not," said D'Amico, "express any gratitude." He earned the thanks of his coworkers, but inadvertently worsened the multilingual mess that, later, doomed the English-language version of the film.

All the while the actor observed Visconti himself, learned his gestures, his stance, the way he dominated others by his assumption of superiority. For the first time since his instinctive beginner's luck on *The Killers*, he did not jump to dominate a role. Clinging to Visconti's one scrap of advice, he waited for the Leopard to inhabit him. "Don't sit on the corn!" the director's voice boomed through the megaphone one day to an extra squatting in the field. "No real worker would ever sit on the corn he has gathered." This was a level of exactitude and artistry the actor soaked in like a sponge. It was agonizing to think he might not meet the standard.

The ostracizing continued into August. The shoot proceeded through the sequences at the Villa Salina (the real-life Villa Boscogrande outside Palermo), the hot dusty journey to Donnafugata (the actual village of Ciminna), and the outdoor scenes at Donnafugata. Not until the long, difficult ball scene, shot at the Palazzo Gangi back in Palermo, did matters improve. "[T]he finest hour of film Visconti ever shot," Pauline Kael wrote much later, a model for *The Deer Hunter* and *The Godfather*, the ball was also Visconti's solution to the problem of how to imply the end of the novel, in which the prince dies, without actually killing him off in the movie. Salina's nephew Tancredi, played by Delon, has fought with Garibaldi, shifted opportunistically with the tide of events to ally himself politically with the forces of the new, national king, Victor Emmanuel II, and no less adroitly secured his financial future by becoming engaged to Cardinale's Angelica, the daughter of the weasly petit-bourgeois mayor of Donnafugata. The ball is to celebrate this coming marriage, to introduce the beautiful fiancée to the Palermo aristocracy (recruited by Palma's wife to play themselves in this scene), and to mark the end of one kind of history and the beginning of another.

Lancaster had not only to personify the change, the bargain with events Salina has so carefully facilitated, but also to show his evolution from youthful vigor to the bone-deep fatigue of too much life, too much history. He walks, wanders, from room to room in the huge ornate palazzo, observing as if for the first and last time all the people he has ever known. Retreating to the library, he sees on the wall a copy of Greuze's *Death of a Just Man* and knows, with the chill pain of revelation, that he will die, that he has always been dying. The peak of the scene and the movie is when Angelica and the prince waltz together, circling alone on the ballroom floor as everyone watches the striking, symbolic pair. When Salina hands Angelica back to Tancredi there is a split-second when the camera rests on the prince's stricken face. He looks one last time at the lovely young woman, at worldly flesh and warmth and energy, and says good-bye to life and his place in it. On that moment the film pivots.

To avoid the ferocious Sicilian August heat, the scene was filmed from eight at night until four in the morning over several weeks. Lancaster hurt his knee, activating an old injury from De Witt Clinton basketball days, and asked Visconti to postpone the waltz segment with Cardinale to give the leg more time to heal. The director refused. Although both stars had taken waltz lessons in preparation, the first take did not go well. "Come, Claudina," said Visconti, according to the recollections of Cardinale in her autobiography, "Mr. Lancaster will let us know when he's ready." It was a publicly humiliating denigration and Lancaster, at last, decided to react. "At the end of the sequence," D'Amico recalled, "he went into the room reserved for Visconti, closed the door behind him and immediately began to bellow." Later he told the screenwriter that, "soured by the pain in his knee and worn out by lack of sleep, he had lost his temper. He felt let down by the treatment of a director he admired greatly, but who only wanted to let him know—without helping him, however—that he didn't consider him up to the job he'd been hired for." In the middle of the "row," the star stopped himself, according to D'Amico, "as if on the edge of a cliff—terrified by the idea that he'd lost all possibility of a calm working relationship with Visconti."

But that is exactly what he gained—and more—by the outburst. From that moment, the two men fell in together, as friendly, said D'Amico, as brothers. "I don't use the word 'brothers' by chance," she explained. "Visconti's relationship with Lancaster often brought to my mind his rapport with his older brother. Real, deep affection, esteem, respect, solidarity—but not closeness." By November 2, the mutual birth date of both men, and after the whole enterprise had moved to Rome for the interior carriage scenes and the Donnafugata interiors, they were on such good terms they shared a party at Visconti's villa on Via Salaria, "grander than usual that year," recalled D'Amico, "and dedicated in part to Burt." For the ideal gift, each researched the other's taste carefully and in secret and, with "reciprocal surprise," gave each other paintings by Renato Guttuso.

The new rapport was an extraordinary breakthrough, marking a major change in Lancaster's sense of himself as an actor and a man of his time. "After working with Visconti," he said in 1976, "one could never be the same again. He was the most important director I worked for because he opened for me a new world and a new way of doing things." After a lifetime of fleeing Stanislavsky in any form, he was now exposed to this director who, according to Tomasi, considered the Russian his "imaginative master." "Visconti had an idea," said Tomasi, "that without the correct ambiance you cannot have real acting. . . . It is not a capricious idea of 'real food' or 'real flowers' or 'real antiques.' It was that if that environment had been a product of the men who lived in it, only a fastidious remodelling of the environment could give us back those men." Even when ignoring his Leopard, Visconti had made sure that Lancaster's on-set chest of drawers was filled with real silk shirts for him "to touch" and that the camera never saw. Similarly, the director spent two hours one night stuffing the prince's mattress to get just the right mixture of lumps. Like the Princess and the Pea, only Lancaster and Rina Morelli, playing the prince's wife, would feel the difference.

Lancaster would have liked to have been a Visconti, a perfectionist in complete control of his vision. Growing up with his head full of Kipling's valedictory poem to Lord Roberts, he was attracted to the idea of himself as a natural aristocrat, noble. He might have been a *gattopardo*, the supple, powerful cat who rules the jungle because he is so strong in his beauty. (A few years later Bruce Dern would say to him, "Burt, you oughta run for King. You'd get elected." And Lancaster, after deliberating a moment, would reply in all seriousness, "Yes. I'd make a good King. I'd be fair.") Tomasi noted that because this New World man, this movie star was "totally of today, totally American, not a man of history," he "liked being put *into* history" by Visconti. The convergence of the two men—one who had, in Tomasi's estimation, "no historical taste, no discrimination," and the other "highly connected to the centuries, to the floor of time"—produced the desired effect: a remarkable performance in which the tireless, exuberant actor held his most defining characteristics in check, simplifying himself into a different form of grace and power. His athlete's economy of gesture became something princely, the mark of Lampedusa's idealized superior being. "I had the luck," he said, "to have an obedient body. I told it to 'March like a prince' and it marched like a prince."

As Lancaster went deeper into these layers of time and snobbery, the ironies of his performance became more complex. The New World man of no taste, as that word is defined by the limitations of Old World parochialism, could yet transform himself into a prince. That the opposite could never happen was the story of the necessary death of an entire way of life.

When a new set of rumors began to circulate, much later, about Lancaster's possible bisexuality, it was often assumed that his exposure to Visconti had been crucial. If he did find some kind of a sexual model in Visconti, it may have been in what Tomasi calls the director's notion of the "hyper-man," derived, D'Amico suggested, from a noble warrior tradition going back, in Visconti's case—and perhaps in Lancaster's—to his ancestors' service in the forces of Charlemagne. "It was the ancient aristocratic sort of strong man," she recalled of the droit du seigneur ideal. "They considered they had the right to do whatever they wanted. But if you told Visconti that it was a homosexual thing, he would have been sincerely surprised. Perhaps it comes out of the aristocrat going to war for years and having the pages and the young men. Maybe it becomes in their blood. I don't know." She insisted that while there was plenty of evidence of Lancaster's pursuit of women, she saw no evidence then or during the years of their friendship of other than heterosexual behavior.

Cardinale also later heard rumors "whispered" of the star, but dismissed them as "not adding up." She admired the "almost maniacal care" he took of his "perfect body." "He was as beautiful," she wrote in her autobiography, "as a Greek hero," a jumble of "that transparent, luminous glance . . . sometimes shocking acts and behaviors." In that attention to his body, Tomasi claims to find a clue to Lancaster's sexual identity. "I believe he was bi-sexual," he said. "He was certainly heterosexual. He had a knowledge of everything sexual! And he had this feeling of himself as a beautiful man and in that there was something narcissistic. He had to look like a sort of youthful god and a god who didn't want that to go away, didn't want that to change. Normally men have the change and it doesn't matter. He felt that very much." To work on *The Leopard*, he told Tomasi, he had put aside another project: the movie version of Irving Stone's 1961 best-selling novel, *The Agony and the Ecstasy*. He had bought the rights to this story of Michaelangelo, who was with equal skill a painter, sculptor, poet, and inventor. "He wanted very much to shoot a film on the Renaissance,"

Tomasi recalled, "that was connected to the high admiration of the homosexual genius. He would have acted Michaelangelo, the great, great man, the man who is extraordinary. Sex is only part of this model of beauty, the idealistic model of life."

In this whirl of ideas which Lancaster absorbed into his skin with the Sicilian sun, there is one beam of sure truth. Like Visconti, he did not wish himself to be defined by vulgar categories, vulgar in the first sense of simplistic, crude, limiting. The same drive to change and risk and test himself that shaped his movies was no less an imperative in his off-screen life. Michaelangelo could write in both directions on a page with both hands simultaneously. Such dexterity was irresistible to Lancaster.

His life assumed another layer of incongruity. Postproduction, back in unaristocratic Hollywood, Schiffer joined the Kibbees one night for dinner at the Lancasters' rented house. Visconti had given the star a set of what Schiffer called "the most beautiful china—blue—you've ever seen," and Norma used the dishes to serve up one of the couple's favorite recipes, chili. Incredulous, Roland Kibbee blurted out, "How can you put chili on a plate like this?"

Coming six months after the shock of the Bel Air fire, the summer in Sicily was one of the last times the Lancaster family would all be in one place, all together. Norma and the children and two friends arrived in Palermo after their summer camp sessions were over and Lancaster rented a yacht for them all. More than thirty years later, shortly after his father died, Billy would tell a family friend that the summer on location for *The Leopard* was the best time the family ever had. Tomasi recalls the children as "not very happy, mentally or physically."

He was not too proud to turn down the chance during a break in filming to make a quick buck in *The List of Adrian Messenger,* a whodunit produced by Kirk Douglas's Joel Productions, a corporate subcompany of Bryna. It was shot in Ireland and England with the added gimmick of a bunch of famous stars—Curtis, Mitchum, Sinatra—artfully disguised in cameo performances. Lancaster appeared briefly in drag as a woman protesting fox hunting. Such vacations from earnestness helped to pay the bills.

In Italy, Lancaster embraced the language, food, smells, the opera, and the gestures of the country whose people had surrounded him at birth. Marriages, relationships, work, and children would come and go, but Italy would remain a constant, his second country. There he was respected as a great man of the cinema, the magically glamorous American star of the Italians' grim postwar recovery years who had transcended himself to become their *gattopardo.*

He hired a genial, energetic Roman, Ivo Palazzi, as guide, sometime cook, procurer of yachts, and general organizer. Over the next thirty years he became a trusted friend and another member of the star's "team" along with Schiffer, Conroy, and wardrobe man Jack Martell. "Ivo!" Lancaster boomed over the telephone from Los Angeles before a trip, "I'm coming!" Eventually the owner of a thriving celebrity limousine service in Rome with clients like Robin Williams, Palazzi would book the hotel in Rome—initially the Grand Hotel and later the Hilton—stock cases of pasta to take on location, and plan the routes and destinations for the friend and boss he affectionately called "the Master." Lancaster ran early each morning before breakfast in the Stadio dei Marmi in Rome, the massive, marble statue–lined stadium built by Mussolini in the Foro Italico, and once told Palazzi that they had probably seen each other in June 1944 when the U.S. Fifth Army had been based there just after the liberation of Rome. As they drove around the countryside, Lancaster sitting in the front seat as "the captain of the road," they tested new restaurants, visited hilltowns in Umbria, and discovered Riccione on the Adriatic where Lancaster pronounced, "I would like to die in this town." Lampedusa's Leopard had died on a seaside hotel balcony, the water crashing down below.

While enmeshed in the intricacies of time past, he was jerked back into the American here and now when Douglas sent him in Italy a copy of a current best-selling novel, *Seven Days in May*. Written by Washington newsmen Fletcher Knebel and Charles Bailey II, the book posed the possibility that a principled and patriotic but fanatic right-wing Chairman of the Joint Chiefs of Staff, General James Muldoon Scott, loosely modeled on General MacArthur, could and would plan an American coup d'état to protect the national security of the country from the dangers of a nuclear disarmament treaty with the Russians. "If the whole point of the functioning of democracy is to have weight and merit," Lancaster wrote back to Douglas in late September 1962, then it was important for any film version to show that the right-wing generals, "however misguided, are more than just power-hungry. . . . In fact," he concluded, "a strong case should be made for them." The two stars had been considering some kind of "loose amalgamation," but when Lancaster decided that after his HHL experience he did not "relish the idea of a partnership with anyone at this stage," Douglas countered with the suggestion that they go in together on a movie version of the book. "I'm glad you liked *Seven Days in May*," he replied to Lancaster on October 8, finding his friend's dismissal of the book's literary merits "a little too harsh" and insisting that the generals are not presented as just power hungry. "They believe in what they are doing—completely—" he wrote, "therein lies the danger." Douglas closed by responding to a different complaint at the end of Lancaster's letter: "the girls," he wrote, "don't look at me anymore either."

With every passing week of that October—what William Manchester later called a "month of unsurpassed autumnal glory"—the book's premise became more plausible. Shortly after the start of Kennedy's term almost three years earlier, the nation had weathered the disastrous Cuban Bay of Pigs "invasion" in April 1961 ("Those sons of bitches with all the fruit salad just sat there nodding, saying it would work," *Washington Post* editor Ben Bradlee recalled Richard Reeves quoting Kennedy's remarks about the real Joint Chiefs after the debacle. "How could I have been so stupid?"). Eighteen months later, two weeks after Douglas wrote to Lancaster in Rome, Kennedy appeared on national television on October 22 to announce evidence of Soviet-supplied missile sites on Cuba. The world then held its breath for six days until the Cuban missile crisis ended with Soviet leader Nikita Khrushchev's order to dismantle what were indeed sites for surface-to-air missiles.

The stupidity of one crisis followed by the potential horror of the next set a perfect stage for *Seven Days in May*, a story of Pentagon intrigue, treachery, bungling, and heroism. As Dwight Macdonald of *Esquire* would write, the movie was "a negative print of *Dr. Strangelove*," the apocalyptic Stanley Kubrick fantasy that was released just before *Seven Days in May*. Or, as Crowther at the *Times* observed, the most overt instance of Hollywood's flirting with the idea of the demagogue since Louis B. Mayer refused to make a movie of the Sinclair Lewis FTP play, *It Can't Happen Here*, and the release of *All the King's Men* in 1949.

Representing the forces of good against Lancaster's General Scott were a peace-mongering president, played by Frederic March, and Douglas's Colonel Jigs Casey, who unravels the whole scary coup scheme. "General Scott, the Joint Chiefs, even the lunatic fringe—they're not the enemy," says March's chief executive. "The enemy is the age, the nuclear age. It happens to have killed man's faith to influence what happens to him. And from this desperation, we look for a champion in red, white, and blue. . . . For some it was a Senator McCarthy. . . . Now, it's a General Scott." The central issue, according to the book's authors, writing in the September 11, 1962, issue of *Look* magazine, was the Constitution: if the United States must keep a "giant military force" constantly at the ready against the Soviet Union, how also to preserve the "constitutional framework which is perhaps the most precious thing we seek to save?"

The movie had to make absolutely clear, if Hollywood and the U.S. military were to get behind it, that checks and balances were in place to ensure that such a takeover would never really happen. Though Paramount eventually financed the movie, UA's Blumofe threw in a key suggestion: get the encouragement of "the Executive Branch." By July, *Newsweek* reported that "the top brass is in an uproar. . . . At least one service, the Army, turned the idea [of cooperating with a movie] down flat, saying it put the military in an undeserved bad light." Douglas, on a trip to Washington to confer with the book's authors, found himself standing at a "fancy buffet dinner" when JFK came up and asked him if he intended to make a movie of *Seven Days in May*. When Douglas replied yes, the President proceeded to tell him why and how it would make an excellent movie.

As Douglas wooed Lancaster, his producer-partner at Bryna, Edward Lewis, approached Frankenheimer to direct the picture. He and Lewis went into partnership and hired writer Rod Serling of television's *Twilight Zone* who had also worked on many shows with Frankenheimer. When Douglas phoned the director to say he preferred Lancaster as General Scott instead of the current choice, Paul Newman, Frankenheimer told him that two pictures in a row with Lancaster was plenty. Douglas insisted he would take care of any problems with the costar. He felt more comfortable with his *Gunfight at the O.K. Corral* pal, plus he felt that Lancaster's presence in the film would ensure its commercial success. Frankenheimer recalled cautioning Douglas that as Casey he was playing, for all practical purposes, an informer, "but Kirk decided to do that part anyway," he said. As Douglas came to see the drawbacks of playing the snoop among titans, Frankenheimer detected that in his chagrin there was not only an irritation at not being properly treated as "a movie star," but also an envy of Lancaster. "He was jealous of Burt Lancaster," the director has said. "He wanted to be Burt Lancaster. He's wanted to be Burt Lancaster all his life." Nevertheless, according to Frankenheimer, the two stars, now working on their fourth movie together, "really liked each other."

Seven Days in May was quickly shot in summer 1963 on the director's signature black-and-white film stock with an assemblage of faces from Lancaster's movie past: Ava Gardner as Eleanor Holbrook, the one-time lover of Scott; Edmond O'Brien, who would get an Oscar nomination for his portrayal of the boozy senator who is sent out to the El Paso desert to find the covert base from which the coup will be launched; and Whit Bissell as a right-wing senator who is in on the plot. Lancaster, recovering from a bout of hepatitis, arrived for the production later than the others and was, perhaps, not his usual adversarial self. He was also preoccupied with postproduction work on *The Leopard*. He and Frankenheimer "really bonded" on the filming and the director has since recalled the experience to be "one of the best I ever had dealing with an actor."

Aware that the director of *The Manchurian Candidate*, a controversial political thriller called by one critic the "un-American film of the year," would now be directing *Seven Days in May*—the "first time," according to the *New York Times*, that a Hollywood movie attacked McCarthyism by name—JFK made what amounted to an ideological choice to cooperate enthusiastically. While the president and his family were in Hyannisport on the weekend of July 27, 1963, the production could use the White House exterior as background for the movie's opening riot scene between pro- and antidisarmament treaty demonstrators. The mansion interior would be made available to sketch, photograph, and "do everything needed to duplicate the set in Hollywood," recalled Frankenheimer. The director was allowed to attend press conferences to observe first-hand the protocol and format. That summer JFK signed a real test-ban treaty.

The key scene, for the movie's makers, was when March's sane, principled president confronts Lancaster's icily unbalanced general with his discovery of the coup and demands his resignation. In response, Scott must articulate his position, defend it, and prepare to act, thereby forcing the plot into the open. Serling spent two weeks writing what he called the "battle of two philosophies"—the American political right versus the left. What about the ballot box? demands the president. We don't have time for the ballot box, snaps back Scott, convinced the Soviet Union will attack under cover of the treaty. If there's a military coup, trumps the commander in chief, they will invade anyway, within hours. Lancaster was in careful awe of March, the great star and actor of *Death of a Salesman* and *The Best Years of Our Lives*. When, on the suggestion of the older actor who knew every line of the script, they rehearsed the weekend before shooting, Lancaster proceeded, according to Frankenheimer, to flub line after line. Slamming down his fist, he yelled, "Goddamn it! I knew these lines in my office!" March coolly asked why he had not brought his office with him. "The next day," said Frankenheimer, "Burt knew every line" of the eight-page scene that was then shot in one day. "I have never seen two actors," he added, "more concentrated. Burt had to show March he could do it; March had to show he was king."

Seven Days in May opened in February 1964, its release delayed a month to avoid any appearance of capitalizing on the national tragedy of Kennedy's assassination. The *New York Herald-Tribune* assured its readers that the movie's scenario "could not happen here, now," for several reasons, one of which being Secretary of Defense Robert S. McNamara, who was "exercising his powers with great decisiveness." In the end, casting the man who had played Sergeant Warden in *From Here to Eternity* gave General Scott whatever measure of sympathy and understanding he has. The pain Warden would have felt at turning against his commander in chief, his Constitution, is not conveyed by Lancaster's sinister performance. It was too late for such evenhandedness. Jamming the familiar signals of stardom, he sacrificed his heroic persona in the service of a movie that was, as Crowther noted, "a hymn to American democracy."

While filming *Seven Days in May* in the summer of 1963, Burt endured what D'Amico believed was "one of the griefs in Lancaster's life." Preoccupied with *Cleopatra*, 20th Century-Fox had insisted the too long, too Italian *Leopard* be cut to 165 minutes, most of it from the ball sequence and battle scenes. For European distribution and screening at the 1963 Cannes Film Festival, Visconti had already edited the movie from a massive 205 minutes to 185 minutes in seventy-millimeter, large-screen Technirama and richly hued Technicolor; Visconti, D'Amico, and Lancaster were all at Cannes when it was announced that the film, to rapturous acclaim, had won the *Palme d'Or*, Visconti's first. Visconti had agreed, even before shooting finished, to give Lancaster charge of the English-language version and the star turned to Pollack to help him with both the cutting and the postsynch dubbing after Cannes. With Emmy nominations now to his credit but still under contract to Universal and "antsy" for the move to feature films, Pollack agreed. In the Titra sound studios in New York during spring 1963 he and Lancaster worked doggedly for about five weeks, all day every day, on what Pollack later called "a hopeless job." "We tried desperately," he said, "because by this time Burt was an expert, a fanatic about it." The American release prints were processed in thirty-five millimeter, thin Deluxe color, and Cinerama.

The end result, disowned by Visconti, was almost universally panned that summer and kept the film, like a sleeping beauty, as good as dead for English-speaking audiences for twenty years. There was the old prejudice against Lancaster overreaching himself, presuming to play a part so utterly dissimilar to anything he had ever done. "Lancaster," said *Newsweek* in August 1963, "looks as if he's playing Clarence Day's *Life With Father* in summer stock." Jonathan Miller in *The New Yorker* jeered that Lancaster was "muzzled by whiskers and clearly stunned by the importance of his role." It was as if he had indeed given the performance Visconti thought him only good for at the beginning. The few who were able to see what the director and actor intended would be vindicated by the very cycle of years the Leopard so trusted and feared: "as the scenes accumulate," reported *Time*, "the character compiles impressive volume and solidity, and by film's end the grand Sicilian stands in the mind as a man whose like men shall not look upon again: one of culture's noblemen, a very imperfect gentle knight."

Lancaster seized on the Bel Air fire as a last chance to salvage his deteriorating family life and suggested they all pack up for Portland or Seattle and vanish into an ordinary life of sidewalks and neighbors. When he was voted down it was as if he gave up and gave in to the glitz. A new house on Linda Flora was finished by spring 1963 and Tinseltown buzzed again about this big, brutal expression of fame from the man who had always claimed to be above all that. A visitor coming down the sloping driveway from the street saw nothing but trees until suddenly the house loomed like a massive rock fortress. The entry walk to the towering front door, lined with stone pillars, was intimidating in its scale. Inside, the ceilings were unnaturally high, making visitors feel like pygmies. The dominant material was hard, cold stone and one craggy wall would prompt a visitor from a later age to say it looked like a big block of rock cocaine.

For clients he described as "delightfully receptive to new ideas," architect Harold Levitt designed a contemporary structure that columnist Sheila Graham described as "plastic modern." Circling out from the central point of the kitchen were a separate wing for the children's suites, a den, an enormous living/screening room opening out to a large bar, plus a dark, formal dining room, a sunken library and atrium, a huge master suite, and a gymnasium. Outside the kitchen doors was a new pool from which a stream fed into and through the house, like the waterfall in Lancaster's old Canon Drive office. The original plan called for a moat.

Friends were baffled at the change in lifestyle, "such a contradiction," Joel Douglas recalled, "to the style we had known." The children stayed upstairs, moving between suites. The clutter of the old house was replaced by designer sterility, even in the children's rooms that had been filled with the posters and personal trinkets Douglas remembered as "wild things." One visitor thought it looked like a museum not a home and predicted it would precede a divorce. Three years after Lancaster moved in, a friend sitting by the edge of the pool looked up at the house and asked Lancaster what style of architecture it was. "Twentieth-century faggot," replied Lancaster, already sick of it.

The new house was ideal for events whose scope and import matched its portentous style. When Martin Luther King Jr. came to Hollywood for the first time in May 1963 to solicit support and funds for his Civil Rights Act "crusade," the Lancaster house was chosen to host the entertainers and industry executives invited to hear the minister speak. Lancaster was in New York working on dubbing *The Leopard* and Norma greeted the guests. Her activist example as what a friend called "a woman without prejudice," brought up in the "fair-shake" philosophy of her father and energized by her consuming work with the League of Women Voters, in turn inspired Lancaster to work together with Paul Newman, Marlon Brando, SAG president Charlton Heston, James Garner, Harry Belafonte, Sidney Poitier, and others of that earliest group of Hollywood celebrities to back King. In the minister's insistence on the redemptive power of suffering for a cause, in his belief that a principled person could transform a jail cell into something noble, the actor who had transformed himself into the Birdman of Alcatraz recognized a kindred passion.

Freedom had become Lancaster's secular religion. The acceleration and intensification of early 1960s American politics matched his own evolution on-screen. By 1963, he was, in the public's mind, Elmer Gantry, the Birdman, the Nazi Janning who accepts his nation's guilt. Youngstein, one of the most active organizers in the industry for an array of progressive causes, recalled Lancaster as "one of the most sensitive men to the race issue I've ever met. I put him up there with anybody. . . . He became a liberal in the best sense of what that means: somebody who wants to improve the status quo for other people." Clarence Jones, an attorney and one of King's principal advisors who dealt with thousands of eager helpers, including an inconsistent Brando, characterized Lancaster's commitment as "serious, very serious." "I remember," he said, "how struck I was by his depth and sincerity. When you're active in the civil rights movement and every day you're talking to large groups of people in churches or one-on-one . . . you can tell by the texture and inflection whether this is the real deal or just contrived."

In June, Kennedy called on Congress to enact a civil rights bill. Days later, Medgar Evers was murdered in Jackson, Mississippi, and King responded with plans for a huge, peaceful march in Washington, D.C., on August 28. He charged Jones to work with point men Belafonte and Poitier to pull together a Hollywood contingent to come to the Washington march. "Because of the power of the movie industry," recalled Jones, "because of the nature, by definition, of who motion picture personalities were, Dr. King felt they could give his moral crusade a certain degree of authenticity and support from the mainstream media. And who better to achieve that," he asked, "than a Burt Lancaster or persons like him?" There had not been such an open demonstration of political advocacy by Hollywood liberals directed at a single issue since the Committee for the First Amendment in 1947, and, as Heston pointed out in his autobiography, *In the Arena*, "there were faint hearts on every side."

At work in France on his next movie project, Lancaster was asked to be the official presenter of a petition signed by fifteen hundred Americans in Europe, some of whom had staged their own minimarch on the American Embassy in Paris. He arrived in Washington with James Baldwin and Josephine Baker to join other Hollywood celebrities including Heston, Brando, Garner, Tony Curtis, Ossie Davis, and Lena Horne, and together they walked with a peaceable quarter of a million people from the Washington Monument to the Lincoln Memorial. At the microphone, dressed in his one tweed sports coat and a tie, his hair blowing in the breeze, Lancaster stood up to speak. Someone unfurled the long petition scroll of paper into the wind where it flapped noisily. "Can I have it, please, fellahs?" he said with easy camaraderie, sounding like the settlement house organizer he had once been. He then spoke, briefly, of the hope that a new civil rights act would "liberate all Americans from the prison of their prejudices and fears" and described the march, the amazing day, as a "stunning example of what America aspires to become." There were other speeches and then King got up to speak his dream of what America might be, his words the pivotal call of the 1960s civil rights movement. CBS correspondent Roger Mudd, headphones clapped on his head, standing in the middle of the crowd, dryly informed the American people that the event was a "new concept in lobbying."

That day Lancaster returned to the old settlement house vision of the *"glorious Golden City of the Light"* where, as the hymn had promised, *"wrong is banished from its borders/Justice reigns supreme o'er all."* He never again appeared in such a mass, celebrity-strewn forum. Some kind of reluctance, a sense of his own limitations, and a respect for the efforts of those much more substantively involved than himself kept him away from the political limelight many of his fellow filmmakers would eagerly court in the tumultuous years to come. He would be no less—in fact, often more—supportive, behind the scenes. In much the same way that he tried to separate facile notions of stardom from the substance of his evolving work, he also separated the glitz of his celebrity from the labor that needed to be done in the real world.

The Train, like many of Lancaster's 1960s projects, took up an inordinate amount of time. Almost a year was spent in France, away from Hollywood, away from his family, using up months he could have spent developing or starring in other projects (*The Agony and the Ecstasy* ended up starring Charlton Heston, was directed by Carol Reed, and flopped in 1965). The movie was not only "the last great black-and-white action-adventure film," Matt Zoller Seitz would write in in 1995, but the precursor, the template of "high-tech shoot-'em-ups" to come. The hero saves the day, stops the train with his bare hands, wits, and a gun or two, paving the way for the *48 Hours, Die Hard, Lethal Weapon,* and *Rambo* series, as well as Arnold Schwarzenegger. Inversely true to type, Lancaster never repeated the formula: "Burt," said Carmichael, "would never have made a *Rambo V.* He'd never even have made a *Rambo II.*" UA's first foray into foreign coproduction, with Les Films Ariane, *The Train* was also the last production Lancaster dominated with quite the same arsenal of personal power. In 1963 he was, recalled Walter Bernstein, one of the movie's original screenwriters, "the gorilla on the bus."

Initially planned as a modest movie, the story was based on a real-life incident during the last days before the Allied forces liberated Paris in August 1944. Under the supervision of an art-loving Nazi officer, a collection of the finest paintings from the Jeu de Paume Impressionist museum was loaded on a train bound for Germany only to be sidetracked for two weeks, thanks to a very French bureaucratic slowdown of bills of lading and invoices masterminded by the Resistance. The train never got more than fifteen miles out of Paris by which time the Allies had arrived. When the German officer got back to Germany he "was so depressed at losing the art," said Lancaster, "he drank poisoned champagne." Screenwriters Franklin Coen, Frank Davis, and Bernstein wrote a script after which the project, according to director Arthur Penn, lay "dormant" at UA until he awakened it. Lancaster was hired to play the Resistance leader, Labiche, as the third of his four UA/HHL payback commitments, and he joined the production in France after finishing work with Pollack on *The Leopard* and just before the March on Washington.

The Academy Award–nominated director of *The Miracle Worker* in 1962 with *Bonnie and Clyde* yet to come, Penn envisioned *The Train* as "an intriguing story about what the Nazis had attempted to do in the French world of art and that particularly French desire to risk their lives for art." The mechanics of the trains would be "only punctuation." He gathered in a carefully chosen group of top European talent: the British stage actor Paul Scofield, as the Nazi Corporal von Waldheim; Jeanne Moreau, the star in 1961 of both *Jules et Jim* and *La Notte,* as the French innkeeper who hides Labiche in her cellar; and, as the big-faced engineer, the great French actor who had worked with Jean Renoir, Marcel Carné, and René Clair—Michel Simon. Penn wanted Lancaster because he felt he could "play the kind of laborer with a certain kind of French sensitivity to the idea of art needing to be protected without really genuinely understanding it himself." Considering the star's level of art collecting, this was an interesting choice. The actor agreed to the project as long as Penn was directing.

UA set the shooting schedule at fifteen weeks, starting in August. Producer Jules Bricken had already arranged with the director of the Louvre, the French Army, and the French National Railways for the use of Paris locations and a full battalion of French soldiers. Preparatory shots of the Nazis in Paris were done at the Place de la Concorde in the very early morning so as not to offend the French by the sight of their World War II occupiers (as a Franco-American production, *The Train* would carefully beg the question of why the nation which let the Nazis march into Paris could then believe that saving a Renoir or two salvaged a national honor worth keeping). With the exception of an abandoned rail yard in Acquigny, near Rouen, complete with some forty rail cars that could be conveniently blown up, the production was based in Vaires-sur-Marne, a village of seven thousand people, in what the *New York Times* called the "limbo-like outer suburbs of Paris."

Walter Bernstein had not worked with Lancaster since *Kiss the Blood Off My Hands* and found that the fresh, eager, overnight discovery of 1947 had utterly vanished. When he began to take the "extremely shy, very pleasant" fifteen-year-old Billy Lancaster out to lunch, the boy said his father had forbidden him to continue. "Why can't you?" asked Bernstein. "Because you're paying for it all the time and I shouldn't be doing this." When the writer reminded Lancaster of a kindness he had once shown his wife when she had been unable, for personal reasons, to test for a part, Lancaster "kind of smiled," remembered Bernstein, "and said, 'You know at some times I'm not such a shit.' "

But he was. The first day of shooting Bernstein observed that when Penn kept trying to get Lancaster to "show some kind of vulnerability and emotion" in the first scene with Simon, the star finally turned to the director and said, "Here I'll give it The Grin." The next day was a holiday with no shooting; about eleven o'clock that night Bernstein got a phone call from Lancaster who told him Penn was fired and Frankenheimer was coming over to take his place; in the meantime Lancaster would direct the picture. He insisted Bernstein come out to the rail yard the next day where he asked him to stay and finish the script. The screenwriter refused, "appalled" at what he felt was "deeply unfair." He remembered both the "real kind of integrity" the early Lancaster had once had, and the golem he had thought the unformed star might be. "When I saw him again in Paris," he recalled, "we came toward each other to say hello, and I was struck by the kind of beauty he had, a male beauty, and a kind of ease with himself physically. . . . I had felt there was a core there, something he wanted to build on that was trustworthy. Now there was a kind of gratuitous cruelty that I hadn't seen. It was fifteen years of Hollywood plus fifteen years of *power.*"

If the switch of directors was in fact cooked up by Lancaster with Frankenheimer, it was with the purpose of making the movie Lancaster wanted to make. As Bernstein was leaving the rail yards that last morning, Lancaster said to him, "Frankenheimer is a bit of a whore, but he'll do what I want." In the suddenness of the decision there was also desperation: if Penn was going to make a quiet, subtle tale about art, Lancaster had to do something, fast. His second chance for an Oscar for *Birdman* had gone to

Gregory Peck's Atticus Finch in *To Kill a Mockingbird* at the ceremonies that spring; *The Leopard,* as doctored by him and Pollack, had just been released and was a huge embarrassment. He needed another major hit, an important movie that could pull in the mainstream audience.

Frankenheimer, still in the middle of a divorce, with a private detective trailing his every step, gladly responded to Lancaster's call to get on the first plane to Paris and help him out. To show its appreciation for his "rescue," UA flew Frankenheimer a Ferrari by chartered plane (a Rolls Royce, the director's preference, was not available). "Aren't you going to send Arthur Krim a thank-you note?" asked Lancaster. "Oh, yeah," said the director, and dictated a fulsome letter on the spot. "No, no, no," said Lancaster. "You'll never learn. Here," he said to the secretary, "take this down: 'Dear Arthur: Why wasn't it the color I wanted?' "

Frankenheimer found a script in which "the train," he recalled, "didn't leave the station until page 90." He and Lancaster closed the production down, losing precious fair weather shooting time, and together reworked the story. The movie was a total joint effort—production, script, direction. Now the train not only left the station, but the station, a truck, a boxcar, three more boxcars, a switch tower, a dozen rail cars, a signal tower, and a seventy-ton locomotive would all get blown to smithereens in a one-minute sequence that took four months to set up, with 140 separate explosions using more than a ton of TNT, two thousand gallons of gas, and twenty-two cameras. In a rehearsal for the sequence, nine cameras were set up with a tenth stuck in the ground by master photographer, Ernst Haas, as an afterthought. When the French stuntman pulled the locomotive's throttle lever too far, sending the machine flying out of control toward Frankenheimer and Lancaster, the two men ran for their lives while the locomotive smashed through all of the cameras, landing, wheels spinning, right over the last, tenth one, producing what Frankenheimer called "one of the great shots ever done."

When autumnal mists fogged up the cameras and a frigid French winter made the ground too hard to safely detonate explosives, *The Train* had to virtually shut down until the following spring. "Shrewder planning," said one report, "might have taken into account the fact that winter has come every year to France." When the leaves came back on the trees new footage had to match what had already been shot and UA—fed up with a production that had doubled its budget to between $6 million and $7 million—stepped in and asserted its completion rights. Producer Bricken blamed Frankenheimer's disregard of costs; Frankenheimer blamed Bricken as "totally irresponsible"; UA suggested that the whole concept had been "ill-conceived." In March it was announced that there would be about seven more weeks of filming, including the addition of a strafing sequence during the filming of which a Spitfire, going three hundred miles per hour, raced after the train zooming at eighty miles per hour for the protective cover of a tunnel. Off-screen, a helicopter, whirring along at eighty miles per hour, from which Frankenheimer was supervising the aerial shot, almost collided with the Spitfire.

Midway into the filming, Lancaster took a day off to play golf, stepped into a hole, and reactivated his old knee injury. Frankenheimer found him in tears with not only the pain, but the quandary of how to continue the movie in which he, as always, did his own stunts. They came up with the idea that Labiche would get shot in the leg as he runs over a wooden railroad bridge, which would allow Lancaster to limp for the rest of the movie.

Even with the real-life injury, *The Train* was a stunning record of Lancaster's physical strength and agility at the age of fifty. There is a proud bravado, even ferocity, in his jumping on and off moving trains, sliding down twenty-foot railroad ladders, scaling walls, tumbling like a human piece of the earth down a hill in a beautifully controlled series of breaks and rolls. "Burt Lancaster," said Frankenheimer, "was the strongest man physically I've ever known. He was one of the best stuntmen who ever lived. I don't think anybody's ever moved as well on the screen."

The relationship of the actor and the director, so felicitous at this point in both of their careers, evolved during *The Train* in complicated ways. On a professional level, Frankenheimer found Lancaster to be "a very dedicated honest man who wanted to do good work in a society where it's very difficult to do good work." He admired the actor's quest for perfection and noted, as an example, that Lancaster's favorite football player was Jim Brown, "probably," he said, "the greatest football player that ever lived—a perfectionist, uncompromising and very positive." But the director had trouble converting that admiration into a personal rapport. "It was very difficult to be a friend of Burt's because he demanded so much," Frankenheimer said. "It was just very difficult to ever relax around him, to ever become vulnerable. I would never want to because he had a habit of being able to pick out your weakness and hone in on it. And I just never let him see stuff. I could never open up." Frankenheimer was not the Brooks or Aldrich kind of personality who relished—or at least bought into—the star's peculiarly masculine testing pattern. "I was never around him when I didn't have to be. He was not the kind of person I wanted to have as my friend. You never knew when his temper was going to flare up," he added. "I saw him blow up at the French production manager once, to the point where I thought he was going to kill him. And after it was over, he just held his head in his hands and said, 'You know, I'm going to die of a stroke. I know it. My mother died of a stroke.' " Looping his anger back to his mother was a provocative connection: Did she die after a fit of rage? Was she angry at him?

During one of the long winter nights over dinner at a Normandy inn, the two men came up with the movie's ending, a scene that inspired many copies. With the train carrying the art finally stopped, Labiche and von Waldheim face off against each other along the tracks. Originally, according to Frankenheimer, Scofield as well as Lancaster had a gun in a kind of *Gunfight at the O.K. Corral*–style of confrontation. Then they realized Scofield would look "ridiculous" with a gun against Lancaster because, said Frankenheimer, "you know Burt Lancaster will gun him down. So we decided that Scofield would talk himself to death and Burt would just pull the trigger." In weather so cold Scofield reportedly had to talk while inhaling to avoid the misty clouds of breath that might mess up the shot, with his voice synched in later, there was a last, bleak shot of Lancaster listening to the Nazi deride his proletarian ignorance. "A painting means as much to you," Scofield sneers, "as pearls to an ape." Lancaster, silent, machine-guns him to bits.

Viewers looked back to Thomas Edison and Buster Keaton for a tradition in which to place Frankenheimer's "steamy, sooty, black-and-silver, hissing-and-hooting" machines when *The Train* opened in March 1965. A sexual connotation in the "masculine drive and power of pistons" was one clue to the movie's fascination for a segment of the audience, but *Newsday*, like many, found the movie "too long" with a train that "pretends it's going somewhere and . . . isn't." Few, however, disputed the thrill of the crashes, derailments, bombings, and strafings; *The Train* was nothing if not a movie. The final cost came in at $6.7 million, but it earned just under $3.5 million in the U.S. In the now-classic pattern of action-adventures, the movie took in much more, $6 million, abroad, where the relatively word-free script could just crash around on the screen, frenetic, apocalyptic, desperate.

Lancaster's Labiche was not a great performance—squint-eyed, Gauloise-smoking, his idea of the stoic, art-ignorant Resistance man is one of his stiff pretendings—but it is a great piece of cinema. He is a human train, a piece of machinery that lives to move and work. For all his intellectual and artistic aspirations, Lancaster was the product of a laboring people. Holding on to the movie with his bare hands, he makes it an artifact that will last. "He is a contemporary Sisyphus," wrote Brendan Gill in *The New Yorker* of his performance, "but he is not resigned, and in a contest between him and any boulder, we are encouraged to suspect that it is the boulder that would crumble first." As he chases the train, he is chasing life itself. Frankenheimer brings the camera in close, sustained and studied, on his hands as they precisely fashion the wires for an explosive device that will stall the train. The long fingers are fastidious and skilled, like the Leopard's, like the Birdman's, like Joe Erin's spinning the gun in *Vera Cruz*.

UA never gave Lancaster quite that much room to play in again. After five years of unrelentingly serious work, he took a mid-decade break to make a couple of lightweight Westerns. His performances would remind the mainstream, ticket-buying audience that he could still be in a good old movie and enjoy himself. And, as he had said years before, when his career was in transition, he could always pull out his grubby old Westerner.

He agreed to make the unlikely Western farce, *The Hallelujah Trail*, for the Mirisch brothers at UA at the last minute, lumping it together as his final HHL payback requirement along with *Khartoum*, with shooting to start on the latter by the fall of 1964. But Paramount had the star lined up for *The Spy Who Came in from the Cold*, also due to start at the end of the year, and he was trying to get Pollack to direct him in a revival of another old HHL project, the African diamond yarn, *Kimberly*. He needed the UA settlement money to finish his house and wanted, Kaplan wrote Krim in January 1964, to "spend part of the summer with his family" after *The Train* wrapped.

It was too many projects but too little time, resulting in a fateful break in what had been an unbroken rhythm of work since 1946: only *The Hallelujah Trail*, released in July 1965, would end up getting made with him. He received his settlement from UA in July—a check for $920,954.85—but did no film work for a year after fall 1964. During that time Charlton Heston was cast in *Khartoum*, and Richard Burton in Le Carré's spy story. Lancaster's mainstream popularity abruptly waned. In 1962, he had come in tenth place in the Motion Picture Herald-Fame poll. In 1963, he was eighteenth. The next year he dropped off the industry popularity barometer forever.

But no one knew that yet. Krim, by now one of President Johnson's closest confidantes and the head of a fabulously successful company poised on the brink of even further popular success (the James Bond and *Pink Panther* series, Clint Eastwood's spaghetti Westerns for Sergio Leone) and artistic respect (*One Flew Over the Cuckoo's Nest, Midnight Cowboy, Last Tango in Paris*) wrote to Lancaster in spring 1964. Dismissing all "the old problems" that had been resolved between them, Krim had the grace to give what, in retrospect, would amount to a farewell to the star on whom he had built the company. "I just want you to know," he wrote, "that whether it be as producer, director, or star or a combination of any two or more of these capacities, we would like to keep doing pictures with you for many years to come. All of us at UA have the greatest respect for your abilities. . . . Also, I need not tell you how much I have always personally valued our relationship."

Lancaster had to go straight from France in June 1964 to Gallup, New Mexico, to make an almost three-hour confused tale of a Denver-bound whiskey wagon train beset by Indians, temperance ladies, and quicksand directed by John Sturges, written by John Gay, and costarring Lee Remick. When *The Hallelujah Trail* opened a year later to tepid reviews and weak box-office receipts, it was inevitably compared with another, better, more successful Western spoof of 1965, *Cat Ballou*, in which Lee Marvin took the role once reserved for Lancaster and won an Oscar for it. Lancaster's body of work was starting to accumulate misses.

A year later, in October 1965, Lancaster was again on Western location, this time with Brooks in Death Valley, the Valley of Fire State Park in Nevada, and at Lake Mead making *The Professionals*. Coming after his *Sweet Bird of Youth* and *Lord Jim*, and in the tradition of Kurosawa's *Seven Samurai* and *The Magnificent Seven*, Brooks's hard-boiled tale of the guys who just do their job and do it well, based on the Frank O'Rourke novel *A Mule for the Marquesa* and featuring brilliant action sequences, would be a big hit and justifiably so.

A wealthy rancher (Ralph Bellamy) hires one-time Pancho Villa revolutionaries-turned-professionals-for-hire (Lee Marvin, Robert Ryan, Lancaster, and Woody Strode) to retrieve his wife (Claudia Cardinale) from Mexican rebel kidnapper Raza (Jack Palance), which latter two turn out to be in love and in cahoots to defraud everybody. The eighty-day shoot became a truly professional endurance test of rain, snow, sleet, desert sun, and a flash flood. Marvin was so drunk during one scene with Lancaster on a rock twenty-five feet in the air—"*stoned!*" said Tom Shaw, assistant director on the film, "I don't think he could tell you his name"—that Shaw had to intervene after forty minutes and three takes for fear the sober, furious star would "take Lee Marvin by the ass and throw him off that mountain."

Lancaster's performance was greeted with welcome relief when the movie opened in November 1966. "[O]ne grin and sinister laugh of his," said one review, "is worth all the art pictures he'd like to act in." The movie, the last together for Brooks and Lancaster, was a valentine to the director's and star's own best notions of each other—by the end, the good guy professionals fall in on the side of true love and leave the money behind—and was the second-highest grossing Western of 1966, after *Nevada Smith*. Brooks's script was full of knowing lines that reflected the amused cynicism of the mid-1960s, in the tradition, it was noted, "of *Vera Cruz* rather than *Shane*." "What were Americans doing in a Mexican Revolution, anyway?" asks Ryan's professional. Lancaster replies, "Maybe there's only one Revolution . . . the Good Guys versus the Bad Guys. The question is: Who are the Good Guys?" In January came the news that over five thousand American soldiers had died in Vietnam during the previous twelve months.

The star's relaxed ease on-screen may have had something to do with a new romance. Along with the usual cadre of his own professionals—Martell, Schiffer—rolling on the movie's credits, there was a new name listed as Hair Designer, Jackie Bone. Mainstream Hollywood would consider her Lancaster's first serious extramarital relationship since Shelley Winters. While checking in at the Los Angeles airport en route to New Mexico to work on *The Hallelujah Trail,* Bone heard Lancaster's "soft padding feet" behind her, like a cat. When they both found themselves in the first-class section, "that," said Bone, "was it."

She was of Irish descent, born in Texas in 1928. Dark-haired, buxom, attractive, tough, relaxed, and gutsy, Bone had been married twice before. Sheilah Graham called her "a very mature woman." Given her easy humor and an independent edge that Lancaster liked, most of the time, the relationship started out passionate, stormy, sometimes violent, and full of arguments—not unlike Lancaster's rapport with his mother. If Norma showed her anger by withdrawing into silence and drinking, Bone did just the opposite. "We were great sparring partners," she told a reporter a few years later, when the dust had settled a bit. Lucy Kibbee became so alarmed watching one of their early fights, the two combatants stopped and burst out laughing. "Jesus!" they told her. "We're not going to kill each other!"

At least one old friend thought Bone was "a tramp"; others found her honest and lacking in any kind of pretension. Though the relationship was kept strictly secret for a few years, columnist Sidney Skolsky later figured out that Lancaster and Norma first separated around the time *The Professionals* wrapped in early 1966. Norma initially stayed in the house and Lancaster moved around between hotels, an apartment in Westwood, another in the Valley, even sleeping in his new office at Goldwyn studios at 1041 North Formosa Avenue. He would try one last time to mend his marriage before settling by the end of the decade into a big, rented Malibu beach house with Bone.

Observing him on a golf course a short time before she met him, Bone recalled that Lancaster had a look, in repose, that made her think, "there is one unhappy man." She provided a diversion from a shifting career, a dying marriage, and needy children. She could also be a guilt-free cover for other, more problematic relationships though, if he was so involved, she claimed she never knew it. "It's not out of the question, though," she said, recalling that there was much sexual experimentation going on at the time. "Maybe in his early life. But I can tell you that he preferred women." Gay men, she observed, were a relief to him as easy company or secretaries or bridge partners because they were "no competition." She caught him out on several female liaisons and asked that he refrain from telling her about his exploits like a buddy but later regretted doing so: "I should have kept that line of communication open." When Nick told his daughter Tina that Jackie reminded him of June Ernst, he may have been recognizing the bigger truth. Lancaster was returning to a semblance of that earlier, grifter life where connections were looser, less formal, less hampering. "He was ripe," Bone recalled, "for an affair."

The romance was not the only indicator of problems in the Lancaster household. Six months before shooting began on *The Professionals*, Billy eloped to Tijuana on June 18, 1965, to marry Kippie Kovacs, the daughter of the late comedian Ernie Kovacs. He was seventeen, she was seventeen (maybe only sixteen), and had endured a harrowing childhood of custody battles and a kidnapping. The teenage couple kept the marriage a secret until a joint Thanksgiving dinner with the two families when they announced the news. In mid-December, the couple was married again at the Beverly Hills Hotel "to resolve any question of whether the Mexican wedding was legal," as the *New York Post* reported. By this time Billy had just turned eighteen. Some family friends saw the marriage as an act of rebellion by Billy against his father or perhaps an attempt to form his own family as his parents' marriage was crumbling. A baby girl, Keigh, Lancaster's first and only grandchild, was born in 1966 and Billy dropped out of high school with plans to be an actor. About the same time, Joanna decided to attend high school in Mexico and Jimmy moved to New York to begin a bachelor's degree in music and piano at the Manhattan School of Music. That November 1965 Thanksgiving dinner was their last one together as the family they had once been.

Out of this sadness and dissolution, Lancaster took on *The Swimmer*. Based on a very short John Cheever story that had appeared in *The New Yorker* in July 1964, the movie followed a Connecticut suburbanite, Ned Merrill, who swims home one afternoon through his neighbors' swimming pools, one after another. When he finally arrives at his front door, the weather has turned cold, the hour is late, the friends are gone. The house is locked, dark, and empty. The story started out as what Cheever biographer Scott Donaldson called "a simple story about Narcissus," the Greek boy beauty who gazed so long at his reflection in a pool of water that he withered away. But the actual writing of it evolved into what Cheever described as "a terrible experience."

Lancaster called the project "*Death of a Salesman* in swimming trunks," and it preoccupied him for the better part of the two years from 1966 to the movie's release in spring 1968. For the first time in his Hollywood life, a year would go by—1967—in which no movie in which he starred was released. Though few realized it at the time, *The Swimmer* crossed a line into a hallucinatory zone where the work of art, the movie, is so much the reality of its time that it is unbearable, unwatchable. The dark side of the turmoil and change of the late 1960s was the death of the grown-ups, or the *idea* of the grown-ups. Families imploded overnight, children disappeared into Canada or drugs, fled the Vietnam draft, the chaos, and were never seen again. When siblings went to find them, they disappeared too. The Moms moved out and what was left for the baffled Dads was the empty house. Watching the movie a generation later, a baby boomer would notice that Lancaster's Irish-American form—on the edge of age, graceful, strong, handsome, with a great smile, corrupted—looked oddly like the older JFK nobody ever got to see.

Though he had been approached by others who saw him as the only star who not only looked the part of the aging suburban stud but could also be persuasive as an athlete, Lancaster felt confident in the hands of Sam Spiegel at Columbia, producer of *On the Waterfront* and *Lawrence of Arabia*, and the director/writer team of Frank and Eleanor Perry, Oscar nominees for *David and Lisa* in 1962. Both Hecht and Kaplan tried to talk him out of the project, the latter feeling he "complicated his professional life by being too partial to intellectual, almost loser-type causes." Frank Perry and John Cheever first thought him miscast in spite of what Perry called his "all-American look," but in fact the incongruity of Lancaster as a smooth Connecticut WASP would contribute to the essential strangeness of his Merrill. In any case, without him, claimed Vincent Canby, film critic for the *New York Times*, the movie "would never have been made."

He accepted the part, he told his swimming coach, Robert Horn, so he would have to learn to swim. It was a characteristic remark: the entire film is nothing *but* swimming (and running) and the star was still afraid of the water. He personally recruited Horn, coach of the hugely successful UCLA men's water polo team. He wanted to learn at this level so he would, as Horn recalled, not "insult" the real swimmers in the audience who, like the *Jim Thorpe* fans fourteen years before, would watch his form with a critical eye. His initial style was what Horn called an "East River crawl, a combination of paddle, sidestroke, and struggle to survive," and during hours of waterlogged practice to improve it the two men developed a friendship that lasted for years. Lancaster introduced Horn to his Hollywood friends as a swimming coach for their children, thereby "keeping me afloat," said Horn, who appreciated the additional income for his family. Sitting happily on the edge of the pool at the end of a swimming lesson, Lancaster said to Horn, about twenty years his junior, "You know, Bob, I could technically be your father. I'd give anything to have had a son like you."

Shooting began in Connecticut in June and Lancaster asked Horn to accompany him to ensure that his new form showed up well on film. Frank Perry had chosen the affluent town of Westport for the location because he had grown up there and knew the local layout, people, and code. A group of seasoned New York actors—Cornelia Otis Skinner, Marge Champion, Kim Hunter, and Barbara Loden—were cast as the largely hungover or drunk pool owners who punctuate each stop on Merrill's journey. Joan Rivers played one of the suburban partygoers.

Cheever had a bit part in a brief exchange with Lancaster and inevitably the prime focus of his observant writer's scrutiny became what his son Benjamin Cheever called "this stylish, lurid, sexual standard playing his Ned Merrill." "Burt Lancaster is fifty-two," was the writer's initial assessment, "lithe, comely and somewhat disfigured by surgical incisions and he looks both young and old, masterful and tearful." Delighted and intrigued with the whole process of moviemaking, Cheever sent bulletins to friend and writer John Weaver describing the encounters between himself, the slight, literary man, and the big movie star: "Anyhow I thought you'd like to know about Burt and me and so forth," he breezily reported in July. "Burt's skin is getting very tough because he's in the water so much. Burt wants me to be in the picture. . . . 'You ought to be in the movies, Cheever,' Burt said, 'because they let you keep the clothes. We've only been shooting eight days and I already got three bathing suits and two bathrobes.' . . . He's very sexy and commanding in the girl scenes but half the time he looks as if he were going to cry which is just right for the part." When Eleanor Perry told Cheever he looked like Lancaster, "that," wrote Cheever in the same letter to Weaver, "did it. I need some new teeth to point up the resemblance but I'm working on my Lancaster walk and I've developed a cute quick sweet sad smile. . . . Burt thinks Norman Mailer is bitter," continued the new *intime*. "Burt thinks Norman Mailer is washed up. Burt doesn't eat anything but cream cheese."

The two men were oddly parallel. Cheever's hunger for the fully lived life and his view of literature as a "vast pilgrimage" were like Lancaster's restless need to absorb new experience and then place it in a meaningful continuum within his work, itself an American narrative. It was an artistic impulse that one man expressed in the natural medium of literature and the other in the not-so-natural battleground of the mainstream movie. *The Swimmer* was also about being the outsider, excluded by class, age, failure, or—implicitly—sexuality, from the center. Cheever was not really the upper-crust WASP his stories seemed to suggest; neither was the ethnically WASP Lancaster the god-like he-man he appeared to be. Lancaster admired the writer as an intellectual, the thing the actor most wanted to be. Cheever, amused, told his son, "He's trying to place me on an island that I've spent most of my adult life trying to get a boat off of." As a man of his generation and would-be class, Cheever admired the athlete enough to make his Ned Merrill a kind of perfection of the type. Lancaster, stuck with the body beautiful, had spent his Hollywood life trying to get off that island too. "They missed each other perfectly," said Benjamin Cheever.

After a honeymoon during which the Perrys, Lancaster, and—from afar in Hollywood—executive producer Spiegel all got along, Lancaster began to feel that Perry's realistic approach was not up to the job of translating Cheever onto the screen. "Film has its own particular life—regardless of what's actually going on in a film," Lancaster said later. "And [*The Swimmer*] needed some kind of strange, weird approach to capture the audience and make them realize that, in a way, they were not looking at anything real. In talking about the script we would say, 'I don't know why two men in white coats don't come take this guy away.' " When Lancaster and Cheever had to block out the movements for Cheever's one brief appearance in the movie—he greets Merrill and a former Merrill-family babysitter (eighteen-year-old Janet Landgard), who joins the swimmer for awhile on his "adventure," at one of the pools—the writer improvised by kissing Landgard instead of shaking her hand. "That son of a bitch is padding his part," Lancaster shouted. On the second take, when Cheever reached out to shake Lancaster's hand, the star—"the bastard," as Cheever wrote to John Weaver—stood with his hands behind his back, claiming he was just improvising too. "Our friendship," concluded Cheever, "is definitely on the rocks."

Temperatures soared to 102°F and the New York newspapers sent reporters on the New Haven commuter line to cover this strange little shoot. Many of them were mesmerized by the equally strange star working in continuity through seventeen pairs of identical navy blue trunks, still looking ten years younger than he was. When Eleanor Perry offered him one of her filter-tipped cigarettes after a take, *Newsday* recorded that after flashing that "piano-keyboard smile," he said, "No, thanks. I like them strong, the kind that leaves your lungs blackened and charred." *The Swimmer* was a break from his "bread-and-butter pictures," he said, and freely offered his interpretations of Cheever's tale to anyone who would listen. Most of the time he churned around on the surface, talking about how the movie was "a mirror of a decadent society . . . a tragedy based on the American way of life, with its emphasis on success and a misguided notion that a man can get by on charm alone."

By mid-August Merrill had begun to get to him. "I'm scared to death of these parts," he said. "Sometimes I know in my heart that I haven't got the right feeling in a particular scene. I know it late in the day when I've finally done it the way I want it." As he must have known when he first read the script, this story of the middle-aged, all-American, successful, 1960s husband with the president of the League of Women Voters wife, the daughters whom he thinks "worship me because I'm their father" but who really laugh at him and think he's a "great big joke," the big expensive house with the tennis courts (but no pool) high up on the hill, the former lover who mocks him for his qualms about leaving his wife and family, the male who yearns for his childhood when he "used to believe in things" and "people seemed happier," who thinks of himself as "a very special human being, noble and splendid," whose whole carefully constructed dream existence life has vanished—who was this if not himself? To take on a project that dealt with regret, the queasy insight that the failure of the life is one's own and the life itself is half over, took courage. It was also the same old seductive flight from life: if he could work it out in a movie, then he'd done it already. A decade after *Sweet Smell of Success*, *The Swimmer* sucked him so far away from the hero business as to return, in its florid surreality, to the despair of his first *noir*.

Merrill literally floats and runs through his life because he cannot face the awful truth he cannot bear to know. The reader, the audience, never really knows Merrill's secret. It can be any secret they want it to be. Cheever also had the "secret," at the time, of his sexuality. As he got older, his forays into homosexuality would become more frequent and open. At the same time, said his son, "he was living the life he was meant to live: the stone house, the dogs, the wife, the kids. It wasn't any more a fraud than the other thing was. The deception, the pretending were essential, so much a part of his character." Lancaster's Merrill, the Narcissus whose body is envied and admired by men and women alike, gives movie flesh to Tomasi's opinion that the star's "narcissistic" preoccupation with his perfect body was a clue to his possible bisexuality. If he balanced children, wife, mistress, occasional bisexual forays, then he too lived a complicated life of layer upon layer connected necessarily by equal layers of deception. What is left is a Cheever-like hall of mirrors that makes *The Swimmer* only more eerie. What mattered to Lancaster was what he made of his life, his work, as he saw fit. In this he was, in the end, very like Cheever.

Spiegel and Columbia took an even more intense dislike to the uncommercial movie when shooting finished, and insisted that certain scenes be reshot. According to Lancaster, some scenes from the story had never been shot at all. The Perrys angrily withdrew and, in any case, the director had relinquished his right of final cut. He would claim that less than fifty percent of what ended up on-screen was his work. Lancaster stepped in, getting Pollack to work with him on another pressure-ridden, compromised fix-it job. During eight weeks of California retakes and recuts, Loden was replaced by Janice Rule and her key scene as the embittered ex-lover was reshot in California. Spiegel washed his hands of the movie after having, seethed Lancaster later, "personally promised me, *personally promised me*," that he would go over the footage. When Columbia cut off further funding, Lancaster came up with $10,000 of his own money for the last day of shooting.

He then reentered the Hollywood fray, picking up the pieces of his interrupted career. In March 1965 he had signed another multipicture deal with UA calling on him to star in four pictures and produce a minimum of six. The following June, *Film Daily* announced that Lancaster, Pollack, writer David Rayfiel, and Roland Kibbee were making plans to form their own production company with headquarters at Goldwyn Studios, its product to be released through UA. After being nominated for five Emmy awards in 1963 and winning one in 1965, Pollack had shifted into feature films, making *The Slender Thread* in 1965 and *This Property Is Condemned* with Natalie Wood and Robert Redford in 1966. "I began getting," he recalled, "a little bit more attention."

As a possible first project with his friend, Lancaster read the early galleys of a World War II novel, *Castle Keep*, by William Eastlake. He "fell crazy in love," recalled Pollack, with the surreal power and black humor of this story of a group of GIs who find themselves defending an art-filled medieval castle from the Germans in the middle of the Ardennes in the last Allied eastward push toward Berlin. He hatched a plan whereby he would star in *Castle Keep*, Pollack would direct, and, since the star did not like two previous draft screenplays done by *From Here to Eternity*'s Daniel Taradash for Columbia and Paramount, Rayfiel and Kibbee could write a new one. As Pollack only had what he called "small interior picture" credits, when Lancaster suggested him as director, producer Martin Ransohoff refused.

"Burt had a lot of control," said Pollack, "but he didn't want to shove me down anybody's throat." Pollack agreed to prove himself by directing another movie—*The Scalphunters*—for UA starring Lancaster with the understanding that if the first two weeks of dailies met with Ransohoff's approval he could then direct *Castle Keep* with a whopping budget of $8 million. The two friends then put in nine months, in between finishing up *The Swimmer*, of preproduction scene-by-scene analysis and construction of a script Pollack initially thought "silly and simplistic." The result was a comic tale shot in Durango and Torreón, Mexico, in spring 1967 and labeled by one critic as "the first black power western." Lancaster plays a fur trapper, Joe Bass, whose dogged efforts to get his pelts back first from the Indians and then from scalphunters (Telly Savalas and Shelley Winters) are the narrative pretext within which Joseph Lee (Ossie Davis), an erudite black slave who just wants his freedom, banters about life and justice with Bass. Their evolving relationship is an unsentimental paradigm of improved race relations in the oblique political tradition of *The Crimson Pirate*. When Bass suggests that maybe Lee had a more comfortable life as a slave, the runaway quotes Aesop back at him.

Unlike Frankenheimer, Pollack owed his entry into Hollywood to Lancaster, a favor that made for a smoother relationship. The star could feel like the father to the son, a relationship he constantly sought in one form or another. He loved to teach and in the Indiana-born Pollack he found an apt, generous, good-humored pupil. "I got to know Burt quite well on *The Scalphunters*," Pollack recalled. "It was like being shipwrecked. We actually lived together: I was by myself and he was with Jackie. When she would go back to the States for a month or so, Burt would just move into the downstairs at my house. We got to be very close." Stories floated around of huge battles on the shoot, but the director insists they got along well with only healthy arguments over the script. Lancaster carefully observed his protégé at work, giving him the room to make mistakes and to learn. "I was setting a scene with Shelley and Telly in the late afternoon," Pollack recalled, "and Burt was standing there, watching and watching as I kept doing something over and over. I said something to an actor and I turned away and then Burt looked at the actor and said, 'Why don't you turn around and . . . ?' I said, 'Just a minute!' And he backed right off and made a little joke of it like this [Pollack tiptoed away, as if walking on eggs]. He knew it was coming from concentration and the work and that was something he had to respect. He knew I wasn't saying, 'Don't you touch my turf. Let's have a turf war.' He had this barometer: He'd learned what he needed to learn."

Pollack claimed Lancaster never became a good director because that same love of the movie process did not extend to the minutiae of directing. What ignited him was the first thrill of the idea. "He would stay up all night and read," recalled Pollack, "and smoke a pack of Camels and then he would love to read it back to you and say, 'God, listen to this hee-ah! This fuckin' guy hee-ah. . . .' He was always saying stuff like, 'This guy Lampedusa, he was. . . .' " When Pollack told him to come out of a wagon in one sequence like *this* and then come down *here*, Lancaster looked at him and, as he had once suggested "the old snake eye" to Dassin, asked, "You want me to do a little bullshit Charlie here? I can get down and fake like I'm crawling on the ground and. . . ."

Though undercut by real-life events—Vietnam, assassinations—breaking in the news during its release in the spring of 1968, *The Scalphunters* was well-received as a lightweight caper. Critic Kael used it as an example of the "skillful" film that, while "one of the few entertaining American movies [of] this past year," was hardly art. In an equation that was fairly typical of the difficulty critics had with appraising Lancaster, she maintained that such distinctions are worth making in the movies, but then mused on how this "undistinguished and too obviously hard-working actor" had an "apparently effortless flair for comedy." Canby decided that Lancaster simply acted with his hair: "While the performances [over the last two decades] haven't differed greatly," he wrote, "the haircuts have—from high, swashbuckling pompadours to plastered-down alcoholic and country-boy bowl cut. In *The Scalphunters* . . . Mr. Lancaster's hair grows as straight up and free as alfalfa."

It would take almost twenty years for many of these same critics to see *The Swimmer*, released six weeks later, as more than a bizarre failure. Opening in May, the movie was largely blasted as incoherent, bad, obviously the work of two directors. What now looks like an appropriately unsteady home movie with lots of water drops on the camera lens, was rejected then as pretentious and uneven, looking, said *Newsweek*, like "a shampoo commercial." The most vicious comments were reserved for Lancaster. *Time:* "Lancaster sounds as if he's reading ingredients from a bread wrapper"; *The New Republic:* "Lancaster, who is supposed to be a Madison Avenue smoothie, looks and sounds like a longshoreman at a union picnic." Judith Crist, one of the very few reviewers who consistently enjoyed the actor's unpredictable work, wrote in *New York* magazine that *The Swimmer* was "a triumph" and the actor's performance "perhaps the best of his career." In the mind of the audience the story stuck like a nightmare, a talisman of its time.

Lancaster and Pollack had by now moved into the making of *Castle Keep*. When Taradash was taken off the project, Lancaster became heavily involved in the crafting of the new script with Pollack and Rayfiel. The gorilla was off the bus but acting up one last time: "If you hired Lancaster in 1968, 1969," recalled Taradash, "you were hiring an actor, a director, a cinematographer, an art director, a costumer, and so forth. He knew everything; he was really impossible." In its juxtaposition of the brutish conquering forces bivouacked amid the accumulated art of centuries, *Castle Keep* was in the tradition of Guy de Maupassant's haunting short story of the Franco-Prussian War, *Mademoiselle Fifi*. Amid growing reaction against the escalating conflict in Vietnam, it was a highly mannered commentary on the spoils of all wars. In its play on the themes of cultured Europeans who know their art and their castles but cannot defend or "keep" them, and the childish, uncultured Americans who can, it was very like *The Train* or even *The Leopard*. Thirty years later, *Il Postino* director Michael Radford would tell Pollack that a class in his London film school devoted an entire year to the study of *Castle Keep*. "Europe is dying," says Patrick O'Neal's Capt. Beckman. "No, Beckman, she's dead," replies Lancaster's Major Falconer. "That's why we're here."

Shooting began in March 1968 on what was supposed to be a three-month stint on the banks of the Danube fifty miles northwest of Belgrade in Novi Sad—"like Pittsburgh in the fifties," said Bruce Dern, cast as Lt. Billy Byron Bix, a demented conscientious objector. The cast—Lancaster, Dern, O'Neal, Peter Falk, Scott Wilson, Astrid Heeren, Tony Bill—and crew were housed in a castle themselves, newly converted into the Petrovaradin Hotel. The movie's tenth-century "castle," a $1 million styrofoam creation, was constructed seven miles away in Kamenica National Park. The structure was to go up in flames as the Germans overwhelm the handful of Americans left defending it, its destruction signaling the end of Europe, culture, art, the war, whatever. The special effects director, Lee Zavits, took an intense dislike to the castle set and, after a few drinks, would fantasize about blowing it up.

After a lot of winter footage had been shot, the weather suddenly became unseasonably warm, melting all the snow. Buds came out on the trees and cameraman Henri Decaë—the French New Wave cinematographer of François Truffaut's *The Four Hundred Blows*—refused to continue because the scenes would not match. Another week passed before he could be persuaded to continue shooting at night with marble dust sprinkled all over for snow. The script was being rewritten as it was shot and the weeks, months, ground on. Pollack later admitted he "wasn't really experienced enough to take on" *Castle Keep*. "We stayed on so long," he recalled of the production that stretched out for six months into the summer, "that people began to behave rather erratically. That's putting it kindly. They drank a lot, they threw bottles and glasses, and got into fights. We lost the snow and had to pretend it was winter in summer. The guys were in hot itchy uniforms pretending they were freezing. It was like a siege, like a war just getting through it. We thought it was never going to end. Making the film became like the film."

Lancaster was on the set all day, every day working with the actors, discussing each scene, deciding with Pollack what was necessary to get each sequence to work. As pressure started building from Ransohoff in Hollywood, the star would buck up his director by quoting Visconti: "You have to be *intransigent!*" Off the set, he had a different set of surreal problems to deal with. When Norma backed out at the last minute from accompanying her husband for the first time in several years on location, he took Bone instead. At the nightly bridge games, Dern noticed that Lancaster, "a highly competitive man," would blame Bone for mistakes that were really his. In the strange rapport of that liaison, the star, according to Dern, "made everybody know that Jackie was his girl, that she was not Mrs. Lancaster, but she was the dearest thing he had in his heart, that she made him tick every day," but he would turn around and "slam her" for not being up to some standard or other of his own devising.

And because she was not Norma, Bone fought back. One night Lancaster asked Wilson to accompany him to the Writer's Club in Novi Sad for dinner with Pollack and Falk. Wilson declined, knowing that Bone was angry with Lancaster and looking for him. "At one point," he recalled of this "tumultuous" relationship, "Jackie bit a big chunk out of Burt's chest." At the club, Bone suddenly appeared at the table. "There you are, you son of a bitch," she said, picking up a wine bottle out of the ice bucket, a "big heavy bottle," recalled Pollack, and hitting the star over the head. Then she put the bottle back down, turned, and walked out, reportedly angry about Lancaster's interest in another woman. "Burt just sat there," said Pollack. "He didn't move and the blood was running down his face. But it didn't bother him; he just shrugged." As the story instantly beamed out on the wire services, misreported as an incident between Lancaster and Norma, the star returned to the hotel and sat down next to Wilson. "What's that brown stuff on your head?" Wilson asked him. "Dried blood," he replied, and proceeded to tell Wilson that a waiter, standing by with a napkin over his arm and serving caviar, had stepped up immediately after the incident and said, "More caviar, Mr. Lancaster?"

Wilson grew fond of the older actor who nicknamed him "Dearboy," after his *Castle Keep* character, Corporal Clearboy, who falls in love with his Volkswagen. "Burt was a very generous actor," he recalled. "I think he thought of me as a kid—at the time I was just about the youngest actor working in serious films—so he had that kind of protective attitude towards me. Even for the smallest role, if he had a scene with you, he was off-camera for you [rather than a substitute] so that you could make that eye contact with him and bring out the best in you." More cynical or insecure up-and-coming costars claimed that Lancaster cleverly used such sessions to distract and manipulate them with the goal of devolving the scene upon himself.

Dern and Lancaster ran together each morning and passed the time with their own version of an American history trivia game in which each would try to trip up the other with the names of famous Americans in history who had done fabulous deeds. One day Dern was sitting in Lancaster's dressing room and said he was thinking of a man who had walked across the country, been a lover of Thomas Jefferson, and blown his brains out. Lancaster, stumped, asked for another clue. Dern said the man had been convinced that once others saw what he had seen, they would destroy it. Still baffled, Lancaster finally gave up and asked who it was. "Merriweather Lewis," said Dern. Enraged at himself, Lancaster shoved his fist through the dressing-room window. Later, back in Malibu, Dern lent him a copy of the diaries of Lewis and Clark, which Lancaster read in a few days and returned, with a note, to Dern's doorstep. "The bullet should have been for me," he wrote and suggested, as he would several times during the coming years, that he and Dern make a "perfect" movie about the expedition, starring themselves.

Castle Keep's American cast and crew, having agreed to a cut in salary to finish the movie, were far out of their native country for the cumulation of events that marked 1968 as the pivotal year of the sixties. They convinced themselves they were contributing to the antiwar effort by making a tale that questioned all wars: "Everyone," said Wilson, "believed in the film." Shortly after the Russians invaded Czechoslovakia in August, the cast and crew were awakened one morning by a strange hubbub and assumed the Soviet army had moved into Yugoslavia. Wilson decided to double-check with Lancaster who pointed to billows of smoke rising in the distance and said, "Lee blew up the fucking castle." During the set-up for the final conflagration, some gasoline in the moat caught fire and instantly engulfed the highly flammable styrofoam. Decaë managed to capture the blaze on film, but production had to stop for another five weeks while the castle was rebuilt for the equivalent of two shots.

"One of the oddest films to come out of Hollywood these twenty years," mused the *London Daily Telegraph* when *Castle Keep* was released a year later in 1969. Between its antiwar, antiart, and antiheroic sensibilities, what now looks like a dream sequence of familiar, plausible attitudes and responses, seemed then like an arty mishmash of quick cuts and exaggerated crazies, with a one-eyed Burt Lancaster riding a white horse through the chaos, pleading with advancing soldiers to stay and keep the castle. The major was in his General Scott tradition: cold, crazy, and obsessed with dreams of messianic victory. Another ambitious failure, *Castle Keep* was the last movie in Lancaster's eager embrace of the 1960s zeitgeist. It would resurface as an acquired-taste favorite that seemed, with some distance, to have been ahead of its time. Within a few years of its release, *Catch 22*, *M.A.S.H.*, and *Slaughterhouse 5* would be big, black-comedy war-movie hits, in step with the mood of the era.

Pollack's career took off with *They Shoot Horses, Don't They?*, *The Way We Were*, *Three Days of the Condor*, *The Electric Horseman*, *Tootsie*, and *Out of Africa*. His main man became Robert Redford. He and Lancaster remained close friends and when Pollack separated from his wife for a year in 1970, he came to live with Lancaster at his house in Malibu. As the director became the success the star had once been, he would tell Lancaster that he and Rayfiel were coming up with a project just for him. Fixing his bright blue gaze on his protégé, the older man would reply, "You'd better hurry up."

Pollack knew and loved Lancaster as well as anyone ever did, which is to say only partially. "Burt was a guy who was loved by men," Bone observed of this and other such relationships. "Men loved him almost better than women. Women would like to use him, put notches in their belts. But men, real men, loved him. He was extraordinary in that way." The director also saw the other side of the man, "a kind of Black Irish mood," though not, he claimed, directed at him: "He was a very troubled guy. He got in terrible depressions sometimes. I saw him in some black rages that were truly terrifying and I said, 'Oh, boy, this is not a guy I would want to plunk heads with.' " But he also saw an authenticity in the anger, perhaps because he was not the brunt of it: "Burt often recognized real feelings towards him as important even if they were feelings of anger. It was more important that you be angry than that you be indifferent." When Pollack's wife, Claire, after years of quietly listening to Lancaster, told him point-blank one night over dinner at Matteo's in Los Angeles that he never let anybody else talk, Lancaster was elated. "Claire!" he said, with what Pollack described as a "wide-eyed expression of delight," and made her sit in his lap in the car all the way home. "You could take that too far and say that's a neurotic thing," said Pollack, and there were many who thought he did so in his relationship with Jackie, "but," he concluded, "who that's not totally boring is not neurotic?"

The same confidence that made Lancaster persist regardless of outside opinion fed the rage within. "If anybody did with him a contest for control, Burt would murder them," Pollack said. "He would murder them emotionally. Or he would murder them physically. Or both. Because he didn't care. You couldn't scare him. He knew who he was, what he was worth—knew himself better than anyone I've ever met. So he was, in a curious sense, fearless: he had no fear. I was always curious: Where'd this guy come from, to be like this? It was because there was nothing at stake for him in terms of his own self-worth.

"If you went on a trip with Burt," Pollack recalled, "he carried less luggage than any human being alive. He had one coat—he called it the 'thousand-miler.' It was a grey herringbone tweed he wore practically every day of his life that I knew him. Khaki pants, black or brown Thom McCann loafers, white sweatsocks, and a Ban-Lon shirt—like the Ralph Lauren polo that you're not supposed to wear a tie with, but he carried a tie in his jacket pocket like a handkerchief and when we would walk into a restaurant he'd pull the tie out, put it under the knit collar and look better than anybody in the room. He shaved with soap, like my father did. He never bought a tube of shaving cream in his life. He would use a Gillette double-edge razor when everybody else was using fancy-this and fancy-that. He smoked Camels years after people were smoking filters. He would drink his protein milkshakes and up until around 1975 when he was in his sixties he was still doing giant swings on the bars. He worked at keeping his body in a whole different way from people today: he drank martinis every night, smoked cigarettes, but three times a week he put on a track suit and jogged. That's all. Once in a while, when he was getting ready to do a picture, he'd say "I gotta lose a few pounds" and he'd drink his protein drink. But it was never a religion with him. It lacked narcissism with him—that's the whole focus of it today. It had to do with either common sense or professionalism. He did as little as he thought he could get away with. As little as interfered with the pleasure of life.

"I never stopped being in awe of him, of how much he learned and continued to learn. If you watch his acting, he got better and better. . . . He was so respected in Europe, much more so than here. The Italians think of him as we think of Barrymore or somebody; they don't think of him as just a movie star with big teeth. They love the *presence* of him. Rayfiel met him in a restaurant in Paris for a drink once and when some women began to make a fuss over him, Burt said to him, 'They think I'm a good actor here.'

"He knew what was bullshit and what wasn't in one second. He had no time for it. He didn't spend his time with movie stars; he just wasn't interested. . . . I came from very simple beginnings too, and I never got used to all this hoopdy-doo and I don't need it either. It didn't matter if he was in a cot at the YMCA or a suite at the Royal Hotel. It's 120 degrees outside and you go in a bush to change clothes. There isn't anything else. . . .

"Rayfiel was staying out at the beach in a hotel once and from the terrace you could look back at the big house Burt had at the beach then. Burt would come out in the mornings to get the newspaper in a nightshirt and Rayfiel said that looking at him was like going to the zoo and you look and there's one animal that just stands out, that's built different and better than anyone else. That's what Burt was like—he was like a better animal. He had a stronger and more integrated character than most people have. He was in one piece."

The most elusive, private element was Lancaster's humor. Far under the megastar carapace was a self-deprecating sense of irony some, notably Frankenheimer, claimed never to see. Indeed, the wit was so dry and deadpan that most people missed it altogether. The East Harlem staccato voice imitated by younger actors and stand-up comics often made him funny in spite of himself. A wit that fed off the foibles of himself and others was, suggested Pollack, a product of Lancaster's "glandular sensitivity to people, situations, and things.

"I remember one guy, an executive at Fox, who hounded me and hounded me because he wanted an appointment with Burt. And I finally said, 'Burt, this guy is driving me crazy, would you . . . ?' 'Yeah,' he says,

'OK.' So we went to lunch and this guy was pitching and Burt is eating and eating, not saying one word, just listening. We got up, said good-bye to the guy and we're walking down the street. It's very quiet, he doesn't look at me, and says, 'When's your birthday, Sydney?' I said, 'July 1.' He says, very quietly, 'I'm gonna give you that guy for your birthday, Sydney.' "

The working relationship with Frankenheimer also ended with the decade. Lancaster joined with the director in fall 1968 near Wichita, Kansas, to make *The Gypsy Moths,* the title taken from the term for skydivers who parachute from planes on Midwestern barnstorming expeditions. Scott Wilson, now known as one of the screen killers in Richard Brooks's *In Cold Blood* (1967), Gene Hackman, also newly famous from *Bonnie and Clyde,* and Lancaster played the skydiving trio who arrive for the July 4 weekend in the little town of Bridgeville. In such company Lancaster's dour portrayal of a sour man is a disappointing end to a decade of impressive work. When his character, Rettig, in stoic despair purposely fails to pull his parachute cord and plunges to his death like a circus aerialist, this demise of the star two-thirds of the way through the movie was, one reviewer suggested when the movie opened at the end of August 1969, "a first for a Hollywood film." Reunited with Lancaster for the first time since *Separate Tables,* Deborah Kerr played her role of the dissatisfied housewife with a pathological repression. Between them, the ritual nude love scene of the era was awkward and creaky, especially in the same movie that featured nude stripper sequences by Sheree North. "We can hear the roar of the surf when they stand on the porch in Kansas," suggested the *Newark Evening News* with a gallant reference to the beach scene of sixteen years before. Wilson thought the movie oddly detached from the chaos of events on the real-life terra firma of the time.

In a year that also saw the release of *Easy Rider,* Richard Schickel writing in *Life* took note of an important, transitional grace in *The Gypsy Moths:* "Mr. Lancaster has developed a capacity, unique in established stars, to give away scenes that his status in the movie pecking order entitles him to dominate . . . and he deserves full credit for his shrewd selflessness."

The bravura days were over. Having spent a decade making movies consistent with the progressive values of his old neighborhood, he knew that the reality of those old streets, his touchstone, was grimmer than ever. The Lancaster house on 106th Street had been torn down in 1959 as part of an urban renewal slum clearance; in its place rose Benjamin Franklin Plaza, a cluster of red-brick residential towers described as "one of the most graceful groups" of its period in Manhattan. But by 1964, what the *New York Herald-Tribune* called "a vast accelerating neighborhood deterioration" had blighted the area. Intended to provide integrated middle-class housing, the new towers—like the other such government "projects" that soon comprised 60 percent of East Harlem's housing—only further undermined the cohesion and human scale of the old slum.

Lancaster's opposition to the Vietnam War was fed by the knowledge that it bled the nation's resources when they were needed for the more immediate needs of places like his old neighborhood. Each year he sent Union Settlement a healthy check, sometimes for a designated project—boy's camp, recreation center, music school—but usually for general needs. As late as 1960, his picture hung in a bakery at 105th Street and Third Avenue, a symbol to his old neighborhood of one kid who had successfully escaped. But escaped into what? More than thirty years later, *The Economist* would look back on the five years in America from 1963 to 1968 as a kind of "devil's litany." The Vietnam War brought moral anguish and inflation, deflating the postwar economic boom on which a Great Society, the shining city, would be built. What had started out with such hope under the Washington Monument in August 1963 had spun into something incomprehensible. Race riots from Watts to the nation's capital plus the disintegration of what the British magazine termed "the uneasy coalition between old-style liberals and the radicals of the New Left," stranded people like Lancaster who needed to believe that somewhere in the confusion a common purpose must be found.

What counted for him within his small world of movie effort was to proceed as if such a purpose still existed—or would be found again: an ideal based on tolerance, diversity, and civil liberties. Like a very thin thread, that assumption kept him on a certain course that avoided the cynical or the reactionary. When he could, he would make movies that addressed the issues of the day as he wished to present them. Otherwise, he would try to avoid—or persuade himself that he was avoiding—junk.

He emerged as one of the most active and vocal of the movie industry's stars in the fractured progressive politics of the late 1960s, a featured speaker at what were called "integration rallies." He and Norma, temporarily reenergizing their marriage with this common cause, became known as what actress Vanessa Sandrich-Brown, active at the time in media liaison for the Democratic Party, called "the big, big generous individuals, the large money donors," the hosts of lavish fund-raising parties. In 1968 Norma organized a program with inner-city parents—later called Transport-A-Child—that prepared the way for the current system of magnet schools in the Los Angeles Unified School District. Black elementary-school children were bused out of overcrowded schools in the southwest section of the city to fill vacancies in the richer, more spacious Bel Air schools.

In May 1969, Lancaster was heavily involved in the Los Angeles mayoral race the *New York Post* described as "surpass[ing] virtually anything this city has ever seen in point of bitterness." City Councilman Tom Bradley, who was black, ran and lost against incumbent mayor Sam Yorty, who had claimed that if Los Angeles elected its first black mayor not only would there be more race riots like those in Watts four years before, but that "militant extremists" would capture control of the city. One of the Bradley supporters so branded was Lancaster.

"The Yorty people brought in John Wayne. The Bradley people brought in Burt Lancaster," recalled Ira B. Cooperman, who left his job as a reporter for the *Los Angeles Times* to write speeches for this first Bradley campaign (four years later the candidate won and served as mayor for twenty years). "In those days, and even now, California politics was all personality, not party politics." One of Cooperman's duties was to write speeches for the stars, most of the names culled from old Robert Kennedy campaign lists, who agreed to support and to make appearances for Bradley. "Lancaster did both at some personal risk," recalled the reporter in a letter to the *Philadelphia Inquirer* after the actor's death. "Many intensely conservative Angelenos admired [Yorty] as a sort of 'man on horseback.' " Unlike many of the celebrity figures in Hollywood and national politics, the star was "amazingly" receptive, Cooperman observed, to the ideas and suggestions of the young people around him and he had an "impatient yearning for information." "Lancaster was always absolutely straight," he said. "He never did the 'Hey, I'm a star and I'm doing you a favor thing.' Peter Lawford and a lot of other people did that. He took time for ideas as opposed to personalities."

The private life was not so engaged or productive. One night in September 1968, during the studio filming at MGM of *The Gypsy Moths,* Lancaster was stopped in his red Mercury for speeding away from the California Highway Patrol while driving north on the Pacific Coast Highway near Big Rock Beach. When he refused to sign a speeding citation, claiming the officers were drunk, he was booked at the Malibu sheriff's station. Bail was posted at $65, which Lancaster, true to his own definition of civic rights, refused to pay because he felt it would have been an admission of guilt. Instead, as the media reported around the world, he spent the night in the County Central Jail in downtown Los Angeles. "I've always wanted to get an education," he said, "and tonight's as good a time as any." Most people assumed he was drunk himself (in a similar arrest three years later in August 1971, he would opt for a trial by jury and be completely exonerated). Concerned friends saw the night in jail as another example, after the headline-making altercation with Bone in Novi Sad, that he was in danger of slipping into a netherworld of has-been embarrassment.

Norma filed for divorce at the beginning of 1969 and in May Lancaster picked up a twelve-month option on the Malibu house of director Charles Walters, where he had been living with Bone. On June 27, after a proceeding that lasted less than five minutes and was kept under tight secrecy, Norma was granted an uncontested divorce in Santa Monica on the grounds of "extreme cruelty" after twenty-two years of marriage. She was granted custody of the three daughters, who were still minors: Susan was attending Pitzer College, Joanna was in college in Mexico, and Sighle was in high school. The two adult boys were not mentioned in the legal action. After completing a bachelor's degree in music and piano, Jimmy had returned to the Manhattan School of Music for a graduate degree in musical education. Billy was trying a brief turn as a Hollywood agent.

The house on Linda Flora, including much of its furniture, was sold for a song. Schiffer says that he would have bought it himself if he had known how little the Lancasters were willing to take. The children, according to Bone, wanted nothing when they left the house except their own immediate belongings; they had all long been living separate lives. Norma immediately left Hollywood with Sighle to live for several years in an apartment Lancaster bought for them in Rome near the Fontana di Trevi, with Sighle continuing her schooling in Italy. Valued at approximately $2 million, the estate was split between the couple, with Norma reportedly getting most of the art collection. Lancaster kept a core for himself, including the Roualt circus drawings, the Thomas Hart Benton painting, the Moore acrobat statuettes, and one Renoir.

It is a measure of how difficult the decision to divorce was that it took so long in coming. "Tormented by guilt for a marriage that died," was a bit of *Modern Screen* reportage that close friends would not have dismissed as hyperbole. "They stayed together long after it was over," recalled Pollack of the couple. "Burt was so good with Norma and her terrible drinking problem. She would fall down but he was never embarrassed for her. He always called her 'Norma-girl': 'Come on, Norma-girl, let's get home,' he would say. He had another part of his life that was going elsewhere, obviously, but he stayed there because he respected her and he was decent to her, in a way. Now you could speculate all sorts of things like, Why did she drink? Did she drink because in some way he was there but he wasn't there? I don't know."

In the constant battle within himself between the settlement house do-gooder and the feckless circus acrobat, the latter won out. "I found marriage somewhat stifling," he told a reporter in July 1969, pausing painfully between phrases. "Frankly, I don't know that I am the kind of man who ought to be married. Mind you, I don't regret it. I've had many happy years in my marriage. My former wife is, in my opinion, a truly wonderful person; so, it's not easy. . . . I'm not sure, either, that I'm the kind of man to live alone." He settled for what seemed to many a destructive relationship with

Bone as much because he didn't think he deserved better or had never known better. Thinking he had put failure behind him long ago in the vaudeville twilight of Kansas City, he was faced with it again. And in the pain and loss there was a sense of bafflement. Life did not always yield to the enormous force of one's willpower and best intentions. Sometimes you can't stop the train.

In the act of pretending on film—finding life, as he once put it, in other people's lives—he hoped to find himself. The search would be visible, as it had always been, like a coded drama on-screen. "Obviously I am not the young man who came to Hollywood in 1946," he said at the end of the decade. "I am continuing on my course, though, a course I had set for myself; and my work, my films, new ideas, new ways to express myself are probably my one true love that keeps me warm."

CHAPTER TEN

Burying the Heroes

I've never really had a consistent image, so I've had no happy fiction to project.

—Burt Lancaster

The antidote of making movies was much harder to achieve as the divorce overlapped with the fading of his career. Coming off ten years of strong, self-propelled work, he was faced with a new set of variables as Hollywood lurched through both internal changes and a major recession that isolated him even more than the natural diminution of age and fame. Gulf & Western had acquired Paramount in 1966, signaling the first entry of huge conglomerates into the movie business. Major layoffs thinned out the industry from stars to grips. "[W]ater is running out of swimming pools all over Beverly Hills," lamented *Films and Filming* in December 1971, "and chances are we shall not see them filled again in our lifetime."

At the creative end of the industry, Penn's *Bonnie and Clyde* had been an early preview in 1967 of what *Easy Rider* in 1969 and *M.A.S.H.* in 1970 confirmed: the beginning of an astonishing American New Wave of movies. Roman Polanski's *Chinatown*, Martin Scorsese's *Mean Streets*, Robert Altman's *McCabe and Mrs. Miller*, Coppola, Penn, Rafelson, Malick, Bogdanovich, Nicholson, Pacino, De Niro—it was a heady time peaking around 1975, the year Saigon fell to the Vietcong and moviegoers spent millions to see Steven Spielberg's *Jaws*. The younger, acid Burt Lancaster of *Sweet Smell of Success* would have fit right in.

He turned down the chance in 1969 to star in *Patton*. The movie that would embolden Nixon to bomb Cambodia was not his kind of project. But when its screenwriter, Francis Ford Coppola, went on to write *The Godfather* for a Hollywood skeptical of Mario Puzo's kitschy best-selling novel that seemed to glorify the Mafia, Lancaster jumped at it. He wanted to play the central character Don Vito Corleone so badly he offered to audition for it, an unheard-of concession for such a star. The Mafia don was a type he had known since the baby massacre on 107th Street; he could do it, he felt, as naturally as Gantry. Paramount was also pushing for Lancaster who, after all, had played the Italian Leopard. When the part went to Brando, the loss marked another twist in the sequence of intersections between the two stars. In 1972 *The Godfather* took in $126 million, then the largest gross in movie history.

Some of the luminaries in the Hollywood New Wave were people he had managed to alienate during his recent past—Penn, Cassavetes, Huston, Barbara Loden, Frank Perry. Actors or directors with whom he had worked well, such as Pollack and Dern, left him behind when they moved on into the new movie world too. As the industry began to give more financial and creative control to directors, his prescient impulse to ally himself with a Frankenheimer or a Pollack fizzled out with no new protégé to showcase him.

He became deeply depressed and questioned the worth of his entire work, speculating that all those cans of celluloid amounted to nothing solid, nothing permanent. He had not made anything, he told Bone, with his hands. "He was really wondering," she said, "what to do with himself. He thought he was just worthless and that all he knew how to do was act." The man who sucked in the ether of power like the early morning air he loved so much covered up his frustration and fear with a trenchant professionalism. When a reporter asked him in 1972 what used to be one of his favorite questions—Can the movies be both commerce *and* art?—he was brutally cynical: "The Hollywood answer to that one is easy," he said. "If you want to get involved with art, and you have the money . . . like the man says, 'Go out and buy a Picasso.' Don't fuck around with the movies."

If he sought professional help, he never told anyone and seemed, finally, to will himself out of his malaise. "Burt was very good at dealing with what came up, facing the music," recalled Bone. "He worked it out on his own—he was like that on almost everything. He might sound somebody out on something, but you wouldn't know for sure. And that would usually happen with his men friends. You know how men get together and they'll air things in their own strange way."

Whether he really solved the core problem was, to him, beside the point: deciding to get himself out of an alien place was good enough. He retreated to what he called his "inner sanctum," his offices on the old Goldwyn studio lot. Since moving in the mid-1960s from "Gower Gulch" next to Paramount, he had constantly improved on the quarters until they were exactly what he wanted: two floors, with the staff and writers downstairs, his cozy and relaxing office upstairs decorated with a Mexican adobe brick fireplace, a Spanish chandelier, Persian rugs, a private gym, and a massive, cluttered desk. He kept a bed in the corner for when he wanted to spend the night, which was often, and the toilet in the bathroom had a wooden privy seat to remind him, he said, of the old days.

When not working on a picture, he showed up at the office every morning between 8:30 and 9:00, driving in from Malibu after his usual early morning jog down the Pacific Coast Highway. He still drove himself around Los Angeles, whizzing down the broad, palm-lined avenues in a succession of brown and black Jaguars, sometimes a Mercedes. He claimed to be in bed each night by nine and devoted weekends to his two enduring, frustrating "diversions"—golf at the Hillcrest Country Club, located southeast of the old 20th Century-Fox studios, and bridge. His upper-body strength was still such that he was able, during a New York–Los Angeles American Airlines flight in 1972, to reach over two airplane passenger seats and lift a heart attack victim up and out to the aisle with one arm. The fights absorbed him and boxing impresario Jerry Perenchio became a good and enduring friend. He gave away impossible-to-get tickets to Edward Albee's hit Broadway play, *Little Alice*, at the last minute in order to stay in his hotel room and watch the Floyd Patterson–George Chuvalo heavyweight fight on TV in 1965. With Don Dunphy, he was a ringside commentator at Madison Square Garden in 1971 for Muhammad Ali's first fight against Joe Frazier.

Both Irving Burns and Thom Conroy were dead by the early seventies but Nick continued to come several times a week to work out on the bars, joke him out of his funk, and bring Marcy and Tina on weekends to play on the beach at Malibu. The two friends cooked spaghetti together like the old days in East Harlem: "It needs salt, Burt"; "No, it doesn't, Nick." The old Burton had a bit of a belly, now, though he liked to pretend he didn't. The balm, as ever, was hours and hours of music—opera, Bach, Brahms, and his favorite, "Mozart the sublime."

That he even considered starring in Ross Hunter's *Airport* indicated to some his state of mind at the turn of the decade. A blockbuster disaster movie that became the biggest hit of 1970 ($45.3 million gross in North America), it was the kind of extravaganza he had successfully avoided for more than twenty years. It was shot at Minneapolis–St. Paul International Airport in Minnesota in the middle of his divorce proceedings during the frigid, snowy winter of 1969. When the movie opened in the spring of 1970, it sucked in an audience eager to see how all the stars—including Dean Martin, Jean Seberg, and Helen Hayes—matched up with their characters in the best-selling novel by Arthur Haley. *Variety* reported that "*Airport* is shaking up Hollywood who thought *Easy Rider* was the wave of the future." Lancaster called the potboiler "the biggest piece of junk ever made" and that was *before* the Oscar ceremonies at which it would win one award (for Hayes) out of ten nominations (*Patton* earned George C. Scott an Oscar for the role Lancaster had turned down; Scott, notoriously, turned down the award).

It was as if he took on the big, tedious movie as some kind of expiation. Though he needed the flood of money that made this the most financially lucrative movie of his entire career, there was a masochistic air to Lancaster's portrayal of airport manager Mel Bakersfeld. For the first time, the shots are not organized around him. The script calls for Bakersfeld to be ridiculed or dismissed by Martin and others and he responds with, for him, an abject cringe. Bakersfeld's marriage is also dissolving under the pressure of an all-consuming job and there are lines that seem to come out of the actor's own life: "I feel like it's [divorce] a failure and I don't like to fail."

For the record, *Airport* was a practical choice: with 10 percent of the profits once the movie hit the $50 million mark, he earned money so he could "do other things"—namely, more problematic pictures. And he began to give more careful time and thought to the altered arena of early 1970s politics. (When Scott Wilson offered to get involved in Pentagon Papers protest rallies in 1971, Lancaster advised the younger, more vulnerable actor, as he had once been advised by Roland Kibbee, "Protect yourself.") Active in George McGovern's 1972 Presidential campaign against Nixon, he joined Warren Beatty, Shirley MacLaine, and other Hollywood Democrats making speeches and appearances across the country as the South Dakota candidate counted on the cachet of Hollywood celebrities to give an instant upgrade to his dark-horse race. "Burt was a straightforward, respected person by his peers," said McGovern, "and I was aware of that and I knew the press admired him. The roles he played were strong roles and I thought that would be helpful." Projecting what Ronald Brownstein called his American sense of "fundamental fairness," Lancaster, like Gregory Peck, was perceived as "compassionate without seeming weak."

As one of the more generous contributors to the candidate's California campaign, he shared a place with Gene Hackman, Hugh Hefner, Norman Lear, and Paul Newman on what came to be known in 1973 as Nixon's list of 575 White House "enemies." (A list of Nixon's seven so-called "friends" included Billy Graham and John Wayne.) Nineteen seventy-three was also the year Bradley, having created a powerful coalition of black and white liberals and moderates, won the race for mayor in Los Angeles decisively against Yorty, a campaign Lancaster actively supported. In a city that was only 15 percent black, the victory was what the *New York Times* called "a significant change in local politics in the United States."

After McGovern's defeat, Lancaster and other liberal stars such as Robert Redford would work more behind the scenes, giving money, the occasional speech, and moral support. At Abby Mann's Malibu house one night in 1970, he had met Luke McKissack, chief counsel to the Black Panthers of Southern California and attorney for Sirhan Sirhan and Charles Manson, who was in the middle of a campaign for California prisoners' rights. At a time when First Amendment rights did not largely apply to the incarcerated, a cause that considered prisoners as human beings rather than "the walking dead" was a natural successor for Lancaster to the earlier campaign for Stroud.

"You're right!" Lancaster told the attorney that night. "But Luke, I'm only an actor. What can I do?" He became known in the activist circles of celebrity involvement as the person who could be counted on with few or no questions asked and no credit claimed or asked for later. In the era of contributor lists—"the Daniel Ellsberg List," "the Chicago 8 List"—that were constantly worked through to drum up money, appearances, and testimonials on behalf of highly publicized and expensive causes, Lancaster was often the first person called because he would not ask who else had signed up.

For the fragging trial of Pvt. Billy Dean Smith, one of the most publicized cases of the Vietnam War, he quietly came through in the fall of 1972. A twenty-four-year-old black draftee from Watts, Smith was accused of killing—"fragging"—two officers with a grenade in Vietnam on March 15, 1971. The case was, with the My Lai massacre trial and conviction of Lt. William L. Calley, also in March 1971, one of the most potent magnets for the antiwar rage that had deepened after the invasion of Cambodia on April 30, 1970, and the murders of four students at Kent State on May 4. Smith was not only the first U.S. soldier to be tried for fragging—at the time of the trial, the Department of Defense reported 551 such incidents of soldiers using fragmentation grenades to kill or maim their superior officers since 1968, resulting in eighty-six deaths—but the dead officers were white and the jury was composed entirely of career combat officers.

McKissack took on Smith's defense, which hinged on the technical question of whether the grenade pin found in Smith's pocket after the explosion matched the fragmentation grenade that killed the officers. The Fort Ord trial was recessed for one day on November 8, the day after Nixon's landslide victory, to give McKissack time to find three expert and expensive ballistics analysts as rebuttal witnesses; after twenty months, the defense team had run out of money with the usual donors leery of putting more money into what looked like a doomed effort. "I sat there in desperation," the attorney recalled, "and said, 'What one person is most likely, if I just tell him I need the money with no questions asked?' And it was Burt Lancaster." He called Lancaster and said, "I hate to trade on our friendship, Burt, but this is desperate." Lancaster asked, "How much do you need right now?" McKissack replied, "Three thousand dollars by tomorrow," and Lancaster said, "You've got it."

Smith was acquitted on November 14 and when McKissack went to thank Lancaster, the actor waved him off and never mentioned the subject again. It was clear he did not wish any "postpublicity." "If Brando had done it," said McKissack, who later worked on behalf of the Native Americans who took over Wounded Knee, South Dakota, in 1973, a well-publicized Brando cause, "everybody would have known about it."

The attorney had also suggested the First Amendment advocacy of the American Civil Liberties Union (ACLU) to Lancaster in 1970 only to find that the organization was already a central focus of Lancaster's life. "Here's this great big aggressive guy," recalled Tony Curtis, "that looks like a ding-dong athlete playing these big tough guys and he has the soul of—who were those first philosophers of equality?—Socrates, Plato. He was a Greek philosopher with a sense that everybody was equal." In the late 1960s the Southern California affiliate of the ACLU was a small, struggling local part of the national organization founded in 1920 by Roger Baldwin. It elected Lancaster to serve as chairman of its newly formed fund-raising arm, the ACLU Foundation of Southern California. In October 1968, he hosted a party at his home to raise money for the ACLU to use for the defense of the more than four hundred people arrested in Chicago at the Democratic National Convention the previous August. In November 1970, he and Sinatra cochaired the Foundation and hosted a $1,000-a-plate dinner to benefit the organization.

In the real world of civil rights and civil liberties—the arena where, as he saw it, the powerless necessarily define the battle—he found the tough, practical work that satisfied his aching need to do something productive, the equivalent of making something with his hands. "A role in the ACLU was a place for Burt," said McKissack. "It wasn't fashionable—the only people from films that you'd see in there would be those who'd suffered so immensely from things like the blacklist." While serving as a member of the five-person ACLU Foundation executive committee, he cast the key vote to retain Ramona Ripston as executive director of the Southern California affiliate, a position she would build into a powerful advocacy force in Los Angeles politics. "The foundation board was all white males," recalled Ripston, who had worked with the Student Non-Violent Coordinating Committee (SNCC), the Mississippi Freedom Party, and the New York Urban Coalition. "There was a feeling that a woman couldn't run the ACLU foundation, nor have access to the books. The vote finally came down to two 'yes' and two 'no.' Who had the deciding vote? Burt. He had a scotch or two and finally he said, 'I think she should be executive director.' I always loved him for that."

. . .

For the actor who called his work his one true love, whose youth and vigor had defined him, he had arrived at *the* crossroads. In 1973 Lancaster would turn sixty. It was time for the stage he talked about all the time to journalists and friends: playing and being the older man. Pushing for the part of Doc Delaney in 1952 when he was thirty-eight had been the free choice of a still-young man. How could he make playing the real thing equally compelling, risky? What were the moves, and how would he block them out? Where was the grace, the fluidity, the energy in being old? If he no longer had the power to push everybody off the bus, what were his career options? Disappear from the screen like Cary Grant? Settle into an avuncular persona that would keep him bankable as a winsome old character actor for years to come? Or pick any one of his previous archetypes—Wyatt Earp, the Leopard, Sgt. Warden, the Swede—and repeat it until he became a caricature?

He followed an intelligent, maybe brilliant instinct. Since he had to play older men, he would do so in a manner and in movies that did not look back to the past with an empty nostalgia. Thus, he would find himself finishing the stories of his own archetypes, one by one. The accumulated weight of his screen years would be brought to bear on a string of performances that buried with scrupulous attention paid the ideas he had developed and refined on-screen since 1946. As the nation more or less matured with time and adversity, so would he, on-screen. It was a version of that old subversive twist, an insistence that his independent, perverse self not be patronized and taken for granted, dressed up like an ape in a zoo. He would still make the lucrative clinkers—he needed the money for Norma, the five children, Nick and his daughters, his grandchild, Bone, his people, and his own love of the life well lived.

In holding to a quixotic integrity that would go its own way even if nobody noticed, he was showing the courage of the artist he had always wanted to be. He didn't care, he said in 1970, if he played a hero or a villain. What mattered was "a satisfying statement." While the best of his movies in this decade are stories of men isolated by circumstance and choice, what continues to distinguish his versions of this all-too-familiar American type is their *wanting* to be connected to the group. As a superstar, he was aware that audiences had grown up with him, watched him change from role to role. He wanted to use that "special place in the public's affections," as he put it, to get them to think a little harder, look a little deeper. He would continue to tell his version of the American story, their story, even if the theater was empty.

Too old to compete with Martin Sheen or Jack Nicholson in a New Wave drama, he could use the form of the Western and shape his role to a contemporary purpose. *Valdez Is Coming, Lawman,* and *Ulzana's Raid,* released from 1971 to 1972, were the third and last trio of horse operas he would make in his career. They form a trilogy united by his evolving presence and by themes uppermost in the minds of what he hoped remained of his audience: law and order and the Vietnam War.

Frustration against a dramatic rise in crime, much of it directed at the police, had fueled a backlash against the iconoclastic sixties and found expression in movies like Clint Eastwood's *Dirty Harry* in 1971. Lancaster turned down the part of Harry Callahan, he told *Lawman* director Michael Winner—another major hit and cultural marker to add to his list of misses. But the plot some called fascist of the lawman who goes beyond the limits of the law to kill the marginalized criminal would have contradicted his belief in a collective responsibility for criminal and social justice and the protection of individual rights. He would tell the story differently, spin it back on itself.

Valdez Is Coming was shot in Almería, Spain, in January 1970, the story a convoluted twisting and turning from wrong to right, a sincere if perplexing attempt to show the moral and strategic dangers of acting alone to right a wrong. It was produced by Lancaster's new company, Norlan Productions, the name a blend of the original "Norma" and "Lancaster," and was the last movie with UA in which he played any significant packager/production role. Kibbee wrote the final script based on an Elmore Leonard novel and Lancaster brought in Ed Sherin, a brand-new screen director, who had just come off directing a Broadway hit, *The Great White Hope* (he would shift to television and eventually produce the popular NBC hit television drama of the 1990s *Law and Order*).

In his segue into grizzled, mature lead character roles, Lancaster plays Bob Valdez, a paunchy, diffident, blue-eyed Mexican constable in the post–Civil War Arizona Territory who is maneuvered into killing a black man by a white rancher. When he tries to raise money for the widow, an Apache, he is tied to a cross by the rancher's men and set out to wander, Christ-like, across the desert in the masochistic tradition of *One-Eyed Jacks* (1961). Debased and angry, he finds his old cavalry uniform, puts it on, is transformed into a vengeance machine, and kills eleven men while eluding capture. Valdez is a man, said Lancaster, with "a compulsion—a kind of bizarre, fanatic drive—to do one good deed."

The question for him and Eastwood and their respective sympathizers was, Who defined the good? All the white men in the movie were racists, some reviewers noted, and all the Mexicans, blacks, and Indians were noble. The violence, cueing off movies such as Peckinpah's *The Wild Bunch* (1969), was graphic. *Women's Wear Daily* sympathized that "[the] competition these days is fierce. What with the [Vietnam] war practically live on TV and the papers full of mayhem on the corner, it's not easy coming up with fictional violence quite as gripping."

The crudely formed ideas of *Valdez* were squeezed into a much tighter and extreme conflict between law and justice in *Lawman*. Lancaster's grimly obsessive U.S. marshal, Jered Maddox, spends the entire movie rounding up a gang of men who inadvertently killed an old man during a drunken shoot-'em-up brawl. By the last scene in a script written by Gerald Wilson, virtually everyone except Maddox is dead, Lee J. Cobb by a horrifying self-inflicted shot into his mouth. Prior to filming near Durango, Mexico, in mid-1970, Lancaster and the director Michael Winner went over the final scene in which the marshal picks off one last man as he runs away. "But why does Maddox shoot the man in the back?" asked Lancaster. "Because he's a bastard, Burt!" replied the ebullient, thirty-five-year-old Winner. A director of BBC TV movies and brittle, clever features like *The Joker*, he was tackling his first Western with the star he liked and respected as a fellow Scorpio and "an American hero of the fifties, when adults could be heroes."

Lancaster in fact relished his portrayal of yet another cold, rigid fanatic. When he played authoritarian bad guys his distaste manifested itself in an extreme containment, à la Hunsecker, of his body. Freedom was *movement*. In one scene where he had to come through the usual barroom swinging doors walking toward the camera, he "moved brilliantly," recalled Winner, and asked at the end of the take, "How was it?" "Well, all I can say, sir," said Winner, "is that it scared the shit out of me."

Justice devours itself with more death and violence in this antibacklash movie and what could have been caricatures—Robert Ryan's faded, complaisant local marshal or Cobb's Big Daddy rancher—are given shadings and complications that intensify the isolation and irrationality of Lancaster's lawman. On its release, *Films and Filming* in April 1971 wondered if an audience accustomed to the mythical variations of Sergio Leone, *Butch Cassidy and the Sundance Kid*, and *The Wild Bunch* would take to *Lawman*: "There is little consolation in this deadly intrusion into the heart of myth . . . everything is dirt, dust, and death."

Lancaster's Western trilogy culminated with *Ulzana's Raid*, not only one of the finest films of his career, but perhaps director Robert Aldrich's masterpiece. Fascinated by the Vietnam echoes in the script by Alan Sharp, Lancaster agreed to work without a salary if necessary to ensure that the movie would be made. "The Western is the most . . . cinematic of experiences," Lancaster told an English audience at the time. "Its simplistic style gives an opportunity for modern parallels." If *Lawman* had implied the link between a deadly complicity in an irreversible chain of events and Vietnam, *Ulzana's Raid* jumped right into what Lancaster's costar Bruce Davison called "the Big Muddy where everybody gets killed."

A cavalry troop led by Davison's inexperienced Lt. DeBuin and guided by Lancaster's seasoned scout McIntosh sets out from a fort to track down a murderous group of Apache tribesmen led by their chief Ulzana. Outwitted by both the guerrilla tactics of the Indians and the lieutenant's fatal misunderstanding of the necessary strategy, the troop are almost all, including McIntosh, killed. Austere, implacable, with an elegant rigor of style and logic, the movie is the story of two utterly different cultures, the white man's and the Indian's, that coexist, barely—except when they are frighteningly the same.

In that revelation, like looking into the mirror-face of the enemy, is the central terror of the movie. *Ulzana's Raid* was released in 1972, a year after Lt. Calley's trial. What stops DeBuin from cracking like Calley when faced with the alien enemy is McIntosh. The scout represents an attitude of vigorous tolerance. He cannot change history, the doomed situation, but he can at least not reduce its complexities to absurd and dangerous postures. Faced with a worthy Apache adversary who is not only brilliant and calculated but desperate to rebuild his diminished power through murdering white men and leaving their women worse than dead, McIntosh proceeds with a knowledge and respect for the enemy that go beyond stereotypes to arrive at the cold exhilaration of reality. The violence on both sides is precise, cold, and horrific, so organic a part of the tighter and tighter circle of action that it is cathartic. Lancaster would have two more fine, minor Western performances before he got off a horse forever, but it is McIntosh who completes his American Western journey. The scout is superb, the man who knows when and how to act, why not to act. Asked some years later which of his roles came closest to himself, Lancaster would say that McIntosh "was a man who reflected my own feelings about life."

He became, in effect, a producer of the Universal movie—shot in ten weeks from January to March 1972 in Nogales, Arizona, and in the Valley of Fire in Overton, Nevada—a situation Aldrich did not like at all. The irascible director, a fat, energetic, brilliant man whose favorite response to the latest Hollywood blindside was *"C'est la goddamn vie!"* had been forced to sell his independent operation when a series of flops followed the success of *The Dirty Dozen* in 1967. Now he needed money, and his complicated latter-day career of horror thrillers such as *Baby Jane* and *Sweet Charlotte* had left him, Sharp recalled, with the opinion that all stars were "cocksuckers" and that the "big cocksucker" was Lancaster.

The two men raged and bellowed back and forth, each rather enjoying the battle over what kind of movie *Ulzana's Raid* was going to be. "Burt was from the outset a principal player in the revisions that went on in the script," said Sharp. "He was intent on what you might call the 'neo-liberal' point of view and I think Bob, who was just as much of a liberal as Burt ever was, just wanted to make his movie which was going to be tough enough, thank you very much, without adding all this other shit." The conflicts usually turned on the nuances of a given scene, how clearly the parallels were portrayed not only between the white men and the Indians but also with Vietnam. "Burt would always seem to be the one who was talking about art," said the screenwriter, "and Bob was talking about nuts and bolts." Never, he claimed, did they actually talk about the movie-as-allegory. They were "too cool" for that.

When Aldrich stonewalled Lancaster's demand that more takes be made of one scene, suggesting, with deliberate irony, that the sets could be kept at Universal, reconstructed, and the scene reshot later, Lancaster burst through the door of Aldrich's Nogales motel room where the director was calmly waiting for what he knew would be vintage "Burt Lancaster." Said Sharp, "It was like *Brute Force*. Burt came storming in and came right up to Bob and said, 'You little fucking cocksucker! What do you think you're doing?' I'd never seen grown men behave like this." Aldrich chuckled, Lancaster made his point that he was not a "fucking fool" who would believe a ploy like that, and the shoot continued—without the extra coverage. Later, Lancaster got the studio to let him recut the final cut over Aldrich's objections. Since the film was already scored, the editing was minor and involved his ongoing preoccupation with nuance and parallels.

Lancaster struck up a smoother rapport with the much younger Davison. These encounters, which rarely lasted longer than the shoot, were more important to him now as his discomfort with his own children grew more obvious and painful; the new acolytes became his temporary offspring. "Burt liked protégés," said Sharp, "young men to stand around in amazement." On the first day of the script reading Davison, just off Daniel Mann's *Willard*, walked up to Lancaster and instead of shaking his hand threw "a fake right" to his chest. "He looked at me with a sort of glee in his eye," recalled Davison, "like 'Ahhh! Let's see if you can do a triple!' " At the end of one day's work, as they moved along side by side on horses for a long shot, chatting out of range of the microphone, the star turned raconteur, reminiscing about Shelley Winters ("hell of a broad, hell of a broad"), Robert Stroud ("a real evil son of a bitch"), and Kirk Douglas ("I'll never forget the time we were getting ready for our big two-shot and I hid his lifts on him. He was so pissed!"). Suddenly Davison realized the wily star was also upstaging him by pulling back, slightly, on his horse. When the younger star did the same, Lancaster looked at him and said, "Now the young lieutenant is not as innocent as he seems, are you, you little son of a bitch?" He could only be challenged so far. "I never would cross him," Davison said. "He'd squash me like a bug."

Although the older star did not look as if he were *doing* anything during filming, when Davison saw the first rushes it was a revelation. "I said, Oh, look at me twitching all over the place like a fly in heat and he's just Burt Lancaster. He's this rock, just sitting there—and he's got all the best lines anyway." Lancaster finally called the young actor over to sit down next to him on one of the desert rocks and hear some advice: "You try to please the director and the cameraman and the sound man," he said, "and you're act- ing and acting and acting and by the time you come to your close-up, you've shot your wad. It's like making love to a woman: you can't try to come all at once, son. A bit of a tit here, a bit of an inner thigh there, and you have a performance!"

The advice stuck with Davison: "That was the Crimson Pirate talking!" He had learned, too, from watching Lancaster that movie acting was not, as he had thought, trying to be Olivier: "When I first met Burt I thought he was no great shakes as an actor. But then I realized that he could play Burt Lancaster better than anyone and he could play it because he had refined it and discovered who he was." In roundabout ways Lancaster asked Sharp if he was being "too Burt Lancaster" in his portrayal of McIntosh. "I think he was aware that he was self-parodic," Sharp said. "I got the sense that the guy knew he inhabited this icon and that sometimes it ruled him. He couldn't help his hands from coming up in a certain way, for example." Since *Vera Cruz,* he had brought to the Western the quick, taunting, What's next? street smarts of the big city. This time, his McIntosh had the freedom to die on-screen without the producers calling foul and he did, burying a screen lifetime of Western heroes and antiheroes. The last freeze-frame catches the dying scout, alone, having failed to save his group, lifting the last, awkwardly rolled cigarette not quite to his mouth. "Burt quite liked the death scene," recalled Sharp.

The result of his reining in the persona was what critic Andrew Sarris called on the movie's release, "the performance of his career" in "the aptest movie yet on the senseless agony of the Vietnam War." *Ulzana's Raid,* reflected Schickel in the *New York Times,* went "beyond the paleface" to a level of brutal rigor in a classic form that might never be seen again, "a bloody but authentically tragic conflict between the races as it was enacted in 'frontiers' all over the globe in the last century." The cumulation of effort once caught by French critic Jean-Claude Missiaen was here brought to one stage of completion: "*un authentique homme de gauche*—if one can be left in Hollywood . . . bent, since adolescence, to the severe discipline of sport, he has visibly conserved to his use the taste of the calculated effort, harmo- niously proportioned to the desired effect."

But nobody came to see it. Like *The Swimmer, Ulzana's Raid* was so true it was unwatchable.

A "winner in the game of survival here in Hollywood," one commentator said of Lancaster's dogged efforts to stay in play. Between making *Lawman* and *Ulzana's Raid,* he returned to the theater stage in spring 1971 at San Francisco's Geary Theater and the Dorothy Chandler Pavilion in Los Angeles to headline in Maxwell Anderson's 1938 musical play *Knickerbocker Holiday.* Strapped into a special peg-leg rigged up by Schiffer, he thrashed about as Peter Stuyvesant, speaking lines punched up by Kibbee with contemporary political references, and singing, after phrasing lessons from Sinatra, "September Song." Reaction included pans for the performance and praise for the fact he was game enough to try. Undeterred, he told Pollack over the phone after opening night, "The critics just *creamed* me, Sydney. And, you know, they were right! I really stunk! But, it's getting way better, Sydney: I'm workin' on the thing." When the Kibbees went backstage one night, worried over what to say to him after a performance they thought was "terrible," he beamed at them: "How did you like me? Wasn't I *great*?"

He made a quick batch of what turned out to be lackluster efforts. *Scorpio,* a contemporary thriller shot in Paris, Vienna, and Washington and directed by Winner, was an attempt to launch him into another movie type suitable for a faded star—the gumshoe. Dressed with obvious discomfort in a suit, bright red tie, and hat, and with a muddy hair dye, he looked bored and irritated. Except for Hunsecker, Lancaster had avoided suits and ties and the roles that went with them. His double agent character dies saying, "The only object of the game is not to win but not to lose, just to stay in the game." The project might have been an acceptable career shift, as *Harper* had been for Paul Newman in 1966, if it had been better than what *Variety* described on its release in 1973 as an "anachronistic emulation of mid-1960s cynical spy mellers [melodramas]." Lancaster growled that, except for working again with *Leopard* costar Alain Delon, making such "purely entertaining" movies "bored the shit" out of him.

His UA contract, which had given him the option to refuse two scripts of every three, was at an end with *Scorpio.* After rejecting Winner's *The Mechanic,* he was briefly considered for the director's Eastwood-esque *Death Wish* before being passed over by Paramount for the more bankable and slightly younger Charles Bronson. It was just as well; *Death Wish,* not to mention its three sequels, was not how he wanted to end his career.

Both to oblige his old friend Kibbee and to take one last crack at directing, he agreed to make in February 1973 what the writer called "pulp fiction" and what Canby would call the "second worst film of 1974," *The Midnight Man*. Norlan produced, and Universal, up to a point, released the tawdry story of murder and incest in which Jim Slade, an ex-con working during his parole as a campus security guard, unravels a murder and blackmail scheme. As Slade, Lancaster looked tired and grumpy, his skin pale as if not quite his own; the patient plodding required of his role left him looking stranded. He was drinking heavily, Lucy Kibbee recalled, staying up late talking endlessly to whomever was around and then getting up at 5 a.m. to work on location at Clemson University in Clemson, South Carolina. He was back to publicly berating Bone and erupted at Susan Clark, his costar in *Valdez Is Coming*, cast as the parole officer with what *Variety* called a "reversible libido."

It was twenty years since Billy—now divorced from Kippie Kovacs and pursuing a brief acting career with a minor part in the movie—Nick Cravat, and Roland and Lucy Kibbee had all been together on location for *The Crimson Pirate*. The behavior tolerated in the 1950s as the prerogative of a megastar at his peak now looked strange and sad. While Roland Kibbee at least had the consolation of winning an Emmy as coexecutive producer of *Columbo* shortly before *The Midnight Man* was released, Lancaster had a very different confirmation: he was finished as a major star or force in Hollywood. "If the studios were still operating as they used to," wrote Howard Kissel in *Women's Wear Daily* of *The Midnight Man*, "there would have been whole departments to tell Burt" that the story had too many holes, his costume too many sags, the movie too many reels. The critic then isolated what kept Lancaster, ethos or politics aside, from becoming some kind of older Eastwood variant—his image was "too heroic" for the "cool, low-keyed style of today." A hero in what he once called "the hero business," he was now an anachronism.

While shooting finished on *The Midnight Man* in March and the Watergate scandal deepened after Nixon's election and the last American ground troops were finally pulled out of Vietnam, Lancaster prepared to star with Robert Ryan in *Executive Action*, the first mainstream JFK assassination conspiracy movie. Its release was timed to coincide with the tenth anniversary of Kennedy's death, its "real purpose," he said, ". . . to make people skeptical."

The movie became for its makers a kind of crusade that developed along a particularly Hollywood activist path. Actor Donald Sutherland—with Lancaster and Ryan, one of the more active Hollywood liberals—initially brought to the attention of producer Edward Lewis a book by Mark Lane and Donald Freed called *Executive Action: Assassination of a Head of State*. Lane was also the author of *Rush to Judgment*, which challenged the conclusions of the official Warren Report on the assassination. Lewis, the producer of *Spartacus* and *Seven Days in May*, and one of the first in the industry to crack the blacklist by revealing Trumbo as the screenwriter of *Spartacus,* assigned the script of *Executive Action* to Trumbo. He may well have recognized a civilian version of Gen. Scott in Lancaster's character of Farrington, the cold, crazy, establishment, right-wing conspirator who masterminds the killing of a liberal president too eager to accommodate the Russians and the civil rights movement. Lancaster accepted the part as another worthy subversion of his WASP persona and a coda to *Seven Days in May,* which had been made with JFK's blessing. A self-described "Kennedy man" who had dined at the Camelot White House, he saw the movie as his tribute to the dead president and a kind of payback to the reactionary crazies he had been bumping up against since the Federal Theater Project.

He immersed himself in the Warren Report and conspiracy "facts" and "evidence" and convinced himself that assassin Lee Harvey Oswald had been set up as a "Communist fall-guy." Lancaster, Ryan, Will Geer, and the rest of the cast worked for scale and the black-and-white movie was shot quickly in Los Angeles and Tulsa, Oklahoma (doubling for Dallas), in May and June 1973 for just under $1 million. It had the desperate, rushed smell of despair: if a right-wing conspiracy eliminated one president only to have another, crooked leader elected not once but twice, what was this country coming to? Reaction in November was immediate and negative. Exception was taken to TV advertisements showing an assassin loading and leveling his rifle when the rest of the media were mounting extensive tributes to the slain president. Some critics found the movie an irresponsible melodrama that cheapened a national tragedy especially when, as Stanley Kauffman pointed out in *The New Republic,* the country "had enough presidential problems now to handle."

It was the beginning of a long revisionist evolution. Joan Mellen, writing in *Cinéaste* in 1974, called *Executive Action* "the first important film dealing with Kennedy's execution and reaching, if not 'the masses,' then a wide range of Americans." For Lancaster, that was success enough. "The dreams have changed," he said a couple of years after the grim anniversary. "It will have to be a whole lot better world before people can sit back and believe the fairy tale again." The movie was generally thought to have been made only because Lancaster agreed to star in it. That it was also considered tasteless, politically dishonest, and fringe screwball only further stripped him of a bankable star presence in the industry that released half as many movies in 1974 as it had in 1946.

It seemed like a good time to be away from Hollywood and the country. Norma had decided to return to Beverly Hills, leaving Sighle behind in the Rome apartment. Lancaster flew to Sinai in fall 1973 to bury the granddaddy of all patriarchs, Moses. The $5-million biblical epic produced for RAI Television and Sir Lew Grade's British ATV-ITC consortium and called, simply, *Moses*, was his first and last venture into bearded, robe-flapping Charlton Heston territory. As preparation, he read the Old Testament and the forty-page entry on Moses in the *Encyclopedia Brittanica*. When a reporter asked if he was following Heston, Lancaster snapped back, "If Charlton was trapped in biblical films, it was his own fault—he accepted the limitation."

The big schism in his life was leaving behind the religious, patriotic passion of the Church of the Son of Man and an old part of him yearned for the "tough customer" God who, as he told one reporter, "made man to torment him with dissatisfaction" until he realized that "only in Me will he be satisfied." Together, Moses and God made a religion from the harsh choices and necessities of survival—a process Lancaster could respect. Bone remains certain he was never the atheist he claimed to be, that "something happened, somewhere—perhaps his mother's death—to turn him off" from what he still, deep down in his Elmer Gantry heart, believed. He tossed off any such identification. The Ten Commandments, he said, were fine—but not for him.

Filming in Jerusalem was briefly interrupted when the Yom Kippur War broke out in December 1973 and Lancaster, Bone, and Palazzi, his Roman driver, plus the rest of the non-Israeli cast and crew—including Billy (now Bill) Lancaster, continuing his desultory acting career as the young Moses—went to Rome, returning as soon as the armistice was signed. The miniseries pulled in the largest audience in Italian television history and was publicized as Lancaster's first venture—aside from a 1969 appearance on the brand-new *Sesame Street*, reciting the alphabet—into American television. But when CBS ran it in the dead of summer 1975 rather than at Easter, it was another humiliating put-down. The production was lackluster, said many reviews, the script often laughable. Lancaster's performance was judged both "magnificent" and "dreadful."

He returned directly from the Middle East to Rome in spring 1974 when Visconti, dying, needed him to play an aging and ineffectual professor in the director's penultimate film, *Conversation Piece*. Sealed up in his hermetic Roman town house, surrounded by exquisite, treasured works of art, the professor is the twentieth-century European intellectual as remote from haphazard egalitarian life as the Leopard gazing out into space with his telescope. The director's thematic requiem, *Conversation Piece* was a paradoxical eulogy to the patriarchs of the Western mind, the keepers of the culture, *their* culture, grounded on Visconti's "floor of time."

Lancaster was necessary to ensure that the movie was made at all. While filming *Ludwig*, Visconti had had a stroke and was now confined to a wheelchair. His friends and associates put together, without his knowledge, what D'Amico called "the secret deal" that would "save him, find a way for him to live, to work": Lancaster would not only star in the picture, he would "guarantee" it by standing as the responsible, insured party, obligated to be on the set at all times in case anything happened to Visconti. "Lancaster would have had to go on [as director]," recalled D'Amico, "so he wanted to know everything, to see, to learn." It was an important, precious task for Lancaster at a time when he needed that kind of affirmation. Who better than Italy's beloved *gattopardo* to "guarantee" a great director's cinematic farewell to life?

The story solution was ingenious. To assure that the director was not overtaxed, the movie had to be shot on one stage set location, indoors. From the model of a genre of eighteenth-century English painting called "conversation pieces"—small pictures in which families of the aristocracy or high bourgeoisie with their children, servants, and dogs are portrayed against the highly detailed background, mise-en-scène, of their cultivated wealth—Enrico Medioli, D'Amico, and Visconti created the real story of temptation, vice, love, and death behind the picture. The professor, isolated with his "conversation pieces," is forced to confront the jagged modern world when a raffish family—Sylvana Magnano, Claudia Marsani, and Stefano Patrizi as mother, daughter, and son as well as a gigolo, Konrad, played by Visconti's real-life lover, the blond, beautiful Helmut Berger—moves in with him and proceeds to tear up his exquisite house and his life. He witnesses their, to him, shocking sexual freedom but, discovering a shared passion for Mozart and art with Konrad, he literally brings real life into his domain when he offers to hide Konrad from political enemies in his apartment. By the end, the gigolo is dead and the professor dying in his violated sanctuary of art and *objets*.

The script was written, according to D'Amico, with Lancaster already in mind as the lead. Although the director denied it, the story was an allegory of his own life, specifically his long relationship with Berger, whom he met shortly after *The Leopard*. Like the professor, he had "rescued" Berger from what the actor described as "the terrible jet set of *La Dolce Vita*—all this noise, new records, the Rolling Stones, tie-dyed jeans, joints, a whole revolution," and hid him in his home to protect him. The younger man became both lover and son, the older man's connection to the modern world and antidote to the weight and obligation of his past.

Berger was playing himself, Lancaster was playing Visconti, and Visconti was watching the two of them. "Two Viscontis, two lions, two teachers," Berger recalled. "Burt directed me. He took over the same rhythm, mentality. They were twins. When one thought something, the other one said it. It was terrible! 'What do you want from me?' I would ask both of them." Lancaster fell into the familiar mode of teacher, the patriarch himself. "Helmut, please don't talk so fast," he would advise, unaware the actor

"Can you hear me, Jesus?" Lancaster in his Oscar-winning role of Elmer Gantry, Sinclair Lewis's wily creature of the heartland. *Elmer Gantry* (1960)

Lancaster never so thoroughly immersed himself in a role as he did in that of Robert Stroud, the killer who transformed himself into the "birdman of Alcatraz." *Birdman of Alcatraz* (1962)

The Leopard (Il Gattopardo) (1963): Lancaster and Claudia Cardinale in the great ball sequence that ends the movie. After an explosive altercation between Lancaster and the movie's director, Luchino Visconti, the two men became very close.

Martin Luther King Jr.'s March on Washington, Aug 28, 1963. Lancaster was part of the Hollywood cont gent that attended the event, which included Sid Poitier, Harry Belafonte, and James Garner.

"The enemy is the age, the nuclear age. It happens to have killed man's faith to influence what happens to him. And from this desperation, we look for a champion in red, white, and blue." Lancaster played right-wing general James Muldoon Scott in Frankenheimer's *Seven Days in May* (1964).

Director John Frankenheimer and Lancaster were in France from 1963 to 1964 for the making of *The Train* (1964), which is considered "the last great black-and-white action-adventure film" and a precursor of "high-tech shoot-'em-ups."

"A painting means as much to you," says Paul Scofield as Nazi Colonel Von Waldheim, "as pearls to an ape"; Lancaster, silent, machine-guns him to bits. This scene in *The Train* inspired many copies.

John Cheever's Ned Merrill thought of himself as "a very special human being, noble and splendid." Lancaster in *The Swimmer* (1968)

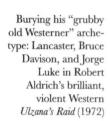

Lancaster and Jackie Bone, his companion for more than fifteen years, attending a Friar's Club dinner. "We were great sparring partners," she said of their long, fractious relationship.

Burying his "grubby old Westerner" archetype: Lancaster, Bruce Davison, and Jorge Luke in Robert Aldrich's brilliant, violent Western *Ulzana's Raid* (1972)

urying the *padrone*, the patriarch: Lancaster as Bertolucci's anguished Parma landowner in *1900* (1976)

"It was the thrill of my life to have invented you." Lancaster's myth-spinning dime novelist Ned Buntline in Robert Altman's *Buffalo Bill and the Indians* (1976)

"This is a sucker's tour, going nowhere, just around and around in circles." Lancaster as Vietnam major Asa Barker in Ted Post's *Go Tell the Spartans* (1978)—"the mind," wrote Bert Cardullo, "to the body of *Platoon.*"

"I know. I did it. They can't take that away from me," said Lancaster after being congratulated on his comeback role—and fourth Oscar nomination—in *Atlantic City* (1981), directed by Louis Malle. Lancaster (left) and Malle on location on the boardwalk in 1979

Local Hero (1983) was one of the most pleasurable movie shoots of Lancaster's career. The part of daffy, star-gazing Felix Happer was written with him and his unique speech cadence clearly in mind by Scottish writer/director Bill Forsyth.

Lancaster and Susie Martin, the woman who would become his third wife, on the set of ABC-TV's feature production *Scandal Sheet* in 1984

May 1986: Lancaster was among the earliest advocates for AIDS awareness in Hollywood. This poster was part of a campaign by Aid for AIDS to increase awareness of the disease among high-risk groups. The organization named him their Man of the Year on July 24, 1987.

ACTOR BURT LANCASTER REMINDS YOU...

"*THINK BEFORE YOU ACT— DON'T GET AIDS!*"

AID AIDS

PHOTOGRAPHY BY: DANIEL ADAMS   PRODUCED BY: MICHAEL JOHN HORNE   GRAPHICS BY: CHRIS McAULIFFE

"Hey, rookie," says Ray Liotta's Shoeless Joe Jackson to Lancaster's Doc Graham, "you were good"—the last line spoken to Lancaster in *Field of Dreams* (1989), and in the movies.

Lancaster and Susie married on September 10, 1990, at the Four Seasons Hotel in Beverly Hills. From left to right: John Scherer (Susie's son), Sighle Lancaster, Susan Lancaster, Mrs. Violet Martin (Susie's mother), Bill Lancaster, Susie, Burt, Joan Lancaster (Jimmy's wife), Jimmy Lancaster, Keigh Lancaster (Bill's daughter), Joanna Lancaster was "so nervous and impressed by Burt that I ate my words." Knowing that Visconti "never, never" did more than three takes, Berger began to calm down and listen. "Take a pause here, Helmut," Lancaster said. "It's your movie. Breathe, take time, show me the feeling." "I showed it to you!" insisted Berger. "No," said Lancaster. "Too early." By the end, Berger was captivated by the star who gave him confidence and peace, who had "enormous humanity." "There was a certain moment," he said, "when I thought, I leave Luchino and go with Burt. Like a little girl, you know? But I cannot leave my old man for the other one, so I take them both, find an island and take care of them, cook for them. A fairy tale! I was really falling in love. Thank God the movie finished—I might have corrupted him." In such a loaded atmosphere, Lancaster's own sexuality was, overtly, not an issue: "He arrived like a father," remembered Berger, "who always had his girlfriends."

Visconti, famous for creating his own "family" of acolytes, fellow filmmakers, and lovers, made what he called "a portrait of a family." Behind that disingenuous comment was perhaps the central sadness of his life. Where did he fit into his own patriarchal tradition that depended on heterosexual unions to endure? How far did his sexuality push him outside the fold, away from the beautifully set family table that repeats like a visual mantra in his films? As Lancaster later said, *Conversation Piece* was "fractured . . . in terms of what Visconti wanted to say and what he was afraid to say." His friend and director had "never," he said, "had the capacity to love. He's always maintained an essential kind of loneliness."

The dilemma was also Lancaster's. He was happiest with his "conversation pieces," his opera, movies, books, ideas, projects—the abstract diversions of the intellect unhampered by messy human connection. He longed for the sustenance of a traditional family but in fact crafted his own assemblage of friends, cronies, lovers, and employees. His constant, almost compulsive generosity kept them all at arm's length, beholden, and, in the end, it corrupted them, especially his children. "I fucked them all up," he once said. Even the delight in physical action verged on a mania that took him further into himself. He would never claim to be a Visconti, with all that that implied of refinement and taste. But an existential detachment of the mind, heart, past, and lived present from the corporal body was something the two men shared. Visconti's gentle, solitary professor was Lancaster's alter ego.

While finishing *Conversation Piece*, Lancaster was asked by Bernardo Bertolucci to incarnate another variation of the patriarch in the director's epic of twentieth-century Italian social and political change, *1900*. For someone so thoroughly American, Lancaster was now an Italian totem, a complex, idealized mix of the best and worst of the country's stratified past.

The *gattopardo* would be placed at the beginning of the century in *1900,* and in another class, as Alfredo Berlinghieri, the *padrone* of the land-owning haute bourgeoisie against whom the peasants revolt to claim the land as their own. With homage to Visconti, the director believed that the great theme of the twentieth century was the unfinished business of the nineteenth: the death of the *padrone.*

Since *The Killers* and *The Crimson Pirate,* Bertolucci had sensed in Lancaster "somebody a bit squashed by his look," his physical image. "As if it were difficult," he recalled, "to pull out of his looks more spirituality. This is what I was always seeing, some untold thing which nobody ever knew." The mystery was ideal for the portrayal of the big, powerful Alfredo, rooted in the soil, an enigma to himself, who has become, in every sense, impotent, whose era is over. His bare feet in the muck of his stables, the center of his ancestral power, he rages, as Bertolucci discussed with Lancaster, like a combination of King Lear and the old man of the Yeats poem that begins, "That is no country for old men. . . ." In one last desperate bid for life he exposes himself to a young peasant girl milking a cow only to have her tell him, "Ah, Signor Alfredo, nobody can milk a bull." Facing a new century in which he will have no meaningful part, the *padrone* hangs himself.

Lancaster agreed to work the few weeks in the late spring required for his small but essential role for no fee, only asking of a delighted and grateful Bertolucci a per diem and expenses. He wanted, very much, to work with the acclaimed director of *Last Tango in Paris,* the explosive X-rated hit of 1972. He was still chasing Brando, whose work in *Tango* had, together with *The Godfather,* resurrected a dead career. Also irresistible was the fact that for Bertolucci, *1900* was an epic about the movies, "the cinema," itself. The two grandfathers who begin and ground the film were deliberately cast with what Bertolucci called "mythological figures, two beautiful aging men of Hollywood"—Lancaster and Sterling Hayden as his peasant counterpart.

When he showed up for his first day on location at the reconstructed Villa Saviola east of Parma for a costume fitting, Lancaster came up quietly behind the director while he was shooting the sylvan picnic sequence in a popular grove that precedes the scene in the stable. He "appeared tiptoeing," recalled Bertolucci, "in order not to bother anybody, almost hiding behind bushes. It was a kind of magic moment—this beautiful light and people dancing a few yards away. He was enchanted. 'Let me watch,' he said to me, 'and enter into the atmosphere.' It was as if he had never been on a set before." Lancaster revealed to the director that so much work had been done on his face, his teeth, his body—some cosmetic, some the scars of injuries and operations—that "the most real thing on my face are my eyes."

Something was happening to him far away from Hollywood on the ancient ground of Italy—a forced confrontation with the ending of life, the beginning of the end of his own personal dream of himself. He was exhilarated to be working at such a pitch, on a politically engagé level for two great directors in a row; but it was also terrifying. Strange and shocking to viewers and critics in their seemingly perverted weaknesses, the professor and the landowner were parts that cut so deep and so close he did not emerge from them the same person. They carried him from the ominous headwaters of middle age down roaring falls to the broader, calmer stream of old age.

At the same time, he was savoring a particular kind of personal achievement. Bertolucci saw in Lancaster's Alfredo, his *gattopardo*, his professor, a kind of grand "social climbing": "Somebody who was born in a slum to become first a Sicilian prince and then a Parma landowner—there was a kind of comprehensible gratification for him in having reached this important position and meantime, taking it to an ending, a kind of metaphorical ending in both cases, of a period, of an era."

A calmer, happier Lancaster returned to the United States in 1975 after almost two years abroad to make a cameo appearance as myth-making dime novelist Ned Buntline in Robert Altman's American bicentennial extravaganza, *Buffalo Bill and the Indians, or Sitting Bull's History Lesson*. Fresh off his success with *Nashville*, Altman's movie was a eulogy of sorts to the overblown, distorted hoopla of William "Buffalo Bill" Cody's Wild West Show. Circus-like precursor to the hype and glamour of Hollywood's star system, Cody's show was the model, in some of Edison's earliest film sequences and in Griffith's first written scenario in 1912, *The Life of Buffalo Bill*, for the Western movie itself. Buntline had modeled his version of Buffalo Bill on the New World new man heroes of James Fenimore Cooper. In the movie, Paul Newman's Cody wrangles with the real-life Sitting Bull, trying to get him to depict Custer's disastrous fate at the Battle of Little Big Horn in a better light—one example of many, according to Joan Mellen, of how *Buffalo Bill and the Indians* unveiled "all the shabby legends and the distortions of our actual history which the American film has perpetuated to foster its unwholesome definitions of masculinity." Newman saw his part simply as the first movie star. In lieu of a feudal *padrone*, that would do as the repository of a new nation's dreams and myths.

Altman sought out Lancaster for Buntline because he wanted someone with the "stature" of a great star who was then "able to play that as a kind of bullshitter." Gantry, Massai, Earp, Scott, Merrill, and McIntosh—Lancaster drew on all of them to make the myth and the mythologizer perfectly, knowingly merge in his Buntline. "Burt Lancaster was a new category," Altman said. "He did *Rose Tattoo* when nobody else would cast him but himself. He was very courageous in that way. . . . He had a very definite persona, but took it to more different kinds of parts than, say, Jimmy Stewart. Gregory Peck and Robert Redford never step too far aside from who they seem to be. Burt bridges the gap between the two kinds of actor. He was very smart, you know," he added. "He understood totally the bullshit factor and what he was playing." Lancaster summed up not only Cody but perhaps himself when he described Buffalo Bill as having "that sycophantic entourage that lived off him and perpetuated his own concept of his legend as a great human being and a great man."

During his two weeks on location in August 1975 at the Stoney Indian Reserve in Alberta, Canada, he was, recalled Altman, "a delight, his own guy, a mensch." No wonder: the director readily took suggestions from his actors. "You know," Lancaster told Altman, "you get out in the West and these guys are always clean-shaven but you never see them shave"—so one scene opened with Lancaster shaving. He even got to use Gantry's censored line, "I'll see you in hell, brother," this time addressed to Newman. Altman's "antinarrator," Buntline settles in and takes a deep, sly delight in observing and undermining his phony creation in action: "It was the thrill of my life," he grins to Newman's Cody, "to have invented you."

It was the thrill of Lancaster's life to have invented himself. The movie's intelligent manipulation of American history and myth in the bicentennial year was one neat culmination of the actor's life, work, and politics. Watergate, Nixon, and the Vietnam War were newly over; McCarthy was in the not-so-distant past. What, exactly, was there to celebrate? Better to find the underlying mythic rhythms that betray and expose them to the light of day.

All three of Lancaster's ambitious, ideological mid-1970s feature films failed spectacularly at the U.S. box office. *Conversation Piece*, with stiff and platitudinous dubbed English dialogue, opened the thirteenth New York Film Festival in October 1975 and giggles turned into what *Variety* called "roars of laughter" and "derision" ending with "boos and catcalls the likes of which haven't been heard at a festival opening night in some time." By the next day, both the *New York Times* and the *New York Post* were calling the film a "disaster"; Kael in *The New Yorker* caught the implied but unfulfilled homosexuality of the story and speculated that an audience "might split its sides if Burt Lancaster"—an actor she admitted she didn't "know the first thing about"—"were to be shown coming out." Stopping to look back at the entire career to date, she admitted that while some of his movies had been "terrible," they were not "complacent choices," but those of "a restless, eager hard worker"; all the more baffling then why anyone would cast him as a "gentle intellectual." The opening night audience was, typically, not made up of enough film true believers like the festival's director, Richard Roud, who admitted that he and the rest of the selection committee were "almost in tears" when they first screened the movie.

Aware that *Conversation Piece* had been a big success in Paris, running twenty-seven weeks at three first-run Paris houses, and that *Le Monde* had found Lancaster *"bouleversant"* as the professor and that Italy awarded Lancaster the Donatello Davidas Award (best foreign actor) for his performance, New Line Cinema picked it up for distribution. Two years later the film was reissued with the original Italian speech and English titles "stripped in like haiku." But not until Visconti came back in favor in the late 1990s would the *New York Times* decide that what had seemed then like one more failure in the director's final slide into mediocrity was, in fact, "excellent . . . brittle, intelligent."

Lancaster was again featured at the New York Film Festival in 1977 in a truncated four-hour and ten-minute version of *1900*, "perhaps," reported the *Times*, "the most eagerly awaited festival debut since Mr. Bertolucci's *Last Tango* was unveiled here five years ago." The movie had run way over its original $6.8 million, three-hour and fifteen-minute U.S. parameter to become, at over $8 million and a running time of five hours and eleven minutes, possibly the most expensive Italian movie ever made. A huge international wrangle ensued between producer, director, and Paramount (the U.S. distributor), resulting in at least three different cut versions and lengths extant at one time. Studio head Barry Diller announced he didn't like any of them. The film was barely seen in the U.S. and, predictably, the reviews of the hacked-up cut acceptable to Paramount were negative. Critics resented what many saw as dressed-up propaganda. Even in Italy, where the first of the two-part director's cut did very well, nothing like the same number of viewers returned for the second half.

Lancaster had got to work with Bertolucci all right, but the director's spectacular setback obscured any appreciation of the actor's own radical departure. Most reviews froze at the shocked stage: Burt Lancaster exposing himself? When *1900* was rereleased in its full form in 1991, Sarris placed it as a (still "much too long") cinema marker between "the euphoric events of 1968 that promised a rejuvenation of Marxism-Leninism . . . and the populist-capitalist upheavals of 1989 that sounded the death knell of Marxism-Leninism as a massive historical force." It was too late, by that time, for Lancaster fully to appreciate that analysis. But, if he were ever to be identified with one epic piece of cinema, that was the kind of significance he would have relished.

Buffalo Bill and the Indians was similarly mired in a series of "disastrous screenings," subsequent interference by executive producer Dino De Laurentiis, and another sorry endgame of multiple cuts. Awaited by the director's avid followers as both a statement of the nation's progress to date and a look back to the beginning of its compulsion to ignore reality and trust the fabrication that had led to the watershed delusion of Vietnam, the movie was too self-consciously antimythic to have broad appeal. It cooked along on the back burner of the culture, a fugitive film rarely screened, not available on video. In 1982 the *Village Voice* would claim that in its depiction of the white man's protective manipulation of history "[n]o more concentrated view of 1970s social politics exists." The irony of casting Lancaster was lost in the movie's general failure.

An elegant coherence of theme in Lancaster's latest work was apparent if anybody had thought to put it together. If control of the intellect (the professor), the land (Alfredo), and celebrity (Buntline) was finally shifting out of the clutch of a small, homogenous, retentive group, this was the great change of history Lancaster had been bred to seek and follow. He was philosophical about the movies' failures; his work would be appreciated eventually. "It shouldn't matter at all whether we get it now," said Alan Rudolph, the screenwriter of *Buffalo Bill,* a few months after the movie's opening failure. "Because it's later that counts. It's Picasso later. And," he added, using a word that defines Lancaster's career, "it's also cumulative."

Lancaster's appearance in the late 1970s took on the style of his own patriarchal prophet wandering in the movie wilderness. He wore the same eccentric assemblage of clothes for several years running, only varying it for special occasions. Each time he appeared on his friend Dinah Shore's television talk show, the outfits were stranger: bright red ties or no ties, rumpled shirts, a necklace—the flamboyant garb of a free-spirit Big Daddy.

Rex Reed, writing for the *New York Daily News,* paid a visit to Lancaster's offices in 1977 and noted with amused wonder the current look. "The door opens," he wrote, "and, as if born on a charge of electric energy—in storms an enormous mass of hair, hide, thongs and fringe." Sneakers with bare feet, tatty terrycloth jogging pants, a big Mexican shawl covering "the huge leonine shoulders," a hat, "equally battered," clamped on top of a "tangle of silver hair," an unkempt beard. When Reed rejected a low-slung chair made out of what looked like leather and bones for something more on the eye level of his subject, he detected a "steely glint" of amused respect from the star. "Perversely and immediately," he concluded, "I know I like Burt Lancaster."

The blazing eyes and Chiclets teeth remained neon-like reminders of the buff beauty he had once been. Steaks on the grill and a very dry Martini made with Bombay gin and a twist of lemon peel had not moved off his list of the Great Pleasures of Life. He jogged five miles to the meeting with

Reed—or claimed he did—on a newly reconstructed knee, a very handsome, fit man in his mid-sixties. Walking down Fifth Avenue in New York City at 4 o'clock in the afternoon still thrilled him. He now projected a bemused geniality, actually chuckling to reporters when reminded of the good old days of *The Crimson Pirate*. He did not obsess about growing old as he had a few years before. The solid work of the strange decade had made him happy, if no one else. When he died, he said, speaking the movie-star unspeakable, he wanted to be able to look a mirror in the face. Clearly he was a man starting to be at peace with himself for the first time since his arrival in Hollywood thirty years before. But only starting. When *Photoplay* asked him in 1975 if he was "fulfilled," the buzz word of the era, he snapped back, "Whether you like it or not, when you're sixty-two you're fulfilled."

The apartment in Rome became a true home base during these years. He had it redecorated to a look *Architectural Digest* would call "calm consistency" by Jim Vance, an artistic director for Altman and Aldrich, and filled it with Turkish rugs, glazed Italian silk pillows, and paintings by Lorenzo Tornabuoni, who had been recommended to him by Guttoso. He entertained frequently, cooking dinners of pasta for six or eight himself, and grew his own herbs in pots with flowers planted in between, just as the Italians did.

The arrangement with Bone was no longer the passionate, fractious union it had once been. The "no questions, no recriminations" rapport had never really worked and could not endure into something more binding. There had been frequent, long separations and friends noted her tendency with time to criticize his children, something he could not tolerate. When she rediscovered her childhood Christianity, he could not share that with her. In 1977, he bought her a house in Malibu, confirming the split. She would still accompany him to social functions and, infrequently, on location.

He had already bought for himself two west-corner condominium units on the eighteenth floor of the Century City apartment towers. His new and last home appropriately overlooked the "New York Street set" on the Fox lot in one direction and the Hillcrest Country Club in the other. Now he could walk across the street to play golf and endlessly practice his swing. Century City had all the amenities—pool, spa, tennis courts, doorman, four parking spaces—he was more than ready to enjoy. With architect Levitt he threw himself into the conversion of the 8,000-square-foot space into one big Leopard-like perch from which he could survey Los Angeles in a big sweep from the Pacific Ocean to the San Gabriel mountains. Spanish-style stucco, exposed beams, arches and columns, red tile floor, and a massive wooden entry door imported from Morocco set a tone of rough-hewn theatricality. The door's frame in turn framed the headboard of his huge bed, which dominated the 800-square-foot bedroom. A living-room display space of white stucco niches was custom-crafted for African sculptures, a bound set of his scripts, books on music and by Hemingway; in one central spot stood his Oscar. On the walls of the den were African spears and groups of pre-Columbian terra-cotta figures and in the living room some of his original art collection hung together with later acquisitions by Braque, Toulouse-Lautrec, and Miró. A magnificently framed fake Gauguin, a prop from the first scene of *The Train* in the Jeu de Paume, was hung near the bridge table behind a couple of hanging plants, positioned to take advantage of the bright Southern California light.

Red, orange, saffron, brown, glints of brass and gold—the range of color had an operatic richness typical of the man. Most surfaces were soft: cream-white walls, Turkish and Moroccan rugs underfoot, pillows made from more rugs, silk-covered sofas, a Kaleme rug so thick and bushy it looked like white water. The end effect was quiet, mostly restful, vaguely Moorish, somewhat overblown, primitive, and warm. He had returned to some sense of the urban compactness with which he had begun life on 106th Street. Houses had never been his natural habitat.

The new place became a refuge for various dependents. When Nick was divorced from Ceil, his second wife, in 1976, he was so distraught and thin that Lancaster let him come live with him for a while. Nick was still brought on location to exercise his friend's knee, which had become more painful with age and mild arthritis, and he often house-sat the apartment and Lancaster's two cats. "Dear Nicodemus," read one instructional note, "I know you know everything about cats but here are a few bits of information which may have escaped you during life." He then described a lavish, loving regimen that indicates where some of his affection was directed at this stage of his life: twice weekly parsley and cod liver oil; liver, chopped fine, once a week; "Fish is OK only if *all* small bones have been carefully removed." The apartment windows could not be opened more than a crack; otherwise the cats could squeeze through and fall to the ground far below.

After grilling Marcy and Tina Cravat about their course plans and budgets, he picked up the bill for their college educations. With the older Marcy especially, he developed the idealized relationship of niece to beloved, benevolent uncle: "He told me that life would bring many challenges," she recalled, "that there would be many lives to live." When she found herself pregnant and unmarried in her early twenties, he took her through the dimensions—practical and emotional—of the situation one by one. Though she later had a miscarriage and happily married someone else, she treasured his open, accepting attitude: "He made me feel free," she said.

The five Lancaster progeny were given much more generous amounts of money, but not always with the same scrutiny paid. Lancaster was often—and publicly—impatient with what looked to him like their suspiciously relaxed attitudes to what he considered work. "Why don't you *do* something? *Steal!*" he'd say, exasperated with one child's chronic student status or another's seeming lack of direction and paycheck. "If you're going to be a bum, be a good bum." At one point he said he had five children and "none of them ever worked. Not sure they're working now." Joanna, briefly married, appeared to conform most to his ideal by eventually working in the movie business, in various production jobs (listed as executive producer of *Ruthless People*, Joanna, said her father, "didn't produce the picture. She produced the script."). With a version of the dazzling good looks of her father, Sighle worked as a model before getting a degree in social work. Susan inherited the social conscience of her parents and spent many volunteer hours at the ACLU. As the years went by, Jim Hill recalled, Lancaster became fixated on building their financial security, doing mediocre movies for just one more fix of cash. When he was gone, his people would at least have money.

Bill Lancaster sold a screenplay—*The Bad News Bears*—to Paramount in 1975, the same year he appeared in *Moses*. A transposition of his own childhood experience as the handicapped kid on a baseball team coached by his father, "*Bad News Bears* was the story of Billy's growing up," said Joel Douglas. "He was Tatum O'Neal, the oddball on the team looking for the break." Presumably Lancaster was some part of Walter Matthau's grumpy old coach. The classic story was so "terrific," critic Joel Siegel has said, that Hollywood has kept on making it in one form or another.

But Bill's bright success quickly faded as much, suggested Douglas, because "Billy never really got the recognition from his dad—and that's what we all do it for." He wrote another screenplay for what some would consider one of the most truly horrifying horror movies of Hollywood—John Carpenter's 1982 remake of *The Thing*—and then withdrew from the fray, an intelligent, black-humor funnyman with, hauntingly, the upper body of his father. Writer Alison Rose lived with Bill in the early seventies and, like most of his friends, called him Billy the Fish. He drank too much, like his mother, and "sometimes," Rose would recall in *The New Yorker*, "blacked out." When they went up to Bel Air to see his father, still living in the Linda Flora house just after the divorce, she listened to the "lilting, authoritative Burt Lancaster cadence" telling her to will herself out of a depression and thought she "wanted to marry *him*." When Joel Douglas would ask him in later years what he was up to, Bill would chortle and say, "I'm NIB—Not In the Business." Jimmy was diagnosed in his early twenties as schizophrenic and, despite the lack of motivation that can be a characteristic of the condition, got a master's degree in music education from the Manhattan School of Music in 1975.

The imperious need to impose himself on dependent creatures, like his cats, took the form with his children of long, boisterous discussions into the night about endless plans and projects, most of which never came to pass. That he could not accept and openly praise them enough for their accomplishments was an old problem rooted in his own typically huge movie-star impatience and child-alienating ego. One friend watched the dynamic, so much like his mother's—"one day he's ready to kill them and the next day he'd be so protective of them"—and decided "part of it was the Irish thing but part of it was that he felt responsible because when they were younger, he was away so much." What had been admiration and fear of him when they were children often turned later to varying degrees of indifference or anger; his money became the mode of communication, the link, and he was saddened at his inability—or theirs—to find another common family thread. One of his closest friends called the Lancaster children "no-goodniks, and Burt knew it"; others give them credit for surviving their childhood—"At ground zero when the bomb went off," said Sharp. Worrying and fussing—"I have a daughter," he said in the late 1970s, "who's living with a guy. That's fine with me. It really is. I am concerned only about whether or not she is living with the *right* guy"—he was happy to see them if they wanted to see him. But that was not the same thing as creating occasions only for them. A shared sense of humor, the sharp wit of survivors, seemed to close observers to indicate some kind of family rapport. Especially with Joanna, who was "plenty, plenty smart," says Sharp, there was "a substantial degree of mutual regard," and she became much closer to her father as an adult than she had ever been as a child.

In one breath he pondered the nature of man, which as a natural democrat he believed sought the good, and then his mind would circle around the idea that maturity might be the ability, after learning to love himself "a little," to love others. If he obsessed a little less about ultimate truths, he could make his own truths and, maybe, be happy. Then, he decided with the old deadpan edge, "I'd be a more giving human being. I would really love my enemy." The warrior in him was ready to put down the sword: "Somewhere," he said, "it has to stop."

There was another archetype to bring to a conclusion before the decade came to a close, but first he crammed three mainstream movie projects into the bicentennial year, all of which opened in 1977: *The Cassandra Crossing* (a star-studded formula disaster movie Frank Rich called "a little gem" of "quintessential trash . . . almost too bad to be true"), *Twilight's Last Gleaming*, and *The Island of Dr. Moreau*. Only the second, directed by Aldrich, fell into his mature pattern of complex, passionate experiments; "I have turned down a lot of garbage lately," he told reporters. He was balancing the risks with commercial sure things that paid him up front and at something close to his peak rate of $750,000. *Variety* noted that "the sun never seems to set on Burt Lancaster."

For *Twilight's Last Gleaming*, the film both director and star hoped would be a "totally honest political film" in that barely post-Vietnam, Jimmy Carter–election year, Lancaster spent March and April 1976 in Munich. (In mid-March he went briefly to Rome for Visconti's funeral and stood beside the coffin looking, still, noted several observers, like their *gattopardo* come to life.) In its frenzied, masterful use of multiple screens for parallel narratives the movie was meant to *be* on-screen the chaotic mess America had become, a "sort of *All the President's Men, Part Two*," said Lancaster. A former air force general played by Lancaster, Lawrence Dell—whom Aldrich called a political "idealistic innocent"—takes over an ICBM launch site in Montana and, finger on the trigger, tries to force the U.S. government to reveal its deception regarding the real reasons for the country's engagement in Vietnam (a foreign war with deliberately high U.S. casualties will "prove" to the Soviets that America can stand up to its enemies). In his apocalyptic attempt to save his country's soul Dell dies and so does the president (Charles Durning), whom his government would rather assassinate than let be the bearer of the truth.

Lancaster and Aldrich reveled in the multiple emotional pairings in the plot characteristic of Aldrich since *Vera Cruz*. Post-Bertolucci, Lancaster chafed under Aldrich's precisely planned scenes, which he thought encouraged a "lack of creative acting." But overall he trusted the director to find his most essential self on camera and use it well. "You are one of the few actors," Aldrich told him, "who when you speak, people believe you say the truth. You're not necessarily the best actor." Lancaster—laughing, bearded, dressed in an outfit in which everything except his shoes was blue—told that story to the National Press Club when the movie premiered in Washington in February 1977. In response to being asked if he wasn't being typecast these days in "government take-over roles," he laughed again and said, "I just choose what's left." The so-called anti-American stance of his recent roles, a pattern since *Seven Days in May* of being the handy icon of liberal Hollywood, had made Lancaster able, wrote Sarris, to use his "Scotch-Irish WASP American Ruling-Class" façade to beat the bad guys at their own game.

Twilight's Last Gleaming came too late to have the shock impact Aldrich wanted on a "ghettos . . . and Sun Belt drive-ins" audience sated with such revelations; American forces were out of Vietnam well before the movie was released. It was a ridiculed flop in the U.S., surviving in various bastardized versions floating around the world, some of them thought to be "brilliant," but was at least given credit by Rich and other critics when it opened for being "the first American pulp movie ever to take a strong stand against the Vietnam War." Only later would the ambition and anguish that inspired the movie find a coterie of admirers. It was Lancaster's final project with Aldrich. Behind the bluster and calculated hardness of both men was a patriotism of which *Twilight's Last Gleaming* in all its frenzied rage was the expression.

As Aldrich wrestled with postproduction editing and distribution problems on *Twilight* at the end of the year, Lancaster flew to St. Croix in the U.S. Virgin Islands and remained there from December to February to play the genetic experimenter, Moreau, in *The Island of Dr. Moreau*. A remake of *Island of Lost Souls,* which had starred Charles Laughton as the doctor, and which Lancaster had undoubtedly seen on its release in 1932, *Moreau* was his last movie with Nick and a final variation on the god and monster theme that had first brought them together in a street-corner discussion of *Franken-stein*. French audiences gave the creepily *grand Guignol* movie what *Variety* called a "torrid box office reception," but American reaction was cooler when it opened in July 1977. Conscious of the limits of his own exploitation—he nixed an opening scene that featured chewed-off human limbs—Lancaster would not venture to such extremes again.

Now he buried Sergeant Warden, grown old and wise. If most of his recent movies had taken him out of the country in quest of lucrative foreign-financed projects in which his stardom was still worth something, this next project was the antithesis of all that. Considered by many to be the best Vietnam movie nobody ever saw, *Go Tell the Spartans* was shot in thirty-one days from October to November 1977 with a constantly shrinking budget of $1.5 million on one square mile of Valencia hillside brush off Interstate 5 in Los Angeles. Keeping the Magic Mountain theme park roller coaster out of the camera frame was an important concern.

In a Hollywood filled with what Dawn Steel called "Baby Moguls," revitalized by a Paramount headed by Michael Eisner and Barry Diller, awaiting both the next "high-concept picture" that could be pitched in one sentence and the release of Coppola's Vietnam epic *Apocalypse Now,* Lancaster returned to the beginnings of his craft. The script was by Wendell Mayes from the Daniel Ford novel *Incident at Muc Wa*. It had kicked around since 1972 when no money could be raised on a pre-*Network* William Holden to star in what was then seen as a too-painfully topical movie budgeted at $7 million. Five years later, Ted Post, director of Eastwood's *Hang 'em High* and *Magnum Force* and Lancaster's old acquaintance from special service days, got Avco Embassy Pictures to agree to piggyback the project onto another cheapie movie as a B picture duo.

Set in 1964 Vietnam when American soldiers were as yet only advisors, the story is an interweaving of Greek and French models of total but heroic defeat with intimations of the modern horror to come. Under orders from Major Asa Barker, the Holden role that went to Lancaster, a group of American and South Vietnamese soldiers sets out into the jungle to reoccupy the former French outpost of Muc Wa. By a tragic sequence of misunderstandings, mistakes, and delusions, the group is trapped and killed by the Vietcong. Craig Wasson's Corporal Courcey, whose faith that he could win the hearts and minds of a Cong family betrayed them all, is the only survivor. At the end of the movie, he is standing in an old cemetery adjacent to Muc Wa in which are buried 302 French soldiers, killed twenty years earlier. They are memorialized with an inscription, in French, of the Simonides couplet that refers to the three hundred Spartans under the command of Leonidas who were betrayed, isolated, trapped, vastly outnumbered, and, after heroic resistance, killed by the Persians in the narrow pass of Thermopylae in the summer of 480 B.C.: "Go tell the Spartans, thou that passeth by,/That here, obedient to their laws, we lie." The last line of the movie is Courcey's. "I'm goin' home, Charlie," he says to a lone, wizened sniper as the date "1964" appears on the last frame. It will be eleven more years before anybody goes home.

In a different way and in a different war, Courcey is another fuck-up like Robert E. Lee Prewitt and no less loved by Barker for that. The McIntosh of *Ulzana's Raid* inhabits Lancaster's major, the utterly realistic colonial who understands and respects the "alien" native. "This is a sucker's tour," Barker says, "going nowhere, just around and around in circles," as McIntosh literally went in circles tracking down the wily Indian chief. A rescue helicopter arrives ready to take the Americans out of Muc Wa and back to safety, the scene suggesting the final abandonment of Saigon in 1975 when choppers whirred the last Americans up and out to safety and left panic-stricken Vietnamese straining at the locked embassy gates. Barker decides to stay with the stubborn Courcey who will not leave their South Vietnamese cofighters stranded in the jungle. Barker is a battle officer, not supposed to go out on patrol. His choice to lead them all out is the action of a Sergeant Warden whose first loyalty is to his community of men. It is also the ancient choice of a Spartan whose model was Achilles, the great hero who stayed with his men to fight at Troy knowing he would surely die.

Post sent the script to Lancaster who was recuperating from a knee operation at the La Costa resort (the temporary limp, as in *The Train*, would be incorporated into his character) and got a phone call from him two days later: "This is a fucking brilliant script. Don't let anybody touch it. I'm coming up and I'm going to do it with you." It was the best American part he had been offered in years. He lined up Nick to be on location to exercise his knee, and agreed to work for much less than his usual salary. In a motel near Magic Mountain, Lancaster appeared at the sliding glass doors of Post's room each morning at dawn. "Teddy, Teddy! Are you awake?" he asked in a loud whisper through a crack in the curtains. "I think I'm awake, now," Post would say to his wife as he got up to join Lancaster at poolside to discuss the coming day's work. "I'm so happy," Lancaster told him. "I don't have to change a word of this script!" The tight, claustrophobic story and the extremely constricted terrain terrified several cast and crew members and one Vietnam vet crew member fled the set. "He couldn't take it," recalled Post. A crew member from Coppola's *Apocalypse Now* visited the shoot one day and told Post, half kidding, "If Francis had seen this, he'd never have gone to the Philippines."

For the last scene, when Courcey finds Barker face down, nude, and dead in the mud, Lancaster arrived clad only in a bathrobe, relaxed. "I thought I was going to have to convince him, let him wear shorts," said Post. "But, no. Burt came on so normal, so natural. There was not a touch of shyness, of modesty. He said, 'Where do you want me?' " He played his Barker quiet and straight: when the major has to send out an emergency transmission requesting air cover, he flicks the Morse Code manual off the desk with a quick sweep of his hand—Barker knows the code. Off-screen, he was happy and mellow. "I'm finished, you know," he would say to the cast and crew, playing up the fading patriarch. "But if the director is ever bothering you, call me!"

Post had observed him over the years since the Second World War and through his wife, a cousin of the actor's advisor, Jack Ostrow, was privy to Lancaster's more private problems. He now saw a "mature, reasonable" man who had ripened after a sequence of hurdles few knew much about. "He had so many problems," recalled Post. "I don't know how the hell he came out of that and didn't die sooner. It would have broken the back of an ordinary guy, destroyed him, decimated him. But with Burt, for some reason, he was able to overcome conflicts—outer and inner—with himself. His life was difficult enough to live and his professional life was not easy. He tried to keep the two of them from colliding because then one would derail. . . . I loved him."

With five days left to shoot in a production that had already been reduced from forty to thirty-one days, Post was suddenly told there was no more money and that the picture would have to be ditched. The producer, Post claimed, used the money to pay off creditors and pocketed the rest. Lancaster told Post to find out how much was needed and when the director came back with a figure of $150,000 Lancaster covered it, as he had helped finance *The Swimmer* ten years before. By the time the picture was released in fall 1978, Avco was up for sale and barely distributed the movie. It only grossed $3 million, sharing the same dismal fate as other Vietnam-related product of the era such as *The Boys in Company C, Coming Home, Heroes,* and *Who'll Stop the Rain.*

But the reviews were extraordinary. "Lancaster's presence," reported *Time,* "carrying with it the memory of other wars (and a different sort of war movie) provides a kind of bench mark against which to measure the distance we have traveled from our former attitudes about the military necessity." Lancaster's hermetic professor in *Conversation Piece* and his Major Barker, the brusque man of action, were yoked together by Kevin Thomas in the *Los Angeles Times* as "both . . . very much of the same world so shrewdly appraised by Burt Lancaster."

Bury the archetypes with honors, but bury them all the same. When Courcey sees Barker's dead body lying in the mud, the audience sitting in the dark, watching, saw the death of an idea of itself, "an era of screen heroism," wrote Michael Sragow in the *Los Angeles Herald Examiner,* ". . . defiled." *Go Tell the Spartans* was a true sequel to *Ulzana's Raid.* The tragic reality in the field of what Pentagon hubris and deception would inflict from far-off Washington, it was the inverse of Achilles. A people abandoned by their leaders to die. For a man who had a vision of America as a community of codependent equals, it was all the more unforgivable if the leaders of such a difficult experiment abused their privilege. That Lancaster chose to channel his anger into disciplined dramas that work out in the classic purity of inevitable action a long American tragedy was a remarkable mastery of himself and the movies.

He was proud of what he called "a good little movie" that "told you in a microcosmic nutshell about Vietnam." The fact that Avco had, as he put it, "left it for dead," was "just part of the business." When *Platoon* came out in 1986, it was recalled that there was "this other Vietnam war movie" that had covered much the same ground and better. A year later, Bert Cardullo wrote in *The Hudson Review,* "*Platoon* is the body to the mind of *Go Tell the Spartans.*"

Lancaster now was more and more tempted to do something completely different—like opera. Pianist Joseph Seiger, Jimmy's teacher at the Manhattan School of Music, had found Lancaster's knowledge of opera "just unbelievable" during their several discussions about Jimmy's progress, conducted over dinner at the Plaza Hotel. After charging backstage at the Dorothy Chandler Pavilion in Los Angeles one night in the early 1960s demanding to meet the director of a New York Metropolitan Opera performance of Massenet's *Manon,* he developed a friendship with Tito Capobianco, a delightfully receptive Argentine opera director. In 1978 Capobianco, who had recently become the director of the San Diego Opera, asked Lancaster to codirect a new production of *Hamlet* with the idea that the star could then solo-direct one of his favorite operas, *I Pagliacci.*

For four weeks he sat next to the director with something of his 1946 neophyte's enthusiasm, "absorbing everything," recalled Capobianco, talking to the crew, studying the movements. He had long wondered how to match the often ponderous bodies of the singers to the expressive line of the music. Indeed, this had been his original, secret dream: to be the opera singer who expressed with his voice *and* his body the ecstasy of the music. But, in the end, even though other opera friends like Beverly Sills urged him on, he pulled back: "I don't know music or Italian well enough," he told Capobianco.

It was another disappointment, a lifelong dream discarded. But the experience of coming so close pulled in more of those disparate threads that had tangled his life. Capobianco saw him at his best, immersed in what he liked to think he would have done with his life if fate had not shoved him in a different direction. The director judged Lancaster a man who had been able to balance "the two extremes" of passion and temperance with the result that he carried into his old age an essential purity and "innocence" of vision. "The miracle of him," recalled Capobianco, "was that he *kept* something great—his intuition. In his enthusiasm, he was like one 'possessed by God.'" The whole man Capobianco saw explains much about Lancaster's rage, frustration, and disappointment at a fabulously successful life that yet fell short of the transcendent synthesis of music and movement he yearned for.

Recognized as an authentic, knowledgeable opera aficionado, longtime member of the board of the Los Angeles Opera, regular Thursday night subscriber to the Los Angeles Philharmonic, Lancaster was asked to MC the San Diego Opera's gala fiftieth birthday celebration for Beverly Sills in March 1979. His Century City apartment was a music-filled eyrie with Mozart's operas the constant background. "He always had that opera *shrieking,*" recalled Lucy Kibbee. Like a crescendo in the long dissonant symphony of his own making, music became the heightened pitch of his now more ordinary daily life.

While *Go Tell the Spartans* was not being released, Lancaster flew to South Africa to make *Zulu Dawn,* a big, two-hour "imperial war epic." His comfortable performance as Colonel Durnford, who is massacred with his troops by Zulu warriors at the 1879 battle of Isandhlwana, was the closest he ever got to portraying a Kiplingesque version of his supposed ancestor, Lord Roberts. Immediately after Sills's birthday party he flew to Durango to make *Cattle Annie and Little Britches,* a delicate Western that took three years to finance, sat on the shelf for two more years, and barely got released to considerable acclaim in 1981.

A de facto postscript to *Buffalo Bill and the Indians,* the movie was based on the true story of two young girls who set out in 1893 to satisfy their Buntline-inflamed dreams of Western outlaw heroes. Amanda Plummer in her screen debut as Annie and Diane Lane as her friend Jenny (Little Britches) come across Lancaster's outlaw Bill Doolin, a little old and sagging but still robbing trains and taking off with his gang for hideouts in the hills. Pursued by a vigilant marshal played by Rod Steiger, the gang rises to the fantasies of the girls and has one last renegade fling of bank robbing before Doolin is arrested, only to escape. Off-screen, the death of the frontier will soon put an end to all such outlaw freedom. The girls become fast-living women, in control of their own manifest destinies. Fond, comic, and elegiac, the production was directed by Lamont Johnson from a script by Robert Ward and David Eyre; critics would note that Larry Pizer's cinematography glowed like a Frederick Remington vision.

Lancaster struck up a friendship with Plummer. The rapport was of teacher and pupil—only this time, the student was a woman. As a self-described "babe in the business," spunky, passionate, and electrically intense, Plummer was struck, the first day on the set, with the older movie star's "stillness." She experienced a Lancaster deeply in tune with her and the payoff was a window on a great movie star in the full, present center of his cinema craft.

"He just brought me in with such gracefulness," she recalled. "There was a youthfulness on top of all that experience—and not a jot of bitterness or ego or anything. This man was unthreatenable by anybody. He understood so much of the business, all aspects of the creative side, that he was incapable of overacting. He got so involved in one scene he started crying and I was looking at his face and he said, 'I have to do that again.' And then he pulled it in a bit and it was spectacular. For him less was more—not as a rule, but thought through, like Giacometti. He was so wanting to teach. Not teach in a preachy way, like 'I've got the right way,' but he wanted to inform, like 'You know what I've discovered through my experience is that if you . . .' It was *technical.*"

If Lancaster was famous for being the supporting actor to Oscar winners, Plummer's insight indicates how that happened. "I know nothing," she recalled of her first day on the set. "He's got it down and effortlessly and he rises in his attention on the other actor, heightens the intelligence and also the spirit within the other characters. You felt this warmth and allowance coming from him. . . . It was a definite playing, like when you're a kid, a charmed existence." She also saw with the eyes of an actress trained to the physical rigors of the stage, the quality of his mobile style. It was, by nature, fluid and expressive to the eye before the brain had a chance to catch up.

She broke down his famous grace into separate frames, like a strip of film. In one scene, much of which was eventually cut into a collage, the Doolin gang play baseball with bats and balls they have stolen off the train and Plummer had to throw the first pitch. "I had to run to get the ball," she recalled, "and pick it up and face the camera and throw it. Burt demonstrated it and it looked at first as if it was done almost in slow motion. That's exploring time and space on film: you set up the beginning with a command of body movement from which you can go into different ripples and then at the end another body movement closes it enough to create a curiosity for the audience to say, 'What's next?' He did a Burt Lancaster thing for me. It was beautiful. He just went down for that ball and then his bum rises and then his back follows and it's turning in to go away from the camera and then surprises the camera with a forward movement towards it because you think he's going to go the other way. And then he throws it and it's just to keep the audience entranced. It was extraordinary. He understood time on film, movement and space on film. How to move and how to work in harmony with the camera so that it wasn't actor-y. He was a mover, he could do anything with his body—therefore he understood music! A lot of film actors are cut off from the head down and their bodies just repeat themselves. He made it so the camera can capture the slightest movement. He knew how to do that. This blows your mind because you work with him in front of the camera and then you see it on film and you go, 'Whoa! This is a master!' All his films—*Birdman*—have been impeccably blocked by him."

Lancaster saw the live audience out there, "always thinking of what secrets to use, involving them, making them present, involved, participators." He was, she said, using the same word Jack Berry had used three decades earlier, "very *generous*. You can be a Burt Lancaster fan or not, but as a worker, you cannot avoid the fact that this man was a master at his craft and loved it, truly loved it and gave it with love. He was a gentle, gentle soul. His work had a purity to it that was not highfalutin. Oh, how I loved him!"

Johnson shuffled *Cattle Annie* around Hollywood for a year before Universal picked it up for distribution in 1981. The movie's fate was an apt example of what had happened to Lancaster and his industry in three decades. In 1978, fed up with the new corporate entity that had been created by their merger in 1967 with Transamerica, Krim and Benjamin had resigned from UA to form Orion Pictures. Without them, filming started in 1979 on Michael Cimino's *Heaven's Gate*, the disastrously over-budget picture that would largely force the sale of UA to Kirk Kerkorian's MGM in 1981. "Independent production on a laissez-faire basis," former UA executive Steven Bach wrote in *Final Cut*, the chronicle of the *Heaven's Gate* folly— "that is, without authentic producers—was breaking down as a reliable method of production." Just how reliable the laissez-faire indie style had ever been was a question that harked back twenty years to the cautionary demise of Hecht-Hill-Lancaster.

Post–*Heaven's Gate*, no one knew quite what to do with a Western, let alone a wry, self-deprecating one like *Cattle Annie and Little Britches*. Marketing was now the big variable and if the "unmarketable" movie got released with no campaign, no art, no bookings, it may as well never have been made. What the *Village Voice* called its "careless release pattern" meant that virtually no one saw the movie except the critics. Canby in the *New York Times* led the way in May, admiring Lancaster's "laid-back, comic self-assurance that comes only after a lifetime on the screen." By June, Pauline Kael in *The New Yorker* pronounced that not only was Lancaster's Doolin "a charmer," with all the old "lithe movements and the rhythmic, courtly delivery" of his Crimson Pirate, he was beyond charm: "The great thing about Lancaster," she wrote, "is that you can see the face of a stubborn, difficult man—a man who is not easy to get along with. He has so much determination that charm doesn't diminish him. . . . And when he's by himself, naked, soaking at the hot springs (where the marshal traps him), he's a magnificent, sagging old buffalo." She heralded Plummer's performance as the most "excitingly, weirdly lyric" screen debut since Katharine Hepburn. But by the time the magazine hit the newsstands, the movie had left its one dinky Times Square theater.

In July, *Rolling Stone* devoted an entire article by Michael Sragow to the movie—"*Cattle Annie:* They Shoot Westerns, Don't They?"—calling it one of the few Westerns worth seeing since Altman's *McCabe and Mrs. Miller.* With Hollywood turning out pop culture dreck, here was a movie exploring that very phenomenon at its Buntline source and "fighting for a chance to be seen." When the movie dribbled through Los Angeles, Kevin Thomas at the *Los Angeles Times* linked the performances in *Go Tell the Spartans* and *Cattle Annie,* concluding that Lancaster "seems to have been liberated . . . once again."

On location at John Wayne's Durango ranch, the cast and crew of *Cattle Annie* had halted work for one minute to pay tribute to Wayne when he died in Los Angeles June 11, 1979. Lancaster had come out on the other side of the "imagined past" that Wayne, Garry Wills would suggest, represented to those who considered him "*the* American." Doolin, Lancaster's last grubby old Westerner, lives in the present. His incredulous reactions to Annie's adoring recounting of his supposed exploits—the imagined past—are the gap between American myth and reality.

CHAPTER ELEVEN

Comebacks

Youth, large, lusty, loving—youth full of grace, force, fascination,
Do you know that Old Age may come after you with equal grace,
force, fascination?

—Walt Whitman, "Youth, Day, Old Age and Night," *Leaves of Grass*

The body that Lancaster had driven hard for so long would begin to break down in the 1980s, just when he needed it for a last lap around the track. He didn't have much time left and he knew it. The zest he always had for the early morning air, the American hum of people at work, the taste, sound, smell, and feel of many pleasures, became even more keen. After taking a speed-reading course, he gobbled up a book a day and then collared a friend, his agent Ben Benjamin, or a golfing partner, with the old, aggressive challenge: "Read the latest Norman Mailer?" Daily crossword puzzles first thing in the morning let him suck in more words, more meanings.

Giant swings were a feat of the past. He walked the track at Beverly Hills High School these days. A regular bridge foursome—including George Burns and Solly Biano, Steve Trilling's assistant at Warner Bros. in 1940 when Lancaster had stormed out of the studio—met at his apartment. He was a more tolerant player, now; it was only a game, not *Gunfight at the O.K. Corral.* In the late afternoon he could often be found with a bucket of balls on the golf course of the Hillcrest Country Club still trying to master the one sport that resisted the force of his willpower. His lifelong immersion in opera distilled down over the decade into a quiet fascination with the intricacies of chamber music. Maybe it was age, but he found that the new voices didn't transport him as Ponselle, McCormack, or Caruso had once done. Beginning with Bach, he worked his way into Bartok.

He shed the eccentric garb of the 1970s. Now he looked like the comfortable, handsome man of substance: herringbone jacket, Nike running shoes, soft polo shirt, and tousled, graying hair—no more Mexican ponchos. The voice softened to a gravelly rumble, the diction still clear and of the streets. The scary blue Lancaster glare was now a knowing, sometimes intensely sad, regretful gaze that looped back to the confused pain of his wounded colossus of 1946. His children were true California creatures of their independent-thinking father, but there was so much, he knew, they had not received from him or anyone.

The seething anger still erupted once in a while, like lava flashes from an old, dormant volcano. Inevitably much of the work was with lesser directors on minor projects—a waste of what he now knew he could do. But it was work nonetheless, the celluloid craft he loved and respected. He joked that what had been aggression in his youth was now masked as the peppy enthusiasm of an old man. He did not like growing old but he accepted it. It helped that he could look back on a span of years fully, exuberantly lived.

In summer 1979 French director Louis Malle and New York playwright John Guare were running through the short list of aging white male Hollywood stars. They needed someone available between October and December to star in *Atlantic City*, which had to be made quickly with Canadian tax-shelter money before the end of the year. Guare had whipped together a story inspired by an old photograph of a 1929 gangsters' convention at the seaside resort in the far left corner of which was a smiling young man. "There's our hero!" he said, launching the odd tale of love, ambition, and rebirth amid the wrecking balls of the new Atlantic City. When he and Malle came to a photograph of Lancaster, they suddenly clicked: "*The Killers! Kiss the Blood Off My Hands!* How could we have been so stupid! Of *course* it's Lancaster!"

In the *noir* antihero of the late forties they found their mobster wannabe lead, Lou Pasco—the beautiful dumb Swede grown old and running numbers in Atlantic City, where Kitty Collins ditched him in 1946 and where an unexpected windfall of drug money gives him one last chance for gangster glory. With gambling newly legal in the state of New Jersey, casinos were rising almost daily on the ashes of the old honky-tonk world of the Steel Pier and Ventnor Avenue that Lancaster had known so well. He would now bury his first archetype, the young American returned from the war, grown old, still handsome, still a sucker. Only this time, in Guare's Runyonesque fairy tale, he finally gets to kill the bad guys, keep the money, and get, if not the best girl, the doll that once looked like Betty Grable.

When Malle and Guare showed him the script, he was immediately enthusiastic, receiving their preview of each potential on-screen humiliation—white hair, paunch, playing gofer for a bed-ridden old gangster moll played by Kate Reid—with what Guare recalled as "absolutely no vanity." Shooting began in Atlantic City at the end of October, continuing on for interiors in Montreal up through the very last day of the tax year on New Year's Eve. Malle, Guare, Lancaster, and his costar, Susan Sarandon, made an intricate movie ménage. The director and actress had been romantically involved since their work on Malle's *Pretty Baby*, with the result that initially Lancaster could not figure out who she was or why she was in the movie. Guare, writing and rewriting as the movie progressed, observed that Lancaster "behaved horribly" to Malle. Sarandon, cast as a woman who shucks oysters by day and takes croupier lessons at night, found herself the designated go-between, Malle's messenger and interpreter to Lancaster.

The star's dilemma was that to play the all-American Pasco to Malle's satisfaction, he had to shed what both Sarandon and Guare recalled as his instinct for the broad, "fifties" overplay. The risk revived the worst of his old antagonism toward directors: to play the loser Pasco *and* be abject to Malle would have been taking this whole thing too far. One observer thought there was a whiff of condescension from Malle toward Lancaster, a scent the actor would have picked up immediately. Although he was working with a European director, he had to play not a powerful leopard but an American character he felt he knew from his own real life and screen life better than anyone on the set. "There's a moment in the script," recalled Guare, "where Pasco yells out, 'I'm a lover, not a gangster!' and Burt was playing the part like Cyrano de Bergerac, to the balcony. Louis said, 'You have to trim it down. You can't do this.' And Burt said, in front of the crew, 'Who knows more, me or you?' and gave a performance that was over the top. Louis then said he wanted something else and Burt said, 'OK, we'll do it the way the little froggie wants it and then we'll do it the way it should be done.' He threw the performance away at Louis with contempt." The throwaway was what Malle really wanted and he continued on more than one take, unbeknownst to Lancaster, to run the camera after he'd called "Cut!" and before the next "Action!"

As the shoot galloped on Lancaster realized the director was right and began to loosen into Pasco. Yet when the time came to shoot the scene in which he reveals to Sarandon that he watches her from his window each evening as she washes herself with lemons and in the telling seduces her with the passion of his attention and the spell of his voice, Sarandon ran smack into the wall of the star's presence at its most monolithic.

"It was very, very difficult for him to understand, to embrace initially that she *gave* herself to him," she recalled. "He saw it as him pretty much taking her clothes off and taking her." Having noticed that his response to Malle's instructions in a given scene was often along the lines of, "Oh, you want me to do number twenty-two"—the old Delsartean menu of antic poses—she also saw that he was very like Pasco in his old-fashioned attitude to women: "He was most comfortable being the guy," she said, "protecting you, educating you, exposing you to different kinds of art or cultural experiences." He was also vain. When she told him that it had been her father, Captain Tomalin, who had interceded for him and Norma with the military police when they had stayed out beyond curfew in wartime Italy, Lancaster was less than thrilled with the coincidence. It only reinforced the fact that he was old enough to be her father.

Sarandon played beyond these limitations by appealing to the curiosity and willingness to expand she saw in the man whose craft she admired as that of a real movie star. "For him the whole thing was a big chance," she insisted. "He was quite game when things weren't figured out, which says something at his age. There isn't a huge range of guys who can do something like this. Either they don't look their age because they've had so many face lifts, or they're very bitter and alcoholic. To his credit, he did a 360—at least a 180!—a complete about-face." For the first time in his screen life—and, for all anybody knew, his real life—he had to let the woman come to him. Not for what Bone had called a notch in the belt, but to encompass another human being. His eyes on Sarandon, her breasts, her youth, are what Guare described as "heart-breaking." In *The Leopard* twenty years before, he had looked at the beautiful young Cardinale dancing away from him with the despairing anguish of life at its end; here his gaze is awestruck at this late chance for the sudden, unexpected joy of life yet to live. The comeback of his *noir* loser as a winner in the postwar game of life.

Pasco's new persona as the tough-guy ladykiller bursts like a boardwalk bubble. Mob thugs knock him to the ground where he lies, a helpless old fake, as they attack and search Sarandon for the missing drug money. When he tries to flee town on a bus, she pursues him to the station and drags him back. But when they are again cornered by the mobsters, Pasco shoots them both dead. Exultant at his first killings, Lancaster gauges his glee like a syncopated beat reverberating off *Brute Force, Vera Cruz, Gunfight at the O.K. Corral.* The odd couple go on the lam, ending up in a motel room south of Atlantic City watching the news of the shooting on TV.

Lying on the bed, the white-haired Pasco suddenly springs up to a standing position, the graceful movement a subliminal shutter click back to *The Crimson Pirate* and *Trapeze.* Peeking through a crack in the bathroom door, he sees Sarandon filch a wad of money out of his wallet so she can split for France and fulfill her dream of being a croupier. When they then go through a short, gentle back-and-forth of who's going out to get the pizza, who's taking off first for good, Lancaster leans against the doorjamb, hands in pockets, one knee bent. It is a striking pose because it is the first time he has stopped to lean against anything in a lifetime of moving with the movies. There is a classical beauty of form, the colossus grown old but the proportions intact and fine. It is the original quietude of his first fresh youth lying on the bed waiting for his killers. The acrobat's instinct for the clean move through space matured into the still confidence of the actor he set out to be.

The shoot wrapped on New Year's Eve with a pizza party in the Montreal hotel room of Guare and his wife, Adele Chatfield-Taylor. Lancaster stood up to give a grandiose toast to Kate Reid, rating her with Magnani and Hepburn as one of the greatest actresses he had ever worked with— only he called her "Kate Fields." The awkward moment was suddenly interrupted when smoke started pouring out of the kitchen. The pizza boxes were on fire in the oven. When the smoke cleared, Lancaster was, recalled Guare, "Poof! Gone!"

The old circus mountebank in him couldn't even remember his costar's name. He had begrudgingly thrown his work at Malle who had in turn forced out of him the chancer that had always lurked behind the megastar bravado. He had arrived at the dimension of the movies that his eager, ego-driven insecurity had often missed, what Sarandon called the "thing beyond what everybody thought, which can be something quite spectacular and unexpected."

Three weeks later, in January 1980, he checked in to Cedars-Sinai Medical Center in Los Angeles to have his gall bladder removed, the source of what was now revealed to the public as a series of attacks over the previous eighteen months. During the filming of *Cattle Annie* Lancaster, accompanied by Joanna, had been flown out by ambulance jet to Los Angeles from Durango, doubled over with pain after two severe attacks of what was initially diagnosed as hepatitis, supposedly contracted in South Africa. Dosed up with painkillers and dismissing the pain as "nothing," he went on to do *Atlantic City* that fall, his condition at age sixty-six undoubtedly a factor in his irritability toward Malle. "Burt always had something wrong, physically," Mickey Knox had observed over the years. "He was internally fragile."

What was supposed to be a five-hour operation turned into a frantic eleven-hour crisis. A team of top doctors, led by Lancaster's friend and ACLU colleague of twenty-five years, Irving Lichtenstein, frantically worked to repair, after the removal of the gall bladder, a malfunctioning and unusually narrow channel from the gall bladder to the intestines. Lancaster later told Knox that a surgeon had cut into a valve by mistake; at least one doctor reportedly got on his knees in the operating room to pray for the actor's life. Bill and Joanna were called to join Bone at the hospital. By 11 p.m. he was stabilized but his life hung in the balance for the next forty-eight hours. On the third day, he was removed from intensive care and only at the end of the week did the hospital feel confident enough to announce that the operation had been a success. The press reported, accurately, that Lancaster had almost died.

Recuperating at home in bed, he had to get up and fly to Florida two weeks after surgery and bring Jimmy home to Century City. His eldest child, now thirty-four, had had difficulties finding a job as a music teacher and reportedly sunk into an emotional breakdown. "Burt was Mom and Pop," recalled Bone. "He sorted it all out with such patience. I'd never seen anything like it." Lancaster got what one family member called "a second chance" with his son. With the help of medication, Jimmy settled into a regular life and married an older woman, Joan Bauser, in 1984; when she died of leukemia in 1993, he would marry Annie Cravat, whose father Lew, Nick's brother, had often been deputized to watch out for Jimmy during difficult times in the past. Of all the children, friends suggested, he seemed in the end to bear the least grudge for all that had gone on before.

A chance to play his vainglorious World War II commander General Mark Clark as well as an eagerness to build on his post–*Atlantic City* sense of new possibilities pushed him by the summer into his next project, considered by many to be his most ignominious, Italian director Liliana Cavani's *La Pelle* (*The Skin*). He returned to Italy in late August 1980 for an eight-week shooting schedule at Cinecittà and in Naples of this Curzio Malaparte tale of 1943 postliberation Naples. Cavani brought the same focus on depravity, violence, and World War II that she had brought to *The Night Porter* in 1974, inflating it to an apocalyptic scale in a bitter story of the vanquished city seducing conquering Yanks in order to survive. Played by Marcello Mastroianni in the film, Malaparte was a Fascist, a communist sympathizer, and a convert to Catholicism just before his death in 1957. He inhabited the "no-man's-land" of ambiguity and controversy that attracted Cavani to satisfy what one Italian journalist called her "hunger for high stakes and difficult projects." Unlike Visconti, whom she knew and admired, and Bertolucci, the director did not look to the past as the ideological seedbed of the present. It was rather a useful canvas, a cinematic pretext.

Disembowelings of soldiers and dogs, GIs lined up to finger-penetrate a virgin, homosexual orgies, crucified prisoners, an enormous phallus "born" of a man—the film was made to be what the director considered a "corrective" to the sentimental "spaghetti and mandolins" image of Italians. Lancaster did not have much to do as the movie's General Mark Cork except be Burt Lancaster in charge, a parody, wrote one reviewer, of himself. But that alone marked a deft convergence of his American and Italian personae, his real and screen stories in a film one of whose themes was what the producer, Renzo Rossellini, called "the plague" of American cultural domination. Lancaster had been in Naples in 1943 and knew, like Malaparte, that it had not all been the brave idealism of *Open City*.

The movie remains the least-seen of all his work. If Malaparte had exaggerated historic reality, Cavani was accused of flagrantly hyping Malaparte. After a showing at the Cannes festival, the movie was barely released in the U.S. in June 1981, dying a quick death after a series of horrified reviews. An "ineptly vicious, fraudulently anti-American film," wrote Jack Kroll in *Newsweek,* calling Cavani "the phoniest filmmaker in the world."

Luckily, *La Pelle* was eclipsed by the ecstatic reviews for *Atlantic City*, released two months earlier. "I don't believe this is the guy I picked up with *Apache*," said Youngstein. Mickey Knox recognized a "great progression of craft," his old friend having "shed all of those gestures and mannerisms he had as a young actor." J.P. Miller picked up the phone: "Old buddy, you did it." Younger viewers and filmmakers rediscovered him. "He really let go of his masculinity," John Turturro recalled, "and softened. He used who he was in a much more sensitive way and really grew as an actor, so it was interesting all over again." To friends like Miller, Lancaster replied, "I know. I did it. They can't take that away from me."

Kael looked back to his 1946 *"hunkus Americanus"* and gave admiring credit for many changes since. "Lancaster uses his big, strong body so expressively," she wrote, "that if this were a stage performance the audience would probably give him a standing ovation. I don't see how he could be any better." Tracing the evolution that had mystified her in the past she acknowledged that "[p]robably no other major star took so many chances." And *Newsweek*'s David Ansen, in a review that captured the particular happy shock to the audience, who greeted an almost forgotten movie memory come back to life, wrote, "the movie's sweet elegiac heart belongs to Lancaster. Lou may be the role of his lifetime, and he carries it gently, obviously cherishing the gift."

Canby pulled out all the stops, stating that "the Lancaster career, more than that of any other actor I can think of, demonstrates the growth of a talent as well as of the intelligence that commands the talent." Admitting "we were all too close to *The Crimson Pirate* to acknowledge the changes that were taking place," the *New York Times* critic revised his original opinion of *The Swimmer* and decided that *Conversation Piece* was a "formidably intelligent piece of work." "If it was initially difficult for us to take him as seriously as he wanted to be taken," he continued, "it was probably because he was obviously trying so hard [and] also because he began making films of so-called social significance, or what he thought to be social significance, films that have never quite regained the vogue they had in the 30's." By the end, Canby wondered whether the coherence of Lancaster's career, what the critic even now assumed was "coincidence"—his playing Buntline and then a Buntline hero, for example—was in fact a sign "that order is demonstrated by Mr. Lancaster's remarkable—though not often remarked about—career."

The New York Film Critics Circle, for the third time, named him Best Actor. In Manhattan with his daughters for the ceremony at Sardi's on January 31, 1982, he was, *New York Post* film critic Stephen Silverman reported, "on the verge of tears." Pointing to his family, he said, "I'm very proud of this award and I'm very proud that my family is here with me tonight." Eventually he would rack up a string of prizes including Best Actor awards from the National Society of Film Critics, the Los Angeles Film Critics, and the British Film Academy. For the last, he turned up at the ceremony in London on March 18 to accept in person. He was savoring every sweet minute.

He was nominated for his fourth Best Actor Oscar in 1982 (Malle, Sarandon, and Guare also earned nominations) and lost to Henry Fonda in *On Golden Pond*. It was generally agreed that without Jane Fonda's vigorous campaign to ensure that her father finally got his first Academy Award, the Oscar would have been his. He showed up for that ceremony too, with granddaughter Keigh: "It might set Norma off if she sees me on television with someone else," he told Bernie Kamber over the phone before the event. If the movie harked back to 1946, so did Norma.

To those who had known, watched, loved, and put up with him for a long time, the movie marked, as Roddy McDowall described it, his "matriculation" from one kind of person to another. Asked how common such an evolution is in Hollywood, the former child star with long memories of the industry and its heroes countered: "How common is it in life for someone to discard what has defined him and change?" Lou Pasco was Burton Stephen Lancaster as he might have ended up if he had never stepped into that elevator in the Royalton Hotel.

Buoyed by his career renaissance, he flew to Scotland in May for what would be one of the most pleasant movie shoots of his career, *Local Hero*. A fey little tale of a Houston oil company's attempt to buy a piece of Scottish beach for a refinery, it was a pet project of producer David Puttnam, whose *Chariots of Fire* had beat out *Atlantic City* for the Best Picture Oscar. A young executive hustler, MacIntyre (Peter Riegert), is dispatched to Scotland to clinch the deal only to succumb to the spell of the little village which is all too eager to make its fortune from the rich Americans. The concept had some rich antecedents: *Brigadoon,* Michael Powell's and Emeric Pressburger's *I Know Where I'm Going,* and Mackendrick's *Whiskey Galore!* (in the U.S., *Tight Little Island*) are all stories of best-laid plans gone askew in the Scottish mists.

Eccentric, star-gazing billionaire Felix Happer, head of Knox Oil and Gas, was created by writer/director Bill Forsyth to function as a literal deus ex machina coming out of the sky in a helicopter to preserve the seaside village as a marine laboratory. He kept hearing the distinctive voice of the star he called his "hero of screen days" and crafted the dialogue "in Lancaster's cadence." To his amazement, his hero loved the script and agreed to the project even though his fee would of necessity be lower than usual because of the production budget of $4.5 million.

After the Knox Oil headquarters scenes had been shot in Houston, Lancaster and Bone joined the production in northeast Scotland, checking into Inverlochy Castle near where the cast and crew were based in the village of Pennan. His scenes were shot first so that he could go on to play golf with friends at the famous courses of Gleneagles, Turnberry, and St. Andrews. The couple had recently lost a son and a granddaughter and Lancaster arranged the golf junket to help them get over their grief.

Not since *Vera Cruz* had Lancaster been given such a chance to be funny on-screen and he took to it with the same precision he had brought to *Atlantic City.* Peter Capaldi, a Glasgow native who played the awkward local Knox representative, recalled that he "was constantly looking for a comedic angle, for delightful funny little things." Like Happer, Lancaster could be supremely detached from anything and anyone but his own sometimes harebrained schemes. And always there was the suspicion that he might be a little crazy. Playing off Capaldi's equally daft character, he formed another of those brief professional liaisons that left a lasting mark on a brand-new talent.

Twenty-three at the time, and in his first movie, Capaldi remembered the star mainly, like Branagh, from *Birdman of Alcatraz.* "No one really believed that this Hollywood star was going to appear in our midst," he said. "And when he did, he exuded such charm and openness that people just fell all over themselves to be around him." He was still the old Lancaster, however. He told Capaldi, who speaks in the film—and less so off-screen—in a distinct Glasgow accent: "I gotta tell you kid, you've fabulous instinct. But I can't understand a fucking word you say." He ribbed Forsyth as the director who spoke "no known language."

He fell right into his teacher mode. The deadpan star of *Animal House,* Riegert was encouraged by the star to speak up for himself when he was made to balance on an unsteady plank during one take: "You comfortable on that thing?" Lancaster asked. "Then don't agree. That's their problem, not yours. . . ." One night Capaldi was in a trailer with a group from the film, all laughing uproariously at "Burt stories," when suddenly Lancaster's face appeared at a window grinning "with that great toothy smile" and beckoning him to come outside. Afraid the star had overheard them and was offended, Capaldi discovered that all he wanted was to go over the lines.

There was in the end indeed a *Brigadoon* aura about the filming of *Local Hero*. Lancaster appeared out of the Hollywood sky, telling Tinseltown tales to a rapt audience, picking up checks, answering questions about *Birdman of Alcatraz* from the locals for whom it was as fresh and vivid as a new release. He liked and trusted Forsyth who in turn claimed to see "a soul crying in there." When he left the production, "we were all quite sad," recalled Capaldi. For better or worse, his type, the patriarch he had so carefully buried the previous decade, would not be seen again.

"They don't make these roles any longer," said Capaldi. "These men who can be trusted to help. We were all brought up with that. The movies told us that there was always a guy who could sort it out. I think it was wrong that it was always a guy, but that's just the way it was." The whiff of Happer-like madness humanized Lancaster's assumption of authority: What father does not appear arbitrary to a child? He probably seemed very like Happer to his own children. The great American star produced in the younger Scotsman an old yearning. "There was always a kind of complexity about Lancaster," Capaldi said. "He began to develop a darkness and it was only towards the end that he developed the sense of trust so that you would really think: I want you to help me. I want you to save me."

Building on Forsyth's previous surprise hit, *Gregory's Girl*, plus Puttnam's *Chariots of Fire*, the movie appeared on its release in February 1983 as the latest in a sort of mini British film revival. Happer's descent out of the sky of shooting stars was described by David Denby in *New York* magazine as "one of the truly magical moments in recent movies." But it was Kael who nailed the cumulative effect: "Lancaster has an imperial romantic aura," she wrote, recalling that the Leopard had also gazed at the stars. The voice, the rhythm of his speech had a "welcome familiarity": "There's nobody else in the world with a voice like that," she concluded, "—the smoothness with the remnant of roughness underneath."

The power of the tale persisted. For years afterward, the red phone booth, MacIntyre's only communication link with Happer in Houston, rang off the hook in Pennan with calls from fans around the world hoping to speak with any local hero who happened to pick up.

.   .   .

Four months after the movie's release, in June 1983, Lancaster checked himself into the fifth-floor cardiac intensive care unit of Cedars-Sinai Medical Center after several days of severe stomach and chest pains, later diagnosed as a possible heart attack. On August 26, another team of surgeons performed a five-and-a-half hour quadruple bypass operation on what had been revealed as a seriously damaged heart with blocked coronary arteries. All those years of steaks, Camels, and Martinis had done their damage. This time there were no emergencies; after a brief period back in intensive care, he recuperated quickly and was released.

But he would never be the same again. The formidable vitality, recalled Bone, "just went right out the window." She believed his vocal cords were damaged after tubes were inserted down his throat during the operation with the result that he lost the roaring power of his old voice and with it, much of his ability to intimidate. "It was really terrible," she said, "because he was a man who was dealt by genetics a great deal of energy. With somebody like that, you can just feel it emanating off him, especially if you sleep next to him. When it is diminished, it's very, very obvious." He hated the change, even more than the average sixty-nine-year-old (he turned seventy that November) because he had once been capable of so much. "Your mind figures up things," said Bone, "your body can't deliver."

The gravity of his condition was minimized to the press and his recovery given a carefully upbeat spin. But bouncing back to a functioning life took time and the timing was devastating for his comeback career. With the exception of a quick turn as ruthless CIA head Maxwell Danforth in director Sam Peckinpah's own last, haphazard comeback attempt, *The Osterman Weekend*, he had been headed in a new direction. Now he had to announce that he was withdrawing from a batch of provocative projects: *Maria's Lovers*, the first American film of Russian director Andrei Konchalovsky, to be replaced by Robert Mitchum; *Gorky Park*, replaced by William Hurt; *The Firestarter*, directed by Mark L. Lester from the Stephen King novel, replaced by Martin Sheen. James Mason took his part of Tiberius in an NBC-TV miniseries "*A.D.*" (*Anno Domini*), cowritten by the *Moses* duo of Anthony Burgess and Vincenzo Labella, which aired in April 1985. The lavish epic would have been Lancaster's third project with Labella: in 1982 he had played Pope Gregory X in the producer's Emmy–award winning miniseries, *Marco Polo*, an RAI production for NBC.

The greatest missed opportunity however, was *Kiss of the Spider Woman*. He was slated to start shooting that summer in the part of Molina, the gentle, flamboyant gay hairdresser, who shares a prison cell somewhere in Argentina with Raul Julia's Valentin, and had carefully nurtured the project, based on the cult novel by Manuel Puig, from its inception with Brazilian director Hector Babenco. The two men first met in Los Angeles in late

1981 when Babenco, in town to receive the Los Angeles Critics Award for *Pixote*, gave Lancaster, a new enthusiast of Latin American literature, a copy of Puig's book. Two weeks later, together again at the New York Film Critics Society ceremony where Lancaster received his award for *Atlantic City*, Babenco was waiting outside Sardi's for a cab when suddenly "a big hand grabbed [his] arm and a voice said, 'Do you think I'm too old to play the part?'" Knees shaking, the director replied, ". . . you look young," and began with Lancaster a months-long process of working on the script and looking for money.

Bone recalled that he was eager to do what he considered "another stretch part." "He'd been around these gay guys like Thom and Irving for all these years," she said. "He could really act like it, do it like falling off a log." There were those who would see his willingness to take on such a part as confirmation of the old rumors about his sexuality. But equally plausible is the old circus instinct for the "ain't seen nothin' yet" topper of the unthinkable novelty. Burt Lancaster as an old queen who can't stop talking about the movies and falls in love with a dying, "straight" leftist! The career strategist in him saw the last screen frontier to be crossed, perhaps the only one left to him now.

Babenco, obsessed with the project for four years, believed the story was really aimed "to destroy the myths of what makes a man a man." Lancaster had to know exactly what he brought to the part of Molina. If he had tried to expand the audience's understanding of a progressive political stance by playing reactionaries, why not use almost thirty years' worth of screen masculinity to suggest a different way to think about sexual stereotypes? It was the same question of freedom—personal, political, sexual. Gays were the latest underdog.

There was an even more fundamental attraction. Molina, the gentle lover of life and the movies, and Valentin, the principled activist in "The Struggle" for human rights, were idealized parts of himself. The two men's love for each other formed a synthesis, a reconciliation of the factions of his nature that had battled it out, given him little psychic rest all his life. He said himself that the story was really about love.

He and Babenco could not find backing from anyone—fifteen years later the *New York Times* would note that playing gay characters on-screen in the early 1980s was considered "one of the last taboos"—and the star decided to come in as a coproducer and make the movie in Brazil. When he withdrew after his heart attack, Babenco gave the part to William Hurt, "the hottest name in America," despite lingering "emotional loyalty" to Lancaster. Even with the bigger name, the project finally had to be largely funded in Brazil at a cost of under $1 million. A special thanks to Lancaster appeared in the credits.

When Hurt won the Oscar in 1985 the victory was a breakthrough for Hollywood and the treatment of gays on-screen. What Lancaster would have made of the part remains a fascinating conjecture. He had already toyed with the idea of remaking *The Crimson Pirate,* casting Mikhail Baryshnikov as the old salt's son—and gay. In 1987 when he was seen in New York at the stage show of *La Cage Aux Folles,* it was reported that his interest gave "rise to speculation again" that he would play the nightclub owner in a movie version. Ten safer years later Robin Williams did the role in *The Birdcage.*

There was one ironic consolation. As he went in for the bypass surgery, a new Technicolor print with a new soundtrack of *The Leopard* was released with twenty-five minutes of footage restored. Now the version that had won the unanimous vote of the *Palme d'Or* jury at Cannes in 1963 was available to viewers and critics. "What other actor," asked the *Times* of London, the city of Olivier, "could incarnate Lampedusa's proud Sicilian prince, who touched chandeliers with his head and bent cutlery by mistake?" Lancaster "looks so majestic," wrote Canby, "—his massive build and his fair coloring set him apart from everyone else in the film—and he moves with such self-assured grace. . . ." Kael, on a Lancaster roll, was the most fulsome: "it has a hero on a grand scale . . . played superlatively well by Burt Lancaster. . . . We know the Prince by his noble bearing and the assurance of his gestures—they're never wasteful. He's at ease with authority: you can believe that he's the result of centuries of aristocratic breeding." She put on Lancaster the center of the film's "intelligent and rapturous" spell. *The New Yorker* in 1990 would elevate his Leopard to "the performance of his career . . . the galvanic center of Visconti's magnum opus." Lancaster had never had much respect for critics and didn't start now. "When *The Leopard* first came out," he recalled, somewhat selectively, "it got good reviews but the critics laughed at me. I was a bum. Twenty years later, they're saying, 'It's his chef d'oeuvre, his great acting piece.' I don't know what happened to these people, but suddenly I've become a hell of a performer."

Nineteen eighty-three ended with an important loss, the death of Robert Aldrich in December. Lancaster sat for an hour and a half at the bedside of the brilliant but erratic director who had jump-started Hecht-Lancaster and United Artists with *Apache* and *Vera Cruz.* He later said of the director's—and his own—career: "We're all forgotten sooner or later. But not the films. . . . That's all the memorial we should need or hope for." Roland Kibbee died eight months later. Lucy Kibbee watched one Hollywood best friend after another fade away and was surprised to find that Lancaster kept in steady touch, including her often in his activities. "I never dreamed," she recalled, "that Burt, whom I'd always considered a kind of misogynist, would be one of the two or three people from that time who remained faithful to me."

A cluster of strong projects like those he had been forced to cancel would never come again. Not to be able to capitalize on another precious chance was an agony. Nevertheless he turned down, "a thousand times," invitations to appear on TV productions like *Dynasty*. He continued to treat even the "phone-in" film jobs with the old insistence on certain values, as when he sent an *Osterman Weekend* preproduction memo to Peckinpah specifying that he wanted "more a) action/movement b) depth to the character c) someone the people will care about."

He agreed to do a favor for Alan Sharp and appear in his first directing venture, a low-budget Tri-Star picture called *Little Treasure*, with Joanna Lancaster hired as coproducer with Richard Wagner. Supporting Lancaster's patriarch character, Teschemacher, was what Sharp considered "an interesting little circle around Burt." Margot Kidder (Lois Lane in *Superman*) was his long-lost daughter—the "little treasure"—and Ted Danson, in his second year on NBC-TV's hit *Cheers*, her companion. The bulk of the story is taken up with the couple's search for robbery loot buried under a tree somewhere in New Mexico that the father has left to the daughter. But "from the beginning," said Sharp of the production that began shooting on location in Tepostlan in Morelos, Mexico, in early 1984, "the problem was that Burt and Margot didn't like each other worth a fucking ha'penny. Basically Margot was pretty straight, wild but straight. She rapidly decided that Burt didn't like her and didn't want to interact with her with a part in which she felt she needed an enormous amount of interaction: he was her father." It didn't help that Kidder's own idolized mining engineer father had been frequently absent during her childhood, that Lancaster's relationships with his children were fraught with issues of absence and loss, and that Bone and he were finally through.

The unresolved emotions lashed out in a literal blow-by-blow blocking out of a key scene. When Teschemacher tells the daughter he abandoned years before that not a day has passed when he hasn't thought of her, she calls him a liar. In rehearsal, Kidder suggested to Lancaster that she grab him by the front of the shirt and force his attention; he replied that he did not think his character would let her do that; Sharp volunteered that Kidder had a point. "So Burt got up to show her how he was going to walk away from her," recalled Sharp, "and Margot grabbed him and he hit her, he slapped her across the face, a big, heavy-handed side-swinging slap. . . . Margot just started to kick him. She just held on to him and kicked him and they fell on the ground in front of the crew. . . . Margot had cut her head a little bit. If I had been Sam Peckinpah, I'd have got a terrific scene out of it."

Danson heard the fracas from the other side of the set and remembered thinking, Wow, rehearsals are going really well. Joanna and Sharp rushed to separate the costars and tried to pretend to reporters that it was all in the script. But it got dubbed a "movie-set brawl" in the press and Lancaster was quoted telling his daughter as she helped him up off the floor, "I don't know what came over me." Both actors continued the rest of Lancaster's two weeks on the production without further incident and settled a potential assault and battery charge quietly with Kidder agreeing to say nothing further, publicly, about the incident.

He had reached another, final limit that Sharp observed carefully. "Burt wasn't a real sadist like John Huston or anything like that," he said. "He wasn't out to hurt people every day just to make himself feel really swishy. But I thought he utilized his Irish temper as an excuse to get shit out. His anger was on a bit of a Rheostat; it was theatrical. . . . He had it when he needed it and he could come on alley, come street on you real quick." His old ambivalence to women had also come to some kind of end point. He had gone too far this time. Even Jim Hill was taken aback and saw the incident as a sign of a more general disintegration: "He'd belted dames before," he said with revealing incredulity, "but not like that, not that had anything to do with his *craft*." While he didn't "dislike women as much as Sam Peckinpah," said Sharp, "there was . . . a crudity to him that was deliberate. He would say the kind of things like men talking about sexual things that would make you say, 'Oh, fuck.' I mean really crude things, cruder than you wanted to hear and yet you knew that this was a guy with culture and sensibility. It was like: 'I just want to let you know that I'm real tough down at the bottom and real smooth at the top.' There was a lot of that. He worked you back and forth." To the question of the actor's sexuality and its role in this long interplay of rage, crudity, and manipulation, the director suggested, "He was smart as a whip . . . but my sense is that if you looked like Burt Lancaster, how could you ever live up to looking like that? If you were so much of a man, you would be running behind yourself all the time. . . . It deserves," he concluded, like many others, "to remain a mystery."

For Lancaster, the old expert at displaced rage, this latest incident was about aging, illness, and the certainty of vanished opportunity: He'd had to pull out of *Kiss of the Spider Woman* for this cockamamie movie? Danson recalled that during a rehearsal Lancaster insisted on hoisting the six-foot two-inch, thirty-seven-year-old Danson up into the air to demonstrate how he should carry the dying Teschemacher. "I sailed up into the air," he recalled. "The physicality, the huge upper body strength, blew me away." Lancaster had made his point. He was still in play, still insurable, not finished yet.

.   .   .

The industry went through its next seismic change in fall 1984, a shift in some ways as significant as the 1948 Paramount antitrust decision that had opened the way for Norma Productions. Michael Eisner was named CEO of Walt Disney Company and the reinvented company would have a power and influence unique in the history of entertainment. Barry Diller left Paramount to run 20th Century-Fox only to spearhead, soon thereafter, the so-called Fourth Network, Fox Television. Japanese conglomerates moved in to invest in the American movies and by the end of the decade Warner Bros. would merge with Time, Inc., to form the giant Time Warner. The Business got Big, more consolidated, more faceless, less quirky. "Things were never the same," wrote Dawn Steel.

Lancaster could have told her there was only change in the movies, like life. His accomplishments at the center of the industry got pushed even further back into the hazy Hollywood past, while the advent of the VCR and cable television meant that anyone could see almost any of his movies anytime. Hollywood's theory, that because he was so many people in one he needed no company, had never been far from the truth, but now he was forced to acknowledge that a dimension of life had been missing for him. He was in danger of fading ignominiously into a void that would negate the crafted accomplishments of decades.

He began to construct a calmer routine with more regular pleasures, a dignified last act. Although making new friends was difficult, he started to invest the time and attention and was asked to join a breakfast golf group of twelve to fourteen Los Angeles businessmen at Hillcrest. Reserved and shy at first, he eventually found that the relaxed but close and loyal camaraderie of men Not In The Business gave him some of the best companionship of his later years. "Burt was a real man's man," recalled Larry Powell, one of the group, "with very down-to-earth values." On Saturday mornings he would show up on the first tee at the last minute, having skipped breakfast at the club, and be dressed so badly the group dubbed him their "Hollywood Scar." "He looked like he got dressed before he woke up," said Al Schaeffer, another golfing buddy. In the high-powered club full of celebrities, Lancaster was different: "Those kind of people," said Schaeffer, "are usually so self-absorbed and egocentric to the point that they're not a lot of fun to be with. But Burt was a no-bullshit kind of guy. If you were trying to use him or blow smoke up his butt—a golf expression—he wouldn't have much time for you. If you were really his friend and tried not to take advantage of him or be something that you weren't, you couldn't have a better friend."

He began to change and old friends noticed. He admitted his regret for the Kidder incident and "started to look around and not just be absorbed in himself," recalled Lucy Kibbee. "He got more tolerant of his kids, their foibles. 'Jesus Christ!,' I said to him. 'What's happened?' He said, 'I've grown up.' There was an inner beauty that had never been there before." Missing was a relationship that could take the place of movies as the latter-day art of his life. His nature needed to be totally absorbed in a project, a focus for a different kind of creativity.

When Henry Winkler approached Ben Benjamin with a script, *Scandal Sheet*, for Lancaster to consider, set to shoot in fall 1984 for ABC-TV, the agent turned it down. Lancaster did not star in made-for-TV movies. But Winkler was persistent. He wanted the real J.J. Hunsecker for this *Sweet Smell of Success*-type melodrama of tabloid publishing and the star finally came around. Based on an article by a former *National Enquirer* reporter, the story revealed the seamy secrets of scandal "fact" gathering with an evil publisher and editor—Lancaster's Harold Fallon—at the dark center. Lancaster now formed a new pattern with television increasingly taking the place of feature films as his big-screen work tapered off with the decade. Short-term projects at home as well as work on foreign locations allowed him to travel and play the international star in places that still remembered and honored him. The fast-paced demands of television were "hard"— *Scandal Sheet* was shot in twenty days—but welcome. "I really felt fulfilled when I got home," he confessed, "tired from a long day."

The two-hour production aired in January 1985 and was well-received. When *New York Daily News* columnist Kay Gardella asked Lancaster if he had ever been "burned by one of those gossip sheets" himself, he looked back to the raunchy days of *Confidential* and claimed that when a woman came in once for a job interview, a meeting witnessed by his secretary and his lawyer, the next thing he knew, he recalled, "it was in the papers that I raped her."

The person assigned to get his coffee and otherwise make sure he was taken care of on the set was a vivacious, attractive, forty-two-year-old woman named Susie Martin, who was also working with the script and extras. When she brought the coffee, she lingered to talk with the seventy-year-old star. The conversations grew so animated and absorbing that when the prop sofa where they usually sat was needed for a scene, it was picked up and moved with both of them still sitting on it, talking away.

He wrote his name and number on her copy of the script and then took off for Germany to make another TV project, *Sins of the Fathers*, a Bavaria Atelier Production miniseries costarring Julie Christie and Bruno Ganz. While filming, he called Susie several times and set up their first date. When the day turned out to be Thanksgiving, they broke it and made another and another. By the new year, each had found in the other what McDowall called "a wonderful partnership."

Susie, born Susan June Martin in 1942, had grown up in Los Angeles, her father, David R. Martin, a publicist for MGM during Dore Schary's tenure and on the board of the industry's Academy of Motion Picture Arts and Sciences. After briefly entering a Roman Catholic convent at the age of twenty-one, she married, had a son John, and was now separated from her husband after twenty-one years of what she termed a "verbally and emotionally abusive marriage." She was working as an extra on shows like *Roseanne* and *Cagney and Lacey*, and as a script supervisor. Lancaster liked straightforward women, without pretensions, and she conformed to the type—but with a key difference. The quality he would most love about her was what he called her "naïveté": she was fresh and trusting and relatively uncomplicated. Her gaze, like his, was wary but direct. Like him, once she decided she liked someone, her generosity was formidable. Pretty, fastidious, moving with alacrity and focus, she was a woman his mother would have called "respectable." Susie would give her best and expect no less from him.

Women who had known him a long time, who knew the best and the worst, were struck by the gentleness and commitment of the new relationship. "I never saw him so dear with any woman," said Lucy Kibbee. Marcy Overway-Cravat feels that he "valued the bond more with a woman in the later years" and she listened to him enthuse about the passionate leap into life he had always been chasing in one form or another: "There's nothing like being in love!" he told her. "I feel so young!" Nick liked Susie, recognizing that his old friend needed what he described to Marcy as "that checkpoint, that balance thing" from women. There was a tinge of sadness, too, for those who had seen so much of the emotional life lived at odds with himself. "By then," Ceil Brink said, "it was going downhill and a little bit too late."

If it was too late, he didn't know it. He seized the chance for love with a calculated zest. He would make this work, leaving nothing to chance. The full focus of his renewed energy was turned on the quotidian details of life with Susie. After she moved into the Century City condominium, their life together settled into a routine that each of them worked to keep fresh and pleasurable. They got up early, walked and ran on the high school track, came home and made fresh orange juice and coffee and then headed out into busy days. They cooked together, tackled the daily crossword puzzle and Jumble word games, took preproduction tune-ups at La Costa, in Mexico or Hawaii, enjoyed lots of golf, music, and reading. The bypass may have slowed him down, but slower for him was still more than most people managed to fit into a day. "There was no idle time. He never stopped," said Susie, recalling hours of reviewing scripts, pursuing projects on the phone, taking in five to nine holes at Hillcrest after lunch, or "matinizing"—what they called catching a movie matinee—often with Bill, after which they would pick the production apart. "He loved Bruce Willis and his sense of humor," she said; *Young Frankenstein* and *Back to the Future* were other favorites. When they attended the sixtieth Academy Awards in 1988, Lancaster told her to buy a new dress because it would make her "feel special." Other years they nested in the den in their pajamas on the floor to watch the Oscars on television, always with the same menu: Caesar salad and hot dogs wrapped in bacon, washed down with gin and tonics.

"He was so easy to be good to," recalled Susie. "He treated me with such respect—he made me feel intelligent, sexy, all the things any human should feel." When she went out to buy some ice cream one afternoon, he gave her a wad of cash totaling $750. "You might see something you like," he said. When she came back with the ice cream and lots of change, he began to cry. "No one ever brought me back any change before." Sexually, she says, he was "fabulous," taking time, talking afterwards until the middle of the night, introducing "something new every six months or so." When flying across the Atlantic to Italy in a first-class section in 1986—empty except for him and Susie due to post-Chernobyl cancellations—he instructed the service staff to turn off the lights and leave them alone for a while, and then made love to her on a jet plane.

He often helped her shop for clothes, suggesting she go for what he called a "classic look." She found him fastidiously clean; when he had to skip a shower he joked about taking "a whore's bath"—a quick splash under the arms and between the legs. Though his shirts were custom-made, he wore them "forever." When he had to, he bought a new Armani tuxedo; even with new Ferragamo and Gucci shoes in the closet, he would keep wearing the old ones because they were "so old and so soft." With the neatness of someone who had once lived years on the road, he put anything he used or wore back where it belonged. He never carried a wallet on his person, preferring to keep it in the car door pocket. Walking into a restaurant, he'd drop a credit card and cash into the pocket of his thousand-miler jacket.

There was little talk of marriage. Susie was enmeshed in a slow divorce and Lancaster was reluctant to enter, again, into an arrangement that had not worked for him in the past. There may have been, too, a reluctance to marry while Norma was still alive. With age she had returned to her Catholic faith and considered herself, according to the family friends who kept in touch with her, still married to Lancaster. He knew that a monogamous alliance was important to Susie. There would be no more indulging in outside liaisons.

More cynical Hollywood observers felt Lancaster was beyond any major philandering. Bone, perhaps the best judge, recognized that Susie "truly adored him" and that he was smart enough to recognize and value the windfall as a gift to be nurtured. "Once I was very upset about something," Susie recalled, "and was telling Burt what was bothering me. He was sitting there, giving me his full attention. I was talking and talking and telling why I felt this way and he just sat there, saying nothing. Finally I said, 'Do you think I'm crazy? Are you trying to control yourself, or what?' And he said, 'I've nothing to say. You're right. I'm sorry.' "

The next five years, with Susie to speed the days, were a happy time of mostly minor, sometimes interesting work taking a backseat to the life. In 1985 the Arts & Entertainment cable network aired a Gordon/Fraser Productions opera feature with Lancaster as host of three televised broadcasts—*La Bohème, Tales of Hoffman,* and *Idomeno.* He played the opera sage/critic to *USA Today.* The ponderous weight of divas like Joan Sutherland still offended his sense of operatic grace and he thought Luciano Pavarotti was overrated. At USC he got to indulge his love of teaching, this time in an academic setting at film seminars. Genuinely stunned by the audiences' enthusiasm, he nonetheless delighted afterward in telling how he had "*killed* them, had them in the *aisles!*" In May Hecht died at the age of seventy-seven in Beverly Hills and the *Los Angeles Times* noted that Hecht-Lancaster had "opened a new era in Hollywood film making." The same month, *Little Treasure,* virtually dumped by Tri-Star, opened in one theater in New York.

Like the rest of Hollywood and the world, he was drawn into the drama of Rock Hudson's announcement in July that he was dying of AIDS, the disease known at the time as the "gay plague." Elizabeth Taylor quickly organized a "Commitment to Life" fund-raising gala dinner at the Bonaventure Hotel in Los Angeles on September 19. For the evening's key event, the reading of a letter from the hospitalized Hudson, it was important to find what Gary Pudney, senior vice president of ABC Entertainment at the time, and executive producer of the dinner, called "a piece of casting for the role." Lancaster, "a friend of Elizabeth's and an acquaintance of Rock Hudson's," he recalled, and "the macho man figure you wouldn't expect," was approached by Pudney and accepted on the spot. "It was the same issue it had always been," recalled Susie. "All people should be treated the same. It was upsetting to him that gay people were shunned." He told her that if anybody should have gotten AIDS from an active sex life, it was he.

Burt Reynolds, Cyndi Lauper, Linda Evans, Shirley MacLaine, and Brooke Shields were among the many who showed up but the top crust of great macho male stars, except for Lancaster, did not. "It was impossible to get people like that to come," recalled Bill Misenheimer, executive director of AIDS Project Los Angeles at the time and later executive director of the American Foundation for AIDS Research (AMFAR). "They were terrified of the stigma." Another person active in the event assessed the "real risk" that Lancaster, in light of the old stories about his sexuality, took when he stood up to read Hudson's letter: "If he was getting involved in this early on, he was one of the few who was willing to be associated with it at all. . . . Even people who were not at risk, not gay—they just didn't want the innuendo. I think from that point of view it was even more courageous for him to get involved."

Despite subsequent controversy about whether Hudson ever publicly acknowledged his disease and admissions that the statement was in fact written by the office of his publicist with, it was claimed, the actor's "complete approval," Lancaster's reading of the statement was a powerful emotional moment in the early history of the disease: "I have . . . been told the media coverage of my own situation," Lancaster read, "has brought enormous international attention to the gravity of this disease in all areas of humanity, and is leading to . . . a better understanding of this disease than ever before. . . ." The identification of Hudson with AIDS humanized the disease virtually overnight and over the next twelve years Taylor's AMFAR would raise $83 million.

Lancaster's restless mind pondered another, more universal problem: the strange state of inhabiting the same mind in an old body. "It seems as if I was thirty-five just yesterday," he said at seventy-three. "And here I am an old codger. What happened?" The indignity and embarrassment of being treated as an old man when he had once been the Body Beautiful of Hollywood put him in the odd position of being his own underdog. And, true to form, he had to do something about it.

When Benjamin sent him a script in mid-1985 for a movie, *Tough Guys*, about two cons out of stir for the first time in thirty years and their adventures facing a changed world as old men, he looked at it carefully. *Cocoon* was playing in theaters across the country; Don Ameche would win an Oscar for his performance in the movie that, according to producer David Brown, made Hollywood more willing to use older stars. He signed only after insisting on script alterations to ensure that his character not be "reduced to a cartoon." The script had been written on spec by two young Canadian writers, James Cruikshank and James Orr, with Lancaster and Kirk Douglas clearly in mind. Returning to the idealized world of their movie youth of the 1950s when the two stars were Tinseltown incarnate, they wrote an updated take-off of the first movie the two stars appeared in together, in 1948, *I Walk Alone*. Harry Doyle (Lancaster) and Archie Long (Douglas) decide the only thing they're good for out of stir is what got them in there in the first place: robbing banks and trains. The "serene, leonine gravity, a force-field of confidence and equipoise" of Lancaster was to be balanced, Michael Wilmington of the *Los Angeles Times* would write, against "the nervy, flawed guy who has to prove himself" of Douglas.

The characterization was accurate and Lancaster thought twice before he agreed to the project. The two stars had appeared in 1981 in a Bernard Sabath play, *Boys in Autumn,* with Lancaster's Huck Finn reunited fifty years later on the banks of the Mississippi with Douglas's Tom Sawyer. Despite weak reviews blaming the script for turning Huck and Tom into "dreadful bores," the four-week run at the Marines Memorial Theater in San Francisco sold out and the play was booked to tour starting with a run in Los Angeles. Lancaster was equivocal about continuing in part because of the stresses associated with working with Douglas. "How come Burt has the best dressing room?" Douglas had asked. "Kirk," said the management, "you have the best dressing room." "I want *Burt's* dressing room." "Give him my dressing room," said Lancaster. During a performance, a ball dropped into the orchestra pit, functioning as the Mississippi, while Douglas was doing a juggling routine. Lancaster quipped, "Oh, one dropped down the river!" The line got a big laugh and he decided a tour might not be so exhausting after all. The next night, Douglas purposely dropped the ball, "took the ad lib" and the laugh, and Lancaster said, "That's it. No tour."

Now, having satisfied himself that *Tough Guys* served a larger purpose and that the old star pairing might bring in audiences, he worked well with Douglas on this, their last picture together. The movie was shot in *noir*-esque Los Angeles spots like Chinatown, Main Street, and the steps of City Hall; for the grand finale train robbery and derailing, the production shifted to the Eagle Mountain railroad line in the desert south of Palm Springs. One of the crew members recalls that, despite the stories of a great friendship, the two stars were "as different as night and day" and did not spend time together off the set. Alexis Smith, on the other hand, playing Lancaster's girlfriend, was a welcome companion to him and seemed to calm him with her graceful manner.

He needed a lot of calming. Ironically, the incapacity of his old age was itself a constant problem on the set. "Burt was just so incredibly gracious and polite and professional and generous and lovely," recalled the production's assistant director, Christopher Griffen. "But he would get so infuriated by the degeneration of his being through old age." Huge cue cards were necessary to aid a fading memory and he had problems reading the cards. Take after take was required for the dance sequence, shot in the ornate Variety Arts Club ballroom, where he slow-danced with Smith to the Red Hot Chili Peppers band. "He had a lot of pride," said Griffen. "You could feel his frustration was just mounting and mounting and yet he just carried on. He didn't stomp off as one of his costars would have. Everybody felt the pain as much as he did. It was just so fucking sad."

When Griffen was deputized to go to Lancaster's Palm Springs hotel room and break the news that the production would go three to four days over schedule, the star "exploded," started screaming, threw an ashtray at him, and then quickly apologized. "There are professionals," he said, "and there is everybody else. Dancing with cue cards—that was infirmities, not lack of professionalism. Oddly enough for a man who was so old and appeared so old, his persona was so strong. Not youthful—it's hard to be youthful in your seventies—but vital, absolutely vital."

When the Touchstone movie was released a few months later in October, *Time* called it "*Cocoon* with cojones" as it grossed $12 million in seventeen days. But critics, reported *Boxoffice*, were "downright angry over seeing two screen greats in such a goofy piece of fluff," despite its moments of sly self-mockery. When asked if there would be a *Tough Guys II*, Lancaster snapped, "The only way there would be a sequel is if this picture goes out and makes $150 million. If it goes out and dies, they'll forget. . . . 'What are those fellows' names?' That's the way it is in this business." The two stars' first producer, Hal Wallis, died that same month, just before the seventy-fifth birthday celebration of Paramount in April 1987.

Douglas continued to cling, admiringly, to his own version of the buddy myth. "I find that I have very few friends," he told the *New York Times*, "whereas Burt has people around him who have been with him for years." What Douglas did have was the ongoing involvement of sons Michael and Joel in the movie industry, keeping the Douglas name in play and enhancing and perpetuating, by association, the father's achievements. Douglas was also willing to branch out into new areas that made Lancaster squirm. His autobiography, *Ragman's Son*, quickly became a best-seller in 1988 and he gave a copy to Lancaster inscribed with a note along the lines of "A lot of these girls will be familiar to you." Lancaster told Schaeffer he was not going to read it and he didn't: "You don't go around banging everybody," he said, "and then talk about it. It's not a nice thing to do and I have no interest in the book." When Douglas tried to get him involved in another movie project Lancaster told Schaeffer, "You're not going to believe this one. Kirk's been calling me thirty times. He's been yelling, 'You've got to come over right away. I've got the perfect script for us!' Finally I had to go over there and he shows me this script and it's about two mercenaries and they're on an island in the Caribbean and they're beating the crap out of all the bad guys and they're banging all the girls and they're swinging from chandeliers and he says, 'Incredible!' I couldn't believe this guy. I said, 'Kirk, for Christ's sake. Don't you know our fans are happy when we wake up in the morning?' "

Lancaster's fans got a rare chance to see him in a prolonged interview when he appeared on *Donahue*, filmed in Los Angeles on September 12, 1985. He had agreed to go on as part of the *Tough Guys* publicity campaign; once there, he captivated the audience with a mix of wit, intelligence, and passion. Allowing for the usual quotient of showman guile, the hour is a revealing picture of the man as himself, mellow and happy. The old herringbone jacket has been replaced by the tan tweed Norfolk jacket he wore on the beach in *Local Hero*. He wears an unremarkable shirt and tie and looks smooth and comfortable.

His energy is limited, so he uses it effectively. As his mind responds to a question from the audience, the body moves to meet it. When a woman stands up to tell him she was in competition for Ava Gardner's part in *The Killers*, he looks at her coldly, his eyes seeming to measure the difference between Gardner then and this old woman now. Then he smiles and tells her, "You should have called me!" Reenacting his huge mother threatening "Shut up or I'll jump down your throat!," Burton's fear and love click forward down the years as he looks up, smiles, and cringes at the same time. The story about the twenty-dollar bill lying on the ground in front of the Corn Exchange Bank gets trotted out for the last time, one of the cluster of morality tales he still calls "the Bible" of his upbringing.

The audience is with him, warm, laughing, charmed. When a telephone caller makes a quip about an earlier anecdote, he automatically shoots out, "You should have called earlier. It would have got a bigger laugh." Timing, reciprocity—the back-and-forth of the living audience he had tried to keep alive in his imagination—is clearly his delight. The raw golem who arrived in Hollywood forty years earlier has become not only an articulate gentleman, but an eloquent one as well, his own favorite dream myth about himself. Someone asks him to do an impression of Frank Gorshin, the comedian known for celebrity impersonations, and he laughs, "I can't even imitate Burt Lancaster!"

The old man he really is breaks through by the end of the hour. The words get jumbled, he has trouble hearing host Phil Donahue. When the show breaks for commercials, he quickly sits down on a director's chair to rest. The subject that elicits the most passion comes toward the end when he is flagging. Asked about Charlton Heston's opposition to a merger of the Screen Actors Guild with the extras union, a red-hot Hollywood issue of the early 1980s, he struggles to summon up the energy and focus in order to do justice to the, for him, bedrock principle of unionism. Reminding the audience that before organizing themselves, "people were shot like dogs" and the wives of Warner Bros. grips had to throw sandwiches over the studio fence in the 1930s to husbands on twenty-four-hour-a-day shifts, he pleads: "We need the help of other people. We need *communion* . . . in order to survive." When Donahue points out that with only one American worker in five belonging to a union, his observation "seems to have less eloquence at this moment of our national life," the old East Harlem warrior rises to the bait. "I don't care," he says, chopping the air with his hand. "These are the ups and downs of life. Because you have trouble at the moment, doesn't mean that by going back to using old methods, you will be better off. . . . I'm not trying to make a brief for the unions," he adds, admitting they need to "clean [their] own house. . . . But this is something we fought for. It's our heritage." The face is angry and insistent; he has found the right words. The applause is sudden and loud.

While Lancaster explained that he had never agreed to do a television series because the pace of the work and the financial constraints of the networks did not suit him as well as movies, the fact was, now, he did not have the stamina. But the medium offered other opportunities in the thriving world of multinational made-for-TV movies and miniseries. He cranked out four television projects through 1986 and 1987. *On Wings of Eagles*, a two-part, five-hour NBC miniseries shot in Mexico City, was based on the Ken Follett best-selling novel about the Ross Perot–backed rescue raid led by Army Lt. Col. Arthur D. "Bull" Simons to free two American businessmen held hostage in an Iranian prison during the 1979 revolution. Lancaster worked the unlikely role into a study of a soldier who had, he said, "a soft, compassionate side that provoked great loyalty," a Warden. His performance was lizard-like, careful in its minimum expenditure of energy. When he's not careful, his movements betray an almost shocking frailty. "I'm not a particularly well man. I have to husband my energies," he said after the production, only to pull himself up with, "You tend to just want to relax. That's the thing you have to fight." After shoulder surgery in May 1986, he went with Susie to New York to start shooting *Barnum*, a two-hour Canadian coproduction CBS-TV television movie of the life of the original impresario with Lancaster in the title role. The part required him to progress from a young to an old man and he looked and moved with uncanny vigor as long as the action was on one plane; steps were more difficult to negotiate. The production continued over July and August outside Montreal and when it aired in November, longtime fan Judith Crist named the carefully produced and detailed saga one of her "Ten Best TV Movies" of 1986.

In the fall, after a brief respite back home, including the appearance on

Donahue, he flew to Italy and Cinecittà to make an appearance as a morally dubious scientist in another Canadian coproduction, *Control.* An antinuclear psychological thriller directed by his *Marco Polo* director, Giuliano Montaldo, it was shot, coincidentally, shortly after the Chernobyl disaster and aired on HBO in February 1987. *The Jeweler's Shop,* a movie based on a play by Pope John Paul II, was probably his most unlikely project—a "sermon on legs," as one review described the original play about the mystical union of marriage. In love himself, he happily rationalized the project at a press conference in Rome as "a story about what love means and the power of love." Between productions, he took Susie up and down Italy showing her the favorite places of his second country. The Rome apartment had been sold in the early 1980s, and the couple stayed at the Cavaleri Hilton, beginning each day with a walk and jog around Lancaster's old favorite, the Stadio dei Marmi. Part of his impatience to finish *Tough Guys* on time was due to fear that a delay would jeopardize reservations for himself and Susie at Marcella Hazan's cooking class in Bologna.

He returned to the U.S. to start work on a movie that went nowhere at the time but that quietly astonishes later. In *Rocket Gibraltar* he gave himself—as Wayne had done in *The Shootist* and Henry Fonda in *On Golden Pond*—his own Hollywood funeral. The supporting cast was a bunch of unknowns who would be some of the best talent of the 1990s: Kevin Spacey, Bill Pullman, Suzy Amis, Sinead Cusack; David Hyde Pierce and James McDaniel in walk-on parts, and an eight-year-old, pre–*Home Alone* Macaulay Culkin.

Writer/director Amos Poe's quirky family reunion plot for this Columbia picture was all too typical, some felt, of David Puttnam's output during his brief stint as head of the studio. One critic renamed it *On Golden Chill.* Lancaster's Levi Rockwell is turning seventy-seven and his children and grandchildren arrive one summer weekend at his Sagaponack, Long Island, house for a big, catered birthday party. Culkin is the youngest grandchild, Blue, and has a psychic rapport with his grandfather. After Rockwell describes to the children a Viking burial at sea with the body put on a flaming ship and pushed off to sail into the sunset, they seize on Blue's idea of fixing up a battered old boat—the *Rocket Gibraltar*—to match a Viking ship model Levi has just given him and present it to their grandfather for his birthday. When a doctor (George Martin) tells Rockwell the day before the party that Rockwell is dying and the children overhear the conversation from their tree house, they concoct a plan to send Grandad out in style with his own Viking funeral.

With his party in full swing outside on the lawn, Rockwell dies alone upstairs on his bed surrounded by his gifts—a book of Jackson Pollack paintings and a video of Rita Hayworth and Fred Astaire dancing. The camera looks out, as if from his eyes, as the book drops back on the bed, the black-and-white television picture of the dancers goes fuzzy, and the big screen dissolves into total black. The children sneak his body out of the house and onto his funeral ship, and then sail him out to sea in flames into the setting sun. Lancaster's gravelly voice intones over an appropriately mythic French horn theme. "By now all that was left was ashes," he reads, diction clear, timbre muted. "Complete obliteration. Carried by the currents to the four corners of the earth. Fresh and beautiful. Vanished completely like a dream."

When he suggested to the cute little Culkin at their first meeting at the Westhampton Beach, Long Island, shoot in August that he might give him some acting tips, the precocious kid shot back, "Just don't step on my lines." "Big Burt," recalled key grip Robert Schulman, "would probably have liked to squash him into the ground." Culkin claimed acting was "too easy," but the old star, who had never found it easy, continued to be plagued with a badly fading memory. It took so much energy to keep doing well the thing he had finally perfected. He joked to a reporter that, at his age, all the director had to do was call, "Action!" and he would start crying. When he blew up at Daniel Petrie one day—after two and a half weeks, Poe was fired as director for budget overruns and replaced by Petrie (*Raisin in the Sun* and *Fort Apache, The Bronx*)—screaming with his hoarse, diminished voice, he later apologized, crying this time in frustration at his inability to control his demon temper.

A dinner-table scene in which Rockwell returns to his old blacklist routine as a stand-up comedian, throwing out favorite bad jokes one after another to his laughing family, took many takes as Lancaster kept flubbing the lines. This time he turned the incapacity into a joke on himself. Spacey would recall on an American Movie Classics television tribute to Lancaster more than ten years later that he had them all laughing so hard "tears [were] streaming out of our eyes." Starting in on the third take of the line, "Thirty years ago, when I was a blacklisted teacher and writer, trying to feed my growing family, . . ." according to Spacey, mimicking the clipped Lancaster style, he suddenly said, "Ah yes, I remember back in the 1950s I was a black male. . . . Wait a minute, that's not right. I wasn't a black male then. Ah, I'd better do this again." Spacey recalled, "We were on the ground."

The comparisons between *Rocket Gibraltar* and his real life were obvious. Spacey would note the many unusually successful transitions Lancaster had made and that he had "just beautifully aged in his career." His own fondest myths were being given a movie send-off: the valiant life well lived; the children and grandchildren gathered around at the end, warm and loving, to say good-bye. If his own life fell short of these, at least he would make it end right in a movie. If his Neddy Merrill had stayed sane and married, he might have ended up Levi Rockwell. If Lancaster's life had been lived differently, *he* might have ended up Levi Rockwell.

By the time of the movie's release in September 1988, Puttnam was out of Columbia and *Rocket Gibraltar* was an embarrassing reminder of his brief time in Hollywood. It was barely seen by anyone but critics. Lancaster's unsentimental presence in the sweet story was considered its saving grace. Lancaster called it a "sleeper" and the movie did eventually gain a following as a rental video taken home as an afterthought and, depending on a tolerance for fable-cliché, embraced. As time and talent caught up with it, it became another, better movie.

Lancaster was back in New York in November for a family celebration of his own that stirred up old feelings he did not bother to hide. Fifty-four years after the fact, New York University decided to honor his late brother, Jim—the "magician" of NYU's 1933–34 basketball season—with induction into the university's sports hall of fame. As Little Dutch, in his dead brother's stead, started to make his speech in front of the audience at the Varsity Club on West Forty-third Street, he admitted he had come with "mixed emotions" because the award had come too late. It was evident the actor was, the *Daily News* reported the next day, "hurting very deeply inside." He finally said he would "cherish" the award as his brother would have and then, still on the podium, cried in earnest.

The public and the industry remained unaware of the rather exquisite balance Lancaster now maintained between his work and his health. He confided to army buddy Boris Barere that he had to take something like twelve pills a day for one condition or another; Susie devised a system of writing down all the drugs and doses on cards that she and Lancaster each carried in their wallets in case of emergencies. "[Y]ou're marking time," he told a reporter. "You're like a fighter. No fights but you keep in great shape." His mind, at least, was "still going like a trip hammer."

At the end of the year he had a real fight for his professional life when Columbia Pictures, having signed him to star with Jane Fonda in *Old Gringo*, told him after he arrived in Mexico City in mid-December to start rehearsals, that he was being replaced by the slightly younger (seventy-two to Lancaster's seventy-five) Gregory Peck. The star, claimed the studio, was too expensive to insure for a project that would require working in high altitudes and blistering temperatures. Kaplan, still Lancaster's attorney, immediately filed a $1.5 million (his full salary) "pay or play" suit in the Los Angeles Superior Court against the studio for damages. "If the industry believes Mr. Lancaster is uninsurable," Kaplan wrote to Columbia's attorneys, "his career will be at an end."

Though the suit was eventually settled privately to Lancaster's satisfaction, the damage was done. He pushed himself even harder to compensate, to keep moving, to keep working. On March 15, 1988, he went to legislative hearings in Washington with James Stewart and other Hollywood professionals to protest the colorization of black-and-white movies and to seek legislation requiring protection under the Berne Copyright Convention. For one week in June he and Susie were in Milan and Yugoslavia to film his scenes as a Cardinal in *I Promesso Sposi* (*The Betrothed*), an RAI-produced Italian miniseries based on Alessandro Manzoni's novel of the same name. News reports claimed he had fallen ill, but Susie recalls that a bad hair-dye job for his role produced an allergic reaction. Countering the rumors was like putting out one fire after another.

To make what would be his last feature movie and biggest box-office hit, *Field of Dreams*, he returned to the U.S. in July. Shot mainly in the Iowa cornfields twenty-five miles west of Dubuque on Don Lansing's farm in Dyersville, the story, taken from W.P. Kinsella's 1982 novel, *Shoeless Joe,* was another 1980s fairy tale. A mystical baseball field, built by Kevin Costner's farmer Ray Kinsella, lures the ghosts of the 1919 Chicago White Sox team, the disgraced World Series fixers, back from the past for a second chance at glory. Lancaster was cast in the small but key role of Doc Graham, the kindly old man who was briefly the team's rookie. In his last scene, he morphs from his past ghost off the baseball field back to his doctor self to save Kinsella's daughter.

It was hot in Iowa that summer. At first the corn would not grow because of a drought and then it grew too fast for camera continuity. Between delays, Lancaster and Susie passed the time by becoming friends with James Earl Jones, the accomplished Tony Award–winning stage actor who had branched out to film and television, cast here as a disaffected writer, and his wife, Cecilia, "Ceci." A star of Lancaster's stature had earned the privilege, felt Jones, of being "very grumpy" while everyone else paid homage. But he also observed that when "Ceci or any nice-looking woman would come on the set, he'd just perk right up and be the best gentleman." Once in costume, he would walk up to the camera and become "the old fit Burt we always knew."

Jones treasured the new friendship because it had no "agendi." "There was nothing we could do for each other," he recalled. "It was just being in touch with somebody of my generation who did the kind of work that I think actors go into acting for. What do you do with your career to make it really worthwhile? For you and for history? Burt exemplified that. . . . That's what was on the line for him: he'd done well, he was proud of that. He could fight like hell over issues, but was never cynical." The actor in Jones saw the connection between Lancaster's life and the long work. "It had to do with the social creature he was," he said. "The word 'liberal' doesn't define him—he was a 'concerned citizen' about all things, all issues. His life had a moral point of view, a very strong one. And it didn't have to. It was his choice. He gave his characters his soul, in a way, even the bad guys, so he made all his characters credible—they had a soul too. Burt was a much simpler man than the star. Burt was basic. He was someone I felt comfortable with and that means he was a simple man because I am a simple man."

The pairing with Costner formed a neat set of post–World War II Hollywood bookends. The younger star was an inheritor of the breakthroughs Lancaster had pushed so hard to achieve. Between *Bull Durham* and his first directing project, *Dances with Wolves,* Costner in 1988 was the new, independent star whom the industry encouraged to branch out, to direct, to experiment. He made a point of bringing his wife and three children on location with him, as Lancaster had done, and talked a lot about "risk," one of the older star's original favorite buzz words. "I kind of march to my own drummer," said Costner, whose career would, like Eastwood's, both benefit and suffer from the freedom and power so readily given to him.

Field of Dreams opened nationally in May 1989 and quickly became the word-of-mouth hit of the year. Critics generally panned its cloying mixture of wishful thinking and idealizing of a crooked, all-white baseball team. The dream-your-dream mystique of the movie seemed emblematic of the fuzzy optimism of the Reagan eighties. Richard Corliss of *Time* wrote that "despite a lovely cameo turn by Burt Lancaster, *Field* is the male weepie at its wussiest." Kael called it "a crock" full of "conformist values" and regretted that Lancaster was "given fourth-rate lines." But by October 1989, five thousand people had made their way to the Lansing farm, pilgrims to a promised heartland. If the movie's otherworldly message was antithetical to Lancaster's lifetime of engaging in the here and now, there were other gratifications in seeing his seventy-third movie not only a hit, but some kind of touchstone of the culture. The movie's catchphrase, "Build it and they will come," was not too far removed from the idealistic push and drive of his own career in the movies.

And there was the added twist of putting in the mouth of one of Hollywood's biggest risk takers musings on the chances *not* taken: "I never got a chance," says Lancaster's Graham, "to bat in the major leagues . . . to run the bases, stretch a double into a triple and flop, face first, into turf, wrap your arms around the bag. . . ." His last line on the big screen is, "Win one for me, will ya boys?" To which Ray Liotta, as Shoeless Joe Jackson, replies, "Hey, rookie! You were good." Lancaster looks back at him as if to say, You don't know the half of it, and walks into the cornfield and out of the movies.

While he was going back and forth to Iowa, waiting for the corn to grow, Norma died on July 21, age seventy-one, of complications from a stroke she had suffered the week before, plus the long-term damage to her liver from a lifetime of drinking. The alcoholism had become even worse with the years, making relations with friends and family difficult if not impossible. There had been frequent falls and dire warnings from her doctors. When one of the children called Lancaster with the news, he took the call privately. She left money in her will for a party at her Beverly Hills home after her death that both Lancaster and Susie attended. Half the guests were African Americans come to honor a woman who had materially helped them—and who was a lifetime member of the NAACP. Lancaster came, briefly, to a small get-together the children held in her memory.

His decade of insisting in various ways that it was not necessary to be a political conservative to qualify as a passionate American was put to a test when Republican candidate George Bush began taunting the ACLU as "un-American" during his 1988 presidential campaign. Lancaster agreed to appear in the first televised ads the organization had ever run, "so glad to do it," recalled Ramona Ripston, "he didn't waver for a second." The media spots ran nationwide showing a venerable Lancaster announcing in his raspy, faded voice: "I'm Burt Lancaster and I have a confession to make: I'm a card-carrying member of the ACLU."

Since Reagan's victory in the presidential election of 1980, Hollywood liberals and progressives had thrown themselves into a "wave of organization building," Ronald Brownstein has written, "more vigorous than anything seen since the 1940s." Skeptical of Reagan's "Morning in America," Lancaster looked for new ways to demonstrate how to be, as Ed Asner put it, a "liberal with balls." Asner's own tempestuous tenure as SAG president in the early 1980s and his campaign to merge actors and extras into one union had attracted what he called Lancaster's "staunch" support. The merger was narrowly rejected, but only after a period when pro- and anti-Reagan politics seemed to find virulent expression on the issue of unionism in a battle soon dubbed "Star Wars." Hollywood polarized between liberal, progressive celebrities such as Asner, Lancaster, Newman, Jack Lemmon, and Carroll O'Connor, who wanted a more aggressive actors' union and an opposing camp made up of Heston, Eastwood, James Stewart, Barbara

Stanwyck, and others who favored retaining a guild. Asner declined to run for a third term as SAG president in 1985 after death threats, the cancellation of his television show, *Lou Grant,* and his alienation of many who thought he had misused his position. In a community where "a lot of people turn out when the water is warm," Lancaster remained for Asner "there, hot or cold."

To fight the Reverend Jerry Falwell's Moral Majority, Norman Lear organized People for the American Way (PAW) in 1981 and immediately roped in Lancaster. The producer/writer devised a number of television ads, directed by Jonathan Demme. Specials studded with stars such as Barbra Streisand and Robin Williams aimed to present an American patriotism no less vigorous for being tolerant. The *Los Angeles Times* called a syndicated fund-raiser narrated by Lancaster and aired by Lear in forty cities in October "as slick and distorted a piece of propaganda" as anything of Falwell's, but with one key difference: "The fundamentalists have the right to believe as they wish, Lancaster notes, but 'no right to stop the rest of us from speaking and believing something different.' Amen." Falwell branded Lear a "hypocrite" and by the late 1980s PAW had shifted its base from Hollywood to Washington and become a major lobbying force for what was now called "progressive" legislation.

A poster with a photograph of Lancaster clutching a rose with the words, "Think before you act—don't get AIDS," attracted nationwide attention in May 1986. It was part of a campaign by Aid for AIDS to increase awareness of the disease among high-risk groups and the organization named him their Man of the Year on July 24, 1987, for his work as a frequent speaker and for the use of his photograph on the organization's Christmas card. Golfing friends Schaeffer and Powell persuaded him to get involved in CONCERN Foundation for Cancer Research, a fund-raising group they had formed in the late 1960s after the death of a friend from cancer. At the annual CONCERN Rodeo Drive block party charity event, he worked as a celebrity bartender and found, to his surprise, that long lines of fans waited at his station wanting a drink mixed by him.

Ripston tried, as she had many times over the years, to get him to agree to let the ACLU honor him for his years of advocacy. And, as he routinely did for any organization in which he was active (Aid for AIDS was an exception because he felt the use of his name would materially benefit the cause), he refused. "Burt's the only one," she said, "who's ever said, 'I don't deserve it.' " In private, he called such awards "the kiss of death." Similarly, he turned down the Film Society of Lincoln Center when he was asked to be the honoree at their annual New York gala recognizing outstanding film careers. Susie recalls that he'd slyly respond to such appeals by suggesting that they call "my good friend Kirk Douglas" instead, knowing the other star would be happier in the limelight. When the ACLU chose to give the award one year to Douglas, Lancaster presented it to him with affection and appreciation.

The ACLU offices at 633 Shatto Place were now a sort of haven for Lancaster, a throwback to the do-good buzz of the settlement house. He brought in cookies and candy for the staff, stayed to bat around ideas and projects. Linda Burstyn, communications director for the organization and, later, California deputy campaign manager for Bill Clinton's 1992 presidential run, helped him with his speeches from late 1988 to 1990 and found in the old man a new friend. "I knew he was a big deal," she recalled, "but I was not fazed by that and that's part of why we became friends. I loved the kinds of things Burt wanted to say, so we really hit it off." Believing that "good relations are made with a little food," Burstyn made sure she had a fresh supply of the star's favorite cookies on hand and that she was available anytime. "He'd come into my office, close the door, and we'd just sit and chat."

His political ideas had now distilled down to what he called a central "simple" belief: the Bill of Rights was what "made this country unique" by empowering the individual while setting limits on government. The balance between them was fragile and too easily lost without the vigilance of a group like the ACLU. In the feel-good ambiance of the Reagan/Bush era, he saw a nostalgic kind of conformity that had, in his opinion, nothing to do with the hard work of tolerating unpopular opinions in a free society. Censorship, discrimination, abortion rights—for him they were issues of personal freedom. "He was a very common-sense kind of guy," said Burstyn, "very aware of his own strength, which made him protective of others who were not so strong—the people other people pushed around." She remembers him making frequent comparisons with McCarthyism. "In a way those days were easier," he said in one speech, "because we could point to the enemy and say, 'Him, that's who the enemy is.' " As he had very clear ideas on what he wished to say for various speeches and television ads, Burstyn helped him smooth and shape text he often blocked out himself. He sent her a bouquet of flowers after the first speech they worked on together, a gesture, she said, "nobody does."

The relationship developed into something Lancaster had rarely if ever had: an easy productive rapport with a woman who was as eager as he to splash around in the rhetoric of good and just causes. "He was such a wonderful guy—a lovely older man," Burstyn recalled, "and so interesting to listen to. His storytelling always felt like he was sharing a secret. He'd tell me about the movies he'd been in and get a faraway look and put me right in the scene: 'And then,' he'd say, 'I'm hiding from the enemy and I knock on a door and there's a woman standing there. We just look at each other and then the longest screen kiss. . . .' He loved that part, playing the role, being the man who sees the woman. He loved being a part of it, never took it for granted at all."

When Burstyn first asked him why he had never written the story of his own life, he said, "Why would anyone want to read about me? It's so boring, everybody talking about themselves." But as he came to trust her, driving one weekend day out to her "tiny, shabby Santa Monica apartment right on the beach" to work on a video for kids about civil liberties, he brought it up again as a project they might do together—perhaps as a work of fiction, so he would not seem to be boasting. She was tempted: "I never had a grandfather. And although I never confided in Burt or asked advice, he touched a little bit of that for me."

Any life story would have to wait a little longer while he embraced two deeply satisfying projects that kept him on the move and far away from home during the last year of the decade. In June he and Susie went to Italy to film *Voyage of Terror: The Achille Lauro Affair* for the new Tribune Premiere Network to be aired in May 1990. It was the second television re-creation of the tragic October 1985 Mediterranean cruise during which four Palestinian hijackers shot the American Jewish passenger Leon Klinghoffer, paralyzed on his right side by an earlier stroke and wheelchair-bound, and threw him overboard. This production's claim to authenticity was that, except for some scenes shot at Cinecittà, most of the story was filmed aboard the original ship, which retraced the voyage's route from Genoa to Alexandria and Port Said, Egypt.

To prepare for the part of Klinghoffer, Lancaster asked to meet in New York with his daughters, Lisa and Else. "I want to do my performance justice," he told them over the phone from Los Angeles, "to get an accurate sense of the man and be proud of it." They met for lunch at Patsy's, one of Lancaster's favorite restaurants, in the theater district. *Field of Dreams* had just been released and the women observed that "everyone knew him." He had already quizzed some friends about what it felt like to have a stroke and proceeded to ask the two sisters a series of specific questions. How was your father's right hand positioned? How did your father sit and move in the wheelchair? How would he have felt if he couldn't see your mother? Klinghoffer's rugged New York City childhood was not unlike his own, he said, and he felt an "affinity" with a tough man who had gone after what he wanted. "Burt didn't want us to be disappointed," recalled Lisa. "He felt it was an incredibly important story."

The sisters, whose lives had been a nightmare of public tragedy, felt Lancaster had a sincere sympathy not only for their loss but for how it had occurred. The great WASP star, they believed, captured their Jewish father's "grittiness" and his "dignity." In terms of his own Hollywood history, it was a gallant crossover, an elevation by the force of his famous presence of Klinghoffer into the fraternity of myth. Propped up against the railing to be shot in the death scene, he stood and flinched and torqued to the bullet with the studied grace of high tragedy.

His next project, *The Phantom of the Opera*, was pure delight, a reward, shot in Paris for NBC-TV, directed by Tony Richardson, the British director of *A Taste of Honey*, *The Loneliness of the Long Distance Runner*, and *Tom Jones*, adapted from the original Gaston Leroux novel ("schlocky even for its time," said Lancaster) by Arthur Kopitt, cast with hit miniseries *Jewel in the Crown* star Charles Dance as the phantom and Lancaster as his father, and budgeted at a lavish $10 million. With the three major television networks under new and increasing pressure from cable TV, Charles Champlin called such blue-chip efforts the new "Gee Whiz route" to lure audiences.

It was all strangely appropriate: the little Burton who had gone with his mother down to the old Met on Thirty-ninth Street was now the father of the Phantom of *the* Opera in Paris. He told Susie he had been running home the night Lizzie threw the pursuing cop down the stairs because he had just seen Lon Chaney in *The Phantom of the Opera* and was terrified. When his eyes had to well up and tears dribble down his face on cue at the sound of a human singing voice, no retakes were needed.

By the middle of 1990, both Ripston and Burstyn noticed that Lancaster was not quite himself. He and Susie had gone to Mona Kai in Hawaii after *Phantom*, then to London in December, and in February to the AT&T Pebble Beach National Pro-Am Tournament (formerly the Bing Crosby Pro-Am Tournament) in Pebble Beach, an event he had played in several times, often with Robert Wagner. He was the keynote speaker in June at a seventieth birthday party for the ACLU in Brentwood; the Southern California affiliate now handled the most cases of any ACLU branch in the country. But he confided to Ripston that he "wasn't feeling the way he had been feeling." Burstyn thought he seemed, for the man who had been "*so* put together," now "starting to go, a little sloppy, befuddled, hair messed up a little." When he ate his cookies, he was messy and didn't notice.

Yet when George Stevens Jr. approached him for *Separate But Equal*, an ABC television drama of the NAACP's legal battle to desegregate the nation's public schools in the 1954 landmark Supreme Court case *Brown v. Board of Education*, he jumped at it. Stevens, founder of the American Film

Institute, whose father had directed classic Hollywood dramas of the 1950s—*A Place in the Sun, Giant*—was writer, producer, and director of this top-quality, four-hour production that *New York* magazine called a "miniseries supreme." He wanted Lancaster to play John W. Davis, a brilliant Wall Street litigator at the very center of the nation's elitist cabal of law, finance, and politics. The 1924 Democratic presidential candidate, Davis had not only pleaded the last stand case for states' rights and segregation, but had also been the attorney for MGM in 1940 when the Justice Department first brought to trial the Paramount antitrust case.

In his first television role in three decades, Sidney Poitier agreed to play the lead part of the NAACP attorney, later to be the first black Supreme Court justice, Thurgood Marshall. He and Lancaster had seen each other over the years since the 1963 March on Washington at political and social functions and on the Hillcrest golf course. By mid-September 1990, as they joined again in Charleston, South Carolina, to start location work, Poitier observed that a development had taken place in the older actor. "We traveled in different circles," he recalled, "but as I got to know him again after the whole civil rights thing, it was borne out to me that when you see substance in an actor's work, it isn't always necessarily there in the unfolding of his personality. In Burt's case, what I saw on the screen—the things I saw *in* him on the screen—were the things I became familiar with *off* the screen. He had a view of life—the word 'fairness' comes to mind. . . . Mind you," he added, "such suspicions on my part, in terms of other people, never bore out."

The effort to make Davis sympathetic came at a cost. Watching Lancaster's calibrated performance, it is evident he is failing. He is thinner, his face often mask-like. A shot over his back as he sits in a garden reveals a bony shoulder jutting up, seemingly held up only by his elbow propped on the arm of a chair. When his Davis scoots around a desk and insists, "We're going to *win!*" with the old diction and punch, the moment stands out. Even so, E. Barrett Prettyman Jr., a young Supreme Court law clerk in 1954, enlisted by Stevens to be an expert advisor on courtroom procedure, observed that the actor was "more alive" than the "stately, formal, self-confident" Davis.

The long Supreme Court summation arguments, filmed at the Disney studios in Orlando, Florida, were potentially a serious problem for Lancaster. Stevens made the process as painless as possible by setting up TelePrompTers within easy view around the courtroom set. "Each of us had an *awful* lot of words, three pages of one speech!" Poitier recalled. "I tried to memorize mine and I worked at it and worked at it and had it pretty OK. . . . Burt came out and had his TelePrompTers there and went right through it and it was a magnificent performance." The point, Poitier said, is that the TelePrompTer was only a tool for Lancaster. "He *knew* what was behind the words, all the subtleties. The monitor only freed him up to know that if he needed it, he just had to look over there. He could give flight to the feeling—the words are the wings."

Separate But Equal ends with Davis, in his garden, hearing that the court has unanimously ruled against his position. Like the Leopard accepting the plebiscite, he takes the news philosophically. In the service of the NAACP triumph, Lancaster gave a depth and humanity to the opposing forces—the portrayal itself a brief for tolerance. "The part speaks," said Poitier, "to the kind of person Burt was. That's what makes him the man."

Out for dinner one night in Florida with Stevens, Lancaster, and Susie, Prettyman observed the woman who clearly "adored" Lancaster watching him "very carefully." She was now his wife. Quietly, in a civil ceremony at the Four Seasons Hotel in Beverly Hills, they had been married in Los Angeles on September 10, the day before leaving for Charleston. Bill and Keigh, Jimmy and his wife, Sighle, Susan, Susie's son John, and her mother, plus Jack Ostrow and his wife Belle, were there for the ceremony. The bride wore a tailored English suit and a veiled hat Lancaster had picked out for her; the groom dressed up in a navy blue cashmere blazer and a tie. When the judge pronounced them married, Lancaster pulled back the veil and kissed his wife.

Stories circulated that Susie had pressured him into marriage after her divorce became final on January 5, 1989, after Norma's death, after his health began to fail. But the impetus, said Susie, came from Lancaster. He suggested the idea in passing a couple of times, then brought it up point-blank three times. Finally, she recalled, he sat her down one day in the den and said, dryly, "Don't act surprised," and asked her to marry him. They went to a jeweler and chose thick, matching gold bands.

The couple threw a big wedding party at the Hillcrest Country Club in October. Lancaster pored over the guest list, the seating ("bridge players with bridge players, golfers with golfers . . ."), the food. Sydney and Claire Pollack, Dinah Shore, Marvin Davis, Don Rickles, Jim Hill, Nick, nuns from Susie's convent, the Hillcrest gang, all the children, Keigh, Ben Benjamin, Ceci and James Earl Jones, Jill and Robert Wagner, Joanna and Sidney Poitier, Jerry Perenchio—250 carefully chosen friends and family members came to hear toasts, to dance, and to celebrate the happy turn in the long life.

George Burns toasted the couple noting he "had never been a good lover" because the only thing he ever "wanted to get into was show business." Rickles roasted the groom and everybody else mercilessly and hilariously, even the dead: "Clark Gable is not here," he said to the assembled group of the once all-Jewish club, "because he's not Jewish." Remembering

Lancaster's power, aloofness, and preoccupation with his appearance in the old days of *Run Silent, Run Deep*—"How do I look?" he mimicked Lancaster as saying, adding that he "didn't talk to anybody in those days"—Rickles finally got serious. "There are many stars in this business," he said, "Peck, Cooper—I've met all of them. But Burt Lancaster had an outstanding class. He has always been kind in a tough business."

Lancaster then rose to give two toasts, the first to his friends at the club who had taken such good care of Susie and himself, and the second to the bride, standing next to him in a bright red dress. His remarks, *Variety* reported, left few in the room, already teary with laughter, with a dry eye—including the groom. "I hope my remaining years will be spent with this woman," he said, "who gives me warmth, joy, friendliness—she's a friend, a *good* friend—all the things a man could hope for at this stage of my life. She makes me young, fills me with ambition to do things. I'm just a lucky fellah."

In his hurly-burly life, it was a refreshingly normal celebration.

PART FOUR

THE END

1990 — 1994

CHAPTER TWELVE

Fade Out

After the party, the newlyweds flew to Italy for ten days. Lancaster finalized arrangements for filming a sequel to *Il Gattopardo,* comprising the book's final death sequence, to be directed by Mauro Bolognini. D'Amico thought the idea was "a great mistake"; Bolognini, who had trained with Luigi Zampa, Yves Allegret, and Jean Delannoy and had directed since 1953, was "good, good," but not Visconti. She understood that Lancaster "could not think that somebody else would play this part." Because he admitted he wasn't feeling "quite right," all efforts were made to make the coming production as pleasant for him as possible.

Back home, on November 20 he decided to take a long-deferred trip to visit Danny Scott, an old bridge friend, at the John Douglas French Center for Alzheimer's Disease in Los Alamitos. Susie offered to drive the fifty-mile trip, but Lancaster told her it would be a long day with lots of freeway changes and he would go by himself. Shortly before noon, he was walking down a hospital corridor when he suddenly felt dizzy and slumped on a chair, saying, "Help me. Please help me." He was taken to nearby Los Alamitos Medical Center and Susie immediately joined him. His children also gathered at the hospital, eventually taking a hotel room. The golf friends came out in a group to see him. Jack Ostrow became the spokesperson to the press, which converged on the hospital when a nurse revealed who the patient was. The hospital phone lines jammed and reporters started stalking the entrance. Like his mother sixty-two years before, Lancaster had had a massive cerebral stroke.

He remained hospitalized until February and then returned home to Century City. As *Separate But Equal* aired that spring to outstanding reviews and an eventual Emmy for Best Mini-Series of 1991, a careful campaign of upbeat bulletins to the public began: the star was recovering well with some unspecified damage to his mobility and speech; he was looking forward to getting back to work and was actively engaged in his physical therapy. The truth was that a partial paralysis of his right side precluded any mobility except in a wheelchair. If his seventy-seven-year-old body—which the Los Alamitos staff, ignorant of who he was on arrival, described as that of a "sixty-year-old man"—had not been, still, so strong, he would have died. Even so, his damaged heart would impede any real recovery. He could make attempts at words, but no one except, eventually, Susie, could understand him. If he worried that the stroke had come too soon for him to rearrange his affairs as a married man, no one knew.

More than death, his first idol, Fairbanks, had feared incapacity. "If God was going to give up on that physique," Carmichael remembered thinking, "then everybody's going to die." Michael Winner came to visit during a trip to Los Angeles and was devastated by the experience. Jim Hill told Carmichael that "Burt's sitting there with a blanket over his legs, looking out the window at Century City" and that he could not face it again, but he did, often. When she heard the news, Claudia Cardinale, thousands of miles away, "immediately thought of that perfect body and I felt a pang in my heart." The Klinghoffer daughters remembered how carefully he had grilled them about the effects of a stroke.

There was some discussion among the Lancaster children, Susie, and the doctors as to whether he should go into a nursing home. Susie insisted he remain at home. A care facility was kept only as a last-resort option and a daily routine of physical therapy and nurses marked his days. In the late afternoons she often took him over to the putting green at Hillcrest where he watched her and other friends hit balls. Dinner at the home of Robert Wagner, and his wife Jill St. John, was one outside social pleasure he would tolerate. He could no longer read. When Marcy Overway-Cravat came into the bedroom during one visit the book on his lap was upside down.

The days turned into years, the experience taking on the endurance of a siege. "His courage at lying there," said Lucy Kibbee, "this great huge physical man to become incapacitated was so tragic." The press bulletins were simple and upbeat. On their first wedding anniversary, Susie told the *Hollywood Reporter,* "There's a lot of laughter going on at the house." To celebrate his eightieth birthday on November 2, 1993, it was reported that he watched a video of *The Rose Tattoo.* But wild rumors kept surfacing. A profile of Hollywood columnist Army Archerd on the front page of the *Wall Street Journal* reported that part of a recent day's work was to respond to a fax from Milan claiming Lancaster had fallen into a coma after saying "goodbye" to his family.

Most people assumed his mind was gone too, but it was not. He knew his own predicament. For this reason, as well as to guard his strength, Susie put strict limits on who was allowed to see him and when. He was in an old-fashioned seclusion, almost like that of a silent screen star. No photograph would reveal to the industry, to the fans who remembered him as he once was, what he looked like now. Many of his older friends, whom Susie did not know as well, felt excluded and resented the lack of access. Douglas was told it would be better if he did not come, at least not yet. Lancaster would be "embarrassed" for Douglas to see him, Susie told him, and Douglas replied, kindly, "That's what I thought." Joel Douglas recalled that his father deeply missed the chance to say good-bye. "It was the right decision for Burt," Susie said, admitting she would handle the situation differently today, "but the wrong thing for Kirk."

The rumor that he was not seeing anybody kept many from even trying. Those who did come kept coming for the almost four years he had left, week in, week out. Ben Benjamin, himself dying from cancer; Schiffer; Asner, whom Lancaster, in his wheelchair, escorted to the door when the TV star arrived late one day from a production; Wagner, who read him the sports page; Pollack, who sat down on the edge of the big bed each time and said, "How are you doing, you bum!" The golf friends made a video of themselves goofing off on the first tee and took turns taking Susie out to dinner. His children were in and out frequently, Bill coming to watch sports on TV with his father, and Jimmy, before he married Annie Cravat in 1993, spending a lot of time at the apartment. George Burns sent bouquets of red roses. Burt's condition, he told Susie, was "too close to home" for him to visit.

In 1991 SAG presented Joanna and Susie, in his absence, with their award for both a distinguished career and a range of humanitarian activities, including the ACLU, Los Angeles Philharmonic, YMCA, YWCA, the John Wayne Cancer Foundation, CONCERN, the Los Angeles Retarded Childrens' Fund, Variety Clubs International, and "a host of other charities." Joanna recalled that evening that her father had grown up "unafraid," thanks in part to the Union Settlement House, and had spent the rest of his life "an enemy of anything that would erode the human spirit," devoted to causes that equipped others to be unafraid. "I've always seen him," she concluded, ". . . as a compassionate anarchist."

The American Museum of the Moving Image in New York presented a Burt Lancaster retrospective that same year that looked back on, now, the whole career: "Unlike . . . most of the other screen tough guys who generally toe the conservative line," read the program note written by curator Richard Koszarski, "Burt Lancaster's films frequently criticize big business, hint at government conspiracies, sympathize with Indians, convicts, and revolutionaries and generally look askance at corporate power and individual acquisitiveness—as an exemplar of screen masculinity, he is clearly unique." It was an assessment that would have pleased him.

There were last grace notes to the life. Arnold Belnick came to play the violin for his old army friend. When he had to stop and restart Fritz Kreisler's "Die Schoen Rosmarin," Lancaster hummed the complex beginning notes himself, getting them exactly right. Poitier, trying "to find a vein of discussion that would be soothing to him," talked about classical music. "His head," he recalled, "was as sharp as ever. . . . He would try to explain to me what a joy it was to have this music and his wife and you could see his eyes and the smile and the way he was listening to the music—it was almost like he was conducting it. He was at one with the music, expressing it with his body."

Ceci and James Earl Jones came to visit Lancaster for what would be the last time. Wanting to be sure he recognized her, Ceci turned to the bed just before leaving and slightly lifted her skirt. "She was wearing a short skirt as it was," said Jones. "Burt raised up in his bed and said, '*Yeah!*' like, 'I remember you and, boy, do I like what I see!' It was the first clear word he uttered without prompting or urging."

He lingered over childhood photographs with Nick's daughters, mumbling and pushing the pages back as if he were "reliving something," Marcy said, "he'd forgotten." He corrected her pronunciation of her name: "*Coo-chia!*" Lucy Kibbee came to read him favorite poems, especially Alfred Noyes's "The Highwayman." "That would break him up completely," she recalled. " 'The road was a ribbon of moonlight over the purple moor/ And the highwayman came riding—riding . . .' and all that. Burt just loved it. I'd shriek at him, 'But I shall be back with the yellow gold . . . !' before I left. I knew he really was fond of me because he would form the word 'darling' to me."

The relationship between Lancaster and Susie was a source of frank amazement to many of this inner circle. "She gave up her life for that guy," said Schaeffer. "She has the respect of everyone around who knows Burt and who lived in that situation." When she walked into a room, friends watched Lancaster's face "light up." Frustrated with his physical therapy, Lancaster yelled at her one day to get out of the way. Later, he apologized. "That takes a man," observed the therapist. In 1992, when the city was engulfed in the riots that broke out after the Rodney King trial verdict, Susie was sitting at the kitchen window, watching smoke rising into the sky three and a half miles away. Lancaster came wheeling up in his chair, put his arm around her and said, clearly, "The city was hit hard." How much he took in of all the other natural and social disasters—floods, wildfires, earthquake—that struck Los Angeles in the last years of his life was difficult to determine.

The one person who wanted, perhaps more than anyone else, to be with him was Nick. When he first heard the news of the stroke and called

Susie, he was so overcome he hung up. She became concerned that Nick's intensity of feeling would only upset Lancaster. But for the two of them the full operatic range of emotion had always been the pitch of life itself. Nick wrote Bill shortly after the stroke: "I've had the feeling that some time in your lives you've must of [*sic*] said to yourselves, What did Dad [Lancaster] ever see in Nick. At times, I wondered, too. I think we both sensed the same thing: trust, love and respect. . . . As for Dad, he's with me right now and will be until I draw my last breath. Who knows, we could still be together in the next world."

What Lancaster wanted or missed, no one, not even Susie, really knew. At the end of 1993, shortly after his eightieth birthday, Nick was diagnosed with lung cancer and died five weeks later on January 29, 1994. Remembering how distraught he had been after the death of Ben Benjamin, Susie kept the news from Burt. If he wondered where his old partner was, his memory, which only worked in brief spurts, protected him.

When Lucy Kibbee came to take Susie out for dinner one evening several months later, he came to the door in his wheelchair and took her hand and would not let go. "I knew he felt death was imminent," she recalled. On October 20, as he sat with Susie quietly in their bed, he had one last heart attack and died.

Tommy Hanneford stopped his circus at the finale for a moment of silence in Lancaster's honor. "The day I found out he died," recalls Turturro, "it was strange. I felt like . . . I fell apart. It was like a family member dying." There were the usual obituaries, career summations. The *New York Times* headlined his death: "Rugged Circus Acrobat Turned Hollywood Star Is Dead at 80," as if the career's development had stopped in 1946.

There was no funeral, no memorial service. He considered all that "bullshit." There is a grave, in Westwood Memorial Park just south of Wilshire Boulevard, with a simple slab: "Burt Lancaster, 1913–1994." A few weeks after his death the *Times* ran an article about production companies owned by actors: Jodie Foster, Clint Eastwood, Meg Ryan, Geena Davis, Tom Hanks, Tim Robbins, Robert Redford. "We are looking," pleaded one studio executive, "for actors who are serious about being producers." Michael Douglas was cited as the last actor to win a Best Picture Oscar for a film—*One Flew Over the Cuckoo's Nest*—that his company produced but in which he did not star or direct. There was no mention of Lancaster or *Marty*. Nor would there be as the next batch of lucrative independent productions captured the imagination of Hollywood as something brand-new.

The city he had once dominated moved on as he had: in the can, on to the next. And not a minute to lose.

Epitaph

Lancaster sat on top of the prickly hide of Shandra, Tommy Hanneford's best elephant. He knew about elephants from his circus days; when they lost interest, they stopped or wandered off. He could feel through his legs that Shandra was getting restless, fed up with the retakes director Lee Phillips kept calling on this unwieldy nineteenth-century circus parade scene. Standing in the sun north of Montreal the cast, crew, elephants, horses, acrobats, and clowns were antsy making *Barnum*, starring Lancaster as old P.T. himself.

He had been grousing for days with Hanneford in his trailer about this "amateur night in Dixie" production. Hanneford remembered Lancaster from 1935 when they had spent a rain-soaked season slogging along the eastern seaboard with the Gorman Bros. Circus. The tall blond New Yorker had been a little big for the bar act he did, in Hanneford's opinion—most gymnasts were little guys—but he'd been good. Not great, but good.

Now he was the seventy-two-year-old Hollywood star, the crabby veteran, but all he wanted to talk about was the circus. Over endless cups of coffee they reminisced about the acts, the performers, the animals, the remembered grit and grind of the Depression-era motorized circus. It was as if all those years spent in front of a camera were a blur compared to the reality of the sawdust trail: a town a day, two shows a day, Sundays off to wash your tights, three dollars a week, pink lemonade, elephant droppings, the ecstasy of the imagined, perfect performance.

The two men did not discuss the appropriateness of Lancaster playing Barnum, the man who may have started the whole infatuation with celebrity and the star system. Lancaster, with his penchant for highfalutin concepts, might have been taken with the idea that the span from Barnum to himself via Buntline makes for an interesting trip down the roller coaster of American entertainment and myth. As it was, he got to look at the camera this time and say: "That's what I invented, the audience. I invented *you*."

The megastar in him had no problem playing the chancer who understood once and for all that the American audience only wants to see what it has never seen before. In this country of inner and outer frontiers, perfection without novelty is no attraction.

For the umpteenth retake, Shandra led the squeaking, clanking horse-drawn wagons of the circus parade down the hill of the historically correct Earle Moore Canadiana Village that, for the purposes of *Barnum*, was nine-teenth-century Bridgeport. Each time the director called "Cut!" the whole lumbering troupe had to turn slowly around, go back up the hill, turn around and head down one more time. Some of the gaudy old circus wagons had no brakes to speak of. The ninety-odd cast members and Han-neford circus performers knew Lancaster well enough by now to know he was fuming.

The parade was about halfway down the hill when Phillips called "Cut!" again. People, animals, wagons halted, again. There was a quick, frozen silence—"you could hear a pin drop," recalled Hanneford—before Lancaster leaned over Shandra's head and called down to the director, "Why'd you call 'cut' *that* time?" Phillips pointed to the sky where a cloud was just heading into the sun, blocking the light. "The sun," he said. Lancaster squinted at the sky, drew himself up, and from the top of the elephant bellowed back down, "Fuck the sun! *Roll 'em!*"

The group fanned out behind Lancaster exploded. "You never heard," said Gary Parkins, executive director of the Royal Hanneford Circus, "such a laugh in your life."

Only a god could get away with cursing the sun. Or an American movie star.

Filmography

(in order of release and all including Lancaster, except as indicated)

THE KILLERS (1946, 105 min., Universal-International)
Producer: Mark Hellinger; Director: Robert Siodmak; Screenplay: Anthony Veiller and John Huston (uncredited), from the short story by Ernest Hemingway; with Ava Gardner, Edmond O'Brien, Albert Dekker, Sam Levene, Jeff Corey.

BRUTE FORCE (1947, 96 min., Universal-International)
Producer: Mark Hellinger; Director: Jules Dassin; Screenplay: Richard Brooks, from the story by Robert Patterson; with Hume Cronyn, Charles Bickford, Yvonne De Carlo, Ann Blyth, Sam Levene, Howard Duff, Jeff Corey.

DESERT FURY (1947, 96 min., Paramount)
Producer: Hal B. Wallis; Director: Lewis Allen; Screenplay: Robert Rossen, from the novel *Desert Town* by Ramona Stewart; with John Hodiak, Lizabeth Scott, Wendell Corey, Mary Astor.

VARIETY GIRL (1947, 83 min., Paramount)
Producer: Daniel Dare; Director: George Marshall; Screenplay: Edmund Hartmann, Frank Tashlin, Robert Welch, and Monte Brice; with Olga San Juan, Mary Hatcher, DeForest Kelley, William Demarest; Paramount "guest stars," with Lancaster, included: Bob Hope, Bing Crosby, William Holden, Lizabeth Scott, Robert Preston, Veronica Lake.

I WALK ALONE (1947, 98 min., Paramount)
Producer: Hal B. Wallis; Director: Byron Haskin; Screenplay: Charles Schnee, from the play *Beggars Are Coming to Town* by Theodore Reeves, adapted by Robert Smith and John Bright; with Lizabeth Scott, Kirk Douglas, Wendell Corey, Mickey Knox.

ALL MY SONS (1948, 94 min., Universal-International)
Producer: Charles Erskine; Director: Irving Reis; Screenplay: Charles Erskine, from

the play by Arthur Miller; with Edward G. Robinson, Mady Christians, Luisa Horton, Howard Duff, Frank Conroy, Arlene Francis.

SORRY, WRONG NUMBER (1948, 89 min., Paramount)
Producer: Hal B. Wallis and Anatole Litvak; Director: Anatole Litvak; Screenplay: Lucille Fletcher, from her radio play; with Barbara Stanwyck, Ann Richards, Wendell Corey, Ed Begley, Lief Erickson, William Conrad, Mickey Knox.

KISS THE BLOOD OFF MY HANDS (1948, 80 min., Universal-International)
Producer: Richard Vernon, Harold Hecht-Norma Productions; Director: Norman Foster; Screenplay: Leonardo Bercovicci, from the novel by Gerald Butler, adapted by Ben Maddow and Walter Bernstein; with Joan Fontaine, Robert Newton, Lewis Russell.

CRISS CROSS (1949, 87 min., Universal-International)
Producer: Michel Kraike; Director: Robert Siodmak; Screenplay: Daniel Fuchs, from the novel by Don Tracy; with Yvonne De Carlo, Dan Duryea, Stephen McNally, Richard Long, Anthony "Tony" Curtis.

ROPE OF SAND (1949, 105 min., Paramount)
Producer: Hal B. Wallis; Director: William Dieterle; Screenplay: Walter Doniger; with Paul Henried, Claude Rains, Corinne Calvet, Peter Lorre, Sam Jaffe.

THE FLAME AND THE ARROW (1950, 88 min., Warner Bros.)
Producer: Harold Hecht and Frank Ross, A Norma F.R. Production; Director: Jacques Tourneur; Screenplay: Waldo Salt; with Virginia Mayo, Robert Douglas, Aline MacMahon, Frank Allenby, Nick Cravat.

MISTER 880 (1950, 90 min., 20th Century-Fox)
Producer: Julian Blaustein; Director: Edmund Goulding; Screenplay: Robert Riskin, from the *New Yorker* story by St. Clair McKelway; with Dorothy McGuire; Edmund Gwenn, Millard Mitchell, Howard St. John.

VENGEANCE VALLEY (1951, 82 min., MGM)
Producer: Nicholas Nayfack; Director: Richard Thorpe; Screenplay: Irving Ravetch, from the novel by Luke Short; with Robert Walker, Joanne Dru, Sally Forrest, John Ireland, Carleton Carpenter, Ray Collins, Hugh O'Brien.

JIM THORPE—ALL AMERICAN (1951, 105 min., Warner Bros.)
Producer: Everett Freeman; Director: Michael Curtiz; Screenplay: Douglas Morrow and Everett Freeman, screen story by Morrow and Vincent X. Flaherty from the autobiography by Russell J. Birdwell with Jim Thorpe; with Charles Bickford, Phyllis Thaxter, Steve Cochran, Dick Wesson, Jack Big Head, Suni Warcloud.

TEN TALL MEN (1951, 97 min., Columbia)
Producer: Harold Hecht, A Norma Production; Director: Willis Goldbeck; Screenplay: Roland Kibbee and Frank Davis from a story by Goldbeck and James Warner Bellah; with Jody Lawrance, Gilbert Roland, Kieron Moore, George Tobias, Mari Blanchard.

THE CRIMSON PIRATE (1952, 104 min., Warner Bros.)
Producer: Harold Hecht, A Norma Production; Director: Robert Siodmak; Screenplay: Roland Kibbee; with Eva Bartok, Nick Cravat, Leslie Bradley, Torin Thatcher, Noel Purcell, Margo Grahame.

COME BACK, LITTLE SHEBA (1952, 99 min., Paramount)
Producer: Hal B. Wallis; Director: Daniel Mann; Screenplay: Ketti Frings, from the play by William Inge; with Shirley Booth, Terry Moore, Richard Jaeckel, Philip Ober.

SOUTH SEA WOMAN (1953, 99 min., Warner Bros.)
Producer: Sam Bischoff; Director: Arthur Lubin; Screenplay: Edwin Blum, from the play *General Court Marshal* by William M. Rankin; with Virginia Mayo, Chuck Connors, Arthur Shields, Veola Vonn.

FROM HERE TO ETERNITY (1953, 118 min., Columbia)
Producer: Buddy Adler; Director: Fred Zinnemann; Screenplay: Daniel Taradash, from the novel by James Jones; with Montgomery Clift, Deborah Kerr, Donna Reed, Frank Sinatra, Philip Ober, Ernest Borgnine, Jack Warden, Mickey Shaughnessy.

THREE SAILORS AND A GIRL (1953, 95 min., Warner Bros.)
Producer: Sammy Cahn; Director: Roy Del Ruth; Screenplay: Roland Kibbee and Devery Freeman, from the play *The Butter and Egg Man* by George S. Kaufman; with Jane Powell, Gordon MacRae, Gene Nelson, Sam Levene, Jack E. Leonard.

HIS MAJESTY O'KEEFE (1954, 90 min., Warner Bros.)
Producer: Harold Hecht, A Norma Production; Director: Byron Haskin; Screenplay: Borden Chase and James Hill, from the novel by Lawrence Kingman and Gerald Green; with Joan Rice, Andre Morrell, Abraham Sofaer, Archie Savage, Benson Fong, Tessa Prendergast, Lloyd Berrell, Charles Horvath.

APACHE (1954, 91 min., United Artists)
Producer: Harold Hecht, A Hecht-Lancaster Production; Director: Robert Aldrich; Screenplay: James R. Webb, from the novel *Broncho Apache* by Paul I. Wellman; with Jean Peters, John McIntire, Charles Buchinsky [Bronson], John Dehner, Paul Guilfoyle, Monte Blue.

VERA CRUZ (1954, 94 min., United Artists)
Producer: James Hill, A Hecht-Lancaster Production; Director: Robert Aldrich; Screenplay: Roland Kibbee and James R. Webb, from a story by Borden Chase; with

Gary Cooper, Denise Darcel, Cesar Romero, Sarita Montiel, Ernest Borgnine, Charles Buchinsky [Bronson], Jack Elam.

THE KENTUCKIAN (1955, 104 min., United Artists)
Producer: Harold Hecht, A Hecht-Lancaster Production; Director: Burt Lancaster; Screenplay: A.B. Guthrie Jr., from the novel *The Gabriel Horn* by Felix Holt; with Diana Lynn, Dianne Foster, John McIntire, Una Merkel, John Carradine, Walter Matthau, Donald MacDonald.

THE ROSE TATTOO (1955, 117 min., Paramount)
Producer: Hal B. Wallis; Director: Daniel Mann; Screenplay: Tennessee Williams, from his play, adapted by Hal Kanter; with Anna Magnani, Marisa Pavan, Ben Cooper, Virginia Grey, Jo Van Fleet, Sandro Giglio.

TRAPEZE (1956, 105 min., United Artists)
Producer: James Hill, A Hecht-Lancaster Production; Director: Carol Reed; Screenplay: James R. Webb, from the novel *The Killing Frost* by Max Catto, adaptation by Liam O'Brien and uncredited rewrites by Wolf Mankowitz; with Tony Curtis, Gina Lollobrigida, Katy Jurado, Thomas Gomez, Johnny Puleo, Minor Watson.

THE RAINMAKER (1956, 121 min., Paramount)
Producer: Hal B. Wallis; Director: Joseph Anthony; Screenplay: N. Richard Nash, from his play; with Katharine Hepburn, Wendell Corey, Lloyd Bridges, Earl Holliman, Cameron Prud'homme.

GUNFIGHT AT THE O.K. CORRAL (1957, 122 min., Paramount)
Producer: Hal B. Wallis; Director: John Sturges; Screenplay: Leon Uris, from the story *The Killer* by George Schullin; with Kirk Douglas, Rhonda Fleming, Jo Van Fleet, John Ireland, Frank Faylen, Earl Holliman, Lyle Bettger, Ted De Corsia, Dennis Hopper.

SWEET SMELL OF SUCCESS (1957, 96 min., United Artists)
Producer: James Hill, A Hecht-Hill-Lancaster Production; Director: Alexander Mackendrick; Screenplay: Clifford Odets and Ernest Lehman; with Tony Curtis, Susan Harrison, Martin Milner, Sam Levene, Barbara Nichols, Jeff Donnell, Edith Atwater, Emile Meyer, Joe Frisco.

RUN SILENT, RUN DEEP (1958, 93 min., United Artists)
Producer: Harold Hecht, A Hecht-Hill-Lancaster Production; Director: Robert Wise; Screenplay: John Gay, from the novel by Edward L. Beach; with Clark Gable, Jack Warden, Brad Dexter, Don Rickles, Nick Cravat.

SEPARATE TABLES (1958, 98 min., United Artists)
Producer: Harold Hecht, A Hecht-Hill-Lancaster Production; Director: Delbert Mann; Screenplay: Terrence Rattigan and John Gay, from the play by Rattigan; with

Rita Hayworth, Deborah Kerr, David Niven, Wendy Hiller, Gladys Cooper, Cathleen Nesbitt, Felix Aylmer, Rod Taylor.

THE DEVIL'S DISCIPLE (1959, 82 min., United Artists)
Producer: Harold Hecht, Hecht-Hill-Lancaster Films Limited and Brynaprod, S.A.; Director: Guy Hamilton; Screenplay: John Dighton and Roland Kibbee, from the play by George Bernard Shaw; with Kirk Douglas, Laurence Olivier, Eva LeGallienne, Harry Andrews, Basil Sydney, George Rose, Janette Scott, Neil McCallum.

THE UNFORGIVEN (1960, 125 min., United Artists)
Producer: James Hill, A Hecht-Hill-Lancaster Production; Director: John Huston; Screenplay: Ben Maddow, from the novel by Alan LeMay; with Audrey Hepburn, Audie Murphy, Lillian Gish, John Saxon, Charles Bickford, Albert Salmi, Joseph Wiseman, Doug McClure, June Walker.

ELMER GANTRY (1960, 146 min., United Artists)
Producer: Bernard Smith, Elmer Gantry Productions; Director: Richard Brooks; Screenplay: Richard Brooks, from the novel by Sinclair Lewis; with Jean Simmons, Arthur Kennedy, Shirley Jones, Dean Jagger, Patti Page, Edward Andrews, John McIntire.

THE YOUNG SAVAGES (1961, 103 min., United Artists)
Producer: Pat Duggan, A Contemporary Production; Director: John Frankenheimer; Screenplay: Edward Anhalt and J.P. Miller, from the novel *A Matter of Conviction* by Evan Hunter; with Dina Merrill, Shelley Winters, Edward Andrews, Telly Savalas.

JUDGMENT AT NUREMBERG (1961, 190 min., United Artists)
Producer and Director: Stanley Kramer, Roxlom Productions; Screenplay: Abby Mann, from his teleplay; with Spencer Tracy, Richard Widmark, Marlene Dietrich, Maximilian Schell, Judy Garland, Montgomery Clift, Werner Klemperer, William Shatner.

BIRDMAN OF ALCATRAZ (1962, 147 min., United Artists)
Producer: Stuart Miller and Guy Trosper, A Norma Production; Director: John Frankenheimer; Screenplay: Guy Trosper, from the book by Thomas E. Gaddis; with Karl Malden, Thelma Ritter, Betty Field, Neville Brand, Edmond O'Brien, Telly Savalas, Whit Bissell.

A CHILD IS WAITING (1963, 104 min., United Artists)
Producer: Stanley Kramer; Director: John Cassavetes; Screenplay: Abby Mann, from his teleplay; with Judy Garland, Gena Rowlands, Steven Hill, Bruce Ritchey, Gloria McGehee, Paul Stewart, Lawrence Tiernay, Elizabeth Wilson.

THE LIST OF ADRIAN MESSENGER (1963, 98 min., Universal-International)
Producer: Edward Lewis, A Joel Production; Director: John Huston; Screenplay: Anthony Veiller, from the novel by Philip MacDonald; with George C. Scott, Kirk

Douglas, Clive Brook, Dana Wynter, Gladys Cooper, Herbert Marshall, John Merivale, and cameos by Tony Curtis, Robert Mitchum, Frank Sinatra.

THE LEOPARD (IL GATTOPARDO) (1963, 205 min. [Italian version], 165 min. [American version], 20th Century-Fox/Titanus/SNPC/GPC)
Producer: Goffredo Lombardo; Director: Luchino Visconti; Screenplay: Suso Cecchi D'Amico, Pasquale Festa Campanile, Massimo Franciosa, Enrico Medioli, and Luchino Visconti, from the novel by Giuseppe de Lampedusa; with Claudia Cardinale, Alain Delon, Paolo Stoppa, Mario Girotti, Pierro Clementi, Rina Morelli, Romolo Valli, Lucilla Morlacchi, Serge Reggiani, Leslie French, Ivo Garranti.

SEVEN DAYS IN MAY (1964, 120 min., Paramount)
Producer: Edward Lewis, A Seven Arts-Joel Production; Director: John Frankenheimer; Screenplay: Rod Serling, from the novel by Fletcher Knebel and Charles W. Bailey II; with Kirk Douglas, Frederic March, Ava Gardner, Edmond O'Brien, Martin Balsam, George Macready, Whit Bissell, Hugh Marlowe, Andrew Duggan, Christopher Todd, John Houseman.

THE TRAIN (1964, 140 min., United Artists)
Producer: Jules Bricken, An Ariane/Dear Production; Director: John Frankenheimer; Screenplay: Franklin Coen and Frank Davis, from the book *Le Front de l'Art* by Rose Valland; with Paul Scofield, Jeanne Moreau, Michel Simon, Suzanne Flon.

THE HALLELUJAH TRAIL (1965, 167 min., United Artists)
Producer and Director: John Sturges, A Mirisch/Kappa Production; Screenplay: John Gay, from the novel by Bill Gulick; with Lee Remick, Jim Hutton, Pamela Tiffin, Donald Pleasance, Brian Keith, Martin Landau, John Anderson, Tom Stern, Whit Bissell.

THE PROFESSIONALS (1966, 117 min., Columbia)
Producer and Director: Richard Brooks, Pax Enterprises; Screenplay: Richard Brooks, from the novel *A Mule for the Marquesa* by Frank O'Rourke; with Lee Marvin, Robert Ryan, Claudia Cardinale, Jack Palance, Ralph Bellamy, Woody Strode.

THE SCALPHUNTERS (1968, 102 min., United Artists)
Producer: Jules Levy, Arthur Gardner, Arnold Laven and Roland Kibbee, A Bristol/Norlan Production; Director: Sydney Pollack; Screenplay: William Norton; with Shelley Winters, Telly Savalas, Ossie Davis, Dabney Coleman, Nick Cravat.

THE SWIMMER (1968, 94 min., Columbia)
Producer: Frank Perry and Roger Lewis, Horizon Pictures; Director: Frank Perry (and Sydney Pollack); Screenplay: Eleanor Perry from the short story by John Cheever; with Janice Rule, Janet Landgard, Marge Champion, Nancy Cushman, Bill Flore, John Garfield Jr., Kim Hunter, Diana Muldaur, Joan Rivers, Cornelia Otis Skinner.

CASTLE KEEP (1969, 106 min., Columbia)
Producer: Martin Ransohoff and John Calley, Filmways; Director: Sydney Pollack; Screenplay: Daniel Taradash and David Rayfiel, from the novel by William Eastlake; with Patrick O'Neal, Jean-Pierre Aumont, Astrid Heeren, Peter Falk, Scott Wilson, Tony Bill, Al Freeman Jr., Bruce Dern, Michael Conrad, James Patterson.

THE GYPSY MOTHS (1969, 110 min., MGM)
Producer: Hal Landers and Bobby Roberts, A Frankenheimer/Lewis Production; Director: John Frankenheimer; Screenplay: William Hanley, from the novel by James Drought; with Deborah Kerr, Gene Hackman, Scott Wilson, Sheree North, William Windom, Bonnie Bedelia.

AIRPORT (1970, 136 min., Universal)
Producer: Jacque Mapes, A Ross Hunter Production; Director: George Seaton; Screenplay: George Seaton, from the novel by Arthur Hailey; with Dean Martin, Jacqueline Bisset, Jean Seberg, George Kennedy, Helen Hayes, Van Heflin, Maureen Stapleton, Barry Nelson, Dana Wynter, Barbara Hale, Lloyd Nolan.

VALDEZ IS COMING (1971, 90 min., United Artists)
Producer: Ira Steiner, A Norlan/Ira Steiner Production; Director: Edwin Sherin; Screenplay: Roland Kibbee and David Rayfiel, from the novel by Elmore Leonard; with Susan Clark, Jon Cypher, Barton Heyman, Richard Jordan, Frank Silvera.

LAWMAN (1971, 99 min., United Artists)
Producer and Director: Michael Winner, A Scimitar Films Production; Screenplay: Gerald Wilson; with Robert Ryan, Lee J. Cobb, Sheree North, Joseph Wiseman, Robert Duvall, Albert Salmi.

ULZANA'S RAID (1972, 103 min., Universal)
Producer: Carter DeHaven, A Carter DeHaven-Robert Aldrich Production; Director: Robert Aldrich; Screenplay: Alan Sharp; with Bruce Davison, Jorge Luke, Richard Jaeckel, Joaquin Martinez, Lloyd Bochner, Karl Swenson.

SCORPIO (1973, 114 min., United Artists)
Producer: Walter Mirisch, A Scimitar/Mirisch Production; Director: Michael Winner; Screenplay: David W. Rintels and Gerald Wilson, from the story by Rintels; with Alain Delon, Paul Scofield, John Colicos, Gayle Hunnicutt, J.D. Canon.

EXECUTIVE ACTION (1973, 91 min., National General Pictures)
Producer: Edward Lewis, An Edward Lewis Production; Director: David Miller; Screenplay: Dalton Trumbo, from the story by Mark Lane and Donald Freed; with Robert Ryan, Will Geer, Gilbert Green, John Anderson, Paul Carr, Colby Chester, Ed Lauter.

THE MIDNIGHT MAN (1974, 117 min., Universal)
Produced, directed, and written by Burt Lancaster and Roland Kibbee, A Norlan

Production, from the novel *The Midnight Lady and the Mourning Man* by David Anthony; with Susan Clark, Cameron Mitchell, Morgan Woodward, Harris Yulin, Robert Quarry, Catherine Bach, William Lancaster, Nick Cravat.

CONVERSATION PIECE (GRUPPO DI FAMIGLIA IN UN INTERNO) (1975, 119 min., Cinema 5)
Producer: Giovanni Bertolucci, Rusconi Film and Gaumont International SARL; Director: Luchino Visconti; Screenplay: Luchino Visconti, Suso Cecchi D'Amico, and Enrico Medioli; with Silvana Mangano, Helmut Berger, Claudia Marsani, Stefano Patrizi, Elvira Cortese, Dominique Sanda, Claudia Cardinale.

1900 (NOVECENTO) (1976, 320 min. [original length shown at 1976 Cannes Film Festival], 310 min. [European release], and 243 min. [print shown at New York Film Festival, 1977, American release], Paramount)
Producer: Alberto Grimaldi, PEA Artistes Associés/Artemis Production; Director: Bernardo Bertolucci; Screenplay: Bernardo Bertolucci, Franco Arcalli, and Giuseppe Bertolucci; with Robert De Niro, Gérard Depardieu, Dominique Sanda, Donald Sutherland, Sterling Hayden.

BUFFALO BILL AND THE INDIANS, OR SITTING BULL'S HISTORY LESSON (1976, 123 min., United Artists)
Producer and Director: Robert Altman, A Dino De Laurentiis Production; Screenplay: Alan Rudolph and Robert Altman, from the play *Indians* by Arthur Kopit; with Paul Newman, Joel Grey, Geraldine Chaplin, Kevin McCarthy, Harvey Keitel, Denver Pyle, John Considine, Pat McCormick, Shelley Duvall, Will Sampson.

THE CASSANDRA CROSSING (1977, 129 min., Avco Embassy Pictures)
Producer: Carlo Ponti and Lew Grade, An Associated General and International Film; Director: George Pan Cosmatos; Screenplay: Robert Katz and George Pan Cosmatos with Tom Mankiewicz; with Sophia Loren, Richard Harris, Ava Gardner, Lee Strasberg, Martin Sheen, Ingrid Thulin, John Phillip Law, Ann Turkel, O.J. Simpson, Lionel Stander.

TWILIGHT'S LAST GLEAMING (1977, 146 min., Allied Artists)
Producer: Merv Adelson, A Lorimar-Bavaria Production; Director: Robert Aldrich; Screenplay: Ronald M. Cohen and Edward Huebsch, from the novel *Viper Three* by Walter Wager; with Richard Widmark, Charles Durning, Melvyn Douglas, Joseph Cotten, Paul Winfield, Burt Young.

THE ISLAND OF DR. MOREAU (1977, 98 min., American International Pictures)
Producer: John Temple-Smith and Skip Steloff, A Cinema 77 Film; Director: Don Taylor; Screenplay: John Herman Shaner and Al Ramrus, from the novel by H.G. Wells; with Michael York, Barbara Carrera, Nigel Davenport, Richard Basehart, Nick Cravat.

GO TELL THE SPARTANS (1978, 114 min., Avco Embassy Pictures)
Producer: Allan F. Bodah and Mitchell Cannold, A Spartan Production/Mar

Vista Productions; Director: Ted Post; Screenplay: Wendell Mayes, from the novel *Incident at Muc Wa* by Daniel Ford; with Craig Wasson, Marc Singer, Jonathan Goldsmith, Joe Unger, Dennis Howard, David Clennon, Evan Kim, John Megna, Dolph Sweet.

ZULU DAWN (1979, 117 min., American Cinema)
Producer: Nate Kohn, A Lamitas Presentation of a Samarkand Production; Director: Douglas Hickox; Screenplay: Cy Endfield and Anthony Sorey; with Peter O'Toole, Simon Ward, Nigel Davenport, Michael Jayston, Denholm Elliott, John Mills, Bob Hoskins.

CATTLE ANNIE AND LITTLE BRITCHES (1981, 95 min., Universal)
Producer: Rupert Hitzig and Alan King, A Hemdale Production; Director: Lamont Johnson; Screenplay: Robert Ward and David Eyre, from the novel by Ward; with Diane Lane, Amanda Plummer, Rod Steiger, John Savage, Scott Glenn.

ATLANTIC CITY (1981, 105 min., Paramount)
Producer: Denis Heroux, An International Cinema Corporation/Selta Films Production; Director: Louis Malle; Screenplay: John Guare; with Susan Sarandon, Kate Reid, Robert Joy, Hollis McLaren, Michel Piccoli, Robert Goulet, Wallace Shawn, Adele Chatfield-Taylor.

LA PELLE (THE SKIN) (1981, 131 min., Gaumont Productions)
Producer: Renzo Rosselini, Opera Film Produzione; Director: Liliana Cavani; Screenplay: Liliana Cavani and Robert Katz, from the novel by Curzio Malaparte; with Claudia Cardinale, Marcello Mastroianni, Ken Marshall, Alexandra King.

LOCAL HERO (1983, 111 min., Warner Bros.)
Producer: David Puttnam, An Enigma Production for Goldcrest; Directed and written by Bill Forsyth; with Peter Riegert, Denis Lawson, Fulton Mackay, Jenny Seagrove, Peter Capaldi.

THE OSTERMAN WEEKEND (1983, 105 min., 20th Century-Fox)
Producer: Peter S. Davis and William N. Panzer, A Panzer-Davis Production; Director: Sam Peckinpah; Screenplay: Alan Sharp, from the novel by Robert Ludlum; with Rutger Hauer, John Hurt, Craig T. Nelson, Dennis Hopper, Chris Sarandon, Meg Foster, Helen Shaver, Cassie Yates.

LITTLE TREASURE (1985, 95 min., A Vista Films/Herb Jaffe Production)
Producer: Herb Jaffe, Tri-Star Pictures (Executive Producer: Joanna Lancaster and Richard Wagner); Director: Alan Sharp; Screenplay: Alan Sharp; with Margot Kidder, Ted Danson, Norman Kane, Malena Doria, John Pearce.

TOUGH GUYS (1986, 104 min., Buena Vista)
Producer: Joe Wizan, Touchstone Pictures/Silver Screen Partner II/Bryna; Director:

Jeff Kanew; Screenplay: James Orr and Jim Cruickshank; with Kirk Douglas, Eli Wallach, Charles Durning, Dana Carvey, Alexis Smith, Darlanne Fluegel.

ROCKET GIBRALTAR (1988, 100 min., Columbia)
Producer: Jeff Weiss, An Ulick Mayo Weiss Production; Director: Daniel Petrie; Screenplay: Amos Poe; with Suzy Amis, Patricia Clarkson, Frances Conroy, Sinead Cusack, John Glover, Bill Pullman, Kevin Spacey, Macauley Culkin, George Martin.

FIELD OF DREAMS (1989, 106 min., Universal)
Producer: Lawrence Gordon and Charles Gordon, Guild/Carolco; Directed and written by Phil Alden Robinson, from the novel *Shoeless Joe* by W.P. Kinsella; with Kevin Costner, Amy Madigan, James Earl Jones, Ray Liotta, Timothy Busfield.

Hecht-Lancaster/Hecht-Hill-Lancaster Films without Lancaster in the Cast

THE FIRST TIME (1952, 89 min., Columbia)
Producer: Harold Hecht, A Hecht-Norma Production; Director: Frank Tashlin; Screenplay: Jean Rouveral, Hugo Butler, Frank Tashlin, and Dane Lussier, from a story by Rouveral and Butler; with Barbara Hale, Robert Cummings, Jeff Donnell, Mona Berrie, Cora Witherspoon.

MARTY (1955, 91 min., United Artists)
Producer: Harold Hecht, A Hecht-Lancaster Production; Director: Delbert Mann; Screenplay: Paddy Chayefsky, from his teleplay; with Ernest Borgnine, Betsy Blair, Joe Mantell, Joe de Santis, Esther Minciotti, Augusta Ciolli, Karen Steele, Jerry Paris, Frank Sutton.

THE BACHELOR PARTY (1957, 93 min., United Artists)
Producer: Harold Hecht, A Hecht-Lancaster Production; Director: Delbert Mann; Screenplay: Paddy Chayefsky, from his teleplay; with Don Murray, Carolyn Jones, E.G. Marshall, Jack Warden, Philip Abbott, Nancy Marchand, Larry Blyden.

CRY TOUGH (1959, 84 min., United Artists)
Producer: Harry Kleiner, A Hecht-Hill-Lancaster Production; Director: Paul Stanley; Screenplay: Harry Kleiner, from the novel by Irving Schulman; with John Saxon, Linda Cristal, Joseph Calleia, Arthur Batanides, Paul Clarke, Joe de Santis.

THE RABBIT TRAP (1959, 72 min., United Artists)
Producer: Harry Kleiner, A Hecht-Hill-Lancaster Production; Director: Philip Leacock; Screenplay: J.P. Miller, from his teleplay; with Ernest Borgnine, David Brian, Bethel Leslie, Kevin Corcoran, June Blair, Jeanette Nolan, Don Rickles.

TAKE A GIANT STEP (1960, 100 min., United Artists)
Producer: Julius Epstein, A Hecht-Hill-Lancaster Production; Director: Philip Leacock; Screenplay: Julius Epstein and Louis S. Peterson, from the play by Peterson; with Johnny Nash, Estelle Hemsley, Ruby Dee, Frederick O'Neal, Beah Richards.

SEASON OF PASSION (1961, 93 min., United Artists)
Producer and Director: Leslie Norman, A Hecht-Hill-Lancaster Production; Screenplay: John Dighton, from the play *The Summer of the Seventeenth Doll* by Ray Lawler; with Ernest Borgnine, Anne Baxter, John Mills, Angela Lansbury, Vincent Ball, Ethel Gabriel.

Television: Movies and Miniseries

MOSES, THE LAWGIVER (June 21, 28; July 5, 12, 16; August 2, 1975; six-hour television format [theatrical/video release: 141 min.]; CBS-TV)
Producer: Vincenzo Labella, An RAI/ITC Co. Production; Director: Gianfranco De Bosio; Teleplay: Anthony Burgess, Vittorio Bonicalle, and Gianfranco De Bosio; with William Lancaster, Anthony Quale, Irene Papas, Ingrid Thulin.

VICTORY AT ENTEBBE (December 13, 1976, 119 min., Warner Bros./ABC-TV)
Producer: Robert Guenette, A David L. Wolper Production; Director: Marvin J. Chomsky; Teleplay: Ernest Kinoy; with Anthony Hopkins, Richard Dreyfuss, Helen Hayes, Linda Blair, Elizabeth Taylor, Kirk Douglas, Harris Yulin, Helmut Berger.

MARCO POLO (May 16–19, 1982, ten-hour television miniseries format, NBC-TV)
Producer: Vincenzo Labella, An RAI Production; Director: Guiliano Montaldo; Teleplay: Guiliano Montaldo, Vincenzo Labella, and David Butler; with Ken Marshall, Denholm Elliott, Tony Vogel, Anne Bancroft, John Gielgud, John Houseman.

SCANDAL SHEET (January 21, 1985, two-hour television format, ABC-TV)
Producer: Roger Birnbaum, A Fair Dinkum Production; Director: David Lowell Rich; Teleplay: Howard Rodman; with Pamela Reed, Lauren Hutton, Robert Urich, Max Wright, Peter Jurasik.

ON WINGS OF EAGLES (May 18, 19, 1986, 225 min. [two-part, five-hour miniseries], NBC-TV)
Producer: Lyn Raynor, An Edgar J. Scherick/Taft Entertainment Production; Director: Andrew V. McLaglen; Teleplay: Sam Rolfe, from the book by Ken Follett; with Richard Crenna, Paul LeMat, Esai Morales, Louis Giambalvo, Jim Metzler.

BARNUM (November 30, 1986, 93 min. [two-hour television format], CBS-TV).
Producer: David J. Patterson, A Robert Halmi, Inc. Production; Director: Lee Phillips; Teleplay: Michael Norell; with Hanna Schygulla, Laura Press, John Roney.

CONTROL (February 14, 1987, 90 min., Cristaldi Films)
Producer: Franco Cristaldi, Alliance Entertainment Corp./Les Films Ariane; Director: Guiliano Montaldo; Teleplay: Brian Moore, Piero Angela, Guilano Montaldo, and Jeremy Hale, from the story by Angela; with Kate Nelligan, Ben Gazzara, Kate Reid, Erland Josephson.

SINS OF THE FATHERS (July 10, 11, 1988, four-hour television format [American debut on Showtime]; 1986, seven-hour format [European release])

Producer: Jorn Schroder and Helmut Krapp, A Bavaria Atelier Production/Bernhard Sinkel Film; Directed and written by Bernhard Sinkel; with Julie Christie, Tina Engel, Bruno Ganz.

THE JEWELER'S SHOP (1989, 90 min.)
Producer: Mario Bregni, PAC/RAI/Alliance Entertainment/IMP; Director: Michael Anderson; Teleplay: Mario de Nardi and Jeff Andrews, from the play by Karol Wojtyla; with Daniel Olbrychski, Ben Cross, Olivia Hussey.

I PROMESSI SPOSI (THE BETROTHED) (November 12, 19, 26; December 3, 10, 1989 [Italy]; five-hour television format)
Executive Producer: Alessandro Calosci and Anna Maria Denza, RAI/UNO/Hermes Film, Bayerischer Rundfunk Gevest Holding B.V./RTV Ljubljana; Director: Salvatore Nocita; Teleplay: Enrico Medioli, Roberta Mazzoni, with assistance of Salvatore Nocita and Pier Emilio Gennarini, from the novel by Alessandro Manzoni; with Helmut Berger, Gary Cady, Mathieu Carriere, Valentina Cortese, Delphine Forest, Danny Quinn, Fernando Rey, Jenny Seagrove, Gisela Steinn, Franco Nero, Alberto Sordi, F. Murray Abraham.

THE PHANTOM OF THE OPERA (March 18, 19, 1990, four-hour television format, NBC-TV)
Executive Producer: Edgar J. Scherick and Haim Saban, Saban Schenck Productions; Director: Tony Richardson; Teleplay: Arthur Kopit, from the novel by Gaston Leroux; with Charles Dance, Teri Polo, Ian Richardson, Adam Storke.

VOYAGE OF TERROR: THE ACHILLE LAURO AFFAIR (May 1, 2, 1990, four-hour television format, Tribune Entertainment)
Executive Producer: Mario Gallo, Fabrizio Castellani, Beta Taurus Group/filmpha Productions/T-F 1; Director: Alberto Negrin; Teleplay: Sergio Donati and Alberto Negrin; with Eva Marie Saint, Robert Culp, Dominique Sanda, Gabrielle Ferzetti, Adriana Innocenti, Said Amadis, Brian Bloom, Jochen Horst, Rebecca Schaeffer.

SEPARATE BUT EQUAL (April 7, 8, 19, 1991, four-hour television format, ABC-TV)
Executive Producer: George Stevens Jr. and Stan Marguilies, New Liberty Production/Republic Pictures Television; Director: George Stevens Jr.; Teleplay: George Stevens Jr.; with Sidney Poitier, Richard Kiley, Clevon Little, Gloria Foster, John McMartin, Graham Beckel, Ed Hall, Lynne Thigpen, Macon McCalman, Cheryl Alynn Bruce, Hallie Foote.

Theater

A SOUND OF HUNTING (Opening date: November 20, 1945, Lyceum Theater, New York, twenty-three performances)
Producer: Irving Jacobs; Director: Anthony Brown; Play: Harry Brown; with Sam Levene, Frank Lovejoy, Carl Frank, George Tyne, Bruce Evans.

KNICKERBOCKER HOLIDAY (Opening date: May 11, 1971, Curran Theater, San Francisco, seven weeks; Dorothy Chandler Pavilion, Los Angeles, eight weeks)
Producer: San Francisco Light Opera Company; General Producer: Edwin Lester; Director: Albert Marre; Music: Kurt Weill; Book and Lyrics: Maxwell Anderson; with Anita Gillette, David Holliday, Jack Collins, Dale Malone, Eric Brotherson.

THE BOYS OF AUTUMN (Opening date: September 3, 1981, Marines Memorial Theater, San Francisco, four weeks)
Producer: James McKenzie, George Stevens Jr., and the John F. Kennedy Center for the Performing Arts; Director: Tom Moore; Play: Bernard Sabath; with Kirk Douglas.

Notes

List of Abbreviations

AFI	American Film Institute
AMPAS	Margaret Herrick Library, Academy of Motion Picture Arts and Sciences
BL FBI	Federal Bureau of Investigation compilation of "see-references" concerning Lancaster, a majority of which were originally in the FBI file titled COMPIC (Communist Infiltration of the Motion Picture Industry); the FBI kept no single file on Lancaster. Collected at author's request under the Freedom of Information Act with the assistance of U.S. Representative Neil Abercrombie (D-HI); a copy of the compilation has been given by the author to the School of Cinema-Television, University of Southern California.
BL PASS	Burt Lancaster Passport File, U.S. Department of State, obtained under the Freedom of Information Act. A copy is filed with the BL FBI materials (see above) in the School of Cinema-Television, University of Southern California.
CMC USC	Constance McCormick Collection, School of Cinema-Television, University of Southern California.
FSC MOMA	The Celeste Bartos International Film Study Center, The Museum of Modern Art
HWC AMPAS	Hal Wallis Collection, AMPAS
MHC USC	Mark Hellinger Collection, School of Cinema-Television, University of Southern California
MPAA AMPAS	Motion Picture Association of America files, AMPAS
NARA	U.S. National Archives and Records Administration
NYPL	Billy Rose Theater Collection, New York Public Library at Lincoln Center
SHSW	State Historical Society of Wisconsin
UAC SHSW	United Artists Collection, Wisconsin Center for Film and Theater Research, State Historical Society of Wisconsin, Madison, Wisconsin. Pending the eventual absorption of the UA materials referenced below into the processed "massive" UA collection,

SHSW Reference Archivist Harold L. Miller suggests adding the following accession number, which will always distinguish these materials from the rest of the UA documents: "UAC Addition MCHC82-046."

UC USC	Universal Collection, School of Cinema-Television, University of Southern California
UCLA	University of California at Los Angeles
USC	School of Cinema-Television, University of Southern California
WB USC	Warner Bros. Archives, School of Cinema-Television, University of Southern California

All interviews were conducted by the author.

vii . . . MR. LANCASTER'S REMARKABLE . . . : Vincent Canby, "Of Time and Talent: The Growth of Burt Lancaster," *New York Times,* May 24, 1981.

Prologue

3 "YOU STAND STILL," HE SUGGESTED: Tony Curtis, Interview. All subsequent quotations of his are drawn from this source.

4 "*SWEET SMELL OF SUCCESS* DESTROYED US ALL,": Alexander Mackendrick, Interview. All subsequent quotations of his, unless otherwise noted, are drawn from this source.

"BEAR WITH ME,": Lancaster quoted in press release, *Come Back, Little Sheba* production file, HWC AMPAS.

5 WHAT ROBERT BRUSTEIN HAS CALLED THE "ZOLA REALISM": Robert Brustein, "The New Hollywood: Myth and Anti-Myth," *Film Quarterly,* Vol. XII, No. 3, 1959, as reprinted in Charles Thomas Samuels, ed., *A Casebook on Film,* 126.

"I HATE LOOKING BACKWARD,": Lancaster quoted in *Boston Globe,* Sept. 28, 1986.

"OUTLANDISHLY POPULAR AND POTENT *MEGA*STARDOM": Roddy McDowall, Interview. All subsequent quotations of his are drawn from this source.

6 "NOTHING MORE THAN A BIG CIRCUS,": Lancaster quoted in Stephen E. Rubin, "The Gentle Side of Burt Lancaster," n.d. [1977], Burt Lancaster clipping file, FSC MOMA.

(WHEN ERNEST LEHMAN TOLD HIM HE WAS AT WORK . . .): Ernest Lehman, Interview. All subsequent quotations of his are from this source.

"THE MOST *PERFECTLY* MYSTERIOUS MAN . . .": Visconti quoted in Shana Alexander, "Will the Real Burt Please Stand Up?" *Life,* Sept. 6, 1963.

7 "SENSE OF WONDER": Amanda Plummer, Interview. All subsequent quotations of hers are drawn from this source.

"BURT DARED US TO DO MORE, BE BETTER . . .": Bruce Dern, Interview. All subsequent quotations of his are drawn from this source.

"WE DON'T KNOW THESE THINGS,": Robert Altman, Interview. All subsequent quotations of his are drawn from this source.

9   I walked out . . . : Minty Clinch, *Burt Lancaster,* 6.

CHAPTER 1: New York City Boy

11   THERE WAS A CHILD WENT FORTH . . . : Walt Whitman, "There Was A Child Went Forth," *Leaves of Grass* (New York: W.W. Norton, 1973), 364.

LATER, EAGER PUBLICISTS: According to Charles Kidd, genealogist at Debrett's Peerage Limited, London, none of the descendants of John of Gaunt, Duke of Lancaster, ever took "Lancaster" as a surname. (Fax from Kidd to author, Aug. 13, 1996.)

HIS FATHER WOULD TELL A TALE: Press release, *Desert Fury* production file, HWC AMPAS.

THE ROBERTS FAMILY: While exploring the possibility of George MacDonald Fraser (screenwriter of Richard Lester's 1973 spoof, *The Three Musketeers*) scripting a sequel to *The Crimson Pirate* in the late 1970s, Lancaster told Fraser his mother's family was from Ulster, specifically Belfast. Fraser overheard him respond at the time to the question of his ethnic origin with "English," then adding, "English-Irish" (Letter to author from George MacDonald Fraser, Sept. 17, 1996). From 1700 to 1900 about 7 million Irish emigrated to North America, of which about 2 million came from the northern Irish province of Ulster. As the "vast majority of Irish Protestants are concentrated in Ulster . . . it is highly probable that Burt Lancaster's Irish Protestant ancestors originated here" (Letter to author from Dr. Brian Trainor, Research Director, Ulster Historical Foundation, Sept. 25, 1996).

12   A SKILLED WORKER, A COOPER: U.S. Federal Census 1880 (E.D. 488, Sheet 25). Although James Lancaster arrived in America in the 1860s, the first U.S. census in which a James Lancaster, married to a "Susan" (derivative of Susannah), with a son James H. Lancaster can be found is that of 1880 where the head of household is listed as a cooper, age forty and born in Ireland. In one interview (*Modern Screen,* Dec. 1969), Lancaster said his father claimed to be the seventh son of a seventh son, a good luck charm in Irish culture, but no such family was found in Manhattan census records and the claim is probably another family embellishment.

JAMES MARRIED: U.S. Federal Census 1880 (E.D. 488, Sheet 25).

THE FAMILY PROUDLY CLAIMED: Press release, *Desert Fury* production file, HWC AMPAS. Early in the actor's Hollywood career publicists made much of the supposed link to Lord Roberts. Lancaster's father brought it up several times in interviews; though the connection was through his wife's family, he was clearly proud of it.

WHAT LAURENCE OLIVIER WOULD DESCRIBE: Laurence Olivier, *Confessions of an Actor,* 226.

13   YEARS LATER HE WOULD REMEMBER: Linda Pomeroy, "Burt & Norma Lancaster to Divorce at Last?" *Modern Screen,* Dec. 1969.

"VERY POOR LITTLE HOUSE,": Burt Lancaster, "Sawdust to Stardust," *Woman* [U.K.], three-part series, Jan. 1970. This is a valuable source of otherwise unrecorded material. At the time of his divorce from his second wife, Lancaster wrote/narrated this detailed history of his life to date for a popular British women's magazine. It was a venue guaranteed to attract little general attention and no distribution—or bibliographic record—in his native country.

14 "LONG, DREARY, ONE ROOM AFTER THE OTHER": Lancaster quoted in Pomeroy, "Burt & Norma."

15 THOUGH THOM WAS A WELL-LOVED DOCTOR: Thom had his office at the corner of York Avenue and East Eighty-sixth Street and was known for his "munificence in the neighborhood from about 1895 until his death in 1933." (Letter to author from Thomas B. Gaines, grandnephew of Dr. Burton P. Thom, June 1, 1995.)
TO USE THE BIBLE TO "POINT THE LESSONS OF BUSINESS . . .": Frederick Lewis Allen, *Only Yesterday,* 127.

16 THE HOUSE ON 106TH STREET: The already crowded flats and tenements of East Harlem were chopped up to make more rentable units when housing construction was suspended for the duration of the First World War. Details of the five families living in the Lancaster house come from the U.S. Federal Census 1920 (E.D. 1263, Sheet 10).

17 A "FUN FATHER": Jim Lancaster, "I'll Bet On Burt," *Photoplay,* Jan. 1953.
"MOTHER BEAT THE HELL OUT OF US,": Lancaster quoted in Helen Itria, "Burt Lancaster: The Story of a Hard Man," *Look,* Oct. 20, 1953.
"GOT THE STRAP.": Lancaster quoted in Louella Parsons, "Burt Lancaster," *Los Angeles Examiner,* Oct. 1, 1950.
IF HE WAS A "TERROR,": Lancaster quoted in Ruth Waterbury, "Don't Run From Yourself," *Photoplay,* Jan. 1956.
TO THE "UTTER DISGUST,": J. Lancaster, "I'll Bet."

18 "BURT ALWAYS LIVED . . .": Tina Cuccia-Cravat, daughter of Nick Cravat, Interview. All subsequent quotations of hers are drawn from this source.
COMING OUT OF THE LOCAL CORN EXCHANGE BANK: J. Lancaster, "I'll Bet." Lancaster told this story many times all his life.
"YOU ARE YOUR OWN SLUM AREA,": Lancaster quoting Lizzie Lancaster in James Robert Parish, *The Tough Guys,* 184.
BURTON LOOKED UP TO HIS OLDER BROTHER JIM: Paul Zimmerman, "From Mosholu to Hollywood," *New York Post,* Nov. 28, 1978.

19 "AW, DAD, ALL I EVER DO . . .": Willie Lancaster quoted in J. Lancaster, "I'll Bet."
"IF YOU WANT TO KNOW ABOUT LOVE,": Lizzie Lancaster as quoted by Lancaster in Pomeroy, "Burt & Norma."
"THE COLD . . . AND THE SCROUNGING FOR JOBS.": Lancaster quoted in Barbara Berch Jamison, "From Here to Maturity," *New York Times Magazine,* Aug. 23, 1953.

20 AT THEIR BEST SUCH EXPERIMENTS: The American settlement house movement was inspired by Arnold Toynbee's Toynbee Hall in the slums of London's East End and launched in the U.S. by Jane Addams when she founded Hull House in Chicago. Background material on Union Settlement and the Church of the Son of Man also came from the Burke Library at Union Theological Seminary in New York.

20 UNION'S "SPECIAL GIFT,": Janet Murray, Interview. All subsequent quotations from her are drawn from this source.

AND THEN HELP THE RESIDENTS: Joined by other neighborhood denominations such as the East Harlem Presbyterian Church, founded by Norman Thomas (another Union graduate and future Socialist Party presidential candidate), reform was a cooperative, neighborhood project.

A LARGE GYM: Union developed one of the first city kindergartens, public baths, and birth control clinics.

"ALL THIS BELONGED TO US,": Lancaster, "Sawdust."

21 "[T]HE RICH FIFTH AVENUE CHURCHES,": Lancaster quoted in Pomeroy, "Burt & Norma."

ONE SUNDAY: Letter from Lancaster to James Adriance, the pastor's son, Feb. 3, 1969, Union Settlement archives.

"SNUFFLE-NOSED LITTLE BOY.": Letter to author from Rebecca W. Corrie, Carrie Nester's niece, March 12, 1996.

"AFTER MUCH EXASPERATED PULLING,": J. Lancaster, "I'll Bet."

THREE PILLS IN A BOTTLE: Rachel Lyman Field, *Six Plays* (New York: Scribner, 1924). Field, the grandniece of Cyrus Field, worked for awhile with Famous Players-Lasky Corporation, wrote children's books (she was the first woman to win the Newbery Medal in 1930, for *Hitty, Her First Hundred Years*) and the best-selling novel, *All This and Heaven Too*, published in 1938; the Warner Bros. movie, starring Bette Davis, was released in 1940. She rewrote the lyrics of Shubert's *Ave Maria* for Walt Disney's *Fantasia* in 1940.

22 "SUDDENLY FRIGHTENED.": Lancaster quoted in Jane Prouty, "Brand-New Star," *Screenland*, Sept. 1946.

A BRAND-NEW THEATER COMPANY: Information about the Lab is from American Laboratory Theater file material and general theater source books, NYPL.

"THE PEAK OF AMERICAN THEATRICAL PRODUCTION . . .": Ann Douglas, *Terrible Honesty: Mongrel Manhattan in the 1920s*, 60.

EVOLVING AWAY FROM THE FIN-DE-SIÈCLE TRADITION: François-Alexandre-Nicolas-Chéri Delsarte (1811–1871) founded his Paris *Cours d'Esthetique Appliqué* (Course of Applied Aesthetics) in 1839. A year after his death, one of his pupils, Steele MacKaye (1842–1894), an American who played with Winslow Homer and William and Henry James as a child, returned to the United States to spread the Delsartean gospel and founded the first dramatic school in America, later named the American Academy of Dramatic Arts, in the Lyceum Theater (not the same one in which Lancaster later debuted) in New York. He believed in the "social value" of drama.

"A SENSE OF THE THEATER IN RELATION TO SOCIETY.": Harold Clurman, *The Fervent Years*, 17.

"THE MOST CELEBRATED THEATER . . .": *New York American*, Jan. 9, 1923.

"THE FRESH VISION OF THE RUSSIAN SOUL.": *New York Globe*, Jan. 16, 1923.

"TRUE AND VIVID AND TELLING": *New York Herald*, Jan. 9, 1923.

23 "PROMISING STUDENTS,": Program prospectus, American Laboratory Theater, 1926–1927, NYPL.

WHEN LAB REPRESENTATIVES CLIMBED: Some accounts claim Boleslavsky and Ouspenskaya came in person; according to one of Lancaster's retellings, Bob Parsons of Columbia University's theater department, and John Martin, one-time dance critic of the *New York Times*—both teachers at the American Lab— were the callers.

"HEY, YOU HEARD?": Basil Natoli, Interview. All subsequent quotations of his are drawn from this source.

"ABOVE ALL," WROTE BOLESLAVSKY: Richard Boleslavsky, *Acting: The First Six Lessons*, 122.

THE LAB'S THEATER OPENED: During its existence from 1925 to 1933, the American Laboratory Theater also produced Thorton Wilder's *The Trumpet Shall Sound* (1926), Clemence Dan's *Granite* (1927), Jean-Jacques Bernard's *Martine* (1928), Arthur Schnitzler's *The Bridal Veil* (1928), among other, largely foreign, plays.

24   "GIVE HER A BIG LOVING KISS,": J. Lancaster, "I'll Bet."

JEFFEREY FARNOL'S 1910 "LONG NOVEL . . .": Lancaster told George MacDonald Fraser of his childhood affection for this book. (Letter to author from Fraser, Sept. 17, 1996.)

"CLEAN, SIMPLE, VALIANT, . . .": Rudyard Kipling, "Lord Roberts," *Collected Poems* (New York: Anchor Books/Doubleday, 1989), 204.

25   ONE NIGHT AT 2 A.M.: *Los Angeles Examiner*, Oct. 1, 1950.

THE MASSIVE DUTCH COLONIAL–STYLE STRUCTURE: When Congressman La Guardia was invited by Leonard Covello, then the chairman of Clinton's Italian department, to address the school's Italian club, a student speaker, Vito Marcantonio, gave such a stirring oration calling for a national pension scheme, he became La Guardia's lifelong protégé and his controversial successor as East Harlem's congressman from 1934 to 1936 and from 1938 to 1950, and chief leader of the American Labor Party (Joseph Lovitz, "East Harlem: Past and Present," *Our Town*, May 9, 1975). According to Thomas Kessner, La Guardia first met "Marc" at a high-school graduation (Thomas Kessner, *Fiorello H. La Guardia and the Making of Modern New York*, 138).

26   "WE [ARE] YOUNG ICONOCLASTS": 1930 De Witt Clinton High School yearbook, DeWitt Clinton High School Alumni Office collection.

HIS COURSE SCHEDULE: Lancaster's high school transcript was kindly furnished to the author by William Wagner.

"HE WAS A STRONG KID . . .": Morris Meislik, De Witt Clinton High School alumnus, Interview.

"SO DAMN WEAK I COULDN'T EVEN CHIN MYSELF,": Lancaster quoted in Zimmerman, "Mosholu."

"LIKE FIFTY POINTS NOWADAYS,": Lancaster quoted in Zimmerman, "Mosholu." In the *Post* article, Lancaster described his basketball style thus: ". . . I could run like hell, and I loved to play defense, and I was a team man. That's what basketball was all about in those days. You'd work the ball around for five minutes to get a layup. Anyone who took two shots in a row was a hot dog and he'd get yanked out of the game."

CHAPTER 2: The Daring Young Man

The principal research on the circus career of Lancaster was done at the Circus World Museum, Robert L. Parkinson Library and Research Center in Baraboo, Wisconsin, with the assistance of Fred Dahlinger, Director; Bill Jackson, Archivist; and Menzi L. Behrnd-Klodt, Archivist. Circus historian John Culhane was a valuable resource and help with American circus history.

28 A CIRCUS IS LIKE A MOTHER . . . : Lancaster quoted in clipping, n.d., Scrapbook, CMC USC.

"BURTON IS ANXIOUS . . .": Union Settlement archives.

"SAVED BURT LANCASTER . . .": Ibid.

"THAT LITTLE INCIDENT ALMOST DID BURT IN,": Recollection of Helen Harris, n.d., Union Settlement archives.

29 IN 1930 AND 1931, CUTTING IN: Stephen Fox, *Blood and Power,* 67.

ONE BLOCK NORTH: *New York Times,* July 29, 1931.

"A DAMNABLE OUTRAGE," Roosevelt quoted in *New York Times,* July 30, 1931.

30 "WE LOVED THE GREAT STAUNCHNESS . . .": James Cagney, *Cagney by Cagney,* 25.

"FLAWLESS ATHLETE,": Ibid., 7.

"BREAK-IN" TO VAUDEVILLE: Ibid., 29.

"UNMISTAKABLE TOUCH OF THE GUTTER": Cagney quoted in Sklar, *City Boys,* 6.

31 THE MOVIE STAR ENGAGÉ: Cagney discarded, as did his fellow Warner Bros. star, Ronald Reagan, his earlier liberal affiliation and became a political conservative.

"BURT KNEW HIS BIRDS,": James Zanghi, East Harlem neighbor, Interview.

"THE ONLY GIRL": Lancaster, "Sawdust."

"I FOUND HIM TO BE A LITTLE CONCEITED,": Emily Hernandez Oster, Interview.

32 "I WISH I COULD DO THAT,": Lancaster, "Sawdust."

"CAN YOU DO BARS?": C.G. Sturtevant, "Can You Do Bars?" *White Tops,* Jan. 1937.

"GREAT CIRCUS IMMORTALS": Robert Lewis Taylor, *Center Ring: The People of the Circus,* 229.

"IN THEIR TIME OF CRISIS, . . .": Ibid.

"TO GROW UP IN AMERICA . . .": Burt Lancaster, "A 'First of May Guy,' " *Ringling Bros. and Barnum & Bailey Circus Magazine and Program,* 1951.

33 "THEY WERE LIKE DAMON AND PYTHIAS,": Tina Cuccia-Cravat, Interview. Two citizens of the Roman state of Syracuse, Damon and Pythias, had a friendship so close they remain a standard of faith and loyalty between friends.

"BURT COULDN'T BE WITHOUT NICK . . .": Frances Cuccia Rossi, sister of Nick Cravat, Interview. All subsequent quotations of hers are drawn from this source.

"ANY LOOK AT BURT . . .": J.P. Miller, Interview. All subsequent quotations of his are drawn from this source.

"NICK HAD A FEW ODD MOMENTS.": Helen White, Union Settlement drama teacher, Interview.

"I THINK MY FATHER . . .": Marcy Overway-Cravat, daughter of Nick Cravat, Interview. All subsequent quotations of hers are drawn from this source.

35 "BEAUTIFUL STYLE AND GRACE.": Lancaster quoted in John Culhane, *The American Circus,* 259.

"THEY WERE VERY POLITE . . .": Mary Ellen and Bob Peters, daughter and son of Bill "Ketrow" Peters, Interview. All subsequent quotations of either Peters are drawn from this source.

"I WAS SO EXCITED,": Lancaster quoted in Dorothy Deere, "Big Guy," *Photoplay,* Jan. 1948; another version of the audition appears in "Kay Bros. Circus," *White Tops,* Sept./Oct. 1995.

36 "BEAUTIFUL BEYOND DESCRIPTION.": Lancaster, "Sawdust."

"THE ONLY ONES WHO HAD TRAVELED . . .": Lancaster quoted in Deere, "Big Guy."

"WHEN YOU'RE NINETEEN . . .": Lancaster, "Sawdust."

37 BURT'S SOLO ROUTINE: Taylor, 181.

"WE WERE A FAMILY GROUP . . .": Lancaster, "First of May."

"THE FUGITIVE BUSTLE": Taylor, 138.

38 GAINED IN "SOLIDARITY AND EMPATHY,": James L. Giorgi, East Harlem neighbor, Interview.

"INCONSIDERATE, ARBITRARY, . . .": La Guardia quoted in August Heckscher with Phyllis Robinson, *When La Guardia Was Mayor,* 152. This book provided much background information about East Harlem in the early Depression.

"ARGUMENTS BASED ON PRECEDENT,": Kessner, *La Guardia,* 141.

HELEN HARRIS DESCRIBED: Notes from Helen M. Harris, Union Settlement archives.

"THE DEPRESSION BROUGHT CHANGE,": Lancaster quoted in *New York World-Telegram,* June 5, 1965.

39 "ADDED ATTRACTION" OF A FOUR-LEGGED GIRL: *Billboard,* May 19, 1934.

"AMERICA'S ETHIOPIA.": Jackson quoted in *New York Times,* July 24, 1996.

"THE ONLY WOMAN . . .": Lancaster quoted in Pete Martin, *Hollywood Without Makeup,* 190.

THE LORETTA TWINS: Steve Gossard, Curator of Circus Collections at the Milner Library Special Collections, Illinois State University, kindly compiled a chronology and a collection of periodical references (ads and articles) to the Ernst family. "The sisters were fantastic," recalled Ernestine Clarke Baer, a niece of "Poodles" Hanneford, a Ringling riding and trapeze star of the 1940s in her own right, and the daughter of Ernest Clarke, the Flying Clarkonian circus flier generally credited for accomplishing the first triple aerial somersault in 1910, though not consistently thereafter, and credited by the Guinness Book of World Records with throwing a quadruple aerial somersault to Charles Clarke in Mexico in 1915 while wearing a safety harness. "The Loretta twins did all the things men did, but pointed their toes and looked beautiful. No women are doing it today or ever will" (Ernestine Clarke Baer, Interview). The Loretta Twins were featured on the April 17, 1917, cover of *Billboard.* "Baby June," born in Australia in 1916, is featured in the December 22, 1917, issue of *Billboard,* sitting in a galvanized metal bucket. The death of Ora's husband, Jack Ernst of the Flying Ernstonians, in San Juan in 1921 was pure circus: making a flying leap from the trapeze to his partner, he miscalculated, fell on his head into the net, died three and a half weeks later, and is buried in San Juan (*Pantagraph,* Apr. 12, 1921, 3; *Billboard,* Apr. 30, 1921, 51).

40   "LOOK AT THE TREES . . .": Ernst quoted in Lancaster, "Sawdust."

"SORT OF LOOKED DOWN ON . . .": Gracie Hanneford, Interview. All subsequent quotations of hers are drawn from this source.

"FOR A BIG GUY, . . .": Tommy Hanneford, Interview. All subsequent quotations of his are drawn from this source.

41   "EVERYBODY WAS ON WPA,": Lancaster quoted in Jamison, "Maturity." For general background on New York theater in the 1930s, see Malcolm Goldstein, *The Political Stage.*

"THE ENTIRE AUDIENCE . . .": Lancaster quoted in Bernard Drew, "Burt Lancaster," in Elisabeth Weis, ed., National Society of Film Critics, *The Movie Star* (New York: Viking/Penguin, 1981), 287.

BECAUSE HE WAS ON RELIEF: Lancaster may have obtained the fiercely contested position—work was virtually guaranteed all year long—with the help of WPA circus manager Burns O'Sullivan, who had just left the Gorman Bros. Circus.

ACROSS THE COUNTRY: There was hope of creating a true national theater but, except for twenty-one simultaneous openings of Sinclair Lewis's antifascist play, *It Can't Happen Here,* in seventeen cities on October 27, 1936, a phenomenon that lasted 260 weeks for a total audience of nearly five hundred thousand people, it didn't happen (Lorraine A. Brown, "Introduction: The Federal Theater Project and Research Collection," *The Federal Theater Project: A Catalog-Calendar of Productions* (New York: Greenwood Press, 1986.)

"AN ASTONISHMENT NEEDLED WITH EXCITEMENT . . .": *Fortune,* July 1937.

42   "BEYOND THE SCALE . . .": *New York Times,* May 2, 1937.

MARY WIGMAN: German modern dancer and choreographer "considered by many the most influential creator of the German expressionist movement" (Barbara Naomi Cohen-Stratyner, *Bibliographical Dictionary of Dance* (New York: Schirmer Books, 1982, 942). June may have seen Wigman's company when it toured the U.S. as a Hurok troupe in 1930.

THE HYPERBOLE OF THE 1937–38 WINTER SEASON PROGRAM: For FTP memorabilia, programs, correspondence see RG [Record Group] 69—WPA—Records of FTP, Correspondence of the NYC Office of the FTP, 1935–1939; and FT 1190—FTP—NYC Circus 1937, NARA, Washington, D.C., Bill Creech, Archivist. See also FTP file materials at NYPL.

43   "DEVOTED, COURAGEOUS AND BOLDLY CREATIVE,": Clurman, 92.

"HOTBED FOR COMMUNISTS.": Thomas quoted in Walter Goodman, *The Committee,* 25.

ROOSEVELT BLASTED THE EFFORT: Roosevelt quote appeared in the *New York Times,* Nov. 15, 1972, at the time of Martin Dies's death.

ONE CONGRESSMAN ASKED FLANAGAN: Flanagan, famously, replied, "Put it in the record that [Marlowe] was the greatest dramatist in the period immediately preceding Shakespeare." Joanne Bentley, *Hallie Flanagan,* 317.

THE "QUICKEST GAME": *TAC* ["a magazine of theater, film, radio, music, dance"], July–Aug. 1939.

44 THE SWAN SONG OF THE NEW YORK CITY FTP: *Sing For Your Supper* did have one hit song, "Ballad for Uncle Sam" by John Latouche and Earl Robinson. It was retitled "Ballad for Americans," recorded by Paul Robeson, and used as the theme song of the 1940 Republican presidential convention as well as for general propaganda purposes during World War II.

AFTER DANCING WITH MIKHAIL MORDKIN: Mordkin (1880–1944), a Russian ballet dancer and choreographer, trained at the Imperial School of Ballet in Moscow and graduated into the Bolshoi Ballet in 1899. He later toured with Anna Pavlova and settled in New York in the mid-1920s, creating a company of American students in the 1930s which later formed the basis of the Ballet Theater. At one time, Mordkin was considered "the better of Balanchine" (Cohen-Stratyner, 633).

HECHT FOLLOWED BOLESLAVSKY: Boleslavsky left New York for Hollywood in 1929 after the invention of talkies and became a feature film director at Columbia and RKO. He then went to MGM and Fox, where he directed *Rasputin and the Empress, Les Misérables, Theodora Goes Wild,* and *The Garden of Allah* before he died suddenly in 1937 at the age of 48. In 1932 Hecht developed a "new screen school of dancing" at Paramount and staged the dances for *Lady and Gent, Devil and the Deep, Horse Feathers,* and *She Done Him Wrong* (*New York Herald Tribune,* July 5, 1931). For Fox, he supervised the dance numbers in *Bottoms Up* in 1934.

"ACE NUMBER": *Billboard,* June 11, 1938.

HIS "RELIGION.": Martin, 198.

45 THE NEWTON BROS. OUTFIT GROUND TO A HALT: Joseph T. Bradbury, "The Old Circus Album: A Historic Look at Shows of the Past," *White Tops,* May-June 1972.

"[N]O RESPONSIBILITIES, NO BILLS TO PAY, . . .": Lancaster quoted in Jamison, "Maturity."

THE LOWEST BOOKINGS: A typical "burly" show might include, as described in various *Billboard* ads of the time, a blond stripper, a brunette "songstress," a range of tawdry predictable skits (the Pullman train honeymoon, the drinking bout), and a "Negro Tom-Tom rhythm" number.

BARNES-CARRUTHERS FAIR BOOKING ASSOCIATION: Claude Crumley, circus performer, Interview. All subsequent quotations of his are drawn from this source.

"A PARTICULARLY REALISTIC . . .": Press release, *Come Back, Little Sheba* production file, HWC AMPAS.

46 THE THREE TOPPERS: Barnes-Carruthers Fair Booking Association, Inc., *1940 Blue Book of Super-Excellent Attractions.* Copies of selected pages kindly provided to author by Steve Gossard (see above).

HARRY JAMES: James once played the trumpet in the Christy Brothers' Circus band (Taylor, 74).

"DRAW [THE AUDIENCE] AWAY . . .": *Billboard,* Dec. 16, 1939.

46 ON NEW YEAR'S EVE: *Billboard,* Jan. 13, 1940.

"SWINGING ON THOSE CRAZY BARS,": Sinatra quoted in Burt Lancaster clipping file, n.d., FSC MOMA.

THE "LAZY TANG": Lancaster, "Sawdust."

47 "WHAT DID YOU DO, . . .": Ibid.

DURING A MATINEE APPEARANCE: *Modern Screen,* July 1957.

ALMOST THIRTY YEARS LATER: Researchers at Photofest in New York claim to have seen early, "meat magazine," pre–WWII photographs of Lancaster; on Jan. 24, 1977, the *New York Post* announced that *Blueboy* magazine "will run the nude photo of Burt Lancaster in its next issue but without identifying the star for legal reasons" (Carol Wells, creative director of *Blueboy* in June, 1996, confirmed to the author on the telephone that *Blueboy* had printed photos of Lancaster in 1977, but no copies remained, twenty years later, of the issue); *Playgirl,* Dec. 1978.

"THERE'S NEVER BEEN A PAYOFF,": Lancaster quoted in Nick Cravat, "My Pal," *Movie Stars Parade,* Nov. 28, 1949.

48 "I . . . LEARNED,": Burt Lancaster, "Selling the Greatest Show on Earth," *Salesman's Opportunity,* Feb. 1957.

"I WAS STARVING,": Ibid.

"SELL YOURSELF FIRST,": Ibid.

"SELLING CULTURE IN LIEU OF SHIRTS,": Lancaster, "Sawdust."

"I BECAME . . . THEIR PAL.": Ibid.

49 "I NEVER LET IT GET UP TO MY CONSCIOUS MIND,": Lancaster quoted in Waterbury, "Run."

THE LONG STRING OF GRUBBY JOBS: There are some unexplained blips in this early 1940s chronology. Some accounts say Lancaster worked for a while as a fireman and/or road gang worker; he claimed to have worked at the Steel Pier in Atlantic City. He was supposed to have done the dinky Poli Circuit, the Bridgeport/New Haven/Scranton/Wilkes-Barre–type of route traditionally the last resort of acts that had no better offer. There is a photograph in the possession of Nick's daughters of an "Oriental" theater somewhere, probably Chicago, with the marquee blazing "Chico Marx and his orchestra in an All Comedy Stage Revue," with Lang & Cravat in lights with three other acts; the band show is opening the 1942 movie *Hello Annapolis,* which starred Tom Brown and Jean Parker, but by 1942 Lang & Cravat was supposed to be long finished. Lancaster never mentioned having appeared with the goofy banana-peeling act of Chico Marx.

"A THOROUGH AND GRUELLING BASIC TRAINING.": Hubert W. Freeman, Captain, Field Artillery, Commanding, Twenty-first Special Service Division, *Historical Record,* 28 Nov. 1945, 2, NARA, College Park, MD.

A BRAND-NEW EXPERIMENT: See John D. Millett, *The Organization and Role of the Army Service Forces.*

THE MAN CHOSEN TO RUN "THE BIGGEST HEADACHE . . .": Somervell—another larger-than-life role model that wove into the fabric of Lancaster's life—transformed the American munitions industry into the "Arsenal of Democracy" that would fuel the war. Not only New York's La Guardia Airport, but also the location, size, shape, and construction of the Pentagon building—"Somervell's Folly," barely completed by April 1942—were his projects. For Operation Torch, the U.S. North African campaign that preceded the July 1943 invasion | of Sicily, he pulled together a convoy of twenty-one ships containing over five thousand trucks, one hundred locomotive engines, and other railway equipment in just two and a half weeks. For general background on the organization of the American effort in World War II, see Geoffrey Perret, *There's a War to Be Won*.

"GIVE ME A THOUSAND MEN . . .": Record Group 160, Records of Headquarters Army Service Forces, Office of the Director of Personnel, Special Services Division, General Records, 1941–1945, Box 246, NARA, College Park, Maryland. Other ASF records consulted, with the assistance of Ken Schlesinger, NARA Archivist at College Park for background data on Special Service Divisions from Record Group 160: Boxes 247, 441, 453, 461, 463, 483, 488; Boxes 485 and 487, also in Record Group 160, contain information specifically about Lancaster's Twenty-first Special Service Division.

"SMART" ARMY: While working with the Civilian Conservation Corps during the Depression, Marshall had noted the adaptable, fast-thinking nature of the new American generation, many educated by some version of the same progressive pedagogy that had guided Lancaster's curriculum at Clinton.

50 "ENTERTAINMENT SPECIALIST.": Burton S. Lancaster, Military Service Record, U.S. Army, Serial/Service Number 32694076, Dates of Service: Jan. 2, 1943–Oct. 14, 1945, National Personnel Records Center, St. Louis, MO.

ARNOLD BELNICK AND PIANIST BORIS BARERE: Arnold Belnick, Interview. Boris Barere, Interview. All subsequent quotations from Belnick or Barere are drawn from these sources.

"HEARTSTOPPING PIANO VIRTUOSO": Sarah Fishgow, Classical music radio show host, WNYC, New York, Interview.

COURT-MARTIALED IN DECEMBER: Lancaster was demoted from Sergeant, Grade T14, back to Private on December 17, 1943 (Service Record, 5).

51 THE ALLIED EFFORT WAS PLAGUED BY FREEZING RAIN: Historian Geoffrey Perret has called Clark's push to Rome in the winter of 1943–44 "one of the most heartbreaking" of the war.

"STARVING, STINKING WINTER,": Lancaster, "Sawdust."

"SENSATIONAL . . . IN THEIR WILL TO LIVE": Lancaster quoted in *Variety*, July 23, 1980.

THE FIRST LIVE SHOW TO PLAY ON THE ANZIO BEACHFRONT: Freeman, 7.

FIRST AMERICAN SHOW TO BE STAGED IN THE NEWLY LIBERATED ROME: Ibid.

52 "COMMENDATIONS FROM GENERALS CLARK . . .": Lancaster quoted in Prouty, "Brand-New." The official history of the Twenty-first confirms: "So many others [commendations] have come in from officers up to and including the Fifth Army Commanding General, that we have a file full of them" (Freeman, 8).

52 THOM CONROY: Background information about Conroy comes from the Conroy

clipping file, NYPL. A July 8, 1946, playbill for the Whalom Drama Festival in Fitchburg, Massachusetts, describes Conroy, playing Sheridan Whiteside in "The Man Who Came to Dinner," as belonging "in that select and limited circle of actors who are directors also" and having "at his fingertips several hundred plays he can put on—and play a leading role—at a moment's notice."

ONE OF THE BEST-LOVED SONGS: The sentimental song, "Sonny Boy," was the climactic number in Al Jolson's second talkie, *The Singing Fool*, in 1928, and perhaps the biggest hit of his career. Coming a year after *The Jazz Singer*, the movie was reportedly Hollywood's top grossing hit until *Gone With the Wind* and pushed its studio, Warner Bros., and the studio's publicity director, Hal Wallis, into the majors.

TED POST: Post was with the Fifth Army's 235th Engineer Combat Battalion in World War II and directed his own soldier show, "By-Pass to Berlin." All subsequent quotations of his are drawn from an interview with Post.

53 "I WAS ALWAYS STICKING UP . . .": Lancaster quoted in Prouty, "Brand-New."

PHILLIP LESLIE TOMALIN: Phillip Leslie Tomalin, Interview. All subsequent quotations of his are drawn from this source. Tomalin started work in the middle of the Depression as a singer with bands when he was sixteen. In 1938 he shifted into more lucrative radio work, singing, announcing, and working his way up to directing. After World War II, he got into the new medium of television, working as what he described as "the first writer, producer, director hired by the old DuMont network in New York" in the early scrambling era of live TV. He recalled trying to get Norma to appear on one of the "awful lot" of shows he had running every day whenever she was in New York, but she would always beg off: "I'm so damn fat! I'm pregnant again." The author wishes to thank Susan Sarandon for kindly providing access to her father for the purposes of this book. Tomalin died in 1999.

FAR NORTHWEST CORNER OF WISCONSIN: Background information on the Anderson family is from interviews with Cora Graham, former neighbor of the Anderson family in Webster, Wisconsin; Fred and Mary Exum, alumni coordinators for Miami Edison High School, Florida; Dorothy Anderson Hall, Norma's sister; and Winifred Amdor of the Opa-locka Historic Preservation Society.

CHARLES ANDERSON: "From 1860 to 1890, the prospect of a better life also attracted nearly 10 million northern European immigrants to American cities. . . . [B]y 1900 . . . nearly a million Scandanavians farmed the rich lands of Wisconsin and Minnesota" (Paul S. Boyer, et al., *The Enduring Vision*, 408).

54 "LOVE HIT ME AGAIN . . .": Lancaster, "Sawdust."

"LOCKED UP FOR THREE WEEKS": Radio interview with Louella Parsons, Sept. 29, 1948.

SHE DUBBED HIM "H.B.L.": Ruth Waterbury, "Soft-Hearted Menace," *Photoplay*, Aug. 1954. There are multiple references to this nickname throughout Lancaster's postwar life.

57 THEY WERE FUN DAYS . . .: Lancaster quoted in William Hall and Tony Crawley, *Game* [U.K.], Feb. 1975.

CHAPTER 3: Discovery

59 NEW YORK, SEPTEMBER 1945, . . .: Irene Mayer Selznick, *A Private View*, 275.
RAYMOND KNIGHT: Obituary, Raymond Knight, *Variety*, Feb. 18, 1953. Knight dreamed up several more zany, popular radio shows throughout the thirties; during the war he was national production manager for the ABC network, writing Broadway musicals and comedies on the side. Before his death in 1953, he was the chief comedy writer for the NBC-TV *Bob & Ray* show.

60 ROYALTON HOTEL: The Manhattan building in which Lancaster was "discovered" has often been claimed, erroneously, to be the RCA Building, among others. Lancaster himself recalled—and emphasized—that his encounter with fate took place in the Royalton, well-known as a "theatrical hotel" at the time. He had a precise memory for such details.
"THE MINCE PIES ON ME,": Lancaster quoted in Martin, 193.
"HE'S HERE RIGHT NOW.": Lancaster, "Sawdust."
"A GOOD ADVANCE JOB OF SELLING": Itria, "Hard Man."

61 "AMONG THE CLASSIC COMEDY PORTRAYALS . . .": *Variety*, Dec. 31, 1980.
AN INTIMATE THEATRICAL SPACE: In 1912, Adolph Zukor challenged the Motion Picture Patents Company by showing the four-reel *Queen Elizabeth*, starring Sarah Bernhardt, at the upscale Lyceum. Riding on the success of what became one of the first international movie hits, the picture that made "cinema interesting to all classes, not just the hoi polloi" (Leslie Halliwell, *Halliwell's Film Guide,* [1991], 891–892), Zukor took over Paramount, the distribution company that he would transform into Paramount Pictures, Lancaster's first studio. Immediately succeeding *A Sound of Hunting*, Garson Kanin's *Born Yesterday* launched another star from the same stage—Judy Holliday.
"BOUNCE OFF THAT STAGE . . .": Max Youngstein, Interview. All subsequent quotations of his are drawn from this source.
GEORGE TYNE: John Guare, Interview. All subsequent quotations of his are drawn from this source.

62 LEVENE, HIS BACK TO THE AUDIENCE: Lancaster, "Sawdust."
"A SMALL-TIME AGENT,": Ruth Waterbury, "Rich Rebel," *The American Weekly*, April 9, 1961.
"DIDN'T TRY TO SELL MYSELF . . .": Lancaster, "Selling."
AFTER MEETING WITH THE PRODUCER: Lancaster and Hecht were probably unaware that even before Wallis saw the play, director Michael Curtiz cabled Wallis, his horseback-riding pal and former Warner Bros. boss, to ask if Lancaster were available as a loanout for Curtiz's next assignment, *Night and Day*, set to roll the last week of December 1945. (Paul Nathan, Paramount's publicity head, to Wallis, Nov. 11, 1945, Burt Lancaster Correspondence file 1946–1950, HWC AMPAS.)

62 "... A BRILLIANT CAST ...": *Cue,* Dec. 1, 1945.

63 "WOUNDED COLOSSUS.": Burt Lancaster clipping file, n.d. [1946], FSC MOMA.
"BACK IN NEW YORK,": Dick Lochte, "Burt Lancaster: One-Half Actor and
One-Half Adding Machine," Los Angeles Free Press, Dec. 8, 1972.
BOX OFFICE GROSSES ... : Arthur Mayer, *Merely Colossal,* 241.
"A PIONEER AMONG INDEPENDENTS ...": *Life,* June 10, 1957.
"VERBAL MESSAGES CAUSE ...": HWC AMPAS.

64 SHEILAH GRAHAM MARKED: Sheilah Graham, "Producer Hal Wallis Packs Much
Into First Year," *The Sun* [Baltimore], Jan. 27, 1946.
"JUTTED LIKE THE TAILFEATHERS ...": Cameron Shipp, "Burt Lancaster," *Cos-
mopolitan,* Aug. 1955.
"COMPLETE NATURALNESS ...": Haskin quoted in press release, *I Walk Alone*
production file, HWC AMPAS.
"A GENE FOR THE SCREEN.": Robert Wise, Interview. All subsequent quotations
of his are drawn from this source.

65 FOR THE FIRST OF A SERIES OF FILMS: Lancaster contract, Jan. 8, 1946, Lancaster
Employment Contracts file, HWC AMPAS.
"STARRED A STATION WAGON.": Shipp, "Burt Lancaster."
MARTIN JUROW: Jurow had worked with the legendary Broadway producer and
director George Abbot, been an MCA agent for big bands, and would go on to
produce such films as *The Fugitive Kind, The Pink Panther,* and *Breakfast at Tiffany's.*
"WHOLE LIBRARIES OF AMERICAN FICTION ...": Michael Gowa, "Supreme Fic-
tions: John Updike selects 100 (well, 85) year's worth of great American short
stories," *New York Times Book Review,* May 9, 1999.
"SHORT, SWIFT, SOBBY LITTLE TALES": Mary Morris, "Crime Does Pay," *PM,*
Nov. 17, 1946.
"THE COCKY STRUT OF GEORGE M. COHAN,": Martin, 88.
"THAT GANGSTER HONOR.": Jules Dassin, Interview. All subsequent quotations of
his are drawn from this source.

66 FOR THE DEATH-BED REVELATIONS: Morris, "Crime."
"[I]T MIGHT BE A VERY GOOD IDEA,": Memorandum to John Joseph at Universal,
May 20, 1946, MHC USC.
THE PRODUCER'S STORY IDEAS: In January 1946, Hellinger sent a cajoling night
letter to Huston at the Weylin Hotel in New York: "... waiting oh so anxiously.
Please phone if there's anything I can do. Mark" (Hellinger to Huston, Jan. 2,
1946, MHC USC). Brooks claimed that while he was starting work on *Brute
Force* for Hellinger, the producer told him to come up with the rest of the story of
The Killers. After "looking up old newspapers and magazines," Brooks said he
came across a story of an ice factory holdup onto which he grafted the invented
character of the insurance inspector (Patrick McGilligan, *Backstory 2,* 42).
"I WAS GOING SLIGHTLY SMORGASBORD,": Mark Hellinger, "The Swede," *Photo-
play,* Mar. 1947.
"I WAS THE CHEAPEST THING IN TOWN, ...": Lancaster quoted in Waterbury,
"Don't Run."

"THIS GUY WAS BIG,": Hellinger, "The Swede."

67 "BIG, BRAWNY BIRD,": Elizabeth Wilson, "Big Guy," *Liberty,* Jan. 1949.

"OVEREMPHASIS ON VIOLENCE AND MURDER": *The Killers,* MPAA AMPAS.

68 *DONAHUE* TELEVISION SHOW: A videotape of the Sept. 12, 1985, ABC-TV Donahue show was kindly lent to the author by Dale Roth, Friars Club, New York
City.

"NOW REGARDED . . .": *Time,* Feb. 4, 1946.

"SO HELP ME,": Jim Bishop, *The Mark Hellinger Story,* 314.

STUART CHASE: Stuart Chase (1888–1985) was an American economist whose
study of the American economic system and methods to revise it, *A New Deal,*
was published in 1932.

69 THE AUTHOR GAVE HIS BLESSING: Hemingway showed up for the screening,
according to Hellinger's biographer, Jim Bishop, wearing a big heavy coat with
two flasks in the deep pockets, one of water, the other of gin. He kept tapping,
but not drinking, the flasks, ready to take a swig if the film went wrong. At the
end he walked up to Hellinger's man and said, "Didn't need 'em" (Bishop,
315). For years thereafter his favorite screening at Finca Vigia, his home in
Cuba, was a Tony Zale versus Rocky Graziano fight and *The Killers.* Gardner
and others would recall that he never stayed awake after the first reel, which
was the only part of the movie he recognized as his own.

PRERELEASE WARMUP TOUR: Details come from Bishop.

"THE BRAWNY APOLLO,": Burt Lancaster clipping file, n.d. [1946], NYPL.

"THE BRUTE WITH THE EYES OF AN ANGEL.": Roland Lacourbe, *Burt Lancaster.*
Translation from the French by the author.

70 "HE CAME OUT OF THAT SCREEN . . .": John Berry, Interview. All subsequent
quotations of his are drawn from the same source.

"FASTER THAN GABLE'S, . . .": Shipp, "Burt Lancaster."

"HIGH PRAISE" FROM FRITZ LANG: File of congratulations for *The Killers,* MHC
USC.

"LANKY, WISTFUL" PRESENCE: *New York Times,* Aug. 29, 1946.

"A FASCINATING, UNSTEREOTYPED . . .": *New Republic,* Sept. 30, 1946.

THE "BEST GANGSTER FILM . . .": *Life,* March 10, 1947.

"THAT PASSIONATE, HUNGRY POSTWAR AUDIENCE . . .": Gore Vidal, *Palimpsest: A
Memoir* (New York: Random House, 1995), 128.

"THE STORY WAS ABOUT COMING BACK FROM THE WAR,": *The Killers* clipping file,
n.d., NYPL.

"LOOKED LIKE A BIRD'S NEST, . . .": Lancaster quoted in Prouty, "Brand-New."

71 WHEN HE WAS ASKED BY LOUELLA PARSONS: Louella Parsons, "Ava Gardner, Burt
Lancaster," *Los Angeles Examiner,* Nov. 24, 1946.

"SHE WOULDN'T HAVE LOOKED AT HIM . . .": Mickey Knox, Interview. All subsequent quotations of his are drawn from this source.

"IMPOSSIBLE TO TAKE . . .": *Time,* Sept. 1, 1947.

"MY BROTHER LOST TO ME.": Waterbury, "Don't Run."

72 TRIED "FRANTICALLY,": Confidential interview.

A CABLE IN EARLY JULY: David Lipton to Marion Pecht, July 5, 1946, MHC USC.

72 WALTER SELTZER: Walter Seltzer, Interview. All subsequent quotations of his are drawn from this source.

"GIVE THE CHILD A NAME,": Cravat quoted in interview with Cuccia-Cravat.

73 "I'VE MADE UP MY MIND . . .": David Ragan, *Movie Stars of the '40's: A Complete Reference Guide for the Film Historian or Trivia Buff* (Englewood Cliffs, NJ: Prentice-Hall, 1985), 111.

"WELL, I WAS LUCKY,": Clyde Murray as quoted in Janet Murray, Interview.

MARTIN SCORSESE: *Los Angeles Times,* Oct. 2, 1997.

74 "THIS ISN'T FUN,": Seymour Peck, "*The Killers* made Burt a Film Star Overnight," *PM,* May 27, 1947.

"WHAT THE HELL, . . .": Ibid.

"IT'S THE OLD FORMULA,": Ibid.

"SAID HE WAS IMPOSSIBLE . . .": Nathan to Wallis, Mar. 24, 1947, HWC AMPAS.

75 WALLIS, MID-ATLANTIC: Cable from Wallis, Apr. 10, 1947, HWC AMPAS.

"HAROLD HAS ASSURED ME . . .": Nathan to Wallis, Apr. 23, 1947, Wallis/Lancaster Correspondence file to end 1950, HWC AMPAS. Bette Davis lost her contract suit against Warner Bros. in 1936, but Cagney, the same year, succeeded in getting his contract "canceled, annulled and terminated" (Sklar, 53). His had been an early, if somewhat inconclusive victory for the idea that the bankable star might control his or her own career.

"I'M GOING TO PICK YOU UP, . . .": Lancaster quoted in Knox, Interview.

WALLIS WAS TERRIFIED OF THE STAR: James Hill, Interview. All subsequent quotations of his are drawn from the same source.

HIS FELLOW INMATES: Looking for real life "convict types," Hellinger claimed to have drafted extras for the prison scenes from what was known as the "slave market"—the corner where day laborers gathered for work—at the corner of Third Street and LaBrea Avenue (Press release, *Brute Force* production file, MHC USC).

76 "HE WASN'T STUPID,": Lancaster quoted in Gordon Gow, "Energy," *Films and Filming,* Jan. 1973.

KNOWING "EXACTLY WHAT HE WANTED, . . .": Yvonne De Carlo, *Yvonne: An Autobiography,* 124.

77 "IF DAUMIER KNOCKS OFF A SKETCH . . .": Lancaster quoted in Peck, "Film Star."

"GAMBLE WITH LANCASTER . . .": *Variety,* June 18, 1947.

"TOO PRETTY.": Peter Manso, *Brando: The Biography,* 221.

"ONLY OTHER PROSPECT,": Selznick, 300.

"YEARNED TO DO THE PART,": Ibid., 301.

"SOUND, . . . SOME KIND OF VISCERAL . . .": William Goldman, "From Brando to Paltrow," *Premiere,* Dec. 1996.

"GENIUS IS A PRETTY DANGEROUS THING . . .": Lancaster clipping file, n.d. [1958], FSC MOMA.

78 KULESHOV'S DICTUM: Kuleshov quoted in James Naremore, *Acting in the Cinema,* 225.

"SUPPLE, DEMONSTRATIVE, . . .": Ibid., 53. Naremore suggests that the Delsartean system was so pervasive up into the 1920s that "a good many actors could be described as Delsartean whether or not they ever studied him—just as middle-class Americans once behaved according to Emily Post whether or not they actually read her advice." He suggests that Cary Grant, another acrobat by training, "could be described as a consummate modern practitioner of vaguely Delsartean technique." So could Lancaster.

"HUNDREDS OF VERY PROMINENT FILM CAPITAL PEOPLE . . .": Thomas quoted in Otto Friedrich, *City of Nets*, 300.

THE FBI HAD BEEN GATHERING: There were many public reasons for what would soon be called a witch hunt. But one root is in the FBI's 1942 initial analysis of the history of the communist movement in the American performing arts. "The makers of the Russian Revolution in 1917," explained the FBI, "were all intellectuals—they never worked a day in their lives of manual labor . . . Marxism involves intense intellectual concentration. It is only on this basis of reasoning that the Communist activities of the highly paid writers, directors, actors and artists, whose salaries in many cases amount to thousands of dollars a week, can be explained." When sound was introduced into movies, the report continued, so was propaganda. After an "initial infiltration" of New York theater groups, the party encouraged converted writers, actors, and directors to take the cause with them to Hollywood. In a loop that goes back to the 1923 appearance in New York of the Moscow Art Theater, the FBI analyst draws a direct connection between the art of theater and Communism: "Young Communists . . . must be perfect in their lives, since a Communist must be always looked up to and thus [be] rigidly rehearsed and given excellent schooling in the matter of dramatics . . . [P]eople in theater become Communists . . . because Russia has theater people on the payroll and offers newcomers security—young people are opportunists and follow those they admire and who will help in their career." *Communist Activity in the Entertainment Industry: FBI Surveillance Files on Hollywood, 1942–1958* (Bethesda, MD: University Publications of America, 1982), Reel 1, NYPL.

THE COMMITTEE HAD HAD ONE BRIEF STAR TURN: Friedrich, 52–53; Sklar, 104–108.

ON AUGUST 7, 1947: "*Brute Force:* Communist Connections with the Production and the Identity of Specific Communist Propaganda Therein," Aug. 7, 1947, *Communist Activity*, Reel 3, NYPL. Thanks to Dassin, who was a member of its Executive Board, the highly suspect Actors' Lab was the source of more than ten of the cast and crew of *Brute Force*, including Hume Cronyn, Sam Levene, Jeff Corey, Whit Bissell, radio's "Sam Spade" Howard Duff, and *The Killers* Art Smith as the prison doctor (Press release, *Brute Force* production file, MHC USC).

79 "THE MISTAKES, CHICANERY . . .": *Variety*, Feb. 5, 1947.

"NO DOUBT ON HIGHER INSTRUCTIONS,": *New York Times*, Mar. 29, 1948.

"LIKE CASTING BORIS KARLOFF . . .": Press release, *All My Sons* production file, UC USC.

"I WANTED TO PLAY CHRIS KELLER,": Lancaster quoted in Allan Hunter, *Burt Lancaster*, 32. Universal paid Wallis $100,000 (to be split with Lancaster) to use Lancaster in a trade-off deal orchestrated by William Dozier, Joan Fontaine's new husband and partner in her equally new Universal-based independent production company, Rampart Productions (Wallis to Dozier, Sept. 2, 1947, Correspondence File, 1946–1950, HWC AMPAS). Dozier and Fontaine were hoping to get Lancaster to costar with Fontaine in *Thunder on the Hill* in 1948 (Universal eventually made the film in 1951 with Claudette Colbert and without Lancaster). Parsons gushed that she had never heard of a star of Fontaine's caliber—winner of the Oscar for *Suspicion* in 1941 and nominated for *Rebecca* in 1940 and *The Constant Nymph* in 1943—waiting that long for a leading man (*Los Angeles Examiner*, July 28, 1947).

79 "AN AVERAGE GUY . . .": Lancaster quoted in Deere, "Big Guy."

"THE HOTTEST THING IN PICTURES": *All My Sons* production file, UC USC.

"OPEN ATTACK" ON THE FAMILY: *Communist Activity*, NYPL.

80 AT 4:30 ON THE AFTERNOON OF OCTOBER 2: Ibid.

ANOTHER MEETING WAS CALLED ON OCTOBER 25: Ibid.

AN INFORMANT TOOK DOWN: Ibid.

"EXCEPT FOR STUDIO COMMITMENTS": Philip Dunne later cited Lancaster as among those in Hollywood who took "a more active part" in the other public activities of the CFA (Philip Dunne, *Take Two*, 201).

81 "THIS IS BURT LANCASTER . . .": Tape of Committee for the First Amendment "Hollywood Fights Back" broadcast, Oct. 26, 1947, Museum of Television and Radio, New York. All quotations from this broadcast are taken from author's transcription from the tape in the museum's collection.

"WALL STREET,": *New York Mirror*, Nov. 29, 1947.

SUDDENLY IT WAS DANGEROUS: Lauren Bacall, *Lauren Bacall: By Myself*, 158.

82 "A NUMBER OF PEOPLE FROM A PREPARED COMMITTEE LIST . . .": "1948 Communist Front Organizations," *4th Report Un-American Activities in California, Report of the Joint Fact-Finding Committee to the 1948 Regular California Legislature*. Sen. Jack Tenny, Chairman (Sacramento, [CA,] 1948), 211.

ONE OF THE SIGNERS: Ibid., 210.

A SPONSOR OF A DINNER: Ibid., 241.

"IN THE PRESENT STATE OF POLITICAL WEATHER . . .": *All My Sons* clipping file, n.d. [Mar. 1948], FSC MOMA.

"FALSE SPRING.": Ronald Brownstein, *The Power and the Glitter*, 115.

CHAPTER 4: Taking Charge of the Asylum

83 THIS KID HAS MADE ONE PICTURE . . . : Hellinger quoted in Mark Hellinger, "Act of Love," *Modern Screen*, n.d., Lancaster clipping file, NYPL.

"CINDERELLA,": Lancaster quoted in Myrtle Gebhart, "Ex-Circus Star-Producer Plans Big Top Picture," *Boston Post Magazine*, Aug. 29, 1948.

"LITTLE VIKINGS": Lancaster quoted in Irene Thirer, "Burt Lancaster Relishes a Challenge in Movies," *New York Post*, Oct. 10, 1948.

"I DIDN'T KNOW WHO HE WAS. . . .": Lucy Kibbee, wife of Roland Kibbee, Interview. All subsequent quotations of hers are drawn from this source.

84 SIDNEY SKOLSKY: Sidney Skolsky, "Hollywood is My Beat . . . Up From the Lingerie Department," *New York Post,* Mar. 15, 1947.

". . . LIKE A MAN . . .": Press release, *The Rose Tattoo* production file, HWC AMPAS.

"FITTING ACTORS, . . .": Letter from Grace Houston Case to author, June 23, 1995.

"THE DREAM—THE LONG, LONG DREAM . . .": Bishop, 343.

ON AUGUST 1: *Los Angeles Examiner,* Aug. 1, 1947.

85 "MAKE ONE MOVIE . . .": Norma Anderson quoted in Confidential Interview.

"I BELIEVE,": Lancaster quoted in Deere, "Big Guy."

"MAKE THE DECISIONS AS TO HOW THEY WANT . . .": Lancaster quoted in Gow, "Energy."

"TAKE THE FEELING OF HUNGER . . .": Lancaster quoted in Thomas M. Pryor, "Leap to Stardom: Burt Lancaster, Ex-Acrobat, Scales Film Heights With the Greatest of Ease," *New York Times,* Oct. 17, 1948.

86 "THE LUNATICS HAVE TAKEN CHARGE . . .": Roland quoted in Mayer, 157.

CAGNEY, PERHAPS THE MOST: See Sklar for an analysis of Cagney's battles with Warner Bros. and his attempts to maintain his own production company.

87 "THE GOOD TRADITION . . .": Walter Bernstein, Interview. All subsequent quotations of his are drawn from this source.

"UNDOUBTEDLY THE FIRST FILM . . .": Press release, *Kiss the Blood Off My Hands* production file, UC USC.

THE END EFFECT: An intricate portable set capable of serving as an entire mile of London limehouse streets was designed by art directors Nathan Juran and Bernard Hezbrun; different combinations of wall and roof were pushed around like Tinkertoys on one sound stage, allowing a long early sequence of Lancaster running desperately up, down, in, and around the murky streets. Fontaine's twinset was her own, as were all her clothes for this production.

"BLOODBATH IN PRODUCTION.": Lancaster quoted in *Los Angeles Times,* May 22, 1955.

"HEY!" CROWED LANCASTER: Burt Lancaster clipping file, n.d., NYPL.

88 "FANCY-PANTS DAME . . .": Lancaster quoted in Martin, 187.

"MOST PEOPLE . . . SEEM TO THINK . . .": Lancaster quoted in Wilson, "Big Guy."

CATCH A 1948 "MOVIE COMET BY THE TAIL,": Martin, 186.

JOHN LE CARRÉ: As quoted in Sydney Pollack, Interview. All subsequent quotations of Pollack's are drawn from this source.

89 "A THING OF BEAUTY,": James Hill, Interview.

"[A] LAVISH AND GRACIOUS GESTURE . . .": Press release, *Kiss the Blood Off My Hands* production file, UC USC.

90 "BIG OUTFIT . . .": Lancaster quoted in Marie Torre, "Lancaster Out-Lancasters Himself," *New York World-Telegram,* Oct. 23, 1948.

NET PROFITS: A. Scott Berg, *Goldwyn,* 431.

91 "THE MOST EXTENDED EMOTIONAL JAG . . .": *Life,* Aug. 23, 1948. *Sorry, Wrong Number* was originally a 1945 half-hour radio play by Lucille Fletcher, starring

Agnes Moorehead. By 1948 it had become enormously popular, rebroadcast seven times and translated into fifteen languages.

"OK, LET'S LEAVE IT UP TO THE STUDIO . . .": Lancaster quoted in Knox, Interview.

HE WAS FORCED: Glad to Lancaster, Feb. 25, 1948, *Criss Cross* production file, MHC USC.

WHEN HE TRIED: Record of the Legal Dept., 20th Century-Fox Film Corporation, Collection 095, Box FX-LR-367-MC 4834861, Theater Arts Library, University of California at Los Angeles Special Collections. There is a flurry of cables and memos as Fox, Lancaster, Universal, and Glad each tried to carve up the best respective deal.

TOOTS SHOR FLEW OUT: Lancaster quoted in (London) *Sunday News,* June 8, 1975.

92 "CELLULOID TRASH.": *Cue,* n.d. [1949], *Criss Cross* clipping file, NYPL.

THE NIGHTCLUB/BAR: At a time when tourists were flocking to Los Angeles, the club was designed to be a realistic example of the polyglot population of the city's midtown area: Mexicans, Chinese, Japanese, Filipinos, Koreans, and South Americans were all represented on the dance floor (Press release, July 13, 1948, *Criss Cross* production file, MHC USC).

"POOR MAN'S BEL AIR.": Ruth Waterbury, "Love Story—Nine Years Young," *Modern Screen,* Jan. 1954.

93 "HEAPING PLATES OF HOT BREAD.": Martin, 197.

"THEY WOULDN'T SLEEP . . .": Lancaster quoted in press release, *Mister 880* clipping file, AMPAS.

THE EARLY EXPERIENCE WITH FOOT CASTS: Itria, "Hard Man."

94 "OUT-AND-OUT ATHLETE . . .": Lancaster quoted in *Los Angeles Examiner,* Oct. 1, 1950.

95 ONE AFTERNOON HE RETURNED: This anecdote, and the direct quotations therein, unless otherwise noted, are from Murray, Interview.

WILLIAM MILLER: *New York Herald Tribune,* May 6, 1949. No record remains of the case other than the final decision. *Miller v. Cuccia,* NYC Special Sessions, 1949.

96 "I COULDN'T STAND THE COMFORT . . .": Lancaster quoted in *Chicago Tribune Magazine,* May 22, 1955.

HANDING OUT MONEY: Cravat, "My Pal."

"BRAVE DAYS OF 1948": Eric Bentley, ed. *Thirty Years of Treason,* 495.

97 "RED STARS . . .": *Red Stars in Hollywood: Their Helpers . . . Fellow Travelers . . . and Co-Conspirators* (St. Louis: Patriotic Tract Society, n.d. [1949]). Attached to letter to J. Edgar Hoover, April 13, 1949 [sender's name and address blacked-out], BL FBI.

"THE CP'S [COMMUNIST PARTY'S] TOP CULTURAL FRONT": *Counterattack: Facts to Combat Communism [Counterattack],* Jan. 21, 1949, BL FBI.

"THE NEW CAVE MAN STAR": *Los Angeles Examiner,* Dec. 31, 1948.

"CAN ANYTHING BE MORE UN-AMERICAN . . .": Lancaster quoted in "Film Star Tells Rally Witchhunts Must Go," *Daily Worker,* Jan. 10, 1949, BL FBI.

BY JANUARY 21: *Counterattack,* Letter No. 87, Jan. 21, 1949, BL FBI.

98 "NOT STRONG ENOUGH": Leon Kaplan, Lancaster's attorney, Interview. All sub-

sequent quotations of his are drawn from this source. Kaplan started as an entertainment lawyer in 1935 and in 1940 formed the firm of Kaplan & Livingston, which ultimately became Kaplan Livingston Goodwin Berkowitz & Selvin, one of the largest Hollywood entertainment law firms. It dissolved in 1980.

"DESTROYED" BY THE MARRIAGE: Confidential Interview.

99 "[BURT] WAS ALWAYS,": Winters quoted in Manso, *Mailer,* 131.

"CHARMING AND FUNNY . . .": Shelley Winters, *Shelley, Also Known as Shirley,* 240.

WHEN THEIR LIAISON: John Berry is the main source of this version of the anecdote.

"LOVELY AND SAD BACKSTREET ROMANCE": Shelley Winters, *Shelley II,* 315.

LANCASTER REPORTEDLY CONTINUED TO BE OBSESSED: Knox, Interview.

"A SWEET TIME, . . .": Norman Mailer, Interview. All subsequent quotations of his are drawn from this source.

CHAPTER 5: The Hero Business

101 "IT WAS THE BEST THING . . .": Lancaster quoted in *New York World-Telegram,* Sept. 19, 1959.

IN 1950, BOX-OFFICE RECEIPTS: Berg, 447.

102 FROM 1946 TO 1962: Tino Balio, *United Artists: The Company That Changed the Film Industry,* 125.

"BY AN ALL-CONSUMING PRE-OCCUPATION . . .": *The New Republic,* n.d. [1948], *All My Sons* clipping file, FSC MOMA.

HE AGREED TO STAR: Lochte, "Adding Machine."

"HAROLD AND I WERE WRACKING OUR BRAINS . . .": Lancaster, "Sawdust."

103 "OUT TO CORNER ALL THE LADS . . .": *Los Angeles Examiner,* Mar. 18, 1949.

"TURBULENT TIMES": Warner quoted in Michael Freedland, *The Warner Brothers,* 200.

"ALMOST EXACTLY DUPLICAT[ING] . . .": Thomas F. Brady, "Lancaster Makes Deal at Warner's," *New York Times,* Mar. 18, 1949.

THERE WERE ACTUALLY TWO: Warner Bros.–Burt Lancaster and Warner Bros.–Norma Production contracts, July 8, 1949, WB USC.

104 "THAT'S THE WAY THEY KILL CATTLE, . . .": Lancaster quoted in press release, *The Flame and the Arrow* production file, WB USC. Production details are also taken from the May 1950 issue of *Argosy.* A list of the movie's acrobatic feats appears in Patricia Clary, "Burt Lancaster Own Stunt Man: Movie Star Gets Affidavits to Prove It," *New York Morning Telegraph,* Aug. 14, 1950.

SHOTSY O'BRIEN: Earl Wilson, "Air Male from Paris," *New York Post,* July 13, 1950. O'Brien became a pal and training consultant for Lancaster for many years.

"WHAT THESE BABIES . . .": Lancaster quoted in press release, *The Flame and the Arrow* production file, WB USC.

"WHAT THE FUCK IS THIS?": Warner quoted in Lochte, "Adding Machine."

"[T]HE PRODUCERS . . .": *New York Times,* July 8, 1950.

TO BACK UP ITS OFFER: *New York Morning Telegraph,* Aug. 14, 1950. One disgruntled bit player later sued Warner Bros., claiming technical fraud; the case was ruled in favor of the studio with the judge commenting that he suspected that the court had been used as a "publicity forum" (*Los Angeles Times*, July 24, 1953).

105 ". . . THE HERO BUSINESS.": Lancaster quoted in (London) *Daily Mail*, July 15, 1970.

"[N]OTHING WAS ABOVE SUSPICION.": William Manchester, *The Glory and the Dream*, 581.

106 "A KIND OF ANTI-COMMUNISTS' *TEN DAYS THAT SHOOK THE WORLD*,": John Cogley, *Report on Blacklisting*, vol. 2, 14.

"COMMUNIST FRONT RECORD.": *Counterattack*, Aug. 4, 1950, BL FBI.

107 THE AMERICAN LEGION: Summary of Trends and Developments exposing the COMMUNIST Conspiracy, Oct.–Nov. 1950 (Indianapolis: National Americanism Commission, Sub-Committee on Subversive Activities, The American Legion Headquarters, 1950), AMPAS.

"BURT IS SLICED . . .": Press release, n.d. [1950], *Mister 880* production file, AMPAS.

HECHT MADE A POINT: *The Hollywood Reporter*, June 17, 1948.

IN OCTOBER 1950, PARSONS ANNOUNCED: *Los Angeles Examiner*, Oct. 12, 1950.

108 *MISTER 880, A* WINSOME DRAMA: *Mister 880* referred to the file number of one of the longest unsolved counterfeiting cases in the history of the U.S. Secret Service, which was published as a true-life story in *The New Yorker* by St. Clair McKelway. Lancaster had originally wanted the property for Norma Productions; it starred Dorothy McGuire and the Santa Claus of *Miracle on Thirty-fourth Street*, Edmund Gwenn, as the old man who printed enough $1 bills each month between 1938 and 1948 to pay his bills and, he figured, save the government the expense of supporting him. Gwenn got an Oscar nomination.

A SOAP-OPERA WESTERN: *Vengeance Valley* was directed by MGM regular Richard Thorpe who had been behind a camera since the early 1920s directing everything from Tarzan to *Lassie* movies.

"I WANT TO CLEAN UP THOSE CONTRACTS . . .": Lancaster quoted in press release, *Mister 880* clipping file, NYPL.

"A NUMBER OF GRIEVANCES.": Lancaster to Wallis, Oct. 2, 1950, Burt Lancaster correspondence file to end Oct. 1950, HWC AMPAS. "Letter, not sent" comes from same source. According to Lancaster, Wallis recovered $37,500 from the $40,000 Lancaster received for *Mister 880* and $25,000 from the $40,000 he received for *Vengeance Valley*—this in addition to the balance of the $150,000 that was paid to Paramount for each of the loanouts.

109 MAKING THE MOVIE: When Thorpe's wife opened a bar during filming, "the producers went crazy," recalled Lancaster, "bought her out" (*New York Times*, Oct. 15, 1982).

"GONE TO POT.": Lancaster quoted in *New York Times*, Oct. 15, 1982.

"STEREOTYPED INDIANS IN EVER CHEAPER . . .": Parish, 201.

110 "NO PEEPS FROM FANS,": William Best, "Sports Experts OK Lancaster," *New York Morning Telegraph*, Sept. 6, 1951. Pop Warner wished to correct the Hollywood version of the history of forward pass, as protrayed in *Knute Rockne: All American*,

Warner's 1940 biopic starring Pat O'Brien and Ronald Reagan: "He wanted to know," wrote Trilling to Freeman, another Warner Bros. executive, "how the hell Rockne could have invented the forward pass when Carlisle was using it ten years before Rockne played football" (Trilling to Freeman, Aug. 3, 1949, *Jim Thorpe* production file, WB USC).

"REALLY WONDERFUL CONDITION.": Lancaster quoted in Wheeler, 252. Lancaster contributed to this biography a section on the making of *Jim Thorpe— All American,* which included a thoughtful analysis of the role of the "amateur" in sports.

"LOOK PRETTY GOOD DOING IT": Lancaster quoted in Wheeler, 252.

"I GET A FUNNY FEELING,": Jim Thorpe quoted in press release, *Jim Thorpe—All American* production file, WB USC.

"WISHED TO HIDE HIS FEELINGS . . .": Ibid.

113 "THESE NORMA PEOPLE,": *New York Times,* Oct. 27, 1951.

"MOST STARS,": Robert Schiffer, Interview. All subsequent quotations of his are drawn from this source.

115 "EMBARRASSED . . . A GREAT DEAL": Siodmak to Trilling, Dec. 3, 1951, *The Crimson Pirate* production file, WB USC.

"WONDERFUL TRAVESTY . . .": Pauline Kael, *5001 Nights at the Movies,* 129. Waldo Salt would later write *Midnight Cowboy, Serpico, The Day of the Locust,* and share an Academy Award for *Coming Home* in 1978.

COSTUMES CLOSELY MODELED: A three-master frigate, also used by the studio that year for *Captain Horatio Hornblower,* and a two-master pirate rig were revamped at Ville-France in the Mediterranean for Caribbean authenticity. What the studio claimed was an exact copy of the first practical balloon made by Jacques and Ettienne Montgolfier in 1783 provided the perfectly improbable escape vehicle (*The Crimson Pirate* production file, WB USC). Other details of *Pirate* production are also drawn from this source.

"UNDERCLASS CHARACTERS": Richard Koszarski quoted in *New York Post,* June 12, 1992.

"THE YOUNG SUN GOD, . . .": *New York Post,* Aug. 28, 1952.

"NOBODY," SAID DIRECTOR JOHN FRANKENHEIMER: John Frankenheimer, Interview. All subsequent quotations of his are drawn from this source.

116 "VIRTUALLY SIMULTANEOUSLY.": *New York Times,* Aug. 19, 1951.

117 THAT WAS THE EASY PART: For a description of the production of *The Crimson Pirate,* see also the *Cleveland Plain Dealer,* Sept. 14, 1952.

118 "EVEN FOR A MILLION DOLLARS,": Siodmak quoted in Lacourbe. Translation by the author.

119 "BORIS," LANCASTER CONFIDED: Lancaster quoted in Barere, Interview.

120 "[H]E COULDN'T WRITE HUMAN DIALOGUE.": Lardner quoted in Victor S. Navasky, "The Hollywood Ten Recalled: To Name or Not to Name," *New York Times,* Mar. 25, 1973.

"BY WAY OF THE HOLLYWOOD ANTI-NAZI LEAGUE . . .": Victor Navasky, *Naming Names,* 274.

IN DECEMBER: J.B. Matthews, "Did the Movies Really Clean House?" *The*

American Legion Magazine, Dec. 1951. (For a discussion of the fascinating J.B. Matthews, who traveled from far left to far right, see Goodman, *The Committee.*)

120 IN JANUARY, *COUNTERATTACK* AGAIN: *Counterattack,* Jan. 11, 1952 BL FBI.

AN INFORMANT WROTE A PERSONAL LETTER: Feb. 16, 1952, FBI document No. 94-38680-14, BL FBI. Except for Lancaster's, names are blacked-out in the FBI copy made available to the author.

121 THOSE LIKE CHARLES KATZ: Navasky, 98.

GANG WAS AN INTEGRAL PART: Linden Productions, another Lancaster subcompany, was named for the street that Gang's partner, Norman Tyre, lived on.

"IT TOOK CASH . . .": Where all the money went remains a mystery. Faith Hubley, film editor and screenwriter whose husband, John Hubley, was blacklisted, told Patrick McGilligan that she believed "there was a foundation of payoffs . . . in the sense that if you gave them money in a brown paper bag, they would lay off the persecution; and that the payoffs underwrote corrupt union, organized crime, and the future of the California Republican Party" (McGilligan and Buhle, 187).

"Z.Z., A TOP-FLIGHT HOLLYWOOD STAR.": Cogley, 131. The first three allegations against "Z.Z."—membership in the CFA, signing the *amici curiae* brief, and sponsorship of the October 28, 1947, *Hollywood Reporter* ad against HUAC—were relatively common and could be claimed by a number of stars. But the fourth charge provides the key clue to the identity of the letter's author. The charged affiliation was erroneous, as the clearance letter affirms, and refers to sponsorship of the dinner benefit rally on March 5, 1948, for the Hollywood Ten that was reported in the 1948 Report of the Committee on Un-American Activities in California, the same annual report which recorded that Ira Gershwin had identified Lancaster as a member of the CFA. Lancaster's is the only sponsor name in that 1948 report listed at the dinner benefit that could be called anything like a "top-flight star," the other Hollywood names being Norman Corwin, Richard Brooks, Joseph DaSilva, John Huston, Garson Kanin, Clifford Odets, and Donald Ogden Stewart. Lancaster is the only person of that small group who also participated in all three other activities listed in the clearance letter. The writer of the legion letter also identifies himself first as "one of the owners of [name of company]" and secondly as "an actor in the motion-picture business." Lancaster, in addition to his own Norma Productions, had contracts with Columbia, Warner Bros., and Paramount; Z.Z. is further identified as a "producer/star."

122 "THEY NEVER GOT A STAR. . . .": For a discussion of why Cagney was neither subpoenaed by the postwar HUAC or blacklisted, see Sklar, 252. Unlike Lancaster, Cagney merited an FBI file, the summary of which, compiled in 1950, is 150 pages long. When Robert Ryan was asked by Montgomery Clift why he, vehemently anti-HUAC, had never been blacklisted, Ryan replied, "I'm a Catholic and an ex-marine. Hoover wouldn't touch that combination" (Robert LaGuardia, *Monty,* 144).

"IT MIGHT BE A GOOD IDEA TO CHECK . . .": *Communist Activity,* NYPL.

123   "DISILLUSIONED EX-ALCOHOLIC . . .": Lancaster quoted in William Brownell Jr.,
"Leaves from Lancaster's Scrapbook," *New York Times*, Jan. 18, 1953.

THE STAR OF THE PLAY WAS SHIRLEY BOOTH: Before *Sheba*, Booth had drawn
acclaim for her portrayal of Cissy in *A Tree Grows in Brooklyn*; the *New York Herald
Tribune* asked in Apr. 23, 1951, "if there were anything she couldn't play" and
labeled her "one of the wonders of the American stage."

THOUGH LANCASTER LATER CLAIMED: Brownell, "Leaves."

WHEN SHOOTING BEGAN: Richard Jaeckel, cast as the boyfriend of the Delaney's
lodger, played by Terry Moore, recalled the rehearsal period of *Come Back, Little
Sheba* as being "warmed up" by director Mann, "like a very expensive, beautiful new car, let out easily, easily, and then zinging it at the end" (Richard
Jaeckel, Interview).

"I GUESS I WANTED TO PLAY [DOC] . . .": Lancaster quoted in Parish, 203. The
aging Bogart of *The African Queen* was one early casting possibility for Doc
Delaney—Booth had made her Broadway debut with him in *Hell's Bells* in
1925—but Warner Bros. would not loan him out.

124   "BURT, ONCE IN A WHILE . . .": Booth quoted in Minty Clinch, *Burt Lancaster*, 42.

"DON'T SELL HIM SHORT . . .": Booth quoted in Kibbee, Interview.

"BURT LANCASTER," REPORTED *THE NEW LEADER*: *New Leader*, Mar. 2, 1953.

"TO MY ASTONISHMENT . . .": *The New Yorker*, Dec. 27, 1952.

"ALAS, FOR THE FIRST TIME . . .": Lancaster quoted in press release, *Come Back,
Little Sheba* production file, HWC AMPAS.

"EXTRAORDINARILY INTERESTING REVIEWS . . .": Lancaster quoted in Gow,
"Energy."

THE AUDIENCE: When Booth's Lola turns on the radio to commune with her
favorite soap opera, "Tabu," the music she writhes to on the sofa is "Brazilian
Rhapsody," the same Esy Morales song De Carlo and Curtis rhumbaed to in
Criss Cross.

125   "THERE WERE TIMES,": Lancaster quoted in *His Majesty O'Keefe* clippings file, n.d.
[1953], AMPAS.

"THE M.O.,": Joe Adamson, *Byron Haskin: A Director Guild of America Oral
History*, 213.

"BURT IS CROWNED.": Ibid., 217. Robert Aldrich later remembered, in response
to a question from Peter Bogdanovich about directing *Vera Cruz*, "the script for
Vera Cruz had many sections that would say: 'And the Arabs took the town,' and
we would shoot for seventeen days." He was evidently confusing *Vera Cruz* with
Ten Tall Men, but the m.o. was the same (Peter Bogdanovich, *Who the Devil Made
It* [New York: Alfred A. Knopf, 1997], 784).

"JUST A NARRATIVE . . .": Adamson, 215.

ZIPPING HIS FINGER: Michael Mindlin, Interview. All subsequent quotations of
his are drawn from this source.

126   "THAT LITTLE TOWHEAD": J. Lancaster, "I'll Bet."

SOUTH SEA WOMAN: The movie's title kept changing, midproduction: *Paradise
Interrupted, Interrupted Paradise, Torrid Island, Torrid Zone, Torrid Woman, Torrid Territory*. In April Lubin wrote Jack Warner to protest the "horrible title,"

suggesting that the typical viewer would ask, "Burt Lancaster in *South Sea Woman?*" (Lubin to J. Warner, Apr. 25, 1953, *South Sea Woman* Correspondence file, WB USC).

126   HE OWED HIS CAREER: David Fury, *Chuck Connors: "The Man Behind the Rifle,"* (Minneapolis, MN: Artist's Press, 1997), 84.

ON A SWELTERING NIGHT: Fred Zinnemann, *Fred Zinnemann: An Autobiography,* 132.

127   "EPIDEMIC OF INVESTIGATIONS": Goodman, 324.

128   "ONE SHOT OF THE WAVES . . .": Cutting note of Harry Cohn, May 28, 1953, "Cutting Notes" File 28-f.353, *From Here to Eternity,* Fred Zinnemann Collection, AMPAS. The cinematographer on *From Here to Eternity,* Burnett Guffey, worked for John Ford and Alfred Hitchcock and was now director of photography at Columbia. His second Oscar after *Eternity* would be for *Bonnie and Clyde.*

CLIFT RESENTED: Clinch, 48.

"HE APPROACHED THE SCRIPT . . .": Lancaster quoted in Clinch, 48.

"THE ONLY TIME I WAS EVER REALLY AFRAID . . .": Lancaster quoted in Kitty Kelley, *His Way,* 197.

WHEN HE TRIED HIS OWN VERSION: LaGuardia, *Monty,* 111. Shortly before his death, Zinnemann would recall of Lancaster "a good working relationship with one or two confrontations which are quite usual under high-pressure working conditions" (Letter from Zinnemann to author, Apr. 26, 1996).

129   LANCASTER GOT SO USED: David Fury, *The Cinema History of Burt Lancaster,* 78.

AND HAVING AN AFFAIR: Sydney Pollack and Lucy Kibbee were each told by Lancaster of the affair with Kerr.

ZINNEMANN'S DETAILED ANALYSIS: Fred Zinnemann's leather-bound script of *From Here to Eternity* is in File 27-f.334 of the Fred Zinnemann Collection, AMPAS.

"THAT SCENE . . .": Daniel Taradash, Interview. All subsequent quotations of his are drawn from this source.

"EITHER KAREN OR WARDEN PUT ON A BEACH ROBE . . .": Production Code Office to Cohn, Aug. 4, 1952, *From Here to Eternity* correspondence File 28-f.346, Fred Zinnemann Collection, AMPAS. *Look* magazine published the censored beach scene stills in its Aug. 25, 1953 issue.

CERTAIN PUBLICITY SHOTS: The still cameraman on the beach was Irving "Lippy" Lippman whose camera made a loud noise with each shot. "He kept clicking this camera," recalled Schiffer, who was told the story by Lancaster, "and Burt would say, 'Don't click the goddamned camera,' but he kept clicking. Finally Burt said, 'I told you not to click it' and he picked him up with the camera and all and he threw him in the water" (Schiffer, Interview).

130   "THE PASSION OF LANCASTER FOR KERR . . .": Joan Mellen, *Big Bad Wolves,* 243.

"IT IS A CURIOUS CONTRIBUTION . . .": Zinnemann, 124.

"AS SERGEANT WARDEN [HE] IS THE MODEL . . .": *Time,* 1953, as quoted in Fury, 79.

ONE FAMILY WAS LASTINGLY: John Turturro, Interview. All subsequent quotations of his are drawn from this source.

ON MARCH 23, HECHT: "Investigation of Communist Activities in the Los Angeles Area"—Part 1, March 23, 24 and 25, 1953. United States Un-American Activities Committee (House) Hearings, 83 Congress, 1 Session, Part I. U.S. Government Printing Office, Washington: 1953. All quoted material from the Hecht hearing comes from this source.

131 HIS ATTORNEY WAS EDWARD BENNETT WILLIAMS: Robert Pack, *Edward Bennett Williams for the Defense,* 139.

"THAT SON OF A BITCH,": Abe Polonsky, Interview.

Chapter 6: Zenith

133 "THE EASY, SURE THING, . . .": Lancaster quoted in Jamison, "Maturity."

"ONE OF THE RUDEST . . .": Itria, "Hard Man."

134 "DOING WHAT MOTHER USED TO DO": Lancaster quoted in Jamison, "Maturity."

HEDDA HOPPER GOT AN EARFUL: Hedda Hopper, "Burt's Tenseness is Characteristic," *Oregon Journal,* Aug. 12, 1951.

"NO. . . . SO FAR THEY HAVE BEEN DETERRED . . .": Lancaster quoted in Inez Robb, "Actor Psychs Himself," *New York Journal-American,* Aug. 13, 1953.

SITTING IN YANKEE STADIUM: John J. O'Connor, "Once a Trapeze Artist, Always a Heart-Stopper," *New York Times,* Feb. 25, 1997.

LESS THAN THREE MONTHS: Release agreement, June 11, 1953, between Norma Productions and Warner Bros. Box #12695B, Norma Productions Collection, WB USC.

135 "THE NEW COIN OF THE REALM.": Neal Gabler, Interview.

"THE MEDICIS OF THE MOVIE BUSINESS.": Jane Mayer, "Krim's Tales: Hollywood Mystery: Woes at Orion Stayed Invisible for Years," *Wall Street Journal,* Oct. 16, 1991.

136 AS SIDNEY LUMET SUMMED UP KRIM'S GOALS: Peter Biskind, "Beneficial Life," *Premiere,* March 1995.

ON JUNE 12: Letter from Lancaster to Wallis, June 12, 1953, Burt Lancaster file #2, Contract Envelope #1, HWC AMPAS.

NORMA WOULD GET 75 PERCENT: Balio, *United Artists: The Company That Changed the Film Industry,* 74.

THE SAMUEL GOLDWYN STUDIOS: Samuel Goldwyn, one-time UA partner, bought the property in 1955.

"NEARLY HAD TO GIVE AWAY THE STORE.": Balio, *United Artists: The Company That Changed the Film Industry,* 74.

EIGHT MONTHS LATER: Edwin Schallert, "Deal for $12,000,000 in New Films Disclosed," *Los Angeles Times,* Feb. 8, 1954.

LANCASTER STOPPED THE PROJECTOR: *Los Angeles Examiner,* Feb. 17, 1954.

137 "THE GRUBBY OLD WESTERNER.": Lancaster quoted in Hall & Crawley, *Game* [U.K.], Feb. 1975.

"MEANT BY ALL INVOLVED,": Lancaster quoted in Edwin T. Arnold and Eugene L. Miller Jr., *The Films and Career of Robert Aldrich,* 24.

"*KILLING* THE *HERO*,": "The Derring-Doers of the Movie Business," *Fortune* 57, May 1958.

137   *APACHE* FINISHED AS THE TOP-GROSSING WESTERN OF 1954: Richard C. Robertson, "Just Dreamin' Out Loud: The Westerns of Burt Lancaster," in Archie P. McDonald, ed., *Shooting Stars: Heroes and Heroines of Western Film*, 168.

138   "ELEGANT ESCAPISM,": Andrew Sarris, *The American Cinema*, 84.

"THE VERY TOP . . .": Harold Hecht, "Location is Broadening," *The Hollywood Reporter*, Nov. 12, 1954.

LANCASTER GAVE THE FIFTY-TWO-YEAR-OLD STAR: Balio, *United Artists: The Company That Changed the Film Industry*, 97.

WHEN THE MPAA CAUTIONED: "MPAA to [HL's] Flora Productions, *Vera Cruz*, May 15, 1954, MPAA AMPAS.

"IF I KNOW ANYTHING ABOUT MOVIE ACTING,": Shepard as quoted on book jacket of Robyn Karney, *Burt Lancaster: A Singular Man* (London: Trafalgar Square, 1996).

139   LOUIS MALLE, AMONG FANS: Philip French, ed., *Malle on Malle*.

COSTS HAD ESCALATED: Rushgram from Seymour Peyser [UA General Counsel] to Krim, Nov. 11, 1955, Box 4, UAC SHSW.

"I HAVE THE COMPLETELY HELPLESS FEELING . . .": Krim to Benjamin, May 5, 1954, Box 4, UAC SHSW.

ASKED UA FOR $100,000: Robert Blumofe to Krim, May 12, 1954, Box 4, UAC SHSW.

140   "THE DECISIVE FACTOR": David Shipman, *The Story of Cinema*, 931.

"WHERE DO I GET OFF . . .": Burt Lancaster, "Actor By Accident," *The Hollywood Reporter*, Nov. 12, 1954.

"THEY'RE THE ONES . . .": Lancaster quoted in Gow, "Energy."

HIS "CONTEMPT" FOR THE DIRECTING PROFESSION: *Variety*, Oct. 5, 1954.

"INCOMPETENT, HIGH-MINDED, SELF-STYLED SUPERMEN": Lancaster quoted in Joe Hyams, "Burt Lancaster to Direct Second Film, Despite Guild Feud," *New York Herald Tribune*, Dec. 10, 1954. *The Kentuckian* (originally titled *Gabriel Horn*) was to have been the third and last of the Warner Bros. productions starring Lancaster (Release Agreement between Warner Bros. and Burt Lancaster, June 11, 1953, Norma Productions, Box # 12695B, WB USC).

141   "I HAD NO ONE TO HELP ME,": Lancaster quoted in Lochte, "Adding Machine."

"YOU DON'T KNOW WHAT THE HELL YOU'RE TALKING ABOUT, . . .": Matthau quoted in Burt Lancaster, "Pre-Filming Warm-Up is Important," *The Hollywood Reporter*, Nov. 14, 1955.

HE WENT TO KANSAS CITY: Benton did at least one head study for the finished *Kentuckian* painting. A photograph of such, misidentified as *Portrait of Burt Lancaster as Robin Hood*, appeared in the March 1999 issue of *House & Garden* (Suzanne Slezin, "Lush Life: A softly rich decor by Sheryl Asklund Rock and Jorge Letelier perfectly complements a spirited collection of American art," *House & Garden*, March 1999).

"YOU OLD REPROBATE,": Lancasater quoted in Joe Creason, "Artist Thomas

Hart Benton Does Thorough Job Sketching Burt Lancaster for *The Kentuckian* Ballyhoo," *Louisville Courier-Journal,* Oct. 17, 1954.

TWEAKING THE MOVIE: *Time,* Sept. 26, 1955.

142 "THE MOST EXPLOSIVE . . .": *Time,* Dec. 12, 1955.

"JESUS CHRIST ALMIGHTY,": Transcribed telephone call, Wallis to Citron, Oct. 27, 1954, *Rose Tattoo* production file, HWC AMPAS. By this point, Wallis was taping and transcribing all telephone calls from and concerning Lancaster.

HIS FEAR OF FLYING: Agreement between Burt Lancaster and Hal Wallis, Jan. 6, 1954, Burt Lancaster contract file, File #2, Envelope #4, HWC AMPAS.

"SHE WOULD WIPE ME OFF THE STAGE,": Brando quoted in Manso, *Brando,* 497.

A "RIOTOUS AND RADIANT THING . . .": Notes of Williams on screen version of *The Rose Tattoo,* Apr. 21, 1952, *Rose Tattoo*-Nathan file, HWC AMPAS.

THE PLAYWRIGHT: Gene D. Phillips, *The Films of Tennessee Williams,* 119.

"LONG ENOUGH TO FINISH . . .": Ibid.

143 "*LO SENTI, NI?*": The author wishes to thank Paola Casella for not only tracking down a copy of *Bellissima* in Rome, but also for watching it and transcribing and translating the dialogue.

"A GREAT CRIMINAL.": *Time,* Dec. 12, 1955.

"[D]ON'T COME IN TIL THE 'THIRD ACT,' ": Lancaster quoted in Philip Scheuer, "Burt Lancaster Takes New Aim. He Aspires to Become a Director," *Los Angeles Times,* n.d. [1954], CMC USC.

144 "WHAT HAVE THE 1950S BROUGHT US . . .": Mailer quoted in Shaun Considine, *Mad As Hell,* 196.

"ALL THE SOULS WERE SINGING . . .": Steiger quoted in Considine, 57. For a recounting of the making of both the TV and movie versions of *Marty,* see chapters 7 and 8 of Considine.

"I'M SURE,": Delbert Mann, Interview. All subsequent quotations of his are drawn from this source.

145 "I THINK YOU GOT THE PART. . . .": Betsy Blair, Interview. All subsequent quotations of hers are drawn from this source. The author wishes to thank John Guare for putting her in touch with Ms. Blair.

"SETTING FORTH WHETHER YOU ARE NOW . . .": R.B. Shipley to Lancaster, Dec. 23, 1953, passport record of Lancaster, U.S. Department of State, Passport Services: PPT/TD/RS/RL—LANCASTER, Burton Stephen, Case Control Number 9502520. Lancaster's passport file was requested from the U.S. Department of State under the Freedom of Information Act and all subsequent references to Lancaster passport-related documents are drawn from that source. BL PASS.

HE MUST PROVIDE ANOTHER MORE DETAILED: Shipley to Lancaster, Feb. 18, 1954. Shipley provided a list of Lancaster's suspect activities: his membership and "active" involvement with the CFA; his signature on a NCASP statement calling for the abolition of HUAC; his speech in January 1949 before the NCASP. BL PASS.

A LENGTHY AFFIDAVIT: Lancaster's affidavit, plus copies of all his passport applications are also in his passport record. BL PASS. In 1958, the Supreme Court ruled that the state department had no authority to withhold the right to travel because of a person's associations or beliefs.

146 TWO YEARS LATER: "Burt Lancaster and Family Request to Meet the Director," FBI Memorandum, June 28, 1957, BL FBI.

"TREMENDOUS OPPORTUNITY . . .": Blumofe to Krim, May 14, 1954, Box 4, UAC SHSW.

"UA WOULD BE IN AN EXTREMELY DISADVANTAGEOUS, . . .": Kaplan to Krim, Nov. 24, 1954, Box 4, UAC SHSW.

"[E]VEN THOUGH THE GUYS AT UA . . .": Lancaster quoted in Lochte, "Adding Machine."

147 WHEN HECHT PROTESTED: Considine, 83.

"IT WAS LIKE A ONE-MAN RELIGIOUS CAMPAIGN . . .": Joe Hyams, Interview. All subsequent quotations of his are drawn from this source.

CHAYEFSKY'S "SENTENCES . . .": As quoted in Considine, 85.

149 "RARELY HAS A SINGLE PICTURE . . .": *Variety*, Feb. 14, 1956.

NEWSWEEK REPORTED: *Newsweek*, April 2, 1956.

150 CHAYEFSKY WROTE *THE BACHELOR PARTY:* David Thomson wrote of *The Bachelor Party*: ". . . a far better film [than *Marty*], beautifully acted and with an accurate sense of American middle-class anxieties, such as only John Cassavetes has since explored" (David Thomson, *A Biographical Dictionary of Film*, 478).

"BROUGHT OUT THE LEDGERS. . . .": Lancaster quoted in Lochte, "Adding Machine."

"AMBITION TO WRITE, PRODUCE OR JUST ACT . . .": Deere, "Big Guy."

151 WHAT THE *LOS ANGELES TIMES* CALLED AN "ASTRONOMICAL": *Los Angeles Times*, May 20, 1956.

"THE GLOBAL LOOK . . .": Newspaper ad, *Trapeze* clipping file, NYPL.

ALMOST 50 PERCENT: *Saturday Review*, Apr. 7, 1956.

A CORPORATE STRUCTURE OF U.S. AND FOREIGN COMPANIES: Confidential memo to files from Peyser, May 15, 1955, Box 4, UAC WSHS.

CHARLES SMADJA: Smadja to Kaplan, May 16, 1955, Box 4, UAC SHSW.

"ESTABLISH SOME BRAKE": Confidential memo to files from Krim, Feb. 21, 1955, Box 4, UAC SHSW.

KRIM WROTE A CONFIDENTIAL MEMO: Ibid.

153 "$160,000 . . . THE LARGEST FILM SALARY . . .": "Lancaster Up to Old Tricks," *Los Angeles Times*, May 20, 1956.

ERNEST CLARKE: Culhane, 178.

LANCASTER SAW TRIPLE MASTER: Ibid., 259.

"ALL FALSE TEETH AND A TERROR OF BEING HIT . . .": Lancaster quoted in Culhane, 259.

"WHAT DOES HE MEAN? . . .": Lollobrigida quoted in Mindlin, Interview.

154 THE ORIGINAL NOVEL: Robert F. Moss, *The Films of Carol Reed*, 216. A 1932 German film, also titled *Trapeze*, may have also been an influence. Wolf Mankowitz gave "uncredited assistance" to the James Webb script for *Trapeze* (Moss, 217). Daniel Fuchs, screenwriter of *Criss Cross*, sued HL, claiming they had plagia-

rized his short story, "The Daring Young Man on the Flying Trapeze"; HL settled, paying Fuchs $50,000 but insisted the movie's source was *The Killing Frost* (Moss, 216).

"I NEED HIM, SO IT'S BETTER . . .": Reed as quoted in Gina Lollobrigida, Interview.

PROCEEDED TO TRASH IT: Youngstein, Interview.

"YOU GET OFF MY HUSBAND'S BACK,": Norma Lancaster quoted in Mindlin, Interview.

155 THERE WAS ONE COMMENTARY: *Saturday Review,* quoted in Fury, 104.

IN TEHRAN, MILITARY POLICE: *Variety,* Mar. 20, 1957.

VARIETY RAVED: *Variety,* May 8, 1957.

AT FOUR O'CLOCK: John Culhane, "Trapeze: The Quest for the 'Impossible' Quadruple Somersault," *New York Times Magazine,* Mar. 19, 1978. The details about Gaona are drawn from this source.

"[T]HE HIGHER THE ACT,": Lancaster quoted in *Hollywood Drama-Logue,* Apr. 2–8, 1981.

WORD OF LANCASTER'S ACTIVITIES: Carl Reinhardt, "He's a star on the flying trapeze, but . . . One night BURT LANCASTER was an acrobat in the BOUDOIR," *Confidential,* n.d. [1956–1957], CMC USC.

156 LANCASTER TOOK MRS. BRUCE CABOT: Charles A. Wright, "The Secret's Out About: Burt Lancaster," *Confidential,* May 1955.

"THAT GREAT ARMY OF DISGRUNTLED MOVIE PEOPLE.": Ezra Goodman, *The Fifty-Year Decline and Fall of Hollywood,* 51.

157 ANOTHER FRIEND SAW THEM BOTH: Ceil Brink, Nick Cravat's second wife, Interview. All subsequent quotations of hers are drawn from this source.

THE PRESS DETAILED: Waterbury, "Menace."

AFTER THE BIRTH: Ruth Waterbury, "The Private World of Burt Lancaster," *Photoplay,* n.d. [1961], CMC USC.

158 THERE WAS A WHIRLWIND: Press release, *The Rainmaker* production file, HWC AMPAS.

"VERY, VERY HAPPY.": Lancaster quoted in Rubin, "Gentle Side."

"YOU STOP THAT!": Joanna Lancaster quoted in Ruth Waterbury, "Burt's Bounding Brood," *Photoplay,* n.d. [1956–1957], CMC USC.

WHEN JIMMY DREW A FANCIFUL MURAL: Waterbury, "Menace."

"NORMA, THEY ARE *OUR* KIDS . . .": Lancaster quoted in Waterbury, "Private World."

160 "AN INTENSE YOUNG COLLEGE INSTRUCTOR . . .": Shipp, "Burt Lancaster."

161 "TOUGH TITTY,": Lancaster quoted in Judith Crist, *Take 22,* 80.

"SLIM, TAUT FIGURE,": Sheila Graham, *New York Mirror,* May 9, 1954.

DID EVERYTHING "HARD.": Sidney Skolsky, "Hollywood Is My Beat," *New York Post,* Aug. 8, 1954.

"BEING THE CARICATURE OF A HE-MAN . . .": Lancaster quoted in Hopper, "Tenseness."

THE RAINMAKER: The play was loosely based on an infamous San Diego water scandal of 1915: Charles Hatfield, a Quaker and self-designated "Moisture

Accelerator," claimed credit for a downpour that, in one month, produced thirty-eight inches of rain, crumbled dams, washed out roads and farms, and drowned twenty people (Tony Perry, "Southland's Water Future May Hinge on Bitter Dispute," *Los Angeles Times*, Aug. 3, 1997).

162   HE WROTE THAT HE WAS "THRILLED": Nash to Wallis, Mar. 8, 1954, N. Richard Nash file, HWC AMPAS.

SHE SIGNED WITH WALLIS: There were a few presigning wrangles. Hepburn found an early version of the script "adolescent" (Hepburn to Wallis, Sept. 9, 1955, *The Rainmaker* production file, HWC AMPAS), then objected to Holden as "wrong for the part" of Starbuck (Hepburn to Wallis, Nov. 28, 1955, *The Rainmaker* production file, HWC AMPAS).

"HE HAS A LOVELY FACE . . .": Hepburn to Wallis, March 1, 1956, *The Rainmaker* production file, HWC AMPAS. Of Magnani, Hepburn wrote in the same letter: "I was thrilled almost out of my skin—my oh my oh my—how remarkable that woman is . . . I hope you don't expect me to be in that class—wow—I felt that she'd picked me up by the seat of the pants, shaken the dust out of me and set me down a bag of bones and sentimentality."

"A HELL-FOR-LEATHER CHALLENGER . . .": Lancaster quoted in *The Rainmaker* clipping file, n.d., NYPL.

"BUNCH OF CRAP": Lancaster quoted in Charles Higham, *Kate*, 170.

163   LANCASTER WAS RUDE AND AGGRESSIVELY IMPATIENT: Higham, *Kate*, 170.

"OVERALL COOPERATIVE SPIRIT AND ENTHUSIASM": Wallis to Nash, Sept. 5, 1956, N. Richard Nash collection, SHSW.

"I NEVER DREAMED,": Wallis to Nash, Sept. 5, 1956, N. Richard Nash collection, SHSW.

"HALF SAY IT WAS A LAY . . .": Nathan to Wallis, n.d., *The Rainmaker*, MPAA AMPAS.

"A GLORIFICATION OF ILLICIT SEX,": Shurlock to Wallis, June 28, 1955, *The Rainmaker*, MPAA AMPAS.

"I AM NOT GOING TO TEAR MY GUTS OUT,": Wallis to Hazan, June 30, 1955, *The Rainmaker* production file, HWC AMPAS.

"[T]HE GRACE HE HAS GIVEN . . .": *Time*, Dec. 31, 1956.

164   WHEN WALLIS FIRST SENT: Wallis to Nathan, July 1954, Nathan file, *Gunfight at the O.K. Corral* production file, HWC AMPAS.

"DOC HOLLIDAY A RUTHLESS BEAST . . .": Nathan to Wallis, Aug. 4, 1954, *Gunfight at the O.K. Corral* production file, HWC AMPAS.

THE ABC TELEVISION NETWORK: Tim Brooks and Earle Marsh, "The Life and Legend of Wyatt Earp," *The Complete Directory to Prime Time Network TV Shows: 1946–Present, Fifth Edition* (New York: Ballantine, 1992), 509–510. Hugh O'Brien's Earp blew away the bad guys with extra-long, barreled Buntline pistols provided by his pal and personal mythologist, dime novelist Ned Buntline, played in the TV series by Lloyd Corrigan. Preproduction notes for *Gunfight at the O.K. Corral* also specified a Buntline pistol and Lancaster would stroke one during a scene in the movie.

A MARCH 1955 ARTICLE: Lynn Rogers, "Ghosts Haunt Tombstone," *Los Angeles*

Times, Mar. 27, 1955. See also Allen Barra, "At the O.K. Corral, They Mythed," *New York Times,* Nov. 1, 1998.

"DESPERADOES": *Denver Post,* July 22, 1956.

165   "SICK, TIRED OLD MAN . . .": Nathan to Wallis, May 6, 1955, Nathan file, *Gunfight at the O.K. Corral* production file, HWC AMPAS.

HE DID NOT LIKE THE SCRIPT: Nathan to Wallis, Dec. 12, 1955, *Gunfight at the O.K. Corral* production file, HWC AMPAS.

AFTER CONSIDERABLE SHUFFLING OF NAMES: Bogart was an early hope to cast as Holliday, seen initially as the major character. In February 1955 Nathan memoed Wallis that Bogart "loves the character and loves the idea of playing it. He also loves the idea of doing a picture with Burt Lancaster as Wyatt Earp" (Nathan to Wallis, Feb. 23, 1955, *Gunfight at the O.K. Corral* production file, HWC AMPAS). There was also talk of casting Bogart's wife, Bacall, as the two stars "want to work together." But in September, Bogart announced the formation of his own independent company, Mapleton Pictures, and rejected *Gunfight.* Bogart's persistent real-life cough at the time (A.M. Sperber and Eric Lax, *Bogart,* 509) would have lent a certain authenticity to his Doc Holliday, who is required by the script to hack away like a frontier Camille. In real life Bogart would never have made it to the Paramount stage set in March: on February 29, he was operated on for cancer of the esophagus and was dead by the following January. In December 1955, Wallis and Nathan were considering whether to shoot for the moon and present a package to John Ford (Nathan to Wallis, Dec. 5, 1955, Nathan file, HWC AMPAS *Gunfight at the O.K. Corral*) with star casting of Lancaster and Richard Widmark. It didn't fly. Michael Curtiz liked the "combo of Lancaster and Kirk Douglas" but passed, finding the script too long and needing to bring into better focus the "unusual relationship between Doc and Wyatt." (Curtiz to Wallis, Jan. 31, 1956, *Gunfight at the O.K. Corral* production file, HWC AMPAS.)

"CERTAIN QUALITIES . . .": Stephen Farber, "Lancaster and Douglas," *New York Times,* Nov. 2, 1986.

166   "TOO MUCH INFORMATION AND UNNECESSARY DIALOGUE.": Script revisions, Feb. 9, 1956, Nathan file, *Gunfight at the O.K. Corral* production file, HWC AMPAS.

URIS THOUGHT IT WAS "PHONEY, . . .": Ibid.

BOBSEY TWINS: Uris to Nathan, June 1956, Nathan file, *Gunfight at the O.K. Corral* production file, HWC AMPAS.

THE COMPANY TRAVELED BACK TO LOS ANGELES: Paramount's Stage 4 was used for the interior of Doc's room at the Astor Hotel in Fort Griffen. Most of the Tombstone scenes were done on the studio's backlot "Western Street." Stages 6 and 7 were Earp's and Holliday's hotel rooms in the early Dodge City scenes as well as the Clanton's kitchen and the Marshall's office in Tombstone. The Long Branch Saloon in Dodge City, where Earp first meets both Holliday and Laura, was set on Stage 11. Some exterior street shots were shot in Tucson with the local Circle Ranch doubling for the Clanton Ranch. The Elgin area of Tucson was used for other exteriors and the Empire Ranch environs served as the road out from Dodge City. (*Gunfight at the O.K. Corral* production file, HWC AMPAS).

166 DEFOREST KELLEY: DeForest Kelley, Interview. All subsequent quotations of his are drawn from this source. Kelley went on to play Dr. Leonard McCoy in the original *Star Trek* TV series.

ONE NIGHT OVER DINNER: Dennis Hopper, Interview. All subsequent quotations of his are drawn from this source.

167 THE FINAL GUNFIGHT SCENE: The summary shot sheet for May 13, 1956, read as follows: "21 set-ups, starting with LONG SHOTS past Ike at burning wagon to Virgil doubled running L to R and getting shot—PAN RT revealing Wyatt as he rescued Virgil and takes him to the side of a small shed—Ike exits L to R after them" and on through the day to "6:15 pm CLOSE PAN SHOT—Ike, Tom and Ringo—PAN RT as they get behind wagon and FIRE OFF R to L at Wyatt as the shotgun is fired" (*Gunfight at the O.K. Corral* production file, HWC AMPAS).

"TOES CROSSED IN DEADLY FEAR . . .": Uris to Nathan, June 1956, Nathan file, *Gunfight at the O.K. Corral* production file, HWC AMPAS.

"THE OLD GAMBLING, BOOZING, . . .": *New York Times,* May 30, 1957.

"LOOKS LIKE A MAN WHO IS HEADING . . .": *Time,* June 17, 1957.

CHAPTER 7: A Cookie Full of Arsenic

"HECHT-LANCASTER PRODUCTIONS IS THE LARGEST . . .": Lancaster quoted in Joe Hyams, "This is Hollywood," *New York Herald Tribune,* Jan. 26, 1956. This Joe Hyams was a Hollywood journalist, biographer, and producer.

170 "LOOKED LIKE A SCENE . . .": Alexander, "The Real Burt."

"IT DOESN'T MATTER . . .": *Time,* Sept. 3, 1956.

HILL WAS SLATED: Ibid.

"EXTRAORDINARILY SUCCESSFUL": *New York Times,* Dec. 31, 1956.

171 "LARGEST INDEPENDENT MOTION PICTURE DEAL . . .": *Variety,* Apr. 13, 1956.

SPECIAL BONUS PROVISION: UA office memo from Krim, Jan. 31, 1956, Box 4, UAC SHSW.

THE NIGGLING ABOUT OVERHEAD: Balio, *United Artists: The Company That Changed the Film Industry,* 149.

A ROSTER OF PROJECTS: Edwin Schallert, "Big Film Producing Program Announced," *Los Angeles Times,* Dec. 31, 1956.

"RULED THE WEST END": Ben Brantley, "Love Invades a Proper English Life," *New York Times,* Mar. 27, 1998.

WHITE HUNTER, BLACK HEART: Huston later said that if a movie was ever made out of *White Hunter, Black Heart,* the one actor he *didn't* want to play him was Lancaster. Eventually Clint Eastwood would produce, direct, and star in the movie, released in 1990.

FOR IRWIN SHAW'S NOVEL: Michael Shnayerson, *Irwin Shaw,* 241.

"NOT VERY INTERESTED IN MOVIE DEALS": Sherlee Lantz, Interview. All subsequent quotations of hers are drawn from this source.

172 AFTER BORGNINE SUED: *Los Angeles Examiner,* Dec. 4, 1956. See Considine for a

more detailed discussion of Borgnine's lawsuit against HL. See also *Los Angeles Examiner*, Sept. 20, 1956; *Los Angeles Examiner*, Dec. 4, 1956; *New York Times*, Nov. 27, 1957.

LANCASTER AND HECHT RESTRUCTURED: *New York Times*, Dec. 31, 1956.

WHAT ARTHUR MAYER CALLED: *The Saturday Review*, Apr. 7, 1956.

"[S]OMEWHERE IN BETWEEN HOLLYWOOD'S SO-CALLED 'BLOCKBUSTER' . . .": *The Hollywood Reporter*, Nov. 14, 1955.

THE OLD CINEMAS: Ronald J. Oakley, *God's Country*, 261.

173 "[T]HE OVERPAID PROFILES": Ezra Goodman, 437.

"YOU EITHER PAY CARY GRANT . . .": *The Saturday Review*, Apr. 7, 1956.

BEGINNING TO EMERGE FROM THE WORST OF THE BLACKLIST: Robert Rich, a.k.a. Dalton Trumbo, won the Oscar for *The Brave One* (1956) and Carl Foreman, blacklisted since 1951, was hired by Columbia in 1957 after an interesting sequence of standoffs (Paul Jacobs, "Good Guys, Bad Guys, and Congressman Walter," *The Hollywood Reporter*, May 15, 1958).

"IF THEY THOUGHT THEY COULD TURN A BUCK . . .": Ibid.

IN 1921 HOLLYWOOD: *The Saturday Review*, Apr. 7, 1956.

DURING 1957, OF 291 PRODUCTIONS: Balio, *United Artists: The Company That Changed the Film Industry*, 87.

ITS LAST FIVE PICTURES: *Time*, Sept. 3, 1956.

"[I]F YOU WANT TO KEEP ON WORKING,": Hecht quoted in Considine, 109.

174 MANAGED TO LEVERAGE RELATIONSHIPS: Yale graduate Vincent Lawrence (1890–1946) began as a Broadway playwright with a flair for snappy dialogue. He went to Hollywood in 1931 and collaborated on *Man-Proof* at MGM (1938) and *Gentleman Jim* at Warner's (1941).

175 "PERFECTLY OPEN ADMIRATION": Waterbury, "Love Story."

"MY HANDS!": Michael Mindlin and press accounts provided details about this incident.

176 AN INFORMANT IN THE BUREAU'S NEW YORK OFFICE: FBI Office Memorandum, M.A. Jones to Mr. DeLoach Re: Burton Stephen Lancaster, July 12, 1963, BL FBI.

"PARTIES AT THE HOME . . .": In the material provided by the FBI in the author's first request under FOIA, this information was blacked-out. On appeal, it was released. BL FBI.

A REPORT WAS FILED: FBI Office Memorandum, SAC [Special Agent "C"] (94-558) to Director, FBI (63-4296), Re: CRIMDEL - CRS, Feb. 16, 1960, BL FBI. In the material provided by the FBI pursuant to the author's first request under FOIA, this information was entirely blacked-out. On appeal, it was released.

NORMA "HATED" HILL: Kamber, Interview.

177 ODETS EVENTUALLY DECIDED: Alexander, "The Real Burt." The author has paraphrased and embellished Alexander's description of Odets's categories.

178 NO PRODUCER—LET ALONE THE CENSORS: Robert Lord to Breen, May 11, 1949, *Sweet Smell of Success*, MPAA AMPAS ("Is it [*Sweet Smell of Success*], by its very

nature, fighting the Code to such an extent that the production of it would become impossible?"). The title of Lehman's original story was "The Sweet Smell of Success"; "The" was eliminated from the movie's title.

178 HE BEGAN WORK: Lehman had one, brief, pre–*Sweet Smell* brush with HL when he was hired to write a script for what became *Trapeze*. He quit out of frustration at both the material and the ambience despite the pleas of Hecht who, according to Lehman, literally went down on his knees and pleaded with him not to leave, claiming Lancaster would blame him (Lehman, Interview).

ONE MORNING, SITTING AT THE TYPEWRITER: Lehman, Interview. Mackendrick's recollections reinforce Lehman's story: "I was testing a lot of people for the Rita role," the director remembered. "They were all very nubile but not all that good as actresses. I wondered, Who the hell is recommending this? So I did a naughty thing. I said, 'Sure, I'll test them, but I want to know which member of the front office is recommending which girl?' There was a dead silence on that one." Mackendrick claimed that he heard of Nichols through New York connections and pushed for casting her as Rita. She remained a family friend of Burt and Norma for several years.

179 "MONSTERS," THE TWO ACTORS CALLED THEM: Philip Kemp, *Lethal Innocence,* 140. See chapter 7 in Kemp, "Sweet Smell of Success," for a discussion of the making of and imagery in *Sweet Smell of Success*.

"HOW ABOUT ME?": Lancaster quoted in Lehman, Interview.

"SOMEDAY WE'LL ALL BE STANDING AROUND . . .": Ibid.

"GEE, ERNIE, . . .": Ibid.

"PERITONITIS OF THE SOUL,": Odets quoted in John Lahr, "Waiting for Odets," *The New Yorker,* Oct. 26, 1992.

180 MANY OF LEHMAN'S LINES: "First Draft Ernest Lehman Script," Mar. 30, 1956, *Sweet Smell of Success* production file, James Wong Howe Collection, AMPAS.

THE GREAT ARTIST OF BLACK-AND-WHITE FILM: "Jimmy [Wong Howe] was of course a tiny little man and the New York crew hated him," said Milner. "He thought they were all lazy louts making twice the money his people were making and doing one-tenth of the work" (Marty Milner, Interview [originally for *Premiere*]. All subsequent quotations of his are drawn from this source).

"SIDNEY'S USE OF THE WORD 'SPIC' . . .": MPAA to Hecht, Jan. 4, 1956, *Sweet Smell of Success,* MPAA AMPAS. The revised Code "lifted the taboos against the treatment of illicit narcotics practices, abortion, prostitution and kidnapping" but specified how they could now be used—and not used.

MUCH OF THE FLUIDITY: "Here we were in a city," Howe recalled, "famed for its magical lights but we were pushing, shoving and hanging equipment, reflecting studio lights from hidden positions in doorways, windows, and even from private apartments, the tenants having gone to a hotel room to sleep. When we were shooting all-night scenes with Burt and Tony on 52nd Street, our worst enemies, although they were unmindful of our existence, were the cleaning women at their jobs in the buildings we were using back of the actors. As the women went about their chores, they'd turn lights on and off in the various offices. It gave us frequent headaches trying to match scenes" (Press book, *Sweet Smell of Success*, NYPL). According to H. Jerome Berns, owner of "21," some of the scenes of the club's interior were done on location, on weekend mornings. (H. Jerome Berns, Interview.)

181 "NEVER QUITE CONNECTED,": Milner, Interview.

"[SANDY] WAS LIKE A MAD PROFESSOR . . .": Lancaster quoted in Kemp, 159.

183 $300,000 ALONE WENT TO ODETS: Lancaster quoted in Crist, 73.

"YOU DIDN'T HAVE TO GO TO TAHITI,": Lancaster quoted in Lehman, Interview.

184 TWO YEARS BEFORE HIS DEATH: Unpublished diary of Clifford Odets, NYPL.

CHAPTER 8: The Fall

185 I BOUGHT A BOAT . . . : Schiffer, Interview.

CLARK GABLE'S AGING COMMANDER RICHARDSON: Gable had a real-life tremor that caused his head to shake slightly; director Wise carefully allowed for that in filming (Wise, Interview).

"ALL-MALE AND ALL-SUBMARINE": *New York Times*, Mar. 28, 1958.

186 ". . . 'WHERE THE HELL IS MY CHECK?' ": Lancaster quoted in Knox, Interview.

TWELVE MOVIES IN 1958: *Variety*, Dec. 18, 1957.

"THIS TV IS BIG,": Lancaster quoted in Cecil Smith, "Fabulous Name for Lancaster," *Los Angeles Times*, Mar. 30, 1958.

NAT PERRIN: *Variety*, Dec. 24, 1958.

"EXCEEDINGLY INTERESTED,": Marc M. Spiegel (HHL Paris publicity rep) to Hecht, Dec. 13, 1957, UAC WSHS.

THE COMPANY'S PLANS: Smith, "Fabulous Name."

RATTIGAN FLOUNDERED: *Variety*, Apr. 10, 1957.

187 "THE LAST GREAT STAND OF THE HOLLYWOOD ENGLISH": Sheridan Morely, *The Other Side of the Moon* (New York: McGraw-Hill, 1979), 251.

188 "[BURT'S] AUTHORITY . . .": Douglas Bell, Interviewer, *An Oral History with Gene Fowler, Jr. and Marjorie Fowler* (Beverly Hills, CA: Academy of Picture Arts and Sciences Foundation, 1993), AMPAS.

189 FOR THE FIRST TIME: Peter Hay, *MGM*, 313.

THE COURTSHIP BEGAN: *New York Times*, June 28, 1957.

"WHY," HE ASKED THE MOVIE'S DIRECTOR, WILLIAM WYLER: Lancaster quoted in Crist, 81.

190 "1958 WILL GO DOWN IN TWENTIETH-CENTURY ANNALS . . .": Leslie Mason, "Stars Tap Golden Vein," *Los Angeles Times*, Jan. 13, 1959.

"ALL MGM FEATURE PRODUCTION.": Alexander, "The Real Burt."

LANCASTER HAD BEEN TALKING: Press release, *The Flame and the Arrow* production file, WB USC.

WORTHY OF THE $600,000: Lochte, "Adding Machine."

191 AT THE 1958 ACADEMY AWARDS CEREMONY: Details taken from a tape of the 1958 30th Annual Academy Awards, Museum of Television and Radio, New York City.

DOUGLAS WROTE TO DICK POWELL: Kirk Douglas Collection, SHSW.

"LIKE BLANCHE DU BOIS IN *STREETCAR*,": Kirk Douglas, *Ragman's Son*, 291.

"I JUST COULDN'T SEEM TO HANDLE . . .": Olivier, 225.

"STRAIGHT AND STEELY-STEADY": Ibid., 226.

191 "SOMEWHERE BETWEEN $150,000 . . .": Lancaster quoted in Fury, 130.

192 BY MARCH 1959 UA HAD MADE AN ACCOUNTING: Hecht-Hill-Lancaster/UA fact sheet, Mar. 30, 1959, UAC SHSW.

"HEAVY NEGOTIATIONS WITH LEW WASSERMAN,": Memo from Krim, April 13, 1959, UAC SHSW.

THE PRESS SCRUPULOUSLY MARKED: *Variety,* July 27, 1959; *New York Times,* Aug. 6, 1959.

193 "CELESTIAL VENGEANCE": John Huston, *An Open Book,* 283.

"WELL, D.W. NEVER DID *THAT*!": Gish as quoted in Tom Shaw, assistant director on *The Unforgiven,* Interview. All subsequent quotations of his are drawn from this source.

194 HILL WOULD WRITE A BOOK: James Hill, *Rita Hayworth.*

WHEN THE MONEY RAN OUT: Hill, Interview.

"A JERK'S IDEA OF AN EPIC,": Kael, *Kiss Kiss Bang Bang,* 43. Robert Aldrich had wanted to make *Taras Bulba* during his association with Hecht-Lancaster. When Billy Lancaster got polio, Lancaster asked him to postpone for a year; Aldrich refused, to his later regret, and sold the property to a company that was in fact representing Hecht, who made the movie in 1962, starring Yul Brynner and Tony Curtis, with a script by Waldo Salt.

STILL-UNMATCHED TRIPLE: Biskind, "Beneficial Life." The three Oscars were *One Flew Over the Cuckoo's Nest* (1975), *Rocky* (1976), and *Annie Hall* (1977).

"THE DOMINATING CENTRAL ISSUE . . .": Steven Bach, *Final Cut,* 29.

THE TRANSITION FROM STUDIOS: Alexander Walker, *Stardom,* 332.

195 "ALL THE GALS IN TOWN . . .": Alexander, "The Real Burt."

"BUT WHAT THE HELL, KIRK,": Lancaster to Douglas, Apr. 16, 1959, Kirk Douglas Collection, SHSW.

PART THREE: THE PAYOFF 1960–1990

197 I ALWAYS TRY TO IMPROVE . . . : Lancaster quoted in John G. Mitchell, "The Amazing Burt Lancaster Story," *New York Journal-American,* Aug. 11, 1961. Five-part series, Aug. 6–10, 1961.

CHAPTER 9: Embracing the Zeitgeist

199 POLITICS WERE NOT ONLY SAFE: See Hy Hollinger, "Mixed Emotions of Disunited Industry Facing Renewed Slurs on Commie-Angled Scripters," *Variety,* Feb. 24, 1960. As signs of a new era Hollinger cites the emergence of "aggressive . . . new executives" in the industry such as "the UA team," the diminishment of the "hysteria" that had marked the nation's dealing with the "so-called Communist menace," the "fight for survival" of movies against TV, and the "unmistakeable signs" that a timorous industry all-too-eager to cave in to pressure groups like the American Legion (whose membership had declined by half a million since 1950) had toughened up.

"[T]HE ORIGINAL MODEL . . .": Alexander, "The Real Burt."

SPRAY-PAINTED GOLD: *Film Calendar,* Oct. 16–Dec. 31, 1983.

"WE IN HOLLYWOOD HAVE A SACRED POSITION,": Lancaster quoted in Mitchell, "Amazing Burt Lancaster."

WHEN RICHARD BROOKS FAILED TO CLEAR HIS WAR NOVEL: Charges against Brooks were dropped and he asked Lewis to meet him for a drink at New York's Astor Bar in 1945. Lewis told Brooks to go back and read all the bad reviews of the novel by Carl Van Doren, H.L. Mencken, and Rebecca West, and learn from them how to make the story better, to make Gantry more sympathetic, more believable. "I liked the big bum," Brooks remembered Lewis saying. "He had a zest for life, a terrific passion for enjoyment. He was kind of a big happy-go-lucky clown. I liked him but hated what he stood for" (*New York Times,* July 3, 1960).

200 TROUBLE FINDING A STUDIO: Cecil B. DeMille and Y. Frank Freeman, vice-president of Paramount, tried to pay off Brooks to prevent him from making a picture that gave the "wrong image of America" (McGilligan, *Backstory 2*, 58).

BEHOLDEN, WITH HECHT, TO UA: The details of the Lancaster-UA arrangement were recalled, in some detail, by Lancaster during an interview by Judith Crist in Tarrytown, October 17–19, 1975, referred to above (Crist, 96 and 99). Although Lancaster told Crist that his salary for each of the pictures included in this arrangement was $185,000, UA records and Frankenheimer's recollections put the amount at $150,000. What Brooks never knew was the "confidential part of this deal" whereby UA worked in the old HHL bonus to Lancaster of $50,000 per $1 million of revenue (Krim and Peyser to Benjamin, Youngstein, Golden, Blumofe, et al., Jan. 15, 1959, *Elmer Gantry* production file, Box 3, UAC SHSW).

"ONE OF THE MOST EXPLOSIVE . . .": Youngstein to Krim, Nov. 21, 1958, Box 3 UAC SHSW.

"BRICK BY BRICK, . . .": *Elmer Gantry* production file, Box 3 UAC SHSW.

THE DIRECTOR HAD AMASSED: Brooks's collection of clippings can be viewed in the Richard Brooks Collection, AMPAS.

MCPHERSON ROARED DOWN THE AISLE: Elmer Gantry press book, Richard Brooks Collection, AMPAS. On top of McPherson's Anglus Temple, which opened in 1923, an electrically illuminated cross rotated in the air and could be seen in then smog-free Los Angeles for fifty miles.

201 BILLY GRAHAM WAS THE OTHER MODEL: Billy Graham file, Richard Brooks Collection, AMPAS.

"SPAWNED SO MANY RELIGIOUS CULTS AND SECTS . . .": *New York Herald Tribune,* June 12, 1960.

"MACHINE-GUN SPEED"; "RESTLESS PACING . . ."; PISTACHIO-GREEN GABARDINE SUIT: *Newsweek,* Feb. 6, 1954.

"STAGGERING DIMENSIONS": *Los Angeles Times,* Aug. 31, 1958. At Madison Square Garden were two thousand ushers, four thousand singers in the choir, and five thousand "trained counselors."

ARTHUR KENNEDY WAS CAST: Kennedy was the star of the last Federal Theater

Project "social drama" production, George Sklar's *Life and Death of an American*, which opened on May 19, 1939, and was still running when the FTP was shut down on June 30.

201 TO FILL THE MOVIE'S REVIVAL TENTS: *Radio Times*, July 19–25, 1975.

". . . WITH THE OLD MAIDENFORM . . .": Hoagy Carmichael Jr., Interview. All subsequent quotations of his are drawn from this source.

202 "I WANTED HIS ADVICE DESPERATELY,": Shirley Jones, Interview. All subsequent quotations of hers are drawn from this source.

203 FIRST "MASS INTERIOR FIRE SCENE.": Brooks quoted in *American Film*, Oct. 1977. Production details come from *Elmer Gantry* press book materials and the *Elmer Gantry* production file, Richard Brooks Collection, AMPAS.

CATHOLICS WERE NOT ALLOWED: *Time*, May 6, 1957.

"EVILS AND SHORTCOMINGS": Isabelle di Cassia to Brooks, Nov. 2, 1959, *Elmer Gantry* production file, Richard Brooks Collection, AMPAS.

"MAKE A SEQUEL . . .": Anonymous letter to Brooks, Oct. 11, 1959, Richard Brooks Collection, AMPAS.

A "BUSINESSMAN" FROM INDIANAPOLIS: Letter to Brooks, Oct. 27, 1959, Richard Brooks Collection, AMPAS.

"THE FIRST TIME . . .": *Variety*, June 15, 1960. UA would keep pushing the boundaries of censorship and Hollywood ratings: in 1969 the company made the X-rated *Midnight Cowboy*, which was an Oscar-winning hit; *Last Tango in Paris* in 1972 was also X-rated and a hit.

204 THE LEGION OBJECTED: *American Film*, Oct. 1977, and McGilligan, *Backstory 2*, 59.

THE LINE WAS CUT: Decades later, when the Christian "Religious Right" came into its own as an organized political force, Elmer Gantry was the name given to an abortive spaceship sabotaged by a fundamentalist crazy in the 1997 movie, *Contact*.

A "NEW BOLDNESS,": *Variety*, n.d. [1960], *Elmer Gantry* clipping file, NYPL.

"FOR ONCE,": *The Hollywood Reporter*, June 24, 1960.

THE "MANNERISMS, . . .": Lancaster quoted in Michael Kearns, "Burt Lancaster: No 'Dumb Actor.'" *Hollywood Drama-Logue*, Apr. 2–8, 1981.

SAID BROOKS, "BURT . . .": Brooks quoted in *Radio Times*, July 19–25, 1975.

205 "WHAT EVERYONE IS SUPPOSED TO WANT . . .": Brooks quoted in *Elmer Gantry* press book, *Elmer Gantry* production file, Richard Brooks Collection, AMPAS.

THE SCRIPT BY EDWARD ANHALT: For further information on the background of *The Young Savages*, see "Recollections of Edward Anhalt Interviewed by Estelle Changas," *An Oral History of the Motion Picture in America* (Los Angeles: The Regents of the University of California), 1969.

206 "VERY SUPPORTIVE AND VERY EASY TO WORK WITH": Dina Merrill, Interview. All subsequent quotations of hers are drawn from this source. Merrill went through what she recalls as multiple challenges to her professionalism and personal equilibrium from Frankenheimer. When her portrayal of a drunk was not satisfactory, the director took her into his trailer and made her drink Scotch at eleven in the morning despite her insistence that it made her sick; after she

threw up and began to stumble over a particularly sibilant word in one scene, "John grabbed me," she said, "and said, 'Either you get this right by five o'clock when Burt leaves or you're fired.' "

THE LANGUAGE WAS "APPALLING,": Winters, *Shelley II: The Middle of My Century,* 319.

FRANKENHEIMER CLAIMED NOT TO REMEMBER: The story may have originated, according to Frankenheimer, with an exchange between him and cameraman Lionel "Curley" Lindon, who had won an Oscar for *Around the World in 80 Days* in 1956 and would work with Frankenheimer on *The Manchurian Candidate* and *Grand Prix:* "I was kind of new," recalled the director, "and I looked through the camera and said, 'You know, Curley, I think this should be about three inches lower.' And Curley looked at me and said, 'Sonny boy, this god-damned picture isn't going to be any better or any worse if this camera is three inches higher or lower. Let's shoot it and get out of here.' "

THE NOTORIOUS STORY: Ed Asner, Interview. All subsequent quotations of his are drawn from this source.

207 "HEY, KID," HE ASKED: Lancaster quoted in Sydney Pollack, Interview. All subsequent quotations of Pollack's are drawn from this source, as is the description of his introduction to Wasserman.

HIS NOW FORMER AGENT: When MCA, through its Revue subsidiary and thanks to a blanket SAG waiver, became the leading television producer as well as talent agency in the 1950s, the Justice Department launched an antitrust investigation; in 1962, MCA signed a consent decree, divesting itself of the talent agency business, and bought Universal Pictures, which became MCA Productions. Ben Benjamin, at International Creative Management, became Lancaster's agent.

208 HECHT AND LANCASTER REVIVED: *Birdman of Alcatraz* was made under an old committment to Norma Productions (UA memo, Mar. 31, 1960, *Birdman of Alcatraz* file, UAC WSHS).

EXCEPT FOR EXTERIOR SCENES: Frankenheimer recalled that to film the exteriors of Alcatraz, Hecht hired a cheap old "Somerset Maugham boat." When the boat's motor failed and it began to drift close to the island, Hecht, believing the prison authorities, utterly uncooperative if not hostile to the movie, had an order to fire on them if they got too close, began to scream, "They're going to shoot at us!" Frankenheimer retorted, "If you'd got us a decent boat, Harold, this would not have happened." A tugboat rescued them (Frankenheimer, Interview).

"STROUD WILL NOT KOWTOW,": Lancaster quoted in Alexander, "The Real Burt."

"A HOMICIDAL THREAT TO SOCIETY": *Time,* Nov. 29, 1963.

"TOOK A MISERABLE, UNNATURAL . . .": Lancaster quoted in "Burt Lancaster Prepares a Message," *Christian Science Monitor,* Jan. 10, 1961.

209 WHEN HECHT CALLED: Frankenheimer, Interview.

TO MAKE THE PROCESS: "Burt had tried to get a hold of Stroud," recalled Schiffer, describing Lancaster's attempt not only to meet the man but to see what he really looked like, "and he wouldn't have anything to do with us" (Schiffer,

Interview). Lancaster eventually visited the Birdman several times in a prison hospital in Springfield, Missouri, just before Stroud's death in 1963.

209 "WHAT THE HELL ARE YOU DOING, . . .": Lancaster quoted in Schiffer, Interview. YEARS LATER: *Los Angeles Times,* Nov. 11, 1989.

210 "AN IMPORTANT FILM.": Joe Hyams, "Prison System Is the Heavy in Alcatraz Film," *New York Herald Tribune,* Dec. 25, 1960.

"OH, NO, JOHN, LET THE AUDIENCE CRY—NOT ME.": Lancaster quoted in Crist, 99. FILMING WAS SUSPENDED: "We greatly truncated the backstory," said Frankenheimer of that six-week effort. "We opened with him right on the train. Where before it was an hour and fifteen minutes before he found the bird, now it was fifteen to twenty minutes. And we made it one bird instead of two. Lotta stuff." THE THIRD ANNUAL RISE IN A ROW: *Variety,* Dec. 27, 1961.

211 "THE VERY PHILOSOPHY THAT ENABLED THE NAZIS TO COME TO POWER": Abby Mann, Notes from the program for the Berlin opening of *Judgment at Nuremberg, Judgment at Nuremberg* file, UAC SHSW.

IT WAS CONSIDERED "A BREACH OF GOOD MANNERS . . .": Ibid. See also "Recollections of Abby Mann Interviewed by Stephen Farber," *An Oral History of the Motion Picture in America* (Los Angeles: The Regents of the University of California, 1969).

UA INSISTED THAT HE GATHER: Balio, *United Artists: The Company That Changed the Film Industry,* 142. Kramer had previously directed two box-office disappointments for UA, *On the Beach* (1959) and *Inherit the Wind* (1960).

212 "IT WAS NOT THE OBVIOUS CHOICE. . . .": Stanley Kramer, Interview. All subsequent quotations of his are drawn from this source.

"IT IS IMPORTANT TO LANCASTER,": Kaplan to Kramer, Dec. 8, 1960, *Judgment at Nuremberg* file, Stanley Kramer Collection, UCLA.

WHEN A JOURNALIST TOLD TRACY: Joe Hyams, "Lancaster's Noble Sacrifice for Art," *New York Herald Tribune,* Dec. 13, 1960.

"THIS," SHE ADDED: Garson as quoted in Pete Martin, "I Call on Burt Lancaster," *Saturday Evening Post,* June 24, 1961.

LATER HE TOLD A FRIEND: Confidential interview.

"I'D EVEN LIKE TO THANK,": Lancaster quoted in Martin, "I Call."

213 "HOLLYWOOD NO LONGER SNICKERS,": *New York Morning Telegraph,* Nov. 20, 1961. SCHELL, WITH WHOM HE HAD WELL-PUBLICIZED CLASHES: Schell, according to Kramer, as described by Steven Bach, "wasn't really German, as he reminded everybody, every day, every hour on the hour"—he was Austrian (Bach, *Marlene Dietrich,* 408). This was the kind of self-justifying behavior that often set Lancaster off and vice-versa. One argument between the two actors reportedly involved Lancaster accusing Schell of missing "an important cue" during filming. Schell denied it and suggested they review the day's rushes to settle the point. Lancaster yelled, "This is a most unprofessional attitude," but when the dailies were shown, they proved Schell was correct (*Family Weekly,* Mar. 18, 1962).

214 "[T]HE LOCALS WERE STUNNED INTO SILENCE,": *Variety,* Dec. 20, 1961. "KRAMER," PRONOUNCED *FILM: Film* (London), Spring 1962.

"SHREWDLY TIMED,": *Time,* Dec. 15, 1961.

GROSSED ONLY $6 MILLION: Balio, *United Artists: The Company That Changed the Film Industry,* 145.

NOMINATED FOR EIGHT OSCARS: Also nominated were: Clift and Garland for Best Supporting Actor/Actress; Kramer for Best Director; Ernest Laszlo for Cinematography; and the movie for Best Picture.

ROBERT F. KENNEDY TURNED DOWN: Kennedy said that he could "not in good conscience recommend" the release of Stroud (UA press release for *Birdman of Alcatraz,* May 5, 1962, Burt Lancaster file, Hedda Hopper Collection, AMPAS).

WHEN TELEVISION NEWSMAN MIKE WALLACE: Bob Williams, "Sequel to a TV Walkout: Lancaster 'Disgusted'—No More Mike Wallace," *New York Post,* Apr. 25, 1962.

"MY TEMPER," HE INSISTED: Lancaster quoted in "Lancaster Walks, Reinvited by Wallace," *New York Post,* Apr. 25, 1962.

IT WAS THE FIRST TIME IN SEVENTEEN YEARS: *New York Herald Tribune,* Apr. 25, 1962.

"MIGHT GET INVOLVED WITH SOME SEXUAL PERVERSION . . .": Lancaster quoted in Crist, 97.

215 AFTER A SCREENING FOR A GROUP OF MEDIA WRITERS: *Variety,* May 2, 1962.

"STROUD HAS INSISTED,": Ibid.

"HIS ONLY REASON FOR HAVING BIRDS . . .": Ida M. Turner to the *Des Moines Register,* Feb. 29, 1956, *Birdman of Alcatraz* file, MPAA AMPAS.

TOWARD THE END OF THE 1960s: Kenneth Branagh, Interview. All subsequent quotations of his are drawn from this source.

216 A "MAMMOTH FIRE": *New York Post,* Nov. 8, 1961.

THE *LOS ANGELES TIMES* RAN A LARGE PHOTOGRAPH: *Los Angeles Times,* Nov. 8, 1961.

"I JUST CAME,": Lancaster quoted in *Variety,* Nov. 8, 1961.

THE LANCASTER COLLECTION: The source of the inventory of the Lancaster art collection in 1961 is the Los Angeles County Art Museum. In addition to the Benton oil painting of Lancaster as *The Kentuckian,* Lancaster and Norma gave Henri Rousseau's *La République Française* to the Museum. At Lancaster's death in 1994, the eleven small Moore sculptures were also left to the Museum in his will.

217 "THE AMBIENCE OF THE THING,": Carmichael, Interview.

"I NEED THIS LIKE A HOLE IN THE HEAD,": Lancaster quoted in Burt Lancaster clipping file, n.d. [1961], FSC MOMA.

"HE HITS LIKE A MULE.": Lancaster quoted in Mitchell, "Amazing Burt Lancaster."

218 "PERIODS OF DEPRESSION": Martin, "I Call."

"OF COURSE, HE'S CHANGED . . .": Brooks quoted in Martin, "I Call."

WHEN SOMEONE ASKED: Lancaster quoted in Harold Hildebrand, "Oscar Rests; Burt Works," *Los Angeles Examiner,* May 21, 1961.

218 MESSAGE-LADEN KRAMER PROJECT: Crist, 92. Lancaster told Crist that each principal on the movie agreed initially to work for about $25,000.

219 BRENDAN GILL WROTE: *The New Yorker,* Feb. 23, 1963.

"SUPPOSE," HE ASKED A REPORTER: Lancaster quoted in *New York Times,* Feb. 18, 1962.

219 "THE FIRST MODERN AMERICAN INDEPENDENT": Thomson, 116. Cassavetes acted in the role of Johnny North in a remake of *The Killers* (1964), directed by Don Siegel.

"AN INORDINATE AMOUNT OF FILM.": *An Oral History with Gene Fowler, Jr. and Marjorie Fowler.*

A "STRETCHING POINT TO CONSIDER . . .": Raymond Carney, *American Dreaming,* 77.

220 WRITING KRAMER FROM SICILY: Lancaster to Kramer, Sept. 28, 1962, *A Child Is Waiting* file, Stanley Kramer Collection, UCLA.

CASSEVETES WOULD BREEZE INTO LANCASTER'S OFFICE: Lochte, "Adding Machine."

"INIMICAL TO ME.": Lancaster quoted in Alexander, "The Real Burt."

221 "A VERY COMPLEX CHARACTER . . .": Visconti quoted in Alexander, "The Real Burt."

222 "THE MOST BLATANT PIECE . . .": Derek Prouse, "Burt Lancaster Discovers a Sicilian Prince," *Christian Science Monitor,* July 18, 1962.

HAVING PREPARED WITH HIS CUSTOMARY EXACTITUDE: Work on *The Leopard* included rebuilding the façade of what was to be the Salina palazzo in Donnafugata in the real-life village of Ciminna, tearing up sections of Palermo to create the necessary nineteenth-century authenticity for the Garibaldi battle scenes, extensively remodeling the Villa Boscogrande in the Comco d'Oro (golden hills) surrounding Palermo as the "Villa Salina," requisitioning 18 of the 128 rooms in the Palazzo Gangi in Palermo for the grand ball scene in the movie's Palazzo Ponteleone, shipping south a technical staff of "twenty electricians, one hundred twenty make-up men, hairdressers, and tailors, one hundred fifty masons, fifteen florists, and ten cooks" (Monica Sterling, *A Screen of Time,* 165). The author would like to thank Christian Scott-Hansen for providing a video copy of *Il Gattopardo.*

"I DIDN'T FOR ONE MOMENT,": Lancaster quoted in Gow, "Energy."

THE DIRECTOR ALREADY HAD A REPUTATION: Gaia Serviado, *Luchino Visconti,* 170.

223 "LANCASTER HAD THE WISDOM,": Suso Cecchi D'Amico, Interview. All subsequent quotations of hers are drawn from this source.

DUBBED HIM "THE ANTI-STAR": Prouse, "Sicilian Prince."

WHEN HE REALIZED: Serviado, 178. According to Serviado, Fox had originally wanted the entire film to be shot in English but, at Visconti's insistence, agreed to an arrangement in which Lancaster's scenes would be shot in English and the rest in Italian, or French, or whatever language a given actor happened to speak, to be dubbed later (postsynched) for the English version.

"DON'T SIT ON THE CORN!": Visconti quoted in *The Times* (London), July 8, 1962.

"[T]HE FINEST HOUR OF FILM . . .": *The New Yorker,* Sept. 19, 1983.

224 TO AVOID THE FEROCIOUS SICILIAN AUGUST HEAT: Schiffer, on hand to do Lancaster's makeup and to apply real gold slivers in his hair, recalls that not only did hair and makeup have to be constantly retouched and freshened, but that,

as the ball progressed in screen time, the redundant aristos, had to look more and more jaded. "We started out with everyone in that ball in absolute splendour," he said, "and as the evening progressed, they got paler, the lips got paler, the hair got a little disheveled and when they struggled out at five or six in the morning, they were absolutely a wreck. That was difficult to do because we had to match it all the time every night. We'd get there and say: Which sequence is this? What did he look like last night? It went on and on" (Schiffer, Interview).

"COME, CLAUDINA," SAID VISCONTI: Visconti quoted in Claudia Cardinale, *Claudia, tu Claudia* (Mondadori, 1996), 104. Translation done by Paola Casella for the author.

225 "VISCONTI'S RELATIONSHIP WITH LANCASTER . . .": History and literature may have been playing a spooky convergence joke on the two men. The director could trace his family back to Desiderius, the father-in-law of Charlemagne; the Prince of Salina boasted in *Il Gattopardo* that his family came to Sicily with Charles of Anjou; Lancaster could have pushed a Plantagenet claim back to Charlemagne not only through the Lancaster name, but also through a Lancaster precursor Norman family name of Taillebois, later anglicized as Preston, which had aristocratic origins in Anjou.

THE DONNAFUGATA INTERIORS: These were shot twenty-six kilometers up the Appian Way from Rome, in the Bernini-remodeled Palazzo Chigi.

"VISCONTI HAD AN IDEA,": Giaocchino Lanza Tomasi, Duke of Palma, Interview. All subsequent quotations of his are drawn from this source.

THE DIRECTOR SPENT TWO HOURS ONE NIGHT: George Waldo, "Burt Lancaster: Circus Acrobat Changes Spots for 'Leopard,' " *Los Angeles Times,* Oct. 21, 1962.

"BURT, YOU OUGHTA RUN FOR KING.": Dern, Interview.

226 "I HAD THE LUCK,": Lancaster quoted in *The Leopard* clipping file, n.d. [1965], NYPL.

WHILE THERE WAS PLENTY OF EVIDENCE: Lancaster was caught twice by the Roman paparazzi that summer, once with Helene Smith, a "British strip-tease artist" (*Modern Screen,* n.d. [1962], *The Leopard* clipping file, NYPL), and on another occasion with Beatrice Altariba, a "starlet." Exiting the Georges Restaurant off the Via Veneto at 2:00 a.m. with Altariba, Lancaster reportedly beat and kicked a six-foot, 260-pound photographer so badly he had to be hospitalized ("Burt Lancaster, Dating a Starlet, Belts Italy Fotog," *New York Daily News,* May 13, 1962).

CARDINALE ALSO LATER HEARD: Cardinale, 191.

227 BILLY WOULD TELL: Ivo Palazzi, Interview. All subsequent quotations of his are drawn from this source. The author would like to thank Scott Wilson for suggesting Mr. Palazzi as a source of information on Lancaster's life in Italy.

228 "IVO!" LANCASTER BOOMED: Lancaster quoted in Palazzi, Interview.

"I WOULD LIKE TO DIE . . .": Ibid.

"IF THE WHOLE POINT OF THE FUNCTIONING OF DEMOCRACY . . .": Lancaster to Douglas, Sept. 28, 1962, *Seven Days in May* file, Kirk Douglas Collection, SHSW.

"I'M GLAD YOU LIKED *SEVEN DAYS IN MAY*,": Douglas to Lancaster, Oct. 8, 1962, *Seven Days in May* file, Kirk Douglas Collection, SHSW.

"A LITTLE TOO HARSH": Ibid.

229 "MONTH OF UNSURPASSED AUTUMNAL GLORY": Manchester, 958.

"THOSE SONS OF BITCHES . . .": Benjamin C. Bradlee, *A Good Life: Newspapering and Other Adventures* (New York: Simon and Schuster, 1995), 219. *Washington Post* editor Bradlee recalled in his autobiography that Kennedy "felt badly used—and that's an understatement—by the Joint Chiefs of Staff, especially General Lyman L. Lemnitzer, their chairman" after the Bay of Pigs invasion. "The Joint Chiefs never trusted Kennedy in the first place, and he never trusted them again."

THE STUPIDITY OF ONE CRISIS: In an eerie bit of overlap, the movie's covert project's code name is "Ecomcon," which is an echo of Ex Comm, the short-hand name of the Executive Committee of the National Security Council, which had navigated the world through the Cuban missile crisis.

"A NEGATIVE PRINT OF *DR. STRANGELOVE*,": *Esquire*, June 1964.

THE MOST OVERT INSTANCE: *New York Times*, Mar. 1, 1964.

UA'S BLUMOFE THREW IN A KEY SUGGESTION: Blumofe to Lewis, June 12, 1962, *Seven Days in May* production file, Kirk Douglas Collection, SHSW.

230 WHEN DOUGLAS PHONED THE DIRECTOR: Frankenheimer, Interview.

"HE WAS JEALOUS OF BURT LANCASTER,": Frankenheimer quoted in Charles Higham, *Ava*, 213.

ON THE DIRECTOR'S SIGNATURE BLACK-AND-WHITE FILM STOCK: At the Paramount studios, the tight, claustrophic Pentagon sets that would enclose Scott and his band of traitorous chiefs of staff like a trap were constructed by designer Cary Odell. Brehon Somervell's original rabbit-warren structure of linear corridors, stark fluorescent lights, and endless doors was recreated in the limited space of a studio stage set by building the halls in forced perspective. Midgets were hired, according to Frankenheimer, and put in uniform to stand and walk at what appeared to be the far end of the building.

"UN-AMERICAN FILM OF THE YEAR,": Penelope Houston, as quoted in Halliwell, 704.

231 "FIRST TIME,": *New York Times*, June 25, 1963

THE WEEKEND OF JULY 27, 1963: Fury, 170.

"COULD NOT HAPPEN HERE, NOW,": *New York Herald Tribune*, Feb. 5, 1964.

232 "A HYMN TO AMERICAN DEMOCRACY.": *New York Times*, Mar. 1, 1964.

SUGGESTED THEY ALL PACK UP: Lorraine Gaugin, "Burt Lancaster," *Movieland*, 1965.

233 "DELIGHTFULLY RECEPTIVE . . .": Harold Levitt, Interview. All subsequent quotations of his are drawn from this source.

"PLASTIC MODERN.": Sheilah Graham, *Confessions of a Hollywood Columnist*, 207.

"TWENTIETH-CENTURY FAGGOT,": Lancaster quoted in Robert Horn, UCLA swimming and water polo coach tapped by Lancaster to coach him for *The Swimmer*, Interview. All subsequent quotations of his are drawn from this source.

"A WOMAN WITHOUT PREJUDICE,": Lucy Kibbee, Interview.

234 "SERIOUS, VERY SERIOUS.": Clarence Jones, attorney and advisor to Dr. Martin Luther King Jr., Interview. All subsequent quotations of his are drawn from this source.

"THERE WERE FAINT HEARTS . . .": Charlton Heston, *In the Arena* (New York: Simon and Schuster, 1995), 315.

AT THE MICROPHONE: The descriptions and transcribed quotations of Lancaster and Roger Mudd are taken from a viewing and transcription by the author of the CBS news broadcast coverage of the March on Washington on August 28, 1963, at the Museum of Television and Radio, New York City.

235 "THE LAST GREAT BLACK-AND-WHITE ACTION-ADVENTURE FILM,": Matt Zoller Seitz, "Those High-Tech Shoot-'em-Ups Got the Formula from *The Train*," *New York Times*, Apr. 30, 1995.

236 "WAS SO DEPRESSED AT LOSING THE ART,": Lancaster quoted in *New York Post*, Mar. 22, 1965.

LAY "DORMANT" AT UA: Arthur Penn, Interview. All subsequent quotations of his are drawn from this source.

237 THE "LIMBO-LIKE OUTER SUBURBS OF PARIS.": Jean-Pierre Lenoir, "Stalling a Great Train Robbery," *New York Times*, Nov. 3, 1963.

238 "AREN'T YOU GOING . . . ": Lancaster quoted in Confidential Interview.

THE STATION, A TRUCK, A BOXCAR: *Newsweek*, n.d. [1964], *The Train* clipping file, AMPAS.

"SHREWDER PLANNING,": Ibid.

240 "STEAMY, SOOTY, BLACK-AND-SILVER, . . .": *The New Yorker*, Mar. 20, 1965.

"MASCULINE DRIVE AND POWER OF PISTONS": *The Saturday Review*, Mar. 13, 1965.

NEWSDAY, LIKE MANY: *Newsday*, Mar. 18, 1965.

THE FINAL COST CAME IN: Balio, *United Artists: The Company That Changed the Film Industry*, 279.

"HE IS A CONTEMPORARY SISYPHUS,": *The New Yorker*, Mar. 20, 1965.

241 "SPEND PART OF THE SUMMER . . .": Kaplan to Krim, Jan. 15, 1964, *The Train* production file, UAC SHSW.

IT WAS TOO MANY PROJECTS: *Kimberly*, according to Pollack, "never had any script" and never got made (Pollack, Interview).

IN 1962, HE HAD COME IN TENTH PLACE: Parish, 228.

WROTE TO LANCASTER: Krim to Lancaster, Apr. 6, 1964, UAC SHSW.

242 A FLASH FLOOD: *New York Herald Tribune*, Dec. 15, 1965

"[O]NE GRIN AND SINISTER LAUGH OF HIS,": Ibid.

"OF *VERA CRUZ* RATHER THAN *SHANE*." *Newsday*, Nov. 3, 1966.

243 "SOFT PADDING FEET": Jackie Bone, Interview. All subsequent quotations of hers are drawn from this source.

"A VERY MATURE WOMAN.": Graham quoted in *Modern Screen Yearbook 1969*, CMC USC.

"WE WERE GREAT SPARRING PARTNERS,": Bone quoted in *National Enquirer*, July 4, 1971.

244 "TO RESOLVE ANY QUESTION . . .": *New York Post,* Dec. 14, 1965.

"A SIMPLE STORY ABOUT NARCISSUS,": Scott Donaldson, *John Cheever: A Biography* (New York: Random House, 1988), 212.

"A TERRIBLE EXPERIENCE.": John Cheever quoted in Donaldson, 212.

244 "*DEATH OF A SALESMAN* IN SWIMMING TRUNKS,": Lancaster quoted in Sidney Skolsky, *New York Post,* June 28, 1968.

245 A BABY BOOMER: Barry Golson, Interview.

"ALL-AMERICAN LOOK,": *New York Daily News,* Aug. 21, 1966.

"WOULD NEVER HAVE BEEN MADE.": *New York Times,* May 16, 1968.

ROBERT HORN: In 1966, Horn was in the middle of a run of three undefeated seasons, which would be succeeded by three NCAA championships in four years and a winning streak of fifty games, a UCLA record that still stands.

"EAST RIVER CRAWL, . . .": Horn quoted in *New York Daily News,* May 5, 1968.

246 "THIS STYLISH, LURID, SEXUAL STANDARD . . .": Benjamin Cheever, Interview. All subsequent quotations of his are drawn from this source.

"BURT LANCASTER IS FIFTY-TWO,": John Cheever to Tanya Litvinov, July 13, 1966, Benjamin Cheever, ed., *The Letters of John Cheever,* 253.

"ANYHOW I THOUGHT YOU'D LIKE TO KNOW . . .": John Cheever to John Weaver [postmarked 11 July 1966], John D. Weaver, ed., *Glad Tidings: A Friendship in Letters,* 189.

"VAST PILGRIMAGE": John Cheever quoted in Donaldson, 350.

"HE'S TRYING TO PLACE ME . . .": John Cheever quoted in Benjamin Cheever, Interview.

247 "FILM HAS ITS OWN PARTICULAR LIFE . . .": Lancaster quoted in Crist, 74.

WHEN LANCASTER AND CHEEVER HAD TO BLOCK: Weaver, 191.

"NO, THANKS. . . .": Lancaster quoted in *Newsday,* July 18, 1966.

"BREAD-AND-BUTTER PICTURES,": Lancaster quoted in *New York Times,* July 16, 1966.

"A MIRROR OF A DECADENT SOCIETY . . .": Lancaster quoted in *Newsday,* July 18, 1966.

"I'M SCARED TO DEATH . . .": Lancaster quoted in *New York Times,* Aug. 14, 1966.

248 HER KEY SCENE AS THE EMBITTERED EX-LOVER: Lancaster later claimed to Crist that this scene later shot with Rule "was simply not done the first time" (Crist, 75), but the *New York Daily News* of Aug. 21, 1966, covered the shooting of the "key mistress scene" in some detail: it was done at a Westport home called "Hillwood" on a closed set in two takes.

249 "PERSONALLY PROMISED ME, . . .": Lancaster as quoted in Crist, 75.

HE HAD SIGNED ANOTHER MULTIPICTURE DEAL WITH UA: *Los Angeles Examiner,* Mar. 17, 1965.

"THE FIRST BLACK POWER WESTERN.": *Cue,* April 6, 1968.

IN THE OBLIQUE POLITICAL TRADITION: If part of King's mission in Hollywood had been to pressure the movie industry to hire more blacks, four years later little progress had been made. When one black writer-director, Charles Washburn, came from Nashville to try his luck in Hollywood in 1965, one of the very few people he was told to see by writer John Bloch was Lancaster. Even when the star personally called around town on Washburn's behalf, he had no luck: "He seemed disappointed with his findings," Washburn would write in a letter to the *Los Angeles Times* after Lancaster's death. "No one he called was willing to meet with the Negro kid he had taken an interest in" (*Los Angeles Times*, Nov. 7, 1994).

AN EXAMPLE OF THE "SKILLFUL" FILM: Pauline Kael, *Going Steady*, 89.

251 "WHILE THE PERFORMANCES . . .": *New York Times*, Apr. 3, 1968.

LIKE "A SHAMPOO COMMERCIAL.": *Newsweek*, May 27, 1968.

"LANCASTER SOUNDS AS IF HE'S READING . . .": *Time*, May 24, 1968.

"LANCASTER, WHO IS SUPPOSED TO BE A MADISON AVENUE . . .": *The New Republic*, June 8, 1968.

"A TRIUMPH": New York, n.d. [1968], *The Swimmer* clipping file, NYPL.

253 "BURT WAS A VERY GENEROUS ACTOR,": Scott Wilson, Interview. All subsequent quotations of his are drawn from this source. According to Wilson, who had just finished shooting *In Cold Blood*, its director, Richard Brooks, told him to "get out of the country" prior to the film's release because he wished to present his two stars of *In Cold Blood*—Wilson and Robert Blake—as if they had emerged from the prairie as fresh and raw as the real-life murderers they portrayed in the movie.

254 "ONE OF THE ODDEST FILMS . . .": *Daily Telegraph* (London), Feb. 20, 1970.

257 "A FIRST FOR A HOLLYWOOD FILM.": *The Villager* (New York), Sept. 4, 1969.

"MR. LANCASTER HAS DEVELOPED A CAPACITY, . . .": *Life*, Sept. 26, 1969.

"ONE OF THE MOST GRACEFUL GROUPS": Elliot Willensky and Norval White, *AIA Guide to New York City*, third ed. (San Diego: Harcourt Brace, 1988), 455.

"A VAST ACCELERATING NEIGHBORHOOD DETERIORATION": *New York Herald Tribune*, Jan. 26, 1964.

258 EACH YEAR HE SENT UNION SETTLEMENT: The proceeds of a special sneak preview of *The Young Savages*, as arranged by Lancaster in 1961, netted Union $3,500; the national premiere of *The Scalphunters* in 1968 was a benefit showing for Union Settlement and produced in that particularly needy year a "top dollar" total of $12,000 (Union Settlement archives).

"DEVIL'S LITANY.": *The Economist*, Sept. 11, 1993.

"THE BIG, BIG GENEROUS INDIVIDUALS, . . .": Vanessa Sandrich-Brown, Interview.

TRANSPORT-A-CHILD: *Los Angeles Times*, July 24, 1988, obituary of Norma Lancaster.

THE CURRENT SYSTEM: Background information on Transport-A-Child was provided by Sherley Braden who drove one of the original buses to the Bel Air schools for Norma's program and is currently a transportation planner for the Los Angeles School District.

259 "SURPASS[ING] VIRTUALLY ANYTHING THIS CITY HAS EVER SEEN . . .": *New York Post*, May 26, 1969.

"MILITANT EXTREMISTS": Ibid.

"THE YORTY PEOPLE BROUGHT IN JOHN WAYNE. . . .": Ira B. Cooperman, Interview.

"LANCASTER DID BOTH . . .": *Philadelphia Inquirer,* Oct. 31, 1994.
This quotation comes from a letter from Cooperman to the editor of the
Inquirer after Lancaster's death. A copy of this longer version was kindly pro-
vided to the author by Mr. Cooperman.

259   "AMAZINGLY"; "LANCASTER WAS ALWAYS ABSOLUTELY STRAIGHT,": Cooperman,
Interview.
ONE NIGHT IN SEPTEMBER 1968: *New York Times,* Sept. 26, 1969; *New York Post,*
Oct. 1, 1968; *Time,* Oct. 4, 1968.
"I'VE ALWAYS WANTED TO GET AN EDUCATION,": Lancaster quoted in *Hollywood
Citizen-News,* Sept. 25, 1968.
NORMA FILED FOR DIVORCE: According to Bone, getting the divorce was pro-
longed from 1963 to 1969 in part because Lancaster did not wish to be the one
to file for divorce against Norma and because Norma did not wish to be
divorced. The couple had tried marital counseling and Norma had tried alco-
hol programs during the 1960s, with no success.

260   AFTER COMPLETING A BACHELOR'S DEGREE: To prepare Jimmy for entry into the
degree program at Manhattan School of Music (which had begun as an adjunct
of Union Settlement), Lancaster called his old army friend, Boris Barere, now a
pianist in New York, and asked him to train his son. Jimmy's teacher at the
Manhattan School of Music, and accompanist to Mischa Elman, was pianist
Joseph Seiger. Although he entered the school "almost totally unequipped to
face the degree," because of poor teaching, said Seiger, Jimmy worked hard,
took an extra year, and finished without having to repeat any courses or his final
recital. "Jimmy had a good sense of humor," Seiger said, "and a little bit of a
temper here and there. I must say he craved affection and understanding."
When Lancaster agreed to let him take an extra year to finish, he visibly
relaxed, Seiger noted, at the knowledge of his father's approval.
"I FOUND MARRIAGE SOMEWHAT STIFLING,": Lancaster quoted in Lancaster clipping file, n.d. [1970], NYPL.

261   "OBVIOUSLY I AM NOT THE YOUNG MAN . . .": Lancaster, "Sawdust."

CHAPTER 10: Burying the Heroes

262   I'VE NEVER REALLY HAD A CONSISTENT IMAGE . . . : Lancaster quoted in *TV Times*
(London), Mar. 15, 1973.
LANCASTER JUMPED AT IT: See Robert Evans, *The Kid Stays in the Picture,* for one
version of Lancaster's interest in *The Godfather.* Evans refers to "Hecht, Hill,
Lancaster" as Lancaster's production company, although it no longer existed
by that time. He claims Lancaster was "desperate" for the title role, wanted to
produce it, and that Paramount was "determined to sell it to [him]" before
being persuaded to have the "Italian" Coppola direct.

263   "THE HOLLYWOOD ANSWER TO THAT ONE IS EASY,": Lancaster quoted in Lochte,
"Adding Machine."

264   HIS UPPER-BODY STRENGTH WAS STILL SUCH: Patt Sklar, Interview. Sklar was the
American Airlines "First Lady" (today's pursar) when Lancaster, traveling first
class, came to the aid of a heart attack victim in tourist class. He performed

CPR, trading off with the airplane staff, but to no avail—the passenger died. Sklar dealt with Lancaster on several New York–Los Angeles flights and recalls that not only was it "very, very unusual for a passenger to become part of the solution," in this case a health crisis, but that he was, in comparison to the other stars who regularly flew the route, "clearly not a celebrity in terms of how he assessed himself."

WITH DON DUNPHY: Lancaster was originally supposed to "handle the color commentary" during the Ali/Frazier fight, but Dunphy, calling the contest "the greatest event in sports history," insisted, "I'm working these rounds solo. Burt Lancaster can talk between rounds" (*New York Times,* July 24, 1998). According to Perenchio, Lancaster came to prefight workouts in February 1971 "with his trunks and tennis shoes" to observe and "work out . . . a couple of rounds" with Ali and Frazier (*New York Post,* Feb. 8, 1971).

BOTH IRVING BURNS AND THOM CONROY: Former *New York Times* reporter Joe Goldberg recalled living in the same apartment building in Hollywood as Burns in the late 1960s. The one-time wardrobe assistant was selling wristwatches out of the back of his car and kept what Goldberg recalled to be "like a religious icon" to Lancaster in his apartment with a huge poster-size photograph and candles. Lancaster frequently came to pick up Burns for a day at the beach in Malibu. When Goldberg noticed the newspapers accumulating outside Burns' apartment, he called the police who found the wardrobe assistant's body inside (Letter to author from Goldberg, June 23, 1995).

"*AIRPORT* IS SHAKING UP HOLLYWOOD . . .": *Variety,* Apr. 15, 1970.

"THE BIGGEST PIECE OF JUNK . . .": Lancaster quoted in Anthony Holden, *Behind the Oscar,* 280.

265 "DO OTHER THINGS": Lancaster quoted in *Boston Globe,* Sept. 28, 1986.

"BURT WAS A STRAIGHTFORWARD, . . .": George McGovern, Interview.

"FUNDAMENTAL FAIRNESS,": Ronald Brownstein, Interview.

AS ONE OF THE MORE GENEROUS CONTRIBUTORS: Lancaster and actor Carroll O'Connor each gave $1,000 to McGovern's campaign; Henry Mancini gave $500, James Garner $200 (*Los Angeles Times,* Feb. 8, 1973).

NIXON'S LIST OF 575 WHITE HOUSE "ENEMIES.": *Los Angeles Times,* Dec. 21, 1973.

"A SIGNIFICANT CHANGE . . .": Jane Fritsch, "Tom Bradley, Mayor in Era of Los Angeles Growth, Dies," *New York Times,* Sept. 30, 1998.

AT ABBY MANN'S MALIBU HOUSE: Luke McKissack, Interview. All subsequent quotations of his are drawn from this source.

266 THE DEPARTMENT OF DEFENSE REPORTED: *New York Times,* Nov. 3, 1972.

267 "THE BOARD WAS ALL WHITE MALES,": Ramona Ripston, Interview. All subsequent quotations of hers are drawn from this source.

268 "A SATISFYING STATEMENT.": Lancaster quoted in *Hollywood Citizen-News,* Apr. 6, 1970.

"SPECIAL PLACE . . .": Lancaster quoted in *Hollywood Citizen-News,* Apr. 6, 1970.

269 TURNED DOWN THE PART OF HARRY CALLAHAN: As told by Lancaster to Michael Winner, Interview. All subsequent quotations of Winner's are drawn from this source.

KIBBEE WROTE THE FINAL SCRIPT: Rayfiel contributed to an earlier verson of the script. Before Lancaster was diverted by *Airport, Valdez Is Coming* was to star Brando as Valdez and Lancaster as the rancher, with Pollack as director and Rayfiel as screenwriter.

269 "A COMPULSION . . .": Lancaster quoted in *Hollywood Citizen-News,* Apr. 6, 1970. "[THE] COMPETITION THESE DAYS IS FIERCE. . . .": *Women's Wear Daily,* Apr. 12, 1971.

270 "THE WESTERN IS THE MOST . . .": Lancaster, as featured speaker at the John Player Lecture, quoted in *Cinema TV Today* (U.K.), Jul. 1972.

271 "THE BIG MUDDY": Bruce Davison, Interview. All subsequent quotations of his are drawn from this source.

"WAS A MAN WHO REFLECTED MY OWN FEELINGS ABOUT LIFE.": Lancaster quoted in *Photoplay,* June 1976.

SHOT IN TEN WEEKS: The Valley of Fire in Overton, Nevada, was the same yellow rocky slash Brooks had used in *The Professionals* for the confrontation scene between Palance and Lancaster.

ALL STARS WERE "COCKSUCKERS": Aldrich quoted in Alan Sharp, Interview. All subsequent quotations of Sharp's are drawn from this source.

273 "THE PERFORMANCE OF HIS CAREER": *Village Voice,* Jan. 30, 1972.

"BEYOND THE PALEFACE"; "A BLOODY BUT AUTHENTICALLY TRAGIC CONFLICT . . .": *New York Times,* Feb. 9, 1975.

"*UN AUTHENTIQUE HOMME DE GAUCHE . . .*": Lacourbe.

274 "WINNER IN THE GAME OF SURVIVAL . . .": *Films and Filming,* Dec. 1971.

AN "ANACHRONISTIC EMULATION . . .": *Variety,* Apr. 11, 1973.

"PURELY ENTERTAINING" MOVIES: Lancaster quoted in Lochte, "Adding Machine."

275 THE "SECOND WORST FILM OF 1974.": *New York Times,* June 15, 1974.

"REVERSIBLE LIBIDO.": *Variety,* Mar. 20, 1974.

"IF THE STUDIOS WERE STILL OPERATING . . .": *Women's Wear Daily,* June 17, 1974.

"REAL PURPOSE,": Lancaster quoted in Hall and Crawley, *Game* [U.K.] Feb. 1975.

276 "COMMUNIST FALL-GUY.": Lancaster quoted in Hunter, 125.

"THE DREAMS HAVE CHANGED,": Lancaster quoted in Hall and Crawley, *Game* [U.K.] Feb. 1975.

277 "IF CHARLTON WAS TRAPPED . . .": Lancaster quoted in Arthur Unger, "Burt Lancaster Talks About His New Role—Moses," *Christian Science Monitor,* n.d. [1975], Museum of Television and Radio.

"MADE MAN TO TORMENT HIM . . .": Lancaster quoted in *Los Angeles Herald-Examiner TV Weekly,* June 22, 1972.

THE YOUNG MOSES: Although Bill Lancaster's limp was usually carefully concealed in *Moses,* there are a couple of shots where it is clearly evident.

"MAGNIFICENT": Judith Crist, *The Saturday Review,* May 1, 1976.

"DREADFUL.": John Simon, *New York,* Apr. 5, 1976.

278 "THE TERRIBLE JET SET . . .": Helmut Berger, Interview. All subsequent quotations of his are drawn from this source.

279   "A PORTRAIT OF A FAMILY.": *L'Avant Scene Cinéma*, no. 159, June 1975. Translation by the author.

"FRACTURED . . . IN TERMS OF WHAT VISCONTI WANTED TO SAY . . .": Lancaster quoted in Crist, 78.

"NEVER," HE SAID: Lancaster quoted in Crist, 78.

280   "SOMEBODY A BIT SQUASHED . . .": Bernardo Bertolucci, Interview. All subsequent quotations of his are drawn from this source.

"THAT IS NO COUNTRY FOR OLD MEN . . .": William Butler Yeats, "Sailing to Byzantium," *Collected Poems of W.B. Yeats* (London: Macmillian, 1963), 217.

281   "ALL THE SHABBY LEGENDS . . .": Mellen, 341.

282   "THAT SYCOPHANTIC ENTOURAGE . . .": Lancaster quoted in Crist, 70.

283   "ALMOST IN TEARS": *Variety*, Oct. 8, 1975.

"BOULEVERSANT": *Le Monde*, Mar. 20, 1975.

"STRIPPED IN LIKE HAIKU.": *Soho Weekly News*, June 30, 1977.

"EXCELLENT . . . BRITTLE, INTELLIGENT.": Philip Lopate, "A Master Who Confounded the Categorizers," *New York Times*, Nov. 16, 1997.

"THE MOST EAGERLY AWAITED FESTIVAL DEBUT . . .": *New York Times*, Oct. 7, 1977.

A HUGE INTERNATIONAL WRANGLE: See chapter 3: "The Formalist's Strategies," in Robert Philip Kokler, *Bernardo Bertolucci*, 68, for a description of the postproduction battles over *1900*.

"THE EUPHORIC EVENTS . . .": *New York Observer*, April 15, 1991.

"DISASTROUS SCREENINGS,": *Christopher Street*, Sept. 1976.

284   "[N]O MORE CONCENTRATED . . .": *Village Voice*, Nov. 23, 1982.

"IT SHOULDN'T MATTER AT ALL WHETHER WE GET IT NOW,": Rudolph quoted in *Film Heritage*, Fall 1976.

"THE DOOR OPENS,": Reprinted in Rex Reed, Travolta to Keaton, 158.

285   "WHETHER YOU LIKE IT OR NOT, . . .": Lancaster quoted in *Photoplay*, June 1975.

LOOK *ARCHITECTURAL DIGEST* WOULD CALL: George Christy, "Architectural Digest Visits: Burt Lancaster," *Architectural Digest*, October, 1982.

"NO QUESTIONS, NO RECRIMINATIONS": Lancaster quoted in *The National Tatler* [U.K.], July 27, 1975.

ONE, BIG LEOPARD-LIKE PERCH: Details of Lancaster's condominium were provided by Levitt and Mrs. Burt "Susie" Lancaster. See also Kate Buford, "Burt Lancaster: *Elmer Gantry*'s Oscar Winner in his Malibu and Century City Residences," *Architectural Digest*, Apr. 1998.

286   "DEAR NICODEMUS,": Letter, n.d. [late 1970s], in private collection of Tina Cuccia-Cravat.

287   "WHY DON'T YOU *DO* SOMETHING? . . .": Lancaster quoted in Bone, Interview.

"NONE OF THEM . . .": Lancaster quoted in *New York Post*, Sept. 29, 1986.

"DIDN'T PRODUCE THE PICTURE. . . .": Lancaster quoted in *New York Post*, Sept. 29, 1986.

"SOMETIMES," ROSE WOULD RECALL: Alison Rose, "How I Became a Single Woman: Scenes from a life of passion and solitude," *The New Yorker*, Apr. 8, 1996. All subsequent quotations of hers are drawn from this source.

DIAGNOSED IN HIS EARLY TWENTIES: Lucy Kibbee, Interview; Jackie Bone, Interview; and several other references from other family friends and colleagues of Lancaster.

288 "ONE DAY HE'S READY . . .": Al Schaeffer, friend and golf partner, Interview. All subsequent quotations of his are drawn from this source.

"I HAVE A DAUGHTER,": Lancaster quoted in *Chicago Tribune*, Mar. 27, 1977.

"I'D BE A MORE GIVING HUMAN BEING. . . .": Lancaster quoted in Rubin, "Gentle Side."

"A LITTLE GEM" OF "QUINTESSENTIAL TRASH . . .": *New York Post*, Feb. 26, 1977.

289 "I HAVE TURNED DOWN . . .": Lancaster quoted in Clinch, 164.

"THE SUN NEVER SEEMS TO SET . . .": *Variety*, n.d. [1977], *The Cassandra Crossing* clipping file, NYPL.

"TOTALLY HONEST POLITICAL FILM": Arnold and Miller, 199.

"SORT OF *ALL THE PRESIDENT'S MEN, PART TWO*": Lancaster as quoted in *Film Today*, May 17, 1976. News clips and production notes on *Twilight's Last Gleaming* are drawn from the Robert Aldrich Collection, AFI.

"A LACK OF CREATIVE ACTING.": Lancaster quoted in *Village Voice*, June 21, 1976.

"YOU ARE ONE OF THE FEW ACTORS,": Aldrich quoted by Lancaster in *Christian Science Monitor*, Feb. 10, 1977.

"I JUST CHOOSE WHAT'S LEFT.": Lancaster quoted in *Christian Science Monitor*, Feb. 10, 1977.

"HIS SCOTCH-IRISH WASP AMERICAN RULING-CLASS": *Twilight's Last Gleaming* production file, n.d. [Feb. 1977], Robert Aldrich Collection, AFI.

"GHETTOS . . . AND SUN BELT DRIVE-INS": Aldrich quoted in Tom Allen, "Soapbox Apocalypse: The Gleam in Robert Aldrich's Eye," *Soho Arts*, Feb. 10, 1977.

290 "THE FIRST AMERICAN PULP MOVIE . . .": *New York Post*, Feb. 10, 1977.

A "TORRID . . .": *Variety*, Aug. 10, 1977.

"BABY MOGULS,": Dawn Steel, *They Can Kill You, But They Can't Eat You*, 98.

291 THE SCENE SUGGESTING: *Go Tell the Spartans* is set in 1964, the year after JFK was assassinated. Declassified Pentagon documents would later show that Kennedy had planned, in spite of the reluctance of the Joint Chiefs of Staff, to start withdrawing all U.S. "special assistance units and personnel" like Barker's by the end of 1965, with the first one thousand to be sent home by the end of 1963; when President Johnson took office after the assassination, he ordered an immediate intensification of covert and overt activity in Vietnam. Also revealed later, of course, was the deception on all levels about the true progress, or lack of it, of the war. *Go Tell the Spartans*, made in 1977, clearly conveys that the official intelligence about Muc Wa had nothing to do with the reality in the field. The scene in which Lancaster's Barker bribes the Vietnamese province chief in order to secure reinforcements and artillery support for Muc Wa deftly suggests a universe of corruption and complicity.

"THIS IS A FUCKING BRILLIANT SCRIPT . . .": Lancaster quoted in *Post*, Interview.

292 "IF FRANCIS HAD SEEN THIS, . . .": *The Hollywood Reporter*, Oct. 28, 1977.

293 "LANCASTER'S PRESENCE,": *Time*, Sept. 25, 1978.

"AN ERA OF SCREEN HEROISM,": *Los Angeles Herald-Examiner,* Sept. 6, 1978.

"A GOOD LITTLE MOVIE": Lancaster quoted in *Boston Globe,* Sept. 28, 1986.

"THIS OTHER VIETNAM WAR MOVIE": *Los Angeles Times,* April 6, 1987.

294   "ABSORBING EVERYTHING,": Tito Capobianco, Interview. All subsequent quotations of his are drawn from this source. Capobianco is currently general director of the Pittsburgh Opera.

297   "INDEPENDENT PRODUCTION ON A LAISSEZ-FAIRE BASIS,": Bach, *Final Cut,* 308.

"CARELESS RELEASE PATTERN": *Village Voice,* June 24–30, 1981.

"SEEMS TO HAVE BEEN LIBERATED . . . ONCE AGAIN.": *Los Angeles Times,* Sept. 14, 1981.

298   THE "IMAGINED PAST": Garry Wills, *The Politics of Celebrity: John Wayne's America* (New York: Simon & Schuster, 1997), 14.

CHAPTER 11: Comebacks

300   "THERE'S OUR HERO!": John Guare, Interview.

301   "IT WAS VERY, VERY DIFFICULT . . .": Susan Sarandon, Interview. All subsequent quotations of hers are drawn from this source.

304   "BURT WAS MOM AND POP,": Bone, Interview.

"NO-MAN'S-LAND": Oct. 30, 1979, *Amica.* Translation by Marisa S. Trubiano for the author. This and subsequent Italian press commentaries on *La Pelle* referred to in these notes were kindly furnished to the author by Gaetana Marrone, Associate Professor of Romance Languages and Literatures, Princeton University. She is the author of a critical work on Cavani, *The Gaze and the Labyrinth: The Cinema of Liliana Cavani,* to be published in 2000 by Princeton University Press. Her critical insights, given during a telephone interview, were very helpful for this section.

"HUNGER FOR HIGH STAKES . . .": Ibid.

"CORRECTIVE": *Europeo,* May 24, 1979. Translation by Marisa S. Trubiano.

305   "THE PLAGUE" OF AMERICAN CULTURAL DOMINATION: *Panorama,* Nov. 24, 1980. Translation by Marisa S. Trubiano.

"*HUNKUS AMERICANUS*": *The New Yorker,* Apr. 6, 1981.

"THE MOVIE'S SWEET ELEGIAC HEART . . .": *Newsweek,* April 6, 1981.

"THE LANCASTER CAREER, . . .": Canby, "Time and Talent."

306   "ON THE VERGE OF TEARS.": *New York Post,* Feb. 1, 1982.

"IT MIGHT SET NORMA OFF . . .": Lancaster quoted in Kamber, Interview.

307   "HERO OF SCREEN DAYS": *Variety,* May 25, 1983.

CRAFTED THE DIALOGUE: Production Information press release, n.d., *Local Hero* clipping file, AMPAS.

THE VILLAGE OF PENNAN: Ibid. The tiny seaside movie village of Ferness was in fact two locations: the east coast village of Banff and Camusdarach Beach near Fort William to the west. Happer's lavish Houston office with the hydraulic glass roof open to the starry sky was constructed in an abandoned Aberdeen distillery. See also Alan Hunter and and Mark Astaire, *Local Hero.*

"WAS CONSTANTLY LOOKING FOR A COMEDIC ANGLE, . . .": Peter Capaldi, Interview. All subsequent quotations of his are drawn from this source.

RIEGERT WAS ENCOURAGED BY THE STAR: Clinch, 172.

308 "A SOUL CRYING IN THERE.": Forsyth quoted in Clinch, 174.

308 "LANCASTER HAS AN IMPERIAL ROMANTIC AURA,": Reprinted in Kael, *Taking It All In*, 465.

309 *THE OSTERMAN WEEKEND:* Alan Sharp described the relationship between the once-great director of *The Wild Bunch* and *Pat Garrett and Billy the Kid* and Lancaster as "two elderly seasoned kind of dudes who'd been through a lot of shit and getting through more shit, you know?" (Sharp, Interview).

    MARIA'S LOVERS: Bill Lancaster reportedly wrote the first script for *Maria's Lovers* with the idea that it would be a family project with his father. When Dino de Laurentiis bought the property, paying Bill a reported $1 million for the rights, the writer withdrew along with his father.

    HE HAD PLAYED POPE GREGORY X: For production information on *Marco Polo*, see Fury, 289–290.

    THE TWO MEN FIRST MET: Dan Yakir, "American Stars Team Up On a Brazilian Movie," *New York Times*, Feb. 26, 1984.

310 "A BIG HAND . . .": Babenco quoted in Yakir, "American Stars."

    "TO DESTROY THE MYTHS . . .": Babenco quoted in Yakir, "American Stars."

    "ONE OF THE LAST TABOOS": Bernard Weinraub, "From Poison Apple to Plum Role: As Taboo Fades, Actors See Little Career Jeopardy in Playing Gay Characters," *New York Times*, Sept. 10, 1997.

    "EMOTIONAL LOYALTY": Helen Dudar, "*Spider Woman:* A Labor of Love," *New York Times*, July 21, 1985.

311 "RISE TO SPECULATION AGAIN": *New York Daily News*, Oct. 5, 1987.

    "WHAT OTHER ACTOR,": *The Times* (London), Sept. 1, 1983. The London newspaper looked back to the "different market forces" at play twenty years before: 20th Century-Fox now had an "International Classics" division from which to rerelease "quality imports"; "fear of subtitles" seemed to have lessened; and Kevin Brownlow's recent restoration of Abel Gance's *Napoleon* had "turned excavation of cinema into something romantic, glamorous—a media event." Critics also remembered the diversion *Cleopatra* had created for Fox in 1963, draining postproduction money and attention from the English-language version of *The Leopard.*

    "LOOKS SO MAJESTIC,": *New York Times*, Sept. 11, 1983.

    "IT HAS A HERO ON A GRAND SCALE . . .": *The New Yorker*, Sept. 19, 1983.

    "THE PERFORMANCE OF HIS CAREER . . .": *The New Yorker*, May 21, 1990.

    "WHEN *THE LEOPARD* FIRST CAME OUT,": *New York Times*, Sept. 2, 1983.

    "WE'RE ALL FORGOTTEN . . .": Lancaster quoted in Alain Silver and James Ursini, *What Ever Happened to Robert Aldrich?*, xvi.

312 "MORE A) ACTION/MOVEMENT . . .": Lancaster to Peckinpah, Sept. 4, 1982. "*Osterman Weekend*—Miscellaneous Correspondence" file, Sam Peckinpah Collection, AMPAS.

    MARGOT KIDDER: Judson Klinger, "Education of Margot Kidder," *Rolling Stone*, July 9, 1981.

    WOW, REHEARSALS ARE GOING REALLY WELL: Ted Danson, Interview.

313　"MOVIE-SET BRAWL": *Los Angeles Times,* Mar. 2, 1984.

DANSON RECALLED: Danson, Interview.

314　"THINGS WERE NEVER . . .": Steel, 188.

"BURT WAS A REAL MAN'S MAN . . .": Larry Powell, Interview. All subsequent quotations of his are drawn from this source.

315　"I REALLY FELT FULFILLED . . .": Lancaster quoted in Kay Gardella, "Burt Sniffs the Sweet Smell" *New York Daily News,* Jan. 16, 1985.

"BURNED BY ONE OF THOSE GOSSIP SHEETS": Lancaster quoted in Gardella, "Burt Sniffs."

COSTARRING JULIE CHRISTIE: Christie recalled Lancaster as "so brave and clear and out of the ordinary. . . . He *minded,* unlike some actors who at that age really just make money." Julie Christie, Interview.

SUSAN JUNE MARTIN: Susie Lancaster, Interview. All subsequent quotations of hers are drawn from this source. Many of the details of Burt and Susie's life together also come from this source. Susie Martin's married name was Scherer.

318　HE PLAYED THE OPERA SAGE/CRITIC: *USA Today,* Feb. 1, 1985.

"*KILLED* THEM, . . .": Lancaster quoted in Confidential Interview.

"OPENED A NEW ERA . . .": *Los Angeles Times,* May 28, 1985.

"A PIECE OF CASTING FOR THE ROLE.": Gary Pudney, Interview.

"A FRIEND OF ELIZABETH'S . . .": Taylor and Lancaster appeared together in 1984 at legislative hearings in Sacramento in favor of a measure to give heirs a veto over use of the photo, voice, or "persona" of deceased celebrities (*New York Daily News,* June 19, 1984). They had also worked together on one project, ABC-TV's *Victory at Entebbe* (1976).

"IT WAS IMPOSSIBLE . . .": Bill Misenheimer, Interview.

319　"REAL RISK": Confidential Interview.

"I HAVE . . . BEEN TOLD THE MEDIA COVERAGE . . .": Hudson quoted in Jerry Oppenheimer and Jack Vitek, *Idol,* 221.

"IT SEEMS AS IF I WAS THIRTY-FIVE JUST YESTERDAY,": Lancaster quoted in Farber, "Lancaster and Douglas."

"REDUCED TO A CARTOON.": Jeffrey Lantos, "The Last Waltz," *American Film,* Oct. 1986.

320　"SERENE, LEONINE GRAVITY, . . .": *Los Angeles Times,* Oct. 2, 1986.

"DREADFUL BORES,": *Los Angeles Herald-Examiner,* Sept. 7, 1981.

"HOW COME BURT HAS THE BEST DRESSING ROOM?": Douglas quoted in Confidential Interview.

"OH, ONE DROPPED DOWN THE RIVER!": Ibid.

"AS DIFFERENT AS NIGHT AND DAY": Christopher Griffen, assistant director, *Tough Guys,* Interview. All subsequent quotations of his are drawn from this source.

321　"DOWNRIGHT ANGRY . . .": *Boxoffice,* Dec. 1986.

"THE ONLY WAY . . .": Lancaster quoted in *Pulse!* (Tower Records), Nov. 1986.

"I FIND THAT I HAVE VERY FEW FRIENDS,": Douglas quoted in Farber, "Lancaster and Douglas."

"A LOT OF THESE GIRLS . . .": As told to Al Schaeffer by Lancaster. Schaeffer, Interview.

323   "A SOFT, COMPASSIONATE SIDE . . .": Lancaster quoted in *On Wings of Eagles* press release, NBC-New York, Apr. 18, 1986.

323   "I'M NOT A PARTICULARLY WELL MAN. . . .": Lancaster quoted in Doug Hill, "How Dare This Young Upstart Tell Burt Lancaster How to Act!" *TV Guide*, May 17–23, 1986.

324   "SERMON ON LEGS,": *London Theater Record*, May 19–June 2, 1982.

    "A STORY ABOUT WHAT LOVE MEANS . . .": Lancaster quoted in *New York Times*, July 9, 1987.

    ONE CRITIC RENAMED IT *ON GOLDEN CHILL*: *Los Angeles Herald-Examiner*, Sept. 2, 1988.

325   "JUST DON'T STEP ON MY LINES.": Culkin quoted in Jeannie Park, " 'Rocket Gibraltar' Journeys From Launch to Apogee," *New York Times*, Sept. 4, 1988.

    "BIG BURT,": Robert Schulman, key grip, *Rocket Gibraltar*, Interview.

    "TOO EASY,": Culkin quoted in *New York Times*, Sept. 4, 1988.

    HE JOKED TO A REPORTER: Ibid.

    WHEN HE BLEW UP AT DANIEL PETRIE: Fishgall, 377.

    "TEARS [WERE] STREAMING . . .": Kevin Spacey interviewed on American Movie Classics tele-biography, "Legendary Lancaster," Feb. 25, 1997. All subsequent quotations of Spacey's come from this source.

326   A "SLEEPER": Lancaster quoted in Ovid Demaris, "He'd Rather Take a Chance," *Parade*, Nov. 6, 1988.

    AS LITTLE DUTCH: *New York Daily News*, Nov. 16, 1987.

    "[Y]OU'RE MARKING TIME,": Lancaster quoted in Charles Champlin, "Burt Lancaster's Undimmed Magic," *Los Angeles Times*, Sept. 10, 1988.

    "STILL GOING LIKE A TRIP HAMMER.": Lancaster quoted in Park, "Launch to Apogee."

    AT THE END OF THE YEAR: *Old Gringo* preproduction information from Nina J. Easton, "The High Cost of Stardom: Lancaster Suit Reveals Role of Insurance in Film Making," *Los Angeles Times*, June 17, 1988, and from Kaplan, Interview.

327   "IF THE INDUSTRY BELIEVES . . .": Easton, "High Cost."

    "VERY GRUMPY": James Earl Jones, Interview. All subsequent quotations of his are drawn from this source.

328   "I KIND OF MARCH . . .": Costner quoted in *Field of Dreams* clipping file, n.d. [1989], AMPAS.

    "DESPITE A LOVELY CAMEO TURN . . .": *Time*, Apr. 24, 1989.

    KAEL CALLED IT "A CROCK": *The New Yorker*, May 1, 1989.

329   "I'M BURT LANCASTER AND I HAVE A CONFESSION . . .": Ramona Ripston kindly let the author view tapes of Lancaster's 1988 ACLU TV spots in her Los Angeles office; from them this transcription was made.

    "WAVE OF ORGANIZATION BUILDING,": Brownstein, 279.

330   "AS SLICK AND DISTORTED . . .": *Los Angeles Times*, Oct. 22, 1982.

    FALWELL BRANDED LEAR: *Newsweek*, Oct. 19, 1982.

    ATTRACTED NATIONWIDE ATTENTION: *New York Post*, May 24, 1986.

    "THE KISS OF DEATH.": Lancaster quoted in Confidential Interview.

331 "I KNEW HE WAS A BIG DEAL,": Linda Burstyn, Interview. All subsequent quotations from Burstyn, unless otherwise noted, come from this source. Burstyn also kindly provided the author, in telephone interviews, with readings from Lancaster's ACLU speeches (dug out of an old computer in a garage), which are the source of the quoted material.

332 IT WAS THE SECOND: In 1989 Karl Malden and Lee Grant had starred in *The Hijacking of the Achille Lauro* for NBC.
"I WANT TO DO MY PERFORMANCE JUSTICE,": Lancaster quoted in Else Klinghoffer and Lisa Klinghoffer, Interview. All subsequent quotations from them are drawn from this source.

333 "SCHLOCKY EVEN FOR ITS TIME,": Lancaster quoted in *Los Angeles Times,* n.d. [1990], CMC USC.
"GEE WHIZ ROUTE": Lancaster quoted in *Los Angeles Times,* n.d. [1990], CMC USC.

334 "MINI-SERIES SUPREME.": John Leonard, "A Mini-Series Supreme," *New York,* Apr. 8, 1991. George Stevens Jr. had won an Emmy for the Outstanding Mini-Series of 1988, NBC's *The Murder of Mary Phagan,* and coproducer Stan Marguiles Jr. had won Emmys for both *Roots* in 1977 and *Roots: The Next Generation* in 1979.
"WE TRAVELED IN DIFFERENT CIRCLES,": Sidney Poitier, Interview. All subsequent quotations of his are drawn from this source.
THE ACTOR WAS "MORE ALIVE": E. Barrett Prettyman Jr., Interview.

335 SHE WAS NOW HIS WIFE: The details about the wedding and wedding party come from Susie Lancaster. Quoted material from same is transcribed from a videotape of the wedding party at Hillcrest, kindly furnished to the author by Mrs. Lancaster.
STORIES CIRCULATED: "Burt Lancaster, 76, secretly weds beauty half his age," *Star,* Sept. 25, 1990.

PART FOUR: THE END 1990–1994

CHAPTER 12: Fade Out

339 LANCASTER HAD HAD A MASSIVE CEREBRAL STROKE: "Burt Lancaster in Hospital; Falls Ill in Los Alamitos," *Los Angeles Times,* Dec. 1, 1990.

340 "IMMEDIATELY THOUGHT OF THAT PERFECT BODY . . .": Cardinale, 191.
BUT WILD RUMORS: *Wall Street Journal,* Jan. 21, 1993.

341 "THAT'S WHAT I THOUGHT.": Douglas quoted in Susie Lancaster, Interview.
IN 1991 SAG: Material and quotations taken from a transcript of the SAG Annual Achievement Award ceremony on Dec. 15, 1991, kindly provided by SAG.

343 "I'VE HAD THE FEELING . . .": Nick Cravat to Bill Lancaster, n.d. [1991]. Copy of letter kindly provided to author by Tina Cuccia-Cravat.
"WE ARE LOOKING,": *New York Times,* Dec. 16, 1994.

Epitaph

346 "YOU NEVER HEARD . . .": Gary Parkins, Executive Director of the Royal Hanneford Circus, Interview.

Selected Bibliography

Adamson, Joe. *Byron Haskin: A Director Guild of America Oral History.* Metuchen, NJ: Scarecrow Press, 1984.

Alicea, Benjamin. *Christian Urban Colonizers: A History of the East Harlem Protestant Parish in New York City, 1948–68.* Submitted in partial fulfillment of the requirements for the degree of Doctor of Philosophy in Church History. Union Theological Seminary, New York City, 1989.

Allanbrook, Alan. *See Naples: A Memoir of Love, Peace, and War in Italy.* Boston: Houghton Mifflin, 1995.

Allen, Frederick Lewis. *Only Yesterday: An Informal History of the Nineteen-Twenties.* New York: Bantam Books, 1959.

Arnold, Edwin T., and Eugene L. Miller Jr. *The Films and Career of Robert Aldrich,* Knoxville: University of Tennessee Press, 1986.

Bacall, Lauren. *Lauren Bacall: By Myself.* New York: Alfred A. Knopf, 1978.

Bach, Steven. *Final Cut: Dreams and Disaster in the Making of "Heaven's Gate."* New York: William Morrow & Company, 1985.

———. *Marlene Dietrich: Life and Legend.* New York: William Morrow & Company, 1992.

Balio, Tino. *United Artists: The Company Built by the Stars.* Madison: University of Wisconsin Press, 1976.

———. *United Artists: The Company That Changed the Film Industry.* Madison: University of Wisconsin Press, 1987.

Bart, Peter. *Fade Out: The Calamitous Final Days of MGM.* New York: William Morrow & Company, 1990.

Behlmer, Rudy, ed., *Memo from Darryl F. Zanuck: The Golden Years at 20th Century-Fox.* New York: Grove Press, 1993.

———. *Inside Warner Brothers (1935–1951).* New York: Viking Press, 1985.

Bentley, Eric, ed. *Thirty Years of Treason: Excerpts From Hearings Before the House Committee on Un-American Activities, 1938–1968.* New York: Viking Press, 1971.

Bentley, Joanne. *Hallie Flanagan: A Life in the American Theater.* New York: Alfred A. Knopf, 1988.

Berg, A. Scott. *Goldwyn: A Biography.* New York: Ballantine Books, 1990.

Bernstein, Walter. *Inside Out: A Memoir of the Blacklist.* New York: Alfred A. Knopf, 1996.

———. *Keep Your Head Down.* New York: Viking Press, 1945.

Bishop, Jim. *The Mark Hellinger Story: A Biography of Broadway.* New York: Appleton-Century-Crofts, 1952.

Biskind, Peter. *Seeing Is Believing: How Hollywood Taught Us to Stop Worrying and Love the Fifties.* New York: Pantheon, 1983.

Boleslavsky, Richard. *Acting: The First Six Lessons.* New York: Theater Arts Books, 1933.

Boyer, Paul S., et al. *The Enduring Vision: A History of the American People.* Lexington, MA: D.C. Heath and Company, 1995.

Branch, Taylor. *Parting the Waters: America in the King Years 1954–63.* New York: Simon & Schuster, 1988.

Brenman-Gibson, Margaret. *Clifford Odets: American Playwright, The Years from 1906 to 1940.* New York: Atheneum, 1981.

Brode, Douglas. *The Films of the Fifties:* Sunset Boulevard *to* On the Beach. New York: A Citadel Press Book, Published by Carol Publishing Group, 1990.

Brown, Peter H., and Jim Pinkston. *Oscar Dearest: Six Decades of Scandal, Politics and Greed Behind Hollywood's Academy Awards, 1927–1986.* New York: Harper & Row, 1987.

Brownlow, Kevin. *The Parade's Gone By . . .* New York: Alfred A. Knopf, 1968.

Brownstein, Ronald. *The Power and the Glitter: The Hollywood-Washington Connection.* New York: Pantheon, 1990.

Cagney, James. *Cagney by Cagney.* Garden City, NY: Doubleday, 1976.

Carney, Raymond. *American Dreaming: The Films of John Cassavetes and the American Experience.* Berkeley: University of California Press, 1985.

Carr, Robert K. *The House Committee on Un-American Activities, 1945–1950.* Ithaca, NY: Cornell University Press, 1952.

Caute, David. *The Great Fear: The Anti-Communist Purge Under Truman and Eisenhower.* New York: Simon & Schuster, 1978.

Ceplair, Larry, and Steven Englund. *The Inquisition in Hollywood: Politics in the Film Community, 1930–1960.* Garden City, NY: Anchor Press/Doubleday, 1980.

Cheever, Benjamin, ed. *The Letters of John Cheever.* New York: Simon & Schuster, 1988.

Clinch, Minty. *Burt Lancaster.* New York: Stein and Day, 1984.

Clurman, Harold, *The Fervent Years: The Story of the Group Theatre and the Thirties.* New York: Alfred A. Knopf, 1945.

Cogley, John. *Report on Blacklisting,* 2 vols. New York: The Fund for the Republic, 1956.

Cole, Lester. *Hollywood Red: The Autobiography of Lester Cole.* Palo Alto, CA: Ramparts Press, 1981.

Conant, Michael. *Antitrust in the Motion Picture Industry: Economic and Legal Analysis.* Berkeley: University of California Press, 1960.

Considine, Shaun. *Mad As Hell: The Life and Work of Paddy Chayefsky.* New York: Random House, 1994.

Cottrell, John. *Laurence Olivier.* Englewood Cliffs, NJ: Prentice-Hall, 1975.

Crist, Judith. *Take 22: Moviemakers on Moviemaking.* New York: Viking Press, 1984.

Culhane, John. *The American Circus: An Illustrated History.* New York: Henry Holt & Co., 1990.

Curtis, Tony, and Barry Parris. *Tony Curtis: The Autobiography.* New York: William Morrow & Company, 1993.

De Carlo, Yvonne, with Doug Warren. *Yvonne: An Autobiography.* New York: St. Martin's Press, 1987.

Douglas, Ann. *Terrible Honesty: Mongrel Manhattan in the 1920's.* New York: Farrar, Straus & Giroux, 1995.

Douglas, Kirk. *Ragman's Son: An Autobiography.* New York: Simon & Schuster, 1988.

———. *Climbing the Mountain: My Search for Meaning.* New York: Simon & Schuster, 1997.

Dunne, Philip. *Take Two: A Life in Movies and Politics.* New York: McGraw-Hill, 1980.

Dyer, Richard. *Heavenly Bodies: Film Stars and Society,* New York, St. Martin's Press, 1986.

Evans, Robert. *The Kid Stays in the Picture.* New York: Hyperion, 1994.

Fine, Marshall. *Bloody Sam: The Life and Films of Sam Peckinpah.* New York: Donald I. Fine, Inc., 1991.

Flanagan, Hallie. *Arena: The Story of the Federal Theatre.* New York: Duell, Sloan & Pearce, 1940.

Fontaine, Joan. *No Bed of Roses.* New York: William Morrow & Company, 1978.

Fox, Stephen. *Blood and Power: Organized Crime in Twentieth-Century America.* New York: William Morrow & Company, 1989.

Freedland, Michael. *Cagney: A Biography.* New York: Stein and Day, 1975.

———. *The Warner Brothers.* New York: St. Martin's Press, 1983.

French, Philip, ed. *Malle on Malle.* London: Faber & Faber, 1993.

Friedrich, Otto. *City of Nets: A Portrait of Hollywood in the 1940s.* New York: Perennial Library/Harper & Row, 1986.

Fury, David. *The Cinema History of Burt Lancaster.* Minneapolis, MN: Artists Press, 1989.

Gabler, Neal. *An Empire of Their Own: How the Jews Created Hollywood.* New York: Anchor Books/Doubleday, 1989.

———. *Walter Winchell: Gossip, Power and the Culture of Celebrity.* New York: Alfred A. Knopf, 1994.

Gansberg, Alan L. *Little Casear: A Biography of Edward G. Robinson.* London: New English Library, 1983.

Gardner, Ava. *Ava: My Story.* New York: Bantam Books, 1990.

Garrow, David J. *Bearing the Cross: Martin Luther King, Jr. and the Southern Christian Leadership Conference.* New York: William Morrow & Company, 1986.

Gilmour, David. *The Last Leopard: A Life of Giuseppe Tomasi de Lampedusa,* New York: Pantheon, 1988.

Gitlin, Todd. *The Sixties: Years of Hope, Days of Rage.* Toronto and New York: Bantam Books, 1987.

Goldstein, Malcolm. *The Political Stage: American Drama and Theater in the Great Depression.* New York: Oxford University Press, 1974.

Goodman, Ezra. *The Fifty-Year Decline and Fall of Hollywood.* New York: Simon & Schuster, 1961.

Goodman, Walter. *The Committee: The Extraordinary Career of the House Committee on Un-American Activities.* New York: Farrar, Straus & Giroux. 1968.

Graham, Sheilah. *Confessions of a Hollywood Columnist.* New York: William Morrow & Company, 1969.

Green, Abel, and Joe Laurie Jr. *Show Biz: From Vaude to Video*. New York: Henry Holt & Co., 1951.

Halliwell, Leslie. *Halliwell's Film Guide*, 8th ed. New York: HarperCollins Publishers, Inc., 1991.

Harding, Bill. *The Films of Michael Winner*. London: Frederick Muller, 1978.

Hay, Peter. *MGM: When the Lion Roars*. Atlanta, GA: Turner Publishing, 1991.

———. *Movie Anecdotes*. New York: Oxford University Press, 1990.

Heckscher, August, with Phyllis Robinson. *When La Guardia Was Mayor: New York's Legendary Years*. New York: W.W. Norton & Company, Inc., 1978.

Henreid, Paul, with Julius Fast. *Ladies Man: An Autobiography*, New York: St. Martin's Press, 1984.

Heymann, David. *Liz: An Intimate Biography of Elizabeth Taylor*. New York: Birch Lane Press, published by Carol Publishing Group, 1995.

Higham, Charles. *Ava: A Life Story*. New York: Delacorte Press, 1974.

———. *Audrey: The Life of Audrey Hepburn*. New York: Macmillan, 1984.

———. *Kate: The Life of Katherine Hepburn*. New York: W.W. Norton & Company, 1975.

———. *Merchant of Dreams: Louis B. Mayer, MGM and the Secret Hollywood*. New York: Donald I. Fine, 1993.

Hill, James. *Rita Hayworth: A Memoir*. New York: Simon & Schuster, 1983.

Hirsch, Foster. *Film Noir: The Dark Side of the Screen*. San Diego: A.S. Barnes, 1981.

Hirschhorn, Clive. *The Columbia Story*. New York: Crown, 1989.

———. *The Universal Story*. New York: Crown, 1983.

Holden, Anthony. *Behind the Oscar: The Secret History of the Academy Awards*. New York: Simon & Schuster, 1993.

———. *Laurence Olivier: A Biography*. New York: Atheneum, 1988.

Hopper, Hedda, and James Brough. *The Whole Truth and Nothing But*. Garden City, NY: Doubleday, 1963.

Hotchner, A.E. *Papa Hemingway: A Personal Memoir*. New York: Random House, 1966.

Hughes, Glenn. *A History of the American Theater, 1700–1950*. New York: Samuel French, 1951.

Hunter, Allen, *Burt Lancaster: The Man and His Movies*. New York: St. Martin's Press, 1984.

Hunter, Allen, and Mark Astaire. *Local Hero: The Making of the Film*. New York: Frederick Ungar, 1983.

Huston, John. *An Open Book: John Huston*. New York: Alfred A. Knopf, 1980.

Kael, Pauline. *5001 Nights at the Movies: A Guide from A to Z*. New York: Holt, Rinehart & Winston, 1982.

———. *Going Steady*. Boston: Little, Brown and Company, 1970.

———. *Taking It All In*. New York: Holt, Rinehart & Winston, 1984.

Kahn, Gordon. *Hollywood on Trial: The Story of the Ten Who Were Indicted*. New York: Boni & Gaer, 1948.

Kaminsky, Stuart. *Coop: The Life and Legend of Gary Cooper*. New York: St. Martin's Press, 1980.

Kartseva, E. *Burt Lancaster*. Moskva: Iskusstvo, 1983.

Katz, Ephraim. *The Film Encyclopedia.* Third Edition. New York: HarperPerennial/ HarperCollins, 1998.

Kelley, Kitty. *His Way: The Unauthorized Biography of Frank Sinatra.* Toronto and New York: Bantam Books, 1986.

Kemp, Philip. *Lethal Innocence: The Cinema of Alexander Mackendrick.* London: Methuen, 1991.

Kessner, Thomas. *Fiorello H. La Guardia and the Making of Modern New York.* New York: McGraw-Hill, 1989.

———. *The Golden Door: Italian and Jewish Immigrant Mobility in New York City, 1880–1915.* New York: Oxford University Press, 1977.

Keyssar, Helene. *Robert Altman's America.* New York: Oxford University Press, 1991.

Kisseloff, Jeff. *You Must Remember This: An Oral History of Manhattan from the 1890's to World War II.* San Diego: Harcourt, Brace, Jovanovich, 1989.

Kline, T. Jefferson. *Bertolucci's Dream Loom: A Psychoanalytic Study of Cinema.* Amherst: University of Massachusetts Press, 1987.

Kolker, Robert Phillip. *Bernardo Bertolucci.* New York: Oxford University Press, 1985.

Kramer, Stanley. *A Mad, Mad, Mad, Mad World: A Life in Hollywood.* New York: Harcourt, Brace, Jovanovich, 1997.

Kyriazi, Gary. *The Great American Amusement Parks: A Pictorial History.* Secaucus, NJ: Castle Books, 1976.

Lacourbe, Roland. *Burt Lancaster.* Paris: Edilig, 1987.

LaGuardia, Robert. *Monty: A Biography of Montgomery Clift.* New York: Avon, 1977.

Lamson, Peggy. *Roger Baldwin: Founder of the ACLU.* Boston: Houghton Mifflin, 1976.

Laurie, Joe, Jr. *Vaudeville: From the Honky-tonks to the Palace.* New York: Henry Holt & Co., 1953.

Leaming, Barbara. *If This Was Happiness: A Biography of Rita Hayworth.* New York: Viking Press, 1989.

Lehman, Ernest. *The Sweet Smell of Success and Other Stories.* New York: Signet, 1956.

Leigh, Janet. *There Really Was a Hollywood: An Autobiography.* Garden City, NY: Doubleday, 1984.

Levy, Emmanuel. *And the Winner Is . . . The History and Politics of the Oscar Awards.* New York: Frederick Ungar, 1987.

Lockwood, Charles. *Manhattan Moves Uptown: An Illustrated History.* Boston: Houghton Mifflin, 1976.

McBride, Joseph, ed. *Filmmakers on Filmmaking: The American Film Institute Seminars on Motion Pictures and Television.* Los Angeles: J.P. Tarcher, 1983.

MacCann, Richard Dyer. *Hollywood in Transition.* Boston: Houghton Mifflin, 1962.

McDonald, Archie P., ed. *Shooting Stars: Heroes and Heroines of Western Film.* Bloomington, IN: Bloomington University Press, 1987.

McGilligan, Patrick. *Backstory: Interviews with Screenwriters of Hollywood's Golden Age.* Berkeley: University of California Press, 1986.

———. *Backstory 2: Interviews with Screenwriters of the 1940s and 1950s.* Berkeley: University of California Press, 1991.

———. *Cagney: The Actor as Auteur.* San Diego: A.S. Barnes, 1982.

————. *Robert Altman: Jumping Off the Cliff, A Biography of the Great American Director*. New York: St. Martin's Press, 1989.

McGilligan, Patrick, and Paul Buhle. *Tender Comrades: A Backstory of the Hollywood Blacklist*. New York: St. Martin's Griffin, 1997.

Madsen, Axel. *Stanwyck*. New York: HarperCollins, 1994.

Manchester, William. *The Glory and the Dream: A Narrative History of America 1932–1972*. Boston: Little, Brown, 1974.

Manso, Peter. *Brando: The Biography*. New York: Hyperion, 1994.

————. *Mailer: His Life and Times*. New York: Simon & Schuster, 1985.

Martin, Pete. *Hollywood Without Makeup*. Philadelphia: J.B. Lippincott, 1948.

Mayer, Arthur. *Merely Colossal: The Story of the Movies from the Long Chase to the Chaise Longue*. New York: Simon & Schuster, 1953.

Mellen, Joan. *Big Bad Wolves: Masculinity in the American Film*. New York: Pantheon, 1977.

Millett, John D. *The Organization and Role of the Army Service Forces*, Office of the Chief of Military History, Department of the Army, Washington, DC, 1954; volume 10 of series, *United States Army in World War II*.

————. *The Works Progress Administration in New York City*. Chicago: Published for the Committee on Public Administration of the Social Science Research Council by Public Administration Service, 1938.

Monroe, Eason. *Safeguarding Civil Liberties*. Los Angeles: UCLA Oral History Project, 1974.

Morella, Joe, and Edward Epstein. *Rebels: The Rebel Hero in Films*. Introduction by Judith Crist. New York: A Citadel Press Book, Published by Carol Publishing Group, 1971.

Morley, Sheridan. *Gladys Cooper: A Biography*. New York: McGraw-Hill, 1979.

Morris, Jan. *Manhattan '45*. New York: Oxford University Press, 1987.

Mosedale, John. *The Men Who Invented Broadway: Damon Runyon, Walter Winchell and Their World*. New York: Richard C. Marek Publishers, 1981.

Moss, Robert F. *The Films of Carol Reed*. New York: Columbia University Press, 1987.

Naremore, James. *Acting in the Cinema*. Berkeley: University of California Press, 1988.

National Society of Film Critics, Elisabeth Weis, ed. *The Movie Star*. New York: Viking/Penguin, 1981.

Navasky, Victor S. *Naming Names*. New York: Viking Press, 1980.

The New York Times Directory of the Film. New York: Arno Press/Random House, 1971.

Nowell-Smith, Geoffrey. *Luchino Visconti*. New York: Viking Press, 1973.

Oakley, J. Ronald. *God's Country: America in the Fifties*. New York: Dembner Books, 1986.

Odets, Clifford. *The Time is Ripe: 1940 Journals*. New York: Grove Press, 1940.

Olivier, Laurence. *Confessions of an Actor: An Autobiography*. New York: Simon & Schuster, 1982.

Oppenheimer, Jerry, and Jack Vitek. *Idol: Rock Hudson, The True Story of An American Film Hero*. New York: Villard, 1986.

Orsi, Robert Anthony. *The Madonna of 115th Street: Faith and Community in Italian Harlem, 1880–1950*. New Haven, CT: Yale University Press, 1985.

Pack, Robert. *Edward Bennett Williams for the Defense*. New York: Harper & Row, 1983.

Parish, James Robert. *Gays and Lesbians in Mainstream Cinema: Plots, Critiques, Casts and Credits for 272 Theatrical and Made-for-television Hollywood Releases.* Jefferson, N.C.: McFarland & Co., 1993.

Perrett, Geoffrey. *There's a War to be Won: The United States Army in World War II.* New York: Random House, 1991.

———. *The Tough Guys.* New Rochelle, NY: Arlington House, 1976.

Phillips, Gene D. *The Films of Tennessee Williams.* Philadelphia: Art Alliance Press, 1980.

Pitiot, Pierre, and Jean-Claude Mirabella. *Sur Bertolucci.* Collection Festival Cinema Mediterranean Montpelier, Castelnau-le-Lez: Editions Climats, 1991.

Ramsaye, Terry. *A Million and One Nights.* New York: Simon & Schuster, 1926.

Reed, Rex. *Travolta to Keaton.* New York: William Morrow & Company, 1979.

Rico, Diana. *Kovacsland: A Biography of Ernie Kovacs.* New York: Harcourt, Brace, Jovanovich, 1990.

Rivers, Joan, with Richard Merryman. *Still Talking.* New York: Turtle Bay Books, Random House, 1991.

Robinson, Edward G., with Leonard Spiegelgass. *All My Yesterdays: An Autobiography.* New York: Hawthorn Books, 1973.

Ross, Lillian. *Picture.* New York: Penguin, 1952.

Roth, Henry. *Call It Sleep.* New York: The Noonday Press/Farrar, Straus & Giroux, 1991.

Russo, Vito. *The Celluoid Closet: Homosexuality in the Movies.* New York: Harper & Row, 1981.

Samuels, Charles Thomas. *A Casebook on Film.* New York: Van Nostrand Reinhold, 1970.

Sarris, Andrew. *The American Cinema: Directors and Directions, 1929–1968.* New York: E.P. Dutton, 1968.

Schary, Dore. *Heyday: An Autobiography.* Boston: Little, Brown, 1979.

Schickel, Richard. *Brando: A Life in Our Times.* New York: Atheneum, 1991.

———. *Movies: The History of an Art and an Institution.* New York: Basic Books, 1964.

———. *Schickel on Film: Encounters—Critical and Personal—with Movie Immortals.* New York: William Morrow & Company, 1989.

Schifano, Laurence. *Luchino Visconti: The Flames of Passion.* London: Collins, 1990.

Schnayerson, Michael. *Irwin Shaw: A Biography.* New York: G.P. Putnam's Sons, 1989.

Schorer, Mark. *Sinclair Lewis: An American Life.* New York: McGraw-Hill, 1961.

Selznick, Irene Mayer. *A Private View.* New York: Alfred A. Knopf, 1983.

Servadio, Gaia. *Luchino Visconti: A Biography.* New York: Franklin Watts, 1983.

Shipman, David. *Judy Garland: The Secret Life of an American Legend.* New York: Hyperion, 1992.

———. *The Story of Cinema: A Complete Narrative History from the Beginnings to the Present.* New York: St. Martin's Press, 1982.

Silver, Alain, and James Ursini. *What Ever Happened to Robert Aldrich? His Life and His Films,* with a foreword by Burt Lancaster. New York: Limelight Editions, 1995.

Sklar, Robert. *City Boys: Cagney, Bogart, Garfield.* Princeton: Princeton University Press, 1992.

Snow, Richard. *Coney Island: A Postcard Journey to the City of Fire.* New York: Brightwaters Press, 1984.

Sperber, A.M., and Eric Lax. *Bogart.* New York: William Morrow & Company, 1997.

Spoto, Donald. *Stanley Kramer: Film Maker.* New York: G.P. Putnam's Sons, 1978.

Steel, Dawn. *They Can Kill You, But They Can't Eat You.* New York: Pocket Books, 1993.

Sterling, Monica. *A Screen of Time: A Study of Luchino Visconti.* New York: Harcourt, Brace, Jovanovich, 1979.

Stern, Robert A.M., Gregory Gilmartin, and John Massengale. *New York 1900: Metropolitan Architecture and Urbanism 1890–1915.* New York: Rizzoli, 1983.

Stern, Robert A.M., Gregory Gilmartin, and Thomas Mellens. *New York 1930: Architecture and Urbanism Between the Two World Wars.* New York: Rizzoli, 1987.

Stewart, Donald. *A Short History of East Harlem.* New York: The Museum of the City of New York, 1972.

Taylor, Robert Lewis. *Center Ring: The People of the Circus.* Garden City, NY: Doubleday, 1956.

Thomas, Bob. *King Cohn: The Life and Times of Harry Cohn.* New York: G.P. Putnam's Sons, 1967.

Thomas, Evan. *The Man to See: Edward Bennett Williams Ultimate Insider; Legendary Trial Lawyer.* New York: Simon & Schuster, 1991.

Thomas, Tony. *Burt Lancaster.* New York: Pyramid, 1975.

Thomson, David. *A Biographical Dictionary of Film.* Third Edition. New York: Alfred A. Knopf, 1994.

Tonetti, Claretta. *Luchino Visconti.* Boston: Twayne Publishers, 1983.

Walker, Alexander. *Stardom: The Hollywood Phenomenon.* New York: Stein and Day, 1970.

Wallis, Hal, and Charles Higham. *Starmaker: The Autobiography of Hal Wallis.* New York: Macmillan, 1980.

Wapshott, Nicholas. *Carol Reed: A Biography.* New York: Alfred A. Knopf, 1994.

Warren, Doug. *James Cagney: The Authorized Biography.* New York: St. Martin's Press, 1983.

Warshow, Robert. *The Immediate Experience: Movies, Comics, Theatre, and Other Aspects of Popular Culture.* Garden City, NY: Doubleday, 1962.

Weaver, John D., ed. *Glad Tidings: A Friendship in Letters. The Correspondence of John Cheever and John D. Weaver, 1945–1982.* New York: HarperCollins, 1993.

Weddle, David. *"If They Move . . . Kill 'Em!": The Life and Times of Sam Peckinpah.* New York: Grove, 1994.

Wheeler, Robert W. *Jim Thorpe: World's Greatest Athlete.* Norman: University of Oklahoma Press, 1975.

Williams, Tennessee. *Memoirs.* Garden City, NY: Anchor Press/Doubleday, 1983.

Windeler, Robert. *Burt Lancaster.* New York: St. Martin's Press, 1984.

Winters, Shelley. *Shelley, Also Known As Shirley.* New York: William Morrow & Company, 1980.

————. *Shelley II: The Middle of My Century.* New York: Simon & Schuster, 1989.

Wood, Michael. *America in the Movies.* New York: Basic Books, 1975.

Yule, Andrew. *Fast Fade: David Puttnam, Columbia Pictures, and the Battle for Hollywood.* New York: Delacorte, 1989.

Zinnemann, Fred. *Fred Zinnemann: An Autobiography: A Life in the Movies.* New York: Charles Scribner's Sons, 1992.

Acknowledgments

The delight of this project has been the support so readily given by so many people. Richard T. Jameson, editor of *Film Comment*, for first letting me loose on Lancaster and for taping all those videos; Kathleen Murphy, New York Film Society Curator for saying "Yes," without hesitation, to the idea of the first major Lancaster film retrospective in New York, at the Walter Reade Theater at Lincoln Center in May 2000; David Thomson and Neal Gabler for essential guidance and much patience; Robert A. M. Stern and Nicholas Stern for putting the pieces together; Amanda Beesley and Sloan Harris, terrific agents both—and Esther Newberg—all at ICM, for immediately seeing the book in Lancaster, a long-time client of the late Ben Benjamin, esteemed ICM agent; Pat McGilligan and Peter Manso, for guidance and access; and Harry Stein for keeping me on track.

Librarians and archivists: Ned Comstock, archivist extraordinaire at the Cinema-Television Library at the University of Southern California, and Howard Prouty at the Margaret Herrick Library of the Academy of Motion Picture Arts and Sciences; the able staffs of the Billy Rose Theatre Collection at the New York Public Library for the Performing Arts at Lincoln Center, the Museum of the City of New York, and Union Theological Seminary; Harry Miller, Reference Archivist at the Wisconsin State Historical Society; Fred Dahlinger at the Circus Museum at Baraboo, Wisconsin; Kenneth Cobb at the New York Municipal Archives; Ken Schlesinger at The National Archives at College Park, Maryland; Pat Sheehan, former head of the Document and Reference Section of the Library of Congress Motion Picture, Broadcasting and Recorded Sound Division; Eugene Sklar, Ramon Rodriguez, and Sally Yarmolinsky at Union Settlement House; Steve Gossard, Curator of Circus Collections at the Milner Library Special Collections, Illinois State University; Jonathan Rosenthal, another researcher extraordinaire, formerly at the Museum of Television and Radio; and Mary Corliss and Charles Silver at the Museum of Modern Art.

A special thanks to: Marcy Overway-Cravat and Tina Cuccia-Cravat, Nick Cravat's daughters, for much help, wonderful photographs, and generous time spent; Nancy Nelson; Lucy Kibbee; Paola Casella and her sister Alessandra Casella, for facilitating my entrée into Lancaster's Italian connections; U.S. Representative Neil Abercrombie for doggedly ensuring that this one citizen's quest for data under the Freedom of Information Act would yield results before the book's deadline.

So many Hollywood and film professionals gave generously of their time to this project and they are credited within. But I would like to thank the following for assistance above and beyond what I had any reason to expect: Sydney Pollack; Susan Sarandon; John Frankenheimer; Sherlee Lantz; Mickey Knox; Tony Curtis; John Guare; Suso Cecchi D'Amico; Giaocchino Tomasi, Duke of Palma; the late Alexander Mackendrick; Joe Hyams; Arnold Belnick; Scott Wilson; Bob Schiffer; Ben Cheever; Ernest Lehman; and John Turturro.

Rob, Lucy, and Will—for their love and support for me and "Buddy Burt." And extended family Gordon Lee, Mark Bonilla, Joe and Pat Drake.

And in the biography business where a catchphrase is "kill the widow," Mrs. Burt "Susie" Lancaster gave enormous, demanding, crucial help with no strings attached.

And to my editor at Alfred A. Knopf, Jon Segal: thank you.

Index

civil rights movement, 233–5, 258
Clair, René, 236
Clark, Gen. Mark, 51, 52, 304
Clark, Susan, 275
Clarke, Ernest, 40, 153
Clift, Montgomery, 127–9, 179, 211
Clurman, Harold, 23, 42
Cobb, Lee J., 270
Codona, Alfredo, 34, 153
Cody, William "Buffalo Bill," 281–2
Coen, Franklin, 236
Cohn, Harry, 106, 113, 128
Cole Bros. Circus, 95–6, 153
Coll, "Mad Dog," 29, 66, 67
Columbia Studios, 102–3, 106, 107, 202, 324, 326; -Lancaster independent production projects, 106, 107, 112–14, 126, 156, 208–10, 245–9, 326–7
Come Back, Little Sheba, 4, 123–4, 130, 180; critical reaction, 124
"Commitment to Life" fundraiser (1985), 318–19
Committee for the First Amendment, 80–2, 120, 121, 234
communism, 43; Hollywood blacklistings, 43–4, 78–82, 96–8, 102, 105–8, 114–15, 119–22, 130–2, 145–6, 173, 201; 1938–39 HUAC hearings, 43–4; 1947–49 HUAC hearings, 78–82, 96–8, 102, 105, 122; 1951 HUAC hearings, 114–15, 122
CONCERN, 330, 341
Confidential, 155–6, 315
Congress, U.S., 43–4, 80–2, 96–8; *see also* House Special Committee on Un-American Activities (HUAC)
Connors, Chuck, 126
Conroy, Thom, 52, 60, 217, 228, 264
Control (TV movie), 324
Conversation Piece, 277–9, 282–3, 293, 305; critical reaction, 282–3, 305; U.S. box-office performance, 282
Cooper, Gary, 62, 141, 167, 171, 183; *Vera Cruz,* 138–9
Cooper, Gladys, 187
Coppola, Francis Ford, 262–3, 290, 292
Corey, Wendell, 64
Corwin, Norman, 120
Cosmopolitan, 70, 160, 178
Costner, Kevin, 328
Counterattack, 97, 106, 120, 122
Cravat, Nick, 33–40, 42–7, 59, 72, 94–6, 102, 104, 115, 119, 165, 175, 185–6, 217, 221, 244, 264, 275, 286, 290, 304, 342–3; death, 343
Crawford, Cheryl, 23

Crichton, Charles, 209
Crimson Pirate, The, 115–18, 122, 124, 125, 215, 249, 275, 280, 285, 302, 305, 311; critical reaction, 115, 118; location shooting, 116
Criss Cross, 90, 91–2
Crist, Judith, 161, 251, 323
Cromwell, Oliver, 11
Cronyn, Hume, 75
Crosby, Bing, 3
Crowther, Bosley, 70, 113, 185, 229, 232
Cuban missile crisis, 229
Cuccia, Nick, *see* Cravat, Nick
Cuccia-Cravat, Tina, 33, 36, 119, 158, 286
Cue, 147
Cukor, George, 26
Culkin, Macaulay, 324, 325
Curtis, Tony, 3, 92, 136, 165, 170, 175, 227, 234, 267; Lancaster and, 152–4; *Sweet Smell of Success,* 178–83; *Trapeze,* 152–5, 185
Curtiz, Michael, 110–11, 123

D'Amico, Suso Cecchi, 232, 339; *The Leopard,* 223–6; *Conversation Piece,* 277–8
Daniels, William, 75, 84
Danson, Ted, 312–13
Dassin, Jules, 65, 78, 114, 209, 250; *Brute Force,* 75, 76
Davis, Bette, 43, 64, 90
Davis, Frank, 236
Davis, John W., 334–5
Davis, Ossie, 234, 249
Davison, Bruce, 271–3
Day, Doris, 104
Death Wish, 274
Decaë, Henri, 252, 254
De Carlo, Yvonne, 76, 91, 92
de Havilland, Olivia, 63, 121
Dekker, Albert, 68, 114, 133
Dekker, Esther, 133
De Laurentiis, Dino, 283
Delon, Alain, 222, 224, 274
Delsarte, François, 22, 24, 78
DeMille, Cecil B., 86
Demme, Jonathan, 330
Denby, David, 308
De Niro, Robert, 262
Depression, 28–9, 34, 35, 37–45
Dern, Bruce, 7, 225; *Castle Keep,* 252–4; Lancaster and, 252–4, 263
Desert Fury, 64–5, 69, 71, 74, 88, 108
Desilu Productions, 172
Devil's Disciple, The, 171, 189, 190–2, 194

De Witt Clinton High School, New York, 25–6
Dies, Martin, 43, 78
Dietrich, Marlene, 53, 113; *Judgment at Nuremberg*, 211, 214; Lancaster and, 71, 116, 126–7
Diller, Barry, 283, 290, 314
Directors Guild of America, 140, 148
Dirty Harry, 269
Disney (Walt) Company, 113, 133, 314
Donahue, Lancaster on, 18, 68, 322–3, 324
Donatello Davidas Award, 283
Dorsey, Tommy, 46
Douglas, Ann, 22
Douglas, Joel, 157–61, 165, 217, 233, 287, 321, 341
Douglas, Kirk, 5, 6, 64, 74, 75, 110, 159, 227, 272; *Boys in Autumn* (play), 320; independent production, 165, 190–1, 227, 230; Lancaster and, 159–60, 165–7, 190–1, 195, 228–30, 319–21, 330–1, 341; *The Devil's Disciple*, 190–1; *O.K. Corral*, 165–7; *Seven Days in May*, 228–32; *Tough Guys*, 319–21
Douglas, Michael, 159, 160, 321, 343
Dowling, Constance, 67
Dreiser, Theodore, 107
Dunne, Philip, 80

Earp, Wyatt, 163–8
East Harlem, New York, 13–35, 37–8, 47, 59, 62, 142, 205–6, 220, 257–8; *see also* Union Settlement House; Church of the Son of Man
Eastlake, William: *Castle Keep*, 249
Eastwood, Clint, 5, 115, 147, 241, 269, 275, 290, 328, 329, 343
Economist, The, 258
Eichmann, Adolf, 214
Eisenhower, Dwight, 127, 133
Eisner, Michael, 290, 340
Eisenstein, Sergei, 222
Elliot, Sumner Locke, 144
Elmer Gantry, 4, 163; casting of Shirley Jones, 201–2; Catholic reaction, 203; critical reaction, 204–5; Lancaster's Academy Award nomination for, 210; Protestant reaction, 203; shooting of, 202–3; success, 212–13
Enright, Ray, 30
Ernst, June, 39–41, 244; marriage to Lancaster, 39–41, 42, 44, 54, 63, 72
Ernst, Ora Blush, 39, 40, 44, 45
Erskine, Chester, 79

Esquire, 229
Executive Action, 275–6; critical reaction, 276

Fairbanks, Douglas, 46–7, 85, 98, 118, 340; *The Black Pirate*, 115; *The Mark of Zorro*, 115
Falk, Peter, 252, 253
Falwell, Jerry, 330
Farber, Manny, 70
Farnol, Jefferey: *The Broad Highway*, 24
FBI, 78–82, 97, 105–6, 114, 120, 122, 146, 176, 214; *see also* House Special Committee on Un-American Activities (HUAC)
Federal Theater Project (FTP), 41–4, 62, 78, 131, 144, 229; communist allegations, 43–4; *Sing for Your Supper*, 43–4
Fellini, Federico, 221
Ferrer, José, 106, 107, 120
Field of Dreams, 22, 327–9, 332; critical reaction, 328
Films and Filming, 270
Film Daily, 249
films, *see* Hollywood film industry; independent production; *specific film titles and genres*
Films Ariane, Les, 236
Firestarter, The, 309
First Love, 171
First Time, The, 126
Flame and the Arrow, The, 107, 113, 115, 117, 138; circus stunts, 104–5; critical reaction, 104–5; shooting of, 103–4; Warner Bros. contract, 103
Flying Concellos, 153
Flynn, Errol, 64, 85, 102, 103, 104, 110
Fonda, Henry, 97, 164, 306, 324
Fonda, Jane, 306, 326
Fontaine, Joan, 85, 87, 90
Foote, Horton, 144
Ford, John, 164, 193
Forsyth, Bill, 307, 308
Fort Riley, Kansas, 49
Fortune, 41, 135, 137
Foster, Norman, 87
Fowler, Gene, 219
Fowler, Marjorie, 188
France, 148, 151, 172, 192, 235–40, 256
Frankenheimer, John, 115, 205, 250, 256, 263; *Birdman of Alcatraz*, 209–10, 214, 215; *The Gypsy Moths*, 257; Lancaster and, 206–7, 209, 231, 239–40; *Seven Days in May*, 230–1; *The Train*, 237–41; *The Young Savages*, 205–7
From Here to Eternity, 4, 113, 126–30, 134, 136, 145, 149, 185, 208, 231, 249; Academy Awards, 128; beach scene, 128,

Viertel, Salka, 145
Vietnam War, 243, 254, 258, 262, 266, 269,
   270–3, 275, 282, 289–93; *see also Castle
   Keep, Go Tell the Spartans, The Professionals,
   Twilight's Last Gleaming, Ulzana's Raid*
Village Voice, 284, 297
Visconti, Luchino, 6, 221, 252, 283, 289,
   304, 339; *Bellissima*, 143, 221; *Conversa-
   tion Piece*, 277–9, 283; *The Leopard*,
   210–11, 221–8, 232, 311; *Rocco and His
   Brothers*, 221, 222; sexuality of, 221, 279
Vogel, Joseph, 189
Voyage of Terror: The Achille Lauro Affair (TV
   movie), 332–3

Wagner, Robert, 335, 340, 341
Wallace, Mike, 214
Wallis, Hal, 30, 61–4, 79, 117, 135, 321;
   Lancaster and, 61–5, 71–5, 90–1, 96,
   103, 106, 107–9, 123, 126, 136, 142,
   162–5; at Warner Bros., 63–4
Wall Street Journal, 340
Wanger, Walter, 66
Warner, Jack, 64, 80, 101, 103, 104
Warner Bros., 30–1, 47, 61, 63–4, 86, 90,
   107, 121, 169, 314; Lancaster contracts,
   103–6, 109–18, 124–6, 134, 136, 144;
   -Lancaster productions, 103–6, 109–18,
   124–6, 134, 136
Wasserman, Lew, 5, 75, 134–6, 207; as
   Lancaster's agent, 136, 151–2, 160, 172,
   189, 192
Waterbury, Ruth, 53, 62, 155, 158, 175
Watts race riots, 258, 259
Wayne, John, 6, 108, 115, 190, 259, 265,
   324; death, 297–8
Way West, The, 171, 192, 194
Webb, James, 153
Welles, Orson, 87, 97, 179, 187
Westerns, 108, 136–9, 162, 163–8, 193,
   241–3, 249–50, 268–73, 295–7

White Hunter, Black Heart, 171
Whitman, Walt: *Leaves of Grass*, 11, 299
Widmark, Richard, 165, 211
Wild Bunch, The, 269, 270
Wilder, Billy, 67, 183
Williams, Edward Bennett, 131, 145–6,
   208
Williams, Robin, 311, 330
Williams, Tennessee, 142; *The Rose Tattoo*,
   142; *A Streetcar Named Desire*, 77–8
Wilson, Gerald, 270
Wilson, Scott, 252, 253, 254, 257, 265
Winchell, Walter, 14, 16, 29, 65, 69, 147,
   178
Winkler, Henry, 315
Winner, Michael, 269, 270, 274, 340
Winters, Shelley, 98–100, 119, 120, 176,
   206, 243, 249, 250, 272
Wise, Robert, 64, 185
Women's Wear Daily, 269, 275
Works Progress Administration (WPA),
   41–4, 45, 49
World War II, 5, 48–55, 60, 127, 128, 185,
   220, 236, 249, 304; Lancaster in, 48,
   49–55
Writer's Guild, 148
Wyler, William, 80, 190

Yorty, Sam, 259, 265
Young Savages, The, 200, 205–7, 209
Youngstein, Max, 61, 64, 65, 112, 114, 135,
   136, 146, 147, 156, 165, 172, 174, 177,
   192, 194, 200, 234, 305

Zanghi, Jim, 31
Zanuck, Darryl, 30, 63, 65, 102, 112
Ziegfeld Follies, 65
Zinnemann, Fred, 126; *From Here to Eternity*,
   126–30
Zulu Dawn, 294–5

Frontispiece   Photofest

Page 9   Private family collection of Nick Cravat

Page 57   Archive Photos

Page 197   Archive Photos

Insert following page 86

Page 1: top left and right, Private family collection of Nick Cravat; bottom, Union Settlement Association archives

Pages 2 and 3: Private family collection of Nick Cravat

Page 4: top, Courtesy of Arnold Belnick; bottom, Photofest

Page 5: top, Stills Collection of the Museum of Modern Art; bottom, Mark Hellinger Collection, USC Cinema-Television Library and Archives of Performing Arts

Page 6: top left, Archive Photos; top right, Photofest; bottom, Gene Lester/Archive Photos

Page 7: top left, Photofest; right, Stills Collection of the Museum of Modern Art; bottom, Private family collection of Nick Cravat

Page 8: top, Stills Collection of the Museum of Modern Art; bottom, Photofest

Insert following page 182

Page 1: top, Archive Photos; bottom, Stills Collection of the Museum of Modern Art

Page 2: top, Stills Collection of the Museum of Modern Art; bottom, Archive Photos

Page 3: top, Archive Photos; bottom, Photofest

Page 4: top, ©1955 E.C. Publications, Inc. All rights reserved. Used with permission of *MAD* Magazine; bottom, *The Kentuckian*, 1954, Thomas Hart Benton, Los Angeles County Museum of Art, gift of Burt Lancaster. © T.H. Benton and R.P. Benton Testamentary Trusts/Licensed by VAGA, New York, NY.

Page 5: top, Archive Photos; bottom, © Al Hirschfeld. Drawing reproduced by special arrangement with Hirschfeld's exclusive representative, The Margo Feiden Galleries Ltd. New York.

Page 6: top, Stills Collection of the Museum of Modern Art; bottom, Kirk Douglas Collection, Wisconsin Center for Film and Theater Research, State Historical Society of Wisconsin, Madison.

Page 7: top and bottom, Courtesy of the Academy of Motion Picture Arts and Sciences

Page 8: top, Photofest; bottom, Express Newspapers/Archive Photos

A NOTE ON THE TYPE

This book was set in Baskerville, a facsimile of the type cast from the original matrices designed by John Baskerville. The original face was the forerunner of the modern group of typefaces.

John Baskerville (1706–1775) of Birmingham, England, was a writing master with a special renown for cutting inscriptions in stone. About 1750 he began experimenting with punch cutting and making typographical material, and in 1757 he published his first work, a Virgil in royal quarto. His types, at first criticized as unnecessarily slender, delicate, and feminine, in time were recognized as both distinct and elegant, and his types as well as his printing were greatly admired.

Four years after his death, Baskerville's widow sold all his punches and matrices to the Société philosophique, littéraire et typographique, which used some of the types for the sumptuous Kehl edition of Voltaire's works in seventy volumes. Eventually the punches and matrices came into the possession of the distinguished Paris typefounders Deberny & Peignot, who, in singularly generous fashion, returned them to Cambridge University Press in 1953.

Composed by North Market Street Graphics, Lancaster, Pennsylvania

Designed by Robert C. Olsson